SOCIAL STRATIFICATION: A Research Bibliography

THE GLENDESSARY PRESS, INC.

2512 Grove Street, Berkeley, California 94704

SOCIAL STRATIFICATION:

A Research Bibliography

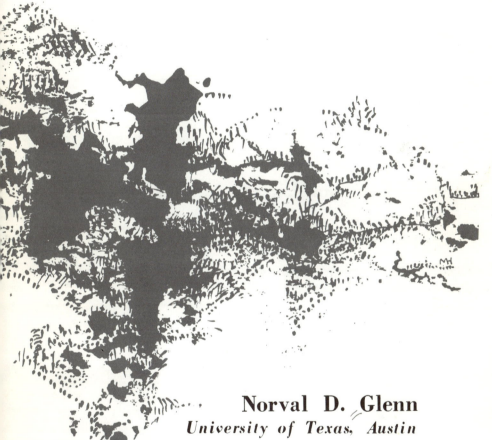

Norval D. Glenn
University of Texas, Austin

Jon P. Alston
University of Georgia

David Weiner
State University of New York, Buffalo

TABLE
of
CONTENTS

PREFACE

If one were to use the volume of literature devoted to each of the substantive areas in sociology as the criterion of their importance, one would conclude that social stratification is the most important and is becoming even more dominant. In 1966 and 1967, 29.9 percent of the articles and research notes in the three leading American sociological journals (the *American Sociological Review*, the *American Journal of Sociology*, and *Social Forces*) dealt primarily with some aspect of stratification. This was a substantial increase from the period of 1961 through 1965, during which 21.5 percent of the articles and research notes in the top three journals focused upon stratification, and it was a marked increase from 1941 through 1945, when only 5.2 percent did so.

The increase in attention to stratification may not have been quite as steep as these data indicate, because the founding of journals to deal with several sociological specialties has tended to draw articles in those areas away from the "big three" journals. However, some of the new specialized journals, such as *Sociology of Education* and *Social Problems,* also devote a large percentage of their space to social stratification. Furthermore, attention to stratification appears to have increased considerably in disciplines other than sociology, including anthropology, political science, and psychology.

The result is such an outpouring of literature that no one can keep abreast of it all without spending most of his time searching for and reading the hundreds of publications that appear each year. At the same time, it has become more important for most social scientists — as well as numerous people in such applied fields as social work, education, and marketing — to be familiar with at least certain segments of this literature. Virtually every social scientist who does any kind of survey research will at least use stratification variables for control purposes, and indeed it seems that a majority of the more prolific social scientific authors eventually deal rather directly with some aspect of stratification.

In view of these conditions, it seems apparent to us that a guide to the literature in this highly important field is needed by numerous students and scholars in the several social sciences and by practitioners in many applied fields. We have compiled this bibliography to fill that need.

However, we must stress the limitations of this work so that it will not be used for purposes for which it is not intended. We wish especially to stress that it does not cover all the literature in the field, nor does it include all the literature related to any one of the topic headings. The user is urged to begin his search of the literature on any topic in stratification with this work but not to end it here. He should assume that important and basic literature is missing from each topical listing (although, of course, we hope this assumption is true of few of the topics). Shortly before this bibliography went to press, we discovered we had overlooked several important and recent articles, including some we had used in our own research. There probably are similar omissions we failed to discover and correct. On the basis of our experience, we are skeptical of any claim that a bibliography covers all the literature on any topic or all the literature on a topic published during a given period of time.

In addition to inadvertent omissions, other literature is deliberately excluded. This compilation is restricted to publications in English, although it includes many works translated from other languages and many articles from journals that also publish articles in other languages. No doctoral dissertations, masters theses, unpublished papers delivered at professional meetings, or book reviews (except review essays) are included. With a few exceptions, articles from mass circulation magazines are not listed, and the large body of fiction that some scholars have found useful for gaining insights into aspects of stratification is excluded. Decennial census reports are not listed, nor are other census publications, with the exception of monographs and a few of the *Current Population Reports,* issued by the U. S. Bureau of the Census, that are of special value.

We did not systematically search issues of periodicals published before 1940 and after April of 1968, although we list many items dated earlier than this period and a few dated later. We did not search journals outside of sociology or published outside of the United States and England as thoroughly as we searched the American and British sociological journals. Inevitably, we compiled more nearly complete lists of literature for some topics than for others, because our specialized interests gave us greater knowledge of the publications on some topics, and we could draw upon recent extensive bibliographies available on some topics but not on others.

Another limitation of this bibliography is that we do not judge the quality of the publications for the user — he must do that for himself. We include many articles and books that we consider mediocre at best; in fact, we exclude no academic publications on the grounds of quality. The reasons for our failure to use quality as a criterion for inclusion are threefold: first, we were unable to read all the literature carefully enough to judge it adequately; second, there is not high consensus on what constitutes quality in this field, and much literature we consider poor is considered excellent by many respectable scholars; and third, many rather poor publications are widely cited and used by researchers, if only because they serve as negative models.

This compilation was developed by expanding upon a bibliography Professor Glenn had compiled over a period of several years for his personal use. Somewhat more than a third of the items finally included came from this original core. Professors Alston and Weiner, who were then graduate students in the Department of Sociology at the University of Texas at Austin, each spent several weeks of intensive searching of journal files, footnotes in articles and books, periodical indexes, and various other sources to make the listing of stratification literature more nearly complete. After Professor Alston joined the faculty of the University of Georgia, he spent part of his time for nine months adding items to the bibliography, including most of the historical material and many of the more obscure publications from outside the American and British sociological literature. The final preparation – including checking the entries for accuracy, expanding the coverage of topics for which few publications had been discovered, and writing the introductions for the topical sections – was done by Professor Glenn. He also assumed responsibility for the final decisions on the classification of items.

Several student assistants helped search the literature and record the entries. These include Ruth Hyland, Linda Wukasch, Ronald Birkelbach, Kenneth Monts, Jay Meddin, and Alan H. Marks. Dianne Monts and Judy Gillham capably handled the tedious job of typing the manuscript. Patricia Ann Glenn, Charlotte Weiner, and Pearl Amster assisted the project in several ways at several of its stages.

Norval D. Glenn
Austin, Texas

David Weiner
Buffalo, New York

Jon P. Alston
Athens, Georgia

Part I

SOCIAL STRATIFICATION

General Works

Most of the publications listed here attempt to summarize the field of social stratification or some broad portion of it. Many are textbooks or chapters in textbooks; several others are statements of the current state of the field and of recent developments. Others are sophisticated theoretical works too broad in scope to be classified under more specific topics. Excluding the latter, the items in this section should be of special interest to laymen, students, and academicians outside of sociology who need an overview of the field.

AUBERT, Vilhelm, *Elements of Sociology,* New York: Scribner's, 1967, Chapter 5, "Social Stratification."

BARBER, Bernard, *Social Stratification: A Comparative Analysis of Structure and Process,* New York: Harcourt, Brace, 1957.

BARBER, Bernard and Elinor G. Barber, editors, *European Social Class: Stability and Change,* New York: Macmillan, 1965.

BENDIX, Reinhard and Seymour M. Lipset, editors, *Class, Status, and Power: A Reader in Social Stratification,* New York: Free Press, 1953.

BENDIX, Reinhard and Seymour M. Lipset, editors, *Class, Status, and Power: Social Stratification in Comparative Perspective,* second edition, New York: Free Press, 1966.

BENDIX, Reinhard and Seymour M. Lipset, "Karl Marx's Theory of Social Classes," in Reinhard Bendix and Seymour M. Lipset, editors, *Class, Status, and Power,* second edition, New York: Free Press, 1966.

BENEDICT, Burton, "Stratification in Plural Societies," *American Anthropologist,* 64 (1962), 1235-1246.

BENSMAN, Joseph and Bernard Rosenberg, *Mass, Class, and Bureaucracy,* Englewood Cliffs, New Jersey: Prentice-Hall, 1963, Chapter 7, "Social Stratification: Differentiation."

BERELSON, Bernard and Gary A. Steiner. *Human Behavior: An Inventory of Scientific Findings,* New York: Harcourt, Brace and World, 1964, Chapter 11, "Social Stratification."

BERGEL, Egon E., *Social Stratification,* New York: McGraw-Hill, 1962.

GENERAL WORKS

BERTRAND, Alvin L., *Basic Sociology,* New York: Appleton-Century-Crofts, 1967, Chapter 10, "Social Stratification and Mobility," and Chapter 11, "Social Power."

BIERSTEDT, Robert, *The Social Order,* second edition, New York: McGraw-Hill, 1963, Chapter 15, "Class and Caste."

BLAU, Peter M. and Otis Dudley Duncan, "Some Preliminary Findings on Social Stratification in the United States," *Acta Sociologica,* 9, 4-24.

BOTTOMORE, T. B., *Classes in Modern Society,* New York: Pantheon, 1966.

BOTTOMORE, T. B., editor, *Karl Marx: Early Writings,* London: Watts, 1963.

BOTTOMORE, T. B., *Sociology: A Guide to Problems and Literature,* London: Allen and Unwin, 1962, Chapter 11, "Social Stratification."

BOYD, Maurice and Donald Worcester, *American Civilization,* second edition, Boston: Allyn and Bacon, 1968, Chapter 16, "Social Stratification."

BREDEMEIER, Harry C. and Richard M. Stephenson, *The Analysis of Social Systems,* New York: Holt, Rinehart, and Winston, 1962, Chapter 11, "Stratification."

BROOM, Leonard and Philip Selznick, *Sociology,* 1st, 2nd, and 3rd editions, New York: Harper and Row, 1955, 1958, and 1963, Chapter 6, "Social Stratification," written in collaboration with Richard T. Morris.

BROOM, Leonard and Philip Selznick, *Sociology,* 4th edition, New York: Harper and Row, 1968, Chapter 6, "Social Stratification," written in collaboration with Norval D. Glenn.

BROWN, Roger, *Social Psychology,* New York: Free Press, 1966.

CARLSSON, Gosta, *Social Mobility and Class Structure,* Lund: Gleerup, 1968.

CHINOY, Ely, "Research in Class Structure," *Canadian Journal of Economics and Political Science,* 16 (May, 1950), 255-263.

CHINOY, Ely, *Society: An Introduction to Sociology,* second edition, New York: Random House, 1967, Chapter 8, "Social Stratification."

COLE, G.D.H., *Studies in Class Structure,* London: Routledge and Kegan Paul, 1955.

COLEMAN, Richard and Bernice L. Neugarten, *Social Class in the City,* New York: Atherton, 1963.

COX, Oliver C., *Caste, Class, and Race,* Garden City, New York: Doubleday, 1948.

COX, Oliver C., "Estates, Social Classes and Political Classes," *American Sociological Review,* 10 (August, 1945), 464-469.

COX, Oliver C., "Max Weber on Social Stratification: A Critique," *American Sociological Review,* 15 (April, 1950), 223-227.

CUBER, John F., *Sociology,* 6th edition, New York: Appleton-Century-Crofts, 1968, Chapter 22, "Social Stratification ."

CUBER, John F. and William F. Kenkel, *Social Stratification in the United States,* New York: Appleton-Century-Crofts,1954.

DAHRENDORF, Ralf, *Class and Class Conflict in Industrial Society,* Stanford: Stanford University Press, 1959.

DAVIS, Kingsley, "A Conceptual Analysis of Stratification," *American Sociological Review,* 7 (June, 1942), 309-321.

ELLIS, Robert A., "The Continuum Theory of Social Stratification: A Critical Note," *Sociology and Social Research,* 42 (March-April,1958), 269-273.

FARIS, Robert E. L., "The Alleged Class System in the United States," *Research Studies of the State College of Washington,* 22 (June, 1954), 77-83.

FOOTE, Nelson N., Walter Goldschmidt, Richard T. Morris, Melvin Seeman, and Joseph Shister, "Alternative Assumptions in Stratification Research," *Transactions of the Second World Congress of Sociology,* 2 (1954), 378-390.

GOLDSCHMIDT, Walter, "America's Social Classes," *Commentary,* 10 (August, 1950), 175-181.

GOLDSCHMIDT, Walter, *As You Sow,* New York: Free Press, 1947.

GOLDSCHMIDT, Walter, "Social Class in America — A Critical Review," *American Anthropologist,* 52 (October-December, 1950), 483-619.

GOLDSCHMIDT, Walter, "Social Class and the Dynamics of Status in America," *American Anthropologist,* (December, 1955), 1209-1217.

GOLDTHORPE, John H., "Social Stratification in Industrial Society," in Paul Halmos, editor, *The Development of Industrial Society,* Sociological Review Monographs, No. 8, Keele, 1964.

GORDON, Milton M., "Social Class in American Sociology," *American Journal of Sociology*, 55 (November, 1949), 262-268.

GENERAL WORKS GORDON, Milton M., *Social Class in American Sociology*, Durham, North Carolina: Duke University Press, 1958.

GOULDNER, Alvin W., and Helen P. Gouldner, *Modern Sociology*, New York: Harcourt, Brace, and World, 1963, Chapter 7, "Stratification: The Distribution of Power, Wealth, and Prestige."

GROSS, Llewellyn, "The Use of Class Concepts in Sociological Research," *American Journal of Sociology*, 54 (March, 1949), 409-421.

HALBWACHS, Maurice, *The Psychology of Social Classes*, New York: Free Press, 1958.

HATT, Paul K., "Stratification in the Mass Society," *American Sociological Review*, 15 (April, 1950), 216-222.

HEBERLE, Rudolph, "Recovery of Class Theory," *Pacific Sociological Review*, 2 (Spring, 1959), 18-24.

HETZLER, Stanley A., "An Investigation of the Distinctiveness of Social Classes," *American Sociological Review*, 18 (October, 1953), 493-497.

HODGES, Harold M., Jr., *Social Stratification: Class in America*, Cambridge, Massachusetts: Schenkman, 1964.

HOLLINGSHEAD, A. B., "Stratification in American Society," in L. Bernstein and B. C. Burris, editors, *The Contribution of the Social Sciences to Psychotherapy*, Springfield, Illinois: Thomas, 1967.

HORTON, Paul B. and Chester L. Hunt, *Sociology*, second edition, New York: McGraw-Hill, 1968, Chapter 11, "Social Class," and Chapter 12, "Social Mobility."

JOHNSON, Harry M., *Sociology*, New York: Harcourt, Brace, 1960, part 7, "Social Stratification."

KAHL, Joseph A., *The American Class Structure*, New York: Holt, Rinehart and Winston, 1957.

KAUFMAN, Harold F., Otis Dudley Duncan, Neal Gross, and William H. Sewell, "Problems of Theory and Method in the Study of Social Stratification," *Rural Sociology*, 18 (March, 1953).

KELLER, Suzanne, "Sociology of Stratification, 1945-1955," in Hans L. Zetterberg, editor, *Sociology in the United States*, Paris: UNESCO, 1956.

KENKEL, William F., "Recent Research in Social Stratification," in Thomas E. Lasswell, John H. Burma, and Sidney H. Aronson, editors, *Life in Society,* Chicago: Scott, Foresman, 1965.

LANDTMAN, Gunnar, *The Origin of the Inequality of the Social Classes,* Chicago: University of Chicago Press, 1938.

LASSWELL, Thomas E., *Class and Stratum: An Introduction to Concepts and Research,* Boston: Houghton Mifflin, 1965.

LASSWELL, Thomas E., "Social Class and Social Stratification: Preface," *Sociology and Social Research,* 50 (April, 1966), 277-279.

LENSKI, Gerhard E., "American Social Classes: Statistical Strata or Social Groups?" *American Journal of Sociology,* 58 (September, 1952), 139-149.

LENSKI, Gerhard E., "Social Stratification," in Joseph Roucek, editor, *Contemporary Sociology,* New York: Philosophical Library, 1958.

LENSKI, Gerhard E., *Power and Privilege: A Theory of Social Stratification,* New York: McGraw-Hill, 1966.

LEWIS, Lionel S., "A Note on the Problem of Classes," *Public Opinion Quarterly,* 27 (Winter, 1963), 599-603.

LIPSET, Seymour M., "Social Class," *International Encyclopedia of the Social Sciences,* 15, New York: Free Press, 1968, 296-316.

LIPSET, Seymour M. and Reinhard Bendix, "Social Status and Social Structure: A Re-examination of Data and Interpretations," *British Journal of Sociology,* 2 (June-September, 1951), 150-168 and 230-254.

LOCKWOOD, David, "Some Remarks on the Social System," *British Journal of Sociology,* 7 (June, 1956), 134-146.

LOEB, Martin, "Social Class and the American Social System," *Social Work,* 6 (April, 1961).

LOOMIS, Charles P., J. A. Beegle, and T. W. Longmore, "Critique of Class as Related to Social Stratification," *Sociometry,* 10 (November, 1947), 319-337.

LUNDBERG, George A., "Occupations and 'Class' Alignments in the United States, 1870-1950," *Social Forces,* 34 (December, 1955), 128-133.

LUNDBERG, George A., Clarence C. Schrag, Otto N. Larsen, and William R. Catton, Jr., *Sociology,* fourth edition, New

York: Harper and Row, 1968, Chapter 12, "Social Stratification: Power, Privilege, Prestige."

LYNES, Russell, *A Surfeit of Honey,* New York: Harper, 1957.

GENERAL WORKS

MACK, Raymond and Kimball Young, *Sociology and Social Life,* fourth edition, New York: American Book Company, 1968, Chapter 9, "Class Structure and its Functions," Chapter 10, "Social Mobility," and Chapter 11, "The Amount of Mobility in the United States."

MARSH, Robert M., *Comparative Sociology: A Codification of Cross-Societal Analyses,* New York: Harcourt, Brace and World, 1962.

MARSHALL, T. H., *Citizenship and Social Class,* Cambridge: Cambridge University Press, 1950.

MARSHALL, T. H., *Class, Citizenship, and Social Development,* Garden City, New York: Doubleday, 1963.

MARTINDALE, Don, *American Social Structure: Historical Antecedents and Contemporary Analysis,* New York: Appleton-Century-Crofts, 1960.

MARX, Karl, "A Note on Classes," in Reinhard Bendix and Seymour M. Lipset, editors, *Class, Status, and Power,* revised edition, Free Press, New York, 1966.

MAYER, Kurt B., *Class and Society,* New York: Random House, 1955.

MAYER, Kurt B., "The Theory of Social Classes," *Harvard Educational Review,* 23 (Summer, 1953), 149-167.

MAYER, Kurt B., "The Theory of Social Classes," in *Transactions of the Second World Congress of Sociology,* 2 (1954).

MENDIETA Y NUNEZ, Lucio, "The Social Classes," *American Sociological Review,* 11 (April, 1946), 166-176.

MILLS, C. Wright and Hans Gerth, translators and editors, *From Max Weber: Essays in Sociology,* New York: Oxford University Press, 1958.

MOMBERT, Paul, "Class," *Encyclopaedia of the Social Sciences,* 13, New York: Macmillan, 1930, 531-536.

MONTAGUE, Joel B., Jr., *Class and Nationality: English and American Studies,* New Haven: College and University Press, 1963.

MONTAGUE, Joel B., Jr., "Class or Status Society," *Sociology and Social Research,* 40 (May-June, 1956), 333-338.

MOTT, Paul E., *The Organization of Society,* Englewood Cliffs,

New Jersey: Prentice-Hall, 1965, Chapter 12, "Social Classes in American Society," and Chapter 13, "Class Differences in American Society."

NISBET, Robert A., "The Decline and Fall of Social Class," *Pacific Sociological Review,* 2 (Spring, 1959), 11-17.

OGBURN, William F. and Meyer F. Nimkoff, *Sociology,* fourth edition, Boston: Houghton-Mifflin, 1964, Chapter 16, "Social Stratification."

OLSEN, Marvin E., *The Process of Social Organization,* New York: Holt, Rinehart and Winston, 1968, Chapter 13, "The Process of Social Allocation or Stratification."

OSSOWSKI, Stanislaw, *Class Structure in the Social Conciousness,* translated by Sheila Patterson, New York: Free Press, 1963.

PACKARD, Vance, *The Status Seekers,* New York: McKay, 1959.

PAGE, Charles H., *Class and American Sociology: From Ward to Ross,* New York: Dial, 1940.

PARSONS, Talcott, "An Analytical Approach to the Theory of Social Stratification," in *Essays in Sociological Theory,* revised edition, New York: Free Press, 1954.

PARSONS, Talcott, "A Revised Analytical Approach to the theory of Social Stratification," in Reinhard Bendix and Seymour M. Lipset, editors, *Class, Status, and Power,* New York: Free Press, 1953.

PARSONS, Talcott, "Social Classes and Class Conflict in the Light of Recent Sociological Theory," *American Economic Review,* 39 (1949), 16-26.

PENNOCK, J. Roland and John W. Chapman, editors, *Equality,* New York: Atherton, 1967.

PORTER, John, *The Vertical Mosaic: An Analysis of Social Class and Power in Canada,* Toronto: University of Toronto Press, 1965.

REISSMAN, Leonard, *Class in American Society,* New York: Free Press, 1960.

REISSMAN, Leonard, "Social Stratification," in Neil J. Smelser, editor, *Sociology,* New York: Wiley, 1967.

ROSE, Arnold M., *Sociology: The Study of Human Relations,* second edition, New York: Knopf, 1965, Chapter 8, "Social Stratification: Castes and Classes."

ROSE, Arnold M., "The Concept of Class and American Sociology," *Social Research,* 25 (Spring, 1958), 53-69.

ROUSSEAU, J. J., "A Dissertation on the Origin and Foundation of the Inequality of Mankind," *The Social Contract and Discourses,* London: Dent and Sons, 1913.

SCHUMPETER, Joseph, "The Problem of Classes," in Reinhard Bendix and Seymour M. Lipset, editors, *Class, Status, and Power,* revised edition, New York: Free Press, 1966.

SJOBERG, Gideon, *The Preindustrial City,* New York: Free Press, 1960, Chapter 5, "Social Class."

SOROKIN, Pitirim A., *Society, Culture, and Personality,* New York: Harper, 1947, Chapter 14, "Differentiation of Population into Multibonded Groups," and Chapter 15, "Social Stratification."

SPEIER, Hans, "Social Stratification," in L. A. Coser and B. Rosenberg, editors, *Sociological Theory,* New York: Macmillan, 1957.

STINCHCOMBE, Arthur L., "The Structure of Stratification Systems," *International Encyclopedia of the Social Sciences,* 15, New York: Free Press, 1968, 325-332.

SVALASTOGA, Kaare, *Prestige, Class, and Mobility,* Copenhagen: Gyldendol, 1959.

SVALASTOGA, Kaare, *Social Differentiation,* New York: McKay, 1965.

SVALASTOGA, Kaare, "Social Differentiation," in Robert E. L. Faris, *Handbook of Modern Sociology,* Chicago: Rand McNally, 1964.

TAUSKY, Curt, "Parsons on Stratification: An Analysis and Critique," *Sociological Quarterly,* 6 (Spring, 1965), 128-138.

TAYLOR, O. H., "Schumpeter and Marx: Imperialism and Social Classes in the Schumpeterian System," *Quarterly Journal of Economics,* 65 (1951), 525-555.

THOMAS, R. Murray, "A Five-Dimension Anatomy of Stratification," *Sociology and Social Research,* 50 (April, 1966), 314-324.

TOBY, Jackson, *Contemporary Society,* New York: Wiley, 1964, Chapter 7, "Social Stratification."

TOENNIES, Ferdinand, "Estates and Classes" in Reinhard Bendix and Seymour M. Lipset, editors, *Class, Status, and Power,* revised edition, New York: Free Press, 1966.

TUMIN, Melvin M., *Social Stratification: The Forms and Functions of Inequality,* Englewood Cliffs, New Jersey: Prentice-Hall, 1967.

VANDER ZANDEN, James W., *Sociology,* New York: Ronald, 1965, Chapter 13, "Social Processes: Stratification."

WARNER, W. Lloyd, "Significance of Caste and Class in a
Democracy," *National Conference of Social Workers,* (1955),
289-301.

WARNER, W. Lloyd, "The Study of Social Stratification," in
Joseph B. Gittler, editor, *Review of Sociology: 1945-1955,*
New York: Wiley, 1957.

WARNER, W. Lloyd, *American Life: Dream and Reality,* revised edition, Chicago: University of Chicago Press, 1962.

WARNER, W. Lloyd, *Structure of American Life,* Edinburgh:
University of Edinburgh Press, 1952.

WARNER, W. Lloyd and M. H. Warner, *What you Should Know
About Social Class,* Chicago: Science Research Associates, 1953.

WEBER, Max, "Class, Status and Party," in Reinhard Bendix
and Seymour M. Lipset, editors, *Class, Status, and Power,*
revised edition, New York: Free Press, 1966.

WILLIAMS, Robin M., Jr., *American Society: A Sociological
Interpretation,* New York: Knopf, 1960, Chapter 5, "Social
Stratification in the United States."

WILSON, Everett K., *Sociology: Rules, Roles, and Relationships,*
Homewood, Illinois: Dorsey, 1966, Chapter 5, "Class Differences in the Transmission of Culture."

ZWEIG, F., "The Theory of Social Classes," *Kyklos,* 11 (1958),
390-404.

Bibliographies

This section includes not only bibliographies dealing specifically with social
stratification or some specific aspect of that field but also a few other bibliographies
containing a significant number of items relevant to stratification.

We have drawn upon many of these bibliographies in preparing this one, and we
acknowledge our indebtedness to their compilers. However, not all the literature
listed in the other bibliographies is included in this one.

ALDOUS, Joan and Reuben Hill, *International Bibliography of
Research in Marriage and the Family, 1900-1964,* Minneapolis,
Minnesota: University of Minnesota Press, 1962.

ASTROM, Sven-Erik, "Literature on Social Mobility and Social

Stratification in Finland: Some Bibliographical Notes," *Transactions of the Westermarck Society,* 2 (1953), 221-227.

BIBLIOGRAPHIES

BERKOWITZ, Morris I. and J. Edmund Johnson, *Social Scientific Studies of Religion: A Bibliography,* Pittsburgh: University of Pittsburgh Press, 1967.

BOALT, G. and C. G. Janson, "A Selected Bibliography of the Literature on Social Stratification and Social Mobility in Sweden," *Current Sociology,* 2 (April, 1954), 111-125.

BOOTH, Robert E., *et al., Culturally Disadvantaged: A Bibliography and Keywood-out-of-Context (KWOC) Index,* Detroit: Wayne State University Press, 1967.

CHILMAN, Catherine, "Economic and Social Deprivation: Its Effects on Children and Families in the United States—A Selected Bibliography," *Journal of Marriage and the Family,* 26, (November, 1964), 495-497.

DEVANANDAN, P. D., *A Bibliography on Hinduism,* Bangalore: Christian Institute for the Study of Religion and Society, 1961.

DIXON, Norman R., "Social Class and Education: An Annotated Bibliography," *Harvard Educational Review,* 23 (Fall, 1953), 330-338.

FREEDMAN, Ronald, "The Sociology of Human Fertility: A Trend Report and Bibliography," *Current Sociology,* 10 (1961-1962), 35-119.

GOLDSTEIN, Bernard, *et al., Low Income Youth in Urban Areas: A Critical Review of the Literature,* New York: Holt, Rinehart, and Winston, 1967.

GORE, William J. and Fred S. Silander, "A Bibliographical Essay on Decision Making," *Administrative Science Quarterly,* 4 (June, 1959).

GOTTLIEB, David and John Reeves, *Adolescent Behavior in Urban Areas: A Bibliographic Review and Discussion of the Literature,* New York: Collier-Macmillan, 1963.

GURSSLIN, Orville R., Jack L. Roach, and Llewellyn Gross, *Social Stratification in the United States: A Classified Bibliography, 1946-1964,* Buffalo: Department of Sociology, State University of New York at Buffalo, 1965.

HIMEOKA, T., K. Ariga, and K. Odaka, "A Select Bibliography on Social Stratification and Social Mobility in Japan Since 1800," *Current Sociology,* 2 (1953-1954), 329-362.

JACOBSEN, R. B., A. L. Flygstad, and R. H. Rodgers, *The Family and Occupational Choice: An Annotated Bibliography,* Eugene, Oregon: University of Oregon Center for Research in Occupational Planning, 1966.

JOHNSON, Benton, C. C. Langford, R. H. White, R. B. Jacobsen, and J. D. McCarthy, *Religion and Occupational Behavior: An Annotated Bibliography,* Eugene, Oregon: University of Oregon, Center for Research in Occupational Planning, 1966.

KUVLESKY, William P. and George W. Ohlendorf, *A Bibliography on Educational Orientations of Youth,* College Station, Texas: Texas A and M University, Department of Agricultural Economics and Sociology, Information Report 65-5, November, 1965.

KUVLESKY, William P. and George W. Ohlendorf, *Occupational Aspirations and Expectations: A Bibliography of Research Literature,* College Station, Texas: Texas A and M University, Department of Agricultural Economics and Sociology, Information Report 66-1, June, 1966.

LASSWELL, Harold D. and C. E. Rothwell, *The Comparative Study of Elites: An Introduction and Bibliography,* Stanford: Stanford University Press, 1952.

MACK, Raymond W., Linton Freeman, and Seymour Yellin, *Social Mobility: Thirty Years of Research and Theory. An Annotated Bibliography,* Syracuse: Syracuse University Press, 1957.

MACRAE, D. G., "Social Stratification—A Trend Report," *Current Sociology,* 2 (1953-1954), 5-74.

MAHAR, James M., *India: A Critical Bibliography,* Tucson: University of Arizona Press, 1964.

MILLER, Elizabeth W., *The Negro in America: A Bibliography,* Cambridge: Harvard University Press, 1966.

MILLER, S. M., "Comparative Social Mobility," *Current Sociology,* 9 (1960), 81-89.

OHLENDORF, George W. and William P. Kuvlesky, *A Bibliography of Literature on Status Aspirations and Expectations: Educational, Residence, Income, and Family Orientations,* College Station, Texas: Texas A and M University, Department of Agricultural Economics and Sociology, 1966.

PALTIEL, Freda L., *Poverty: An Annotated Bibliography and References,* Ottowa, Canada: The Canadian Welfare Council, 1966.

PATTERSON, Maureen L. P., and Ronald B. Inden, *Introduction to the Civilization of India. An Introductory Bibliography.* Chicago: University of Chicago Press, 1962.

PELLEGRIN, Roland J., "Selected Bibliography on Community Power Structure," *Southwestern Social Science Quarterly,* 48 (December, 1967), 451-465.

PFAUTZ, H., "The Current Literature on Social Stratification: Critique and Bibliography," *American Journal of Sociology*, 58 (January, 1963), 401-404.

SCHLESINGER, Benjamin, *Poverty in Canada and the United States: Overview and Annotated Bibliography*, Toronto: University of Toronto Press, 1966.

SEWELL, William H., *A Bibliography on Social Class and Childhood Personality*, University of Wisconsin, Department of Sociology, 1961.

SRINIVAS, M. N., Y. B. Damle, S. Shahani, and Andre Beteille, "Caste: A Trend Report and Bibliography," *Current Sociology*, 8 (No.3, 1959), 157-183.

TREGWORGY, Mildred L. and Paul B. Foreman, *Negroes in the United States: A Bibliography of Materials for School*, University Park, Pennsylvania: Pennsylvania State University Libraries, 1967.

WASSERMAN, Paul, *Decision-Making: An Annotated Bibliography*, Ithaca: Graduate School of Business and Public Administration, Cornell University, 1958.

WIRTH, L., "Social Stratification and Social Mobility in the United States," *Current Sociology*, 2 (1953-1954), 279-303.

Functions and Dysfunctions of Inequality

Perhaps the liveliest topic of debate in social stratification in recent years concerns the extent to which inequality is beneficial and the extent to which it is detrimental to societies and groups considered as wholes. A related question concerns whether or not inequality is functionally necessary for the maintenance of social systems, and if so, how much and what kind. Much of the important literature on these and closely related topics is listed below.

ANDERSON, C. Arnold, "The Need for a Functional Theory of Social Class," *Rural Sociology*, 19 (June, 1954), 152-160.

BARBER, Bernard, *Social Stratification*, New York: Harcourt Brace, 1957, Chapters 1-4.

BUCKLEY, Walter, "A Rejoinder to Functionalists Dr. Davis and Dr. Levy," *American Sociological Review*, 24 (February, 1959), 84-86.

BUCKLEY, Walter, "On Equitable Inequality," *American Sociological Review,* 28 (October, 1963), 799-801.

BUCKLEY, Walter, "Social Stratification and the Functional Theory of Social Differentiation," *American Sociological Review,* 23 (August, 1958), 369-375.

BURNSTEIN, Eugene, Robert Moulton, and Paul Liberty, Jr., "Role vs. Excellence as Determinants of Role Attractiveness," *American Sociological Review,* 28 (April, 1963), 212-219.

CATTELL, Raymond B., "The Cultural Functions of Social Stratification: I. Regarding the Genetic Bases of Society," *Journal of Social Psychology,* 21 (1945), 3-23.

CATTELL, Raymond B., "The Cultural Functions of Social Stratification: II. Regarding Individual and Group Dynamics," *Journal of Social Psychology,* 21 (1945), 25-55.

COHN, Werner, "Reply to Sgan," *American Sociological Review,* 26 (February, 1961), 104-105.

COHN, Werner, "Social Status and the Ambivalence Hypothesis: Some Critical Notes and a Suggestion," *American Sociological Review,* 25 (August, 1960), 508-513.

DAVIS, Kingsley, "The Abominable Heresey: A Reply to Dr. Buckley," *American Sociological Review,* 24 (February, 1959), 82-83.

DAVIS, Kingsley, *Human Society,* New York: Macmillan, 1948, Chapter 14, "Caste, Class, and Stratification."

DAVIS, Kingsley, "Reply to Tumin," *American Sociological Review,* 18 (August, 1953), 394-397.

DAVIS, Kingsley and Wilbert E. Moore, "Some Principles of Stratification," *American Sociological Review,* 10 (April, 1945), 242-249.

GOULD, H. A., "The Adaptive Functions of Caste in Contemporary Indian Society," *Asian Survey,* 3 (1963), 427-438.

HARRIS, Edward E., "Research Methods, Functional Importance, and Occupational Roles," *Sociological Quarterly,* 8 (Spring, 1967), 255-259.

HUACO, George A., "A Logical Analysis of the Davis-Moore Theory of Stratification," *American Sociological Review,* 28 (October, 1963), 801-804.

HUACO, George A., "The Functionalist Theory of Stratification: Two Decades of Controversy," *Inquiry,* 9 (Autumn, 1966), 215-240.

HUNTER, Floyd, *The Big Rich and the Little Rich,* Garden City, New York: Doubleday, 1965.

JOHNSON, Harry M., *Sociology,* New York: Harcourt Brace, 1960, Chapter 19, "The Functions and Dysfunctions of Social Stratification."

**FUNCTIONS
AND DYSFUNCTIONS
OF INEQUALITY**

LEWIS, Lionel S. and Joseph Lopreato, "Functional Importance and Prestige of Occupations," *Pacific Sociological Review,* 6 (Fall, 1963), 55-59.

LOPREATO, Joseph and Lionel S. Lewis, "An Analysis of Variables in the Functional Theory of Stratification," *Sociological Quarterly,* 4 (Autumn, 1963), 301-310.

MACK, Raymond W., "Race, Class, and Power in Barbados: A Study of Stratification as an Integrating Force in a Democratic Revolution," in Herbert R. Barringer, George Blankensten and Raymond W. Mack, editors, *Social Change in Developing Areas,* Cambridge: Schenkman, 1966.

MOORE, Wilbert E., "But Some Are More Equal than Others," *American Sociological Review,* 28 (February, 1963), 13-18.

NORTH, C. C., *Social Differentiation,* Chapel Hill: University of North Carolina Press, 1926.

PORTER, James M., Jr., "Consumption Patterns of Professors and Businessmen: A Pilot Study of Conspicuous Consumption and Status," *Sociological Inquiry,* 37 (Spring, 1967), 255-265.

QUEEN, Stuart A., "The Function of Social Stratification: A Critique," *Sociology and Social Research,* 46 (July, 1962), 412-415.

REISSMAN, Leonard, *Class in American Society,* New York: Free Press, 1959, 69-94.

ROSENFELD, Eva, "Social Stratification in a 'Classless Society,'" *American Sociological Review,* 16 (December, 1951), 766-774.

SCHWARTZ, Richard D., "Functional Alternatives to Inequality," *American Sociological Review,* 20 (August, 1955), 424-430.

SEEMAN, Melvin and John W. Evans, "Stratification and Hospital Care: I. The Performance of the Medical Intern," *American Sociological Review,* 26 (February, 1961), 67-80.

SEEMAN, Melvin and John W. Evans, "Stratification and Hospital Care: II. The Objective Criteria of Performance," *American Sociological Review,* 26 (April, 1961), 193-204.

SGAN, Mathew, "On Social Status and Ambivalence," *American Sociological Review,* 26 (February, 1961), 104.

SIMPSON, Richard L., "A Modification of the Functional Theory of Social Stratification," *Social Forces,* 35 (December, 1956), 132-137.

STINCHCOMBE, Arthur L., "Some Empirical Consequences of the Davis-Moore Theory of Stratification," *American Sociological Review,* 28 (October, 1963), 805-808.

TAUSKY, Curt, "Parsons on Stratification: An Analysis and Critique," *Sociological Quarterly,* 6 (Spring, 1965), 128-138.

TUMIN, Melvin M., "Competing Status Systems," in Arnold

FUNCTIONS AND DYSFUNCTIONS OF INEQUALITY

S. Feldman and Wilbert E. Moore, editors, *Labor Commitment and Social Change in Developing Areas,* New York: Social Science Research Council, 1960.

TUMIN, Melvin M., "Obstacles to Creativity," *Review of General Semantics,* 11 (Summer, 1954), 261-271.

TUMIN, Melvin M., "On Inequality," *American Sociological Review,* 28 (February, 1963), 19-26.

TUMIN, Melvin M., "Reply to Kingsley Davis," *American Sociological Review,* 18 (December, 1963), 672-673.

TUMIN, Melvin M., "Rewards and Task-Orientations," *American Sociological Review,* 20 (August, 1955), 419-423.

TUMIN, Melvin M., "Social Conditions for Effective Community Development," *Community Development Review,* (December, 1958), 1-39.

TUMIN, Melvin M., *Social Stratification: The Forms and Functions of Inequality,* Englewood Cliffs, New Jersey: Prentice-Hall, 1967.

TUMIN, Melvin M., "Some Dysfunctions of Institutional Imbalance," *Behavioral Science,* 1 (July, 1956), 218-223.

TUMIN, Melvin M., "Some Principles of Stratification: A Critical Analysis," *American Sociological Review,* 18 (August, 1953), 387-394.

TUMIN, Melvin M. and Arnold S. Feldman, *Social Class and Social Change in Puerto Rico,* Princeton University Press, 1961.

WATSON, Walter B. and Ernest A. T. Barth, "Questionable Assumptions in the Theory of Social Stratification," *Pacific Sociological Review,* 7 (Spring, 1964), 10-16.

WESOTOWSKI, Wtodzimierz, "Some Notes on the Functional Theory of Stratification," in Reinhard Bendix and Seymour M. Lipset, editors, *Class, Status, and Power,* New York: Free Press, 1966. Reprinted from *Polish Sociological Bulletin,* 5-6 (1962), 28-38.

WRONG, Dennis H., "Social Inequality without Social Stratification," *Canadian Review of Sociology and Anthropology,* 1 (Spring, 1964), 5-16.

WRONG, Dennis H., "The Functional Theory of Stratification: Some Neglected Considerations," *American Sociological Review,* 24 (December, 1959), 772-782.

Measurement

The scientific study of social stratification is highly dependent upon techniques of measurement; therefore, this is one of the more important sections of this bibliography. Problems of measurement of stratification variables are especially knotty and will not soon be solved—a fact revealed by examination of almost any of the more recent selections listed here. However, a survey of this literature also reveals substantial progress in the past decade or so.

Since problems of measurement are inextricably linked with other methodological problems and with problems of conceptualization, several publications dealing primarily with these other topics are included in this section. In each case, the relevance to measurement is very direct.

ABU-LABAN, Baha, "The Reputational Approach to the Study of Community Power: A Critical Evaluation," *Pacific Sociological Review,* 8 (Spring, 1965), 35-42.

ADRIAN, Charles R. and David A. Booth, *Simplifying the Discovery of Elites,* East Lansing: Institute for Community Development and Services, Michigan State University.

ALFORD, Robert R., "A Suggested Index of the Association of Social Class and Voting," *Public Opinion Quarterly,* 26 (Fall, 1962) 417-425.

BASSETT, Raymond E., "Sampling Problems in Influence Studies," *Sociometry,* 12 (November, 1948), 320-328.

BECK, James D., "Limitations of One Social Class Index When Comparing Races with Respect to Indices of Health," *Social Forces,* 45 (June, 1967), 586-588.

BELCHER, John C., "Evaluation and Restandardization of Sewell's Socio-economic Scale," *Rural Sociology,* 16 (September, 1951), 246-255.

BELCHER, John C. and E. Sharp, *A Short Scale for Measuring Farm Family Level of Living,* Stillwater: Oklahoma Agricultural Experimental Station Technical Bulletin, 1952.

BILLEWICZ, W. Z., "Some Remarks on the Measurement of Social Mobility," *Population Studies,* 9 (July, 1955), 96-100.

BLALOCK, H. M., Jr., "Comment: Status Inconsistency and the Identification Problem," *Public Opinion Quarterly,* 30 (Spring, 1966), 130-132.

BLALOCK, H. M., Jr., "Status Inconsistency and Interaction: Some Alternative Models," *American Journal of Sociology,* 73 (November, 1967), 305-315.

BLALOCK, H. M., Jr., "Status Inconsistency, Social Mobility, Status Integration and Structural Effects," *American Sociological Review,* 32 (October, 1967), 790-801.

MEASUREMENT

BLALOCK, H. M., Jr., "Tests of Status Inconsistency Theory: A Note of Caution," *Pacific Sociological Review,* 10 (Fall, 1967), 69-74.

BLANKENSHIP, Vaughn, "Community Power and Decision-Making: A Comparative Evaluation of Measurement Techniques," *Social Forces,* 43 (December, 1964), 207-216.

BLAU, Peter M., "Inferring Mobility Trends From a Single Study," *Population Studies,* 16 (July, 1962), 79-85.

BLISHEN, Bernard R., "The Construction and Use of an Occupational Class Scale," *Canadian Journal of Economic and Political Science,* 25 (1958), 519-531.

BLISHEN, Bernard R., "A Socio-Economic Index for Occupations in Canada," *Canadian Review of Sociology and Anthropology,* 4 (1967), 41-53.

BONJEAN, Charles M., "Community Leadership: A Case Study and Conceptual Refinement," *American Journal of Sociology* 68 (May, 1963), 672-681.

BONJEAN, Charles M., Richard J. Hill, and S. Dale McLemore, *Sociological Measurement: An Inventory of Scales and Indices,* San Francisco: Chandler, 1967.

BOOTH, David A. and Charles R. Adrian, "Simplifying the Discovery of Elites," *American Behavioral Scientist,* 5 (October, 1961), 14-16.

CARLSSON, Gosta, *Social Mobility and Class Structure,* Lund: Gleerup, 1958.

CATTELL, Raymond B., "New Concepts for Measuring Leadership in Terms of Group Syntality, *Human Relations,* 4 (1951), 161-184.

CENTERS, Richard, "Toward an Articulation of Two Approaches to Social Class Phenomena: I. Similarities and Differences in Theoretical Formulation, Methods and Results," *International Journal of Opinion and Attitude Research,* 4 (1950), 499-514.

CENTERS, Richard, "Toward an Articulation of Two Approaches to Social Class Phenomena, II: The Index of Status Characteristics and Class Identification," *International Journal of Opinion and Attitude Research,* 5 (1951), 159-178.

CHAPIN, Stuart F., *The Measurement of Social Status by the Use of the Social Status Scale,* Minneapolis: University of Minnesota Press, 1933.

CHAPIN, Stuart F., "A Quantitative Scale for Rating the Home and Social Environments of Middle Class Families in an Urban Community," *Journal of Educational Sociology,* 19 (February, 1928), 99-111.

MEASUREMENT

CLARK, Rodney A. and Carson McQuire, "Sociographic Analysis of Sociometric Valuation," *Child Development,* 23 (1952), 129-140.

COLEMAN, James S., "Foundations for a Theory of Collective Decisions," *American Journal of Sociology,* 71 (May, 1966), 615-627.

COLEMAN, John A., "A Paradigm for the Study of Social Strata," *Sociology and Social Research,* 50 (April, 1966), 338-350.

DALE, George A., "Correlation of Scores Secured by Interview with Scores Based on Observation, For the Sewell Farm Family Socio-Economic Status Scale," *Rural Sociology,* 19 (September, 1954), 291.

D'ANTONIO, William V. and Eugene C. Erickson, "The Reputational Technique for the Study of Community Power," *American Sociological Review,* 27 (June, 1962), 362-375.

DAVIS, James A., "Status Symbols and the Measurement of Status Perception," *Sociometry,* 19 (September, 1956), 154-175.

DEASY, Leila C., "An Index of Social Mobility," *Rural Sociology,* 20 (June, 1955), 149-151.

DICK, Harry R., "A Method for Ranking Community Influentials, *American Sociological Review,* 25 (June, 1960), 395-399.

DUNCAN, Otis Dudley, "Methodological Issues in the Analysis of Social Mobility," in Neil J. Smelser and Seymour M. Lipset, editors, *Social Structure and Mobility in Economic Development,* Chicago: Aldine, 1966.

DUNCAN, Otis Dudley, "A Socioeconomic Index for all Occupations," and "Properties and Characteristics of the Socioeconomic Index," in Albert J. Reiss, Jr., *Occupations and Social Status,* New York: Free Press, 1961.

EDINGER, Lewis J. and Donald D. Searing, "Social Background in Elite Analysis: A Methodological Inquiry," *American Political Science Review,* 61 (June, 1967), 428-445.

EHRLICH, Howard, "The Reputational Approach to the Study of Community Power," *American Sociological Review,* 26 (December, 1961), 926-927.

ELLIS, Robert A., "The Prestige Rating Technique in Community Stratification Research," in Richard N. Adams and Jack J. Preiss, editors, *Human Organization Research: Field Relations and Techniques,* Homewood, Illinois: Dorsey, 1960.

ELLIS, Robert A., W. Clayton Lane, and Virginia Olesen, "The Index of Class Position: An Improved Intercommunity Measure of Stratification," *American Sociological Review,* 28 (April, 1963), 271-277.

EMPEY, LaMar T., "Social Class and Occupational Aspiration: A Comparison of Absolute and Relative Measurement," *American Sociological Review,* 21 (December, 1956), 703-709.

MEASUREMENT

FINCH, F. H. and A. J. Hoechn, "Measuring Socio-Economic or Cultural Status: A Comparison of Methods," *Journal of Social Psychology,* 33 (1951), 51-67.

FREED, Stanley A., "An Objective Method For Determining the Collective Caste Hierarchy of an Indian Village," *American Anthropologist,* 65 (August, 1963), 879-891.

FREEMAN, Howard E. and Camille Lambert, Jr., "The Identification of 'Lower-Class' Families in an Urban Community," in Arthur B. Shostak and William Gomberg, editors, *Blue-Collar World: Studies of the American Worker,* Englewood Cliffs, New Jersey: Prentice-Hall, 1964.

FREEMAN, Linton C., T. J. Fararo, W. J. Bloomberg, and M. H. Sunshine, "Locating Leaders in Local Communities: A Comparison of Some Alternative Approaches," *American Sociological Review,* 28 (October, 1963), 791-798.

FRENCH, Robert M. and Michael Aiken, "Community Power in Cornucopia: A Replication in A Small Community of the Bonjean Technique of Identifying Community Leaders," *Sociological Quarterly,* 9 (Spring, 1968), 261-270.

GABOR, Andre, "The Concept of Statistical Freedom and its Application ot Social Mobility," *Population Studies,* 9 (July, 1955) 82-95.

GESCHWENDER, James A., "On the Proper Use of the GOMS," *Social Forces,* 46 (June, 1968), 545-546.

GESCHWENDER, James A., "Theory and Measurement of Occupational Mobility: A Re-Examination," *American Sociological Review,* 26 (June, 1961) 451-452.

GORDON, Milton M., "The Logic of Socio-Economic Status Scales," *Sociometry,* 15 (August, 1952), 342-353.

GORDON, Milton M., "A System of Social Class Analysis," *Drew University Studies,* No. 2 (August, 1951).

GOUGH, Harrison G., "A New Dimension of Status: I, Development of a Personality Scale," *American Sociological Review,* 13 (August, 1948), 401-409.

GOUGH, Harrison G., "A New Dimension of Status: II, Relationship of the St Scale to Other Variables," *American Sociological Review,* 13 (October, 1948), 543-537.

GOUGH, Harrison G., "A New Dimension of Status: III, Discrepancies Between the St Scale and 'Objective' Status," *American Sociological Review,* 14 (April, 1949), 275-281.

GOUGH, Harrison G., "A Short Social Inventory," *Journal of Educational Psychology,* 40, (January, 1949), 52-56.

GUTTMAN, Louis, "A Revision of Chapin's Social Status Scale," *American Sociological Review,* 7 (June, 1942), 362-369.

MEASUREMENT

HAER, John L. "Predictive Utility of Five Indices of Social Stratification," *American Sociological Review,* 22 (October, 1957) 541-546.

HAER, John L., "A Test of the Unidimensionality of the Index of Status Characteristics," *Social Forces,* 34 (October, 1955) 56-58.

HAGOOD, Margaret J. and Louis J. Ducoff, "What Level of Living Indexes Measure," *American Sociological Review,* 9 (February, 1944), 78-84.

HALLER, Archie O. and Irwin W. Miller, *The Occupational Aspiration Scale,* East Lansing: Michigan State University Technical Bulletin 288, 1963.

HATCH, David L. and Mary A. Hatch, "Criteria of Social Status as Derived from Marriage Announcements in the New York *Times,*" *American Sociological Review,* 12 (August, 1947), 396-403.

HILL, Mozell C. and A. N. Whiting, "Some Theoretical and Methodological Problems in Community Studies," *Social Forces,* 29 (1950), 117-124.

HOCHBAUM, Godfrey, John G. Darley, E. D. Monochesi, and Charles Bird, "Socio-Economic Variables in a Large City, *American Journal of Sociology,* 61 (July, 1955), 31-38.

HODGE, Robert W. and Paul M. Siegel, "The Measurement of Social Class," *International Encyclopedia of the Social Sciences,* 15, New York: Free Press, 1968, 316-325.

HOLLINGSHEAD, August B., "Two Factor Index of Social Position," New Haven: Privately Mimeographed, 1957.

HYMAN, Martin D., "Determining the Effects of Status Inconsistency," *Public Opinion Quarterly,* 30 (Spring, 1966), 120-129.

KAUFMAN, Harold F., "Members of a Rural Community as Judges of Prestige Rank," *Sociometry,* 9 (February, 1946), 71-85.

KAHL, Joseph A., "Some Measurements of Achievement Orientation," *American Journal of Sociology,* 70 (May, 1965), 669-681.

KAHL, Joseph A. and James A. Davis, "A Comparison of Indexes of Socio-Economic Status," *American Sociological Review,* 20 (June, 1955), 317-325.

KAUFMAN, Harold F., *Prestige Classes in a New York Rural Community,* Ithaca: Cornell University Agricultural Experimental Station, 1944.

KAUFMAN, Harold F., Otis Dudley Duncan, Neal Gross, and William H. Sewell, "Problems of Theory and Method in the Study of Social Stratification," *Rural Sociology,* 18 (March, 1953).

KAUFMAN, Harold F. and John E. Dunkleberger, "Classifying Families in Low-Income Rural Areas," *Sociologia,* 22 (June, 1960).

KIMBALL, Solon T. and M. Pearsall, "Event Analysis as an Approach to Community Study," *Social Forces,* 34 (October, 1955), 58-63.

KINCAID, Harry V. and Margaret Bright, "Interviewing the Business Elite," *American Journal of Sociology,* 63 (November, 1957), 304-311.

LARSON, Richard and James L. Olson, "A Method of Identifying Culturally Deprived Kindergarten Children," *Exceptional Children,* 3 (November, 1963), 130-137.

LASSWELL, Thomas E. and Peter F. Parshall, "The Perception of Social Class from Photographs," *Sociology and Social Research,* 45 (July, 1961), 407-414.

LAWSON, Edwin D. and Walter E. Boek, "Correlations of Indexes of Families' Socio-Economic Status," *Social Forces,* 39 (December, 1960), 149-152.

LENSKI, Gerhard E., "Comment on 'Methodological Notes on a Theory of Status Crystallization'," *Public Opinion Quarterly,* 28 (Summer, 1964), 326-330.

LIPSET, Seymour M., "Research Problems in the Comparative Analysis of Mobility and Development," *International Social Science Journal,* 16 (1964), 35-48.

LONGMORE, T. Wilson, "A Matrix Approach to the Analysis of Rank and Status in a Community in Peru," *Sociometry,* 11 (August, 1948), 192-206.

LUNDBERG, George A., "The Measurement of Socioeconomic Status," *American Sociological Review,* 5 (February, 1940), 29-39.

LUNDBERG, George A. and Pearl Freedman, "A Comparison of Three Measures of Socioeconomic Status," *Rural Sociology,* 8 (September, 1943), 227-242.

MACK, Raymond W., "Housing as an Index of Social Class," *Social Forces,* 29 (May, 1951), 391-400.

MAHAR, P. M. A., "A Multiple Scaling Technique for Caste Ranking," *Man in India,* 39 (1959), 127-147.

MAHAR, P. M. A. "A Ritual Pollution Scale for Ranking Hindu Castes," *Sociometry,* 23 (1960), 292-306.

MARCH, James G., "An Introduction to the Theory and Measurement of Influence," *American Political Science Review,* 49 (June, 1955), 431-451.

MARCH, James G., "Measurement Concepts in the Theory of Influence," *Journal of Politics,* 19 (May, 1957), 202-226.

MAU, James A., Richard J. Hill and Wendell Bell, "Scale Analysis of Status Perception and Status Attitude in Jamaica and the United States," *Pacific Sociological Review,* 4 (Spring, 1961) 33-40.

MCQUIRE, Carson and George D. White, "The Measurement of Social Status," *Research Paper in Human Development,* No. 3, revised, Department of Educational Psychology, The University of Texas, March, 1955.

MCTAVISH, Donald G., "A Method for More Reliably Coding Detailed Occupations into Duncan's Socioeconomic Categories," *American Sociological Review,* (June, 1964), 402-406.

MICHEL, Jerry, "Measurement of Social Power on the Community Level," *American Journal of Economics and Sociology,* 23 (April, 1964), 189-196.

MILLER, Andreas, "The Problem of Class Boundaries and its Significance for Research into Class Boundaries," *Transactions of the Second World Congress of Sociology,* 2 (1954), 343-352.

MILLER, Delbert C., *Handbook of Research Design and Social Measurement,* New York: McKay, 1964.

MILLER, Delbert C. and James L. Dirksen, "The Identification of Visible, Concealed, and Symbolic Leaders in a Small Indiana City: A Replication of the Bonjean-Noland Study of Burlington, North Carolina," *Social Forces,* 43 (December, 1964), 207-216.

MILLER, Delbert C. and William H. Form, "Measuring Patterns of Occupational Security," *Sociometry,* 10 (November, 1947), 362-375.

MILLER, Irwin W. and Archie O. Haller, "A Measure of Level of Occupational Aspirations," *Personnel and Guidance Journal,* 42 (January, 1964), 448-455.

MILLER, S. M., "The Concept and Measurement of Mobility," *Transactions of the Third World Congress of Sociology,* 3 (1956), 144-154.

MITCHELL, Robert E., "Methodological Notes on a Theory of Status Crystallization," *Public Opinion Quarterly,* 28, (Summer, 1964), 315-325.

MORRISON, Denton E., "Achievement Motivation of Farm Operators: A Measurement Study," *Rural Sociology,* 29 (December, 1964), 367-384.

MUKHERJEE, Ramkrishna and John R. Hill, "A Note on the Analysis of Data on Social Mobility," in David V. Glass, editor, *Social Mobility in Britain,* London: Routledge and Kegan Paul, 1954.

MURRAY, Walter, "Measuring the Social-Class Status of Negro Children in the Elementary and High School," *Journal of Educational Sociology,* 25 (October, 1951), 102-111.

NELSON, Harold A. and Thomas E. Lasswell, "Status Indices, Social Stratification, and Social Class," *Sociology and Social Research,* 44 (July-August, 1960), 410-413.

NELSON, Harold A. and Edward C. McDonagh, "Perception of Statuses and Images of Selected Professions," *Sociology and Social Research,* 46 (October, 1961), 3-16.

PAYNE, Raymond, "An Approach to the Study of Relative Prestige of Formal Organizations," *Social Forces,* 32 (March, 1954),244-247.

POLSBY, Nelson W. "How to Study Community Power: The Pluralist Alternative," *Journal of Politics,* 22 (August, 1960), 474-484.

PORTER, John, "Elite Groups: A Scheme for the Study of Power in Canada," *Canadian Journal of Economics and Political Science,* 21 (November, 1955), 498-512.

PRAIS, S. J., "Measuring Social Mobility," *Statistical Journal,* 118 (1955), 56-66.

REISS, Albert J. Jr., *Occupations and Social Status,* New York: Free Press, 1962.

REISS, Albert J. Jr., "Some Logical and Methodological Problems in Community Research," *Social Forces,* 33 (October, 1954), 51-57.

ROSSI, Peter H. and Alex Inkeles, "Multidimensional Ratings of Occupations," *Sociometry,* 20 (September, 1957), 234-251.

SARIOLA, Sakari, "Defining Social Class in Two Finnish Communities," *Transactions of the Second World Congress of Sociology,* 2 (1954), 108-118.

SARIOLA, Sakari, "Defining Social Class in Two Finnish Localities," *Transactions of the Westermarck Society,* 11 (1953), 134-147.

SCHEUCH, Erwin K. and Dietrich Ruschemeyer, "Scaling Social Status in Western Germany," *British Journal of Sociology,* 9 (June, 1960), 151-168.

SCHULZE, Robert O. and Leonard U. Blumberg, "The Determination of Local Power Elites," *American Journal of Sociology,* 63 (November, 1957), 290-296.

SCOTT, W., "Some Remarks on the Measurement of Social Mobility—A Reply," *Population Studies,* 9 (July, 1955), 102-103.

SCUDDER, Richard and C. Arnold Anderson, "Range of Acquaintance and of Repute as Factors in Prestige Rating: Methods of Studying Social Status," *Social Forces,* 32 March, 1954) 248-253.

SCUDDER, Richard and C. Arnold Anderson, "The Relation of Being Known to Status Rating," *Sociology and Social Research,* 38 (March-April, 1954), 239-241.

MEASUREMENT

SEEMAN, Melvin, J. W. Evans, and L. E. Rogers, "The Measurement of Stratification In Formal Organizations," *Human Organization,* 19 (1960), 90-96.

MEASUREMENT

SEWELL, William H., *The Construction and Standardization of a Scale for the Measurement of Socio-Economic Status of Oklahoma Farm Families,* Stillwater: Oklahoma Agricultural Experiment Station Technical Bulletin, No. 9, 1940.

SEWELL, William H., "A Scale for the Measurement of Farm Family Socio-Economic Status," *Southwestern Social Science Quarterly,* 21 (September, 1940), 125-137.

SEWELL, William H., "A Short Form of the Farm Family Socioeconomic Status Scale," *Rural Sociology,* 8 (June, 1943), 161-170.

SHIMBORI, Michiya, Hideo Ikeda, Tsuyoshi Ishida, and Moto Kondo, "Measuring a Nation's Prestige," *American Journal of Sociology,"* 69 (July, 1963), 63-68.

SILVERMAN, Sydel, "An Ethnographic Approach to Social Stratification: Prestige in a Central Italian Community," *American Anthropologist,* 68 (August, 1966), 899-921.

SIMON, Herbert, "Notes on the Observation and Measurement of Political Power," *Journal of Politics,* 15 (November, 1953), 500-516.

SIMPSON, Richard L. and Ida Harper Simpson, "Correlates and Estimation of Occupational Prestige," *American Journal of Sociology,* 66 (September, 1960), 135-140.

SIMS, V. M., *Manual for SCI Occupational Rating Scale,* Yonkers-on-Hudson: World Book Company, 1952.

SMITH, J. and T. Hood, "The Delineation of Community Power Structure by a Reputational Approach," *Sociological Inquiry,* 36 (Winter, 1966), 3-14.

SNYDER, Richard C., H. W. Bruck, and Burton Sapin, "The Decision-Making Approach," in H. Eulau, S. J. Eldersveld, and M. Janowitz, editors, *Political Behavior,* New York: Free Press, 1956.

SOLLIE, Carlton R., "A Comparison of Reputational Techniques for Identifying Leaders," *Rural Sociology,* 31 (September, 1966), 301-309.

SVALASTOGA, Kaare, "Measurement of Occupational Prestige: Field Techniques," *Transactions of the Second World Congress of Sociology,* 2 (1954), 403-413.

SVALASTOGA, Kaare, *Social Differentiation,* New York: McKay, 1965.

TANNENBAUM, Arnold, "An Event Structure Approach to Social Power and to the Problem of Power Comparability," *Behavioral Science,* 7 (July, 1962), 315-331.

TUMIN, Melvin M. and Arnold S. Feldman, "Theory and Measurement of Occupational Mobility," *American Sociological Review*, 22 (June, 1957), 281-288.

U. S. BUREAU OF THE CENSUS, *Methodology and Scores of Socioeconomic Status, Working Paper 15,* Washington, D. C., Government Printing Office, 1963.

VAN HEEK, F., "The Method of Extreme Types as a Tool for the Study of the Causes of Vertical Mobility," *Transactions of the Second World Congress of Sociology,* 2 (1954), 391-395.

VAUGHAN, Charles L., "A Scale for Assessing Socio-Economic Status in Survey Research," *Public Opinion Quarterly,* 22 (Spring, 1958), 19-34.

WALLIN, Paul, and Leslie C. Waldo, "Indeterminancies in Ranking of Father's Occupations," *Public Opinion Quarterly,* 28 (Summer, 1964) 287-292.

WALTON, John, "Discipline, Method and Community Power: A Note on the Sociology of Knowledge," *American Sociological Review,* 31 (October, 1966), 684-689.

WARNER, W. Lloyd, "A Methodology for the Study of Social Class," in Meyer Fortes, editor, *Social Structure,* New York: Oxford University Press, 1949.

WARNER, W. Lloyd, Marchia Meeker and Kenneth Eells, *Social Class in America: A Manual of Procedure for the Measurement of Social Status,* New York: Science Research Associates, 1949.

WESTIE, Frank R., "Social Distance Scales: A Tool for the Study of Stratification," *Sociology and Social Research,* 43 (March-April, 1959), 251-258.

WHITE, Harrison C., "Cause and Effect in Social Mobility Tables," *Behavioral Science,* 8 (1963), 14-27.

WHITE, James E., "Theory and Method for Research in Community Leadership," *American Sociological Review,* 15 (February, 1950), 50-60.

WILENSKY, Harold L., "Measures and Effects of Mobility," in Neil J. Smelser and Seymour M. Lipset, editors, *Social Structure and Mobility in Economic Development,* Chicago: Aldine, 1966.

WITHEY, Stephen B., "Reliability of Recall of Income," *Public Opinion Quarterly,* 18 (Summer, 1954), 197-204.

WOLFINGER, Raymond, "A Plea for a Decent Burial," *American Sociological Review,* 27 (December, 1962), 841-847.

WOLFINGER, Raymond, "Reputation and Reality in the Study of 'Community Power,' " *American Sociological Review,* 25 (October, 1960), 636-644.

YASUDA, Saburo, "A Methodological Inquiry into Social Mobility," *American Sociological Review,* 29 (February, 1964), 16-23.

YAUKEY, David, "A Metric Measurement of Occupational Status," *Sociology and Social Research,* 39 (May-June, 1955), 317-323.

ZELENY, Leslie D., "Measurement of Social Status," *American Journal of Sociology,* 45 (January, 1940), 576-582.

ZELENY, Leslie D., "Status: Its Measurement and Control in Education," *Sociometry,* 4 (May, 1941), 193-204.

Class Conflict and Other Aspects

of Inter-Class Relations

The term class as used in the stratification literature has a variety of meanings; therefore, relations between and among several kinds of entities are treated in the publications in this section. A few of the publications deal with relations among Asiatic castes. A very large portion of the stratification literature deals at least incidentally with inter-class relations, but we include here only publications focused quite specifically upon those relations. Furthermore, we list little of the vast body of literature on labor-management relations found outside the sociological journals.

Many closely related publications are found under the topic "Correlates of Stratification: Class Consciousness and Related Psychological Correlates."

AGGER, Robert E., Daniel Goldrich, and Bert E. Swanson, *The Rulers and the Ruled,* New York: Wiley, 1964.

ANDERSON, Dewey and Percy E. Davidson, *Ballots and the Democratic Class Struggle: A Study in the Background of Political Education,* Stanford: Stanford University Press, 1943.

ANDERSON, Elin, *We Americans: A Study of Cleavage in an American City,* Cambridge: Harvard University Press, 1938.

ANDRESKI, Stanislav, *Partisanism and Subversion: The Case of Latin America,* New York: Pantheon, 1967.

ARENDT, Hannah, *On Revolution,* New York: Viking, 1965.

BENDIX, Reinhard and Seymour M. Lipset, "Karl Marx's Theory of Social Classes," in Reinhard Bendix and Seymour M. Lipset, editors, *Class, Status, and Power,* 2nd edition, New York: Free Press, 1966.

BEQIRAJ, Mehmet, *Peasantry in Revolution,* Ithaca, New York: Center for International Studies, Cornell University, 1966.

BLUM, Jerome, *Lord and Peasant in Russia from the Ninth to the Nineteenth Century,* Princeton: Princeton University Press, 1961.

BOTTOMORE, T. B., editor, *Karl Marx: Early Writings*, London: Watts, 1963.

BURNS, Tom, "The Cold Class War," *New Statesman and Nation*, (April 7, 1956).

COLE, G. D. H. and A. W. Filson, editors, *British Working Class Movements*, New York: Macmillan, 1965.

COX, Oliver C., "Modern Democracy and the Class Struggle," *Journal of Negro Education*, 16 (1947), 155-164.

CROOK, Isabel and David Crook, *Revolution in a Chinese Village: Ten Mile Inn*, London: Routledge and Kegan Paul, 1959.

CURTIS, Richard F., "Differential Association and the Stratification of the Urban Community," *Social Forces*, 42 (October, 1963), 68-77.

DAHRENDORF, Ralf, *Class and Class Conflict in Industrial Society*, Stanford: Stanford University Press, 1959.

DAHRENDORF, Ralf, "Conflict and Liberty: Some Remarks on the Social Structure of German Politics," *British Journal of Sociology*, 14 (September, 1963), 197-211.

DAHRENDORF, Ralf, "Social Structure, Class Interests and Social Conflict," *Transactions of the Third World Congress of Sociology*, 3 (1956), 291-296.

DE KADT, Emanuel J., "Conflict and Power in Society," *International Social Science Journal*, 17 (1965), 454-471.

DE TOCQUEVILLE, Alexis, "How Democracy Affects the Relations of Masters and Servants," in Reinhard Bendix and Seymour M. Lipset, editors, *Class, Status, and Power*, revised edition, New York: Free Press, 1966.

DICK, Harry R., "The Office Worker: Attitudes Toward Self, Labor, Management," *Sociological Quarterly*, 3 (January, 1962), 45-56.

EVAN, William M., "Power, Bargaining, and Law: A Preliminary Analysis of Labor Arbitration Cases," *Social Problems*, 7 (Summer, 1959), 4-15.

FEI, Hsiao-Tung, "Peasantry and Gentry: An Interpretation of Chinese Social Structure and Its Changes," in Reinhard Bendix and Seymour M. Lipset, editors, *Class, Status, and Power*, New York: Free Press, 1953.

GRIMSHAW, Allen D., "Three Views of Urban Violence: Civil Disturbance, Racial Revolt, Class Assault," *American Behavioral Scientist*, 11 (March-April, 1968), 2-7.

GUIDON, Hubert, "Social Unrest, Social Class and Quebec's Bureaucratic Revolution," *Queen's Quarterly*, 71 (Summer, 1964), 150-162.

GUPTA, Raghuraj, "Caste Ranking and Inter-Caste Relations Among Muslims of a Village in Northwestern Uttar Pradesh," *Eastern Anthropologist,* 10 (1956), 30-42.

CLASS CONFLICT

HILDEBRAND, George H., "American Unionism, Social Stratification, and Power," *American Journal of Sociology,* 58 (January, 1953), 381-390.

INKELES, Alex, "Images of Class Relations Among Former Soviet Citizens," *Social Problems,* 3 (January 1956), 180-196.

JANOWITZ, Morris and David R. Segal, "Social Cleavage and Party Affiliation: Germany, Great Britain, and the United States," *American Journal of Sociology,* 72 (May, 1967), 601-618.

JONES, Alfred W., "Class Consciousness and Property," in Reinhard Bendix and Seymour M. Lipset, *Class, Status, and Power,* New York: Free Press, 1953.

JONES, Alfred W., *Life, Liberty, and Property,* Philadelphia: Lippincott, 1941.

KAUTSKY, Karl, *The Social Revolution,* Chicago: Kerr, 1903.

KING, C. Wendell, "Social Cleavage in a New England Community," *Social Forces,* 24 (1945-1946), 322-327.

LEVENTMAN, Seymour, "Class and Ethnic Tensions: Minority Group Leadership in Transition," *Sociology and Social Research,* 50 (April, 1966), 371-376.

LEWIS, Lionel S., "Class Consciousness and Inter-Class Sentiments," *Sociological Quarterly,* 6 (Autumn, 1965), 325-338.

LEWIS, Ralph, "Officer-Enlisted Men's Relationships," *American Journal of Sociology,* 52 (March, 1947), 410-419.

LIPSET, Seymour M., *Revolution and Counterrevolution: Change and Persistence in Social Structures,* New York: Basic Books, 1968.

LIPSET, Seymour M., "Trade Unions and Social Structure," *Industrial Relations,* 1 (October, 1961), 75-89.

LOPREATO, Joseph, "Authority Relations and Class Conflict," *Social Forces,* 47 (December, 1968), 70-79.

LYND, Robert S. and Helen M. Lynd, *Middletown,* New York: Harcourt Brace, 1929.

LYND, Robert S. and Helen M. Lynd, *Middletown in Transition,* New York: Harcourt Brace, 1937.

LYND, Staughton, *Class Conflict, Slavery, and the United States Constitution,* Indianapolis: Bobbs-Merrill, 1967.

MACK, Raymond W., "Race, Class, and Power in Barbados: A Study of Stratification as an Integrating Force in a Democratic Revolution," in Herbert R. Barringer, George Blanksten, and

Raymond W. Mack, editors, *Social Change in Developing Areas*, Cambridge: Schenkman, 1966.

MACRAE, Donald G., "Class Relationships and Ideology," *Sociological Review*, 6 (December, 1958), 261-272.

MAJUMDAR, D. N., "Inter-Caste Relations in Gohanakallan, A Village Near Lucknow," *Eastern Anthropologist*, 8 (1955) 191-214.

MANDELBAUM, D. G., "Role Variation in Caste Relations," in T. N. Madan and G. Sarana, editors, *Indian Anthropology: Essays in Honor of D. N. Majumdar*, Bombay: Asia Publishing House, 1962.

MARSHALL, T. H., editor, *Class, Conflict and Social Stratification*, Ledbury: Institute of Sociology, Le Play House, 1938.

MARSHALL, T. H., "The Nature of Class Conflict," in his *Class, Citizenship, and Social Development*, Garden City, New York: Doubleday, 1965.

MARX, Karl, *Captial, The Communist Manifesto, and Other Writings*, edited by Max Eastman, New York: Modern Library, 1932.

MARX, Karl, *Class Struggles in France, 1848-1850*, New York: International Publishers, 1964.

MARX, Karl, *Karl Marx, Early Writings*, translated and edited by T. B. Bottomore, London: Watts, 1963.

MARX, Karl, *Selected Works*, edited by V. Adoratsky, London: Lawrence and Wishart, 1942.

MARX, Karl, *Selected Works of Karl Marx*, New York: International Publishers, 1933.

MARX, Karl, *Selected Writings in Sociology and Social Philosophy*, edited by T. B. Bottomore and Maximillien Rubel, London: Watts, 1956.

MARX, Karl and Friedrich Engels, *Basic Writings on Politics and Philosophy*, edited by Lewis S. Feuer, Garden City, New York: Doubleday, 1959.

MARX, Karl and Friedrich Engels, *The Communist Manifesto*, New York: Washington Square Press, 1964.

MARX, Karl and Friedrich Engels, *The German Ideology*, edited by R. Pascal, New York: International Publishers, 1947.

MARX, Karl and Friedrich Engels, *On Britain*, Moscow: Foreign Publishing House, 1953.

MARX, Karl and Friedrich Engels, *Selected Correspondence: 1846-1895*, translated by Dona Torr, New York: International Publishers, 1942.

MATSUSHIMA, Shizuo, "Labour Management Relations," in Joseph Kahl, editor, *Comparative Perspectives on Stratification,* Boston: Little, Brown, 1968.

CLASS CONFLICT

MEUSEL, A., "Revolution and Counter-Revolution," in *Encyclopedia of the Social Sciences,* New York: Macmillan, 13 (1930), 367-376.

MOORE, Barrington, Jr., "A Comparative Analysis of the Class Struggle," *American Sociological Review,* 10 (February, 1945), 31-37.

MOORE, Barrington, Jr., *Social Origins of Dictatorship and Democracy: Lord and Peasant in the Making of the Modern World,* Boston: Beacon Press, 1966.

O'NEILL, J., "Alienation, Class Struggle, and Marxian Anti-Politics," *Review of Metaphysics,* 17 (March, 1964), 462-471.

PARSONS, Talcott, "Social Classes and Class Conflict in the Light of Recent Sociological Theory," *American Economic Review,* 39 (1949), 16-26.

PARSONS, Talcott, "Voting and the Equilibrium of the American Political System," in E. Burdick and A. Brodbeck, editors, *American Voting Behavior,* New York: Free Press, 1959.

PIKE, F. B., "Aspects of Class Relations in Chile," *Hispanic American Historical Review,* 43 (1963), 14-33.

PINARD, Maurice, "Poverty and Political Movements," *Social Problems,* 15 (Fall, 1967), 250-263.

RATH, R. and N. C. Sicar, "Intercaste Relationship as Reflected in the Study of Attitudes and Opinions of Six Hindu Caste Groups," *Journal of Social Psychology,* 51 (1960), 3-25.

REED, Nelson, *The Caste War of Yucatan,* Stanford: Stanford University Press, 1964.

REISSMAN, Leonard, "Class and Power: The Sacred and the Profane," *Views,* 6 (Autumn, 1964), 46-51.

RIESMAN, David, "The Intellectuals and the Discontented Classes: Some Further Reflections," *Partisan Review,* 29 (Spring, 1962), 250-262.

ROBERTS, John M. and Fredrick Koenig, "Focused and Distributed Status Affinity," *Sociological Quarterly,* 9 (Spring, 1968), 150-157.

SABOUL, A., "Classes and Class Struggles during the French Revolution," *Science and Society,* 17 (Summer, 1953), 238-257.

SCHUMPETER, Joseph A., *Imperialism and Social Class,* New York: Kelley, 1951, 131-221.

SIMPSON, George Eaton, "The Ras Tafari Movement in Jamaica:

A Study of Race and Class Conflict," *Social Forces,* 34 (December, 1955), 167-171.

SINGH, Kailash K., *Inter-Caste Tension in Two Villages in North India,* Ithaca: Cornell University Press, 1957.

SOREL, Georges, *Reflections on Violence,* New York: Free Press, 1950.

SPINRAD, William, "Blue-Collar Workers as City and Suburban Residents—Effects on Union Membership," in Arthur B. Shosak and William Gomberg, editors, *Blue-Collar World: Studies of the American Worker,* Englewood Cliffs, New Jersey: Prentice-Hall 1964.

STONE, Robert C., "Conflicting Approaches to the Study of Worker-Manager Relations," *Social Forces,* 31 (December, 1952), 117-124.

SUMNER, William Graham, *What Social Classes Owe to Each Other,* New York: Harper, 1883.

ULC, Otto, "Class Struggle and Socialist Justice: The Case of Czechoslovakia," *American Political Science Review,* 56, 727-743.

VARMA, V. P., "Class Struggle and Democratic Dynamics," *Indian Journal of Political Science,* 14 (July-September, 1953), 172-187.

WINGFIELD, Roland and Vernon J. Parenton, "Class Structure and Class Conflict in Haitian Society," *Social Forces,* 43 (March, 1965), 338-347.

ZEIGLER, Harmon, *Interest Groups in American Society,* Englewood Cliffs, New Jersey: Prentice-Hall, 1964.

ZEITLIN, Maurice, *Revolutionary Politics and the Cuban Working Class,* Princeton; Princeton University Press, 1967.

Community Studies and Critiques
and Summaries of Community Studies

The era of community stratification studies in American sociology has ended. Most of the publications listed in this section date from the 1940's and early 1950's. However, they remain of interest to students of social stratification in the United States, if only because they dominated stratification research when sociologists in this country first developed a major interest in "class" and related phenomena. There is still a lively interest in community power studies, but the publications reporting those studies are listed in a separate section.

ALLAH, I., "Caste, Patti and Faction in the Life of a Punjab Village," *Sociologus*, 8 (1958), 170-186.

ANDERSON, E. L., *We Americans: A Study of Cleavage in an American City*, Cambridge: Harvard University Press, 1937.

ARENSBERG, Conrad M., "American Communities," *American Anthropologist*, 57 (December, 1955), 1143-1162.

BALTZELL, E. Digby, *An American Business Aristocracy*, New York: Collier, 1962.

BALTZELL, E. Digby, *Philadelphia Gentlemen*, New York: Free Press, 1958.

BERGER, Bennett, *Working-Class Suburb*, Berkeley: University of California Press, 1960.

BLUMENTHAL, Albert, *Small Town Stuff*, Chicago: University of Chicago Press, 1932.

CANCIAN, Frank, *Economics and Prestige in a Maya Community: The Religious Cargo System in Zinacantan*, Stanford: Stanford University Press, 1965.

CROOK, Isabel and David Crook, *Revolution in a Chinese Village, Ten Mile Inn*, London: Routedge and Kegan Paul, 1959.

CUBER, John F. and William Kenkel, *Social Stratification in the United States*, New York: Appleton-Century-Crofts, 1954.

DANIELS, John, *In Freedom's Birthplace*, Boston: Houghton Mifflin, 1914.

DARELY, John G., E. D. Monachesi, and Charles Bird, "Socio-Economic Variables in a Large City," *American Journal of Sociology*, 61 (July, 1955), 31-38.

DAVIS, Allison, Burleigh Gardner, and Mary R. Gardner, *Deep South*, Chicago: University of Chicago Press, 1941.

DEAN, Lois, "Minersville: A Study in Socioeconomic Stagnation," *Human Organization*, 24 (Fall, 1965), 254-261.

DOBRINER, William M., *Class in Suburbia*, Englewood Cliffs, New Jersey: Prentice-Hall, 1963.

DOLLARD, John, *Caste and Class in a Southern Town*, New Haven: Yale University Press, 1937.

DRAKE, St. Clair and Horace R. Cayton, *Black Metropolis*, New York: Harcourt, Brace, 1945.

DUBE, S. C. *Indian Village*, New York: Harper and Row, 1967.

DUBOIS, W. E. B., *The Philadelphia Negro*, Philadelphia: University of Pennsylvania Press, 1901.

DUNCAN, Otis Dudley and Jay W. Artis, *Social Stratification in* a *Pennsylvania Rural Community,* Pennsylvania State College, School of Agriculture, Bulletin 543, October, 1951.

DUNCAN, Otis Dudley and Jay W. Artis, "Some Problems of Stratification Research," *Rural Sociology,* 16 (March, 1951), 17-29.

ELLIS, Robert A., "The Prestige Rating Technique in Community Stratification Research," in Richard N. Adams and Jack J. Preiss, editors, *Human Organization Research: Field Relations and Techniques,* Homewood, Illinois: Dorsey, 1960.

FAUNCE, William A. and Donald A. Clelland, "Professionalization and Stratification Patterns in an Industrial Community," *American Journal of Sociology,* 72 (January, 1967), 341-350.

FAUNCE, William A. and M. Joseph Smucker, "Industrialization and Community Status Structure," *American Sociological Review,* 31 (June, 1966), 390-399.

FORM, William H., "Status Stratification in a Planned Community," *American Sociological Review,* 10 (October, 1945), 605-613.

FOSTER, Philip J., "Status, Power and Education in a Traditional Community," *School Review,* 72 (Summer, 1967), 158-182.

GALLAHER, Art, Jr., *Plainville Fifteen Years Later,* New York: Columbia University Press, 1961.

GANS, Herbert J., *The Levittowners: Ways of Life and Politics in a New Suburban Community,* New York: Pantheon, 1967.

GANS, Herbert J., *The Urban Villagers: Group and Class in the Life of Italian-Americans,* New York: Free Press, 1962.

GOLDSCHMIDT, Walter, "America's Social Classes," *Commentary,* 10 (August, 1950), 175-181.

GOLDSCHMIDT, Walter, *As You Sow,* New York: Free Press, 1947.

GOLDSCHMIDT, Walter, "Social Class and the Dynamics of Status in America," *American Anthropologist,* 57 (December, 1955), 1209-1217.

GOLDSCHMIDT, Walter, "Social Class in America—A Critical Review," *American Anthropologist,* 52 (October-December, 1950), 483-619.

GORDON, Milton M., *Social Class in American Sociology,* Durham, North Carolina: Duke University Press, 1958.

GULICK, John, *Tripoli: A Modern Arab City,* Cambridge: Harvard University Press, 1967.

HALPERN, Joel M., *A Serbian Village,* revised edition, New York; Harper and Row, 1967.

HAMMOND, S. B., "Stratification in an Australian City," in Guy

E. Swanson, T. M. Newcomb, and E. L. Hartley, editors, *Readings in Social Psychology,* revised edition, New York: Holt, 1952.

COMMUNITY STUDIES

HATT, Paul K. "Stratification in the Mass Society," *American Sociological Review,* 15 (April, 1950), 216-222.

HAVIGHURST, Robert J., Robert H. Bowman, Gordon P. Liddle, Charles V. Matthews, and James V. Pierce, *Growing Up in River City,* New York: Wiley, 1962.

HICKEY, Gerald Cannon, *Village in Vietnam,* New Haven: Yale University Press, 1967.

HILL, Mozell C., "A Comparative Analysis of the All-Negro Society in Oklahoma," *Social Forces,* 25 (October, 1946), 70-77.

HILL, Mozell C. and Bevode C. McCall, "Social Stratification in 'Georgia Town'," *American Sociological Review,* 15 (December, 1950), 721-729.

HILL, Mozell C. and A. N. Whiting, "Some Theoretical and Methodological Problems in Community Studies," *Social Forces,* 29 (1950), 117-124.

HOLLINGSHEAD, August B., "Class and Kinship in a Middle Western Community," *American Sociological Review,* 14 (August, 1949), 469-475.

HOLLINGSHEAD, August B., "Community Research: Development and Present Condition," *American Sociological Review,* 13 (April, 1948), 136-146.

HOLLINGSHEAD, August B., *Elmtown's Youth: The Impact of Social Classes on Adolescents,* New York: Wiley, 1949.

HOLLINGSHEAD, August B., "Selected Characteristics of Classes in a Middle Western Community," *American Sociological Review,* 12 (1947), 385-395.

HUMPHREY, Norman D., "Social Stratification in a Mexican Town," *Southwestern Journal of Anthropology,* 5 (1949), 138-146.

IVERSON, Noel, *Germania, U. S. A.: Social Change in New Ulm, Minnesota,* Minneapolis: University of Minnesota Press, 1967.

JONES, Alfred Winslow, *Life, Liberty, and Property,* Philadelphia: Lippincott, 1941.

JONES, Clifton R., "Social Stratification in the Negro Population: A Study of Social Classes in South Boston, Virginia," *Journal of Negro Education,* 15 (Winter, 1946), 4-12.

KAUFMAN, Harold F., "An Approach to the Study of Urban

Stratification," *American Sociological Review,* 17 (August, 1952), 430-437.

KAUFMAN, Harold F., "Defining Prestige Rank in a Rural Community," *Sociometry,* 8 (May, 1945), 199-207.

KAUFMAN, Harold F., "Members of a Rural Community as Judges of Prestige Rank," *Sociometry,* 9 (February, 1946), 71-85.

KAUFMAN, Harold F., *Prestige Classes in a New York Rural Community,* Ithaca: Cornell University Agricultural Experiment Station, Memoir 260, March, 1944.

KING, Charles E., "The Process of Social Stratification Among an Urban Minority Population," *Social Forces,* 31 (May, 1953), 352-355.

KING, C. Wendell, "Social Cleavage in a New England Community," *Social Forces,* 24 (1945-1946), 322-327.

KORNHAUSER, Ruth Rosner, "The Warner Approach to Social Stratification" in Reinhard Bendix and Seymour M. Lipset, editors, *Class, Status, and Power,* New York: Free Press, 1953.

KORSON, J. Henry, "Dower and Social Class in an Urban Muslim Community," *Journal of Marriage and the Family,* 29 (August, 1967), 527-533.

LANTZ, Herman R., *People of Coal Town,* New York: Columbia University Press, 1958.

LANTZ, Herman R., "Resignation, Industrialization, and the Problem of Social Change: A Case History of a Coal-Mining Community," in Arthur B. Shostak and William Gomberg, editors, *Blue-Collar World: Studies of the American Worker,* Englewood Cliffs, New Jersey: Prentice Hall, 1964.

LASSWELL, Thomas E., "A Study of Social Stratification Using An Area Sample of Raters," *American Sociological Review,* 19 (June, 1954), 310-313.

LAUMANN, Edward O., *Prestige and Association in an Urban Community: An Analysis of An Urban Stratification System,* Indianapolis: Bobbs-Merrill, 1966.

LAUMANN, Edward O. and Louis Guttman, "The Relative Associational Contiguity of Occupations in an Urban Setting," *American Sociological Review,* 31 (April, 1966), 169-178.

LENSKI, Gerhard E., "American Social Classes: Statistical Strata or Social Groups?" *American Journal of Sociology,* 58 (September, 1952), 139-149.

LEWIS, Hylan, *Blackways of Kent,* Chapel Hill: University of North Carolina Press, 1955.

LEWIS, Lionel S., "A Note on the Problem of Classes," *Public Opinion Quarterly,* 27 (Winter, 1963), 599-603.

LIEBOW, Elliot, *Tally's Corner: A Study of Negro Street-corner Men,* Boston: Little, Brown, 1968.

COMMUNITY STUDIES

LIPSET, Seymour M. and Reinhard Bendix, "Social Status and Social Structure: A Re-examination of Data and Interpretations I and II," *British Journal of Sociology,* 2 (1951) 150-168 and 230-254.

LISON-TOLOSANA, Carmelo, *Belmonte de los Caballeros: A Sociological Study of a Spanish Town,* New York: Oxford University Press, 1966.

LONGMORE, T. Wilson, "A Matrix Approach to the Analysis of Rank and Status in a Community in Peru," *Sociometry* 11 (August, 1948), 192-206.

LOOMIS, Charles P. and Reed M. Powell, "Sociometric Analysis of Class Status in Rural Costa Rica—A Peasant Community Compared with an Hacienda Community," *Sociometry,* 12 (February, 1949), 144-157.

LUNDBERG, George A., "Social Attraction Patterns in a Rural Village: A Preliminary Report," *Sociometry,* 1 (July-October, 1937), 77-80.

LUNDBERG, George A. and Margaret Lawsing, "The Sociography of Some Community Relations," *American Sociological Review,* 2 (June, 1937), 318-335.

LUNDBERG, George A. and Mary Steele, "Social Attraction Patterns in a Village," *Sociometry,* 1 (January-April, 1938), 375-419.

LYND, Robert S. and Helen Merrell Lynd, *Middletown,* New York: Harcourt, Brace, 1929.

LYND., Robert S. and Helen Merrell Lynd, *Middletown in Transition,* New York: Harcourt, Brace, 1937.

MARANELL, Gary M., "Stratification in a Small Town: An Attempt to Replicate," *Sociological Quarterly,* 8 (Spring, 1967), 259-263.

MATHIESON, Thomas, "Aspects of Social Stratification in a Changing Community," *Acta Sociologica,* 4, 42-54.

MILLER, S. M., "Social Class and the 'Typical' American Community," *American Sociological Review,* 15 (April, 1950), 294-295.

MILLS, C. Wright, "The Middle Classes in Middle-Sized Cities: The Stratification and Political Position of Small Business and White Collar Strata," *American Sociological Review,* 11 (October, 1946), 520-529.

MORLAND, J. Kenneth, "Kent Revisited: Blue-Collar Aspirations and Achievements," in Arthur B. Shostak and William Gomberg, editors, *Blue-Collar World: Studies of the American Worker,* Englewood Cliffs, New Jersey: Prentice Hall, 1964.

MORLAND, J. Kenneth, *Millways of Kent,* Chapel Hill: University of North Carolina Press, 1958.

PFAUTZ, Harold W. and Otis Dudley Duncan, "A Critical Evaluation of Warner's Work in Community Stratification," *American Sociological Review,* 15 (April, 1950), 205-215.

POWDERMAKER, Hortense, *After Freedom,* New York: Viking, 1939.

RENNIE, Douglas, "A Rejoinder to 'Stratification in a Small Town: An Attempt to Replicate'," *Sociological Quarterly,* 8 (Spring, 1967), 263-264.

RENNIE, Douglas and Robert Hilgendorf, "Stratification in a Small Town," *Sociological Quarterly,* 1 (April, 1960), 117-128.

RESEARCH COMMITTEE, Japan Sociological Society, "Social Stratification and Mobility in the Six Large Cities of Japan," *Transactions of the Second World Congress of Sociology,* 2 (1954), 414-431.

ROHRER, John H. and Munro S. Edmonson, editors, *The Eighth Generation,* New York: Harper and Row, 1960.

SARIOLA, Sakari, "Defining Social Class in Two Finnish Communities," *Transactions of the Second World Congress of Sociology,* 2 (1954), 108-118.

SARIOLA, Sakari, *Social Class and Social Mobility in a Costa Rican Town,* Turrialba: Inter-American Institute of Agricultural Sciences, 1954.

SCHULER, Edgar A., "Social and Economic Status in a Louisiana Hills Community," *Rural Sociology,* 5 (March, 1940), 69-89.

SEELEY, John, R. A. Sim, and E. W. Loosley, *Crestwood Heights: A Study of the Culture of Suburban Life,* New York: 1956.

SILVERMAN, Sydel, "An Ethnographic Approach to Social Stratification: Prestige in a Central Italian Community," *American Anthropologist,* 68 (August, 1966), 899-921.

SPECTORSKY, A. C., *The Exurbanites,* Philadelphia: Lippincott, 1955.

SPEIER, Hans, "Social Stratification in the Urban Community," *American Sociological Review,* 1 (April, 1936), 193-202.

COMMUNITY
STUDIES

STEIN, Maurice R., *The Eclipse of Community*, Princeton: Princeton University Press, 1960.

STONE, Gregory P. and William H. Form, "Instabilities in Status: The Problem of Hierarchy in the Community Study of Status Arrangements," *American Sociological Review*, 18 (April, 1953), 149-162.

THERNSTROM, Stephan, *Poverty and Progress: Social Mobility in a Nineteenth Century City*, Cambridge: Harvard University Press, 1964.

THERNSTROM, Stephan, " ' Yankee City' Revisited: The Perils of Historical Naivete," *American Sociological Review*, 30 (April, 1965), 234-242.

USEEM, John, Pierre Tangent, and Ruth Useem, "Stratification in a Prairie Town," *American Sociological Review*, 7 (June, 1942), 331-342.

VAN DER MERWE, Hendrick W., "Social Stratification in a Cape Colored Community," *Sociology and Social Research*, 46 (April, 1962), 302-311.

VIDICH, Arthur J. and Joseph Bensman, *Small Town in Mass Society: Class, Power and Religion in a Rural Community*, Garden City, New York: Doubleday, 1960.

VIDICH, Arthur J., Joseph Bensman, and Maurice Stein, editors, *Reflections on Community Studies*, New York: Wiley, 1964.

WARNER, Robert A., *New Haven Negroes*, New Haven: Yale University Press, 1940.

WARNER, W. Lloyd, "Life in Suburbia," *Saturday Review*, 39 (October, 1956).

WARNER, W. Lloyd, *American Life: Dream and Reality*, revised edition, Chicago: University of Chicago Press, 1962.

WARNER, W. Lloyd, *The Living and the Dead*, New Haven: Yale University Press, 1959.

WARNER, W. Lloyd, *Yankee City*, one volume paperback edition, New Haven: Yale University Press, 1963.

WARNER, W. Lloyd and associates, *Democracy in Jonesville: A Study in Quality and Inequality*, New York: Harper and Row, 1949.

WARNER, W. Lloyd, Buford Junker and Walter A. Adams, *Color and Human Nature*, Washington, D.C.: American Council on Education, 1941.

WARNER, W. Lloyd and J. O. Low, *The Social System of the Modern Factory*, New Haven: Yale University Press, 1947.

WARNER, W. Lloyd and J. O. Low, "Yankee City Loses Control if Its Factories," in Roland L. Warren, editor, *Perspectives on the American Community,* Chicago: Rand McNally, 1965.

WARNER, W. Lloyd and Paul S. Lunt, *The Social Life of a Modern Community,* New Haven: Yale University Press, 1941.

WARNER, W. Lloyd and Paul S. Lunt, *The Status System of a Modern Community,* New Haven: Yale University Press, 1942.

WARNER, W. Lloyd, Marchia Meeker, and Kenneth Eells, *Social Class in America,* New York: Science Research Associates, 1949.

WARNER, W. Lloyd and Leo Srole, *The Social Systems of American Ethnic Groups,* New Haven: Yale University Press, 1945.

WEST, James (Carl Withers), *Plainville, U.S.A.,* New York: Columbia University Press, 1945.

WHYTE, William F., *Street Corner Society: The Social Structure of an Italian Slum,* Chicago: University of Chicago Press, 1955.

WILLMOTT, Peter, *Adolescent Boys of East London,* New York: Humanities Press, 1967.

WOOD, Robert C., *Suburbia,* Boston: Houghton Mifflin, 1958.

YOUNG, Michael and Peter Willmott, *Family and Kinship in East London,* Baltimore: Penguin, 1960.

ZORBAUGH, Harvey W., *The Gold Coast and the Slum,* Chicago: University of Chicago Press, 1929.

Stratification in Suburbia

In general, the literature in this section is more relevant to understanding stratification in contemporary industrial societies than are the numerous studies of stratification in small, independent communities. Not surprisingly, most of it appeared in the 1950's and 1960's.

BAZELON, David T., "The New Class," *Commentary,* 42 (August, 1966), 48-53.

BEEGLE, J. Allen, "Characteristics of Michigan's Fringe Population," *Rural Sociology,* (September, 1947), 254-263.

BERGER, Bennett, *Working-Class Suburb,* Berkeley: University of California Press, 1960.

BLOOMBERG, Warner and Morris Sunshine, *Suburban Power Structures and Public Education,* Syracuse: Syracuse University Press, 1963.

BOGGS, Stephen T., "Family Size and Social Mobility in a California Suburb," *Eugenics Quarterly,* 4 (December, 1957), 208-213.

CLARK, S. D., *The Suburban Society,* Toronto: University of Toronto Press, 1966.

DOBRINER, William M., *Class in Suburbia,* Englewood Cliffs, New Jersey: Prentice-Hall, 1963.

DOBRINER, William M., editor, *The Suburban Community,* New York: Putnam, 1958.

DYE, Thomas, "Popular Images of Decision-Making in Suburban Communities," *Sociology and Social Research,* 47 (October, 1962), 75-85.

FARLEY, Reynolds, "Suburban Persistence," *American Sociological Review,* 29 (February, 1964), 38-47.

FAVA, Sylvia Fleis, "Suburbanism as a Way of Life," *American Sociological Review,* 21 (February, 1956), 34-37.

GANS, Herbert J., *The Levittowners: Ways of Life and Politics in a New Suburban Community,* New York: Pantheon, 1967.

GERSH, Harry, "The New Suburbanites of the 50's" *Commentary,* (March, 1954), 209-221.

GOLDSTEIN, Sidney and Kurt B. Mayer, "The Impact of Migration on the Socio-economic Structure of Cities and Suburbs," *Sociology and Social Research,* 50 (October, 1965), 5-23.

GREER, Scott, "The Social Structure and Political Process of Suburbia," *American Sociological Review,* 25 (August, 1960), 514-526.

LAZERWITZ, Bernard, "Metropolitan Residential Belts," *American Sociological Review,* 25 (April, 1960), 245-252.

LUNDBERG, George A., Mirra Komarovsky, and M. A. McInery, *Leisure: A Suburban Study,* New York: Columbia University Press, 1934.

MARTIN, Walter T., *The Rural-Urban Fringe,* Eugene: University

SUBURBIA

of Oregon Press, 1953.

MARTIN, Walter T., "The Structuring of Social Relationships Engendered by Suburban Residence," *American Sociological Review,* 21 (August, 1956), 446-453.

SCHNORE, Leo F., "City-Suburban Income Differentials in Metropolitan Areas," *American Sociological Review,* 27 (April, 1962), 252-255.

SCHNORE. Leo F., "The Socio-economic Status of Cities and Suburbs," *American Sociological Review,* 28 (February, 1963), 76-85.

SEELEY, John, R. A. Sim, and E. W. Loosley, *Crestwood Heights: A Study of the Culture of Suburban Life,* New York: 1956.

SMITH, Ted C., "The Structuring of Power in a Suburban Community," *Pacific Sociological Review,* 3 (Fall, 1960), 83-88.

SOWER, Christopher, "Social Stratification in Suburban Communities," *Sociometry,* 11 (August, 1948), 235-243.

SPECTORSKY, A. C., *The Exurbanites,* Philadelphia: Lippincott, 1955.

SPINRAD, William, "Blue-Collar Workers as City and Suburban Residents—Effects on Union Membership," in Arthur B. Shostak and William Gomberg, editors, *Blue-Collar World: Studies of the American Worker,* Englewood Cliffs, New Jersey: Prentice-Hall, 1964.

TAEUBER, Karl E. and Alma F. Taeuber, "White Migration and Socio-economic Differences Between Cities and Suburbs," *American Sociological Review,* 29 (October, 1964), 718-729.

UDRY, J. Richard, "The Importance of Social Class in a Suburban School," *Journal of Educational Sociology,* 33 (April, 1960), 307-310.

WARNER, W. Lloyd, "Life in Suburbia," *Saturday Review,* 39 (October 20, 1956).

WHYTE, William H., Jr., *The Organization Man,* New York: Simon and Schuster, 1956.

WILLMOTT, Peter and Michael Young, *Family and Class in a London Suburb,* New York: Humanities Press, 1961.

WINCH, Robert F., Scott Greer, and R. L. Blumberg, "Ethnicity and Extended Familism in an Upper-Middle-Class Suburb," *American Sociological Review,* 32 (April, 1967), 265-272.

WIRT, Frederick, "The Political Sociology of American Suburbia: A Reinterpretation," *Journal of Politics,* 27 (August, 1965), 647-666.

WOOD, Robert C., *Suburbia,* Boston: Houghton Mifflin, 1958.

ZIMMER, Basil G. and Amos H. Hawley,"Opinions on School District Reorganization in Metropolitan Areas: A Comparative Analysis of the Views of Citizens and Officials in Central City and Suburban Areas," *Southwestern Social Science Quarterly,* 48 (December, 1967), 311-324.

Stratification and Residential Patterns

In spite of the considerable body of literature in this field, it is one of the several areas of social stratification in which some of the most crucial questions are virtually unresearched. For example, our survey of the literature fails to reveal any adequate empirical evidence on trends in industrial societies in the degree of residential segregation by occupational or economic level.

Much of the literature deals with the Burgess zonal hypothesis and similar descriptive schemes devised in the 1920's and 1930's. Few new questions seem to have been raised in this area in recent years.

We exclude the many studies dealing with Negro-white segregation unless they also deal specifically with segregation by occupational or economic level.

ANDERSON, Theodore R. and Janice A. Egeland, "Spatial Aspects of Social Area Analysis," *American Sociological Review,* 26 (June, 1961), 392-398.

BESHERS, James M., *Urban Social Structure,* New York: Free Press, 1962.

BOWERS, Raymond V., "Ecological Patterning of Rochester, New York," *American Sociological Review,* 4 (April, 1939), 180-189.

BURGESS, Ernest W., "Residential Segregation in American Cities," *Annals of the American Academy of Political and Social Science,* 140 (1928), 105-115.

BURGESS, Ernest W., "The Determination of Gradients in the Growth of Cities," *Publications of the American Sociological Society,* 21 (1927).

BURGESS, Ernest W., "The Growth of the City: An Introduction to a Research Project," *Publications of the American Sociological Society,* 18 (1924), 85-97.

BURGESS, Ernest W., "Urban Areas," in T. V. Smith and L. D. White, editors, *Chicago, An Experiment in Social Science Research,* Chicago: University of Chicago Press, 1929.

CAPLOW, Theodore, "Recent Research on the Ecology of Paris," *Midwest Sociologist,* 16 (1954), 19-21.

CAPLOW, Theodore, "The Social Ecology of Guatemala City," *Social Forces,* 28 (December, 1949), 113-133.

CAPLOW, Theodore, "Urban Structure in France," *American Sociological Review,* 17 (1952), 544-549.

COLLISON, Peter, "Occupation, Education, and Housing in an English City," *American Journal of Sociology,* 65 (May, 1960), 588-597.

COLLISON, Peter and John Mogey, "Residence and Social Class in Oxford," *American Journal of Sociology,* 64 (May, 1959), 599-605.

COWHIG, James D., "Early Occupational Status as Related to Education and Residence," *Rural Sociology,* 27 (March, 1962), 18-27.

CRESSEY, Paul F., "Ecological Organization of Rangoon," *Sociology and Social Research,* 40 (1956), 166-169.

DOTSON, Floyd and Lillian Dotson, "Ecological Trends in Guadalajara, Mexico," *Social Forces,* 32 (May, 1954), 367-374.

DUNCAN, Beverly, "Devolution of an Empirical Generalization," *American Sociological Review,* 29 (December, 1964), 855-862.

DUNCAN, Otis Dudley, "Population Distribution and Community Structure," *Cold Spring Harbor Symposia on Quantitative Biology,* 22 (1957).

DUNCAN, Otis Dudley and Beverly Duncan, "Residential Distribution and Occupational Stratification," *American Journal of Sociology,* 60 (March, 1955), 493-503.

ENGELS, Friedrich, *The Condition of the Working Class in England,* New York: Macmillan, 1958.

FARLEY, Reynolds, "Suburban Persistence," *American Sociological Reveiw,* 29 (February, 1964), 38-47.

FELDMAN, Arnold S. and Charles Tilly, "The Interaction of Social and Physical Space," *American Sociological Review,* 25 (December, 1960), 877-884.

FIREY, Walter, *Land Use in Central Boston,* Cambridge: Harvard University Press, 1947.

FRAZIER, E. Franklin, "Negro Harlem: An Ecological Study," *American Journal of Sociology,* 43 (July, 1937), 72-88.

GIBBARD, Harold A., "The Status Factor in Residential Succession," *American Journal of Sociology,* 46 (May, 1941), 835-842.

GIST, Noel P., "The Ecology of Bangalore, India: An East-West Comparison," *Social Forces,* 35 (May, 1957), 356-365.

GOLDSTEIN, Sidney and Kurt Mayer, "Population Decline and the Social and Demographic Structure of an American City," *American Sociological Review,* 29 (February, 1964), 48-54.

GOLDSTEIN, Sidney and Kurt B. Mayer, "The Impact of Migration on the Socio-Economic Structure of Cities and Suburbs," *Sociology and Social Research,* 50 (October, 1965), 5-23.

HANSEN, Asael T., "The Ecology of a Latin American City," in Edward B. Reuter, editor, *Race and Culture Contracts,* New York: McGraw-Hill, 1934.

HAWLEY, Amos H., *Human Ecology: A Theory of Community Structure,* New York: Ronald, 1950.

HAWLEY, Amos H., "Land Value Patterns in Okayama, Japan, 1940 and 1952," *American Journal of Sociology,* 60 (March, 1955), 487-492.

HAWLEY, Amos H., "Some Observations on the Land Use Patterns in Manila," in *Papers in Demography and Public Administration,* revised edition, Manila: Institute of Public Administration, University of the Philippines, 1954.

HAWLEY, Amos H., *The Changing Shape of Metropolitan America,* New York: Free Press, 1956.

HAWTHORN, Harry B. and Audrey E. Hawthorn, "Stratification in a Latin American City," *Social Forces,* 27 (October, 1948), 19-29.

HAWTHORN, Harry B. and Audrey E. Hawthorn, "The Shape of a City: Some Observations on Sucre, Bolivia," *Sociology and Social Research,* 33 (1948), 87-91.

HAYNER, Norman S., "Oaxaca: City of Old Mexico," *Sociology and Social Research,* 29 (1944), 87-95.

HAYNER, Norman S., "Mexico City: Its Growth and Configuration," *American Journal of Sociology,* 50 (January, 1945), 295-304.

HOYT, Homer, "The Residential and Retail Patterns of Leading Latin American Cities," *Land Economics,* 39 (1963).

HOYT, Homer, "The Structure and Growth of American Cities Contrasted with the Structure and Growth of European Cities," *Urban Land,* 18 (1959), 3-8.

RESIDENTIAL
PATTERNS

HOYT, Homer, *The Structure and Growth of Residential Neighborhoods in American Cities,* Washington: Federal Housing Administration, 1939.

LAZERWITZ, Bernard, "Metropolitan Community Residential Belts," *American Sociological Review,* 25 (February, 1960), 245-252.

LEONARD, Olen E., "La Paz, Bolivia: Its Population and Growth," *American Sociological Review,* 13 (August, 1948), 448-454.

LOBB, John, "Caste and Class in Haiti," *American Journal of Sociology,* 46 (July, 1940).

LOCKWOOD, David, *The Blackcoated Worker,* London: Unwin, 1958, Appendix B, "The Dwelling Areas of Clerks in Greater London."

MAYER, Kurt and Sidney Goldstein, "Interelationships Between Social and Demographic Processes in an American City, *Transactions of the International Population Conference,* Vienna, (1959), 92-105.

McELRATH, Dennis C., "The Social Areas of Rome: A Comparative Analysis," *American Sociological Review,* 27 (June, 1962), 376-391.

MEHTA, Surinder K., "Patterns of Residence in Poona (India) by Income, Education, and Occupation (1937-1965), *American Journal of Sociology,* 73 (January, 1968), 496-508.

MILLER, Alden D., *Principal Components and Curvature in Occupational Stratification,* Chapel Hill: University of North Carolina Press, 1967.

MORSE, Richard M., "Latin American Cities: Aspects of Function and Structure," *Comparative Studies in Society and History,* 4 (1962).

QUINN, James A., *Human Ecology,* Englewood Cliffs: Prentice-Hall, 1950.

QUINN, James A., "The Burgess Zonal Hypothesis and Its Critics," *American Sociological Review,* 5 (April, 1940), 210-218.

REDICK, Richard W., "Population Growth and Distribution in Central Cities, 1940-50," *American Sociological Review,* 21 (February, 1956), 38-43.

SCHMID, Calvin F., "Generalizations Concerning the Ecology of the American City," *American Sociological Review,* 15 (April, 1950), 264-281.

SCHMID, Calvin F., Earle H. McCannell, and Maurice D. Van Arsdol, Jr., "The Ecology of the American City: Further Comparison and Validation of Generalizations," *American Sociological Review,* 23 (August, 1958), 392-401.

SCHNORE, Leo F., "City-Suburban Income Differentials in Metropolitan Areas," *American Sociological Review,* 27 (April, 1962), 252-255.

SCHNORE, Leo F., "On the Spatial Structure of Cities in the Two Americas," in Philip M. Hauser and Leo F. Schnore, *The Study of Urbanization,* New York: Wiley, 1965.

SCHNORE, Leo F., "Social Class Segregation Among Nonwhites in Metropolitan Centers," *Demography,* 2 (1965), 126-133.

SCHNORE, Leo F., "The Socio-economic Status of Cities and Suburbs," *American Sociological Review,* 28 (February, 1963), 76-85.

SCHNORE, Leo F., *The Urban Scene,* New York: Free Press, 1965.

SHEVKY, Eshref and Marilyn Williams, *The Social Areas of Los Angeles,* Berkeley: University of California Press, 1949.

SJOBERG, Gideon, *The Pre-Industrial City: Past and Present,* New York: Free Press, 1960.

TAEUBER, Karl E. and Alma F. Taeuber, *Negroes in Cities,* Chicago: Aldine, 1965.

TAEUBER, Karl E. and Alma F. Taeuber, "White Migration and Socio-economic Differences Between Cities and Suburbs," *American Sociological Review,* 29 (October, 1964), 718-729.

UYEKI, Eugene S., "Residential Distribution and Stratification, 1950-60," *American Journal of Sociology,* 69 (March, 1964), 491-498.

WARNER, W. Lloyd and Paul S. Lunt, *The Social Life of a Modern Community,* New Haven: Yale University Press, 1942.

WARNER, W. Lloyd, Marchia Meeker, and Kenneth Eells, *Social Class in America,* New York: Science Research Associates, 1949.

WILLIE, C. V., "Age, Status and Residential Stratification," *American Sociological Review,* 25 (April, 1960), 260-264.

WILSON, Alan B., "Residential Segregation of Social Classes and Aspirations of High School Boys," *American Sociological Review,* 24 (December, 1959), 836-845.

ZORBAUGH, Harvey W., *The Gold Coast and the Slum,* Chicago: University of Chicago Press, 1929.

ZORBAUGH, Harvey W., "The Natural Areas of the City," in Ernest W. Burgess, editor, *The Urban Community,* Chicago: University of Chicago Press, 1926.

Recent Trends in Stratification

The literature listed in this section deals with changes that have occurred during the past few years and decades. Most of it concerns what happens to the distribution of rewards and resources and to the correlates of stratification in advanced industrial societies.

ABRAMS, Mark, "Press, Polls and Votes in Britain since the 1955 General Elections," *Public Opinion Quarterly,* 21 (1957-1958), 543-547.

ADAMS, Stuart, "Trends in Occupational Origins of Business Leaders," *American Sociological Review,* 19 (October, 1954), 541-548.

ADAMS, Stuart, "Trends in Occupational Origins of Physicians," *American Sociological Review,* 18 (August, 1953), 404-409.

ALFORD, Robert, *Party and Society,* Chicago: Rand McNally, 1963.

ANDERSON, C. Arnold and Mary Jean Bowman, "The Vanishing Servant and The Contemporary Status System of the American South," *American Journal of Sociology,* 59 (November, 1953), 215-230.

ANTONOVSKY, A., "Social Class, Life Expectancy and Overall Mortality," *Milbank Memorial Fund Quarterly,* 45 (April, 1967), 31-73.

BARBER, Bernard and Elinor G. Barber, editors, *European Social Class: Stability and Change,* New York: Macmillan, 1965.

BAZELON, David T., "The New Class," *Commentary,* 42 (July, 1966), 48-53.

BECKER, Howard, "Changes in the Social Stratification of Contemporary Germany," *American Sociological Review,* 15 (June, 1950), 333-342.

BERNARD, Jessie, "Class Organization in an Era of Abundance:

A New Principle of Class Organization," *Transactions of the Third World Congress of Sociology,* 3 (1956), 26-31.

BLAU, Peter M. and Otis Dudley Duncan, *The American Occupational Structure,* New York: Wiley, 1967.

BONNE, A., "Trends in Occupational Structure and Distribution of Income Among the Jewish Population in Israel," *Jewish Journal of Sociology,* 1 (1959), 242-249.

BROOM, Leonard and Norval D. Glenn, *Transformation of the Negro American,* New York: Harper and Row, 1965.

BROOM, Leonard and Norval D. Glenn, "When Will America's Negroes Catch Up?" *New Society,* (March 25, 1965), 6-7.

BURNHAM, James M., *The Managerial Revolution,* New York: Day, 1941.

CARTER, Cedric O., "Changing Patterns of Differential Fertility in Northwest Europe and North America," *Eugenics Quarterly,* 9 (September, 1962), 147-150.

CARTTER, Allan M., *The Redistribution of Income in Postwar Britain,* New Haven: Yale University Press, 1955.

CHEN, Theodore Hsi-en, "The Marxist Remolding of Chinese Society," *American Journal of Sociology,* 58 (January, 1953), 340-346.

COHN, Bernard S., "Changing Traditions of a Low Caste," *Journal of American Folklore,* 71 (1958), 413-421.

COSTA, L. A. Pinta, "Social Stratification in Brazil: A General Survey of Some Recent Changes," *Transactions of the Third World Congress of Sociology,* 3 (1956), 54-65.

CUTRIGHT, Phillips, "Income Redistribution: A Cross-National Analysis," *Social Forces,* 46 (December, 1967), 180-190.

DAHRENDORF, Ralf, "Recent Changes in the Class Structure of European Societies," *Daedalus,* (Winter, 1964), 225-270.

DEEG, M. E. and D. G. Patterson, "Changes in Social Status of Occupations," *Occupations,* 25 (1947), 205-208.

DINITZ, Simon, Franklin Banks, and Benjamin Pasamanick, "Mate Selection and Social Class: Changes During the Past Quarter Century," *Marriage and Family Living,* 22 (November, 1960), 348-351.

DRUCKER, Peter F., "The Employee Society," *American Journal of Sociology,* 58 (January, 1953), 358-362.

EDINGER, Lewis J., "Continuity and Change in the Background of German Decision-Makers," *Western Political Quarterly,* 14 (March, 1961), 17-36.

EDWARDS, Alba M., *Comparative Occupational Statistics for the United States, 1970-1940,* Washington, D. C.: United States Department of Commerce, Bureau of the Census, U. S. Government Printing Office, 1943.

FARIS, Robert E. L., "The Middle Class from a Sociological Viewpoint," *Social Forces,* 39 (October, 1960), 1-5.

FARRAG, A. M., "The Occupational Structure of the Labour Force: Patterns and Trends in Selected Countries," *Population Studies,* 18 (July, 1964), 17-34.

FELDT, Allan G. and Robert H. Weller, "The Balance of Social, Economic, and Demographic Change in Puerto Rico—1950-60," *Demography,* 2 (1965), 474-489.

FITZPATRICK, Joseph R., "Toward a White Collar Society," *Thought,* 35 (Summer, 1960), 369-389.

FOLGER, John K. and Charles B. Nam, *Education of the American Population,* Washington, D. C.: Government Printing Office, 1967.

FOLGER, John K. and Charles B. Nam, "Trends in Education in Relation to the Occupational Structure," *Sociology of Education,* 38 (Fall, 1964), 19-33.

HANDEL, Gerald and Lee Rainwater, "Persistence and Change in Working-Class Life Styles," *Sociology and Social Research,* 48 (April, 1964), 281-283.

GILBERT, Claire W., "Some Trends in Community Politics: A Secondary Analysis of Power Structure Data from 166 Communities," *Southwestern Social Science Quarterly,* 48 (December, 1967), 373-381.

GLAZER, Nathan "The American Jew and the Attainment of Middle-Class Rank: Some Trends and Explorations," in Marshall Sklare, editor, *The Jews,* New York: Free Press, 1958.

GLENN, Norval D., "Massification Versus Differentiation: Some Trend Data from National Surveys," *Social Forces,* 46 (December, 1967), 172-180.

GLENN, Norval D., "Social Security and Income Redistribution," *Social Forces,* 46 (June, 1968).

GLENN, Norval D., "Some Changes in the Relative Standing of American Nonwhites," *Phylon,* 24 (Summer, 1963), 109-122.

GLENN, Norval D., "The Trend in Differences in Attitudes and Behavior by Educational Level," *Sociology of Education,* 39 (Summer, 1966), 255-275.

GLENN, Norval D. and Ruth Hyland, "Religious Preference and Worldly Success: Some Evidence from National Surveys," *American Sociological Review,* 32 (February, 1967), 73-85.

GOLDSMITH, Selma F., "Changes in the Size Distribution of Income," *American Economic Review Papers and Proceedings,* 47 (May, 1957), 504-511.

GOLDTHORPE, John H., David Lockwood, Frank Bechhofer, and Jennifer Platt, "The Affluent Worker and the Thesis of Embourgeoisement: Some Preliminary Research Findings," in Joseph Kahl, editor, *Comparative Perspectives on Stratification,* Boston: Little, Brown, 1968.

GUTTSMAN, W. L., "The Changing Social Structure of the British Political Elite, 1886-1935," *British Journal of Sociology,* 2 (June, 1951), 122-134.

GUTTSMAN, W. L., "Social Stratification and Political Elite," *British Journal of Sociology,* 11 (June, 1960), 137-150.

HAMILTON, Richard F., "Affluence and the Worker: The West German Case," *American Journal of Sociology,* 71 (September, 1965), 144-152.

HAMILTON, Richard F., *Class and Politics in the United States,* New York: Wiley, 1969.

HAMILTON, Richard F., "The Marginal Middle Class: A Reconsideration," *American Sociological Review,* 31 (April, 1966), 192-199.

HARE, Nathan, "Recent Trends in the Occupational Mobility of Negroes, 1930-1960: An Intra-cohort Analysis," *Social Forces,* 44 (December, 1965), 166-173.

HAVIGHURST, Robert J., "The Influence of Recent Social Changes on the Desire for Mobility in the United States," in Lyman Bryson, Louis Finkelstein, and R. M. McIver, editors, *Conflicts of Power in Modern Culture,* New York: Harper, 1947.

HEBERLE, Rudolf, "Changes in the Social Stratification of the South," *Transactions of the Third World Congress of Sociology,* 3 (1956), 96-105.

HEBERLE, Rudolf, "The Changing Social Stratification of the South," *Social Forces,* 38 (October, 1959), 42-50.

HERTZLER, J. O., "Some Tendencies toward a Closed Class System in the United States," *Social Forces,* 30 (March, 1952), 313-323.

HODGE, Robert W., Paul M. Siegel, and Peter H. Rossi, "Occupational Prestige in the United States, 1925-1963," *American Journal of Sociology,* 70 (November, 1964), 286-302.

HOLLINGSHEAD, August B., "Trends in Social Stratification: A Case Study," *American Sociological Review,* 17 (December, 1952), 679-686.

JAFFE, A. J. and Walter Adams, "College Education for United States Youth: The Attitudes of Parents and Children," *American Journal of Economics and Sociology,* 23 (July, 1964), 269-283.

JOHNSON, John J., *Political Change in Latin America: The Emergence of the Middle Sectors,* Stanford: Stanford University Press, 1958.

KAPADIA, K. M., "Caste in Transition," *Sociological Bulletin,* 11 (1961), 73-90.

KARIEL, Henry, *The Decline of American Pluralism,* Stanford: Stanford University Press, 1961.

KELSALL, R. K., "The Social Origin of Higher Civil Servants in Great Britain, Now and in the Past," *Transactions of the Second World Congress of Sociology,* 2 (1954), 131-142.

KNOWLES, K. G. J. and D. J. Robertson, "Differences between the Wages of Skilled and Unskilled Workers, 1880-1950," *Bulletin of the Oxford Institute of Statistics,* 1951.

KOLKO, Gabriel, *Wealth and Power in America: An Analysis of Social Class and Income Distribution,* New York: Praeger, 1962.

KUZNETS, Simon, *Shares of Upper Income Groups in Income and Savings,* New York: National Bureau of Economic Research, 1953.

LAMPMAN, Robert J., "Income Distribution and Poverty," in Margaret S. Gordon, editor, *Poverty in America,* San Francisco: Chandler, 1965.

LAMPMAN, Robert J., *The Share of Top Wealth-Holders in National Wealth: 1922-1956.,* Princeton: Princeton University Press, 1962.

LENSKI, Gerhard, *Power and Privilege,* New York: McGraw-Hill, 1966.

LIPMAN, V. D., "Trends in Anglo-Jewish Occupations," *Jewish Journal of Sociology,* 2 (1960), 202-218.

LIPSET, Seymour M., "The Changing Class Structure and Contemporary European Politics," *Daedalus,* (Winter, 1964), 271-303.

LITTLE, Alan and John Westergaard, "The Trend in Class Differentials in Educational Opportunity in England and Wales," *British Journal of Sociology,* 15 (December, 1964), 301-316.

MacIVER, Robert M., "The New Social Stratification," in R. N. Anshen, editor, *Our Emergent Civilization,* New York: Harper, 1947.

MAHAR, P. M., "Changing Caste Ideology in a North Indian Village," *Journal of Social Issues,* 14 (1958), 51-65.

MARSH, D. C., *The Changing Social Structure of England and Wales,* London: Routledge and Kegan Paul, 1958.

MARSHALL, T. H., "Changes in Social Stratification in the Twentieth Century," in *Class, Citizenship, and Social Development,* Garden City, New York: Doubleday, 1965.

MARSHALL, T. H., "General Survey of Changes in Social Stratification in the Twentieth Century," *Transactions of the Third World Congress of Sociology,* 3 (1956), 1-17.

MAYER, Kurt B., "The Changing Shape of the American Class Structure," *Social Research,* 30 (Winter, 1963), 458-468.

MAYER, Kurt B., "Class and Status in the United States," *Quarterly Review,* 303 (October, 1965), 450-459.

MAYER, Kurt B., "Diminishing Class Differentials in the United States," *Kyklos,* 12 (October, 1959), 605-628.

MAYER, Kurt B., "Recent Changes in the Class Structure of the United States," *Transactions of the Third World Congress of Sociology,* 3 (1956), 66-80.

METROPOLITAN LIFE INSURANCE COMPANY, "Occupational Mortality Diminishing," *Statistical Bulletin,* 49 (April, 1968), 3-4.

MILLER, Herman P., "Annual and Lifetime Income in Relation to Education: 1939-1959," *American Economic Review,* 50 (December, 1960), 962-986.

MILLER, Herman P., "Changes in the Number and Composition of the Poor," in Margaret S. Gordon, editor, *Poverty in America,* San Francisco: Chandler, 1965.

MILLER, Herman P., *Income Distribution in the United States,* Washington, D. C.: U. S. Department of Commerce, 1966.

MILLER, Herman P., *Rich Man, Poor Man,* New York: Crowell, 1964.

MILLER, Herman P., "What's Happening to Our Social Revolution?" in Reinhard Bendix and Seymour M. Lipset, *Class, Status, and Power,* second edition, New York: Free Press, 1966.

MILLER, S. M. and Frank Riessman, "Are Workers Middle Class?" *Dissent,* (Autumn, 1961), 507-516.

MOGEY, John, "A Century of Declining Paternal Authority," *Marriage and Family Living,* 19 (August, 1957), 234-239.

NEMCHINOV, V. S., "Changes in the Class Structure of the Population of the Soviet Union," *Transactions of the Third*

World Congress of Sociology, 8 (1957).

PASHKOV, A. I., "Radical Changes in Property in the U.S.S.R. in the Twentieth Century," *Transactions of the Third World Congress of Sociology,* 2 (1956), 213-219.

PENALOSA, Fernando, "The Changing Mexican-American in Southern California," *Sociology and Social Research,* 51 (July, 1967), 405-417.

PERLO, Victor, *The Income 'Revolution",* New York: International Publishers, 1954.

PRICE, Daniel O., "Occupational Changes in the Negro Population," *Social Science Quarterly,* 49 (December, 1968).

RAINWATER, Lee and Gerald Handel, "Changing Family Roles in the Working Class," in Arthur B. Shostak and William Gomberg, editors, *Blue-Collar World: Studies of the American Worker,* Englewood Cliffs, New Jersey: Prentice-Hall, 1964.

REID, Margaret G., "Changing Income Patterns," in Elizabeth A. Hoyt, *et al.,* editors, *American Income and Its Use,* New York: Harper and Row, 1954.

RIPPY, J. Fred, *Latin America: A Modern History,* Ann Arbor: University of Michigan Press, 1958.

RYAN, B., *Caste in Modern Ceylon: The Sinhalese System in Transition,* New Brunswick, New Jersey: Rutgers University Press, 1953.

SANGANE, Vilas A., "Changing Pattern of Caste Organization in Kolhapur City," *Sociological Bulletin,* 11 (March-September), 36-61.

SCHMID, Calvin F. and Charles E. Nobbe, "Socio-economic Differentials Among Non-white Races," *American Sociological Review,* 30 (December, 1965), 909-922.

SCHNORE, Leo F., *The Urban Scene,* New York: Free Press, 1965.

SILVERTSEN, Dagfinn, *When Caste Barriers Fall: A Study of Social and Economic Change in a South Indian Village,* New York: Humanities Press, 1963.

SJOBERG, Gideon, "Are Social Classes in America Becoming More Rigid?" *American Sociological Review,* 16 (December, 1951), 775-783.

SMYTHE, Hugh H. and Mabel Smythe, "Africa's New Class," *Queen's Quarterly,* 68 (Summer, 1960), 225-231.

SOLOW, Robert M., "Income Inequality Since the War," in Rolf E. Freeman, editor, *Postwar Economic Trends in the United States,* New York: Harper and Row, 1960.

SOLTOW, Lee, *Toward Income Equality in Norway,* Madison: University of Wisconsin Press, 1965.

SOROKIN, Pitirim A., "War and Post-War Changes in Social Stratifications of the Euro-American Population," *American Sociological Review,* 10 (April, 1945), 294-303.

SPENGLER, Joseph L., "Changes in Income Distribution and Social Stratification: A Note," *American Journal of Sociology,* 59 (November, 1953), 247-259.

SRINIVAS, M. N., *et al.,* "Caste: A Trend Report and Bibliography," *Current Sociology,* 8 (1959), 133-184.

STOCKWELL, Edward G., "Infant Mortality and Socio-Economic Status: A Changing Relationship," *Milbank Memorial Fund Quarterly,* 40 (January, 1962), 101-111.

TAEUBER, Karl E. and Alma F. Taeuber, "White Migration and Socio-Economic Differences Between Cities and Suburbs," *American Sociological Review,* 29 (October, 1964), 718-729.

THOMPSON, F. M. L., "The Social Distribution of Landed Property in England Since the Sixteenth Century," *Economic History Review,* 19 (December, 1966), 505-517.

TITMUSS, Richard M., *Income Distribution and Social Change,* Toronto: University of Toronto Press, 1962.

TROW, Martin, "The Second Transformation of American Secondary Education," in Reinhard Bendix and Seymour M. Lipset, editors, *Class, Status, and Power,* 2nd edition, New York: Free Press, 1966.

TUCKER, Charles W., "A Comparative Analysis of Subjective Social Class: 1945-1963," *Social Forces,* 46 (June, 1968), 508-514.

TURNER, H. A., "Trade Unions, Differentials and the Levelling of Wages," *Manchester School,* (September, 1952).

U. S. BUREAU OF THE CENSUS, *Current Population Reports,* Series P-20, No. 54, "The Extent of Poverty in the United States: 1959 to 1966," U. S. Government Printing Office, Washington, D. C., 1968.

U. S. BUREAU OF THE CENSUS, "Educational Change in a Generation: March, 1962," *Current Population Reports,* Series P-20, No. 132, September 22, 1964.

VAN DOORN, Jacques A., "The Changed Positions of Unskilled Workers in the Social Structure of the Netherlands," *Transaction of the Third World Congress of Sociology,* 3 (1956), 113-125.

WARNER, W. Lloyd, *The Corporation in the Emergent American Society,* New York: Harper and Row, 1961.

WARNER, W. Lloyd, *et al., The Emergent American Society: Volume I. Large-Scale Organizations,* New Haven: Yale University Press, 1967.

WESTERGAARD, J. H., "The Withering Away of Class: A Contemporary Myth," in P. Anderson and R. Blackburn, editors, *Toward Socialism,* Fontana, 1965.

WESTOFF, Charles F., "Differential Fertility in the United States: 1900 to 1952," *American Sociological Review,* 19 (October, 1954), 549-561.

WHYTE, William H., Jr., *The Organization Man,* Garden City, New York: Doubleday, 1956.

WILLIE, Charles V., "A Research Note on the Changing Association Between Infant Mortality and Socioeconomic Status," *Social Forces,* 37 (1958-1959), 221-227.

WRONG, Dennis H., "Trends in Class Fertiltiy in Western Nations," *Canadian Journal of Economics and Political Science,* 24 (May, 1958), 216-229.

YANOWITCH, Murray, "The Soviet Income Revolution," *Slavic Review,* 23 (December, 1963).

Income Distribution

The literature listed here deals primarily with the overall extent of inequality in the distribution of income within societies. Literature dealing with other aspects of income distributions can be found under other topics, including especially "The Role of Minorities in the Stratification of Societies." No attempt is made to include the vast number of census publications dealing with income distributions in the United States and in other countries.

ANDERSON, C. Arnold, "Economic Status Differentials Within Southern Agriculture," *Rural Sociology,* 19 (March, 1954), 50-67.

ANDERSON, C. Arnold, "Regional and Racial Differences in Relations between Income and Education," *School Review,* 63 (Spring, 1955), 38-45.

BOONE, Alfred, "Trends in Occupational Structure and Distribution of Income Among the Jewish Population in Israel," *Jewish Journal of Sociology,* 1 (1959), 242-249.

BOWLEY, A. L., *Wages and Income in the United Kingdom Since 1860,* London: 1937.

BROWN, E. H. Phelps and Sheila V. Hopkins, "The Course of Wage-Rates in Five Countries, 1860-1939," *Oxford Economic Papers,* 2 (June, 1950).

CARTTER, Allan M., *The Redistribution of Income in Post-war Britain,* New Haven: Yale University Press, 1955.

CENTERS, Richard and Hadley Cantril, "Income Satisfaction and Income Aspiration," *Journal of Abnormal and Social Psychology,* 41 (January, 1946), 64-69.

CHAMPERNOWNE, D. C., "The Graduation of Income Distributions," *Econometrica,* 20 (1952), 591-615.

CHANG, Chung-li, *The Income of the Chinese Gentry,* Seattle, University of Washington Press, 1962.

COLM, Gerhard and Theodor Geiger, *The Economy of the American People,* Washington, D. C.: National Planning Association, 1967.

CUTRIGHT, Phillips, "Inequality: A Cross-National Analysis," *American Sociological Review,* 32 (August, 1967), 562-578.

CUTRIGHT, Phillips, "Income Redistribution: A Cross-National Analysis," *Social Forces,* 46 (December, 1967), 180-190.

CUTRIGHT, Phillips, "Reply to Glenn," *Social Forces,* 46 (June, 1968), 539-540.

DAMLE, Y. B., *Social Differentiation and Differentiation in Emoluments,* Poona, India: Deccan College, 1955.

DERKSEN, J. B. D., "Statistics of the Distribution of Family Incomes by Size," *Milbank Memorial Fund Quarterly,* 27 (July, 1949), 324-331.

DORNBUSCH, Sanford M., "Correlations between Income and Labor-Force Participation by Race," *American Journal of Sociology,* 61 (January, 1956), 340-344.

EPSTEIN, Lenore, "Income of the Aged," in Robert E. Will and Harold G. Vatter, editors, *Poverty in Affluence,* New York: Harcourt, Brace and World, 1965.

FERNBACH, Frank L., "Policies Affecting Income Distribution," in Margaret S. Gordon, editor, *Poverty in America,* San Francisco: Chandler, 1965.

GALBRAITH, John K., *The Affluent Society,* Boston: Houghton-Mifflin, 1958.

GLENN, Norval D., "Social Security and Income Redistribution,"
Social Forces, 46 (June, 1968), 538-539.

GOLDSMITH, Selma F., "Changes in the Size Distribution of
Income," *American Economic Review Papers and Proceedings,*
47 (May, 1957), 504-511.

GOLDSMITH, Selma F., "Income Distribution in Depression,
War, and Peace," in Robert E. Will and Harold G. Vatter,
editors, *Poverty in Affluence,* New York: Harcourt, Brace
and World, 1965.

GOLDSMITH, Selma F., George Jaszi, Hyman Kaitz, and Maurice
Liebenberg, "Size Distribution of Income Since the Mid-
Thirties," *Review of Economics and Statistics,* 36 (February,
1954), 1-32.

GOLDSTEIN, Sidney, "The Effect of Income Level on the
Consumer Behavior of the Aged," *Proceedings of the
Seventh International Congress of Gerontology,* Vienna,
Austria, 8, 1-6.

HAMILTON, Richard F., "Income, Class, and Reference
Groups," *American Sociological Review,* 29 (August, 1964),
576-578.

HAMILTON, Richard F., "The Income Differences Between
Skilled and White Collar Workers," *British Journal of
Sociology,* 14 (December, 1963), 363-373.

HARRINGTON, Michael, *The Other America: Poverty in the
United States,* New York: Macmillan, 1963.

HARRIS, Mary Jordon and Josephine Staab, "The Relationship of Current Net Income to the Socioeconomic Status
of Southern Farm Families," *Rural Sociology,* 16 (December,
1951), 353-358.

JOHANSEN, Leif, "Death Rates, Age Distribution and Average
Income in Stationary Populations," *Population Studies,* 11
(July, 1957), 64-77.

KATONA, George and John Lansing, "The Wealth of the Wealthy,"
Review of Economics and Statistics, 46 (February, 1964), 1-13.

KNOWLES, K. G. J. C. and D. J. Robertson, "Differences Between the Wages of Skilled and Unskilled Workers, 1880-1950,"
Bulletin of the Oxford Institute of Statistics, 1951.

KOLKO, Gabriel, *Wealth and Power in America: An Analysis
of Social Class and Income Distribution,* New York: Praeger,
1962.

KRAVIS, Irving B., "International Differences in the Distribution
of Income," *Review of Economics and Statistics,* 42 (November, 1960), 408-416.

INCOME
DISTRIBUTION

KRAVIS, Irving B., *The Structure of Income,* Philadelphia: University of Pennsylvania Press, 1962.

KUVLESKY, William P. and David E. Wright, *Poverty in Texas: The Distribution of Low Income Families,* College Station: Texas Agricultural Experiment Station, Texas A and M University, 1965.

KUZNETS, Simon S., "Economic Growth and Income Inequality," *American Economic Review,* 45 (March, 1955), 18-19.

KUZNETS, Simon S., "Population, Income and Capital," *International Social Science Bulletin,* 6, No. 2, (1954), 165-170.

KUZNETS, Simon S., "Quantitative Aspects of the Economic Growth of Nations: VIII, The Distribution of Income by Size," *Economic Development and Cultural Change,* 11 (January, 1963).

KUZNETS, Simon S., *Shares of Upper Income Groups in Income and Savings,* New York: National Bureau of Economic Research, 1953.

LAMPMAN, Robert J., "Income Distribution and Poverty," in Margaret S. Gordon, editor, *Poverty in America,* San Francisco: Chandler, 1965.

LAMPMAN, Robert J., *The Share of Top Wealth-Holders in the National Wealth, 1922-1956,* Princeton: University of Princeton Press, 1962.

LENSKI, Gerhard E., *Power and Privilege,* New York: McGraw-Hill, 1966.

LYDALL, H. F., *British Incomes and Savings,* London: Oxford University Institute of Statistics, 1955.

MILLER, Herman P., "Changes in the Number and Composition of the Poor," in Margaret S. Gordon, editor, *Poverty in America,* San Francisco: Chandler, 1965.

MILLER, Herman P., *Income Distribution in the United States,* Washington, D. C.: U.S. Department of Commerce, Bureau of Census, 1966.

MILLER, Herman P., *Income of the American People,* New York: Wiley, 1955.

MILLER, Herman P., *Rich Man, Poor Man,* New York: Crowell, 1964.

MILLER, Herman P., "What's Happening to Our Social Revolution?" in Reinhard Bendix and Seymour M. Lipset, editors, *Class, Status, and Power,* 2nd edition, New York: Free Press, 1966.

MORGAN, James, Martin David, Wilbur Cohen, and Harvey Brazer, *Income and Welfare in the United States,* New York: McGraw-Hill, 1962.

OSHIMA, H., "The International Comparison of Size Distribution of Family Income with Special Reference to Asia," *Review of Economics and Statistics,* 44 (August, 1962), 439-445.

PEACOCK, Alan, editor, *Income Redistribution and Social Policy,* London: Cape, 1954.

PERLO, Victor, *The Income "Revolution,"* New York: International Publishers, 1954.

PORTER, John, *The Vertical Mosaic: An Analysis of Class and Power in Canada,* Toronto: University of Toronto Press, 1965, Chapter 4, "Classes and Income."

REID, Margaret G., "Changing Income Patterns," in Elizabeth A. Hoyt, *et al., American Income and Its Use,* New York: Harper and Row, 1954.

ROBERTS, David R., *Executive Compensation,* New York: Free Press, 1953.

SCHMITT, Robert C., "Interracial Households and Family Income Differentials," *Sociology and Social Research,* 46 (January, 1962), 203-206.

SEXTON, Patricia Cayo, *Education and Income,* New York, Viking, 1961.

SIMPSON, Alan, *The Wealth of the Gentry, 1540-1660,* London, Cambridge University Press, 1961.

SOLOW, Robert M., "Income Inequality Since the War," in Rolf E. Freeman, editor, *Postwar Economic Trends in the United States,* New York: Harper and Row, 1960.

SOLTOW, Lee, *Toward Income Equality in Norway,* Madison: University of Wisconsin Press, 1965.

SPENGLER, Joseph L., "Changes in Income Distribution and Social Stratification: A Note," *American Journal of Sociology,* 59 (November, 1953), 247-259.

TAWNEY, R. H., *Equality,* Fourth edition, London: Allen and Unwin, 1964.

THOMPSON, F. M. L., "The Social Distribution of Landed Property in England Since the Sixteenth Century," *Economic History Review,* 19 (December, 1966), 505-517.

TITMUSS, Richard M., *Income Distribution and Social Change,* London: Allen and Unwin, 1962.

TITMUSS, Richard M., "The Role of Redistribution in Social Policy," *Social Security Bulletin,* (June, 1965), 14-20.

TURNER, H. A., "Trade Unions, Differentials and the Leveling of Wages," *Manchester School,* 20 (September, 1952), 227-282.

YANOWITCH, Murray, "The Soviet Income Revolution," *Slavic Review,* 23 (December, 1963), 683-697.

INCOME
DISTRIBUTION

Prestige, Other than Occupational

Prestige is one of the major dimensions of stratification, and thus a concern with it pervades the literature. The publications listed here focus rather specifically upon prestige, or upon "social status," when that term is used more or less synonymously with prestige. A large number of publications not listed here deal to some extent with prestige.

ABBOTT, Joan ,"Students' Social Class in Three Northern Universities," *British Journal of Sociology,* 16 (September, 1965), 206-220.

ANASTASI, Anne and Shirley Miller, "Adolescent 'Prestige Factors' in Relation to Scholastic and Socio-Economic Variables," *Journal of Social Psychology,* 29 (1949), 43-50.

ANDERSON, Ronald E., "Status Structures in Coalition Bargaining Games," *Sociometry,* 30 (December, 1963), 393-403.

BABCHUK, Nicholas, Ruth Marsey, and C. Wayne Gordon, "Men and Women in Community Agencies: A Note on Power and Prestige," *American Sociological Review,* 25 (June, 1960), 399-403.

BARBER, Bernard, "Family Status, Local Community Status, and Social Stratification: Three Types of Social Ranking," *Pacific Sociological Review,* 4 (Spring, 1961), 3-10.

BARBER, Bernard and L. S. Lobel, " ' Fashion' in Woman's Clothes and the American Social System," *Social Forces,* 31 (December, 1952), 124-131.

BERELSON, Bernard, *Graduate Education in the United States,* New York: McGraw-Hill, 1960.

BESHERS, James M., Ephraim H. Mizruchi and Robert Perrucci, "Social Distance Strategies and Status Symbols: An Approach to the Study of Social Structure," *Sociological Quarterly,* 4 (Autumn, 1963), 311-324.

BESHERS, James M., *Urban Social Structure,* New York: Free Press, 1962.

BESHERS, James M., "Urban Social Structure as a Single Hierarchy," *Social Forces,* 41 (March, 1963), 233-239.

BONJEAN, Charles M., "Class, Status, and Power Reputation," *Sociology and Social Research,* 49 (October, 1964), 69-75.

BURNSTEIN, Eugene, Robert Moulton, and Paul Liberty, Jr., "Role vs. Excellence as Determinants of Role Attractiveness," *American Sociological Review,* 28 (April, 1963), 212-219.

CANCIAN, Frank, *Economics and Prestige in a Maya Community: The Religious Cargo System in Zinacantan,* Stanford: Stanford University Press, 1965.

CAPLOW, Theodore, and Reece J. McGee, *The Academic Marketplace,* New York: Basic Books, 1958.

CATTELL, Raymond B., "The Concept of Social Status," *Journal of Social Psychology,* 25 (May, 1942), 293-308.

COHN, Werner, "Social Status and the Ambivalence Hypothesis," *American Sociological Review,* 25 (August, 1960), 508-513.

COLE, Stephan and Jonathan R. Cole, "Scientific Output and Recognition: A Study in the Operation of the Reward System in Science," *American Sociological Review,* 32 (June, 1967), 377-390.

COLE, Stephen and Jonathan R. Cole, "Visibility and the Structural Bases of Awareness of Scientific Research," *American Sociological Review,* 33 (June, 1968), 397-413.

CRAIN, Robert L. and Donald B. Rosenthal, "Community Status as a Dimension of Local Decision-Making," *American Sociological Review,* 32 (December, 1967), 970-985.

CRANE, Diana, "Scientists at Major and Minor Universities: A Study of Productivity and Recognition," *American Sociological Review,* 30 (October, 1965), 699-714.

CUBER, John F. and William F. Kenkel, *Social Stratification in the United States,* New York: Appleton-Century-Crofts, 1954.

DANIELS, John, *In Freedom's Birthplace,* Boston: Houghton Mifflin, 1914.

DAVIS, Allison, Burleigh Gardner, and Mary R. Gardner, *Deep South,* Chicago: University of Chicago Press, 1941.

DAVIS, James A., "Status Symbols and the Measurement of Status Perception," *Sociometry,* 19 (September, 1956), 154-165.

DAVIS, Kingsley, "A Conceptual Analysis of Stratification," *American Sociological Review,* 7 (June, 1942), 309-321.

DAVIS, Kingsley, *Human Society,* New York: Macmillan, 1948, Chapter 24, "Caste, Class, and Stratification."

DINITZ, Simon, Mark Lefton, and Benjamin Pasamanick, "Status

Perceptions in a Mental Hospital," *Social Forces,* 38 (December, 1959), 124-128.

DOLLARD, John, *Caste and Class in a Southern Town,* New Haven: Yale University Press, 1937.

PRESTIGE

DRAKE, St. Clair and Horace R. Cayton, *Black Metropolis,* New York: Harcourt Brace, 1945.

DREYFUSS, C., "Prestige Grading: A Mechanism of Control," in Robert K. Merton, *et al.,* editors, *Reader in Bureaucracy,* New York: Free Press, 1952.

DUNCAN, Otis Dudley and J. W. Artis, *Social Stratification in a Pennsylvania Rural Community,* Pennsylvania State College, School of Agriculture, Bulletin 543, October, 1951.

DURHAM, R. and E. S. Cole, "Social Class Structure in Emporia Senior High School," *Midwest Sociologist,* 19 (May, 1957).

ELLIS, Robert A., "Social Status and Social Distance," *Sociology and Social Research,* 40 (March-April, 1956), 240-246.

ELLIS, Robert A., "The Prestige Rating Technique in Community Stratification Research," in Richard N. Adams and Jack J. Preiss, editors, *Human Organization Research: Field Relations and Techniques,* Homewood, Illinois: Dorsey, 1960.

ELLIS, Robert A. and Thomas C. Reedy, Jr., "Three Dimensions of Status: A Study of Academic Prestige," *Pacific Sociological Review,* 3 (Spring, 1960), 23-28.

FAUNCE, William A. and M. Joseph Smucker, "Industrialization and Community Status Structure," *American Sociological Review,* 31 (June, 1966), 390-399.

FLIEGEL, Frederick C., "Differences in Prestige Standards and Orientation to Change in a Traditional Agricultural Setting," *Rural Sociology,* 30 (September, 1965), 278-290.

FORM, William H., "Status Stratification in a Planned Community," *American Sociological Review,* 10 (October, 1945), 605-613.

FOSTER, Philip J., "Status, Power and Education in a Traditional Community," *School Review,* 72 (Summer, 1964), 158-182.

FREEDMAN, Howard E., J. Michael Ross, David Armor, and Thomas F. Pettigrew, "Color Gradation and Attitudes Among Middle-Income Negroes," *American Sociological Review,* 31 (June, 1966), 365-374.

FREIDMAN, N. L., "German Lineage and Reform Affiliation: American Jewish Prestige Criteria in Transition," *Phylon,* 26 (Summer, 1965), 140-147.

GALLAHER, Art, Jr., *Plainville Fifteen Years Later,* New York: Columbia University Press, 1961.

GANS, Herbert J., *The Urban Villagers: Group and Class in the Life of Italian Americans,* New York: Free Press, 1962.

GLENN, Norval D., "Negro Prestige Criteria: A Case Study in the Bases of Prestige," *American Journal of Sociology,* 68 (May, 1963), 645-657.

GOFFMAN, Erving, *Stigma: Notes on the Management of Spoiled Identity,* Englewood Cliffs, New Jersey: Prentice-Hall, 1963.

GOLDHAMER, Herbert and Edward A. Shils, "Types of Power and Status," *American Journal of Sociology,* 45 (September, 1939), 171-182.

GOLDSCHMIDT, Walter, "Social Class in America—A Critical Review," *American Anthropologist,* 52 (October-December, 1950), 483-498.

GOLDSCHMIDT, Walter, "Social Class and the Dynamics of Status in America," *American Anthropologist,* (December, 1955), 1209-1217.

GORDON, Milton M., *Social Class in American Sociology,* Durham, North Carolina: Duke University Press, 1958.

HAAS, Mary R., "The Declining Descent Rule for Rank in Thailand: A Correction," *American Anthropologist,* 53 (1951), 585-587.

HAER, John L., "A Test of the Unidimensionality of the Index of Status Characteristics," *Social Forces,* 34 (October, 1955), 56-58.

HAER, John L., "Predictive Utility of Five Indices of Social Stratification," *American Sociological Review,* 22 (October, 1957), 541-546.

HARGENS, Lowell L. and Warren O. Hagstrom, "Sponsored and Contest Mobility of American Academic Scientists," *Sociology of Education,* 40 (Winter, 1967), 24-38.

HARRIS, Edward E., "The Generalizability of Prestige Ratings in Cross-Cultural Perspective," *Australian and New Zealand Journal of Sociology,* 4 (April, 1968), 63-67.

HATCH, D. L. and M. A. Hatch, "Criteria of Social Status as Derived from Marriage Announcements in the *New York Times,*" *American Sociological Review,* 12 (August, 1947), 396-403.

HATT, Paul K., "Stratification in the Mass Society," *American Sociological Review,* 15 (April, 1950), 216-222.

HATT, Paul K., "The Prestige Continuum," in R. W. O'Brien, *et al.,* editors, *Readings in General Sociology,* New York: Houghton Mifflin, 1951.

HAVIGHURST, Robert J., Robert H. Bowman, Gordon P. Liddle, Charles V. Matthews, and James V. Pierce, *Growing Up in River City,* New York: Wiley, 1962.

HEBER, Rick F. and Mary E. Heber, "The Effect of Group Failure and Success on Social Status," *Journal of Educational Psychology,* 48 (March, 1957), 129-134.

PRESTIGE

HILL, Mozell C., "Social Status and Physical Appearance Among Negro Adolescents," *Social Forces,* 22 (May, 1944), 443-448.

HILL, Mozell C. and Bevode C. McCall, "Social Stratification in 'Georgia Town'," *American Sociological Review,* 15 (December, 1950), 721-729.

HOLLINGSHEAD, August B., "Class and Kinship in a Middle Western Community," *American Sociological Review,* 14 (August, 1949), 469-475.

HOLLINGSHEAD, August B., *Elmtown's Youth: The Impact of Social Classes on Adolescents,* New York: Wiley, 1949.

HOLLINGSHEAD, August B., "Selected Characteristics of Classes in a Middle Western Community," *American Sociological Review,* 12 (August, 1947), 385-395.

HOMANS, George C., "Status among Clerical Workers," *Human Organization,* 12 (1953), 5-10.

HOULT, T. F., "Experimental Measurement of Clothing as a Factor in Some Social Ratings of Selected American Men," *American Sociological Review,* 19 (June, 1954), 324-328.

JONES, Clifton R., "Social Stratification in the Negro Population: A Study of Social Classes in South Boston, Virginia," *Journal of Negro Education,* 15 (Winter, 1946), 4-12.

KAUFMAN, Harold F., "An Approach to the Study of Urban Stratification," *American Sociological Review,* 17 (August, 1952), 430-437.

KAUFMAN, Harold F., "Defining Prestige Rank in a Rural Community," *Sociometry,* 8 (May, 1945), 199-207.

KAUFMAN, Harold F., *Defining Prestige in a Rural Community,* Sociometry Monograph No. 10, Beacon House, 1946.

KAUFMAN, Harold F., "Members of a Rural Community as Judges of Prestige Rank," *Sociometry,* 9 (February, 1946), 71-85.

KAUFMAN, Harold F., *Prestige Classes in a New York Rural Community,* Ithaca: Cornell University Agricultural Experiment Station, Memoir 260, March, 1944.

KEPHART, William M., "Status after Death," *American Sociological Review,* 15 (October, 1950), 635-643.

KOLAJA, Jiri and Ali Paydarfar, "A Note on the Concepts of Esteem and Prestige," *Sociological Review,* 12 (November, 1964), 283-292.

KORNHAUSER, Ruth Rosner, "The Warner Approach to Social

Stratification," in Reinhard Bendix and Seymour M. Lipset, editors, *Class, Status, and Power,* New York: Free Press, 1953.

LASSWELL, Thomas E., "A Study of Social Stratification Using an Area Sample of Raters," *American Sociological Review,* 19 (June, 1954), 310-313.

LASSWELL, Thomas E., "The Perception of Social Status," *Sociology and Social Research,* 45 (January, 1961), 170-174.

LAUMANN, Edward O., *Prestige and Association in an Urban Community: An Analysis of an Urban Stratification System,* Indianapolis: Bobbs-Merrill, 1966.

LAZARSFELD, Paul F. and Wagner Thielans, Jr., *The Academic Mind,* New York: Free Press, 1958.

LENSKI, Gerhard E., "American Social Classes: Statistical Strata or Social Groups," *American Journal of Sociology,* 58 (September, 1952), 139-149.

LEVINE, Gene Norman and Leila A. Sussman, "Social Class and Sociability in Fraternity Pledging," *American Journal of Sociology,* 65 (January, 1960), 391-399.

LIPSET, Seymour M. and Reinhard Bendix, "Social Status and Social Structure: A Re-examination of Data and Interpretations, I and II," *British Journal of Sociology,* 2 (June and September, 1951), 150-168 and 230-254.

LOCKWOOD, David, *The Blackcoated Worker,* London: Unwin, 1958, Chapter 4, "The Modern Office: Status Situation."

LONGMORE, T. Wilson, "A Matrix Approach to the Analysis of Rank and Status in a Community in Peru," *Sociometry,* 11 (August, 1948), 192-206.

LOOMIS, Charles P. and Reed M. Powell, "Sociometric Analysis of Class Status in Rural Costa Rica—A Peasant Community Compared with an Hacienda Community," *Sociometry,* 12 (February, 1949), 144-157.

MANHEIM, Henry L., "Intergroup Interaction as Related to Status and Leadership Differences between Groups," *Sociometry,* 23 (December, 1960), 415-427.

MARGOLIN, Edythe, "Group Context and Concepts of Social Status," *Sociology and Social Research,* 48 (April, 1964), 324-329.

MARSHALL, T. H., "The Nature and Determinants of Social Status," in *Class, Citizenship, and Social Development,* Garden City, New York: Doubleday, 1965.

MAU, James A., Richard J. Hill, and Wendell Bell, "Scale Analysis of Status Perception and Status Attitude in Jamaica and the

United States," *Pacific Sociological Review,* 4 (Spring, 1961), 33-40.

McDILL, Edward L., and James Coleman, "High School Social Status, College Plans, and Interest in Academic Achievement: A Panel Analysis, *American Sociological Review,* 28 (December, 1963), 905-918.

McGUIRE, Carson, "Social Status," in J. Olsen, editor, *School and Community,* New York: Prentice-Hall, 1954.

McGUIRE, Carson and Rodney A. Clark, "Age-Mate Acceptance and Indices of Peer Status," *Child Development,* 23 (1952), 141-154.

MERTON, Robert K., "Recognition and Excellence: Instructive Ambiguities," in Adam Yarmolinsky, editor, *Recognition of Excellence,* New York: Free Press, 1960.

MITCHELL, J. Clyde and A. L. Epstein, "Occupational Prestige and Social Status Among Urban Africans in Northern Rhodesia," *Africa,* 29 (January, 1959), 22-40.

MONTAGUE, Joel B., Jr., "Class or Status Society," *Sociology and Social Research,* 40 (May-June, 1956), 333-338.

MOOS, Malcolm and Bertram Kaslin, "Prestige Suggestion and Political Leadership," *Public Opinion Quarterly,* 16 (Spring, 1952), 77-93.

OPPENHEIMER, F., "Pamela: A Case Study in Status Symbols," *Journal of Abnormal and Social Psychology,* 40 (April, 1945), 187-194.

PAYNE, Raymond, "An Approach to the Study of Relative Prestige of Formal Organizations," *Social Forces,* 32 (March, 1954), 244-247.

PERROW, Charles, "Organizational Prestige: Some Functions and Dysfunctions," *American Journal of Sociology,* 66 (January, 1961, 335-341.

PERRUCCI, Robert, "Social Distance Strategies and Intra-Organizational Stratification: A Study of the Status System on a Psychiatric Ward," *American Sociological Review,* 28 (December, 1963), 951-962.

PFAUTZ, Harold W. and Otis Dudley Duncan, "A Critical Evaluation of Warner's Work in Community Stratification," *American Sociological Review,* 15 (April, 1950), 205-215.

POPE, B., "Socioeconomic Contrasts in Children's Peer Culture Prestige Values," *Genetic Psychology Monographs,* 48 (1953), 157-220.

POWDERMAKER, Hortense, *After Freedom,* New York: Viking, 1939.

PRICE, Derek, *Little Science, Big Science,* New York: Columbia University Press, 1963.

PUTNEY, Snell and Gladys J. Putney, "Radical Innovation and Prestige," *American Sociological Review,* 27 (August, 1962), 548-551.

RADIN, Max, "Status," *Encyclopedia of the Social Sciences,* 14, New York: Macmillan, 1930, 373-378.

RECORD, Jane Cassels, "The Marine Radioman's Struggle for Status," *American Journal of Sociology,* 62 (January, 1957), 353-359.

RODNICK, David, "Status Values Among Railroadmen," *Social Forces,* 20 (October, 1941), 89-96.

ROGERS, Everett M. and A. Eugene Havens, "Prestige Rating and Mate Selection on a College Campus," *Journal of Marriage and the Family,* 22 (February, 1960), 55-59.

ROHRER, John H. and Munro S. Edmonson, editors, *The Eighth Generation,* New York: Harper and Row, 1960.

ROUCEK, Joseph S., "Age as a Prestige Factor," *Sociology and Social Research,* 42 (May-June, 1958), 349-352.

SCHNEIDER, Joseph, "Class of Origin and Fame: Eminent English Women," *American Sociological Review,* 5 (October, 1940), 700-712.

SCHNEIDER, Joseph, "Social Origin and Fame: The United States and England," *American Sociological Review,* 10 (February, 1945), 52-60.

SCHNEIDER, Joseph, "The Definition of Eminence and the Social Origins of Famous Men of Genius," *American Sociological Review,* 3 (December, 1938), 834-849.

SCHOENBAUM, David, *Hitler's Social Revolution: Class and Status in Nazi Germany, 1933-1939,* Garden City, New York: Doubleday, 1967.

SCUDDER, Richard and C. Arnold Anderson, "Range of Acquaintance and of Repute as Factors in Prestige Rating: Methods of Studying Social Status," *Social Forces,* 32 (March, 1954), 248-253.

SCUDDER, Richard and C. Arnold Anderson, "The Relation of Being Known to Status Rating," *Sociology and Social Research,* 38 (March-April, 1954), 239-241.

SHERIF, Muzafer, B. Jack White, and O. J. Harvey, "Status in Experimentally Produced Groups," *American Journal of Sociology,* 60 (January, 1955), 370-379.

SHIMBARI, Michiya, Hideo Ikeda, Tsuyoshi Ishida, and Moto Kondo, "Measuring a Nation's Prestige," *American Journal of*

Sociology, 69 (July, 1963), 63-68.

SCHULER, Edgar A., "Social and Economic Status in a Louisiana Hills Community," *Rural Sociology,* 5 (March, 1940), 69-89.

PRESTIGE

SILVERMAN, Sydel, "An Ethnographic Approach to Social Stratification: Prestige in a Central Italian Community," *American Anthropologist,* 68 (August, 1966), 899-921.

SMITH, M. G., "The Hausa System of Social Status," *Africa,* 19 (July, 1959), 239-251.

SPEIER, Hans, "Social Stratification in the Urban Community," *American Sociological Review,* 1 (April, 1936), 193-202.

STAGNER, Ross, "The Prestige Value of Different Types of Leadership," *Sociology and Social Research,* 25 (May-June, 1941), 403-413.

STEVENSON, H. N. C., "Status Evaluation in the Hindu Caste System," *Journal of the Royal Anthropological Institute,* 84 (1954), 45-65.

STONE, Gregory P. and William H. Form, "Instabilities in Status: The Problem of Hierarchy in the Community Study of Status Arrangements," *American Sociological Review,* 18 (April, 1953), 149-162.

SVALASTOGA, Kaare, *Prestige, Class, and Mobility,* Copenhagen: Gyldendal, 1959.

SVALASTOGA, Kaare, *Social Differentiation,* New York: McKay, 1965.

TRIANDIS, Harry C., Vasso Vassiliou, and Erich Thomanek, "Social Status as a Determinant of Respect and Friendship Acceptance," *Sociometry,* 29 (December, 1966), 396-405.

USEEM, John, Pierre Tangent, and Ruth Useem, "Stratification in a Prairie Town," *American Sociological Review,* 7 (June, 1942), 331-342.

VAN DER MERWE, Hendrick W., "Social Stratification in a Cape Colored Community," *Sociology and Social Research,* 46 (April, 1962), 302-311.

VEBLEN, Thorstein, *The Theory of the Leisure Class,* New York: Macmillan, 1899.

WARNER, Robert A., *New Haven Negroes,* New Haven: Yale University Press, 1940.

WARNER, W. Lloyd, *American Life: Dream and Reality,* revised edition, Chicago: University of Chicago Press, 1962.

WARNER, W. Lloyd, *The Living and the Dead,* New Haven: Yale University Press, 1959.

WARNER, W. Lloyd, *Yankee City*, one volume paperback edition, New Haven: Yale University Press, 1963.

WARNER, W. Lloyd and Associates, *Democracy in Jonesville: A Study in Quality and Inequality*, New York: Harper, 1949.

WARNER, W. Lloyd, Marchia Meeker, and Kenneth Eells, *Social Class in America*, New York: Science Research Associates, 1949.

WARNER, W. Lloyd and Paul S. Lunt, *The Social Life of a Modern Community*, New Haven: Yale University Press, 1941.

WARNER, W. Lloyd and Paul S. Lunt, *The Status System of a Modern Community*, New Haven: Yale University Press, 1942.

WEST, James, (Carl Withers), *Plainville, U. S. A.*, New York: Columbia University Press, 1945.

WHYTE, William F., *Street Corner Society: The Social Structure of an Italian Slum*, Chicago: University of Chicago Press, 1955.

WILLARD, Walter, "The Rating and Dating Complex," *American Sociological Review*, 2 (October, 1937), 727-734.

WILSON, Logan, "Prestige Patterns in Scholarship and Science," *Southwestern Social Science Quarterly*, 23 (1943), 305-319.

WILSON, Logan, *The Academic Man: Sociology of a Profession*, London: Oxford University Press, 1958.

WISPE, Lauren G., "Some Social and Psychological Correlates of Eminence in Psychology," *Journal of the History of the Behavioral Sciences*, 1 (January, 1965).

YARMOLINSKY, Adam, editor, *Recognition of Excellence*, New York: Free Press, 1960.

YOUNG, Michael and Peter Willmott, "Social Grading by Manual Workers," *British Journal of Sociology*, 7 (December, 1956), 337-345.

ZELDITCH, Morris, "Status, Social," *International Encyclopedia of the Social Sciences*, 15, New York: Free Press, 1968, 250-257.

ZUCKERMAN, Harriet, "Nobel Laureates in Science: Patterns of Productivity, Collaboration, and Authorship," *American Sociological Review*, 32 (June, 1967), 391-403.

Occupational Prestige

The literature in this section covers not only studies of occupational prestige but also rankings of occupations in terms of such ambiguously defined variables as "socio-economic status."

ALZOBAIE, Abdul Jalil and Mohammed Ahmed El-Ghannam, "Iraqi Student Perceptions of Occupations," *Sociology and Social Research,* 52 (April, 1968), 231-236.

ANDERSON, C. Arnold, "The Social Status of University Students in Relation to Type of Economy: An International Comparison," *Transactions of the Third World Congress of Sociology,* 5 (1956), 51-63.

ANDERSON, W. A., "The Occupational Attitudes of College Men," *Journal of Social Psychology,* 5 (1934), 435-466.

ARMER, J. Michael, "Intersociety and Intrasociety Correlations of Occupational Prestige," *American Journal of Sociology,* 74 (July, 1968), 28-36.

BAUDLER, Lucille and D. G. Patterson, "Social Status of Women's Occupations," *Occupations,* 26 (1947-1948), 421-424.

BLAU, Peter M., "Occupational Bias and Mobility," *American Sociological Review,* 22 (August, 1957), 392-399.

BROWN, Morgan C., "The Status of Jobs and Occupations as Evaluated by an Urban Negro Sample," *American Sociological Review,* 20 (October, 1955), 561-566.

CARLSON, Richard O., "Variation and Myth in Social Status of Teachers," *Journal of Educational Sociology,* 35 (November, 1961), 104-120.

CARLSSON, Gosta, *Social Mobility and Class Structure,* Lund: C. W. K. Gleerup, 1958, 145-155.

CARTER, Roy E., Jr. and Orlando Sepulveda, "Occupational Prestige in Santiago, Chile," *American Behavioral Scientist,* 8 (September, 1964), 20-24.

CONGALTON, Athol A., *Occupational Status in Australia,* Kensington: University of New South Wales, School of Sociology, 1963.

CONGALTON, Athol A., "Social Grading of Occupations in New Zealand," *British Journal of Sociology,* 4 (March, 1953), 45-59.

COOK, David R., "Prestige of Occupations in India," *Psychological Studies,* 7 (January 1962), 31-37.

COOPER, James G., "The Social Status of Occupations in Micronesia," *Personnel and Guidance Journal,* 41 (November, 1962), 267-269.

COUNTS, George S., "The Social Status of Occupations," *School Review,* 33 (January, 1925), 16-27.

COUTU, W., "The Relative Prestige of Twenty Professions as Judged by Three Groups of Professional Students," *Social Forces,* 14 (May, 1936), 522-529.

DAVIDSON, Percy E. and H. Dewey Anderson, "Are Edwards' Socio-Economic Levels Economic?" *School and Society,* 48 (July, 1938), 153-156.

DAVIES, A. F., "Prestige of Occupations," *British Journal of Sociology,* 3 (June, 1952), 134-147.

DAVIS, Jerome, "Testing the Social Attitudes of Children in the Government Schools of Russia," *American Journal of Sociology,* 32 (May, 1927), 947-952.

DEEG, M. E. and D. G. Patterson, "Changes in Social Status of Occupations," *Occupations,* 25 (January, 1947), 205-208.

DeFLEUR, Melvin L., "Occupational Roles as Portrayed on Television," *Public Opinion Quarterly,* 28 (Spring, 1964), 57-74.

DEVEREUX, George and Florence R. Weiner, "The Occupational Status of Nurses," *American Sociological Review,* 15 (October, 1950), 628-634.

D'SOUZA, Victor S., "Social Grading of Occupations in India," *Sociological Review,* 10 (July, 1962), 145-159.

DUNCAN, Otis Dudley, "A Socioeconomic Index for All Occupations," and "Properties and Characteristics of the Socioeconomic Index," in Albert J. Reiss, Jr., *Occupations and Social Status,* New York: Free Press, 1961.

EDWARDS, Alba M., "A Social-Economic Grouping of the Gainful Workers of the United States," *Journal of the American Statistical Association,* 28 (December, 1933), 377-387.

EDWARDS, Alba M., *A Social-Economic Grouping of the Gainful Workers of the United States,* Washington, D. C., U. S. Government Printing Office, 1938.

EPSTEIN, A. L., "Occupational Prestige on the Gazelle Peninsula, New Britain," *Australian and New Zealand Journal of Sociology,* 3 (October, 1967), 111-121.

GAMSON, William A. and Howard Schuman, "Some Undercurrents in the Prestige of Physicians," *American Journal of Sociology,* 68 (January, 1963), 463-470.

GARBIN, Albeno P. and Frederick L. Bates, "Occupational Prestige: An Empirical Study of its Correlates," *Social Forces,* 40 (December, 1961), 131-136.

GARBIN, Albeno P. and Frederick L. Bates, "Occupational Prestige and its Correlates: A Re-examination," *Social Forces,* 44 (March, 1966), 295-302.

GERSTL, Joel E. and Lois K. Cohen, "Dissensus, Situs, and Egocentrism in Occupational Ranking," *British Journal of Sociology,* 15 (September, 1964), 254-261.

GROFF, Patrick J., "The Social Status of Teachers," *Journal of Educational Sociology,* 36 (September, 1962), 20-25.

GUSFIELD, Joseph R. and Michael Schwartz, "The Meanings of Occupational Prestige: Reconsideration of the NORC Scale," *American Sociological Review,* 28 (April, 1963), 265-271.

HALL, J. R., and D. C. Jones, "The Social Grading of Occupations," *British Journal of Sociology,* 1 (March, 1950), 31-55.

HALLER, Archibald O. and David M. Lewis, "The Hypothesis of Intersocietal Similarity in Occupational Prestige Hierarchies," *American Journal of Sociology,* 72 (September, 1966), 210-216.

HARRIS, Edward E., "The Generalizability of Prestige Ratings in Cross-Cultural Perspective," *Australian and New Zealand Journal of Sociology,* 4 (April, 1968), 63-67.

HARTMANN, George W., "The Prestige of Occupations," *Personnel Journal,* 13 (October, 1934), 144-152.

HARTMANN, George W., "The Relative Social Prestige of Representative Medical Specialties," *Journal of Applied Psychology,* 20 (1936), 659-663.

HATT, Paul K., "The Prestige Continuum," in R. W. O'Brien, *et al.,* editors, *Readings in General Sociology,* New York: Houghton Mifflin, 1951.

HODGE, Robert W., Donald J. Treiman, and Peter H. Rossi, "A Comparative Study of Occupational Prestige," in Reinhard Bendix and Seymour M. Lipset, editors, *Class, Status and Power,* revised edition, New York: Free Press, 1966.

HODGE, Robert W., Paul M. Siegel, and Peter H. Rossi, "Occupational Prestige in the United States, 1925-1963," in Reinhard Bendix and Seymour M. Lipset, editors, *Class, Status and Power,* New York: Free Press, 1966.

HODGE, Robert W., Paul M. Siegel, and Peter H. Rossi, "Occupational Prestige in the United States, 1925-1963," *American Journal of Sociology,* 70 (November, 1964), 286-302. This is an abridged version of the preceding item.

HUTCHINSON, Bertram, "Social Grading of Occupations in Brazil," *British Journal of Sociology,* 8 (June, 1957), 176-189.

INKELES, Alex and Peter H. Rossi, "National Comparisons of Occupational Prestige," *American Journal of Sociology,* 61 (January, 1956), 329-339.

KRIESBERG, Louis, "The Bases of Occupational Prestige: The Case of Dentists," *American Sociological Review,* 27 (April, 1962), 238-244.

KRISHNAN, B., "Regional Influences on Occupational Preferences," *Psychological Studies,* 6 (July, 1961), 66-70.

KRISHNAN, B., "Social Prestige of Occupations," *Journal of Vocational and Educational Guidance,* 3 (August, 1956), 18-22.

LEHMAN, H. C. and P. A. Witty, "Further Study of the Social Status of Occupations," *Journal of Educational Sociology,* 5 (1931), 101-112.

LEWIS, David M., "Perception of Entrepreneurial Prestige by Japanese Boys," *Rural Sociology,* 33 (March, 1968), 71-79.

LEWIS, Lionel S. and Joseph Lopreato, "Functional Importance and Prestige of Occupations," *Pacific Sociological Review,* 6 (1963), 55-59.

McDONAGH, Edward C., Sven Wermlund, and John F. Growther, "Relative Professional Status as Perceived by American and Swedish University Students," *Social Forces,* 38 (October, 1959), 65-69.

McTAVISH, Donald G., "The Differential Prestige of Situs Categories," *Social Forces,* 41 (May, 1963), 363-368.

MITCHELL, J. Clyde and A. L. Epstein, "Occupational Prestige and Social Status Among Urban Africans in Northern Rhodesia," *Africa,* 29 (January, 1959), 22-40.

MITCHELL, J. Clyde, "The Differences in an English and an American Rating of the Prestige of Occupations: A Reconsideration of Montague and Pustilnik's Study," *British Journal of Sociology,* 15 (June, 1964), 166-173.

MITCHELL, William C., "The Ambivalent Social Status of the American Politician," *Western Political Quarterly,* 12 (September, 1959), 683-698.

MOSER, C. A. and J. R. Hall, "The Social Grading of Occupations," in David V. Glass, editor, *Social Mobility in Britain,* London: Routledge and Kegan Paul, 1954.

NATIONAL OPINION RESEARCH CENTER; "Jobs and Occupations: A Popular Evaluation," *Opinion News,* 9 (September 1, 1947), 3-13. Authorship of this article is usually attributed to Paul K. Hatt and C. C. North.

OCCUPATIONAL PRESTIGE

NELSON, Harold A. and Edward C. McDonagh, "Perception of Statuses and Images of Selected Professions," *Sociology and Social Research,* 46 (October, 1961), 3-16.

PINEO, Peter C. and John C. Porter, "Occupational Prestige in Canada," *Canadian Review of Sociology and Anthropology,* 4 (1967), 24-40.

RAMSEY, Charles E. and Robert J. Smith, "Japanese and American Perceptions of Occupations," *American Journal of Sociology,* 65 (March, 1960), 475-482.

REISS, Albert J., Jr., Otis Dudley Duncan, Paul K. Hatt, and Cecil C. North, *Occupations and Social Status,* New York: Free Press, 1961.

RESEARCH COMMITTEE, Japan Sociological Society, "Social Stratification and Mobility in Six Large Cities of Japan," *Transactions of the Second World Congress of Sociology,* 2 (1954), 414-431.

ROSSI, Peter H. and Alex Inkeles, "Multidimensional Ratings of Occupations," *Sociometry,* 20 (September, 1957), 234-251.

SARAPATA, Adam and Wlodzimierz Wesolowski, "The Evaluation of Occupations by Warsaw Inhabitants," *American Journal of Sociology,* 66 (May, 1961), 581-591.

SIMENSON, William and Gilbert Geis, "A Cross-cultural Study of University Students," *Journal of Higher Education,* 26 (January, 1955), 21-24.

SIMPSON, Richard L. and Ida Harper Simpson, "Correlates and Estimates of Occupational Prestige," *American Journal of Sociology,* 66 (September, 1960), 135-140.

SIMS, V. M., "Social Class Affiliation of a Group of Public School Teachers," *School Review,* 59 (September, 1951).

SMITH, Mapheus, "An Empirical Scale of Prestige Status of Occupations," *American Sociological Review,* 8 (April, 1943), 185-192.

SMITH, M. G., "The Hausa System of Social Status," *Africa,* 29 (July, 1959), 239-251.

STRODTBECK, Fred L., Margaret R. McDonald, and Bernard C. Rosen, "Evaluation of Occupations: A Reflection of Jewish and Italian Differences," *American Sociological Review,* 22 (October, 1957), 546-553.

SVALASTOGA, Kaare, "Measurement of Occupational Prestige: Field Techniques," *Transactions of the Second World Congress of Sociology,* 2 (1954), 403-413.

SVALASTOGA, Kaare, *Prestige, Class, and Mobility,* Copenhagen: Glydendal, 1959.

TAFT, Ronald, "The Social Grading of Occupations in Australia," *British Journal of Sociology,* 4 (March, 1953), 181-188.

THOMAS, Murray, "Occupational Prestige: Indonesia and America," *Personnel and Guidance Journal,* 41 (January, 1963), 430-434.

THOMAS, Murray, "Reinspecting a Structural Position on Occupational Prestige," *American Journal of Sociology,* 67 (March, 1962), 561-565.

TIRYAKIAN, Edward A., "The Prestige Evaluation of Occupations in an Underdeveloped Country: The Philippines," *American Journal of Sociology,* 63 (January, 1958), 390-399.

TUCKMAN, Jacob, "Social Status of Occupations in Canada," *Canadian Journal of Psychology,* 1 (June, 1947), 71-74.

VAN DER VEUR, Paul W., "Occupational Prestige Among Secondary School Students in West New Guinea (West Irian)," *Australian and New Zealand Journal of Sociology,* 2 (October, 1966), 107-110.

WALLIN, Paul and Leslie C. Waldo, "Indeterminacies in Ranking of Fathers' Occupations," *Public Opinion Quarterly,* 28 (Summer, 1964), 287-292.

WELCH, M. K., "The Ranking of Occupations on the Basis of Social Status," *Occupations,* 26 (January, 1949), 237-241.

XYDIAS, N., "Prestige of Occupations," in C. Daryl Forde, editor, *Social Implications of Industrialization and Urbanization in Africa South of the Sahara,* Paris: UNESCO, Tension and Technology Series, 1956.

Power, Authority, and Leadership:

General Treatments

The material under this topic is generally theoretical and conceptual. Examination of almost any two or three of the publications reveals that the conceptual problems are complex and not highly tractable. In spite of the considerable body of literature, there is still room for many important contributions in this area.

ABRAMSON, E., H. A. Cutter, R. W. Kautz and M. Mendelson, "Social Power and Commitment: A Theoretical Statement," *American Sociological Review,* 23 (February, 1958), 15-22.

ADAMS, Richard N., *The Second Sowing: Power and Secondary Development in Latin America,* San Francisco: Chandler, 1967.

AGGER, Robert E., Daniel Goldrich and Bert E. Swanson, *The Rulers and the Ruled,* New York: Wiley, 1964.

BACHRACH, Peter and Morton S. Baratz, "Two Faces of Power," *American Political Science Review,* 56 (December, 1962), 947-952.

BANFIELD, Edward C., *Political Influence,* New York: Free Press, 1960.

BAUER, Raymond A., "Communications as a Transaction: A Comment on 'On the Concept of Influence,'" *Public Opinion Quarterly,* 27 (Spring, 1963), 83-86.

BAUER, Raymond A., "Social Psychology and the Study of Policy Formation," *American Psychologist,* 21 (1966), 933-942.

BAUER, Raymond A. and Kenneth J. Gergen, editors, *The Study of Policy Formation,* New York: Free Press, 1968.

BENDIX, Reinhard, "Social Stratification and Political Power," *American Political Science Review,* 46 (June, 1952), 357-375.

BERTRAND, Alvin L., *Basic Sociology,* New York: Appleton-Century-Crofts, 1967, Chapter 11, "Social Power."

BIERSTEDT, Robert, "An Analysis of Social Power," *American Sociological Review,* 15 (December, 1950), 730-738.

BIERSTEDT, Robert, "The Problem of Authority," in Morroe Berger, Theodore Abel, and Charles H. Page, editors, *Freedom and Control in Modern Society,* New York: Van Nostrand, 1954.

BLAU, Peter M., "Critical Remarks on Weber's Theory of Authority," *American Political Science Review,* 57 (June, 1963), 305-316.

BLAU, Peter M., *Exchange and Power in Social Life,* New York: Wiley, 1964.

BORGATTA, E. F., R. F. Bales, and A. S. Couch, "Some Findings Relevant to the Great Man Theory of Leadership," *American Sociological Review,* 19 (December, 1954), 755-759.

BUCKLEY, Walter, *Sociology and Modern Systems Analysis,* Englewood Cliffs, New Jersey: Prentice-Hall, 1967, Chapter 6.

CARTWRIGHT, D., editor, *Studies in Social Power,* Ann Arbor: University of Michigan, Institute for Social Research, 1959.

COLEMAN, James S., "Comment on 'On the Concept of Influence,'" *Public Opinion Quarterly,* 27 (Spring, 1963), 63-82.

COLEMAN, James S., "Foundations for a Theory of Collective Decisions," *American Journal of Sociology,* 71 (May, 1966), 615-627.

DAHL, Robert A., "The Concept of Power," *Behavioral Science,* 2 (July, 1957), 201-215.

DAHL, Robert A., "Power," *International Encyclopedia of the Social Sciences,* 12, New York: Free Press, 1968, 405-414.

DAHLSTROM, Edmund, "Exchange, Influence and Power," *Acta Sociologica,* 9, 237-284.

DUBIN, Robert, "Power, Function, and Organization," *Pacific Sociological Review,* 6 (Spring, 1963), 16-24.

EMERSON, Richard M., "Power-Dependence Relations," *American Sociological Review,* 27 (February, 1962), 31-41.

FRENCH, John R. P. and Bertram Raven, "The Bases of Social Power," in D. Cartwright, editor, *Studies in Social Power,* Ann Arbor: University of Michigan, Institute for Social Research, 1959.

FRENCH, John R. P. and R. Snyder, "Leadership and Interpersonal Power," in D. Cartwright, editor, *Studies in Social Power,* Ann Arbor, Michigan: University of Michigan Institute for Social Research, 1959.

FRIEDRICH, Carl J., "Political Leadership and Charismatic Power," *Journal of Politics,* 23 (February, 1961).

GIBB, C. A., "Leadership," in Gardner Lindzey, editor, *Handbook of Social Psychology,* Cambridge: Addison-Wesley, 1954.

GENERAL TREATMENTS

GIBB, C. A., "The Principles and Traits of Leadership," in A. Paul Hare, E. F. Borgatta, and R. F. Bales, editors, *Small Groups: Studies in Social Interaction,* New York: Knopf, 1955.

GENERAL TREATMENTS

GOLDHAMER, Herbert and Edward A. Shils, "Types of Power and Status," *American Journal of Sociology,* 45 (September, 1939), 171-182.

HELLER, Hermann, "Power, Political," *Encyclopaedia of the Social Sciences,* 7, New York: Macmillan, 1930, 301-305.

HOLLANDER, Edwin P., *Leaders, Groups, and Influence,* New York: Oxford University Press, 1964.

HOLLANDER, E. P. and James W. Julian, "Leadership," in Edgar F. Borgatta and William W. Lambert, editors, *Handbook of Personality Theory and Research,* Chicago: Rand McNally, 1968.

HOVLAND, C. I., I. L. Janis, and H. H. Kelley, *Communication and Persuasion,* New Haven: Yale University Press, 1953.

JENNINGS, Eugene E., *The Anatomy of Leadership: Princes, Heroes, and Supermen,* New York: Harper and Row, 1960.

KAUFMAN, Herbert and Victor Jones, "The Mystery of Power," *Public Administration Review,* 14 (Summer, 1954), 205-212.

KELLER, Suzanne, *Beyond the Ruling Class,* New York: Random House, 1963.

LASSWELL, Harold D., *Politics: Who Gets What, When, and How,* New York: McGraw-Hill, 1936.

LASSWELL, Harold D., *Power and Personality,* New York: Norton, 1948.

LASSWELL, Harold D. and Abraham Kaplan, *Power and Society: A Framework for Political Inquiry,* New Haven: Yale University Press, 1950.

LIPPITT, Ronald, Norman Polansky, Fritz Redl, and Sidney Rosen, "The Dynamics of Power," *Human Relations,* 5 (February, 1952), 37-64.

LOEWENSTEIN, Karl, *Max Webers' Political Ideas in the Perspective of Our Time,* Amherst: University of Massachusetts Press, 1966.

MARCH, James G., "An Introduction to the Theory and Measurement of Influence," *American Political Science Review,* 49 (June, 1955), 431-451.

MARVICK, Dwaine, editor, *Political Decision-Makers,* New York: Free Press, 1961.

McINTOSH, Donald S., "Power and Social Control," *American Political Science Review,* 57 (September, 1963), 619-631.

MICHELS, Robert, "Authority," *Encyclopaedia of the Social Sciences,* 2, New York: Macmillan, 1930, 319-321.

MILLER, Walter B., "Two Concepts of Authority," *American Anthropologist,* 57 (April, 1955), 271-289.

MOORE, Barrington Jr., *Political Power and Social Theory,* New York: Harper and Row, 1965.

MORGENTHAU, Hans, "Power as a Political Concept," in Roland Young, editor, *Approaches to the Study of Politics,* Evanston: Northwestern University Press, 1958.

MORRIS, Richard T. and Melvin Seeman, "The Problem of Leadership: An Interdisciplinary Approach," *American Journal of Sociology,* 56 (September, 1950), 149-155.

MURPHY, Albert J., "A Study of the Leadership Process," *American Sociological Review,* 6 (October, 1941), 674-687.

OLSEN, Marvin E., *The Process of Social Organization,* New York: Holt, Rinehart and Winston, 1968. Chapter 12, "The Process of Social Power."

PARSONS, Talcott, "On the Concept of Influence," *Public Opinion Quarterly,* 27 (Spring, 1963), 37-62.

PARSONS, Talcott, "On the Concept of Political Power," *Proceedings of the American Philosophical Society,* 107 (June, 1963).

PEABODY, Robert L., "Authority," *International Encyclopedia of the Social Sciences,* 1, New York: Free Press, 1968, 473-477.

PIGORS, P., *Leadership or Domination,* Boston: Houghton Mifflin, 1935.

PLESSNER, Helmuth, "The Emancipation of Power," *Social Research,* 31 (Summer, 1954), 155-174.

RAVEN, Bertram H., and John R. P. French, Jr., "Legitimate Power, Coercive Power and Observability in Social Influence," *Sociometry,* 21 (June, 1958), 83-97.

RIKER, William H., "Some Ambiguities in the Notion of Power," *American Political Science Review,* 58 (June, 1964), 341-349.

RUSTOW, Dankwart A., "Introduction to Issue on 'Philosophers and Kings:' Studies in Leadership," *Daedalus,* 97 (Summer, 1968), 683-694.

SCHERMERHORN, Richard A., *Society and Power,* New York: Random House, 1961.

SHKLAR, Judith N., "Rousseau's Images of Authority," *American Political Science Review,* 58 (December, 1964), 919-932.

GENERAL
TREATMENTS

TANNENBAUM Arnold, "An Event Structure Approach to Social Power and to the Problem of Power Comparability," *Behavioral Science,* 7 (July, 1962), 315-331.

WASSERMAN, Paul, *Decision-Making: An Annotated Bibliography,* Ithaca: Graduate School of Business and Public Administration, Cornell University, 1958.

WEBER, Max, *The Theory of Social and Economic Organization,* New York: Oxford University Press, 1947.

WEBER, Max., "The Three Types of Legitimate Rule," *Berkeley Publications in Society and Institutions,* 4 (Summer, 1958).

WESTIN, Alan, *Uses of Power,* New York: Harcourt, Brace, 1962.

WRONG, Dennis H., "Some Problems in Defining Social Power," *American Journal of Sociology,* 73 (May, 1968), 673-681.

Power, Authority, and Leadership:

at the Community Level

This has been an unusually active area of research and controversy since the publication in 1953 of Floyd Hunter's *Community Power Structure.* The past few years have been marked by important refinements in measurement and conceptualization and at least partial resolution of earlier heated debates concerning measurement and whether or not the distribution of power in communities in the United States is typically monolithic or pluralistic.

In compiling this list of publications, we drew so heavily upon a bibliography prepared by Roland J. Pellegrin and published in the December, 1967, issue of the *Southwestern Social Science Quarterly* that a special acknowledgement is due. Pellegrin's bibliography contains almost 90 percent of the items included here, plus a few publications we do not list.

ABRAMSON, E., H. A. Cutter, R. W. Kautz, and M. Mendelson, "Social Power and Commitment: A Theoretical Statement," *American Sociological Review,* 23 (February, 1958), 15-22.

ABU-LABAN, Baha, "Leader Visibility in a Local Community," *Pacific Sociological Review,* 4 (Fall, 1961), 73-78.

ABU-LABAN, Baha, "Self-Conception and Appraisal by Others: A Study of Community Leaders," *Sociology and Social Research,* 48 (October, 1963), 32-37.

ABU-LABAN, Baha, "Social Origins and Occupational Career Patterns of Community Leaders," *Sociological Inquiry,* 33 (Spring, 1963), 131-140.

ABU-LABAN, Baha, "The Reputational Approach in the Study of Community Power: A Critical Evaluation," *Pacific Sociological Review,* 8 (Spring, 1965), 35-42.

ADRIAN, Charles R., "Leadership and Decision-Making in Manager Cities: A Study of Three Communities," *Public Administration Review,* 18 (Summer, 1958), 208-213.

ADRIAN, Charles R., editor, *Social Science and Community Action,* East Lansing: Institute for Community Development and Services, Michigan State University, 1960.

ADRIAN, Charles R. and David A. Booth, *Simplifying the Discovery of Elites,* East Landing: Institute for Community Development and Services, Michigan State University.

AGGER, Robert E., "The Politics of Local Education: A Comparative Study of Community Decision-Making," in Donald E. Tope, editor, *A Forward Look: The Preparation of School Administrators, 1970,* Eugene: Bureau of Educational Research, University of Oregon, 1960.

AGGER, Robert E., "Power Attributions in the Local Community: Theoretical and Research Considerations," *Social Forces,* 34 (May, 1956), 322-331.

AGGER, Robert E. and Daniel Goldrich, "Community Power Structures and Partisanship," *American Sociological Review,* 23 (August, 1958), 383-392.

AGGER, Robert E. and Vincent Ostrom, "Political Participation in a Small Community," in Heinz Eulau, *et al.,* editors, *Political Behavior,* New York: Free Press, 1957.

AGGER, Robert E. and Vincent Ostrom, "The Political Structure of a Small Community," *Public Opinion Quarterly,* 20 (Spring, 1956), 81-89.

AGGER, Robert E., Bert E. Swanson, Daniel Goldrich, and Marshall N. Goldstein, "Empirical Considerations," in Bert E. Swanson, editor, *Current Trends in Community Studies,* Public Affairs Monograph Series, No. 1, Kansas City: Community Studies, Inc., 1962, 81-88.

AGGER, Robert E., Daniel Goldrich, and Bert E. Swanson, *The Rulers and the Ruled: Political Power and Impotence in American Communities,* New York: Wiley, 1964.

ALFORD, Robert R. and Harry M. Scoble, "Community Leadership, Education, and Political Behavior," *American Sociological Review,* 33 (April, 1968), 191-209.

ANTON, Thomas J., "Power, Pluralism, and Local Politics," *Administrative Science Quarterly,* 7 (March, 1963), 425-457.

COMMUNITY
LEVEL

BABCHUK, Nicholas, Ruth Marsey, and C. Wayne Gordon, "Men and Women in Community Agencies: A Note on Power and Prestige," *American Sociological Review,* 25 (June, 1960), 399-403.

BACHRACH, P., "Elite Consensus and Democracy," *Journal of Politics,* 24 (August, 1962), 439-452.

BACHRACH, P. and M. Baratz, "Two Faces of Power," *American Political Science Review,* 51 (December, 1962), 947-952.

BAILEY, Stephen K., "Leadership in Local Government," *Yale Review,* 45 (June, 1956), 563-573.

BANFIELD, Edward C., *Political Influence,* New York: Free Press, 1960.

BANFIELD, Edward C. and James Q. Wilson, *City Politics,* Cambridge: Harvard University Press and MIT Press, 1963.

BARKLEY, R., "Theory of the Elite and the Mythology of Power," *Science and Society,* 19 (Spring, 1955), 97-106.

BARTH, Ernest A. T., "Community Influence Systems: Structure and Change," *Social Forces,* 40 (October, 1961), 58-63.

BARTH, Ernest A. T. and Baha Abu-Laban, "Power Structure and the Negro Sub-Community," *American Sociological Review,* 24 (February, 1959), 69-76.

BARTH, Ernest A. T. and Stuart D. Johnson, "Community Power and a Typology of Social Issues," *Social Forces,* 38 (October, 1959), 29-32.

BASSETT, Raymond E., "Sampling Problems in Influence Studies," *Sociometry,* 12 (November, 1948), 320-328.

BELKNAP, George M. and Ralph Smuckler, "Political Power Relations in a Mid-West City," *Public Opinion Quarterly,* 20 (Spring, 1956), 73-81.

BELKNAP, George M. and Ralph Smuckler, *Leadership and Participation in Urban Political Affairs,* East Lansing: Government Research Bureau, Michigan State University, 1956.

BELKNAP, Ivan and John G. Steinle, *The Community and Its Hospitals,* Syracuse: Syracuse University Press, 1963.

BELL, Daniel, "The Power Elite—Reconsidered," *American Journal of Sociology,* 64 (November, 1958), 238-250.

BELL, Wendell, Richard J. Hill, and Charles R. Wright, *Public Leadership,* San Francisco: Chandler, 1961.

BENNEY, Mark and Phyllis Geiss, "Social Class and Politics in

Greenwich," *British Journal of Sociology,* 1 (December, 1950), 310-327.

BERELSON, Bernard R., Paul Lazarsfeld, and William N. McPhee, *Voting: A Study of Opinion Formation in a Presidential Campaign,* Chicago: University of Chicago Press, 1954.

BETH, Marian W., "The Elite and the Elites," *American Journal of Sociology,* 47 (March, 1942), 746-755.

BIERSTEDT, Robert, "An Analysis of Social Power," *American Sociological Review,* 15 (December, 1950), 730-738.

BIRCH, A. H., *Small-Town Politics: A Study of Political Life in Glossop,* New York: Oxford University Press, 1959.

BLACKWELL, Gordon W., "Community Analysis," in Roland Young, editor, *Approaches to the Study of Politics,* Evanston: Northwestern University Press, 1958.

BLANKENSHIP, Vaughn, "Community Power and Decision-Making: A Comparative Evaluation of Measurement Techniques," *Social Forces,* 43 (December, 1964), 207-216.

BLOOMBERG, Warner and Morris Sunshine, *Suburban Power Structures and Public Education,* Syracuse: Syracuse University Press, 1963.

BONJEAN, Charles M., "Class, Status, and Power Reputation," *Sociology and Social Research,* 49 (October, 1964), 69-75.

BONJEAN, Charles M., "Community Leadership: A Case Study and Conceptual Refinement," *American Journal of Sociology,* 68 (May, 1963), 672-681.

BONJEAN, Charles M. and Lewis F. Carter, "Legitimacy and Visibility: Leadership Structures Related to Four Community Systems," *Pacific Sociological Review,* 8 (Spring, 1965), 16-20.

BONJEAN, Charles M. and David M. Olson, "Community Leadership: Directions of Research," *Administrative Science Quarterly,* 9 (December, 1964), 278-300.

BOOTH, David A. and Charles R. Adrian, "Elections and Community Power," *Journal of Politics,* 25 (February, 1963), 107-118.

BOOTH, David A., "Power Structure and Community Change: A Replication Study of Community A," *Midwest Journal of Political Science,* 6 (August, 1962), 277-296.

BOOTH, David A. and Charles R. Adrian, "Simplifying the Discovery of Elites," *American Behavioral Scientist,* 5 (October, 1962), 14-16.

BRADLEY, Donald and Mayer Zald, "From Commercial Elite to Political Administrator: The Recruitment of the Mayors of Chicago," *American Journal of Sociology,* 71 (September, 1965), 153-167.

BROWN, Bernard, "Municipal Finances and Annexation: A Case Study of Post-War Houston," *Southwestern Social Science Quarterly,* 48 (December, 1967),339-351.

COMMUNITY LEVEL

BURGESS, M. Elaine, *Negro Leadership in a Southern City,* Chapel Hill: University of North Carolina Press, 1962.

CLARK, Terry N., editor, *Community Structure and Decision Making: Comparative Analyses,* San Francisco: Chandler, 1968.

CLARK, Terry N., "The Concept of Power: Some Overemphasized and Underrecognized Dimensions—An Examination with Special Reference to the Local Community," *Southwestern Social Science Quarterly,* 48 (December, 1967), 271-286.

CLARK, Terry N., "Power and Community Structure: Who Governs, Where, and When?," *Sociological Quarterly,* 8 (Summer, 1967), 291-316.

CLELLAND, Donald and William Form, "Economic Dominants and Community Power: A Comparative Analysis," *American Journal of Sociology,* 69 (March, 1964), 511-521.

COLCORD, Frank C., Jr., "Decision-Making and Transportation Policies: A Comparative Analysis," *Southwestern Social Science Quarterly,* 48 (December, 1967), 383-397.

COLEMAN, James S., *Community Conflict,* New York: Free Press, 1957.

CRAIN, Robert L. and Donald B. Rosenthal, "Community Status as a Dimension of Local Decision Making," *American Sociological Review,* 32 (December, 1967), 970-985.

CRAIN, Robert L., Elihu Katz, and Donald Rosenthal, *The Politics of Community Conflict: The Floridation Decision,* Indianapolis: Bobbs-Merrill, 1968.

DAHL, Robert A., "The Analysis of Influence in Local Communities," in Charles R. Adrian, editor, *Social Science and Community Action,* East Lansing: Institute for Community Development and Services, Michigan State University, 1961.

DAHL, Robert A., "The Concept of Power," *Behavioral Science,* 2 (July, 1957), 201-215.

DAHL, Robert A., "A Critique of the Ruling Elite Model," *American Political Science Review,* 52 (June, 1958), 463-469.

DAHL, Robert A., *Who Governs?: Power and Democracy in America,* New Haven: Yale University Press, 1961.

DAKIN, Ralph E., "Variations in Power Structures and Organizing Efficiency: A Comparative Study of Four Areas," *Sociological Quarterly,* 3 (July, 1962), 228-250.

D'ANTONIO, William V., "Community Leadership in an Economic Crisis: Testing Ground for Ideological Cleavage," *American Journal of Sociology,* 71 (May, 1966), 688-700.

D'ANTONIO, William V., Howard J. Ehrlich, and Eugene C. Erickson, "Further Notes on the Study of Community Power," *American Sociological Review,* 27 (December, 1962), 848-853.

D'ANTONIO, William V., Howard H. Ehrlich, and Eugene C. Erickson, editors, *Power and Democracy in America,* Notre Dame: University of Notre Dame Press, 1961.

D'ANTONIO, William V., and Eugene C. Erickson, "The Reputational Technique for the Study of Community Power," *American Sociological Review,* 27 (June, 1962), 362-375.

D'ANTONIO, William V. and William H. Form, *Influentials in Two Border Cities,* Notre Dame: University of Notre Dame Press, 1965.

D'ANTONIO, William V., Charles P. Loomis, William H. Form, and Eugene C. Erickson, "Institutional and Occupational Representations in Eleven Community Influence Systems," *American Sociological Review,* 26 (June, 1961), 440-446.

DANZGER, M. Herbert, "Community Power Structure: Problems and Continuities," *American Sociological Review,* 29 (October, 1964), 707-717.

DICK, Harry R., "A Method for Ranking Community Influentials," *American Sociological Review,* 25 (June, 1960), 395-399.

DYE, Thomas, "Popular Images of Decision-Making in Suburban Communities," *Sociology and Social Research,* 47 (October 1962), 75-85.

DYE, Thomas, "The Local-Cosmopolitan Dimension and the Study of Urban Politics," *Social Forces,* 41 (March, 1963), 239-246.

EHRLICH, Howard, "The Reputational Approach to the Study of Community Power," *American Sociological Review,* 26 (December, 1961), 926-927.

EHRLICH, Howard, "The Social Psychology of Reputations for Community Leadership," *Sociological Quarterly,* 8 (Autumn, 1967), 514-530.

EULAU, Heinz, Samuel J. Eldersveld, and Morris Janowitz, editors, *Political Behavior,* New York: Free Press, 1956.

FANELLI, A. Alexander, "A Typology of Community Leadership Based on Influence and Interaction within the Leader Sub-System" *Social Forces,* 34 (May, 1956), 332-338.

FISHER, Sethard, "Community Power Studies: A Critique," *Social Research,* 29 (Winter, 1962), 449-466.

COMMUNITY LEVEL

FORM, William H., "Organized Labor's Place in Community Power Structure," *Industrial and Labor Relations Review,* 12 (July, 1959), 526-539.

FORM, William H., "Labor and Community Influentials: A Comparative Study of Participation and Imagery," *Industrial and Labor Relations Review,* 17 (October, 1963), 3-19.

FORM, William H. and Warren L. Sauer, "Organized Labor's Image of Community Power Structure," *Social Forces,* 38 (May, 1960), 332-341.

FORM, William H. and William V. D'Antonio, "Integration and Cleavage among Community Influentials in Two Border Cities: A Comparative Study of Social Relations and Institutional Perspectives," *American Sociological Review,* 24 (December, 1959), 804-814.

FORM, William H. and Warren L. Sauer, *Community Influentials in a Middle-Sized City,* East Lansing: Michigan State University Labor and Industrial Relations Center, General Bulletin No. 5, 1960.

FOSKETT, John M. and Raymond Hohle, "The Measurement of Influence in Community Affairs," *Research Studies of the State College of Washington,* 25 (June, 1957), 148-154.

FOWLER, Irving A., "Local Industrial Structures, Economic Power, and Community Welfare," *Social Problems,* 6 (Summer, 1958), 41-51.

FREEMAN, Charles and Selz C. Mayo, "Decision Makers in Rural Community Action," *Social Forces,* 35 (May, 1957), 319-322.

FREEMAN, Linton C., *Patterns of Local Community Leadership,* Indianapolis: Bobbs-Merrill, 1968.

FREEMAN, Linton C., *et al., Local Community Leadership,* Syracuse: University College, Syracuse University, 1960.

FREEMAN, Linton C., T. J. Fararo, W. J. Bloomberg, and M. H. Sunshine, "Locating Leaders in Local Communities: A Comparison of Some Alternative Approaches," *American Sociological Review,* 28 (October, 1963), 791-798.

FREEMAN, Linton C., *et al., Metropolitan Decision-Making: Further Analysis from the Syracuse Study of Local Community Leadership,* Syracuse: University College, Syracuse University, 1962.

GAMSON, William A., "Rancorous Conflict in Community Politics," *American Sociological Review,* 31 (February, 1966), 71-81.

GAMSON, William A., "Reputation and Resources in Community

Politics," *American Journal of Sociology,* 72 (September, 1966), 121-131.

GILBERT, Claire W., "Some Trends in Community Politics: A Secondary Analysis of Power Structure Data from 166 Communities," *Southwestern Social Science Quarterly,* 48 (December, 1967), 373-381.

GITLIN, Todd, "Local Pluralism As Theory and Ideology," *Studies on the Left,* 5 (1965), 21-45.

GOLDHAMMER, Keith, "Community Power Structure and School Board Membership," *American School Board Journal,* 130 (March, 1955), 23-25.

GOLDSTEIN, Marshall N., "Absentee Ownership and Monolithic Power Structures: Two Questions for Community Studies," in Bert E. Swanson, editor, *Current Trends in Comparative Community Studies,* Public Affairs Monograph Series, No. 1, Kansas City, Missouri: Community Studies, Inc., 1962.

GORE, William J. and Robert L. Peabody, "The Functions of the Political Campaign," *Western Political Quarterly,* 11 (March, 1958), 55-70.

GORE, William J. and Fred S. Silander, "A Bibliographical Essay on Decision Making," *Administrative Science Quarterly,* 4 (June, 1959).

GREER, Scott, "Individual Participation in Mass Society," in R. Young, editor, *Approaches to the Study of Politics,* Evanston: Northwestern University Press, 1958, 324-342.

GREER, Scott, "The Social Structure and Political Process of Suburbia," *American Sociological Review,* 25 (August, 1960), 514-526.

HAER, John L. "Social Stratification in Relation to Attitude toward Sources of Power in a Community," *Social Forces,* 35 (December, 1956), 137-142.

HANSON, Robert C., "Predicting a Community Decision: A Test of the Miller-Form Theory," *American Sociological Review,* 24 (October, 1959), 662-671.

HARRIS, R., "The Selection of Leaders in Ballybeg, Northern Ireland," *Sociological Review,* 9 (July, 1961), 137-149.

HAWKINS, Brett W., "Life Style, Demographic Distance and Voter Support of City-County Consolidation," *Southwestern Social Science Quarterly,* 48 (December, 1967), 325-337.

HAWLEY, Amos, "Community Power and Urban Renewal Success," *American Journal of Sociology,* 68 (January, 1963), 422-431.

HAWLEY, Willis D. and Frederick Wirt, editors, *The Search For Community Power*, Englewood Cliffs, New Jersey: Prentice-Hall, 1968.

HERSON, Lawrence J., "In the Footsteps of Community Power," *American Political Science Review*, 55 (December, 1961), 817-830.

HUNTER, Floyd, *Community Power Structure: A Study of Decision Makers*, Chapel Hill: University of North Carolina, 1953.

HUNTER, Floyd, "Decision Makers," *Nation*, 179 (August 21, 1954), 148-150.

HUNTER, Floyd, *Top Leadership, U.S.A.*, Chapel Hill: University of North Carolina, 1959.

HUNTER, Floyd, Ruth C. Schaffer, and Cecil G. Sheps, *Community Organization: Action and Inaction*, Chapel Hill: University of North Carolina, 1956.

JANOWITZ, Morris, "Community Power and 'Policy Science' Research," *Public Opinion Quarterly*, 26 (Fall, 1962), 398-410.

JANOWITZ, Morris, editor, *Community Political Systems*, New York: Free Press, 1960.

JENNINGS, M. Kent, *Community Influentials: The Elites of Atlanta*, New York: Free Press, 1964.

JENNINGS, M. Kent, "Public Administrators and Community Decision-Making," *Administrative Science Quarterly*, 8 (June, 1963), 18-43.

JENNINGS, M. Kent, "Study of Community Decision-Making," in Bert E. Swanson, editor, *Current Trends in Comparative Community Studies*, Public Affairs Monograph Series, No. 1, Kansas City, Missouri: Community Studies, Inc., 1962.

KAMMERER, Gladys M. and J. M. DeGrove, "Urban Leadership During Change," *The Annals of the American Academy of Political and Social Science*, 353 (May, 1964), 95-106.

KAMMERER, Gladys M., *et al.*, *The Urban Political Community: Profiles in Town Politics*, Boston: Houghton Mifflin, 1963.

KAMMERER, Kenneth, "Community Homogeneity and Decision-Making," *Rural Sociology*, 20 (September, 1963), 238-245.

KARIEL, Henry, *The Decline of American Pluralism*, Stanford: Stanford University Press, 1961.

KELLER, Suzanne, *Beyond the Ruling Class*, New York: Random House, 1963.

KILLIAN, Lewis M., and Charles U. Smith, "Negro Protest

Leaders in a Southern Community," *Social Forces,* 38 (March, 1960), 253-257.

KIMBALL, S. T. and M. Pearsall, "Event Analysis as an Approach to Community Study," *Social Forces,* (October, 1955), 58-63.

KIMBROUGH, Ralph B., *Political Power and Educational Decision Making,* Chicago: Rand McNally, 1964.

KLAPP, Orrin E. and L. Vincent Padgett, "Power Structure and Decision-Making in a Mexican Border City," *American Journal of Sociology,* 65 (January, 1960), 400-406.

KORNHAUSER, Arthur, editor, *Problems of Power in American Society,* Detroit: Wayne State University Press, 1957.

KURODA, Yasumasa, "Psychological Aspects of Community Power Structure: Leaders and Rank-and-File Citizens in Reed Town, Japan," *Southwestern Social Science Quarterly,* 48 (December, 1967), 433-442.

LANE, Robert E., *Political Life,* New York: Free Press, 1959.

LASKIN, Richard, *Leadership of Voluntary Organizations in a Saskatchewan Town,* Saskatoon: Centre for Community Studies, 1962.

LASSWELL, Harold D. and Abraham Kaplan, *Power and Society,* New Haven: Yale University Press, 1960.

LOWE, Francis E. and Thomas C. McCormick, "A Study of the Influence of Formal and Informal Leaders in an Election Campaign," *Public Opinion Quarterly,* 20 (Winter, 1956-1957), 651-662.

LOWRY, Ritchie P., *Who's Running This Town?,* New York: Harper and Row, 1962.

LYND, Robert S., "Power in American Society as Resource and Problem," in Arthur Kornhauser, editor, *Problems of Power in American Democracy,* Detroit: Wayne State University Press, 1957.

LYND, Robert S., "Power in the United States," *Nation,* 182 (May 12, 1956), 408-411.

LYND, Robert S. and Helen M. Lynd, *Middletown,* New York: Harcourt, Brace, and Co., 1929.

LYND, Robert S. and Helen M. Lynd, *Middletown in Transition,* New York: Harcourt, Brace, and Co., 1937.

MARSH, C. Paul, Margaret Marsh, and Selz C. Mayo, "Tentative Hypotheses Concerning Designated Leaders in Two Rural Locality Groups in North Carolina," *Rural Sociology,* 16 (September, 1951), 273-275.

COMMUNITY LEVEL

MARTIN, Roscoe C., *et al., Decisions in Syracuse,* Bloomington: Indiana University Press, 1961.

McCLAIN, Jackson M. and Robert Highsaw, *Dixie City Acts: A Study in Decision Making,* Birmingham: Bureau of Public Administration, University of Alabama, 1962.

McKEE, James B., "Community Power and Strategies in Race Relations: Some Critical Observations," *Social Problems,* 6 (Winter, 1958-59), 195-203.

McKEE, James B., "Status and Power in the Industrial Community: A Comment on Drucker's Thesis," *American Journal of Sociology,* 58 (January, 1953), 364-370.

MERRIAM, Charles, *Political Power,* New York: Collier, 1964.

MERTON, Robert K., "Patterns of Influence: A Study of Interpersonal Influence and of Communications Behavior in a Local Community," in P. F. Lazarsfeld and F. N. Stanton, editors, *Communications Research, 1948-49,* New York: Harper, 1949.

MICHEL, Jerry, "Measurement of Social Power on the Community Level," *American Journal of Economics and Sociology,* 23 (April, 1964), 189-196.

MILLER, Delbert C., "Decision-Making Cliques in Community Power Structures: A Comparative Study of an American and an English City," *American Journal of Sociology,* 64 (November, 1958), 299-310.

MILLER, Delbert C., "Industry and Community Power Structures: A Comparative Study of an American and an English City," *American Sociological Review,* 23 (February, 1958), 9-15.

MILLER, Delbert C., "The Prediction of Issue Outcome in Community Decision-Making," *Research Studies of the State College of Washington,* 25 (June, 1957), 137-147.

MILLER, Delbert C., "Town and Gown: The Power Structure of a University Town," *American Journal of Sociology,* 68 (January, 1963), 432-443.

MILLER, Delbert C. and James L. Dirkson, "The Identification of Visible, Concealed and Symbolic Leaders in a Small Indiana City: A Replication of the Bonjean-Nolan Study of Burlington, North Carolina," *Social Forces,* 43 (May, 1965), 548-555.

MILLER, Delbert C. and William H. Form, *Industry, Labor and Community,* New York: Harper and Row, 1960.

MILLER, Paul A., *Community Health Action,* East Lansing: Michigan State College Press, 1953.

COMMUNITY
LEVEL

MILLER, Paul A., "The Process of Decision-Making Within the Context of Community Organization," *Rural Sociology,* 17 (June, 1952), 153-161.

MONSEN, J. and M. Cannon, *The Makers of Public Policy: American Power Groups and Their Ideologies,* New York: McGraw-Hill, 1965.

MORGENTHAU, Hans, "Power as a Political Concept," in Roland Young, editor, *Approaches to the Study of Politics,* Evanston: Northwestern University Press, 1958.

MULFORD, Charles L., "Considerations of the Instrumental and Expressive Roles of Community Influentials and Formal Organizations," *Sociology and Social Research,* 51 (January, 1967), 141-147.

MULFORD, Charles L., "On Role Consensus about Community Leaders," *Sociological Inquiry,* 36 (Winter, 1966), 15-18.

NAVILLE, Pierre, "Technical Elites and Social Elites," *Sociology of Education,* 37 (Fall, 1963), 27-29.

NIX, Harold L., Jennie McIntyre, and Charles J. Dudley, "Bases of Leadership: Cultural Ideal and Estimates of Reality," *Southwestern Social Science Quarterly,* 48 (December, 1967), 423-432.

PADOVER, Saul, "Lasswell's Impact on the Study of Power in a Democracy," *Social Research,* 29 (Winter, 1962), 489-494.

PARENTON, V. J. and Roland J. Pellegrin, "Social Structure and the Leadership Factor in a Negro Community in South Louisiana," *Phylon,* 17 (March, 1956), 74-78.

PARSONS, Talcott, "The Distribution of Power in American Society," *World Politics,* 10 (October, 1957), 123-143.

PAYNE, Raymond, "Leadership and Perception of Change in a Village Confronted with Urbanism," *Social Forces,* 41 (March, 1963), 264-269.

PELLEGRIN, Roland J. and Charles H. Coates, "Absentee-Owned Corporations and Community Power Structure," *American Journal of Sociology,* 61 (March, 1956), 413-419.

PFAUTZ, Harold, "The Power Structure of the Negro Sub-Community: A Case Study and a Comparative View," *Phylon,* 23 (Summer, 1962), 156-166.

POLSBY, Nelson W., *Community Power and Political Theory,* New Haven: Yale University Press, 1963.

POLSBY, Nelson W., "Community Power: Some Reflections on the Recent Literature," *American Sociological Review,* 27 (December, 1962), 838-840.

POLSBY, Nelson W., "How to Study Community Power: The Pluralist Alternative," *Journal of Politics,* 22 (August, 1960), 474-484.

POLSBY, Nelson W., "Power in Middletown: Fact and Value in Community Research," *Canadian Journal of Economics and Political Science,* 26 (November, 1960), 592-603.

POLSBY, Nelson W., "The Sociology of Community Power: A Reassessment," *Social Forces,* 37 (March, 1959), 232-236.

POLSBY, Nelson W., "Three Problems in the Analysis of Community Power," *American Sociological Review,* 24 (December, 1959), 796-803.

POLSBY, Nelson W., *Community Power and Political Theory,* New Haven: Yale University Press, 1963.

PORTER, John, "Elite Groups: A Scheme for the Study of Power in Canada," *Canadian Journal of Economics and Political Science,* 21 (November, 1955), 498-512.

PRESENT, Phillip Edward, "Defense Contracting and Community Leadership: A Comparative Analysis," *Southwestern Social Science Quarterly,* 48 (December, 1967), 399-410.

PRESTHUS, Robert, *Men at the Top: A Study in Community Power,* New York: Oxford University Press, 1964.

PRINCE, Julius S., "The Health Officer and Community Power Groups," *Health Education Monographs,* 2 (1958), 16-31.

REID, Ira De A. and Emily L. Ehle, "Leadership Selection in Urban Locality Areas," *Public Opinion Quarterly,* 14 (Summer, 1950), 262-284.

REISS, Albert J., Jr., "Some Logical and Methodological Problems in Community Research," *Social Forces,* 33 (October, 1954), 51-57.

RHYNE, Edwin H., "Political Parties and Decision-Making in Three Southern Counties," *American Political Science Review,* 52 (December, 1958), 1091-1107.

RIKER, William H., *The Study of Local Politics,* New York: Random House, 1959.

ROGERS, David, "Community Political Systems: A Framework and Hypothesis for Comparative Studies," in Bert E. Swanson, editor, *Current Trends in Comparative Community Studies,* Public Affairs Monograph Series, No. 1, Kansas City, Missouri: Community Studies, Inc., 1962.

ROGERS, Everett M. and George M. Beal, "The Importance of Personal Influence in the Adoption of Technological Changes," *Social Forces,* 36 (May, 1958), 329-335.

ROSE, Arnold M., "Power Distribution in the Community Through Voluntary Association," in J. E. Hulett, Jr., and Ross Stagner, editors, *Problems in Social Psychology,* Urbana: University of Illinois Press, 1952.

ROSE, Arnold M. and Caroline Rose, "Communication and Participation in a Small City as Viewed by its Leaders," *International Journal of Opinion and Attitude Research,* 5 (Fall, 1951), 367-390.

ROSSI, Peter H., "Community Decision-Making," *Administrative Science Quarterly,* 1 (March, 1957), 415-443.

ROSSI, Peter H., "Power and Community Structure," *Midwest Journal of Political Science,* 4 (November, 1960), 390-401.

ROSSI, Peter H., *Power and Politics: A Road to Social Reform,* Chicago: National Opinion Research Center, 1961.

ROSSI, Peter H. and Robert Dentler, *Politics of Urban Renewal,* New York: Free Press, 1961.

SCHERMERHORN, Richard A., *Society and Power,* New York: Random House, 1961.

SCHULZE, Robert O., "The Bifurcation of Power in a Satellite City," in Morris Janowitz, editor, *Community Political Systems,* New York: Free Press, 1961.

SCHULZE, Robert O., "The Role of Economic Dominants in Community Power Structure," *American Sociological Review,* 23 (February, 1958), 3-9.

SCHULZE, Robert O. and Leonard U. Blumberg, "The Determination of Local Power Elites," *American Journal of Sociology,* 63 (November, 1957), 290-296.

SCOBLE, Harry, "Leadership Hierarchies and Political Issues in a New England Town," in Morris Janowitz, editor, *Community Political Systems,* New York: Free Press, 1961.

SIMON, Herbert, "Notes on the Observation and Measurement of Political Power," *Journal of Politics,* 15 (1953), 500-516.

SIMON, Herbert, "Theories of Decision-Making in Economics and Behavioral-Science," *American Economic Review,* 49 (June, 1959), 253-283.

SMITH, Christopher, "Social Selection in Community Leadership," *Social Forces,* 15 (May, 1937), 530-535.

SMITH, J. and T. Hood, "The Delineation of Community Power Structure by Reputational Approach," *Sociological Inquiry,* 36 (Winter, 1966), 3-14.

SMITH, L., "Political Leadership in a New England Community," *Review of Politics,* 17 (July, 1955), 292-309.

SMITH, Lincoln, "Power Politics in Brunswick: A Case Study," *Human Organization,* 22 (Summer, 1963), 152-158.

SMITH, P. A., "The Game of Community Politics," *Midwest Journal of Political Science,* 9 (February, 1965), 37-60.

COMMUNITY LEVEL

SMITH, Ted C., "The Structuring of Power in a Suburban Community," *Pacific Sociological Review,* 3 (Fall, 1960), 83-88.

SNYDER, Richard C., H. W. Bruck, and Burton Sapin, "The Decision-Making Approach," in H. Eulau, S. J. Eldersveld, and M. Janowitz, editors, *Political Behavior,* New York: Free Press, 1956.

SOFEN, Edward, "Problems of Metropolitan Leadership: The Miami Experience," *Midwest Journal of Political Science,* 5 (February, 1961), 18-38.

SOLLIE, Carlton R., "A Comparison of Reputational Techniques for Identifying Leaders," *Rural Sociology,* 31 (September, 1966), 301-309.

SPINRAD, William, "Power in Local Communities," *Social Problems,* 12 (Winter, 1965), 335-356.

STEWART, Frank, "A Sociometric Study of Influence in Southtown," *Sociometry,* 10 (February, 1947), 11-31, 273-286.

STONE, Gregory P. and William H. Form, "Instabilities in Status: The Problem of Hierarchy in the Community Study of Status Arrangements," *American Sociological Review,* 18 (April, 1953), 149-162.

STONE, Robert C., "Power and Values in Trans-Community Relations," in Bert E. Swanson, editor, *Current Trends in Comparative Community Studies,* Kansas City, Missouri: Community Studies, Inc., 1962.

SRAUSZ-HUPE, Robert, *Power and Community,* New York: Praeger, 1956.

SUSSMAN, Marvin B., editor, *Community Structure and Analysis,* New York: Crowell, 1959.

SWEEZY, Paul M., "Power Elite or Ruling Class," *Monthly Review,* 8 (September, 1956), 138-150.

TANNENBAUM, Arnold, "An Event Structure Approach to Social Power and to the Problem of Power Comparability," *Behavioral Science,* 7 (July, 1962), 315-331.

THOMETZ, Carol Estes, *The Decision-Makers: The Power Structure of Dallas,* Dallas: Southern Methodist University Press, 1963.

THOMPSON, Daniel, *The Negro Leadership Class,* Englewood Cliffs, New Jersey: Prentice-Hall, 1963.

VERNEY, Douglas V., *The Analysis of Political Systems,* New York: Free Press, 1960.

VIDICH, Arthur and Joseph Bensman, *Small Town in Mass Society,* Princeton: Princeton University Press, 1958.

VOGT, Evon Z. and Thomas F. O'Dea, "A Comparative Study of the Role of Values in Social Action in Two South-Western Communities," *American Sociological Review,* 18 (December, 1953), 645-654.

WALKER, Jack L., "Protest and Negotiation: A Case Study of Negro Leadership in Atlanta," *Midwest Journal of Political Science,* 7 (May, 1963), 99-124.

WALTON, John, "Discipline, Method and Community Power: A Note on the Sociology of Knowledge," *American Sociological Review,* 31 (October, 1966), 684-689.

WALTON, John, "Substance and Artifact: The Current Status on Research of Community Power Structure," *American Journal of Sociology,* 71 (January, 1966), 403-438.

WALTON, John, "The Vertical Axis of Community Organization and the Structure of Power," *Southwestern Social Science Quarterly,* 48 (December, 1967), 353-368.

WARNER, W. Lloyd, *et al., Democracy in Jonesville,* New York: Harper, 1949.

WARREN, Roland L., "Toward a Typology of Extra-Community Controls Limiting Local Community Autonomy," *Social Forces,* 34 (May, 1956), 338-341.

WARREN, Roland L., "A Note on Walton's Analysis of Power Structure and Vertical Ties," *Southwestern Social Science Quarterly,* 48 (December, 1967), 369-372.

WATSON, James B. and Julian Samora, "Subordinate Leadership in a Bi-cultural Community: An Analysis," *American Sociological Review,* 19 (August, 1954), 413-421.

WEBB, Harold Vernon, *Community Power Structure Related to School Administration,* Laramie: University of Wyoming, 1956.

WELLS, Lloyd M., "Social Values and Political Orientations of City Managers: A Survey Report," *Southwestern Social Science Quarterly,* 48 (December, 1967), 443-450.

WEST, James, *Plainville, U. S. A.,* New York: Columbia University Press, 1945.

WESTIN, Alan, *et al.,* editors, *Centers of Power,* New York: Atherton, 1964.

WESTIN, Alan, *Uses of Power,* New York: Harcourt, Brace, 1962.

WHITE, James E., "Theory and Method for Research in Community Leadership," *American Sociological Review,* 15 (February, 1950), 50-60.

WILDAVSKY, Aaron, *Leadership in a Small Town,* Totowa, New Jersey: Bedminister Press, 1964.

WILLIAMS, Oliver P., "Life Style Values and Political Decentralization in Metropolitan Areas," *Southwestern Social Science Quarterly,* 48 (December, 1967), 299-310.

WILLIE, Charles, Herbert Notkin, and Nicholas Rezak, "Trends in the Participation of Businessmen in Local Community Voluntary Affairs," *Sociology and Social Research,* 48 (April, 1964), 289-300.

WILSON, Everett K., "Determinants of Participation in Policy Formation in a College Community," *Human Relations,* 7 (1954), 287-312.

WILSON, James Q., *Negro Politics: The Search for Leadership,* New York: Free Press, 1960.

WINGFIELD, C. J., "Power Structure and Decision-Making in City Planning," *Public Administration Review,* 23 (June, 1963), 74-80.

WOLFINGER, Raymond, "A Plea for a Decent Burial," *American Sociological Review,* 27 (December, 1962), 841-847.

WOLFINGER, Raymond, "Reputation and Reality in the Study of 'Community Power'," *American Sociological Review,* 25 (October, 1960), 636-644.

WOOD, Thomas J., "Dade County: Unbossed, Erratically Led," *Annals of the American Academy of Political and Social Science,* (May, 1964), 64-71.

WORSLEY, Peter, "The Distribution of Power in Industrial Society," *Sociological Review Monograph,* 8 (October, 1964), 15-41.

WRONG, Dennis, "Who Runs American Cities?," *New Society,* 27 (April, 1963), 16-17.

ZIMMER, Basil G. and Amos H. Hawley, "Opinions on School District Reorganization in Metropolitan Areas: A Comparative Analysis of the Views of Citizens and Officials in Central City and Suburban Areas," *Southwestern Social Science Quarterly,* 48 (December, 1967), 311-324.

ZURCHER, Louis A., "Functional Marginality: Dynamics of a Poverty Intervention Organization," *Southwestern Social Science Quarterly,* 48 (December, 1967), 411-421.

Power, Authority, and Leadership:

at the National Level

This may well be the area of social stratification least amenable to rigorous research techniques and precise measurement. For this reason, it is not surprising that the empirical study of power and leadership has been highly concentrated at the community level. However, impressions and speculations about the society-wide distribution of power abound, and there are more than a few insightful and judicious treatments, largely by political scientists.

A large and important literature deals with the distribution of power *among* nation-states, but it is beyond the scope of this bibliography.

AARONOVITCH, Sam, *The Ruling Class: A Study of British Finance Capital*, London: Lawrence and Wishart, 1961.

ABEGGLEN, James and Hiroshi Mannari, "Leaders of Modern Japan," *Economic Development and Cultural Change*, 9 (1960), 109-134.

ADAMS, Richard N., *The Second Sowing: Power and Secondary Development in Latin America*, San Francisco: Chandler, 1967.

APTER, David E., "Nkrumah, Charisma, and the Coup," *Daedelus*, 97 (Summer, 1968), 757-792.

ARENDT, Hannah, *The Origins of Totalitarianism*, New York: Harcourt Brace, 1951.

ARON, Raymond, "Social Class, Political Class, Ruling Class," in Reinhard Bendix and Seymour M. Lipset, editors, Class, *Status and Power*, 2nd edition, New York: Free Press, 1966.

ARON, Raymond, "Social Structure and Ruling Class," *British Journal of Sociology*, 1 (March, 1950), 1-16 and (June, 1950), 126-130.

BARATZ, Morton, "Corporate Giants and the Power Structure," *Western Political Quarterly*, 9 (June, 1956), 406-415.

BARKIN, Solomon, *The Decline of the Labor Movement*, Santa Barbara: Center for the Study of Democratic Institutions, 1961.

BAUER, Raymond, Alex Inkeles and Clyde Kluckhohn, *How the Soviet System Works*, New York: Vintage, 1960.

BECK, Hubert, *Men Who Control Our Universities,* New York: King's Crown Press, 1947.

BELL, Daniel, *End of Ideology,* New York: Free Press, 1960.

BELL, Daniel, "The Power Elite — Reconsidered," *American Journal of Sociology,* 64 (November, 1958), 238-250.

BELL, Wendell, editor, *The Democratic Revolution in the West Indies: Studies in Nationalism, Leadership, and Belief in Progress,* Cambridge: Schenkman, 1967.

BERLE, A. A., Jr., *Economic Power and the Free Society: A Preliminary Discussion of the Corporation,* New York: Fund for the Republic, 1958.

BERLE, A. A. Jr., *Power Without Property,* New York: Harcourt Brace, 1959.

BLAISDELL, D. C., *Economic Power and Political Pressures,* Washington D. C.: United States Government Printing Office, 1941.

BLONDEL, Jean, *Voters, Parties, and Leaders: The Social Fabric of British Politics,* London: Pelican, 1963.

BRADY, Robert A., *Business as a System of Power,* New York: Columbia University Press, 1943.

BRANDENBURG, Frank, *The Making of Modern Mexico,* Englewood Cliffs, New Jersey: Prentice Hall, 1965.

BRETTON, Henry L., *Power and Stability in Nigeria,* New York: Praeger, 1962.

BRZEZINSKI, Zbigniew K., *Ideology and Power in Soviet Politics,* London: Thames and Hudson, 1962.

BURNHAM, James, *The Managerial Revolution,* New York: Day, 1941.

BURNHAM, Walter Dean, "The Changing Shape of the American Political Universe," *American Political Science Review,* 59 (March, 1965), 7-28.

CANTRIL, Hadley, *Soviet Leaders and Mastery Over Man,* New Brunswick, New Jersey: Rutgers University Press, 1960.

CATER, Douglass, *Power in Washington,* New York: Random House, 1964.

CODERE, Helen, "Power in Ruanda," *Anthropologica,* 4 (1962), 42-85.

COLLINS, N. R. and L. E. Preston, "The Size Structure of the Largest Industrial Firms, 1909-1958," *American Economic Review,* 51 (December 1961), 986-1003.

COOK, Fred, *The Warfare State,* New York: Collier Books, 1964.

COPEMAN, George H., *Leaders of British Industry,* London: Business Publications, 1955.

CRANKSHAW, Edward, *Khrushchev's Russia,* London: Penguin, 1959.

DAHL, Robert A., "A Critique of the Ruling Elite Model," *American Political Science Review,* 52 (June, 1958), 463-469.

DAHL, Robert A., *A Preface to Democratic Theory,* Chicago: University of Chicago Press, 1956.

DAHL, Robert A., "Business and Politics: A Critical Appraisal of Political Science," *Social Science Research on Business: Product and Potential,* New York: Columbia University Press, 1959.

DE KADT, Emanuel J., "Conflict and Power in Society," *International Social Science Journal,* 17 (1965), 454-471.

DEMERATH, Nicholas J., Richard W. Stephens and R. Robb-Taylor, *Power, Presidents, and Professors,* New York: Basic Books, 1967.

DOMHOFF, G. William, *Who Rules America?* Englewood Cliffs, New Jersey: Prentice Hall, 1967.

DOUMAS, C. L., "A Tentative Analysis of the Power Elite of Greece," *Southern Quarterly,* 4 (July, 1966), 374-408.

EBERHARD, Wolfram, *Conquerors and Rulers: Social Forces in Medieval China,* second edition, Leiden, Netherlands: Brill, 1965.

EDELMAN, Murray, "Governments' Balance of Power in Labor-Management Relations," *Labor Law Journal,* (January, 1951).

EDINGER, Lewis J., "Continuity and Change in the Background of German Decision-Makers," *Western Political Quarterly,* 14 (March, 1961), 17-36.

EDINGER, Lewis J., editor, *Political Leadership in Industrialized Societies: Studies in Comparative Analysis,* New York: Wiley, 1967.

EISENSTADT, S. N., "Changes in Patterns of Stratification Attendant on Attainment of Political Independence," *Transactions of the Third World Congress of Sociology,* 3 (1950), 32-41.

ENGLER, Robert, *The Politics of Oil,* New York: Macmillan, 1961.

FAINSOD, Merle, *How Russia is Ruled,* Cambridge: Harvard University Press, 1953.

FAINSOD, Merle, *How Russia is Ruled,* revised edition, Cambridge: Harvard University Press, 1963.

NATIONAL LEVEL

GALBRAITH, John Kenneth, *American Capitalism: The Concept of Countervailing Power,* Boston: Houghton Mifflin, 1952.

GORDON, Robert, *Business Leadership in the Large Corporation,* Berkeley: University of California Press, 1966.

GUBIN, K., "The Supreme Soviet of the U. S. S. R. and Its Members," *International Social Science Journal,* 13 (1961), 635-640.

GUTTSMAN, W. L., *The British Political Elite,* London: MacGibbon and Kee, 1963.

HACKER, Andrew, "Liberal Democracy and Social Control," *American Political Science Review,* 51 (1957), 1009-1026.

HACKER, Andrew, "Power to Do What?" in Irving L. Horowitz, editor, *The New Sociology,* New York: Oxford University Press, 1964.

HACKER, Andrew, editor, *The Corporation Takes Over,* New York: Harper and Row, 1964.

HANKS, L. M., Jr., "Merit and Power in the Thai Social Order," *American Anthropologist,* 64 (December, 1962), 1247-1261.

HOLLANDER, Paul, editor, *American and Soviet Society: A Reader in Comparative Sociology and Perception,* Englewood Cliffs, New Jersey: Prentice Hall, 1968.

HOROWITZ, Irving L., editor, *Power, Politics and People: The Collected Essays of C. Wright Mills,* New York: Oxford University Press, 1965.

HUGHES, Emmet, *The Ordeal of Power,* New York: Atheneum, 1963.

HUNTER, Floyd, *Top Leadership, U. S. A.,* Chapell Hill: University of North Carolina Press, 1959.

HUNTINGTON, Samuel, *The Soldier and the State,* Cambridge: Harvard University Press, 1957.

JENKINS, C., *Power at the Top,* London: MacGibbon and Kee, 1959.

KARIEL, Henry, *The Decline of American Pluralism,* Stanford: Stanford University Press, 1961.

KAYSEN, Carl, "The Corporation: How Much Power? What Scope?" in Reinhard Bendix and Seymour M. Lipset, editors, *Class, Status and Power,* 2nd edition, New York: Free Press, 1966.

KEFAUVER, Estes, *In a Few Hands,* New York: Pantheon, 1965.

KELLER, Suzanne, *Beyond the Ruling Class: Strategic Elites in Modern Society,* New York: Random House, 1963.

KELLY, Sir David, *The Ruling Few,* London: Hollis and Carter, 1952.

KELSALL, R. K., D. Lockwood, and A. Trapp, "The New Middle Class in the Power Structure of Great Britain," *Transactions of the Third World Congress of Sociology,* 3 (1956), 320-329.

KEY, V. O., *Politics, Parties, and Pressure Groups,* New York: Crowell, 1958.

KOLKO, Gabriel, *Wealth and Power in America: An Analysis of Social Class and Income Distribution,* New York: Praeger, 1962.

KORNHAUSER, Arthur, editor, *Problems of Power in American Society,* Detroit: Wayne State University Press, 1957.

KORNHAUSER, William, *Politics in Mass Society,* New York: Free Press, 1959.

KORNHAUSER, William, " 'Power Elite' or 'Veto Groups'," in Reinhard Bendix and Seymour M. Lipset, editors, *Class, Status, and Power,* 2nd edition, Free Press, New York: 1966.

LANE, Robert E., *Political Life,* New York: Free Press, 1959.

LASSWELL, Harold D. and Abraham Kaplan, *Power and Society,* New Haven ; Yale University Press, 1950.

LASSWELL, Harold D., *Politics: Who Gets What, When, How,* New York: McGraw-Hill, 1936.

LEE, Shu-Ching, "Administration and Bureaucracy: The Power Structure in Chinese Society," *Transactions of the Second World Congress of Sociology,* 2 (1954), 3-15.

LENSKI, Gerhard, *Power and Privilege,* New York: McGraw-Hill, 1966.

LEVINE, Gene, *When Workers Vote,* Totowa, New Jersey: Bedminister, 1963.

LEWIS, John Wilson, *Leadership in Communist China,* Ithaca: Cornell University Press, 1963.

LIPSET, Seymour M., *Political Man,* Garden City, New York: Doubleday Anchor, 1963.

LUNDBERG, Ferdinand, *The Rich and The Super-Rich: A Study in the Power of Money Today,* New York: Lyle Stuart, 1968.

LYNCH, David, *The Concentration of Economic Power,* New York: Columbia University Press, 1946.

NATIONAL LEVEL

LYND, Robert S., "Power in American Society as Resource and Problem," in Arthur Kornhauser, editor, *Problems of Power in American Society,* Detroit: Wayne State University Press, 1957.

LYND, Robert S., "Power in the United States," *Nation,* 182 (May 23, 1956), 408-411.

MANNHEIM, Karl, *Freedom, Power, and Democratic Planning,* New York: Oxford University Press, 1950.

MARSHALL, T. H., "Class and Power in Canada," *Canadian Review of Sociology and Anthropology,* 2 (November, 1966), 215-222.

McCONNELL, Grant, *Private Power and American Democracy,* New York: Knopf, 1966.

MEISEL, James H., *The Myth of the Ruling Class: Gaetano Mosca and the Elite,* Ann Arbor: University of Michigan Press, 1958.

MERRIAM, Charles, *Political Power,* New York: Collier, 1964.

MICHELS, Robert, *Political Parties,* New York: Dover, 1959.

MILLS, C. Wright, *The Causes of World War Three,* New York: Simon and Schuster, 1958.

MILLS, C. Wright, "The Labor Leaders and the Power Elite," in Arthur Kornhauser, Robert Dubin, and Arthur M. Ross, *Industrial Conflict,* New York: McGraw-Hill, 1954.

MILLS, C. Wright, *The New Men of Power,* New York: Harcourt Brace, 1948.

MILLS, C. Wright, *The Power Elite,* New York: Oxford University Press, 1956.

MILLS, C. Wright, "The Power Elite," in Arthur Kornhauser, editor, *Problems of Power in American Society,* Detroit: Wayne State University Press, 1957.

MILLS, C. Wright, *White Collar,* New York: Oxford University Press, 1951.

MONSEN, J., and M. Cannon, *The Makers of Public Policy: American Power Groups and Their Ideologies,* New York: McGraw-Hill, 1965.

MONTAGUE, Joel B., Jr., "Some Aspects of Class, Status, and Power Relations in England," *Social Forces,* 30 (December, 1951), 134-140.

MOORE, Barrington, Jr., *Political Power and Social Theory,* New York: Harper and Row, 1965.

MOSCA, Gaetano, *The Ruling Class,* New York: McGraw-Hill, 1939.

NEUMAN, Franz, *The Democratic and Authoritarian State,* New York: Free Press, 1957.

NOSSITER, Bernard, *The Mythmakers,* Princeton: Van Nostrand, 1964.

OXAAL, Ivar, *Black Intellectuals Come to Power: The Rise of Creole Nationalism in Trinidad and Tobago,* Cambridge: Schenkman, 1967.

PADOVER, Saul, "Lasswell's Impact on the Study of Power in a Democracy," *Social Research,* 29 (Winter, 1962), 489-494.

PARETO, Vilfredo, *The Mind and Society,* edited and translated by Arthur Livingston and A. Bongiorno, New York: Harcourt Brace, 1935.

PARSONS, Talcott, "The Distribution of Power in American Society," *World Politics,* 10 (October, 1957), 123-143.

PARSONS, Talcott, *Structure and Process in Modern Societies,* New York: Free Press, 1960.

PECK, Sidney M., *The Rank-and-File Leader,* New Haven: College and University Press, 1966.

PERLO, Victor, *The Empire of High Finance,* New York: International Publishers, 1957.

PILISUK, Marc and Tom Hayden, "Is There a Military Industrial Complex That Prevents Peace?" *Journal of Social Issues,* 21 (July, 1965), 67-117.

PORTER, John, "Elite Groups: A Scheme for the Study of Power in Canada," *Canadian Journal of Economics and Political Science,* 21 (November, 1955), 498-512.

PORTER, John, *The Vertical Mosaic: An Analysis of Social Class and Power in Canada,* Toronto: University of Toronto Press, 1965.

POTTER, Allen, "The American Governing Class," *British Journal of Sociology,* 13 (December, 1962), 309-319.

RAYMOND, Jack, *Power at the Pentagon,* New York: Harper and Row, 1964.

RIESMAN, David, in collaboration with Reuel Denney and Nathan Glazer, *The Lonely Crowd,* New Haven: Yale University Press, 1950.

RODELL, Fred, "An American View of the Power Elite," *Saturday Review,* (April 28, 1956), 9-10.

ROSE, Arnold M., *The Power Structure: Political Process in American Society,* New York: Oxford University Press, 1967.

NATIONAL LEVEL

ROSENBERG, Hans, *Bureaucracy, Aristocracy and Autocracy: The Prussian Experience, 1660-1815,* Cambridge: Harvard University Press, 1958.

ROVERE, Richard, *The American Establishment,* New York: Harcourt, Brace, and World, 1962.

NATIONAL LEVEL

SAWYER, Jack, "Dimensions of Nations: Size, Wealth, and Politics," *American Journal of Sociology,* 73 (September, 1967), 145-172.

SCHAPIRO, Leonard, "The Nature of Total Power," *Political Quarterly,* 29 (1958), 105-113.

SCHAPIRO, L., *The Communist Party of the Soviet Union,* London: Eyre and Spottiswoode, 1960.

SCHERMERHORN, Richard A., *Society and Power,* New York: Random House, 1961.

SCHOENBAUM, David, *Hitler's Social Revolution: Class and Status in Nazi Germany 1933-1939,* Garden City, New York: Doubleday, 1968.

SCHUMPETER, Joseph, *Imperialism and Social Classes,* New York: Meridian, 1955.

SOELAEMAN, Soemardi, "Some Aspects of the Social Origins of Indonesian Political Decision Makers," *Transactions of the Third World Congress of Sociology,* 3 (1956), 338-348.

STOKES, Donald and Warren Miller, "Party Government and the Saliency of Congress," *Public Opinion Quarterly,* 26 (Winter, 1962), 531-546.

SUTTON, Francis X., *et al, The American Business Creed,* Cambridge: Harvard University Press, 1956.

SWEEZY, Paul M., "The American Ruling Class," in *The Present as History,* New York: Monthly Review Press, 1953.

SWEEZY, Paul M., "Power Elite or Ruling Class," *Monthly Review,* 8 (September, 1956), 138-150.

TOWNSEND, James R., *Political Participation in Communist China,* Berkeley: University of California Press, 1967.

TRUMAN, David, *The Governmental Process,* New York: Knopf, 1951.

USEEM, John, "Structure of Power in Palau," *Social Forces,* 29 (December, 1950), 141-148.

VILLAREJO, Don, "Stock Ownership and Control of Corporations," *New University Thought,* 2 (Autumn, 1961), 33-77 and (Winter, 1962), 47-65.

WALKER, Jack, "A Critique of the Elitist Theory of Democracy,"

American Political Science Review, 60 (June, 1966), 285-305.

WILEY, Norbert, "America's Unique Class Politics: The Interplay of the Labor, Credit and Commodity Markets," *American Sociological Review,* 32 (August, 1967), 529-541.

WILKINSON, Rupert, *Gentlemanly Power: British Leadership and the Public School Tradition,* New York: Oxford University Press, 1964.

WITTFOGEL, K. A., *Oriental Despotism,* New Haven: Yale University Press, 1957.

WORSLEY, Peter, "The Distribution of Power in Industrial Society," *Sociological Review Monograph,* 8 (October, 1964), 15-41.

ZEIGLER, Harmon, *Interest Groups in American Society,* Englewood Cliffs, New Jersey: Prentice Hall, 1964.

ZEITLIN, Maurice, *Revolutionary Politics and the Cuban Working Class,* Princeton: Princeton University Press, 1967.

Power, Authority, and Leadership:

Special Treatments

This is a residual category containing treatments of power, authority, and leadership that do not fit, or do not fit solely, under one of the three preceding topics. The publications here deal with power (or related phenomena) within small groups, nuclear families, formal organizations, educational institutions, economic institutions, and racial and ethnic minority populations, among other categories and groups of people. Several items deal with relationships between power, authority, or leadership and other stratification variables.

ADAMS, Stuart, "Trends in Occupational Origins of Business Leaders," *American Sociological Review,* 19 (October, 1954), 541-548.

ANDERSON, Ronald E., "Status Structure in Coalition Bargaining Games," *Sociometry,* 30 (December, 1967), 393-403.

ANDREWS, R. E., *Leadership and Supervision: A Survey of Research Findings,* Personnel Management Series No. 9, Washington, D. C.: United States Civil Service Commission, 1955.

BABCHUK, Nicholas, Ruth Marsey, and C. Wayne Gordon, "Men and Women in Community Agencies: A Note on Power and Prestige,"*American Sociological Review,* 25 (June, 1960), 399-403.

SPECIAL TREATMENTS

BARKLEY, R., "Theory of the Elite and the Mythology of Power," *Science and Society,* 19 (Spring, 1955), 97-106.

BARTH, Ernest A. T. and Baha Abu-Laban, "Power Structure and the Negro Sub-Community," *American Sociological Review,* 24 (February, 1959) 69-76.

BARTOS, Otomar J., and Richard A. Kalsih, "Sociological Correlates of Student Leadership in Hawaii," *Journal of Educational Sociology,* 35 (October, 1961), 65-72.

BASS, B. M., editor, *Leadership and Interpersonal Behavior,* New York: Holt, Rinehart and Winston, 1961.

BASS, B. M., *Leadership, Psychology and Organizational Behavior,* New York: Harper and Row, 1960.

BASS, B. M., Margaret W. Pryer, E. L. Gailer, and A. W. Flint, "Interacting Effects of Control, Motivation, Group Practice, and Problem Difficulty on Attempted Leadership," *Journal of Abnormal and Social Psychology,* 56 (May, 1958), 352-358.

BECKER, Howard S., "The Teacher in the Authority System of the Public School," *Journal of Educational Sociology,* 27, (November, 1953), 128-141.

BELL, G. B. and R. L. French, "Consistency of Individual Leadership Position in Small Groups of Varying Membership," *Journal of Abnormal and Social Psychology,* 45 (1950), 764-767.

BELOFF, Halla, "Two Forms of Social Conformity: Acquiescence and Conventionality," *Journal of Abnormal and Social Psychology,* 56 (January, 1958), 99-104.

BENSMAN, J. and A. Vidich, "Power Cliques in Bureaucratic Society," *Social Research,* 29 (Winter, 1962), Number 4, 467-474.

BERNARD, Jessie, "The Power of Science and the Science of Power," *American Sociological Review,* 14 (October, 1949), 575-584.

BERNARD, Jessie, "Scientists and the Paradox of Power," *Social Forces,* 31 (October, 1952), 14-20.

BIERSTEDT, Robert, "Power and Social Class," in Anthony Leeds, editor, *Seminar on Social Structure, Stratification and Mobility with Special Reference to Latin America,* Washington, D. C.: Pan American Union, 1966.

BLOOD, Robert O., Jr., and Robert L. Hamblin, "The Effect

of the Wife's Employment on the Family Power Structure," *Social Forces,* 36 (May, 1958), 347-352.

BOUMA, Donald H., "Analysis of the Social Power Position of a Real Estate Board," *Social Problems,* 10 (Fall, 1962), 121-132.

BOWERMAN, Charles E. and Glen H. Elder, Jr., "Variation in Adolescent Perception of Family Power Structure," *American Sociological Review,* 29 (August, 1964), 551-567.

BRESSLER, Marvin, and Charles F. Westoff, "Leadership and Social Change: The Reactions of a Special Group to Industrialization and Population Influx," *Social Forces,* 32 (December, 1953), 235-243.

BRONFENBRENNER, Urie, "Some Familial Antecedents of Responsibility and Leadership in Adolescents," in Luigi Petrullo and B. M. Bass, editors, *Leadership and Interpersonal Behavior,* New York: Holt, Rinehart and Winston, 1961.

BROTZ, Howard M., "Social Stratification and the Political Order," *American Journal of Sociology,* 64 (May, 1964), 571-578.

BROWNING, Rufus P. and Herbert Jacob, "Power Motivation and the Political Personality," *Public Opinion Quarterly,* 28 (Spring, 1964), 75-90.

BRYSON, Lyman, Louis Finkelstein, and R. M. McIver, editors, *Conflicts of Power in Modern Culture,* New York: Harper, 1947.

BURMA, John H., "Current Leadership Problems Among Japanese Americans," *Sociology and Social Research,* 37 (January-February, 1953), 157-163.

CAMILLERI, Santo F. and Joseph Berger, "Decision-Making and Social Influence: A Model and an Experimental Design," *Sociometry,* 30 (December, 1967), 365-378.

CANNETTI, Elias, *Crowds and Power,* second edition, translated from the German by Carol Stewart, New York: Viking Press, 1966.

CAPLAN, Gerald, "Some Comments on 'Community Psychiatry and Social Power,' " *Social Problems,* 14 (Summer, 1966), 23-25.

CARTER, Roy E., Jr. and Peter Clarke, "Public Affairs Opinion Leadership Among Educational Television Viewers," *American Sociological Review,* 27 (December, 1962), 792-799.

CATTELL, Raymond B., "New Concepts for Measuring Leadership in Terms of Group Syntality," *Human Relations,* 4 (1951), 161-184.

CHARTERS, W. W., Jr., "Social Class Analysis and the Control of Public Education," *Harvard Educational Review,* 23 (Fall, 1953), 268-283.

SPECIAL TREATMENTS

CIRCOUREL, Aaron V. and John I. Kitsuse, *The Educational Decision-Makers,* Indianapolis: Bobbs-Merrill, 1963.

CLARK, Kenneth B., *Dark Ghetto: Dilemmas of Social Power,* New York: Harper, 1965.

COHEN, Arthur R., *Attitude Change and Social Influence,* New York: Basic Books, 1964.

COHEN, Julius, Reginald Robson, and Alan Bates, *Parental Authority,* New Brunswick: Rutgers University Press, 1958.

COHN, Werner, "Social Stratification and the Charismatic," *Midwest Sociologist,* 21 (December, 1958), 12-18.

COTHRAN, Tilman C. and William M. Phillips, Jr., "Negro Leadership in a Crisis Situation," *Phylon,* 22 (Summer, 1961), 107-118.

COUSENS, F. R., "Indigenous Leadership in Two Lower-Class Neighborhood Organizations," in Arthur B. Shostak and William Gomberg, editors, *Blue-Collar World: Studies of the American Worker,* Englewood Cliffs, New Jersey: Prentice Hall, 1964.

CUNNISON, Ian, *Baggara Arabs: Power and the Lineage in a Sudanese Nomad Tribe,* New York: Oxford University Press, 1966.

DAHRENDORF, Ralf, *Class and Class Conflict in Industrial Society,* Stanford, California: Stanford University Press, 1959.

DAKIN, Ralph E., "Variations in Power Structures and Organizing Efficiency: A Comparative Study of Four Areas," *Sociological Quarterly,* 3 (July, 1962), 228-250.

DE GRAZIA, Alfred, "The Limits of External Leadership Over a Minority Electorate," *Public Opinion Quarterly,* 20 (Spring, 1956), 113-128.

EARLE, John R., "Parent-Child Communication, Sentiment, and Authority," *Sociological Inquiry,* 37 (Spring, 1967), 275-282.

EISENSTADT, S. N., "Social Mobility and the Evaluation of Intergroup Leadership," *Transactions of the Second World Congress of Sociology,* 2 (1954), 218-230.

ELDER, Glen H., Jr., "Parental Power Legitimation and Its Effect on the Adolescent," *Sociometry,* 26 (March, 1963), 50-65.

ETZIONI, Amitai, "Dual Leadership in Complex Organizations," *American Sociological Review,* 30 (October, 1965), 688-698.

EVAN, William M., "Power, Bargaining, and Law: A Preliminary Analysis of Labor Arbitration Cases," *Social Problems,* 7 (Summer, 1959), 4-15.

FORD, Clelland S., "The Role of the Fijian Chief," *American Sociological Review,* 3 (August, 1938), 542-550.

FOSTER, Philip, "Status, Power and Education in a Traditional Community," *School Review,* 72 (Summer, 1964), 158-182.

GAMSON, William A., *Power and Discontent,* Homewood, Illinois: Dorsey, 1968.

GARCEAU, Oliver and Corinne Silverman, "A Pressure Group and the Pressured," *American Political Science Review,* 48 (September, 1954), 672-691.

GODFREY, Gardner, "Functional Leadership and Popularity in Small Groups," *Human Relations,* 9 (1956), 491-504.

GOSS, Mary E., "Influence and Authority Among Physicians in an Outpatient Clinic," *American Sociological Review,* 26 (February, 1961), 39-50.

GROSS, Bertrand M., *The Managing of Organizations: The Administrative Struggle,* New York: Free Press, 1964.

GRUSKY, Oscar, "Organizational Goals and the Behavior of Informal Leaders, *American Journal of Sociology,* 65 (July, 1959), 59-67.

HAGGSTROM, Warren C., "The Power of the Poor," in Frank Riessman, Jerome Cohen, and Arthur Pearl, editors, *Mental Health of the Poor,* New York: Free Press, 1964.

HANSEN, Donald A., "Personal and Positional Influence in Formal Groups: Propositions and Theory for Research on Family Vulnerability to Stress," *Social Forces,* 44 (December, 1965), 202-210.

HARRISON, Paul M., *Authority and Power in the Free Church Tradition,* Princeton: Princeton University Press, 1959.

HARTER, Carl L., "The Power Roles of Intellectuals: An Introductory Statement," *Sociology and Social Research,* 48 (January, 1964), 176-186.

HERMAN, Melvin and Michael Munk, *Decision-Making in Poverty Programs,* New York: Columbia University Press, 1968.

HESS, Robert D. and Judith V. Torney, "Religion, Age, and Sex in Childrens' Perceptions of Family Authority," *Child Development,* 33 (December, 1962), 781-789.

HILDEBRAND, George H., "American Unionism, Social Stratification, and Power," *American Journal of Sociology,* 58 (January, 1953), 381-390.

HIRSCHMAN, Albert O., "Underdevelopment, Obstacles to the Perception of Change, and Leadership," *Daedelus,* 97 (Summer, 1968), 925-937.

SPECIAL
TREATMENTS

HODGES, Harold M., Jr., "Campus Leaders and Nonleaders," *Sociology and Social Research,* 37 (March-April, 1953), 251-255.

HOLLANDER, E. P., *Leaders, Groups, and Influence,* New York: Oxford University Press, 1964.

HOLMES, Roger, "Freud, Piaget, and Democratic Leadership," *British Journal of Sociology,* 16 (June, 1965), 123-138.

HOLMES, Roger, "Freud and Social Class," *British Journal of Sociology,* 16 (March, 1965), 48-67.

HOLT, Robert T., "Age as a Factor in the Recruitment of Communist Leadership," *American Political Science Review,* 48 (June, 1954), 486-499.

HOPKINS, Terence K., *The Exercise of Influence in Small Groups,* Totowa, New Jersey: Bedminister Press, 1965.

HOROWITZ, Irving L., editor, *Power, Politics and People: The Collected Essays of C. Wright Mills,* New York: Oxford University Press, 1965.

JAMES, Ralph and Estell James, *Hoffa and the Teamsters: A Study of Union Power,* Princeton, Van Nostrand, 1965.

JOHANNIS, Theodore B. and James M. Rollins, "Teenager Perception of Family Decision Making," *The Coordinator,* 7 (1959), 70-74.

JANOWITZ, Morris, "Changing Patterns of Organizational Authority: The Military," *Administrative Science Quarterly,* 4 (March, 1959), 473-493.

JANOWITZ, Morris, "Hierarchy and Authority in the Military Establishment," in Amitai Etzioni, editor, *Complex Organizations,* New York: Holt, Rinehart and Winston, 1961.

KARL, Barry D., "The Power of Intellect and the Politics of Ideas," *Daedelas,* 97 (Summer, 1968), 1002-1035.

KATZ, E., Peter M. Blau, M. Brown, and Fred L. Strodtbeck, "Leadership Stability and Social Change," *Sociometry,* 20 (March, 1957), 36-50.

KATZ, E. and Paul F. Lazersfeld, *Personal Influence: The Part Played by People in the Flow of Mass Communication,* New York: Free Press, 1955.

KLAPP, Orrin E., *Symbolic Leaders: Public Dramas and Public Men,* Chicago: Aldine, 1965.

KILLIAN, Lewis M., "Community Structure and the Role of the Negro Leader-Agent," *Sociological Inquiry,* 35 (Winter, 1965).

KOHN, Melvin L., and John A. Clausen, "Parental Authority Behavior and Schizophrenia," *American Journal of Ortho-psychiatry,* 26 (April, 1956), 297-313.

LADD, Everett C., Jr., *Negro Political Leadership in the South,* Ithaca: Cornell University Press, 1966.

LAMMERS, C. J., "Power and Participation in Decision-Making in Formal Organizations," *American Journal of Sociology,* 79 (September, 1967), 201-216.

LARSON, Lyle E. and Theodore B. Johannis, Jr., "Religious Perspective and the Authority Structure of the Family," *Pacific Sociological Review,* 10 (Spring, 1967), 13-24.

LASKIN, Richard, *Leadership of Voluntary Organizations in a Saskatchewan Town,* Saskatoon: Centre for Community Studies, 1962.

LEIFER, Ronald, "Community Psychiatry and Social Power," *Social Problems,* 14 (Summer, 1966), 16-22.

LEVENTMAN, Seymour, "Class and Ethnic Tensions: Minority Group Leadership in Transition," *Sociology and Social Research,* 50 (April, 1966), 371-376.

LHOMME, Jean, "Reflections on the Nature of Economic Power," *Political Research: Organization and Design,* 3 (December, 1959), 10-18.

LINTON, Thomas E. and Jack L. Nelson, *Patterns of Power: Social Foundations of Education,* New York: Pitman, 1968.

LIPPITT, R. O. and R. K. White, "An Experimental Study of Leadership and Group Life," in Eleanor Maccoby, T. M. Newcomb, and E. L. Hartley, editors, *Readings in Social Psychology,* 3rd edition, New York: Holt, Rinehart and Winston, 1958.

LOPREATO, Joseph, "Authority Relations and Class Conflict," *Social Forces,* 47 (December, 1968), 70-79.

LOWE, Francis E., and Thomas C. McCormick, "A Study of the Influence of Formal and Informal Leaders in an Election Campaign," *Public Opinion Quarterly,* 20 (Winter, 1956-1957), 651-662.

MACAULEY, Stewart, *Law and the Balance of Power: The Automobile Manufacturers and Their Dealers,* New York: Russell Sage Foundation, 1966.

MANHEIM, Henry L., "Intergroup Interaction as Related to Status and Leadership Differences between Groups, *Sociometry,* 23 (December, 1960), 415-427.

MANNHEIM, Karl, *Freedom, Power, and Democratic Planning,* New York: Oxford University Press, 1950.

MATTHEWS, Donald R. and James W. Prothro, *Negroes and the New Southern Politics,* New York: Harcourt, Brace and World, 1966.

McWORTER, Gerald, and Robert L. Crain, "Subcommunity Gladiatorial Competition: Civil Rights Leadership as a Competitive Process," *Social Forces,* 46 (September, 1967), 8-21.

MEREI, F., "Group Leadership and Institutionalization," *Human Relations,* 2 (1949), 23-39.

MERTON, Robert K., "Patterns of Influence: Local and Cosmopolitan Influentials," in his *Social Theory and Social Structure,* revised edition, New York: Free Press, 1957.

MERTON, Robert K., "The Provisional Concept of Interpersonal Influence," in Paul F. Lazarsfeld and F. N. Stanton, editors, *Communications Research, 1948-1949,* New York: Harper, 1949.

MIDDLETON, Russell and Snell Putney, "Dominance in Decisions in the Family: Race and Class Differences," *American Journal of Sociology,* 65 (May, 1960), 605-609.

MOGEY, John, "A Century of Declining Paternal Authority," *Marriage and Family Living,* 19 (August, 1957), 234-239.

MOORE, Barrington, Jr., "The Relation between Social Stratification and Social Control," *Sociometry,* 5 (August, 1942), 230-250.

MOOS, Malcolm, and Bertram Kaslin, "Prestige Suggestion and Political Leadership," *Public Opinion Quarterly,* 16 (Spring, 1952), 77-93.

NOSSITER, Bernard, *The Mythmakers: An Essay in Power and Wealth,* Boston: Houghton Mifflin, 1964.

NUQUIST, Joseph E., "Contemporary Trends in Rural Leadership," *Rural Sociology,* 12 (September, 1947), 273-284.

OLMSTEAD, Donald, "Organizational Leadership and Social Structure in a Small City," *American Sociological Review,* 19 (June, 1954), 273-281.

OPPENHEIM, Felix E., "Degrees of Power and Freedom," *American Political Science Review,* 54 (June, 1960), 437-446.

PAREEK, U., editor, *Studies in Rural Leadership,* Delhi, India: Behaviour Science Centre, 1966.

PEABODY, Robert L., *Organizational Authority: Superior-Subordinate Relations in Three Public Service Organizations,* New York: Atherton, 1964.

PECK, Sidney, *The Rank-and-File Leader,* New Haven: College and University Press, 1963.

PELLEGRIN, Roland J., "The Achievement of High Statuses and Leadership in the Small Group," *Social Forces, 32* (October, 1953), 10-16.

PETRULLO, Luigi and B. M. Bass, editors, *Leadership and Interpersonal Behavior,* New York: Holt, Rinehart and Winston, 1961.

RAFFAELE, Joseph A., *Labor Leadership in Italy and Denmark,* Madison: University of Wisconsin Press, 1962.

RATHS, Louis, "Power in Small Groups," *Journal of Educational Sociology,* 28 (November, 1954, 97-103.

RAVEN, B. H. and J. R. P. French, "Group Support, Legitimate Power, and Social Influence," *Journal of Personality,* 26 (September, 1958), 400-409.

REDL, Fritz, "Group Emotion and Leadership," in A Paul Hare, E. F. Borgatta, and R. F. Bales, editors, *Small Groups,* New York: Knopf, 1955.

REISSMAN, Leonard, "Class and Power: The Sacred and the Profane," *Views,* 6 (Autumn, 1964), 46-51.

ROSENBERG, Morris, "Power and Desegregation," *Social Problems,* 3 (April, 1956), 215-223.

ROSS, Aileen D., "Control and Leadership in Women's Groups: An Analysis of Philanthropic Money-raising Activity," *Social Forces,* 3 (December, 1958), 124-131.

ROUCEK, Joseph S., "Minority-Majority Relations in Their Power Aspects," *Phylon,* 17 (First Quarter, 1956), 24-30.

RUSHING, William A., *The Psychiatric Professions: Power, Conflict, and Adoptation in a Psychiatric Hospital Staff,* Chapel Hill: University of North Carolina Press, 1964.

SANFORD, F. H., *Authoritarianism and Leadership,* Philadelphia: Stevenson, 1950.

SCHEFF, Thomas J., "Negotiating Reality: Notes on Power in the Assessment of Responsibility," *Social Problems,* 16 (Summer, 1968), 3-17.

SCHERMERHORN, Richard A., "Power as a Primary Concept in the Study of Minorities," *Social Forces,* 35 (October, 1956), 53-56.

SCHLESINGER, Arthur, Jr., "On Heroic Leadership," *Encounter,* 15 (December, 1960), 3-11.

SCHOENFELD, Benjamin N., "The Psychological Characteristics of Leadership," *Social Forces,* 26 (May, 1948), 391-396.

SCHRAG, Clarence, "Leadership Among Prison Inmates," *American Sociological Review,* 19 (February, 1954), 37-42.

SEIDMAN, Joel, Jack London, and Bernard Karsh, "Leadership in a Local Union," *American Journal of Sociology,* 56 (November, 1950), 229-237.

SELZNICK, Philip, *Leadership in Administration,* New York: Harper and Row, 1957.

SELZNICK, Philip, *TVA and the Grass Roots,* Berkeley: University of California Press, 1949.

SHILS, Edward, "Charisma, Order, and Status," *American Sociological Review,* 30 (April, 1965), 199-213.

SIMPSON, George, "Ethnic Groups, Social Mobility and Power in Latin America," *Seminar on Social Structure, Stratification and Mobility, with Special Reference to Latin America,* Washington, D. C.: Pan American Union, 1966.

SKINNER, G. William, *Leadership and Power in the Chinese Community of Thailand,* Ithaca: Cornell University Press, 1958.

SMITH, Claggett and Michael Brown, "Communication Structure and Control Structure in a Voluntary Association," *Sociometry,* 27 (December, 1964), 449-468.

SMITH, Lincoln, "Power Politics in Brunswick: A Case Study," *Human Organization,* 22 (Summer, 1963), 152-158.

SMITH, Luke M., "The Clergy: Authority Structure, Ideology, Migration," *American Sociological Review,* 18 (June, 1953), 242-248.

SMYTHE, Hugh H., "Changing Patterns in Negro Leadership," *Social Forces,* 29 (December, 1950), 191-197.

SMYTHE, Hugh H., "Negro Masses and Leaders: An Analysis of Current Trends," *Sociology and Social Research,* 35 (September-October, 1950), 31-37.

SOKOL, Robert, "Power Orientation and McCarthyism," *American Journal of Sociology,* 73 (January, 1968), 443-452.

SOROKIN, Pitirim A., *Power and Morality,* Boston: Porter Sargent, 1959.

STAGNER, Ross, "The Prestige Value of Different Types of Leadership," *Sociology and Social Research,* 25 (May-June, 1941), 403-413.

STONE, Robert C., "Status and Leadership in a Combat Fighter Squadron," *American Journal of Sociology* 51 (March, 1946), 388-394.

SPECIAL TREATMENTS

STRAUS, Murray A., "Conjugal Power Structure and Adolescent Personality," *Marriage and Family Living,* 24 (February, 1962), 17-25.

TANNENBAUM, Arnold S. and Basil S. Georgopoulos, "The Distribution of Control in Formal Organizations," *Social Forces,* 36 (October, 1957), 44-50.

TANNENBAUM, Robert, Irving R. Weschler, and Fred Massarik, *Leadership and Organization: A Behavioral Science Approach,* New York: McGraw-Hill, 1961.

TARCHER, Martin, *Leadership and the Power of Ideas,* New York: Harper and Row, 1966.

THIBAUT, J. and H. H. Kelley, *The Social Psychology of Groups,* New York: Wiley, 1959.

THOMPSON, Daniel C., *The Negro Leadership Class,* New York: Prentice Hall, 1963.

THOMPSON, James D., "Authority and Power in 'Identical' Organizations," *American Journal of Sociology,* 62 (November, 1956), 290-301.

TRAPP, P., "Leadership and Popularity as a Function of Behavioral Predictions," *Journal of Abnormal and Social Psychology,* 51 (November, 1955), 452-457.

TUCKER, Robert C., "The Theory of Charismatic Leadership," *Daedelus,* 97 (Summer, 1968), 731-756.

TURK, Herman and G . Robert Wills, "Authority and Interaction," *Sociometry,* 27 (March, 1964), 1-18.

TURK, Herman, Eugene L. Hartley, and David M. Shaw, "The Expectation of Social Influence," *Journal of Social Psychology,* 58 (October, 1962), 23-29.

WALKER, Jack L., "Protest and Negotiation: A Case Study of Negro Leadership in Atlanta," *Midwest Journal of Political Science,* 7 (May, 1963), 99-124.

WALTER, E. V., " 'Mass Society': The Late Stages of an Idea," *Social Research,* 31 (Winter, 1964), 391-410.

WATSON, J. B. and Julian Samora, "Subordinate Leadership in a Bicultural Society," *American Sociological Review,* 19 (August, 1954), 413-421.

WILLER, David E., "Weber's Missing Authority Type," *Sociological Inquiry,* 37 (Spring, 1967), 231-239.

WILLNER, Ann Ruth and Dorothy Willner, "The Rise and Role of Charismatic Leaders," *Annals of the American Academy of Political and Social Science,* 358 (March, 1965), 77-88.

SPECIAL
TREATMENTS

WEINBERG, Carl, "Institutional Differences in Factors Associated with Student Leadership," *Sociology and Social Research,* 49 (July, 1965), 425-436.

WILSON, C. S. and T. Lupton, "The Social Background and Connections of Top Decision Makers," *Manchester School,* 27 (January, 1959), 30-46.

WILSON, James Q., *Negro Politics: The Search for Leadership,* New York: Free Press, 1960.

ZALD, Mayer N., "Who Shall Rule? A Political Analysis of Succession in a Large Welfare Organization," *Pacific Sociological Review,* 8 (Spring, 1965), 52-60.

ZANDER, Alvin and Arthur R. Cohen, "Attributed Social Power and Group Acceptance," *Journal of Abnormal and Social Psychology,* 51 (November, 1955), 490-492.

ZANDER, Alvin and Theodore Curtis, "Effects of Social Powers on Aspiration Setting and Striving," *Journal of Abnormal and Social Psychology,* 64 (January, 1962), 63-74.

ZELENY, L. D., "Characteristics of Group Leaders," *Sociology and Social Research,* 24 (November-December, 1939), 140-149.

ZURCHER, Louis A., "The Leader and the Lost: A Case Study of Indigenous Leadership in a Poverty Program Community Action Committee," *Genetic Psychology Monographs,* 76 (1967), 23-93.

Status Consistency and Inconsistency

Perusal of this section reveals that most of the publications in it are very recent; status inconsistency has been one of the most fashionable research topics in social stratification during the 1960's. In spite of refractory methodological problems in determining the effects of status inconsistency (see the several publications by Blalock), there is a continuing strong interest in research in this area.

ABRAMSON, J. H., "Emotional Disorder, Status Inconsistency and Migration," *Milbank Memorial Fund Quarterly,* 44 (January, 1966), 23-48.

ADAMS, Stuart, "Status Congruency as a Variable in Small Group Performance," *Social Forces,* 32 (October, 1953), 16-22.

ANDERSON, Bo and Morris Zelditch, "Rank Equilibration and Political Behavior," *Archives europennes de Sociologie,* 5 (1964), 112-125.

BAUMAN, Karl E., "Status Inconsistency, Satisfactory Social Interaction, and Community Satisfaction in an area of Rapid Growth," *Social Forces,* 47 (September, 1968), 45-52.

BELL, Inge Powell, "Status Discrepancy and the Radical Rejection of Non-violence," *Sociological Inquiry,* 38 (Winter, 1968), 51-63.

BENOIT-SMULLYAN, Emile, "Status, Status Types, and Status Interrelations," *American Sociological Review,* 9 (April, 1944), 151-161.

BERNARD, Jessie, "Marital Stability and Patterns of Status Variables," *Journal of Marriage and the Family,* 28 (November, 1966), 421-439.

BLALOCK, Hubert M., Jr., "Comment: Status Inconsistency and the Identification Problem," *Public Opinion Quarterly,* 30 (Spring, 1966), 130-132.

BLALOCK, Hubert M., Jr., "Status Inconsistency and Interaction: Some Alternative Models," *American Journal of Sociology,* 73 (November, 1967), 305-315.

BLALOCK, Hubert M., Jr., "Status Inconsistency, Social Mobility, Status Integration and Structural Effects," *American Sociological Review,* 32 (October, 1967), 790-801.

BLALOCK, Hubert M., Jr., "Tests of Status Inconsistency Theory: A Note of Caution," *Pacific Sociological Review,* 10 (Fall, 1967), 69-74.

BLALOCK, Hubert M., Jr., "The Identification Problem and Theory Building: The Case of Status Inconsistency," *American Sociological Review,* 31 (February, 1966), 52-61.

BLOOMBAUM, Milton, "The Mobility Dimensions of Status Consistency," *Sociology and Social Research,* 48 (April, 1964), 340-347.

BOGUE, Donald, *Principles of Demography,* New York: Wiley, Chapter 14.

BOHLKE, Robert H., "Social Mobility, Stratification Inconsistency, and Middle Class Delinquency," *Social Problems,* 8 (Spring, 1961), 351-363.

BRADBURN, Norman M. and David Caplovitz. *Reports on Happiness,* Chicago: Aldine, 1965.

BRANDMEYER, Gerard, "Status Consistency and Political Behavior: A Replication and Extension of Research," *Sociological Quarterly,* 6 (Summer, 1965), 241-256.

STATUS BRANDON, Arlene C., "Status Congruence and Expectations," *Sociometry,* 28 (September, 1965), 272-288.

BROOM, Leonard, "Social Differentiation and Stratification," in Robert K. Merton, Leonard Broom, and Leonard S. Cottrell, Jr., editors, *Sociology Today,* New York: Basic Books, 1959.

BURNSTEIN, Eugene and Robert B. Zajonc, "The Effect of Group Success on the Reduction of Status Incongruence in Task-Oriented Groups," *Sociometry,* 28 (December, 1965), 349-362.

CURTIS, Richard F., "Differential Association and the Stratification of the Urban Community," *Social Forces,* 42 (October, 1963), 68-77.

DEMERATH, N. J., III, *Social Class in American Protestantism,* Chicago: Rand McNally, 1965, Chapter VI, "Status Discrepancy and Religious Commitment," and Chapter VII, "Status Discrepancy under Harsher Light."

EXLINE, Rolf V. and Robert C. Ziller, "Status Congruency and Interpersonal Conflict in Decision-Making Groups," *Human Relations,* 12 (May, 1959), 147-160.

FAUMAN, S. Joseph, "Status Crystallization and Interracial Attitudes," *Social Forces,* 47 (September, 1968), 53-60.

FENCHEL, G. H., Jack H. Monderer, and Eugene L. Hartley, "Subjective Status and the Equilibration Hypothesis," *Journal of Abnormal and Social Psychology,* 46 (October, 1951), 476-479.

GESCHWENDER, James A., "Civil Rights Protest and Riots: A Disappearing Distinction," *Social Science Quarterly,* 49 (December, 1968), 474-484.

GESCHWENDER, James A., "Social Structure and the Negro Revolt: An Examination of Some Hypotheses," *Social Forces,* 43 (December, 1964), 248-256.

GESCHWENDER, James A., "Status Inconsistency, Social Isolation, and Individual Unrest," *Social Forces,* 46 (June, 1968), 477-483.

GOFFMAN, Irving W., "Status Consistency and Preference for Change in Power Distribution," *American Sociological Review,* 22 (June, 1957), 275-281.

HODGE, Robert W., "The Status Consistency of Occupational Groups," *American Sociological Review,* 27 (June, 1962), 336-343.

HOMANS, George C., "Status Among Clerical Workers," *Human Organization,* 12 (Spring, 1953), 5-10.

HOMANS, George C., "The Cash Posters: A Study of a Group of Working Girls," *American Sociological Review,* 19 (December, 1954), 724-733.

HUGHES, Everett C., "Dilemmas and Contradictions of Status," *American Journal of Sociology,* 50 (March, 1945), 353-359.

HUGHES, Everett C., "Social Change and the Marginal Man," *Phylon,* 10 (First Quarter, 1949), 58-65.

HYMAN, Herbert H., "Reflections on Reference Groups," *Public Opinion Quarterly,* 24 (Fall, 1960), 383-396.

HYMAN, Martin D., "Determining the Effects of Status Inconsistency," *Public Opinion Quarterly,* 30 (Spring, 1966), 120-129.

JACKSON, Elton F., "Status Consistency and Symptoms of Stress," *American Sociological Review,* 27 (August, 1962), 469-480.

JACKSON, Elton F. and Peter J. Burke, "Status and Symptoms of Stress: Additive and Interaction Effects," *American Sociological Review,* 30 (August, 1965), 556-564.

KELLY, K. Dennis and William J. Chambliss, "Status Consistency and Political Attitudes," *American Sociological Review,* 31 (June, 1966), 375-382.

KENKEL, William F., "The Relationship Between Status Consistency and Politico-Economic Attitudes," *American Sociological Review,* 21 (June, 1956), 365-368.

KIMBERLY, James C., "A Theory of Status Equilibration," in Joseph Berger, Morris Zelditch, Jr., and Bo Anderson, *Sociological Theories in Progress,* New York: Houghton Mifflin, 1966.

KOLACK, Shirley, "Status Inconsistency Among Social Work Professionals," *Social Problems,* 15 (Winter, 1968), 365-376.

LANDECKER, Werner S., "Class Boundaries," *American Sociological Review,* 25 (December, 1960), 868-877.

LANDECKER, Werner S., "Class Crystallization and Class Consciousness," *American Sociological Review,* 28 (April, 1963), 219-229.

LANDECKER, Werner S., "Class Crystallization and Its Urban Pattern," *Social Research,* 27 (Autumn, 1960), 308-320.

LENSKI, Gerhard E., "Comment on 'Methodological Notes on a Theory of Status Crystallization,'" *Public Opinion Quarterly,* 28

(Summer, 1964), 326-330.

LENSKI, Gerhard E., "Social Participation and Status Crystallization," *American Sociological Review,* 21 (August, 1956), 458-464.

LENSKI, Gerhard E., "Status Crystallization: A Non-Vertical Dimension of Social Status," *American Sociological Review,* 19 (August, 1954), 405-413.

LENSKI, Gerhard E., "Status Inconsistency and the Vote: A Four Nations Test," *American Sociological Review,* 32 (April, 1967), 288-301.

LOPREATO, Joseph, "Upward Social Mobility and Political Orientation," *American Sociological Review,* 32 (August, 1967), 586-592.

MALEWSKI, Andrzij, "The Degree of Status Incongruence and its Effects," in Reinhard Bendix and Seymour M. Lipset, editors, *Class, Status and Power,* revised edition, New York: Free Press, 1966.

MITCHELL, Robert Edward, "Methodological Notes on a Theory of Status Crystallization," *Public Opinion Quarterly,* 28 (Summer, 1964), 315-325.

NAGI, Saad Z., "Status Profile and Reactions to Status Threats," *American Sociological Review,* 28 (June, 1963), 440-443.

NAM, Charles B. and Mary G. Powers, "Variations in Socioeconomic Structure by Race, Residence, and the Life Cycle," *American Sociological Review,* 30 (February, 1965), 97-103.

PELLEGRIN, Roland J. and Frederick L. Bates, "Congruity and Incongruity of Status Attributes within Occupations and Work Positions," *Social Forces,* 38 (October, 1959), 23-28.

PORTER, James M., "Consumption Patterns of Professors and Businessmen: A Pilot Study of Conspicuous Consumption and Status," *Sociological Inquiry,* 37 (Spring, 1967), 255-265.

RUSH, Gary B., "Status Consistency and Right-Wing Extremism," *American Sociological Review,* 32 (February, 1967), 86-92.

SAMPSON, Edward E., "Status Congruence and Cognitive Consistency," *Sociometry,* 26 (June, 1963), 146-162.

SCHMITT, David R., "An Attitudinal Correlate of the Status Congruency of Married Women," *Social Forces,* 44 (December, 1965), 190-195.

SEEMAN, Melvin, *Social Status and Leadership: The Case of the School Executive,* Columbus: Bureau of Educational Research and Service, Ohio State University, Monograph No. 35, 1960.

STATUS

SHERIF, Muzafer and Carolyn W. Sherif, *Groups in Harmony and Tension,* New York: Harper, 1953, 383-396.

TREIMAN, Donald J., "Status Discrepancy and Prejudice," *American Journal of Sociology,* 72 (March, 1966), 651-664.

TROW, Donald B., "Status Equilibration in the Laboratory," *Pacific Sociological Review,* 10 (Fall, 1967), 75-80.

Interrelations Among Stratification Variables

In recent years an increasing proportion of the research in stratification has dealt in some way with the interrelations among the major stratification variables: wealth, power, prestige, and education. Both this change and the increased interest in status inconsistency exemplify the fact that both research and theory in the field increasingly utilize a multi-dimensional view of stratification, and efforts are now more often made to keep the dimensions analytically and operationally distinct.

This is one of several topics included in this bibliography in which a complete and comprehensive coverage of all the relevant publications would include too large a percentage of the total stratification literature to be of much value. Therefore, we list only publications in which the main contribution is the illumination of aspects of the interrelations among the stratification variables.

ANASTASI, Anne and Shirley Miller, "Adolescent 'Prestige Factors' in Relation to Scholastic and Socio-Economic Variables," *Journal of Social Psychology,* 29 (February, 1949), 43-50.

ANDERSON, C. Arnold, "Regional and Racial Differences in Relation Between Income and Education," *School Review,* 63 (January, 1955), 38-45.

ANDERSON C. Arnold, "Social Class Differentials in the Schooling of Youth Within the Regions and Community-Size Groups of the United States," *Social Forces,* 25 (May, 1947), 434-440.

BARBER, Bernard, "Family Status, Local-Community Status, and Social Stratification: Three Types of Social Ranking," *Pacific Sociological Review,* 4 (Spring, 1961), 69-75.

BONJEAN, Charles M., "Class, Status, and Power Reputation," *Sociology and Social Research,* 49 (October, 1964), 69-75.

BROTZ, Howard M., "Social Stratification and the Political Order," *American Journal of Sociology,* 64 (May, 1964), 571-578.

BRUNNER, Edmund deS. and Sloan Wayland, "Education and Income," *Journal of Educational Sociology,* 32 (September, 1958), 21-27.

BRUNNER, Edmund deS. and Sloan Wayland, "Occupation, Labor Force Status, and Education," *Journal of Educational Sociology,* 32 (September, 1958), 8-20.

BURNS, Hobert W., "Social Class and Education in Latin America," *Comparative Education Review,* 6 (February, 1963), 230-237.

BURTON, William H., "Education and Social Class in the United States," *Harvard Educational Review,* 23 (Fall, 1953), 243-256.

COWHIG, James D., "Early Occupational Status as Related to Education and Residence," *Rural Sociology,* 27 (March, 1962), 18-27.

CLELLAND, Donald A. and William H. Form, "Economic Dominants and Community Power: A Comparative Analysis," *American Journal of Sociology,* 69 (March, 1964), 511-521.

COTGROVE, Stephen, "Education and Occupation," *British Journal of Sociology,* 13 (March, 1962), 33-42.

CRAIN, Robert L. and Donald B. Rosenthal, "Community Status as a Dimension of Local Decision Making," *American Sociological Review,* 32 (December, 1967), 970-985.

DAILEY, John T., "Education and Emergence from Poverty," *Journal of Marriage and the Family,* 26 (November, 1964), 430-434.

DUNCAN, Otis Dudley, "Occupational Components of Educational Differences in Income," *Journal of the American Statistical Association,* 56 (December, 1961) 783-792.

FLOUD, Jean, "Social Class Factors in Educational Achievement," in Joseph Kahl, editor, *Comparative Perspectives on Stratification,* Boston: Little, Brown, 1968.

FLOUD, Jean, A. H. Halsey and F. M. Martin, *Social Class and Educational Opportunity,* London: 1956.

FOLGER, John K. and Charles B. Nam, *Education of the American Population,* Washington, D. C.: United States Government Printing Office, 1967.

FOLGER, John K. and Charles B. Nam, "Trends in Education in Relation to the Occupational Structure," *Sociology of Education,* 38 (Fall, 1964), 19-33.

FOSTER, Philip, "Status, Power and Education in a Traditional Community," *School Review,* 72 (Summer, 1967), 158-182.

GLENN, Norval D., "Negro Prestige Criteria: A Case Study in the Bases of Prestige," *American Journal of Sociology,* 68 (May, 1963), 645-657.

GLICK, Paul C. and Herman P. Miller, "Educational Level and Potential Income," *American Sociological Review,* 21 (June, 1956), 307-312.

GOUGH, Harrison G., "A New Dimension of Status, III: Discrepancies between the St Scale and 'Objective' Status," *American Sociological Review,* 14 (April, 1949), 275-281.

HALSEY, A. H., Jean Floud, and C. Arnold Anderson, editors, *Education, Economy, and Society,* New York: Free Press, 1961.

HATT, Paul K., "Occupation and Social Stratification," *American Journal of Sociology,* 55 (May, 1950), 533-543.

HAVEMANN, Ernest and Patricia Salter West, *They Went to College,* New York: Harcourt Brace, 1952.

HILGARD, E. R., "Success in Relation to Level of Aspiration," *School and Society,* 55 (April 11, 1942), 423-428.

HOUTHAKKER, H. S., "Education and Income," *Review of Economics and Statistics,* 61 (February, 1959).

HOCHBAUM, Godfrey, John G. Darley, E. D. Monachesi, and Charles Bird, "Socio-Economic Variables in a Large City," *American Journal of Sociology,* 61 (July, 1955), 31-38.

KNOX, John B., "Occupation and Education in a Democracy," *Social Forces,* 20 (October, 1941), 109-115.

LUNDBERG, George A., "Occupations and 'Class' Alignments in the United States, 1870-1950," *Social Forces,* 34 (December, 1955), 128-130.

MARKS, J. B., "Interests, Leadership and Sociometric Status Among Adolescents," *Sociometry,* 17 (November, 1954), 340-349.

MILLER, Alden D., *Principal Components and Curvature in Occupational Stratification,* Chapel Hill: Institute for Research in Social Science, University of North Carolina, 1967.

MILLER, Herman P., "Annual and Lifetime Income in Relation to Education: 1939-1959," *American Economic Review,* 50 (December, 1960), 962-986.

MILLER, Herman P., *Rich Man, Poor Man,* New York: Crowell, 1964.

MOOS, Malcolm and Bertram Kaslin, "Prestige Suggestion and Political Leadership," *Public Opinion Quarterly,* 16 (Spring, 1952), 77-93.

INTERRELATIONS AMONG VARIABLES

PERRUCCI, Robert, "Education, Stratification, and Mobility," in Donald A. Hansen and Joel Gerstl, editors, *On Education— Sociological Perspectives,* New York: Wiley, 1967.

PUNKE, Harold H., "Economic Status and High School Attendance," *Social Forces,* 19 (March, 1941), 365-368.

REISSMAN, Leonard, "Class and Power: The Sacred and the Profane," *Views,* 6 (Autumn, 1964), 46-51.

RENSHAW, Edward F., "Estimating the Returns to Education," *Review of Economics and Statistics,* 62 (August, 1960), 318-324.

SCHULTZ, Theodore, *Economic Value of Education,* New York: Columbia University Press, 1963.

SCHULZE, Robert O., "The Role of Economic Dominants in Community Power Structure," *American Sociological Review,* 23 (February, 1958), 3-9.

SEXTON, Patricia Cayo, *Education and Income,* New York: Viking, 1961.

SHANNON, Lyle W., and Elaine Krass, "The Urban Adjustment of Immigrants: The Relationship of Education to Occupation and Total Family Income," *Pacific Sociological Review,* 6, (Spring, 1963), 37-42.

SMYTHE, Hugh H., "Nigerian Elite: Role of Education," *Sociology and Social Research,* 45 (October, 1960), 71-73.

STAGNER, Ross, "The Prestige Value of Different Types of Leadership," *Sociology and Social Research,* 25 (May-June, 1941), 403-413.

STEPHENSON, Richard, "Education and Stratification," *Journal of Educational Research,* 25 (September, 1951), 34-41.

STEPHENSON, Richard, "Status Achievement and the Occupational Pyramid," *Social Forces,* 31 (October, 1952), 75-77.

THOMAS, Lawrence G., *The Occupational Structure and Education,* Englewood Cliffs, New Jersey: Prentice-Hall, 1956.

WARNER, W. Lloyd, Marchia Meeker, and Kenneth Eells, *Social Class in America,* New York: Science Research Associates, 1949.

Stratification and Religion

This section includes publications in which dimensions of stratification are treated as independent variables, publications in which stratification phenomena are treated as dependent variables, and publications in which interaction between stratification and religious phenomena is emphasized. Those users of this bibliography who are interested only in publications in which stratification phenomena are treated as independent variables are referred to the section entitled "Correlates of Stratification: Religious Phenomena." The effects of religious phenomena upon social mobility are also treated in a separate section (see "Religion and Social Mobility"). Some of the items listed here also appear under one of the more specific topics dealing with religion, but many do not.

ANDRESKI, Stanislav, "Method and Substantive Theory in Max Weber," *British Journal of Sociology,* 15 (March, 1964), 1-18.

BELL, Wendell and Maryanne Force, "Religious Preference and the Class Structure," *Midwest Sociologist,* 19 (May, 1957), 79-86.

BOGUE, Donald J., "Religious Affiliation," *The Population of the United States,* New York: Free Press, 1959, 688-709.

BOISEN, A. T., "Economic Distress and Religious Experience," *Psychiatry,* (May, 1939), 185-194.

BOISEN, A. T., "Religion and Hard Times: A Study of the Holy Rollers," *Social Action,* (March 15, 1939), 8-35.

BRADEN, Charles S., *These Also Believe: A Study of Modern American Cults and Minority Religious Movements,* New York: Macmillan, 1949.

BRESSLER, Marvin and Charles F. Westoff, "Catholic Education, Economic Values, and Achievement," *American Journal of Sociology,* 69 (November, 1963), 225-233.

BREWER, E. D. C., "Sect and Church in Methodism," *Social Forces,* 30 (May, 1952), 400-408.

BROOM, Leonard and Norval D. Glenn, "Religious Differences in Reported Attitudes and Behavior," *Sociological Analysis,* 27 (Winter, 1966), 187-209.

BROWN, James Stephen, "Social Class, Intermarriage, and Church Membership in a Kentucky Community," *American Journal of Sociology,* 57 (November, 1951), 232-242.

BULTENA, Louis, "Church Membership and Church Attendance in Madison, Wisconsin," *American Sociological Review,* 14 (June, 1949), 384-389.

BURCHINAL, Lee G., "Some Social Status Criteria and Church Membership and Church Attendance," *Journal of Social Psychology,* 49 (February, 1959), 53-64.

RELIGION

BURCHINAL, Lee G. and William F. Kenkel, "Religious Identification and Occupational Status of Iowa Grooms, 1953-1957," *American Sociological Review,* 27 (August, 1962), 526-5:

CANCIAN, Frank, *Economics and Prestige in a Maya Community: The Religious Cargo System in Zinacantan,* Stanford: Stanford University Press, 1965.

CANTRIL, Hadley, "Education and Economic Composition of Religious Groups: An Analysis of Poll Data," *American Journal of Sociology,* 47 (March, 1943), 574-579.

CARNEY, Richard E. and Wilbert J. McKeachie, "Religion, Sex, Social Class, Probability of Success and Student Personality," *Journal for the Scientific Study of Religion,* 3 (Fall, 1963), 32-41.

CLARK, Elmer T., *The Small Sects in America,* second edition, New York: Adingdon-Cokesbury Press, 1949.

CLARK, S. D., "The Religious Sect in Canadian Economic Development," *Canadian Journal of Economics and Political Science,* 12 (1946), 439-453.

COHN, W., "Jehovah's Witnesses as a Proletarian Movement," *American Scholar,* 24 (1955), 281-298.

CRAMER, Carl, "The Peculiar People Prosper," *New York Times Magazine,* (April 15, 1962).

CURTIS, Richard F., "Occupational Mobility and Church Participation," *Social Forces,* 38 (May, 1960), 315-319.

DALTON, Melville, "Worker Response and Social Background," *Journal of Political Economy,* 55 (August, 1947), 323-332.

DATTA, Lois-ellin, "Family Religious Background and Early Scientific Creativity," *American Sociological Review,* 32 (August, 1967), 626-635.

DAVIES, J. K., "The Morman Church: Its Middle-Class Propensities," *Review of Religious Research,* 4 (1963), 84-95.

De JONG, Gordon F., "Religious Fundamentalism, Socio-Economic Status, and Fertility Attitudes in the Southern Appalachians," *Demography,* 2 (1965), 540-548.

DEMANT, V. A., *Religion and the Fall of Capitalism,* London: Faber, 1952.

DEMERATH, N. J., III, "Social Stratification and Church Involvement: The Church-Sect Distinction Applied to Individual Participation," *Review of Religious Research,* 2 (1961), 146-154.

DEMERATH, N. J., III, *Social Class in American Protestantism,*
Chicago: Rand McNally, 1965.

DILLINGHAM, Harry C., "Protestant Religion and Social
Status," *American Journal of Sociology,* 70 (January, 1965),
416-422.

DOUGLASS, H. P., "Cultural Differences and Recent Religious
Divisions," *Christendom,* (Winter, 1945), 89-105.

DRAKE, St. Clair and Horace R. Cayton, *Black Metropolis,* New
York: Harcourt Brace, 1945.

DYNES, Russell, "Church-Sect Typology and Socio-Economic
Status," *American Sociological Review,* 20 (October, 1955),
555-560.

FANFANI, Amintore, *Catholicism, Protestantism, and Capitalism,*
New York: Sheed and Ward, 1955.

FAUCET, Arthur H., *Black Gods of the Metropolis,* Philadelphia:
University of Pennsylvania Press, 1949.

FRAZIER, E. Franklin, *Negroes in the United States,* revised
edition, New York: Macmillan, 1957.

FUKUYAMA, Yoshio, *Styles of Church Membership,* New York:
United Church Board for Homeland Ministries, 1961.

GLAZER, Nathan, "The American Jew and the Attainment
of Middle-Class Rank: Some Trends and Explanations," in
Marshall Sklare, editor, *The Jews,* New York: Free Press, 1958.

GLENN, Norval D., "Negro Religion and Negro Status in the
United States," in Louis Schneider, editor, *Religion, Culture
and Society,* New York: Wiley, 1964.

GLENN, Norval D. and Jon P. Alston, "Cultural Distances Among
Occupational Categories," *American Sociological Review,* 33
(August, 1968), 365-382.

GLENN, Norval D. and Jon P. Alston, "Rural-Urban Differences
in Reported Attitudes and Behavior," *Southwestern Social
Science Quarterly,* 47 (March, 1967), 381-400.

GLENN, Norval D. and Ruth Hyland, "Religious Preference and
Worldly Success: Some Evidence from National Surveys,"
American Sociological Review, 32 (February, 1967), 73-85.

GLOCK, Charles Y., "The Role of Deprivation in the Origin and
Evolution of Religious Groups," in Robert Lee and Martin E.
Marty, *Religion and Social Conflict,* New York: Oxford
University Press, 1964.

GLOCK, Charles Y. and Rodney Stark, *Religion and Society in
Tension,* Chicago: Rand McNally, 1965.

GOLDSCHMIDT, Walter R., "Class Denominationalism in Rural California Churches," *American Journal of Sociology,* 49 (January, 1944), 348-355.

RELIGION

GOODE, Erich, "Social Class and Church Participation," *American Journal of Sociology,* 72 (July, 1966), 102-111.

GREELEY, Andrew M., "Influence of the 'Religious Factor' on Career Plans and Occupational Values of College Graduates," *American Journal of Sociology,* 68 (May, 1963), 658-671.

GREELEY, Andrew M., "The Protestant Ethic: Time for a Moratorium," *Sociological Analysis,* 25 (Spring, 1964), 20-33.

GREELEY, Andrew M., *Religion and Career: A Study of College Graduates,* New York: Sheed and Ward, 1963.

GREELEY, Andrew and Peter Rossi, *The Education of Catholic Americans,* Chicago: Aldine, 1966.

GRONER, F., "The Social Standing of Catholics in the Federal Republic of German," *Social Compass,* 9 (1962), 348-355.

HADDEN, Jeffrey K., "An Analysis of Some Factors Associated with Religious and Political Affiliations in a College Population," *Journal for the Scientific Study of Religion,* 2 (Spring, 1963), 209-216.

HARROLD, H., "Religious Institutions and the Culture of Poverty," *Journal of Religious Thought,* 21 (1964), 81-94.

HERBERG, Will, *Protestant, Catholic, Jew,* Garden City, New York: Doubleday, 1956.

HODGES, D. C., "The Class Significance of Ethical Traditions," *American Journal of Economics and Sociology,* 20 (1963), 241-252.

HOLLINGSHEAD, August B., *Elmtown's Youth,* New York: Wiley, 1949.

HOLT, John B., "Holiness Religion: Cultural Shock and Social Reorganization," *American Sociological Review,* 5 (October, 1940), 740-747.

HOULT, Thomas Ford, "Economic Class Consciousness in American Protestantism," *American Sociological Review,* 15 (February, 1950), 97-100.

HOULT, Thomas Ford, "Economic Class Consciousness in American Protestantism: II," *American Sociological Review,* 17 (June, 1952), 349-350.

HURVITZ, Nathan, "Sources of Middle-Class Values of American Jews," *Social Forces,* 37 (December, 1958), 117-123.

HURVITZ, Nathan, "Sources of Motivation and Achievement of

American Jews," *Jewish Social Studies,* 23 (1961), 217-234.

INGLIS, K. S., *Churches and the Working Classes in Victorian England,* London: Routledge and Kegan Paul, 1963.

ISAMBERT, Francois-Andre, "Is the Religious Abstention of the Working Classes a General Phenomenon?" in Louis Schneider, editor, *Religion, Culture and Society,* New York: Wiley, 1964.

ISRAEL, Herman, "Religious Basis for Solidarity in Industrial Society," *Social Forces,* 45 (September, 1966), 84-95.

ISRAEL, Herman, "Some Religious Factors in the Emergence of Industrial Society in England," *American Sociological Review,* 31 (October, 1966), 589-599.

JOHNSON, Benton, "Do Holiness Sects Socialize in Dominant Values?" *Social Forces,* 39 (May, 1961), 309-316.

JOHNSON, Benton, "Theology and Party Preference Among Protestant Clergymen," *American Sociological Review,* 31 (April, 1966), 200-208.

JOHNSON, Benton, C. C. Langford, R. H. White, R. B. Jacobsen, and J. D. McCarthy, *Religion and Occupational Behavior: An Annotated Bibliography,* Eugene, Oregon: University of Oregon, Center for Research in Occupational Planning, 1966.

JONES, Peter, *The Christian Socialist Revival, 1877-1914: Religion, Class, and Social Conscience in Late-Victorian England,* Princeton: Princeton University Press, 1968.

KAUFMAN, Harold, "Prestige Classes in a New York Rural Community," *Cornell University Experiment Station Bulletin,* (March, 1944).

KNIGHT, F. H. and T. W. Merriam, *The Economic Order and Religion,* London: Routledge and Kegan Paul, 1947.

KOGAN, Norman, "Italian Communism, the Working Class and Organized Catholicism," *Journal of Politics,* 28 (August, 1966), 531-555.

KOSA, J., "Patterns of Social Mobility Among American Catholics," *Social Compass,* 9 (1962), 361-371.

LANE, Ralph, Jr., "Research on Catholics as a Status Group," *Sociological Analysis,* 26 (Summer, 1965), 110-112.

LANGDON, Frank C., "The Catholic Anti-Communist Role Within Australian Labor," *Western Political Quarterly,* 9 (December, 1956), 884-899.

LAZERWITZ, Bernard, "A Comparison of Major United States Religious Groups," *Journal of the American Statistical Association,* 56 (September, 1961), 568-579.

LAZERWITZ, Bernard, "Religion and Social Structure in the United States," in Louis Schneider, editor, *Religion, Culture and Society,* New York: Wiley, 1964.

RELIGION LAZERWITZ, Bernard, "Some Factors Associated with Church Attendance," *Social Forces,* 39 (May, 1961), 306-308.

LENSKI, Gerhard E., "Social Correlates of Religious Interest," *American Sociological Review,* 18 (October, 1953), 533-544.

LENSKI, Gerhard E., *The Religious Factor: A Sociological Study of Religion's Impact on Economics, Politics, and Family Life,* New York: Doubleday, 1961.

LENSKI, Gerhard, *The Religious Factor,* revised edition, Garden City, New York: Doubleday, 1963.

LINCOLN, C. Eric, *The Black Muslims in America,* Boston: Beacon Press, 1961.

LIPMAN, V. D., "Trends in Anglo-Jewish Occupations," *Jewish Journal of Sociology,* 2 (November, 1960), 202-218.

LIPSET, Seymour Martin and Reinhard Bendix, *Social Mobility in Industrial Society,* Berkeley: University of California Press, 1959, 48-56.

MACK, Raymond W., Raymond J. Murphy, and Seymour Yellin, "The Protestant Ethic, Level of Aspiration, and Social Mobility: An Empirical Test," *American Sociological Review,* 21 (June, 1956), 295-300.

MARX, Gary T., "Religion: Opiate or Inspiration of Civil Rights Militancy Among Negroes," *American Sociological Review,* 32 (February, 1967), 64-72.

MARX, Karl and Friedrich Engels, *On Religion,* Moscow: Foreign Languages Publishing House, 1957.

MAYER, Albert J. and Harry Sharp, "Religious Preference and Worldly Success," *American Sociological Review,* 27 (April, 1962), 218-227.

McDONAGH, Edward C., "Status Levels of American Jews," *Sociology and Social Research,* 32 (July-August, 1948), 944-953.

MOBERG, D. O., "Does Social Class Shape the Church?" *Review of Religious Research,* 1 (1960), 110-115.

MULLEN, Robert, *The Latter-Day Saints: The Mormans Yesterday and Today,* Garden City, New York: Doubleday, 1966.

NIEBUHR, H. Richard, *The Social Sources of Denominationalism,* New York: Holt, 1929.

OBENHAUS, Victor W., W. Widick Schroeder, and Charles D.

England, "Church Participation Related to Social Class," *Rural Sociology,* 23 (September, 1958), 298-308.

O'DEA, Thomas F., *American Catholic Dilemma,* New York: Sheed and Ward, 1958.

O'DEA, Thomas F., *The Mormons,* Chicago: University of Chicago Press, 1957.

O'DONOVAN, Thomas and Arthur X. Deegan, "A Comparative Study of the Orientations of a Selected Group of Church Executives," *Sociology and Social Research,* 48 (April, 1964), 330-339.

PIKE, E. Royston, *Jehovah's Witnesses,* London: Watts, 1954.

PIN, Emile, "Social Classes and Their Religious Approaches," in Louis Schneider, editor, *Religion, Culture and Society,* New York: Wiley, 1964.

POPE, Liston, *Millhands and Preachers,* New Haven: Yale University Press, 1942.

POPE, Liston, "Religion and the Class Structure," *Annals of the American Academy of Political and Social Science,* (March, 1948), 84-91.

ROBERTS, Bryan R., "Protestant Groups and Coping with Urban Life in Guatemala City," *American Journal of Sociology,* 73 (May, 1968), 753-767.

ROBERTSON, H. M., *Aspects of the Rise of Economic Individualism: A Criticism of Max Weber and His School,* Cambridge: Cambridge University Press, 1933.

ROSEN, Bernard C., "Race, Ethnicity, and the Achievement Syndrome," *American Sociological Review,* 24 (February, 1959), 47-60.

ROSSI, Peter H. and Andrew M. Greeley, "The Impact of the Roman Catholic Denominational School," *School Review,* 72 (Spring, 1964), 34-51.

SAMUELSSON, Kurt, *Religion and Economic Action: The Protestant Ethic, the Rise of Capitalism, and the Abuses of Scholarship,* New York: Basic Books, 1961.

SHIPPEY, Frederick A., "Social Class in Philadelphia Methodism," *Sociology and Social Research,* 43 (September-October, 1958), 23-27.

SMITH, James Otis and Gideon Sjoberg, "Origins and Career Patterns of Leading Protestant Clergyman," *Social Forces,* 39 (May, 1961), 290-296.

SOMBART, Werner, *The Jews and Modern Capitalism,* translated by M. Epstein, London: Unwin, 1913.

STARK, Rodney, "Class, Radicalism, and Religious Involvement in Great Britain," *American Sociological Review,* 29 (October, 1964), 698-706.

RELIGION

STRODTBECK, Fred L., "Family Interaction, Values, and Achievement," in Marshall Sklare, editor, *The Jews,* New York: Free Press, 1958.

STRODTBECK, Fred L., Margaret R. McDonald, and Bernard C. Rosen, "Evaluation of Occupations: A Reflection of Jewish and Italian Differences," *American Sociological Review,* 22 (October, 1957), 546-553.

STROUP, H. H., *Jehovah's Witnesses,* New York: Columbia University Press, 1945.

TAWNEY, R. H., *Religion and the Rise of Capitalism,* New York: Harcourt Brace, 1926.

TROELTSCH, Ernst, *The Social Teaching of the Christian Churches,* London: George Allen and Unwin, 1930.

VERNON, Glenn M., "Religious Groups and Social Class—Some Inconsistencies," *Papers of the Michigan Academy of Science, Arts, and Letters,* 45 (1960), 295-301.

VEROFF, Joseph, Sheila Feld, and Gerald Gurin, "Achievement Motivation and Religious Background," *American Sociological Review,* 27 (April, 1962), 205-217.

WACH, Joachim, *Sociology of Religion,* Chicago: University of Chicago Press, 1944.

WARNER, W. Lloyd and Paul S. Lunt, *The Social Life of a Modern Community,* New Haven: Yale University Press, 1941.

WEBER, Max, *The Protestant Ethic and the Spirit of Capitalism,* translated by Talcott Parsons, New York: Scribners, 1958.

WHITLEY, Oliver R., "The Sect to Denomination Process in an American Religious Movement: The Disciples of Christ," *Southwestern Social Science Quarterly,* 36 (December, 1955), 275-282.

WILSON, Bryan, "An Analysis of Sect Development," *American Sociological Review,* 24 (February, 1959), 3-15.

WILSON, Bryan, *Minority Religious Movements in Modern Britain,* London: Heinemann, 1960.

WILSON, Bryan, *Sects and Society,* London: Heinemann, 1961.

WRONG, Dennis H., "Jews, Gentiles and the New Establishment," *Commentary,* 39 (June, 1965), 83-86.

YINGER, J. Milton, *Religion in the Struggle for Power,* Durham, North Carolina: Duke University Press, 1946.

YINGER, J. Milton, *Religion, Society and the Individual,* New York: Macmillan, 1957, Chapter 7, "Religion and Social Status," and "Religion and Economics."

Role of Minorities in the Stratification

of Societies

The publications included here focus specifically upon social stratification; literature dealing only with the social psychology of discrimination and prejudice is excluded. The amount of recent literature on this topic is so great that we attempt to cover only the studies we judge to be of greatest value to social science researchers.

ANDERSON, C. Arnold, "Regional and Racial Differences in Relations Between Income and Education," *School Review,* 63 (January, 1955), 38-45.

ANDERSON, C. Arnold and Philip J. Foster, "Discrimination and Inequality in Education," *Sociology of Education,* 38 (Fall, 1964), 1-18.

ANDERSON, Elin, *We Americans: A Study of Cleavage in an American City,* Cambridge: Harvard University Press, 1938.

ANTONOVSKY, Aaron and Melvin J. Lerner, "Occupational Aspirations of Lower Class Negro and White Youth," *Social Problems,* 7 (Fall, 1959), 132-138.

BAHR, Howard M. and Jack P. Gibbs, "Racial Differentiation In American Metropolitan Areas," *Social Forces,* 45 (June, 1967), 521-532.

BANTON, Michael, "The Economic and Social Position of Negro Immigrants in Britain," *Sociological Review,* 1 (December, 1953), 43-62.

BARRON, Milton L., editor, *Minorities in a Changing World,* New York: Knopf, 1967.

BELCHER, John C. and Carolyn N. Allman, *The Non-White Population of Georgia,* Athens: University of Georgia, Institute of Community and Area Development, 1967.

BERREMAN, Gerald D., "Caste in India and the United States," *American Journal of Sociology,* 66 (September, 1960), 120-127.

BLALOCK, H. M., Jr., "Economic Discrimination and Negro Increase," *American Sociological Review,* 21 (October, 1956), 484-588.

BLALOCK, H. M., Jr., "Occupational Discrimination: Some Theoretical Propositions," *Social Problems,* 9 (Winter, 1962), 240-247.

BLALOCK, H. M., Jr., "Per Cent Non-White and Discrimination in the South," *American Sociological Review,* 22 (December, 1957), 677-682.

BLALOCK, H. M., Jr., *Toward a Theory of Minority-Group Relations,* New York: Wiley,1967.

BLAU, Peter M. and Otis Dudley Duncan, *The American Occupational Structure,* New York: John Wiley, 1967.

BLOCH, H. D., "The New York City Negro and Occupational Eviction, 1860-1910," *International Review of Social History,* 5 (1960), 26-38.

BLOOM, Richard, Martin Whiteman, and Martin Deutsch, "Race and Social Class as Separate Factors Related to Social Environment," *American Journal of Sociology,* 70 (January, 1965), 471-476.

BOGARDUS, Emory S., "Comparing Racial Distance in Ethiopia, South Africa and the United States," *Sociology and Social Research,* 52 (January, 1963), 149-156.

BOGUE, Donald J., *The Population of the United States,* New York: Free Press, 1959.

BOSKIN, Joseph, "The Origins of American Slavery: Education as an Index of Early Differentiation," *Journal of Negro Education,* 35 (Spring, 1966), 125-133.

BOYD, George Felix, "The Levels of Aspiration of White and Negro Children in a Non-Segregated Elementary School," *Journal of Social Psychology,* 36 (August, 1952), 191-196.

BROOKS, Maxwell R., "American Class and Caste: An Appraisal," *Social Forces,* 25 (December, 1946), 207-211.

BROOM, Leonard and Norval D. Glenn, *Transformation of the Negro American,* New York: Harper and Row, 1965.

BROOM, Leonard and Norval D. Glenn, "When Will America's Negroes Catch Up?" *New Society,* (March 25, 1965), 5-6.

BROOM, Leonard and Ruth Reimer, *Removal and Return: The Socio-Economic Effects of the War on Japanese Americans,* Berkeley: University of California Press, 1949.

BROTZ, Howard, "The Position of the Jews in English Society," *Jewish Journal of Sociology,* 1 (April, 1959), 94-113.

BROWNING, Harley L. and S. Dale McLemore, *A Statistical Profile of the Spanish-Surname Population of Texas,* Austin: Bureau of Business Research, University of Texas, 1964.

BULLOCK, Henry Allen, "A Comparison of the Academic Achievements of White and Negro High School Graduates," *Journal of Educational Research,* 44 (November, 1950), 179-192.

BULLOCK, Henry Allen, "Racial Attitudes and the Employment of Negroes," *American Journal of Sociology,* 56 (March, 1951), 448-457.

BURGIN, Trevor and Patricia Edson, *Spring Grove: The Education of Immigrant Children,* New York: Oxford University Press, 1967.

BURMA, John H., "The Present Status of the Spanish-Americans of New Mexico," *Social Forces,* 28 (December, 1949), 133-138.

CARSTENS, Peter, *The Social Structure of a Cape Coloured Reserve: A Study of Racial Integration and Segregation in South Africa,* New York: Oxford University Press, 1966.

CASE, Fred E., *Minority Families in the Metropolis. Profile of the Los Angeles Metropolis: Its People and Its Homes,* Graduate School of Business Administration, Division of Research, University of California, 1966.

CAUDILL, William and George DeVos, "Achievement, Culture and Personality: The Case of the Japanese Americans," *American Anthropologist,* 58 (December, 1956), 47-51.

CAYTON, Horace R. and George S. Mitchell, *Black Workers and the New Unions,* Chapel Hill: University of North Carolina Press, 1939.

CHAPLIN, David, "Domestic Service and the Negro," in Arthur B. Shostak and William Gomberg, editors, *Blue-Collar World: Studies of the American Worker,* Englewood Cliffs, New Jersey: Prentice-Hall, 1964.

CHRISTIANSEN, John R., "Estimation of the Socio-Economic Status of Spanish-Americans in Atascosa and Bexar Counties, Texas," *Rocky Mountain Social Science Journal,* 2 (March, 1965), 215-222.

CLARK, Kenneth B., *Dark Ghetto: Dilemmas of Social Power,* New York: Harper and Row, 1965.

COLEMAN, James S., Ernest Q. Campbell, Carol J. Hobson, James McPartland, Alexander M. Mood, Frederick D. Weinfeld, and

Robert L. York, *Equality of Educational Opportunity,* Washington D. C.: U. S. Government Printing Office, 1966.

COLEMAN, James S., *et al., Supplemental Appendix to the Survey on Equality of Educational Opportunity,* Washington, D. C.: Government Printing Office, 1966.

COSTELLO, B. D., "Catholics in American Commerce and Industry," *American Catholic Sociological Review,* 17 (1956), 219-233.

COUGHLIN, Richard J., "The Chinese in Bangkok: A Commercial-Oriented Minority," *American Sociological Review,* 20 (June, 1955), 311-316.

COWHIG, James D. and Calvin L. Beale, "Relative Socioeconomic Status of Southern Whites and Nonwhites," *Southwestern Social Science Quarterly,* 45 (September, 1964), 113-124.

COX, Oliver C., *Class, Caste and Race,* Garden City, New York: Doubleday, 1948.

COX, Oliver C., "The Modern Caste School of Race Relations," *Social Forces,* 21 (December, 1942), 218-226.

COX, Oliver C., "Race and Caste: A Distinction," *American Journal of Sociology,* 50 (March, 1945), 360-368.

CRAMER, Carl, "The Peculiar People Prosper," *New York Times Magazine,* (April 15, 1962).

DAVIE, Maurice R., *Negroes in American Society,* New York: McGraw-Hill, 1949.

DAVIS, Allison, "Caste, Economy, and Violence," *American Journal of Sociology,* 51 (July, 1945), 7-15.

DAVIS, Allison, Burleigh B. Gardner, and Mary R. Gardner, *Deep South,* Chicago: University of Chicago Press, 1941.

DECTER, Moshe, "The Status of the Jews in the Soviet Union," *Foreign Affairs,* (January, 1963), 420-430.

DeGRAZIA, Alfred, "The Limits of External Leadership over a Minority Electorate," *Public Opinion Quarterly,* 20 (Spring, 1956), 113-128.

DESAI, Rashmi, *Indian Immigrants in Britain,* New York: Oxford University Press, 1963.

DICKIE-CLARK, H. F., *The Marginal Situation: A Sociological Study of a Coloured Group,* New York: Humanities Press, 1967.

DOLLARD, John, *Caste and Class in a Southern Town,* New Haven: Yale University Press, 1937.

DONOGHUE, John D., "An Eta Community in Japan: The Social Persistence of Outcaste Groups," *American Anthropologist,* 59 (December, 1957), 1000-1017.

DOYLE, Bertram, *The Etiquette of Race Relations in the South: A Study in Social Control,* Chicago: University of Chicago Press, 1937.

DRAKE, St. Clair, "The Social and Economic Status of the Negro in the United States," in Talcott Parsons and Kenneth B. Clark, editors, *The Negro American,* Boston: Houghton Mifflin, 1966.

DRAKE, St. Clair and Horace R. Cayton, *Black Metropolis,* Harcourt, Brace and World, 1945.

DUNCAN, Otis Dudley, and Beverly Duncan, "Minorities and the Process of Stratification," *American Sociological Review,* 33 (June, 1968), 365-382.

EDWARDS, G. Frankin, "Community and Class Realities: The Ordeal of Change," in Talcott Parsons and Kenneth B. Clark, editors, *The Negro American,* Boston: Houghton Mifflin, 1966.

ELKHOLY, Abdo A., *The Arab Moslems in the United States: Religions and Assimilation,* New Haven: College and University Press, 1966.

ELLIS, Robert, A., "Color and Class in a Jamaican Market Town," *Sociology and Social Research,* 41 (May-June, 1957), 354-360.

FARLEY, Reynolds, "The Demographic Rates and Social Institutions of the Nineteenth-Century Negro Population: A Stable Population Analysis," *Demography,* 2 (1965), 386-398.

FOGEL, Walter, *Education and Income of the Mexican-American in the Southwest,* Los Angeles: Mexican-American Project, Advance Report No. 7, Division of Research, Graduate School of Business Administration, University of California, 1966.

FOSTER, Philip, "Ethnicity and the Schools in Ghana," *Comparative Education Review,* 6 (October, 1962), 127-135.

FRAZIER, E. Franklin, *The Negro in the United States,* revised edition, New York: Macmillan, 1957.

GESCHWENDER, James A., "Social Structure and the Negro Revolt: An Examination of Some Hypotheses," *Social Forces,* 43 (December, 1964), 248-256.

GHAI, Dharam P., editor, *Portrait of a Minority: Asians in East Africa,* New York: Oxford University Press, 1966.

GIBBS, Jack P., "Occupational Differentiation of Negroes and Whites in the United States," *Social Forces,* 44 (December, 1965), 159-165.

GILMORE, Harlan and Logan Wilson, "The Employment of Negro Women as Domestic Servants in New Orleans," *Social Forces,* 22 (March, 1944), 318-323.

GINZBERG, Eli, *The Middle-Class Negro in the White Man's World,* New York: Columbia University Press, 1967.

GINZBERG, Eli, *The Negro Potential,* New York: Columbia University Press, 1956.

GIPSON, Theodore H., "Educational Status of the Negro Family in Louisiana," *Journal of Educational Sociology,* 32 (October, 1958), 83-89.

GLASS, Ruth (assisted by Harold Pollins), *London's Newcomers: The West Indian Migrants,* Cambridge: Harvard University Press, 1961.

GLAZER, Nathan, "The American Jew and the Attainment of Middle-Class Rank," in Marshall Sklare, editor, *The Jews,* New York: Free Press, 1958.

GLENN, Norval D., "Changes in the American Occupational Structure and Occupational Gains of Negroes During the 1940's," *Social Forces,* 41 (December, 1962), 443-448.

GLENN, Norval D., "Negro Population Concentration and Negro Status," *Journal of Negro Education,* 36 (Fall, 1967), 353-361.

GLENN, Norval D., "Negro Religion and Negro Status in the United States," in Louis Schneider, editor, *Religion, Culture and Society,* New York: Wiley, 1964.

GLENN, Norval D., "Occupational Benefits to Whites from the Subordination of Negroes," *American Sociological Review,* 28 (June, 1963), 443-448.

GLENN, Norval D., "The Role of White Resistance and Discrimination in the Negro Struggle for Equality," *Phylon,* 26 (Summer, 1965), 105-116.

GLENN, Norval D., "Some Changes in the Relative Status of American Nonwhites, 1940 to 1960," *Phylon,* 24 (Summer, 1963), 109-122.

GLENN, Norval D., "The Relative Size of the Negro Population and Negro Occupational Status," *Social Forces,* 43 (October, 1964), 42-49.

GLENN, Norval D., "White Gains from Negro Subordination," *Social Problems,* 14 (Fall, 1966), 159-178.

GLENN, Norval D. and Ruth Hyland, "Religious Preference and Worldly Success: Some Evidence from National Surveys," *American Sociological Review,* 32 (February, 1967), 79-85.

GLICK, Clarence, "The Position of Racial Groups in Occupational Structures," *Social Forces,* 26 (December, 1947), 206-211.

ROLE OF MINORITIES

GRAVES, Theodore, "Psychological Acculturation in a Tri-Ethnic Community," *Southwestern Journal of Anthropology,* 23 (Winter, 1967), 337-350.

GREER, Scott, *Last Man In: Racial Access to Union Power,* New York: Free Press, 1959.

GUIDON, Hubert, "Social Unrest, Social Class and Quebec's Bureaucratic Revolution," *Queen's Quarterly,* 71 (Summer, 1964), 150-162.

HANDLIN, Oscar, *The Newcomers: Negroes and Puerto Ricans in a Changing Metropolis,* Cambridge: Harvard University Press, 1959.

HARE, Nathan, "Recent Trends in the Occupational Mobility of Negroes, 1930-1960: An Intracohort Analysis," *Social Forces,* 44 (December, 1965), 166-173.

HARRIS, Marvin, "Caste, Class, and Minority," *Social Forces,* 37 (March, 1959), 248-254.

HENDERSON, Vivian W., *The Economic Status of Negroes: In the Nation and in the South,* Atlanta: Southern Regional Council, 1963.

HIESTAND, Dale, *Economic Growth and Employment Opportunities for Minorities,* New York: Columbia University Press, 1964.

HILL, Herbert, "Racial Inequality in Employment: The Patterns of Discrimination," *Annals of the American Academy of Political and Social Science,* 357 (January, 1965), 30-47.

HODGE, Robert W. and Patricia Hodge, "Occupational Assimilation as a Competitive Process," *American Journal of Sociology,* 70 (November, 1965), 249-264.

HOETINK, H., *The Two Variants in Caribbean Race Relations: A Contribution to the Sociology of Segmented Societies,* Translated by Eva M. Hooykaas, New York: Oxford University Press, 1967.

HOLLOWAY, Robert G. and Joel V. Berreman, "The Educational and Occupational Aspirations and Plans of Negro and White Male Elementary School Students," *Pacific Sociological Review,* 2 (Fall, 1959), 56-60.

HOPE, John, II and Edward E. Shelton, "The Negro in the Federal Government," *Journal of Negro Education,* 32 (Fall, 1963), 367-374.

HUGHES, Everett C., "Queries Concerning Industry and Society Growing Out of Study of Ethnic Relations in Industry," *American Sociological Review,* 14 (April, 1949), 211-220.

HUGHES, Everett, "The Knitting of Racial Groups in Industry," *American Sociological Review,* 11 (October, 1946), 512-519.

HUGHES, Julius H. and George G. Thompson, "A Comparison of Value Systems of Southern Negro and Northern White Youth," *Journal of Educational Psychology,* 45 (May, 1954), 300-309.

HURVITZ, Nathan, "Sources of Middle-Class Values of American Jews," *Social Forces,* 37 (December, 1958), 117-123.

HURVITZ, Nathan, "Sources of Motivation and Achievement of American Jews," *Jewish Social Studies,* 23 (1961), 217-234.

IANNI, Octavio, "Race and Class," *Educacao e Ciencias Sociais,* 7 (1962), 88-111.

ISAACS, Harold R., *The New World of Negro Americans,* New York: Day, 1963.

JACKSON, John Archer, *The Irish in Britain,* London: Routledge and Kegan Paul, 1963.

JACOBSON, Alan and Lee Rainwater, "A Study of Management Representative Evaluations of Nisei Workers," *Social Forces,* 32 (October, 1953), 35-41.

KEPHART, William M., "What is the Position of Jewish Economy in the United States?" *Social Forces,* 28 (December, 1949), 153-164.

KEPHART, William M., "Minority Group Discrimination In Higher Education," *Journal of Educational Sociology,* 23 (September, 1949), 52-57.

KINZER, Robert H. and Edward Sagarin, *The Negro in American Business: The Conflict Between Separation and Integration,* New York: Greenberg, 1950.

KNOWLTON, Clark S., "A Study of Social Mobility Among the Syrian and Lebanese Community of Sao Paulo," *Rocky Mountain Social Science Journal,* 2 (October, 1965), 174-192.

KOENIG, Samuel, "Ethnic Groups in Connecticut Industry," *Social Forces,* 20 (October, 1941), 96-105.

KOENIG, Samuel, "Ethnic Factors in the Economic Life of Urban Connecticut," *American Sociological Review,* 8 (April, 1943), 193-197.

KRISLOV, Samuel, *The Negro in Federal Employment: The Quest for Equal Opportunity,* Minneapolis: University of Minnesota, 1967.

KUPER, Leo, *An African Bourgeoisie: Race, Class, and Politics in South Africa,* New Haven: Yale University Press, 1965.

KUPER, Leo, "The South African Native: Caste, Proletariat, or Race?" *Social Forces,* 28 (December, 1949), 146-153.

KWOH, Beulah Ong, "The Occupational Status of American-Born Chinese Male College Graduates," *American Journal of Sociology,* 53 (November, 1947), 192-200.

LANDIS, Judson R., Darryl Datwyler, and Dean S. Dorn, "Race and Social Class as Determinants of Social Distance," *Sociology and Social Research,* 51 (October, 1966), 78-86.

LAZERWITZ, Bernard, "A Comparison of Major Religious Groups," *Journal of the American Statistical Association,* 56 (September, 1961), 568-579.

LAZERWITZ, Bernard, "Religion and Social Structure in the United States," in Louis Schneider, editor, *Religion, Culture and Society,* New York: Wiley, 1964.

LEGGETT, John C., *Class, Race and Labor: Working-Class Consciousness in Detroit,* New York: Oxford University Press, 1968.

LEGGETT, John C. and David Street, "Economic Crisis and Expectations of Violence: A Study of Unemployed Negroes," in Arthur B. Shostak and William Gomberg, editors, *Blue Collar World: Studies of the American Worker,* Englewood Cliffs, New Jersey: Prentice Hall, 1964.

LENSKI, Gerhard, *The Religious Factor,* revised edition, Garden City, New York: Doubleday, 1963.

LIEBERSON, Stanley and Glenn V. Fuguitt, "Negro-White Occupational Differences in the Absence of Discrimination," *American Journal of Sociology,* 73 (September, 1967), 188-200.

LIPMAN, V. D., "Trends in Anglo-Jewish Occupations," *Jewish Journal of Sociology,* 2 (November, 1960), 202-218.

LITTLE, Kenneth, "The Position of Colored People in Britain," *Phylon,* 15 (Spring, 1954), 58-64.

LOTT, Albert J. and Bernice E. Lott, *Negro and White Youth: A Psychological Study in a Borderstate Community,* New York: Holt, Rinehart and Winston, 1963.

LYSTAD, Mary H., "Family Patterns, Achievements and Aspirations of Urban Negroes," *Sociology and Social Research,* 45 (April, 1961), 281-288.

MACK, Raymond, editor, *Race, Class, and Power,* second edition, New York: American Book Company, 1968.

MADSEN, William, *The Mexican-Americans of South Texas,* New York: Holt, Rinehart and Winston, 1964.

MARDEN, Charles F. and Gladys Meyer, *Minorities in American Society,* third edition, New York: American Book Company, 1968.

MARSHALL, Ray, *The Negro and Organized Labor,* New York: Wiley, 1965.

MARSHALL, Ray, "The Negro and Organized Labor," *Journal of Negro Education,* 32 (Fall, 1963), 375-389.

MARSHALL, Ray, *The Negro Worker,* New York: Random House, 1967.

MATTHEWS, Donald R. and James W. Prothro, *Negroes and the New Southern Politics,* New York: Harcourt, Brace and World, 1966.

MAYER, Albert J. and Harry Sharp, "Religious Preference and Worldly Success," *American Sociological Review,* 27 (April, 1962), 218-227.

McDONAGH, Edward C., "Status Levels of American Jews," *Sociology and Social Research,* 32 (July-August, 1948), 944-953.

McDONAGH, Edward C., "Status Levels of Mexicans," *Sociology and Social Research,* 33 (July-August, 1949), 449-459.

McKEE, James B., "Community Power and Strategies In Race Relations: Some Critical Observations," *Social Problems,* 6 (Winter, 1958-59), 195-203.

MEADOWS, Paul, "Insiders and Outsiders: Toward a Theory of Overseas Cultural Groups," *Social Forces,* 46 (September, 1967), 61-71.

MEIER, August, and Elliott M. Rudwick, *From Plantation to Ghetto: An Interpretive History of American Negroes,* New York: Hill and Wang, 1966.

MELTZER, Milton and August Meier, *Time of Trial, Time of Hope: The Negro in America, 1919-1941,* Garden City, New York: Doubleday, 1966.

MEMMI, Albert, *The Colonizer and the Colonized,* Boston: Beacon, 1967.

MEYER, Peter, *Jews in the Soviet Satellites,* Syracuse: Syracuse University Press, 1953.

MITCHELL, Richard H., *The Korean Minority in Japan,* Berkeley: University of California Press, 1967.

MONTAGUE, Joel B. and Edgar G. Epps, "Attitudes Toward Social Mobility as Revealed By Samples of Negro and White Boys," *Pacific Sociological Review,* 1 (Fall, 1958), 81-84.

MOYNIHAN, Daniel Patrick, "The Irish of New York," *Commentary,* 36 (August, 1963), 93-107.

MULLEN, Robert, *The Latter-Day Saints: The Mormons Yesterday and Today,* Garden City, New York: Doubleday, 1966.

ROLE OF
MINORITIES

MYRDAL, Gunnar, *An American Dilemma: The Negro Problem and Modern Democracy,* New York: Harper and Row, 1944.

NAM, Charles B., "Nationality Groups and Social Stratification in America," *Social Forces,* 37 (May, 1959), 328-333.

NAM, Charles B. and Mary G. Powers, "Variations in Socioeconomic Structure by Race, Residence, and the Life Cycle," *American Sociological Review,* 30 (February, 1965), 97-103.

NEAL, Ernest E. and Lewis W. Jones, "The Place of the Negro Farmer in the Changing Economy of the Cotton South," *Rural Sociologist,* 15 (March, 1950), 30-41.

NORTHRUP, Herbert R., *Organized Labor and the Negro,* New York: Harper and Row, 1944.

O'BRIEN, Robert W., "Status of Chinese in the Mississippi Delta," *Social Forces,* 19 (March, 1941), 386-390.

O'DEA, Thomas F., *The Mormons,* Chicago: University of Chicago Press, 1957.

PADILLA, Elena, *Up from Puerto Rico,* New York: Columbia University Press, 1958.

PARSONS, Talcott and Kenneth B. Clark, editors, *The Negro American,* Boston: Houghton Mifflin, 1966.

PELLEGRIN, Roland J. and Vernon J. Parenton, "The Impact of Socio-Economic Change on Racial Groups in a Rural Setting," *Phylon,* 23 (Spring, 1962), 56-60.

PENALOSA, Fernando, "The Changing Mexican-American in Southern California," *Sociology and Social Research,* 51 (July, 1967), 405-417.

PENALOSA, Fernando and Edward C. McDonagh, "Education, Economic Status and Social Class Awareness of Mexican-Americans," *Phylon,* 29 (Summer, 1968), 119-126.

PENALOSA, Fernando and Edward C. McDonagh, "Social Mobility in a Mexican-American Community," *Social Forces,* 44 (June, 1966), 498-505.

PERLO, Victor, "Trends in the Economic Status of the Negro People," *Science and Society,* 16 (1952), 115-150.

PETTIGREW, Thomas F., *A Profile of the Negro American,* Princeton: Van Nostrand, 1964.

PIERSON, Donald, *Negroes in Brazil: A Study of Race Contact at Bahia,* Carbondale: Southern Illinois Press, 1967.

POHLMAN, Edward W., "Semantic Aspects of the Controversy over Negro-White Caste in the United States," *Social Forces,* 30 (May, 1952), 416-419.

PORTER, John, *The Vertical Mosaic: An Analysis of Social Class and Power in Canada,* Toronto: University of Toronto Press, 1965, Chapter 3, "Ethnicity and Social Class."

POWDERMAKER, Hortense, *After Freedom: A Cultural Study in the Deep South,* New York: Viking, 1939.

PRENTICE, N. M., "The Influence of Ethnic Groups," *Journal of Abnormal and Social Psychology,* 55 (July-November, 1957), 270-272.

PRICE, Daniel O., "Occupational Changes in the Negro Population," *Social Science Quarterly,* 49 (December, 1968), 563-572.

PURCELL, Theodore V., "The Hopes of Negro Workers for Their Children," in Arthur B. Shostak and William Gomberg, editors, *Blue-Collar World: Studies of the American Worker,* Englewood Cliffs, New Jersey: Prentice Hall, 1964.

RECORD, C. Wilson, "Negroes in the California Agriculture Labor Force," *Social Problems,* 6 (Spring, 1959), 354-361.

REX, John and Robert Moore, *Race, Community and Conflict: A Study of Sparbrook,* London: Oxford University Press, 1967.

RICHMOND, Anthony H., "Education, Social Mobility and Racial Relations in the Union of South Africa," *Transactions of the Third World Congress of Sociology,* 5 (1956), 105-114.

ROBERTS, R. E. T., "Comparison of Ethnic Relations in Two Guatemalan Communities," *Acta Americana,* 6 (1958), 135-151.

ROSEN, Bernard C., "Race, Ethnicity, and the Achievement Syndrome," *American Sociological Review,* 24 (February, 1959), 47-60.

ROSS, Arthur M. and Herbert Hill, editors, *Employment, Race and Poverty,* New York: Harcourt, Brace and World, 1967.

ROUCEK, Joseph S., "Minority-Majority Relations in Their Power Aspects," *Phylon,* 17 (First Quarter, 1956).

RUBIN, Morton, "Resident Response to Urban Rehabilitation in a Negro Working-Class Neighborhood," in Arthur B. Shostak and William Gomberg, editors, *Blue-Collar World: Studies of the American Worker,* Englewood Cliffs, New Jersey: Prentice Hall, 1964.

SAMORA, Julian, *La Raza: Forgotten Americans,* Notre Dame, Indiana: University of Notre Dame Press, 1966.

SCHERMERHORN, R. A., "Power as a Primary Concept in the Study of Minorities," *Social Forces,* 35 (October, 1956), 53-56.

SCHERMERHORN, R. A., *These Our People: Minorities in American Culture,* Boston: Heath, 1949.

SCHMID, Calvin F. and Charles E. Nobbe, "Socioeconomic Differentials among Nonwhite Races," *American Sociological Review,* 30 (December, 1965), 909-922.

SCHMID, Calvin F. and Charles E. Nobbe, "Socio-Economic Differentials Among Nonwhite Races in the State of Washington," *Demography,* 2 (1965), 549-566.

SCHMITT, Robert C. and Robert A. Souza, "Social and Economic Characteristics of Interracial Households in Honolulu," *Social Problems,* 10 (Winter, 1963), 264-268.

SCHWARTZ, Michael and George Henderson, "The Culture of Unemployment: Some Notes on Negro Children," in Arthur B. Shostak and William Gomberg, editors, *Blue-Collar World: Studies of the American Worker,* Englewood Cliffs, New Jersey: Prentice Hall, 1964.

SCHWARTZ, Solomon, *Jews in the Soviet Union,* Syracuse: Syracuse University Press, 1951.

SEXTON, Patricia, "Negro Career Expectations," *Merrill-Palmer Quarterly,* 9 (October, 1963), 303-316.

SEXTON, Patricia, *Spanish Harlem: Anatomy of Poverty,* New York: Harper and Row, 1965.

SHANNON, Lyle W. and E. M. Krass, "Economic Absorption of Immigrant Laborers in a Northern Industrial Community," *American Journal of Economics and Sociology,* 23 (January, 1964), 65-84.

SHANNON, Lyle and Patricia Morgan, "The Prediction of Economic Adoption and Cultural Integration among Mexican-Americans, Negroes, and Anglos in a Northern Industrial Community," *Human Organization,* 25 (1966), 154-162.

SHARP, Dan C. and Colin M. Tatz, editors, *Aborigines in the Economy: Employment, Wages and Training,* Melbourne, Australia: Jaconda Press, 1966.

SHERMAN, C. Bezalel, *The Jew Within American Society,* Detroit: Wayne State Press, 1961.

SHIBUTANI, Tamotsu and Kian M. Kwan, *Ethnic Stratification: A Comparative Approach,* New York: Macmillan, 1965.

SIEGEL, Paul, "On the Cost of Being a Negro," *Sociological Inquiry,* 35 (Winter, 1965), 41-57.

SILBERMAN, Charles E., "The City and the Negro," *Fortune,* 65 (March, 1962), 88-154.

SIMPSON, George E., "Ethnic Groups, Social Mobility and

Power in Latin America," *Seminar on Social Structure, Stratification and Mobility, with Special Reference to Latin America,* Washington, D. C., Pan American Union, 1966.

ROLE OF MINORITIES

SIMPSON, George E., "The Ras Tafari Movement in Jamaica: A Study of Race and Class Conflict," *Social Forces,* 34 (December, 1955), 167-171.

SIMPSON, George E. and J. Milton Yinger, *Racial and Cultural Minorities,* 3rd edition, New York: Harper and Row, 1965, Chapter 11, "Majority-Minority Relations and Social Stratification," and Chapters 12 and 13, "Minorities in the Economy of the United States."

SKLARE, Marshall, editor, *The Jews: Social Patterns of an American Group,* New York: Free Press, 1958.

SMYTHE, H. H. and T. Gershuny, "Jewish Castes of Cochin, India," *Sociology and Social Research,* 41 (1956), 108-111.

SMYTHE, H. H. and Mabel M. Smythe, "The Non-African Minority in Modern Africa: Social Status," *Sociology and Social Research,* 45 (April, 1961), 310-315.

SPREY, Jetse, "Sex Differences in Occupational Choice Patterns Among Negro Adolescents," *Social Problems,* 10 (Summer, 1962), 11-23.

STAMLER, Rose, "Acculturation and Negro Blue-Collar Workers," in Arthur B. Shostak and William Gomberg, editors, *Blue-Collar World: Studies of the American Worker,* Englewood Cliffs, New Jersey: Prentice-Hall, 1964.

STERNER, Richard, *The Negro's Share,* New York: Harper and Row, 1943.

STRIZOWER, S., "Jews as an Indian Caste," *Jewish Journal of Sociology,* 1 (April, 1959), 43-57.

ST. JOHN, Nancy Hoyt, "The Effect of Segregation on the Aspirations of Negro Youths," *Harvard Educational Review,* 36 (Summer, 1966), 284-294.

STRODTBECK, Fred L., "Family Interaction, Values, and Achievement," in Marshall Sklare, editor, *The Jews,* New York: Free Press, 1958.

TOBIN, James, "On Improving the Economic Status of the Negro," in Talcott Parsons and Kenneth B. Clark, *The Negro American,* Boston: Houghton Mifflin, 1966.

TURNER, Ralph H., "The Expected-Cases Method Applied to the Nonwhite Male Labor Force," *American Journal of Sociology,* 55 (September, 1949), 146-156.

TURNER, Ralph H., "Foci of Discrimination in the Employment

of Nonwhites," *American Journal of Sociology,* 58 (November, 1952), 247-256.

TURNER, Ralph H., "Negro Job Status and Education," *Social Forces,* 32 (October, 1953), 45-52.

TURNER, Ralph H., "Occupational Patterns of Inequality," *American Journal of Sociology,* 59 (March, 1954), 437-447.

TURNER, Ralph H., "The Nonwhite Male in the Labor Force," *American Journal of Sociology,* 54 (January, 1949), 356-362.

TURNER, Ralph H., "The Nonwhite Female in the Labor Force," *American Journal of Sociology,* 56 (March, 1951), 438-447.

TURNER, Ralph H., "The Relative Position of the Negro Male in the Labor Force of Large American Cities," *American Sociological Review,* 16 (August, 1951), 524-529.

UNESCO, *Apartheid: Its Effects on Education, Science, Culture and Information,* Paris: UNESCO, 1967.

UPHAM, W. Kennedy and David E. Wright, *Poverty Among Spanish Americans in Texas: Low Income Families in a Minority Group,* College Station: Texas A&M University Experiment Station, 1966.

UZELL, O., "Occupational Aspirations of Negro Male High School Students," *Sociology and Social Research* 45 (January, 1961), 202-204.

U. S. BUREAU OF LABOR STATISTICS, *Social and Economic Conditions of Negroes in the United States,* Washington, D. C.: U. S. Government Printing Office, 1967.

U. S. COMMISSION ON CIVIL RIGHTS, *Racial Isolation in the Public Schools,* Washington, D. C.: U. S. Government Printing Office, 1967.

VALIEN, Preston, "The 'Mentalities' of Negro and White Workers: An 'Experimental School' Interpretation of Negro Trade Unionism," *Social Forces,* 27 (May, 1949), 433-438.

VAN DEN BERGHE, Pierre L., *Race and Racism: A Comparative Perspective,* New York: Wiley, 1967.

VAN DEN BERGHE, Pierre L., *South Africa: A Study in Conflict,* Middleton: Wesleyan University Press, 1965.

VANDER ZANDEN, James W., *American Minority Relations: The Sociology of Race and Ethnic Groups,* second edition, New York: Ronald, 1966, Chapter 9, "Stratification."

WAGLEY, Charles, editor, *Race and Class In Rural Brazil,* Paris: UNESCO, 1952.

WARNER, W. Lloyd, "American Caste and Class," *American Journal of Sociology,* 42 (September, 1936), 234-237.

ROLE OF
MINORITIES

WARNER, W. Lloyd, "Significance of Caste and Class in a Democracy," *National Conference of Social Workers,* (1955), 289-301.

WARNER, W. Lloyd and Leo Srole, *The Social Systems of American Ethnic Groups,* New Haven: Yale University Press, 1945.

WAX, Murray L., Rosalie H. Wax, and Robert V. Dumont, Jr., "Formal Education in an Indian Community: Ecology, Economy, and Educational Achievement; Blood, Color, Custom, and Social Acceptance," *Social Problems,* 11 (Spring, 1964), 15-41.

WEAVER, Robert C., "The Economic Status of the Negro in the United States," *Journal of Negro Education,* 19 (Summer, 1950), 232-243.

WEAVER, Robert C., *Negro Labor: A National Problem,* New York: Harcourt, Brace, and World, 1946.

WESTIE, Frank R., "Negro-White Status Differentials and Social Distance," *American Sociological Review,* 17 (October, 1952), 550-558.

WESTIE, Frank R. and Margaret L. Westie, "The Social-Distance Pyramid: Relationships between Caste and Class," *American Journal of Sociology,* 63 (September, 1957), 190-196.

WILLIAMS, Robin M., Jr., *Strangers Next Door,* Englewood Cliffs, New Jersey: Prentice-Hall, 1964.

WRONG, Dennis H., "Jews, Gentiles and the New Establishment," *Commentary,* 39 (June, 1965), 83-86.

YARBROUGH, C. L., "Age-Grade Status of Texas Children of Latin American Descent," *Journal of Educational Research,* 40 (September, 1946), 14-27.

YOUNG, Donald, *American Minority Peoples,* New York: Harper and Brothers, 1932.

ZIMMER, Basil G., "The Adjustment of Negroes in a Northern Industrial Community," *Social Problems,* 9 (Spring, 1962), 378-386.

ZENTNER, Henry, "Factors in the Social Pathology of the North American Indian Society," *Anthropologica,* 5 (1963), 119-130.

Internal Stratification of Minorities

Whereas the preceding section deals with the place of racial and ethnic minorities in the society-wide pattern of stratification, this section focuses upon inequality within the minority population.

ANDERSON, C. Arnold, "Regional and Racial Differences in Relations Between Income and Education," *School Review,* 63 (January, 1955), 38-45.

BARTH, Ernest A. T. and Baha Abu-Laban, "Power Structure and the Negro Sub-Community," *American Sociological Review,* 24 (February, 1959), 69-76.

BEEBE, Gilbert W., "Differential Fertility by Color for Coal Miners in Logan County, West Virginia," *Milbank Memorial Fund Quarterly,* 19 (April, 1941), 189-195.

BENNETT, John W., *Hutterian Brethren: The Agricultural Economy and Social Organization of a Communal People.* Stanford: Stanford University Press, 1967.

BERNARD, Jessie, *Marriage and Family Among Negroes,* Englewood Cliffs, New Jersey: Prentice-Hall, 1966.

BLOOM, Leonard and Eshref Shevky, "The Differentiation of an Ethnic Group," *American Sociological Review,* 14 (August, 1949), 476-481.

BOSKOFF, Alvin, "Negro Class Structure and the Technicways," *Social Forces,* 29 (December, 1950), 124-131.

BOWMAN, Lewis, "Racial Discrimination and Negro Leadership Problems: The Case of 'Northern Community'," *Social Forces,* 44 (December, 1965), 173-186.

BOYKIM, Leander, "Differentials in Negro Education," *Journal of Educational Research,* 43 (March, 1950), 533-540.

BROOM, Leonard and Norval D. Glenn, *Transformation of the Negro American,* New York: Harper and Row, 1965.

BROWNING, Harley L. and S. Dale McLemore, *A Statistical Profile of the Spanish-Surname Population of Texas,* Austin: Bureau of Business Research, The University of Texas, 1964.

BURMA, John H., "Current Leadership Problems Among Japanese Americans," *Sociology and Social Research,* 37 (January-February, 1953), 157-163.

BURMA, John H., *Spanish-Speaking Groups in the United States,* Durham, North Carolina: Duke University Press, 1954.

CAHNMAN, W. J., "Role and Significance of the Jewish Artisan Class," *Jewish Journal of Sociology,* 7 (Dec., 1965), 207-214.

CARSTENS, Peter, *The Social Structure of a Cape Coloured Reserve,* New York: Oxford University Press, 1967.

COTHRAN, Tilman C. and William M. Phillips, Jr., "Negro Leadership in a Crisis Situation," *Phylon,* 22 (Summer, 1961), 107-118.

DANIEL, V. E., "Ritual and Stratification in Chicago Negro Churches," *American Sociological Review,* 7 (June, 1942), 352-361.

DANIELS, John, *In Freedom's Birthplace,* Boston: Houghton Mifflin, 1914.

DAVIE, Maurice, *Negroes in American Society,* New York: McGraw-Hill, 1949.

DAVIS, Allison, Burleigh Gardner, and Mary Gardner, *Deep South,* Chicago: University of Chicago Press, 1941.

DOLLARD, John, *Caste and Class in a Southern Town,* New Haven: Yale University Press, 1937.

DRAKE, St. Clair and Horace R. Cayton, *Black Metropolis,* New York Harcourt Brace, 1945.

DU BOIS, W. E., *The Philadelphia Negro,* Philadelphia: University of Pennsylvania Press, 1899.

EDWARDS, G. Franklin, *The Negro Professional Class,* New York: Free Press, 1959.

FAUMAN, S. Joseph, "Occupational Selection Among Detroit Jews," in Marshall Sklare, editor, *The Jews,* New York: Free Press, 1958.

FRAZIER, E. Franklin, *Black Bourgeoisie,* New York: Free Press, 1947.

FRAZIER, E. Franklin, *Negro Youth at the Crossways,* Washington, D. C.: American Council on Education, 1940.

FRAZIER, E. Franklin, *Negroes in the United States,* revised edition, New York: Macmillan, 1957.

FRAZIER, E. Franklin, "The Negro Middle Class and Desegregation," *Social Problems,* 4 (April, 1957), 291-301.

FRAZIER, E. Franklin and Eleanor H. Bernert, "Children and Income in Negro Families," *Social Forces,* 25 (December, 1946), 178-182.

FREEMAN, Howard E., J. Michael Ross, David Armor, and Thomas F. Pettigrew, "Color Gradation and Attitudes Among Middle-Income Negroes," *American Sociological Review,* 31 (June, 1966), 365-374.

FREIDMAN, N. L., "German Lineage and Reform Affiliation: American Jewish Prestige Criteria in Transition," *Phylon,* 26 (Summer, 1965), 140-147.

GANS, Herbert J., *Urban Villagers: Group and Class in the Life of Italian-Americans,* New York: Free Press, 1962.

GLENN, Norval D., "Negro Prestige Criteria: A Case Study in the Bases of Prestige," *American Journal of Sociology,* 68 (May, 1963), 645-657.

GLENN, Norval D., "Negro Religion and Negro Status in the United States," in Louis Schneider, editor, *Religion, Culture and Society,* New York: Wiley, 1964.

GLENN, Norval D. and Ruth Hyland, "Religious Preference and Worldly Success: Some Evidence from National Surveys," *American Sociological Review,* 32 (February, 1967), 73-85.

GOLDSTEIN, Sidney, "The Changing Socio-Demographic Structure of an American Jewish Community," *Jewish Journal of Sociology,* 8 (June, 1966), 11-30.

HAPGOOD, Hutchins, *The Spirit of the Ghetto: Studies of the Jewish Quarter of New York,* New York: Schocken, 1966.

HILL, Mozell C., "Social Status and Physical Appearance Among Negro Adolescents," *Social Forces,* 22 (May, 1944), 443-448.

HILL, Mozell C. and Thelma D. Ackiss, "Social Classes: A Frame of Reference for the Study of Negro-Society," *Social Forces,* 22 (October, 1943), 92-98.

HILL, Mozell C. and Bevode C. McCall, "Social Stratification in 'Georgia Town'," *American Sociological Review,* 15 (December, 1950), 721-729.

HUNTER, Floyd, *Community Power Structure: A Study of Decision Makers,* Chapel Hill: University of North Carolina Press, 1954.

JOHNSON, Charles S., *Growing Up in the Black Belt,* Washington, D. C.: American Council on Education, 1941.

JONES, Clifton R., "Social Stratification in the Negro Population: A Study of Social Classes in South Boston, Virginia," *Journal of Negro Education,* 15 (Winter, 1946), 4-12.

KATZ, Jacob, *Tradition and Crisis: Jewish Society at the End of the Middle Ages,* New York: Free Press, 1961.

KILLIAN, Lewis M. and Charles U. Smith, "Negro Protest Leaders in a Southern Community," *Social Forces,* 38 (March, 1960), 253-257.

KING, Charles E., "The Process of Social Stratification among an Urban Southern Minority Population," *Social Forces,* 31 (May, 1953), 352-363.

KISER, Clyde V., "Fertility Trends and Differentials Among Non-whites in the United States," *Milbank Memorial Fund Quarterly,* 36 (April, 1958), 149-197.

LADD, Everett C., Jr., *Negro Political Leadership in the South,* Ithaca: Cornell University Press, 1966.

LAZERWITZ, Bernard, "A Comparison of Major United States Religious Groups," *Journal of the American Statistical Association,* 56 (September, 1961), 568-579.

LAZERWITZ, Bernard, "Jews In and Out of New York City," *Jewish Journal of Sociology,* 3 (December, 1961), 254-260.

LAZERWITZ, Bernard, "Religion and Social Structure in the United States," in Louis Schneider, editor, *Religion, Culture and Society,* New York: Wiley, 1964.

LEVENTMAN, Seymour, "Class and Ethnic Tensions: Minority Group Leadership in Transition," *Sociology and Social Research,* 50 (April, 1966), 371-376.

LEWIS, Hylan, *Blackways of Kent,* Chapel Hill: University of North Carolina Press, 1955.

LIEBOW, Elliot, *Tally's Corner: A Study of Negro Streetcorner Men,* Boston: Little, Brown, 1967.

LIPMAN, V. D., "Trends in Anglo-Jewish Occupations," *Jewish Journal of Sociology,* 2 (November, 1960), 202-218.

LUCHTERHAND, Elmer and Leonard Weller, "Social Class and the Desegregation Movement: A Study of Parents' Decisions in a Negro Ghetto," *Social Forces,* 13 (Summer, 1965), 83-88.

MADSEN, William, *Mexican-Americans of South Texas,* New York: Holt, Rinehart and Winston, 1964.

MARSHALL, Ray, *The Negro Worker,* New York: Random House, 1967.

MARX, Gary T., *Protest and Prejudice: A Study of Belief in the Black Community,* New York: Harper and Row, 1967.

MATTHEWS, Donald R. and James W. Prothro, *Negroes and the New Southern Politics,* New York: Harcourt, Brace and World, 1966.

MATTHEWS, Donald R. and James W. Prothro, "Social and Economic Factors and Negro Voter Registration in the South," *American Political Science Review,* 57 (March, 1963), 24-44.

MEIER, August and Elliott M. Rudwick, *From Plantation to Ghetto: An Interpretive History of American Negroes,* New York: Hill and Wang, 1966.

MURRAY, Walter, "Measuring The Social-Class Status of Negro Children In the Elementary and High School," *Journal of Educational Sociology,* 25 (October, 1951), 102-111.

MYRDAL, Gunnar, with the assistance of Richard Sterner and Arnold Rose, *An American Dilemma,* New York: Harper and Row, 1944.

ORBELL, John M., "Protest Participation Among Negro College Students," *American Political Science Review,* 61 (June, 1967), 446-456.

ORUM, Anthony M. and Amy W. Orum, "The Class and Status Bases of Negro Student Protest," *Social Science Quarterly,* 49 (December, 1968), 521-533.

PARENTON, V. J. and Roland J. Pellegrin, "Social Structure and the Leadership Factor in a Negro Community in South Louisiana," *Phylon,* 17 (March, 1956), 74-78.

PENALOSA, Fernando, "The Changing Mexican-American in Southern California," *Sociology and Social Research,* 51 (July, 1967), 405-417.

PENALOSA, Fernando and Edward C. McDonagh, "Education, Economic Status and Social Class Awareness of Mexican-Americans," *Phylon,* 29 (Summer, 1968), 119-126.

PETTIGREW, Thomas F., *A Profile of the Negro American,* Princeton: Van Nostrand, 1964.

PFAUTZ, Harold, "The Power Structure of the Negro Sub-Community: A Case Study and a Comparative View," *Phylon,* 23 (Summer, 1962), 156-166.

ROHRER, John H. and Munro S. Edmonson, editors, *The Eighth Generation,* New York: Harper and Row, 1960.

ROMANO, V., "Donship in a Mexican-American Community in Texas," *American Anthropologist,* 62 (December, 1960), 966-976.

POWDERMAKER, Hortense, *After Freedom,* New York: Viking, 1939.

SAMORA, Julian and Richard A. Lamanna, *Mexican-Americans in a Midwest Metropolis: A Study of East Chicago,* Advance Report 8, Los Angeles: University of California, 1967.

SCHNORE, Leo F., "Social Class Segregation among Nonwhites in Metropolitan Centers," *Demography,* 2 (1965), 126-133.

SEARLES, Ruth and J. Allen Williams, Jr., "Negro College Students' Participation in Sit-Ins," *Social Forces,* 40 (March, 1962), 215-220.

SIMPSON, George E. and J. Milton Yinger, *Racial and Cultural Minorities,* third edition, New York: Harper and Row, Chapter 11, Majority-Minority Relations and Social Stratification."

SKINNER, G. William, *Leadership and Power in the Chinese Community of Thailand,* Ithaca: Cornell University Press, 1958.

SMYTHE, Hugh H., "Changing Patterns in Negro Leadership," *Social Forces,* 29 (December, 1950), 191-197.

SMYTHE, Hugh H., "Negro Masses and Leaders: An Analysis of Current Trends," *Sociology and Social Research,* 35 (September-October, 1950), 31-37.

SPEAR, Allan H., *Black Chicago: The Making of a Negro Ghetto, 1890-1920,* Chicago: University of Chicago Press, 1967.

SUTKER, Solomon, "The Jewish Organizational Elite of Atlanta, Georgia," *Social Forces,* 31 (December, 1952), 136-143.

SUTKER, Solomon, "The Role of Social Clubs in the Atlanta Jewish Community," in Marshall Sklare, editor, *The Jews,* New York: Free Press, 1958.

TAEUBER, Karl E. and Alma F. Taeuber, *Negroes in Cities,* Chicago: Aldine, 1965.

THOMPSON, Daniel C., *The Negro Leadership Class,* Englewood Cliffs: New Jersey, Prentice-Hall, 1963.

VANDER ZANDEN, James W., *American Minority Relations: The Sociology of Race and Ethnic Groups,* second edition, 1966, Chapter 9, "Stratification."

WALKER, Harry J., "The Nature and Characteristics of the Negro Community," *Journal of Negro Education,* 19 (Summer, 1950), 219-231.

WALKER, Jack L., "Protest and Negotiation: A Case Study of Negro Leadership in Atlanta," *Midwest Journal of Political Science,* 7 (May, 1963), 99-124.

WARNER, Robert A., *New Haven Negroes,* New Haven: Yale University Press, 1940.

WARNER, W. Lloyd, "American Caste and Class," *American Journal of Sociology,* 42 (September, 1936), 234-237.

WARNER, W. Lloyd, Buford H. Junker, and Walter A. Adams,

Color and Human Nature, Washington, D. C.: American
Council on Education, 1941.

WATSON, J. B. and Julian Samora, "Subordinate Leadership in
a Bicultural Society," *American Sociological Review,* 19
(August, 1954), 413-421.

WHITTEN, Norman E., Jr., *Class, Kinship, and Power in an
Ecuadorian Town: The Negroes of San Lorenzo,* Stanford:
Stanford University Press, 1955.

Stratification in Societies
Other than the United States

Since this bibliography is prepared primarily for the use of social scientists in the
United States, and since there is a more voluminous literature about stratification in
the United States than in any other country, a large percentage of the publications
listed deal with one society. However, social scientists increasingly understand that
no society can be adequately understood except from a comparative and historical
perspective. For this reason, we list considerable historical material in several
sections of this bibliography, and we include this section especially to help users in
the United States gain the needed comparative perspective. Also, some users will
have a specific interest in some of the countries and continents for which we include
material.

Since we list no publications in languages other than English and include few of
the more obscure items in English published outside the United States, this section
contains a smaller percentage of the relevant publications than any other section of
the bibliography.

United Kingdom

AARONOVITCH, Sam, *The Ruling Class: A Study of British
Finance Capital,* London: Lawrence and Wishart, 1961.

ABBOTT, Joan, "Students' Social Class in Three Northern
Universities," *British Journal of Sociology,* 16 (September,
1965), 206-220.

ABRAMS, Mark, *Class Distinctions in Britain,* London: Con-
servative Political Centre, 1958.

ABRAMS, Mark, "Press, Polls and Votes in Britain since the 1955 General Elections," *Public Opinion Quarterly,* 21 (1957-1958), 543-547.

ABRAMS, Mark, "Social Class and British Politics," *Public Opinion Quarterly,* 25 (Fall, 1961), 342-350.

ANDERSON, C. Arnold, *School and Society in England: Social Backgrounds of Oxford and Cambridge Students,* Annals of American Research, 1952.

ARNAN, N. G., "The Intellectual Aristocracy," in J. H. Plumb, editor, *Studies in Social History,* London: Longmans Green, 1955.

BAMFORD, T. W., "Public Schools and Social Class, 1801-1850," *British Journal of Sociology,* 12 (September, 1961), 224-235.

BANKS, J. A. and Olive Banks, *Feminism and Family Planning in Victorian England,* New York: Schocken, 1964.

BANTON, Michael, "The Economic and Social Position of Negro Immigrants in Britain," *Sociological Review,* 1 (December, 1953), 43-62.

BARR, F., "Urban and Rural Differences in Ability and Attainment," *Educational Research,* 1 (February, 1959), 49-60.

BEER, Samuel M., *British Politics in the Collectivist Age,* New York: Knopf, 1965.

BENDIX, Reinhard, "The Self-Legitimation of an Entrepreneurial Class: The Case of England," *Transactions of the Second World Congress of Sociology,* 2 (1954), 259-282.

BENE, Eva, "Some Differences Between Middle-Class Grammar School Boys in Their Attitude toward Education," *British Journal of Sociology,* 10 (June, 1959), 148-152.

BENJAMIN, B., "Inter-Generation Differences in Occupation: a Sample Comparison, in England and Wales, of Census and Birth Registration Records," *Population Studies,* 11 (March, 1958), 262-268.

BENNETT, H. S., *Life on the English Manor: A Study of Peasant Conditions, 1150-1400,* London: Cambridge University Press, 1960.

BENNEY, Mark and Phyllis Geis, "Social Class and Politics in Greenwich," *British Journal of Sociology,* 1 (December, 1950), 310-327.

BENNEY, Mark, A. P. Gray, and H. Pear, *How People Vote,* London: Routledge and Kegan Paul, 1956.

BEREDAY, George Z., "The Problem of Social Equality in English Education," *Harvard Educational Review,* 23 (Summer, 1953), 228-242.

BIRCH, A. H., *Small-Town Politics,* London: Oxford University Press, 1959.

BIRCH, A. H. and Peter Campbell, "Voting Behavior in a Lancashire Constituency," *British Journal of Sociology,* 1 (September, 1950), 197-208.

BLONDEL, Jean, *Voters, Parties, and Leaders,* Baltimore: Penguin, 1963.

BLOOMFIELD, Paul, *Uncommon People: A Study of England Elite,* London: Hamish Hamilton, 1955.

BONHAM, J., *The Middle Class Vote,* London: Faber and Faber, 1954.

BOTTOMORE, T. B., *Classes in Modern Society,* New York: Pantheon, 1966.

BOWLEY, A. L., *Wages and Income in the United Kingdom Since 1860,* London, 1937.

BRENNAN, T., "The Working Class in the British Social Structure," *Transactions of the Third World Congress of Sociology,* 3 (1956), 96-105.

BUCHANAN, William and Hadley Cantril, *How Nations See Each Other,* Urbana: University of Illinois Press, 1953.

BURNS, Tom, "The Cold Class War," *New Statesman and Nation,* (April 7, 1956).

BUTLER, D. E., *The British General Election of 1951,* London: Macmillan, 1951.

CARLSSON, Gosta, *Social Mobility and Class Structure,* Lund: Gleerup, 1958.

CARR-SAUNDERS, A. G. and P. A. Wilson, *The Professions,* London: Oxford University Press, 1933.

CARTER, Michael, *Into Work,* Baltimore: Penguin, 1966.

CARTTER, Allan M., *The Redistribution of Income in Postwar Britain,* New Haven: Yale University Press, 1955.

CHAPMAN, Dennis, *The Home and Social Status,* London: Routledge and Kegan Paul, 1955.

CLAYTON, L. W., "The British Administrative Class," *Personnel Administration,* 14 (July, 1951), 41-45.

COLE, G. D. H., *Studies in Class Structure,* London: Routledge and Kegan Paul, 1955.

COLE, G. D. H. and A. W. Filson, editors, *British Working Class Movements,* New York: Macmillan, 1965.

COLE, G. D. H. and Raymond Postgate, *The Common People,* London: Methuen, 1948.

COLLISON, Peter, "Occupation, Education, and Housing in an English City," *American Journal of Sociology,* 65 (May, 1960), 588-597.

COLLISON, Peter and John Mogey, "Residence and Social Class in Oxford," *American Journal of Sociology,* 64 (May, 1959), 599-605.

COPEMAN, G. H., *Leaders of British Industry,* London, 1955.

DESAI, Rashmi, *Indian Immigrants in Britain,* New York: Oxford University Press, 1963.

DUBLIN, Louis I. and Bessie Bunzel, *To Be or Not to Be,* New York: Smith and Haas, 1933.

ELDER, Glen H., Jr., "Life Opportunity and Personality--Some Consequences of Stratified Secondary Education in Great Britain," *Sociology of Education,* 38 (Spring, 1965), 173-202.

ENGELS, Friedrich, *The Condition of the Working Class in England,* New York: Macmillan, 1958.

EYSENCK, H. J., *The Psychology of Politics,* London: Routledge and Kegan Paul, 1954.

FLORENCE, P. Sargant, *Ownership, Control, and Success of Large Companies: An Analysis of English Industrial Structure and Policy, 1936-1951,* London: Street and Maxwell, 1961.

FLOUD, Jean E., "Social Class Factors in Educational Achievement," in Joseph Kahl, editor, *Comparative Perspectives on Stratification,* Boston: Little, Brown, 1968.

FLOUD, Jean E., A. H. Halsey, and F. M. Martin, editors, *Social Class and Educational Opportunity,* London: Heinemann, 1956.

GLASS, David V., editor, *Social Mobility in Britain,* London: Routledge, 1954.

GLASS, David V. and E. Grebenik, *The Trend and Pattern of Fertility in Great Britain,* London: Royal Commission on Population, 1954.

GLASS, Ruth, *London's Newcomers: The West Indian Migrants,* Cambridge: Harvard University Press, 1961.

GOLDTHORPE, John H. and David Lockwood, "Affluence and the British Class Structure," *Sociological Review,* 11 (July, 1963), 133-163.

GOLDTHORPE, John H., David Lockwood, Frank Bechhofer, and Jennifer Platt, "The Affluent Worker and the Thesis of Embougeoisement: Some Preliminary Research Findings," in

Joseph Kahl, editor, *Comparative Perspectives on Stratification,* Boston: Little, Brown, 1968.

GUTTSMAN, W. L., *The British Political Elite,* London: MacGibbon and Kee, 1963.

GUTTSMAN, W. L., "The Changing Social Structure of the British Political Elite, 1886-1935," *British Journal of Sociology,* 2 (June, 1951), 122-134.

HABAKKUK, H. J., "England," in A. Goodwin, editor, *The European Nobility in the Eighteenth Century,* London: Black, 1953.

HALL, J. R. and W. A. Ziegel, "A Comparison of Social Mobility Data for England, Wales, Italy, France, and the U.S.A.," in David V. Glass, editor, *Social Mobility in Britain,* London: Routledge and Kegan Paul, 1954.

HALSEY, A. H., "Social Mobility in Britain--A Review," *Sociological Review,* 2 (December, 1954), 169-177.

HARRIS, R., "The Selection of Leaders in Ballybeg, Northern Ireland," *Sociological Review,* 9 (July, 1961), 137-149.

HASKINS, W. G., *The Midland Peasant: The Economic and Social History of a Leicestershire Village,* London: Macmillan, 1957.

HAVIGHURST, Robert J., "Education, Social Change in Four Societies: Great Britain, U.S.A., Brazil, Australia," *International Review of Education,* 4 (1958), 167-185.

HOGGART, Richard, *The Uses of Literacy,* London: Chatto and Windus, 1957.

HOLLY, D. N., "Profiting from a Comprehensive School: Sex, Class, and Ability," *British Journal of Sociology,* 16 (June, 1965), 150-158.

HOPKIN, W. A. and J. Haunol, "Analysis of the Births in England and Wales, 1939, by Father's Occupation. Part I," *Population Studies,* 1 (September, 1947), 187-203.

ILLSLEY, R., "Social Class Selection and Class Differences in Relation to Stillbirth and Infant Deaths," *British Medical Journal,* (December 24, 1955), 1520-1524.

INGLIS, K. S., *Churches and the Working Classes in Victorian England,* London: Routledge and Kegan Paul, 1963.

INNES, J. W., "Class Birth Rates in England and Wales, 1921-1931," *Milbank Memorial Fund Quarterly,* 19 (January, 1941), 72-96.

INNES, J. W., *Class Fertility Trends in England and Wales, 1876-1934,* Princeton: Princeton University Press, 1938.

JACKSON, Brian, *Streaming: An Education System in Miniature,* London: Routledge and Kegan Paul, 1964.

JACKSON, Brian, *Working Class Community,* London: Routledge and Kegan Paul, 1968.

JACKSON, Brian and Dennis Marsden, *Education and the Working Class,* London: Routledge and Kegan Paul, 1962.

JANOWITZ, Morris and David R. Segal, "Social Change and Party Affiliation: Germany, Great Britain, and the United States," *American Journal of Sociology,* 72 (May, 1967), 601-618.

JENKINS, C., *Power at the Top,* London: MacGibbon and Kee, 1959.

JENKINS, Hester and D. C. Jones, "Social Class of Cambridge University Alumni of the 18th and 19th Centuries," *British Journal of Sociology,* 1 (June, 1950), 93-116.

JONES, Peter, *The Christian Socialist Revival, 1877-1914: Religion, Class, and Social Conscience in Late-Victorian England,* Princeton: Princeton University Press, 1968.

KAHL, Joseph A., *Comparative Perspectives on Stratification: Mexico, Great Britain, Japan,* Boston: Little, Brown, 1968.

KELLY, Sir David, *The Ruling Few,* London: Hollis and Carter, 1952.

KELSALL, R. K., *Higher Civil Servants in Britain,* London: Routledge and Kegan Paul, 1955.

KELSALL, R. K., "The Social Origin of Higher Civil Servants in Great Britain, Now and in the Past," *Transactions of the Second World Congress of Sociology,* 2 (1954), 131-142.

KELSALL, R. K., David Lockwood, and A. Tropp, "The New Middle Class in the Power Structure of Great Britain," in *Transactions of the Third World Congress of Sociology,* 3 (1956).

KNOWLES, K. G. and D. J. Robertson, "Differences between the Wages of Skilled and Unskilled Workers, 1880-1950," *Bulletin of the Oxford Institute of Statistics,* 1951.

LAWTON, Denis, *Social Class, Language and Education,* London: Routledge and Kegan Paul, 1968.

LEWIS, R. and A. Maude, *The English Middle Classes,* New York: Knopf, 1950.

LEWIS, R. and Rosemary Stewart, *The Managers: A New Examination of the English, German and American Executive,* New York: Mentor Books, 1961.

LIPSET, Seymour M., "The British Voter, II: Sex Age and Education," *New Leader,* (November 21, 1960).

LITTLE, Alan and John Westergaard, "The Trend of Class Differentials in Educational Opportunity in England and Wales," *British Journal of Sociology,* 15 (December, 1964), 301-316.

LITTLE, Kenneth, "The Position of Colored People in Britain," *Phylon,* 15 (Spring, 1954), 58-64.

LOCKWOOD, David, "Sources of Variation in Working Class Images of Society," *Sociological Review,* 14 (November, 1966), 249-267.

LOCKWOOD, David, *The Blackcoated Worker,* London: Unwin, 1958.

LYDALL, H. F., *British Incomes and Savings,* London: 1955.

MacPHERSON, J, S., *Eleven-Year-Olds Grow Up,* London: University of London Press, 1958.

MARSH, D. C., *The Changing Social Structure of England and Wales,* London: Routledge and Kegan Paul, 1958.

MARSHALL, T. H., *Citizenship and Social Classes,* Cambridge, England: Cambridge University Press, 1950.

MARSHALL, T. H., *Class, Citizenship, and Social Development,* Garden City, New York: Doubleday, 1963.

MAXWELL, James, "Intelligence, Fertility and the Future: A Report on the 1947 Scottish Mental Survey," *Proceedings of the World Population Conference,* New York: United Nations, 1954.

MAXWELL, James, "The Level and Trend of National Intelligence," *Publications of the Scottish Council for Research in Education,* 1961.

McKENZIE, R. T. and A. Silver, "Conservatism, Industrialism, and the Working Class Today in England," *Transactions of the Fifth World Congress of Sociology,* Louvain, 3 (1964), 191-202.

MILLAR, Robert, *The New Classes,* London: Longmans Green, 1966.

MILLER, Delbert C., "Decision-Making Cliques in Community Power Structures: A Comparative Study of an American and an English City," *American Journal of Sociology,* 64 (November, 1958), 299-310.

MILLER, Delbert C., "Industry and Community Power Structure: A Comparative Study of an American and an English City," *American Sociological Review,* 23 (February, 1958), 9-15.

UNITED KINGDOM

MOGEY, J. M., "Changes in Family Life Experienced by English Workers Moving From Slums to Housing Estates," *Marriage and Family Living,* 17 (May, 1953), 123-128.

MOGEY, J. M., *Family and Neighborhood,* New York: Oxford University Press, 1956.

MONTAGUE, Joel B., Jr., *Class and Nationality: English and American Studies,* New Haven: College and University Press, 1963.

MONTAGUE, Joel B., Jr., "Research Related to Social Class in England," *American Sociological Review,* 17 (April, 1952), 192-196.

MONTAGUE, Joel B., Jr., "Social Class Status of the Small Farm Freeholder in the English Midlands," *Rural Sociology,* 23 (December, 1958), 401-403.

MONTAGUE, Joel B., Jr., "Some Aspects of Class, Status, and Power Relations in England," *Social Forces,* 30 (December, 1951), 134-140.

MORRIS, Terence, *The Criminal Area: A Study in Social Ecology,* London: Routledge and Kegan Paul, 1957.

MUSGROVE, F., "Middle Class Families and Schools, 1780-1880," *Sociological Review,* 7 (December, 1959), 169-178.

NOEL, Edward, "Sponsored and Contest Mobility in America and England," *Comparative Education Review,* 6 (October, 1962), 148-151.

PEAR, H., *English Social Differences,* London: Allen and Unwin, 1935.

RAINWATER, Lee, "Marital Sexuality in Four Cultures of Poverty," *Journal of Marriage and the Family,* 26 (November, 1964), 457-466.

RAZZELL, P. E., "Social Origins of Officers in the Indian and British Home Army: 1758-1962," *British Journal of Sociology,* 14 (September, 1963), 248-260.

REX, John and Robert Moore, *Race, Community and Conflict: A Study of Sparbrook,* London: Oxford University Press, 1967.

ROSE, Richard, "Class and Party Divisions: Britain as a Test Case," *Occasional Paper Number One,* (1968), Survey Research Centre, University of Strathclyde, Glasgow, Scotland.

ROSS, Alan S. C., *Noblesse Oblige: An Inquiry into the Identifiable Characteristics of the English Aristocracy,* London: Hamilton, 1956.

RUNCIMAN, W. G., *Relative Deprivation and Social Justice:*

A Study of Attitudes to Social Inequality in Twentieth-Century England, Berkeley: University of California Press, 1966.

SAINSBURY, Peter, *Suicide in London,* London: Chapman and Hall, 1955.

SCHNEIDER, Joseph, "Class Origin and Fame: Eminent English Women," *American Sociological Review,* 5 (October, 1940), 700-712.

SCHNEIDER, Joseph, "Social Origin and Fame: The United States and England," *American Sociological Review,* 10 (February, 1945), 52-60.

SCHNEIDER, Joseph, "The Definition of Eminence and the Social Origins of Famous English Men of Genius," *American Sociological Review,* 3 (December, 1938), 834-849.

SCOTT, Eileen M., R. Illsely, and A. M. Thomson, "A Psychological Investigation of Primigravidae. II: Maternal Social Class, Age, Physique and Intelligence," *Journal of Obstetrics and Gynaecology of the British Empire,* 63 (1956).

SEAGER, C. P. and R. A. Flood, "Suicide in Bristol," *British Journal of Psychiatry,* 3 (October, 1965).

SIMPSON, Alan, *The Wealth of the Gentry: 1540-1660,* London: Cambridge University Press, 1961.

SPINLEY, B. M., *The Deprived and the Privileged: Personality Development in English Society,* London: Routledge and Kegan Paul, 1953.

STARK, Rodney, "Class, Radicalism, and Religious Involvement in Great Britain," *American Sociological Review,* 29 (October, 1964), 698-706.

STEWART, Rosemary G. and Paul Duncan-Jones, "Educational Background and Career History of British Managers, with Some American Comparisons," *Explorations in Entrepreneurial History,* 9 (December, 1956), 61-71.

SWIFT, D. F., "Meritocratic and Social Class Selection at Age Eleven," *Educational Research,* 8 (November, 1965), 65-72.

SWIFT, D. F., "Social Class and Achievement Motivation," *Educational Research,* 8 (February, 1966), 83-95.

TAWNEY, R. H., *Equality,* London: Allen and Unwin, 1931, fourth edition, 1952.

THOMPSON, E. P., *The Making of the English Working Class,* New York: Vintage, 1963.

THOMPSON, F. M., "The Social Distribution of Landed Property in England since the Sixteenth Century," *Economic History Review,* 19 (December, 1966), 505-517.

THOMSON, Sir Godfrey, "Intelligence and Fertility: The Scottish 1947 Survey," *Eugenics Review,* 41 (January, 1950), 163-170.

THRUPP, Sylvia L., *The Merchant Class of Medieval London, 1300-1500,* Chicago: University of Chicago Press, 1948.

TIETZE, Christopher, "Life Tables for Social Classes in England," *Milbank Memorial Fund Quarterly,* 21 (April, 1943), 182-187.

TINGSTEN, Herbert, *Political Behavior: Studies in Election Statistics,* London: King, 1937.

TITMUSS, Richard M., "Goals of Today's Welfare State," in Joseph Kahl, editor, *Comparative Perspectives on Stratification,* Boston: Little, Brown, 1968.

TITMUSS, Richard M., *Income Distribution and Social Change,* Toronto: University of Toronto Press, 1962.

TOWNSEND, Peter, *The Family Life of Old People,* London: Routledge and Kegan Paul, 1957.

TREVOR-ROPER, H. R., *The Gentry: 1540-1640,* London: Cambridge University Press, 1953.

TURNER, H. A., "Trade Unions, Differentials and the Levelling of Wages," *Manchester School,* 20 (September, 1952), 227-282.

TURNER, Ralph H., "Acceptance of Irregular Mobility in Britain and the United States," *Sociometry,* 29 (December, 1966), 334-352.

WEINBERG, Ian, *The English Public Schools: The Sociology of Elite Education,* New York: Atherton, 1967.

WILLMOTT, Peter, *Adolescent Boys of East London,* New York: Humanities Press, 1967.

WILLMOTT, Peter and Michael Young, *Family and Class in a London Suburb,* New York: Humanities Press, 1961.

WILLOUGHBY, Gertrude, "The Working Class Family in England," *Transactions of the Third World Congress of Sociology,* 4 (1956), 155-160.

WILSON, Bryan, *Minority Religious Movements in Modern Britain,* London: Heinemann, 1960.

WILSON, C. S. and T. Lupton, "The Social Background and Connections of Top Decision Makers," *Manchester School,* 27 (January, 1959), 30-46.

WRONG, Dennis H., "Class Fertility Differentials in England and Wales," *Milbank Memorial Fund Quarterly,* 38 (January, 1960), 37-47.

YOUNG, Michael and Peter Willmott, *Family and Kinship in*

East London, New York: Free Press, 1957.

YOUNG, Michael and Peter Willmott, "Social Grading by Manual Workers," *British Journal of Sociology,* 7 (December, 1956), 337-345.

ZWEIG, F., *The British Worker,* London: 1952.

Soviet Union

ARMSTRONG, John A., *The Soviet Bureaucratic Elite: A Case Study of the Ukranian Apparatus,* London: Stevens and Sons, 1959.

ARON, Raymond, "Social Structure and the Ruling Class," *British Journal of Sociology,* 1 (March, 1950 and June, 1950), 1-16, 126-143.

BAUER, Raymond, Alex Inkeles, and Clyde Kluckhohn, *How the Soviet System Works,* New York: Vintage Books, 1960.

BERLINER, Joseph S., *Factory and Manager in the U.S.S.R.,* Cambridge: Harvard University Press, 1957.

BERLINER, Joseph S., "The Situation of Plant Managers," in Alex Inkeles and Kent Geiger, *Soviet Society: A Book of Readings,* Boston: Houghton-Mifflin, 1961.

BILL, Valentine, *The Forgotten Class: The Russian Bourgeoisie from the Earliest Beginnings to 1900,* New York: Praeger, 1959.

BLUM, Jerome, *Lord and Peasant in Russia from the Ninth to the Nineteenth Century,* Princeton: Princeton University Press, 1961.

BOTTOMORE, T. B., *Classes in Modern Society,* New York: Pantheon, 1966, 56-75.

BRODERSEN, Arvid, *The Soviet Worker: Labor and Government in Soviet Society,* New York: Random House, 1966.

BRUTZHUS, Boris, "The Historical Peculiarities of the Social and Economic Development of Russia," in Reinhard Bendix and Seymour M. Lipset, editors, *Class, Status, and Power,* revised edition, New York: Free Press, 1966.

BRZEZINSKI, Zbigniew K., *Ideology and Power in Soviet Politics,* London: Thames and Hudson, 1962.

CANTRIL, Hadley, *Soviet Leaders and Mastery Over Man,* New Brunswick, New Jersey: Rutgers University Press, 1960.

CRANKSHAW, Edward, *Krushchev's Russia,* London: Penguin, 1959.

DALLIN, David, *The Real Soviet Russia,* New Haven: Yale University Press, 1944.

DAVIS, Jerome, "Testing the Social Attitudes of Children in the Government Schools of Russia," *American Journal of Sociology,* 32 (May, 1927), 947-952.

DECTER, Moshe, "The Status of the Jews in the Soviet Union," *Foreign Affairs,* (January, 1963), 420-430.

FAINSOD, Merle, *How Russia is Ruled,* revised edition, Cambridge: Harvard University Press, 1963.

FAIRCHILD, Mildred, "Social-Economic Classes in Soviet Russia," *American Sociological Review,* 9 (June, 1944), 236-241.

FELDMESSER, Robert A., "Social Status and Access to Higher Education: A Comparison of the United States and the Soviet Union," *Harvard Educational Review,* 27 (Spring, 1957), 92-106.

FELDMESSER, Robert A., "The Persistence of Status Advantages in Soviet Russia," *American Journal of Sociology,* 59 (July, 1953), 19-27.

FELDMESSER, Robert A., "Toward the Classless Society?" in Reinhard Bendix and Seymour M. Lipset, editors, *Class, Status and Power,* revised edition, New York: Free Press, 1966.

FISCHER, George, *The Soviet System and Modern Society,* New York: Atherton, 1968.

FRANKEL, Max, "The 8,708,000 Elite of Russia," *New York Times Magazine,* (May 29, 1960).

GRANICK, David, *The Red Executive,* Garden City, New York: Doubleday, 1961.

HOLLANDER, Paul, editor, *American and Soviet Society: A Reader in Comparative Sociology and Perception,* Englewood Cliffs: Prentice-Hall, 1958.

INKELES, Alex, "Images of Class Relations Among Former Soviet Citizens," *Social Problems,* 3 (January, 1956), 181-196.

INKELES, Alex, "Social Stratification and Mobility in the Soviet Union: 1940-1950," *American Sociological Review,* 15 (August, 1950), 465-479.

INKELES, Alex and R. A. Bauer, *The Soviet Citizen: Daily Life in a Totalitarian Society,* Cambridge: Harvard University Press, 1959.

KOROL, Alexander G., *Soviet Education for Science and*

Technology, Cambridge: M. I. T. Press, 1957.

MEDYNSKY, Eugene, "Schools and Education in the U.S.S.R.," *American Sociological Review,* 9 (June, 1944), 287-295.

MILLER, S. M., "Comparative Social Mobility," *Current Sociology,* 9 (1960).

NEMCHINOV, V. S., "Change in the Class Structure of the Population of the Soviet Union," *Transactions of the Third World Congress of Sociology,* 8 (1957).

OSSOWSKI, Stanislaw, *Class Structure in the Social Consciousness,* translated by Sheila Patterson, New York: Free Press, 1963.

PASHKOV, A. I., "Radical Changes in Property in the U.S.S.R. in the Twentieth Century," *Transactions of the Third World Congress of Sociology,* 2 (1956), 213-219.

RIGSBY, T. H., "Social Characteristics of the Party Membership," in Alex Inkeles and Kent Geiger, editors, *Soviet Society,* Boston: Houghton Mifflin, 1961.

SCHAPIRO, Leonard, *The Communist Party of the Soviet Union,* London: Eyre and Spottiswoods, 1960.

SCHAPIRO, Leonard, "The Nature of Total Power," *Political Quarterly,* 29 (January-March, 1958), 105-113.

SCHLESINGER, Rudolph, *The Spirit of Post-War Russia,* London: Dobson, 1947.

SCHWARTZ, Solomon, *Jews in the Soviet Union,* Syracuse: Syracuse University Press, 1951.

SCHWARTZ, Solomon, *Labor in the Soviet Union,* New York: 1952.

TIMASHEFF, Nicholas S., *The Great Retreat,* New York: Dutton, 1946.

TIMASHEFF, Nicholas S., "Vertical Social Mobility in Communist Society," *American Journal of Sociology,* 50 (July, 1944), 9-21.

TOWSTER, Julian, *Political Power in the U.S.S.R., 1917-1947,* New York: Oxford University Press, 1948.

UTECHIN, S. V., "Social Stratification and Social Mobility in the U.S.S.R., *Transactions of the Second World Congress of Sociology,* 2 (1954), 55-63.

VIGOR, P. H., *A Guide to Marxism and its Effects on Soviet Development,* New York: Humanities Press, 1966.

YANOWITCH, Murray, "The Soviet Income Revolution," *Slavic Review,* 22 (December, 1963), 683-697.

YUGOW, A., *Russia's Economic Front for War and Peace,* New York: Harper, 1942.

ALLARDT, Erik and Kettil Bruun, "Characteristics of the Finnish Non-Voter," *Transactions of the Westermarck Society,* 3 (1956), 55-76.

ANDERSON, C. Arnold, "Lifetime Inter-Occupational Mobility Patterns in Sweden," *Acta Sociologica,* 1 (1955), 168-202.

ANDERSON, C. Arnold, "Social Class as a Factor in the Assimilation of Women into Higher Education," *Acta Sociologica,* 4 (1959), 27-32.

ASTROM, Sven-Erik, "Literature on Social Mobility and Social Stratification in Finland: Some Bibliographical Notes," *Transactions of the Westermarck Society,* 2 (1953), 221-227.

BANFIELD, Edward C., *The Moral Basis of a Backward Society,* New York: Free Press, 1958. Deals with Italy.

BARBER, Bernard and Elinor G. Barber, editors, *European Social Class: Stability and Change,* New York: Macmillan, 1965.

BARBER, Elinor G., *The Bourgeoisie in 18th Century France,* Princeton: Princeton University Press, 1955.

BAUMAN, Zygmunt, "Economic Growth, Social Structure, Elite Formation: The Case of Poland," *International Social Science Journal,* 16 (1964), 203-216.

BECKER, Howard, "Changes in the Social Stratification of Contemporary Germany," *American Sociological Review,* 15 (June, 1950), 333-342.

BELOFF, M., "Intellectual Classes and Ruling Classes in France," *Occidente,* 10 (January-February, 1954), 54-65.

BLACKER, J.G.C., "Social Ambitions of the Bourgeoisie of 18th Century France and Their Relation to Family Limitation," *Population Studies,* 11 (July, 1957), 46-53.

BOALT, Gunnar, "Social Mobility in Stockholm: A Pilot Investigation," *Transactions of the Second World Congress of Sociology,* 2 (1954), 67-73.

BOLTE, Karl M., "Some Aspects of Social Mobility in Western Europe," *Transactions of the World Congress of Sociology,* 3 (1956), 183-190.

BOTTOMORE, T. B., "Higher Civil Servants in France," *Transactions of the Second World Congress of Sociology*, 2 (1954), 143-152.

BUCHANAN, William and Hadley Cantril, *How Nations See Each Other*, Urbana: University of Illinois Press, 1953.

CANCIAN, Frank, "The Southern Italian Peasant: World View and Political Behavior," *Anthropological Quarterly*, 34 (1961), 1-18.

CAPLOW, Theodore, "Recent Research on the Ecology of Paris," *Midwest Sociologist*, 16 (1954), 19-21.

CAPLOW, Theodore, "Urban Structure in France," *American Sociological Review*, 17 (October, 1952), 544-549.

CARLSSON, Gosta, *Social Mobility and Class Structure*, Lund: Gleerup, 1958.

CARLSSON, Gosta and Bengt Gresser, "Universities as Selecting and Socializing Agents: Some Recent Swedish Data," *Acta Sociologica*, 9, 25-39.

CARTER, Cedric O. "Changing Patterns of Differential Fertility in Northwest Europe and North America," *Eugenics Quarterly*, 9 (September, 1962), 147-150.

CLIFFORD-VAUGHN, Michalina, "Some French Concepts of Elites," *British Journal of Sociology*, 11 (December, 1960), 319-332.

DAHRENDORF, Ralf, "Recent Changes in the Class Structure of European Societies," *Daedalus*, (Winter, 1964), 225-270.

DJILAS, Milovan, *The New Class: An Analysis of the Communist Systems*, New York: Praeger, 1959.

DOBLIN, E. M. and C. Pohly, "The Social Composition of the Nazi Leadership," *American Journal of Sociology*, 51 (July, 1945), 42-49.

DOOGHE, Gilbert, "Premarital Conceptions with Married Couples According to Socio-Professional Status," *Journal of Marriage and the Family* 30 (May, 1968), 324-328. Deals with Denmark.

DOUMAS, C. L., "A Tentative Analysis of the Power Elite of Greece," *Southern Quarterly*, 4 (July, 1966), 374-408.

EDINGER, Lewis J., "Continuity and Change in the Background of German Decision-Makers," *Western Political Quarterly*, 14 (March, 1961), 17-36.

FLOUD, Jean, "Social Stratification in Denmark," *British Journal of Sociology*, 3 (June, 1952), 173-177.

GALLAGHER, Orvoell R., "Voluntary Associations in France," *Social Forces,* 36 (December, 1957), 153-160.

EUROPE

GALESKI, B., "Social Stratification In Rural Areas: Research Problems," *International Social Science Bulletin,* 9 (1957), 193-211. Deals with Poland.

GEIGER, Theodor, "A Dynamic Analysis of Social Mobility," *Acta Sociologica,* 1 (1955), 26-38. Deals with Denmark.

GEIGER, Theodor, "An Historical Study of the Origins and Structure of the Danish Intelligentsia," *British Journal of Sociology,* 1 (September, 1950), 209-220.

GIROD, Robert and Firouz Tofigh, "Family Background and Income, School Career and Social Mobility of Young Males of Working-Class Origin—A Geneva Survey," *Acta Sociologica,* 9, 94-109.

GOODWIN, A., editor, *The European Nobility in the Eighteenth Century,* London: Black, 1953.

GOUDSBLOM, Johan, *Dutch Society,* New York: Random House, 1967.

HALL, J. R. and W. A. Ziegel, "A Comparison of Social Mobility Data for England, and Wales, Italy, France, and the U.S.A.," in David V. Glass, editor, *Social Mobility in Britain,* London: Routledge and Kegan Paul, 1954.

HAMILTON, Richard F., *Affluence and the French Worker in the Fourth Republic,* Princeton: Princeton University Press, 1967.

HAMILTON, Richard F., "Affluence and the Worker: The West German Case," *American Journal of Sociology,* 71, (September, 1965), 144-152.

HAMON, Leon, "The Members of the French Parliament," *International Social Science Journal,* 13 (1961), 545-567.

HOFSTEE, E. W., "Changes in Rural Social Stratification in the Netherlands," *Transactions of the Second World Congress of Sociology* 2 (1954), 74-80.

HONKALA, Kanko, "Social Class and Visiting Patterns in Two Finish Villages," *Acta Sociologica,* 5, 42-49.

HOYT, Homer, "The Structure and Growth of American Cities Contrasted with the Structure and Growth of European Cities," *Urban Land,* 18 (1959), 3-8.

JANOWITZ, Morris, "Social Stratification and Mobility in West Germany," *American Journal of Sociology,* 64 (July, 1958), 6-24.

JANOWITZ, Morris and David R. Segal, "Social Change and

Party Affiliation: Germany, Great Britain, and the United States," *American Journal of Sociology,* 72 (May, 1967), 601-618.

JANUSCHKA, Emmanuel, *The Social Stratification of the Austrian Population,* New York: Columbia University Press, 1939.

KARLSSON, Georg, "Voting Participation Among Male Swedish Youth," *Acta Sociologica,* 3 (1958), 98-111.

KLOSKOWSKA, Antonina, "Attitudes Toward the Status of Women in Polish Working Class Families: General Attitudes Toward the Respective Roles and the Equality of the Two Sexes, and Towards Children," *International Social Science Journal,* 14 (1962), 66-79.

KOGAN, Norman, "Italian Communism the Working Class and Organized Catholicism," *Journal of Politics,* 28 (August, 1966), 531-555.

KUIPER, G., "The Recruitment of the Learned Professions in the Netherlands," *Transactions of the Third World Congress of Sociology,* 3 (1956), 230-238.

LANDES, David, "French Business and the Businessman: A Social and Cultural Analysis," in Edward M. Earle, editor, *Modern France,* Princeton: Princeton University Press, 1951.

LEWIS, R. and Rosemary Steward, *The Managers: A New Examination of the English, German and American Executive,* New York: Mentor, 1961.

LIPSET, Seymour M., "The Changing Class Structure and Contemporary European Politics," *Daedalus,* 93 (Winter, 1964).

LIPSET, Seymour M. and Natalie Rogoff, "Class and Opportunity in Europe and the U. S.," *Commentary,* 18 (December, 1954), 562-568.

LOPREATO, Joseph, "How Would You Like to be a Peasant?" *Human Organization,* 24 (Winter, 1965), 298-307.

LOPREATO, Joseph, "Interpersonal Relations in Peasant Society: The Peasant's View," *Human Organization,* 21 (Spring, 1962), 21-24.

LOPREATO, Joseph, *Peasants No More: Social Class and Social Change in Southern Italy,* San Francisco: Chandler, 1967.

LOPREATO, Joseph, "Social Classes in an Italian Farm Village," *Rural Sociology,* (September, 1961), 266-281.

LOPREATO, Joseph and Janet Saltzman, "Descriptive Models of Peasant Society: A Reconciliation from Southern Italy," *Human Organization,* 27 (Summer, 1968), 132-142.

LUIJCKX, A. W. "Inquiry into the Mobility of Employment in the Dutch Middle Class," *Transactions of the Second World Congress of Sociology,* 2 (1954), 89-90.

EUROPE   MacRAE, Duncan, Jr., "Religious and Socioeconomic Factors in the French Vote, 1946-1956," *American Journal of Sociology,* 64 (November, 1958), 290-298.

MARX, Karl, *Class Struggles in France, 1848-1850,* New York: International Publishers, 1964.

MATHIESEN, Thomas, "Aspects of Social Stratification in a Changing Community," *Acta Sociologica,* 4 (1959), 42-54.

MAYER, Kurt B., *The Population of Switzerland,* New York: Columbia University Press, 1952.

McDONAGH, Edward C., Sven Wermlund, and John F. Crowther, "Relative Professional Status as Perceived by American and Swedish University Students," *Social Forces,* 38 (October, 1959), 65-69.

McELRATH, Dennis C., "The Social Areas of Rome: A Comparative Analysis," *American Sociological Review,* 27 (June, 1962), 376-391.

MEYER, Peter, *Jews in the Soviet Satellites,* Syracuse: Syracuse University Press, 1953.

MILIC, Vojin, "General Trends in Social Mobility in Jugoslavia," *Acta Sociologica,* 9 (1965), 116-136.

MOBERG, Sven, "Marital Status and Family Size Among Matriculated Persons in Sweden," *Population Studies,* 4 (June, 1950), 115-127.

MOSKOS, Charles C., Jr., "Social Transformation of the Albanian Elite: From Monarchy to Communism," in Herbert R. Barringer, George Blanksten, and Raymond W. Mack, editors, *Social Change in Developing Areas,* Cambridge: Schenkman, 1966.

MOSS, Leonard W. and Stephen C. Cappannari, "Estate and Class in a South Italian Hill Village," *American Anthropologist,* 64 (April, 1962), 287-300.

NORDAL, Johannes, "The Recruitment of the Professions in Iceland," *Transactions of the Second World Congress of Sociology,* 2 (1954), 153-165.

NOWAKOWSKI, Stefan, "Peasant-Workers: Some Aspects of Social Mobility in Post-War Poland," *Transactions of the Third World Congress of Sociology,* 3 (1956), 330-337.

PEARLIN, Leonard I. and Melvin L. Kohn, "Social Class, Occupation, and Parental Values: A Cross National Study," *American Sociological Review,* 31 (August, 1966), 466-479.

174

PERROY, E., "Social Mobility Among the French *Noblesse* in the Later Middle Ages," *Past and Present,* 21 (1962), 25-38.

RAFFAELE, Joseph A., *Labor Leadership in Italy and Denmark,* Madison: University of Wisconsin Press, 1962.

ROGOFF, Natalie, "Social Stratification in France and in the United States," *American Journal of Sociology,* 58 (January, 1953), 347-357.

ROSENBERG, Hans, *Bureaucracy, Aristocracy and Autocracy: The Prussian Experience, 1660-1815,* Cambridge: Harvard University Press, 1958.

SARAPATA, Adam and Wlodzimierz Wesolowski, "The Evaluation of Occupations by Warsaw Inhabitants," *American Journal of Sociology,* 66 (May, 1961), 581-591.

SARIOLA, Sakari, "Defining Social Class in Two Finnish Communities," *Transactions of the Second World Congress of Sociology,* 2 (1954), 108-118.

SCHEUCH, Erwin K. and Dietrich Ruschemeyer, "Scaling Social Status in Western Germany," *British Journal of Sociology,* 11 (June, 1960) 151-168.

SCHOENBAUM, David, *Hitler's Social Revolution: Class and Status in Nazi Germany, 1933-1939,* Garden City, New York: Doubleday, 1967.

SCHWARZWELLER, Harry K., "Community of Residence and Career Choices of German Youth," *Rural Sociology,* 33 (March, 1968), 46-63.

SEEMAN, Melvin, Dennis Rohan, and Milton Argeriou, "Social Mobility and Prejudice: A Swedish Replication," *Social Problems,* 14 (Fall, 1966), 188-197.

SEGERSTEDT, Torgny T., "An Investigation of Class Consciousness Among Office Employees and Workers in Swedish Factories," *Transactions of the Second World Congress of Sociology,* 2 (1954), 298-308.

SILVERMAN, Sydel, "An Ethnographic Approach to Social Stratification: Prestige in a Central Italian Community," *American Anthropologist,* 68 (August, 1966), 899-921.

SMITH, Lincoln, "Power Politics in Brunswick: A Case Study," *Human Organization,* 22 (Summer, 1963), 152-158.

SOLTOW, Lee, *Toward Income Equality in Norway,* Madison: University of Wisconsin Press, 1965.

STAFILIOS-ROTHSCHILD, Constantina, "Class Position and Success Stereotypes in Greek and American Cultures," *Social Forces,* 45 (March, 1967), 374-383.

EUROPE

STODDARD, Lothrop, *Social Classes in Post-War Europe*, London: 1925.

STOETZEL, Jean, "Voting Behavior in France," *British Journal of Sociology,* 6 (June, 1955), 104-122.

EUROPE   SURACE, Samuel J., *Ideology, Economic Change and the Working Classes: The Case of Italy,* Berkeley: University of California Press, 1966.

SVALASTOGA, Kaare, "Social Mobility: The Western European Model," *Acta Sociologica,* 9, 175-182.

SVALASTOGA, Kaare, and Gosta Carlsson, "Social Stratification and Social Mobility in Scandinavia," *Sociological Inquiry,* 31 (1961), 23-46.

SVALASTOGA, Kaare, E. Hogh, M. Pederson, and E. Schild, "Differential Class Behavior in Denmark," *American Sociological Review,* 21 (August, 1956), 435-439.

SWEETSER, Dorrian A., "Intergenerational Ties in Finnish Urban Families," *American Sociological Review,* 33 (April, 1968), 236-246.

SYME, Ronald, *Colonial Elites: Rome, Spain, and the Americas,* London: Oxford University Press, 1958.

SZCZEPANSKI, J., "Changes in the Structure and the Function of the Intelligentsia," *International Social Science Bulletin,* 9 (1957), 180-192. Deals with Poland.

THOENES, P., *The Elite in the Welfare State,* New York: Free Press, 1966.

TINGSTEN, Herbert, *Political Behavior: Studies in Election Statistics,* London: King, 1937.

VAN DOORN, Jacques A. A., "The Changed Position of Unskilled Workers in the Social Structure of the Netherlands," *Transactions of the Third World Congress of Sociology,* 3 (1956), 113-125.

VAN HULTEN, Ida, "Summary of a Study of Social Mobility at the Philips Works, Edinhoven," *Transactions of the Second World Congress of Sociology,* 2 (1954), 81-88.

VAN TULDER, J.J.M., "Occupational Mobility in the Netherlands from 1919 to 1954,"' *Transactions of the Third World Congress of Sociology,* 3 (1956), 209-218.

ULC, Otto, "Class Struggle and Socialist Justice: The Case of Czechoslovakia," *American Political Science Review,* 56 (September, 1967), 727-743.

VINKE, P., "The Vertical Social Mobility of the Chief Executive Groups in the Netherlands," *Transactions of the Third World Congress of Sociology,* 3 (1956), 219-229.

VON FERBER, C., "The Social Background of German University and College Professors Since 1864," *Transactions of the Third World Congress of Sociology* 3 (1956), 239-244.

WILKENING, Eugene A. and C. Van Es, "Aspirations and Attainments Among German Farm Families," *Rural Sociology,* 32 (December, 1967), 435-445.

WOLF, P., "Crime and Social Class in Denmark," *British Journal of Criminology,* 3 (1962), 5-17.

WUNDERLICH, Frieda, "Fascism and the German Middle Class," *Antioch Review,* 5 (1945), 56-67.

China

CHANG, Chung-li, *The Chinese Gentry: Studies on their Role in Nineteenth-Century Chinese Society,* Seattle: University of Washington Press, 1955.

CHANG, Chung-li, *The Income of the Chinese Gentry,* Seattle: University of Washington Press, 1962.

CHEN, Ta., "Basic Problems of the Chinese Working Classes," *American Journal of Sociology,* 53 (November, 1947), 184-191.

CHEN, Theodore Hsi-en, "The Marxist Remolding of Chinese Society," *American Journal of Sociology,* 58 (January, 1953), 340-346.

CHO, Yung-Teh, *Social Mobility in China: Status Careers Among the Gentry in a Chinese Community,* New York: Atherton, 1966.

CROOK, Isabel and David Crook, *Revolution in a Chinese Village Ten Mile Inn,* London: Routledge and Kegan Paul, 1959.

DENLINGER, P. B., "Report from Communist China," *Contemporary Japan,* 22 (1953), 431-471.

EBERHARD, Wolfram, *Conquerors and Rulers: Social Forces in Medieval China,* Leiden, Netherlands: Brill, 1952.

EBERHARD, Wolfram, *Conquerors and Rulers: Social Forces in Medieval China,* second edition, Leiden, Netherlands: Brill, 1965.

CHINA

EBERHARD, Wolfram, *Social Mobility in Traditional China,* Leiden, Netherlands: Brill, 1962.

EBERHARD, Wolfram, "Social Mobility and Stratification in China," in Reinhard Bendix and Seymour M. Lipset, editors, *Class, Status, and Power,* revised edition, New York: Free Press, 1966.

FEI, Hsiao-Tung, *China's Gentry,* Chicago: University of Chicago Press, 1953.

FEI, Hsiao-Tung, "Peasantry and Gentry: An Interpretation of Chinese Social Structure and Its Changes," in Reinhard Bendix and Seymour M. Lipset, editors, *Class, Status and Power,* New York: Free Press, 1953.

FRIED, M. H., *The Fabric of Chinese Society: A Study of the Social Life of a Chinese County Seat,* New York: Praeger, 1953.

HO, Ping-Ti, *The Ladder of Success in Imperial China: Aspects of Social Mobility, 1368-1911,* New York: Columbia University Press, 1962.

HSU, Francis L. K., "Social Mobility in China," *American Sociological Review,* 14 (December, 1949), 764-771.

HUANG, Lucy Jin, "Attitude of the Communist Chinese Toward Inter-Class Marriage," *Marriage and Family Living,* 24 (November, 1962), 389-392.

KRACKE, E. A., Jr., "Family Versus Merit in Chinese Civil Service Examinations Under the Empire," *Harvard Journal of Asiatic Studies,* 10 (1947), 103-123.

LEE, Shu-Ching, "Administration and Bureaucracy: The Power Structure in Chinese Society," *Transactions of the Second World Congress of Sociology,* 2 (1954), 3-15.

LEE, Shu-Ching, "Intelligentsia of China," *American Journal of Sociology,* 52 (May, 1947), 489-497.

LEWIS, John Wilson, *Leadership in Communist China,* Ithaca: Cornell University Press, 1963.

LIU, William T., editor, *Chinese Society Under Communism: A Reader,* New York: Wiley, 1967.

MARSH, Robert M., *The Mandarins: The Circulation of Elites in China, 1600-1900,* New York: Free Press, 1961.

NORTH, Robert C., "The Chinese Communist Elite," *Annals of the American Academy of Political and Social Science,* (September, 1951), 67-75.

ORLEANS, Leo A., *Professional Manpower and Education in Communist China,* Washington, D. C.: National Science Foundation, 1961.

TIMASHEFF, N. S., "Vertical Social Mobility in Communist Society," *American Journal of Sociology,* 50 (July, 1944), 9-21.

TOWNSEND, James R., *Political Participation in Communist China,* Berkeley: University of California Press, 1967.

Japan

ABEGGLEN, James C. and H. Mannari, "Leaders of Modern Japan: Social Origins and Mobility," *Economic Development and Cultural Change,* 9 (October, 1960), 109-134.

CORNELL, John B., "Outcaste Relations in a Japanese Village," *American Anthropologist,* 63 (April, 1961), 282-296.

DeVOS, George, "Motivational Components of Caste," in George DeVos and H. Wagatsuma, editors, *Japan's Invisible Race: Caste in Culture and Personality,* Berkeley; University of California Press, 1966.

DeVOS, George and H. Wagatsuma, editors, *Japan's Invisible Race: Caste in Culture and Personality,* Berkeley: University of California Press, 1966.

DONOGHUE, John D., "An Eta Community in Japan: The Social Persistence of Outcaste Groups," *American Anthropologist,* 59 (December, 1957), 1000-1017.

HAWLEY, Amos H., "Land Value Patterns in Okayoma, Japan, 1940 and 1952," *American Journal of Sociology,* 60 (March, 1955), 487-492.

JAPAN SOCIOLOGICAL SOCIETY, Research Committee, *Social Mobility in Japan: An Interim Report on the 1955 Survey of Social Stratification and Social Mobility in Japan,* Tokyo: 1956.

JAPAN SOCIOLOGICAL SOCIETY, Research Committee, "Social Stratification and Mobility in the Six Large Cities of Japan," *Transactions of the Second World Congress of Sociology,* 2 (1954), 414-431.

KAHL, Joseph A., *Comparative Perspectives on Stratification: Mexico, Great Britain, Japan,* Boston: Little, Brown, 1968.

KIDO, Kotaro and Masataka Sugi, "A Report of Research on Social Stratification and Mobility in Tokyo, *Japanese Sociological Review,* 4 (1954), 74-100.

JAPAN

KURODA, Yasumasa, "Measurement, Correlates, and Significance of Political Participation in a Japanese Community," *Western Political Quarterly,* 20 (September, 1967), 660-668.

KURODA, Yasumasa, "Psychological Aspects of Community Power Structure: Leaders and Rank-and-File Citizens in Reed Town, Japan," *Southwestern Social Science Quarterly,* 48 (December, 1967), 433-442.

LEWIS, David M., "Perception of Entrepreneurial Prestige by Japanese Boys," *Rural Sociology,* 33 (March, 1968), 71-79.

MATSUSHIMA, Shizuo, "Labour Management Relations," in Joseph Kahl, editor, *Comparative Perspectives on Stratification,* Boston: Little, Brown, 1968.

MITCHELL, Richard H., *The Korean Minority in Japan,* Berkeley: University of California Press, 1967.

NATIONAL PUBLIC OPINION INSTITUTE OF JAPAN, *A Survey Concerning the Protection of Civil Liberties,* Tokyo, 1951.

ODAKA, Kunio, "The Middle Classes in Japan," in Reinhard Bendix and Seymour M.Lipset, editors, *Class, Status and Power,* rev. edition, New York: Free Press, 1966.

ODAKA, Kunio and Sigeki Nishihira, "Social Mobility in Japan: A Report on the 1955 Survey," *East Asian Cultural Studies,* 4 (March, 1965), 83-126.

ODAKA, Kunio and Sigeki Nishihira, "Some Factors Related to Social Mobility in Japan," *Annals of the Institute of Statistical Mathematics,* 10 (1959), 283-288.

PASSIN, Herbert, *Society and Education in Japan,* New York: Teachers College Press, 1967.

PELZEL, John C., "The Small Industrialist in Japan," *Explorations in Entrepreneurial History,* 7 (1954), 79-93.

RAMSEY, Charles E., and Robert J. Smith, "Japanese and American Perception of Occupations," *American Journal of Sociology,* 65 (March, 1960), 475-482.

SMITH, Robert J., "Aspects of Mobility in Pre-Industrial Japanese Cities," *Comparative Studies in Society and History,* 5 (July, 1963), 416-423.

SMITH, Thomas C., "Japan's Aristocratic Revolution," *Yale Review,* 50 (Spring, 1960-1961), 370-383.

SMYTHE, Hugh H., "The Eta: A Marginal Japanese Caste," *American Journal of Sociology,* 58 (September, 1952), 194-196.

TAEUBER, Irene, *The Population of Japan,* Princeton: Princeton University Press, 1958.

TOMINAGA, Kenichi, "Occupational Mobility in Tokyo," in Joseph Kahl, editor, *Comparative Perspectives on Stratification,* Boston: Little, Brown, 1958.

VOGEL, Ezra F., *Japan's New Middle Class: The Salary Man and his Family in a Tokyo Suburb,* Berkeley: University of California Press, 1963.

YAMAMURA, Koso, "The Role of Samurai in the Development of Modern Banking in Japan," *Journal of Economic History,* 27 (June, 1967), 198-220.

Asiatic Caste

ABERLE, E. K. G., "Criteria of Caste Ranking in South India," *Man in India,* 39 (1959), 115-126.

ALLAH, I., "Caste, Patti and Faction in the Life of a Punjab Village," *Sociologus,* 8 (1958), 170-186.

AMBEDKAR, B. R., *What Congress and Gandhi Have Done to the Untouchables,* Bombay: Thacker, 1945.

ANSARI, G., *Muslim Caste in Uttar Pradesh,* Lucknow: Ethnographic and Folk Culture Society, 1960.

AROKIASWANI, M., "Castes in South India," *Tamil Culture,* 3 (October, 1954), 326-330.

BAHADUR, R. P., "The Economics of Casteism," *Indian Journal of Economics,* 36 (1956), 325-336.

BAILEY, F. G., *Caste and Economic Frontier,* Manchester: Manchester University Press, 1957.

BAILEY, F. G., "Closed Social Stratification in India," *Archives of European Sociology,* 4 (1963), 107-124.

BAILEY, F. G., *Tribe, Caste, and Nation,* Manchester: Manchester University Press, 1960.

BANKS, Michael, "Caste in Jaffna," in E. R. Leach,

editor, *Aspects of Caste in South India, Ceylon and Northwest Pakistan,* Cambridge: Cambridge University Press, 1962.

BARTH, Fredrik, "The System of Social Stratification in Sevat, North Pakistan," in E. R. Leach, editor, *Aspects of Caste in South India, Ceylon and Northwest Pakistan,* Cambridge: Cambridge University Press, 1962.

BASHAM, A. L., *The Wonder That Was India,* New York: Grove, 1954.

BEALS, Alan R., *Gopalpur: A South Indian Village,* New York: Holt, Rinehart and Winston, 1963.

BEIDELMAN, Thomas O., *A Comparative Analysis of the Jajmani System,* Locust Valley, New York: Augustin, 1959.

BURTON, Benedict, "Caste in Mauritius," in Barton M. Schwartz, editor, *Caste in Overseas Indian Communities,* San Francisco: Chandler, 1967.

BERREMAN, Gerald D., "Caste and Community Development," *Human Organization,* 22 (Spring 1963), 90-94.

BERREMAN, Gerald D., "Caste in India and the United States," *American Journal of Sociology,* 66 (September, 1960), 120-127.

BERREMAN, Gerald D., "Caste, Racism and Stratification," *Contributions to Indian Sociology,* 6 (1962), 122-125.

BERREMAN, Gerald D., "Caste as a Social Process," *Southwestern Journal of Anthropology,* 23 (Winter, 1967), 351-370.

BERREMAN, Gerald D., "The Concept of Caste," in *International Encyclopedia of the Social Sciences,* New York: Macmillan, 1967.

BERREMAN, Gerald D., "The Study of Caste Ranking in India," *Journal of Anthropology,* 21 (1965), 115-129.

BETEILLE, Andre, *Caste, Caste, and Power: Changing Patterns of Stratification in a Tanjore Village,* Berkeley: University of California Press, 1965.

BHARATI, Agehananda, "Ideology and Content of Caste Among the Indians in East Africa," in Barton M. Schwartz, editor, *Caste in Overseas Indian Communities,* San Francisco: Chandler, 1967.

BHAT, J. H., "Untouchability in India," *Civilizations,* 4 (1954), 565-570.

BHOWMICK, P. K. and B. Bhattacharya, "Caste, Occupation and Status," *Man in India,* 37 (1957), 81-83.

BOSE, N. K., "Who Are the Backward Classes?" *Man in India,* 34 (April-June, 1954), 89-98.

BOSE, N. K., "Some Aspects of Caste in Bengal," *Journal of American Folklore,* 71 (1958), 397-412.

BOSE, N. K., "Some Observations on Nomadic Castes in India," *Man in India,* 36 (1956), 1-6.

BOUGLE, C., "The Essence and Reality of the Caste System," *Contributions to Indian Sociology,* 2 (1958), 7-30.

CARSTAIRS, G. Morris, *The Twice-Born: A Study of a Community of High-Caste Hindus,* London: Hogarth, 1957.

CHANDRASHEKHARAIYAH, K., "Mobility Patterns Within the Caste," *Sociological Bulletin,* 11 (1961), 62-67.

CHATTOPADHYAYA, B., "Caste in the Vedas," *Calcutta Review,* 145 (1957), 237-242.

COHN, Bernard S., "Changing Traditions of a Low Caste," *Journal of American Folklore,* 71 (1958), 413-421.

CLARKE, Colin, "Caste Among Hindus in a Town in Trinidad: San Fernando," in Barton M. Schwartz, editor, *Caste in Overseas Indian Communities,* San Francisco: Chandler, 1967.

COUGH, E Kathleen, "Caste in a Tanjore Village," in E. R. Leach, editor, *Aspects of Caste in South India, Ceylon, and Northwest Pakistan,* Cambridge: Cambridge University Press, 1962.

COX, Oliver Cromwell, *Caste, Class and Race: A Study in Social Dynamics,* Garden City, New York: Doubleday, 1948.

COX, Oliver Cromwell, "Race and Caste: A Distinction," *American Journal of Sociology,* 50 (March, 1945), 360-368.

DAMLE, Y. B., "Caste in Maharashtra," *Journal of the University of Poona,* 9 (1958), 87-98.

DAMLE, Y. B., "Reference Group Theory With Regard to Mobility in Caste," *Social Action,* 13 (1963), 190-199.

DAVIS, Kingsley, "Intermarriage in Caste Societies," *American Anthropologist,* 43 (July-September, 1941), 376-395.

DAVIS, Kingsley, *The Population of India and Pakistan,* Princeton: Princeton University Press, 1951.

DESAI, I. P., "Caste and Family," *Economic Weekly,* 6 (February, 1954), 249-254.

DEVANANDAN, P. D., *A Bibliography on Hinduism,* Dangalore: Christian Institute for the Study of Religion and Society, 1961.

DeVOS, George, "Motivational Components of Caste," in George

DeVos and H. Wagatsuma, editors, *Japan's Invisible Race: Caste in Culture and Personality,* Berkeley: University of California Press, 1966.

DRIVER, Edwin D., "Caste and Occupational Structure in Central India," *Social Forces,* 41 (October, 1962), 26-31.

DRIVER, Edwin D., "Family Structure and Socio-Economic Status in Central India," *Sociological Bulletin,* 11 (March-September, 1962), 112-120.

D'SOUZA, Victor S., "Caste and Endogamy: A Reappraisal of the Concept of Caste," *Journal of the Anthropological Society of Bombay,* 11 (1959), 11-42.

D'SOUZA, Victor S., "Social Grading of Occupations in India," *Sociological Review,* 10 (July, 1962), 145-159.

DUBE, S. C., *Indian Village,* Ithaca: Cornell University Press, 1955.

DUBE, S. C., "Ranking Castes in Telengana Villages, *Eastern Anthropologist,* 8 (1955), 182-190.

DUBE, S. C., "Social Structure and Change in Indian Peasant Communities," *Transactions of the Third World Congress of Sociology,* 2 (1956), 259-266.

DUMONT, Louis, *Hierarchy and Marriage Alliance in South Indian Kinship,* London: Occasional Papers of the Royal Anthropological Institute, 1957.

DUMONT, Louis " ' Tribe and Caste' in India," *Contributions to Indian Sociology,* 6 (1962), 120-122.

FREED, S. A., "An Objective Method for Determining the Collective Caste Hierarchy of an Indian Village," *American Anthropologist,* 65 (1963), 879-891.

GHURYE, G. S., *Caste and Class in India,* Bombay: Popular Book Depot, 1957.

GHURYE, G. S., *Caste, Class, and Occupation,* 4th Edition, Bombay: Popular Book Depot, 1961.

GIST, Noel P., "Caste in Transition: South India," *Phylon,* 15 (Second Quarter, 1954), 155-164.

GOUGH, Kathleen, "Brahman Kinship in a Tamil Village," *American Anthropologist,* 58 (October, 1956), 826-853.

GOUGH, Kathleen, "Criteria of Caste Ranking in South India," *Man in India,* 39 (1959), 15-17.

GOULD, H. A., "Castes, Outcastes, and the Sociology of Stratification," *International Journal of Comparative Sociology,* 1 (1960), 220-238.

GOULD, H. A., "The Adaptive Functions of Caste in Contemporary Indian Society," *Asian Survey,* 3 (1963), 427-438.

GREENE, Fred, *The Far East,* New York: Rinehart and Company, 1957.

GUHA, U., "Caste Among Rural Bengali Muslims," *Man in India,* 45 (1965), 167-169.

GUMPERZ, John J., "Dialect Differences and Social Stratification in a North Indian Village," *American Anthropologist,* 60 (August, 1958), 668-692.

GUPTA, B. K. D., "Caste-Mobility Among the Mahato of South Manbhum," *Man in India,* 42 (1962), 228-236.

GUPTA, Raghuraj, "Caste Ranking and Inter-Caste Relations among Muslims of a Village in Northwestern Uttar Pradesh," *Eastern Anthropologist,* 10 (1956), 30-42.

HANSEN, A. T., "Teaching About Caste in Intracaste and Cross-Caste Situations," *Human Organization,* 19 (Sum., 1960), 77-81.

HARDGRAVE, Robert L., "Caste in India: A Preface to the Elections," *Economic Weekly,* (November 21, 1964).

HARDGRAVE, Robert L., "Caste, Class, and Politics in Kerala," *Political Science Review,* 3 (May, 1964), 120-126.

HARDGRAVE, Robert L., *The Political Culture of a Community in Change: The Nadars of Tamilnard,* Berkeley: University of California Press, 1968.

HARDGRAVE, Robert L., "Varieties of Political Behavior Among Nadars of Tamilnard," *Asian Survey,* 6 (November, 1966), 614-621.

HARPER, E. B., "Ritual Pollution as an Integrator of Caste and Religion," *Journal of Asian Studies,* 23 (1964), 151-197.

HARRISON, Selig S., "Caste and the Andhra Communists," *American Political Science Review,* 50 (June, 1956), 378-404.

HORART, A. M., *Caste: A Comparative Study,* London: Methuen, 1950.

HSU, Francis L. K., *Clan, Caste, and Club,* Princeton: Van Nostrand, 1963.

HUTTON, John H., *Caste in India: Its Nature, Function, and Origins,* London: Oxford University Press, 1951.

ISAACS, Harold R., *India's Ex-Untouchables,* New York: Day, 1965.

JASHI, G. N., *The Constitution of India,* London: Macmillan, 1954.

KANNAN, C. T., "Intercaste Marriage in Bombay," *Sociological Bulletin,* 10 (September, 1961), 53-68.

KAPADIA, K. M., "Caste in Transition," *Sociological Bulletin,* 11 (March-September, 1962), 73-90.

KARVE, Irawati, *Hindu Society: An Interpretation,* Poona: Deccan College Postgraduate and Research Institute, 1961.

KHATRI, A. A., "Social Change in the Caste Hindu Family and its Possible Impact on Personality and Mental Health," *Sociological Bulletin,* 11 (March-September, 1962), 146-165.

KUMAR, D., "Caste and Landlessness in South India," *Comparative Studies in Society and History,* 4 (1962), 337-363.

KUPER, Hilda, "Changes in Caste of the South African Indian," in Barton M. Schwartz, editor, *Caste in Overseas Indian Communities,* San Francisco: Chandler, 1967.

LAMBERT, R. D., "Untouchability As a Social Problem: Theory and Research," *Sociological Bulletin,* 7 (1958), 55-61.

LEACH, E. R., editor, *Aspects of Caste in South India, Ceylon and Northwest Pakistan,* Cambridge: Cambridge University Press, 1962.

LEACH, E. R., "What Should We Mean by Caste?" in E. R. Leach, editor, *Aspects of Caste in South India, Ceylon and Northwest Pakistan,* Cambridge: Cambridge University Press, 1962.

LEWIS, Oscar, and V. Barnouw, "Caste and the Jajmani System in a North Indian Village," *Scientific Monthly,* 83 (1956), 66-79.

LEWIS, Oscar, *Village Life in Northern India,* Urbana: University of Illinois Press, 1958.

MADGE, C., "Caste and Community in India and Thailand—A Contrast," *Indian Journal of Adult Education,* 19 (1958), 127-147.

MAHAR, James M., *India: A Critical Bibliography,* Tucson: University of Arizona Press, 1964.

MAHAR, P. M., "A Multiple Scaling Technique for Caste Ranking," *Man in India,* 39 (1959), 127-147.

MAHAR, P. M., "A Ritual Pollution Scale for Ranking Hindu Castes," *Sociometry,* 23 (September, 1960), 292-306.

MAHAR, P. M., "Changing Caste Ideology in a North Indian Village," *Journal of Social Issues,* 14 (1958), 51-65.

MAHAR, P. M., "Changing Religious Practices of an Untouchable Caste," *Economic Development and Cultural Change,* 8 (April, 1960), 279-287.

MAJUMDAR, D., *Caste and Communication in an Indian Village,* Bombay: Asia Publishing House, 1958.

MAJUMDAR, D., *et al.,* "Inter-Caste Relations in Gohanakollan– A Village near Lucknow," *Eastern Anthropologist,* 8 (1955), 191-214.

MANDELBAUM, D. G., "Role Variation in Caste Relations," in T. N. Madan and G. Sarana, editors, *Indian Anthropology: Essays in Honor of D. N. Majumdar,* Bombay: Asia Publishing House, 1962.

MANN, H. H., "The Untouchable Classes of an Indian City," *Sociological Review,* 5 (1912), 42-55.

MARRIOT, McKim, *Caste Ranking and Community Structure in Five Regions of India and Pakistan,* Poona: Deccan College Postgraduate and Research Institute, 1960.

MARRIOT, McKim, "Interactional and Attributional Theories of Caste Ranking," *Man in India,* 39 (1959), 92-107.

MATHUR, K. S., "Caste and Occupation in a Malwa Village," *Eastern Anthropologist,* 12 (1958), 47-61.

MATHUR, K. S., "Caste and Occupation in a Malwa Village," *Eastern Anthropologist,* 12 (September-November, 1958), 47-61.

MAYER, Adrian C., *Caste and Kinship in Central India: A Village and Its Region,* Berkeley: University of California Press, 1960.

MAYER, Adrian C., "Introduction," in Barton M. Schwartz, editor, *Caste in Overseas Indian Communities,* San Francisco: Chandler, 1967.

MAYER, Adrian C., "Some Hierarchical Aspects of Caste," *Southwestern Journal of Anthropology,* 12 (1956), 117-144.

MAYER, Adrian C., "The Dominant Caste in a Region of Central India," *Southwestern Journal of Anthropology,* 14 (1958), 407-427.

MEHTA, S. K., "Patterns of Residence In Poona (India) by Income, Education, and Occupation (1937-65)," *American Journal of Sociology,* 73 (January, 1968), 496-508.

MILLER, Eric J., "Caste and Territory in Malabar," *American Anthropologist,* 56 (June, 1954), 410-420.

MILLER, F. Max, *The Laws of Manu,* London: Oxford University Press, 1886.

MISRA, B. B., *The Indian Middle Classes: Their Growth in Modern Times,* London: Oxford University Press, 1961.

MORAY, V. E., "The Patterns of Caste and Family in Wai

Taluka," *Journal of the University of Bombay,* 28 (1959), 74-75.

MORRIS, H. S., "Caste Among the Indians of Uganda," in Barton M. Schwartz, editor, *Caste in Overseas Indian Communities,* San Francisco: Chandler, 1967.

NADEL, S. F., "Caste and Government in Primitive Society," *Journal of the Anthropological Society of Bombay,* 8 (1954), 9-22.

NAIR, B. N., *The Dynamic Brahmin,* Bombay: Popular Book Depot, 1959.

NANAVATTY, M. C., "Casteism and Social Education: Role of the Social Education Worker," *Indian Journal of Adult Education,* 19 (1958), 47-61.

NANAVATTY, M. C., "Seminar on Casteism and Removal of Untouchability: A Review," *Indian Journal of Adult Education,* 16 (1955), 41-56.

NAYAR, Baldev Raj, *Minority Politics in the Punjab,* Princeton: Princeton University Press, 1966.

NEWELL, W. H., "Inter-Caste Marriage in Kugti Village, Uper Budl, Brahmour Tahsil, Chamba District, Miachel Pradesh, India," *Man,* 63 (1963), 55-57.

NIEHOFF, Arthur, "The Junction of Caste Among the Indians of the Oropuche Lagoon," in Barton M. Schwartz, editor, *Caste in Overseas Indian Communities,* San Francisco: Chandler, 1967.

NIMBARK, A., "Status Conflicts Within a Hindu Caste," *Social Forces,* 43 (October, 1964), 50-57.

OLCOTT, Mason, "The Caste System of India," *American Sociological Review,* 9 (December, 1944), 648-657.

O'MALLEY, L. S. S., *Indian Caste Customs,* London: Cambridge University Press, 1932.

ORENSTEIN, H., "Caste and the Concept of 'Moratha' in Maharashtra," *Eastern Anthropologist,* 16 (1963), 1-9.

ORENSTEIN, H., *Gaon: Conflict and Cohesion in an Indian Village,* Princeton: Princeton University Press, 1965.

ORENSTEIN, H., "The Structure of Hindu Caste Values: A Preliminary Study of Hierarchy and Ritual Defilement," *Ethnology,* 4 (January, 1965), 1-15.

ORENSTEIN, H., "Village, Caste, and the Welfare State," *Human Organization,* 22 (Spring, 1963), 83-89.

PATNAIK, N., "Caste and Occupation in Rural Orissa," *Man in India,* 34 (1954), 257-270.

PAULUS, Caleb R., "A Study of Social Stratification in Bangalore City," *Pacific Sociological Review,* 11 (Spring, 1968), 49-56.

POCOCK, David F., "Differences in East Africa: A Study of Caste and Religion in Indian Society," *Southwestern Journal of Anthropology,* 13 (Winter, 1957), 289-300.

POCOCK, David F., "Inclusion and Exclusion: A Process in the Caste System of Gujarat," *Southwestern Journal of Anthropology,* 13 (Spring, 1957), 19-31.

POCOCK, David F., "The Movement of Castes," *Man in India,* 79 (1955), 71-72.

PRABHU, P. N., *Hindu Social Organization,* Bombay: Popular Book Depot, 1954.

PRASAD, I., "A Brief Note on the Methodological Aspect of Studies in Caste Stereotypes," *Man in India,* 4 (1961), 204-214.

PUNDALIK, V. G. and S. S. Patwardhan, "A Note on the Behavior of the Caste in a Crisis-Situation," *Sociological Bulletin,* 11 (March-September, 1962), 68-72.

RATH, R. and N. C. Sircar, "Intercaste Relationship as Reflected in the Study of Attitudes and Opinions of Six Hindu Caste Groups," *Journal of Social Psychology,* 51 (February, 1960), 3-25.

ROSS, Aileen D., *et al.,* Symposium on Caste and Joint Family," *Sociological Bulletin,* 4 (September, 1955), 85-146.

ROSSER, Colin, "Social Mobility in the Newar Caste System," in Christoph von Furer-Haimendorf, editor, *Caste and Kin in Nepal, India and Ceylon,* Bombay: Asia Publishing House, 1966.

ROWE, William L., "Changing Rural Class Sturcture and the Jajmani System," *Human Organization,* 22 (Spring, 1963), 41-44.

RUDOLPH, L. I., "The Modernity of Traditions: The Democratic Incarnation of Castes in India," *American Political Science Review,* 59 (December, 1965), 975-989.

RUDOLPH, L. I. and S. Rudolph, "The Political Role of India's Caste Associations," *Pacific Affairs,* 33 (1960), 5-22.

RYAN, B., *Caste in Modern Ceylon: The Sinhalese System in Transition,* New Brunswick, New Jersey: Rutgers University Press, 1953.

SANGAVE, Vilas A., "Changing Pattern of Caste Organization in Kolhapur City," *Sociological Bulletin,* 11 (March-September, 1962), 36-61.

SARMA, J., "The Secular Status of Castes," *Eastern Anthropologist,* 12 (December, 1958-January, 1959), 87-106.

SCHWARTZ, Barton M., editor, *Caste in Overseas Indian Communities,* San Francisco: Chandler, 1967.

SCHWARTZ, Barton M., "Caste and Endogamy in Fiji," in Barton M. Schwartz, editor, *Caste in Overseas Indian Communities,* San Francisco: Chandler, 1967.

SCHWARTZ, Barton M., "The Failure of Caste in Trinidad," in Barton M. Schwartz, editor, *Caste in Overseas Indian Communities,* San Francisco: Chandler, 1967.

SHAH, B. V., "Gujarati College Students and Caste," *Sociological Bulletin,* 10 (March, 1961), 41-60.

SHARMA, K. N., "Occupational Mobility of Castes in a North Indian Village," *Southwestern Journal of Anthropology,* 17 (Summer, 1961), 146-164.

SILVERBERG, James, "Caste-Ascribed 'Status' Versus Caste-Irrelevant Roles," *Man in India,* 39 (1959), 148-162.

SIGNER, Philip, "Caste and Identity in Guyana," in Barton M. Schwartz, editor, *Caste in Overseas Indian Communities,* San Francisco: Chandler, 1967.

SINGH, Kailash K., *Inter-Caste Tension in Two Villages in North India,* Ithaca, New York: Cornell University Press, 1957.

SINHA, G. S., and R. C. Sinha, "Exploration in Caste Stereotypes," *Sociological Bulletin,* 46 (September, 1967), 42-47.

SILVERTSEN, Dagfinn, *When Caste Barriers Fall: A Study of Social and Economic Change in a South Indian Village,* New York: Humanities Press, 1963.

SMITH, Raymond T. and Chandra Jayawardena, "Caste and Social Status Among the Indians of Gyana," in Barton M. Schwartz, editor, *Caste in Overseas Indian Communities,* San Francisco: Chandler, 1967.

SMYTHE, H. H. and T. Gershuny, "Jewish Castes in Cochin, India," *Sociology and Social Research,* 41 (1956), 108-111.

SOVANI, N. V. and Kusum Pradham, "Occupational Mobility in Poona City Between Three Generations," *Indian Economic Review,* 2 (1955), 23-36.

SPECKMAN, Johan D., "The Caste System and the Hindustani Group in Surinam," in Barton M. Schwartz, editor, *Caste in Overseas Indian Communities,* San Francisco: Chandler, 1967.

SRINIVAS, M. N., "A Note of Sanskritization and Westernization," *Far Eastern Quarterly,* 15 (1956), 481-496.

SRINIVAS, M. N., *et al.,* "Caste: A Trend Report and Bibliography," *Current Sociology,* 8 (1959), 133-184.

SRINIVAS, M. N., "Caste in Modern India," *Journal of Asian Studies,* 16 (1957), 529-548.

SRINIVAS, M. N., *Caste in Modern India and Other Essays,* Bombay: Asia Publishing House, 1962.

SRINIVAS, M. N., editor, *India's Villages,* Calcutta: West Bengal Government Press, 1955.

SRINIVAS, M. N., *Religion and Society Among the Coorgs of South India,* London: Oxford University Press, 1952.

SRINIVAS, M. N., *Social Change in Modern India,* Berkeley: University of California Press, 1966.

SRINIVAS, M. N., "The Dominant Caste in Rampura," *American Anthropologist,* 61 (February, 1959), 1-16.

SRIVASTAVA, Ram P., "Tribe-Caste Mobility in India and the Case of Kumaon Bhatias," in Christoph von Furer-Haimendorf, editor, *Caste and Kin in Nepal, India and Ceylon,* Bombay: Asia Publishing House, 1966.

STEVENSON, H. N. C., "Status Evaluation in the Hindu Caste System," *Journal of the Royal Anthropological Institute,* 84 (1954), 45-65.

STRIZOWER, S., "Jews as an Indian Caste," *Jewish Journal of Sociology,* 1 (April, 1959), 43-57.

STROUP, H., "The Caste System in Hinduism," *Journal of Human Relations,* 5 (1947), 64-79.

THAKKAR, K. K., "The Problem of Casteism and Untouchability," *Indian Journal of Social Work,* 17 (1956), 44-49.

THOMAS, P. J. and K. C. Ramakrishnan, editors, *Some South Indian Villages Resurveyed,* Madras, India: 1940.

VENKATARAMAN, S. R., "Seminar on Casteism and Untouchability--Report," *Indian Journal of Social Work,* 16 (1956), 305-309.

VIDYARTHI, L. P., "The Extensions of an Indian Priestly Caste," *Man in India,* 39 (1959), 28-35.

VON FURER-HAMIMENDORF, Christoph, "Caste Concepts and Status Distinctions in Buddhist Communities of Western Nepal," in Christoph Von Fuer-Haimendorf, editor, *Caste and Kin in Nepal, India and Ceylon,* Bombay: Asia Publishing House, 1966.

VON FURER-HAIMENDORF, Christoph, editor, *Caste and Kin in Nepal, India and Ceylon: Anthropological Studies in Hindu-Buddist Contact Zones,* Bombay: Asia Publishing House, 1966.

VON FURER-HAIMENDORF, Christoph, "Caste in the Multi-

Ethnic Society of Nepal," *Contributions to Indian Sociology,* 4 (1940), 12-32.

VON FURER-HAIMENDORF, Christoph, "Status Differences in a High Hindu Caste of Nepal," *Eastern Anthropologist,* 12 (1959), 223-233.

VON FURER-HAIMENDORF, Christoph, "Unity and Diversity in Chetri Caste of Nepal," in Christoph Von Furer-Haimendorf, editor, *Caste and Kin in Nepal, India and Ceylon,* Bombay: Asia Publishing House, 1966.

WATSON, James B., "Caste as a Form of Acculturation," *Southwestern Journal of Anthropology,* 19 (1963), 356-379.

WEBER, Max, "The Development of Caste," in Reinhard Bendix and Seymour M. Lipset, editors, *Class, Status, and Power,* revised edition, New York: Free Press, 1966.

WEBER, Max, *The Religion of India: The Sociology of Hinduism and Buddhism,* translated and edited by Hans H. Gerth and Don Martindale, New York: Free Press.

WOOD, E., "Caste Ranking," *Man in India,* 42 (1962), 247-249.

YALMAN, N., "On the Purity of Women in the Castes of Ceylon and Malabar," *Journal of the Royal Anthropological Institute of Great Britain and Ireland,* 93 (1963), 25-58.

YALMAN, N., "The Flexibility of Caste Principles in a Kandyan Community," in E. R. Leach, editor, *Aspects of Caste in South India, Ceylon and Northwest Pakistan,* Cambridge: Cambridge University Press, 1962.

ZINKIN, Taya, *Caste Today,* London: Oxford University Press, 1962.

Asia, Excluding China, Japan, The Soviet Union and Specific Treatments of Caste

ABRAMSON, J. H., "Emotional Disorder, Status Inconsistency and Migration: A Health Questionnaire Survey in Jerusalem," *Milbank Memorial Fund Quarterly,* 44 (January, 1966), 23-44.

ARMSTRONG, L. and G. Hirabayoshi, "Social Differentiation in Selected Lebanese Villages," *American Sociological Review,* 21 (1956), 425-434.

AURBACH, Herbert A., "Social Stratification in the Collective Agricultural Settlements in Israel," *Rural Sociology,* 18 (March, 1953), 25-34.

BAALI, Fuad, "Educational Aspirations Among College Girls in Iraq," *Sociology and Social Research,* 51 (July, 1967), 485-493.

BAALI, Fuad, *Relation of the People to the Land in Southern Iraq,* Gainesville: University of Florida Press, 1966.

BEN-DAVID, J., "The Rise of a Salaried Professional Class in Israel," *Transactions of the Third World Congress of Sociology,* 3 (1956), 302-310.

BETEILLE, André,*Class, Status, and Power: Changing Patterns of Stratification in a Tanjore Village,* Berkeley: University of California Press, 1965.

BONNE, Alfred, "The Adjustment of Oriental Immigrants to Industrial Employment in Israel," *International Social Science Bulletin,* 8 (1956), 12-35.

BONNE, Alfred, "Trends in Occupational Structure and Distribution of Income Among the Jewish Population in Israel," *Jewish Journal of Sociology,* 1 (1959), 242-249.

CHANDRASEKARAN, C. and M. V. George, "Mechanisms Underlying the Differences in Fertility Patterns of Bengalee Women from Three Socio-Economic Groups," *Milbank Memorial Fund Quarterly,* 40 (January, 1962), 59-89.

COOK, David R., "Prestige of Occupations in India," *Psychological Studies,* 7 (January, 1962), 31-37.

CRESSEY, Paul F., "Ecological Organization of Rangoon," *Sociology and Social Research* 40 (1956), 166-169.

DRIVER, Edwin, "Family Structure and Socioeconomic Status in Central India," *Sociological Bulletin,* 11 (March-September, 1962), 112-120.

D'SOUZA, Victor S., "Restriction on Admissions to Higher Education: The Criterion of Selection," *Sociological Bulletin,* 10 (March, 1961), 82-91.

EISENSTADT, S. N., "The Place of Elites and Primary Groups in the Absorption of New Immigrants in Israel," *American Journal of Sociology,* 57 (November, 1951), 222-231.

ETZIONI, Amitai, "Functional Differentiation of Elites in the Kibbutz," *American Journal of Sociology,* 64 (March, 1959), 476-487.

EVERS, Hans-Dieter, "The Formation of a Social Class Structure: Urbanization, Bureaucratization and Social Mobility in Thailand," *American Sociological Review,* 31 (August, 1966), 480-488.

FAIGIN, Helen, "Social Behavior of Young Children in the Kibbutz," *Journal of Abnormal and Social Psychology*, 56 (1958), 117-129.

FREY, Frederick W., "Surveying Peasant Attitudes in Turkey," *Public Opinion Quarterly*, 27 (Fall, 1963), 335-355.

GASTIL, Raymond, D., "Middle Class Impediments to Iranian Modernization," *Public Opinion Quarterly*, 22 (Fall, 1958), 325-329.

GIST, Noel P., "The Ecology of Bangalore, India: An East West Comparison," *Social Forces*, 35 (1957), 356-365.

GIST, Noel P., "Educational Differentials in South India," *Journal of Educational Sociology*, 28 (March, 1955), 315-324.

GUMPERZ, John J., "Dialect Differences and Social Stratification in a North Indian Village," *American Anthropologist*, 60 (August, 1958), 668-682.

HAAS, Mary R., "The Declining Descent Rule for Rank in Thailand: A Correction," *American Anthropologist*, 53 (1951), 585-587.

HANKS, L. M., Jr., "Merit and Power in the Thai Social Order," *American Anthropologist*, 64 (December, 1962), 1247-1261.

HAWLEY, Amos H., "Some Observations on the Land Use Patterns in Manila," in *Papers in Demography and Public Administration*, revised edition, Manila: Institute of Public Administration, University of the Philippines, 1954.

HIRABAYASHI, Gordon K. and Lincoln Armstrong, "Social Structure and Differentiation in Rural Lebanon," *Transactions of the Third World Congress of Sociology*, 3 (1956), 349-356.

KALELKAR, K., "The Backward Classes Problems," *Careers and Courses*, 5 (September, 1953), 805-807. Deals with India.

KERSTIENS, T., *The New Elite in Asia and Africa: A Comparative Study of Indonesia and Ghana*, New York: Praeger, 1966.

KRISHNAN, B., "Regional Influences on Occupational Preferences," *Psychological Studies*, 6 (July, 1961), 66-70. Deals with India.

KRISHNAN, B., "Social Prestige of Occupations," *Journal of Vocational and Educational Guidance* (India), 3 (August, 1956), 18-22.

MATRAS, Judah, "Some Data on Intergenerational Occupational Mobility in Israel," *Population Studies*, 17 (November, 1963), 167-186.

MEHTA, Surinder K., "Patterns of Residence in Poona (India) by

ASIA

Income, Education, and Occupation, (1937-1965), *American Journal of Sociology,* 73 (January, 1968), 496-508.

MISRA, B. B., *The Indian Middle Classes,* London: Oxford University Press, 1960.

MUKERJEE, Radhakamal, "Social Structure and Stratification of the Indian Nation," *Transactions of the Second World Congress of Sociology,* 2 (1954), 16-25.

OSHIMA, H., "The International Comparison of Size Distribution of Family Income with Special Reference to Asia," *Review of Economics and Statistics,* 44 (August, 1962), 439-445.

PHILLIPS, Herbert, "Personality and Social Structure in a Siamese Community, *Human Organization,* 22 (Summer, 1963), 105-108.

POTI, S. J. and D. Subodh, "Pilot Study on Social Mobility and its Association with Fertility in West Bengal in 1956," *Artha Vijnana,* 2 (June, 1960), 85-95.

RIELE, J. R., "Fertility Differentials in India—Evidence from a Rural Background," *Milbank Memorial Fund Quarterly,* 41 (April, 1963), 183-199.

ROBINS, Robert S., "Political Elite Formation in Rural India: The Uttar Pradesh *Panchayat* Elections of 1949, 1956, and 1961," *Journal of Politics,* 29 (November, 1967), 838-860.

ROSENFELD, Eva, "Social Stratification in a Classless Society," *American Sociological Review,* 16 (1951), 766-774. Deals with Israel.

ROWE, W. L., "Changing Rural Class Structure and the Jajmani System," *Human Organization,* 22 (1963), 41-44.

SCHWARTZ, Richard D., "Functional Alternatives to Inequality," *American Sociological Review,* 20 (August, 1955), 424-430. Deals with Israel.

SHOLAM, Shlomo and Meir Horav, "'B' Nei Tavim"—Middle and Upper Class Delinquency in Israel, *Sociology and Social Research,* 48 (July, 1964), 454-468.

SINGH, Mohinder, *The Depressed Classes: Their Economic and Social Conditions,* Bombay: Hind Kitabs, 1947. Deals with India.

SINHA, B., "Disintegration of the Middle Class: Another Indication of West Bengal's Decay," *Modern Review,* 93 (March, 1953), 189-194.

SINHA, J. N., "Differential Fertility and Family Limitation in an Urban Community of Uttar Pradesh," *Population Studies,* 11 (November, 1957), 157-169.

SKINNER, G. William, *Leadership and Power in the Chinese Community of Thailand,* Ithaca: Cornell University Press, 1958.

SOELAEMAN, Soemardi, "Some Aspects of the Social Origins of Indonesian Political Decision Makers," *Transactions of the Third World Congress of Sociology,* 3 (1956), 338-348.

SPIRO, Melford E., *Children of the Kibbutz: A Study in Child Training and Personality,* New York: Schocken, 1958.

SPIRO, Melford E., *Kibbutz—Venture in Utopia,* New York, Schocken, 1956.

THOMAS, Murray, "Occupational Prestige: Indonesia and America," *Personnel and Guidance Journal,* 41 (January, 1963), 430-434.

THOMAS, Murray and W. Surachmad, "Social Class Differences in Mothers' Expectations for Children in Indonesia," *Journal of Social Psychology,* 57 (August, 1962), 303-307.

TIRYAKIN, Edward A., "The Prestige Evaluation of Occupations in an Underdeveloped Country: The Philippines," *American Journal of Sociology,* 63 (January, 1958), 390-399.

VAN NIEL, R., *The Emergence of the Modern Indonesian Elite,* The Hague: Van Hoewe, 1960.

WEINBERG, A. A., "Acculturation and Integration of Immigrants in Israel," *International Social Science Bulletin,* 5 (1953) 702-710.

WINDLE, Charles and Georges Sabagh, "Social Status and Family Size of Iranian Industrial Employees," *Milbank Memorial Fund Quarterly,* 41 (October, 1963), 436-443.

WOOD, Arthur L., "A Socio-Structural Analysis of Murder, Suicide, and Economic Crime in Ceylon," *American Sociological Review,* 26 (October, 1961), 744-753.

YAP, Pow Meng, *Suicide in Hong Kong,* Hong Kong: Hong Kong University Press, 1958.

ZWEIG, Ferdinand, "Working Classes and the Social Framework in Israel," *Sociological Review,* 5 (December, 1957), 191-206.

Africa

ABU-LUGHOD, Janet, "The Emergence of Differential Fertility in Urban Egypt," *Milbank Memorial Fund Quarterly,* 43 (April, 1965), 235-253.

APTER, David E., "Nkrumah, Charisma, and the Coup," *Daedelus,* 97 (Summer, 1968), 757-792.

BASCOM, William R., "Social Status, Wealth and Individual Differences Among the Yoruba," *American Anthropologist,* 53 (October-December, 1951), 490-505.

BLACKER, J. G. C., "Population Growth and Differential Fertility in Zanzibar Protectorate," *Population Studies,* 15 (March, 1962), 258-266.

BRETTON, Henry L., *Power and Stability in Nigeria,* New York: Praeger, 1962.

CLIGNET, Remi and Philip Foster, *The Fortunate Few: A Study of Secondary Schools and Students in the Ivory Coast,* Evanston: Northwestern University Press, 1966.

CODERE, Helen, "Power in Ruanda," *Anthropologica,* 4 (1962), 42-85.

ELKAN, Walter, *Migrants and Proletarians: Urban Labour in the Economic Development of Uganda,* New York: Oxford University Press, 1960.

FALLERS, Lloyd A., "Social Stratification and Economic Processes in Africa," in Melville J. Herskovits and Mitchell Harwitz, editors, *Economic Transition in Africa,* Evanston: Northwestern University Press, 1964.

FOSTER, Philip J., "Ethnicity and the Schools in Ghana," *Comparative Education Review,* 6 (October, 1963, 127-135.

FOSTER, Philip J., "Secondary Schooling and Social Mobility in a West African Nation," *Sociology of Education,* 37 (Winter, 1963), 150-171.

FOSTER, Philip J., "Secondary School Leavers in Ghana: Expectations and Reality," *Harvard Educational Review,* 34 (Fall, 1964), 537-558.

FOSTER, Philip J., "Status, Power and Education in a Traditional Community," *School Review,* 72 (Summer, 1967), 158-182.

FRAENKEL, Merran, *Tribe and Class in Monrovia,* New York: Oxford University Press, 1965.

FRAZIER, E. Franklin, "Education and the African Elite," *Transactions of the Third World Congress of Sociology,* 5 (1956), 90-96.

GHAI, Dharam P., editor, *Portrait of a Minority: Asians in East Africa,* New York: Oxford University Press, 1966.

GOLDTHORPE, J. E., "Social Class and Education in East Africa," *Transactions of the Third World Congress of Sociology,* 5 (1956), 1115-1122.

KERSTIENS, T., *The New Elite in Asia and Africa: A Comparative Study of Indonesia and Ghana,* New York: Praeger, 1966.

KUPER, Leo, *An African Bourgeoisie: Race, Class, and Politics in South Africa,* New Haven: Yale University Press, 1965.

KUPER, Leo, "The South African Native: Caste, Proletariat, or Race?" *Social Forces,* 28 (December, 1949), 146-153.

MESSING, Simon D., "Group Therapy and Social Status in the Zar Cult of Ethiopia," *American Anthropologist,* 60 (December, 1958), 1120-1126.

MITCHELL, J. Clyde and A. L. Epstein, "Occupational Prestige and Social Status Among Urban Africans in Northern Rhodesia," *Africa,* 29 (January, 1959), 22-40.

RICHMOND, Anthony H., "Education, Social Mobility and Racial Relations in the Union of South Africa," *Transactions of the Third World Congress of Sociology,* 5 (1956), 105-114.

SEPMEYER, Inez and Martena Sasnett, *Educational Systems of Africa,* Berkeley: University of California Press, 1966.

SMITH, M. G., "Kebbi and Hausa Stratification," *British Journal of Sociology,* 12 (March, 1961), 52-64.

SMITH, M. G., "The Hausa System of Social Status," *Africa,* 29 (July, 1959), 239-251.

SMYTHE, Hugh H., "Nigerian Elite: Role of Education," *Sociology and Social Research,* 45 (October, 1960), 71-73.

SMYTHE, Hugh H., "Social Stratification in Nigeria," *Social Forces,* 37 (December, 1958), 168-171.

SMYTHE, Hugh H. and Mabel Smythe, "Africa's New Class," *Queen's Quarterly,* 68 (Summer, 1960), 225-231.

SMYTHE, Hugh H. and Mabel Smythe, "The Nigerian Elite: Some Observations," *Sociology and Social Research,* 44 (September-October, 1959), 42-45.

SMYTHE, Hugh H. and Mabel Smythe, "The Non-African Minority in Modern Africa: Social Status," *Sociology and Social Research,* 45 (April, 1961), 310-315.

UNESCO, *Apartheid: Its Effects on Education, Science, Culture and Information, Paris:* UNESCO, 1967.

UNESCO, "Symposium on African Elites," *International Social Science Bulletin,* 8 (1956), 413-488.

VAN DEN BERGHE, Pierre, *South Africa: A Study in Conflict,* Middletown: Wesleyan University Press, 1965.

VAN DER MERWE, Hendrick W., "Social Stratification in a Cape Colored Community," *Sociology and Social Research,* 46 (April, 1962), 302-311.

AFRICA

XYDIAS, N., "Prestige of Occupations," in C. Daryl Forde, editor, *Social Implications of Industrialization and Urbanization in Africa South of the Sahara,* Paris: UNESCO, Tension and Technology Series, 1956.

YELD, E. R., "Islam and Social Stratification in Northern Nigeria," *British Journal of Sociology,* 11 (June, 1960), 112-128.

Latin America

ADAMS, Richard N., "A Change from Caste to Class in a Peruvian Sierra Town," *Social Forces,* 31 (March, 1953), 238-244.

ADAMS, Richard N., *The Second Sowing: Power and Secondary Development in Latin America,* San Francisco: Chandler, 1967.

ADAMS, Richard N., "Cultural Components of Central America," *American Anthropologist,* 58 (October, 1956), 881-907.

ANDRESKI, Stanislav, *Parasitism and Subversion: The Case of Latin America,* New York: Pantheon, 1967.

BASTIDE, Roger, "The Negro in Latin America," *International Social Science Bulletin,* 4 (1952), 435-441.

BEALS, Ralph, "Social Stratification in Latin America," *American Journal of Sociology,* 58 (November, 1953), 327-339.

BEHRENDT, Richard R. W., "Factors that Affect the Present Economic Status of the Indian in Latin America," *America Indigena,* 10 (1950), 195-214.

BELL, Wendell, editor, *The Democratic Revolution in the West Indies: Studies in Nationalism, Leadership, and Belief in Progress,* Cambridge: Schenkman, 1967.

BERGSTEN, D. F., "Social Mobility and Economic Development: The Vital Parameters of the Bolivian Revolution," *Journal of Inter-American Studies,* 6 (1964), 367-375.

BIERSTEDT, Robert, "Power and Social Class," in Anthony Leeds, editor, *Seminar on Social Structure, Stratification and Mobility with Special Reference to Latin America,* Washington, D. D.: Pan American Union, 1966.

BORAH, Woodrow, "Race and Class in Mexico," *Pacific Historical Review,* 23 (1954), 331-342.

BOUGUIGNON, E. E., "Class Structure and Acculturation in Haiti," *Ohio Journal of Science,* 52 (1952), 317-320.

BRAITHWAITE, Lloyd, "Social Stratification in Trinidad," *Social and Economic Studies,* 2 (1953), 5-175.

BRANDENBURG, Frank, *The Making of Modern Mexico,* Englewood Cliffs, New Jersey: Prentice-Hall, 1965.

BROOM, Leonard, "Social Differentiation of Jamaica," *American Sociological Review,* 19 (April, 1954), 115-125.

BUCHANAN, William and Hadley Cantril, *How Nations See Each Other,* Urbana: University of Illinois Press, 1953.

BUCKLEY, W., "Continuity and Discontinuity in Social Classes," in Anthony Leeds, editor, *Seminar on Social Structure, Stratification and Mobility with Special Reference to Latin America,* Washington, D. C.: Pan American Union, 1966.

BURMA, John H., *Social Class in Latin America,* Grinnell, Iowa: 1959.

BURNS, Hobert W., "Social Class and Education in Latin America," *Comparative Education Review,* 6 (1963), 230-237.

CAPLOW, Theodore, "The Social Ecology of Guatamala City," *Social Forces,* 28 (December, 1949), 113-133.

CARLETON, Robert O., "Fertility Trends and Differentials in Latin America," *Milbank Memorial Fund Quarterly,* 43 (October, 1965), 15-35.

COLLINS, Sydney, "Social Mobility in Jamacia, with Reference to Rural Communities and the Teaching Profession," *Transactions of the Third World Congress of Sociology,* 3 (1956), 267-276.

COMBS, Jerry W., Jr. and Kingsley Davis, "Differential Fertility in Puerto Rico," *Population Studies,* 5 (November, 1951), 104-116.

COMHAIRE-SYLVAN, J. and S. Comhaire-Sylvan, "Urban Stratification in Haiti," *Social and Economic Studies,* 8 (1959), 179-189.

CROWLEY, D. J., "Plural and Differential Acculturation in Trinidad," *American Anthropologist,* 59 (October, 1957), 817-824.

DOTSON, Floyd and Lillian Ota Dotson, "Ecological Trends in the City of Guadalajara, Mexico," *Social Forces,* 32 (May, 1954), 367-374.

ELLIS, Robert A., "Color and Class in a Jamaican Market Town," *Sociology and Social Research,* 41 (May-June, 1957), 345-360.

ELMER, M. C., "The Growth of a Middle Class in Venezuela," *Social Science,* 38 (1963), 145-147.

FELDT, Allan G. and Robert H. Weller, "The Balance of Social, Economic, and Demographic Change in Puerto Rico–1950-60," *Demography,* 2 (1965), 475-489.

FORM, William H. and William V. D'Antonio, "Integration and Cleavage Among Community Influentials in Two Border Cities," *American Sociological Review,* 24 (December, 1959), 804-814.

GANON, Issaac, "Social Stratification in Uruguay," *Transactions of the Second World Congress of Sociology,* 2 (1954), 26-33.

GERMANI, Gino, "Social Stratification and Social Mobility in Four Latin American Cities: A Note on the Research Design," *America Latina,* 6 (1963), 91-94.

GOLDRICH, Daniel, *Sons of the Establishment: Elite Youth in Panama and Costa Rica,* Chicago: Rand McNally, 1966.

GONZALEZ-CASONOVA, Pablo, "Dynamics of the Class Structure (in Mexico)," in Joseph Kahl, editor, *Comparative Perspectives on Stratification,* Boston: Little, Brown, and Co., 1968.

HANSEN, Asael T., "The Ecology of a Latin-American City," in Edward B. Reuter, editor, *Race and Culture Contacts,* New York: McGraw-Hill, 1934.

HARRIS, M., "The Classification of Stratified Groups," in Anthony Leeds, editor, *Seminar on Social Structure, Stratification and Mobility with Special Reference to Latin America,* Washington, D. C.: Pan American Union, 1966.

HAVIGHURST, Robert J., "Education, Social Mobility, and Social Change in Four Societies: Great Britain, U. S. A., Brazil, Australia," *International Review of Education,* 4 (1958), 167-185.

HAVIGHURST, Robert J., "Secondary Schooling and Socio-Economic Structure in Brazil," *Social and Economic Studies,* 14 (1965), 106-117.

HAWTHORN, Harry B. and Audrey E. Hawthorn, "The Shape of a City: Some Observations on Sucre, Bolivia," *Sociology and Social Research,* 33 (November-December, 1948), 87-91.

HAWTHORN, Harry B. and Audrey E. Hawthorn, "Stratification in a Latin American City," *Social Forces,* 27 (October, 1948), 19-29.

HAYNER, Norman S., "Mexico City: Its Growth and Configuration," *American Journal of Sociology,* 50 (January, 1945), 295-304.

HAYNER, Norman S., "Oaxaca: City of Old Mexico," *Sociology and Social Research,* 29 (November-December), 1944, 87-95.

HERMANN, Lucille, "The Middle Class in Guaratingueta," *Economic Development and Cultural Change,* 2 (1953), 83-108.

HILL, Reuben, J. M. Stycos, and K. W. Back, *The Family and Population Control: A Puerto Rican Experiment in Social Change,*

Chapel Hill: University of North Carolina Press, 1959.

HOETINK, H., *The Two Variants in Carribbean Race Relations: A Contribution to the Sociology of Segmented Societies,* New York: Oxford University Press, 1967.

HOYT, Homer, "The Residential and Retail Patterns of Leading Latin American Citles," *Land Economics,* 39 (1963).

HUMPHREY, Norman D., "Social Stratification in a Mexican Town," *Southwestern Journal of Anthropology,* 5 (Sum, 1949), 138-146.

HUTCHINSON, Bertram, "Class Self-Assessment in a Rio de Janeiro Population," *America Latina,* 6 (1963), 53-64.

HUTCHINSON, Bertram, "Fertility, Social Mobility and Urban Migration in Brazil," *Population Studies,* 14 (March, 1961), 182-189.

HUTCHINSON, Bertram, "Social Grading of Occupations in Brazil," *British Journal of Sociology,* 8 (June, 1957), 176-189.

HUTCHINSON, Bertram, "Social Mobility Rates in Buenos Aires, Montevideo, and Sao Paulo: A Preliminary Comparison," *America Latina,* 5 (1962), 3-20.

HUTCHINSON, Bertram, "Urban Mobility Rates in Brazil Related to Migration and Changing Occupational Structure," *America Latina,* 6 (1963), 47-60.

IANNI, Octavio, "Race and Class," *Educacao e Ciencias Sociais,* 7 (1962), 88-111.

IUTAKA, Sugiyama, "Social Status and Illness in Urban Brazil," *Milbank Memorial Fund Quarterly,* 44 (April, 1966), 97-110.

JAFFE, A. J., *People, Jobs and Economic Development: A Case History of Puerto Rico,* New York: Free Press, 1959.

JOHNSON, John J., "Middle Groups in National Politics in Latin America," *Hispanic American Historical Review,* 37 (1957), 313-329.

JOHNSON, John J., *Political Change in Latin America: The Emergence of the Middle Sectors,* Stanford, California: Stanford University Press, 1958.

JOHNSON, John J., "The Political Role of the Latin American Middle Sectors," *Annals of American Academy of Political and Social Science,* 334 (1961), 20-29.

KAHL, Joseph A., *Comparative Perspectives on Stratification: Mexico, Great Britain, Japan,* Boston: Little, Brown, and Co., 1968.

KAHL, Joseph A., "Social Stratification and Values in Metropoli and Provinces; Brazil and Mexico," *America Latina,* 8 (January-March, 1965), 25-35.

KAHL, Joseph A., "Three Types of Mexican Industrial Workers," *Economic Development and Cultural Change,* 8 (January, 1960), 164-169.

KLAPP, Orrin, and L. Vincent Padgett, "Power Structure and Decision-Making in a Mexican Border City," *American Journal of Sociology,* 65 (January, 1960), 400-406.

KNOWLTON, Clark S., "A Study of Social Mobility Among the Syrian and Lebanese Community of Sao Paulo," *Rocky Mountain Social Science Journal,* 2 (October, 1965), 174-192.

LEEDS, Anthony, editor, *Seminar on Social Structure, Stratification and Mobility with Special Reference to Latin America,* Washington, D. C.: Pan American Union, 1966.

LEEDS, Anthony, "Some Problems in the Analysis of Class and Social Order," in Anthony Leeds, editor, *Seminar on Social Structure, Stratification and Mobility with Special Reference to Latin America,* Washington, D. C.: Pan American Union, 1966.

LEEDS, Anthony, "Brazilian Careers and Social Structure: An Evolutionary and Case Study," *American Anthropologist,* 66 (December, 1964), 1321-1347.

LEONARD, Olen E., "La Paz, Bolivia: Its Population and Growth," *American Sociological Review,* 13 (August, 1948), 448-454.

LEONARD, Olen E. and Charles P. Loomis, editors, *Readings in Latin American Social Organizations and Institutions,* East Lansing: Michigan State University Press, 1953.

LEWIS, Oscar, *The Children of Sanchez,* New York: Random House, 1961.

LEWIS, Oscar, *Five Families: Mexican Case Studies in the Culture of Poverty,* New York: Basic Books, 1959.

LEWIS, Oscar, *La Vida: A Puerto Rican Family in the Culture of Poverty—San Juan and New York,* New York: Random House, 1966.

LEWIS, Oscar and Ruth Lewis, "A Day in the Life of a Mexican Peasant Family," *Marriage and Family Living,* 18 (February, 1956), 3-13.

LEYBURN, James G., *The Haitian People,* New Haven: Yale University Press, 1966.

LIPSET, Seymour Martin and Aldo Solari, editors, *Elites in Latin America;* New York: Oxford University Press, 1967.

LOBB, John, "Caste and Class in Haiti," *American Journal of Sociology,* 46 (July, 1940), 23-34.

LONGMORE, T. Wilson, "A Matrix Approach to the Analysis of

Rank and Status in a Community in Peru," *Sociometry,* 11 (August, 1948), 192-206.

LOOMIS, Charles P. and Reed M. Powell, "Sociometric Analysis of Class Status in Rural Costa Rica—A Peasant Community Compared with an Hacienda Community," *Sociometry,* 12 (February, 1949), 144-157.

LOOMIS, Charles P. and J. C. McKinney, "Systemic Differences between Latin American Communities of Family Farms and Large Estates," *American Journal of Sociology,* 61 (March, 1956), 404-412.

MacGAFFEY, Wyatt, "Social Structure and Mobility in Cuba," *Anthropological Quarterly,* 34 (1961), 94-109.

MAU, James A., Richard J. Hill, and Wendell Bell, "Scale Analysis of Status Perception and Status Attitude in Jamaica and the United States," *Pacific Sociological Review,* 4 (Spring, 1961), 33-40.

MAYNITY, R., "Methodological Problems in the Study of Stratification," in Anthony Leeds, editor, *Seminar on Social Structure, Stratification and Mobility with Special Reference to Latin America,* Washington, D. C.: Pan American Union, 1966.

McGINN, Noel F., "Marriage and Family in Middle-Class Mexico," *Journal of Marriage and the Family,* 28 (August, 1966), 305-313.

MOREIRA, J. Roberto, "Rural Education and Socioeconomic Development in Brazil," *Rural Sociology,* 25 (March, 1960), 38-50.

MOREIRA, J. Roberto, "Some Social Aspects of Brazilian Education," *Comparative Education Review,* 4 (October, 1960), 93-97.

MORSE, Richard M., "Latin American Cities: Aspects of Function and Structure," *Comparative Studies in Society and History,* 4 (July, 1962), 473-493.

OBERG, K., "Some Historical Aspects of Rural to Urban Class Conversion," in Anthony Leeds, editor, *Seminar on Social Structure, Stratification and Mobility with Special Reference to Latin America,* Washington, D. C.: Pan American Union, 1966.

OXAAL, Ivar, *Black Intellectuals Come to Power: The Rise of Creole Nationalism in Trinidad and Tobago,* Cambridge: Schenkman, 1967.

PETERSON, Robert L., "Social Structure and the Political Process in Latin America: A Methodological Re-examination," *Western Political Quarterly,* 16 (December, 1963), 885-896.

PETRAS, James and Maurice Zeitlin, "Miners and Agrarian Radicalism," *American Sociological Review,* 32 (August, 1967), 578-586.

PIERSON, Donald, *Negroes in Brazil: A Study of Race Contact at Bahia,* Carbondale: Southern Illinois University Press, 1967.

PIKE, F. B., "Aspects of Class Relations in Chile," *Hispanic American Historical Review,* 43 (1963), 14-33.

PINTO, L. A. Costa, "Social Stratification in Brazil: A General Survey of Some Recent Changes," *Transactions of the Third World Congress of Sociology,* 3 (1956), 54-65.

RAINWATER, Lee, "Marital Sexuality in Four Cultures of Poverty," *Journal of Marriage and the Family,* 26 (November, 1964), 457-466.

REED, Nelson, *The Caste War of Yucatan,* Stanford: Stanford University Press, 1964.

RIPPY, J. Fred, *Latin America: A Modern History,* Ann Arbor: University of Michigan Press, 1958.

ROBERTS, R. E. T., "Comparison of Ethnic Relations in Two Guatemalan Communities," *Acta Americana,* 6 (1958), 135-151.

ROEMER, Milton I., "Medical Care and Social Class in Latin America," *Milbank Memorial Fund Quarterly,* 42 (July, 1964, Part 1), 54-64.

ROSEN, Bernard, "Socialization and Achievement Motivation in Brazil," *American Sociological Review,* 27 (1962), 612-624.

ROSEN, Bernard, "The Achievement Syndrome and Economic Growth in Brazil," *Social Forces,* 42 (March, 1964), 341-354.

ROSENTHAL, Celia Stopnicka, "Lower Class Family Organization on the Carribean Coast of Columbia," *Pacific Sociological Review,* 3 (Spring, 1960), 12-17.

SARIOLA, S., *Social Class and Social Mobility in a Costa Rican Town,* Turrialba: Inter-American Institute of Agricultural Sciences, 1954.

SIMPSON, George E., "Ethnic Groups, Social Mobility and Power in Latin America," *Seminar on Social Structure, Stratification and Mobility with Special Reference to Latin America,* Washington, D. C.: Pan American Union, 1966.

SIMPSON, George E., "The Ras Tafari Movement in Jamaica: A Study of Race and Class Conflict," *Social Forces,* 34 (December, 1955), 167-171.

SMITH, M. G., *Stratification in Grenada,* Berkeley: University of California Press, 1965.

SMITH, M. G., *The Plural Society in the British West Indies,* Berkeley: University of California Press, 1965.

SMITH, T. Lynn, "Observations on the Middle Class in Columbia," *Materiales para el Estudia de la clase Media en la America Latina,* 6 (1951), 1-15.

SOARES, Glaucio, "Economic Development and Class Structure," in Reinhard Bendix and Seymour M. Lipset, editors, *Class, Status, and Power,* second edition, New York: Free Press, 1966.

SOARES, Glaucio and Robert L. Hamblin, "Socio-economic Variables and Voting for the Radical Left: Chile, 1952," *American Political Science Review,* 61 (December, 1967), 1053-1065.

STAVENHAGEN, Rodolfo, "Classes, Colonialism, and Acculturation (in Mexico)," in Joseph Kahl, editor, *Comparative Perspectives on Stratification,* Boston: Little, Brown, and Co., 1968.

STERN, Claudio and Joseph A. Kahl, "Stratification Since the Revolution (in Mexico)," in Joseph Kahl, editor, *Comparative Perspectives on Stratification,* Boston: Little, Brown, and Co., 1968.

STRICKON, Arnold, "Folk Models of Stratification, Political Ideology, and Socio-Cultural Systems," in Paul Halmos, editor, *Latin American Sociological Studies,* Sociological Review Monograph No. 11, 1967.

STYCOS, J. M. "Culture and Differential Fertility in Peru," *Population Studies,* 16 (March, 1963), 257-270.

STYCOS, J. M., *Family and Fertility in Puerto Rico: A Study of the Lower Income Group,* New York: Columbia University Press, 1955.

TANNENBAUM, F., "The Future of Democracy in Latin America," *Foreign Affairs,* 33 (1955), 429-444.

TUMIN, Melvin M., *Caste in a Peasant Society: A Case Study in the Dynamics of Caste,* Princeton:Princeton University Press, 1952.

TUMIN, Melvin M., "Reciprocity and Stability of Caste in Guatemala," *American Sociological Review,* 14 (1949), 17-25.

TUMIN, Melvin M. and Arnold S. Feldman, *Social Class and Social Change in Puerto Rico,* Princeton: Princeton University Press, 1960.

TUMIN, Melvin M. and Arnold S. Feldman, "Status, Perspective, and Achievement: Education and Class Structure in Puerto Rico," *American Soliological Review,* 21 (August, 1956), 464-472.

WAGLEY, Charles, editor, *Race and Class in Rural Brazil,* Paris: UNESCO, 1952.

WHITEFORD, A. H., *Two Cities of Latin America: A Comparative Description of Social Classes,* New York: Doubleday, 1964.

WILLIAMSON, Robert C., "Social Class and Orientation to Change: Some Relevant Variables in a Bogota Sample," *Social Forces,* 46 (March, 1968), 317-328.

WILLIAMSON, Robert C., "Some Variables of Middle and Lower Class in Two Central American Cities, *Social Forces,* 41 (December, 1962), 195-207.

WINGFIELD, Roland and Vernon J. Parenton, "Class Structure and Class Conflict in Haitian Society," *Social Forces,* 43 (March, 1965), 338-347.

WOLF, Eric R., "Aspects of Group Relations in a Complex Society: Mexico," *American Anthropologist,* 58 (1956), 1065-1078.

WOLF, Eric R., "Types of Latin American Peasantry: A Preliminary Discussion," *American Anthropologist,* 57 (June, 1955), 452-471.

ZEITLIN, Maurice, "Revolutionary Workers and Individual Liberties," *American Journal of Sociology,* 72 (May, 1967), 619-632.

Australia

ALLINGHAM, John D., "Class Regression: An Aspect of the Social Stratification Process," *American Sociological Review,* 32 (June, 1967), 443-449.

BASSETT, G. W., "The Occupational Background of Teachers," *Australian Journal of Education,* 2 (1958),

BROOM, Leonard and Richard J. Hill, "Opinion Polls and Social Rank in Australia: Method and First Findings," *Australian and New Zealand Journal of Sociology,* 1 (October, 1965), 97-106.

BROOM, Leonard, F. Lancaster Jones, and Jerzy Zubrzycki, "An Occupational Classification of the Australian Workforce," *Australian and New Zealand Journal of Sociology,* 1 (October, 1965), supplement.

BROOM, Leonard, F. Lancaster Jones, and Jerzy Zubrzycki, "Social Stratification in Australia," *Sociological Studies,* Cambridge University Press, 1, 1968.

BUCHANAN, William and Hadley Cantril, *How Nations See Each Other,* Urbana: University of Illinois Press, 1953.

CONGALTON, Athol A., *Occupational Status in Australia,* Kensington: University of New South Wales, School of Sociology, 1963.

CONNELL, W. F., "Education and Social Mobility in Australia," *Transactions of the Third World Congress of Sociology,* 5 (1956),

DAVIES, Alan F., *Images of Class: An Australian Study,* Sydney: Sydney University Press, 1967.

DAVIES, Alan F. and S. Encel, *Australian Society: A Sociological Introduction,* Melmourne: F. W. Chesire, 1965.

HAMMOND, S. B., "Stratification in an Australian City," in Guy E. Swanson, T. M. Newcomb, and E. L. Hartley, editors, *Readings in Social Psychology,* revised edition, New York: Holt, 1952.

HARDEE, J. Gilbert, "Social Structure and Participation in an Australian Community," *Rural Sociology,* 26 (September, 1961), 240-251.

HAVIGHURST, Robert J., "Education, Social Mobility, and Social Change in Four Societies: Great Britain, United States of America, Brazil, Australia," *International Review of Education,* 4 (1958), 167-185.

KRUPINSKI, Jerzy and Alan Stoller, "Occupational Hierarchy of First Admissions to the Victorian Mental Health Department, 1962-1965," *Australian and New Zealand Journal of Sociology,* 4 (April, 1968), 55-63.

LANDON, Frank C., "The Catholic Anti-Communist Role Within Australian Labor," *Western Political Quarterly,* 9 (December, 1956), 884-899.

MARTIN, Jean I., "Marriage, the Family and Class," in A. P. Elkin, editor, *Marriage and the Family in Australia,* Sydney: Angus and Robertson, 1957.

MAYER, Kurt B., "Social Stratification in Two Equalitarian Societies: Australia and the United States," *Social Research,* 31 (Winter, 1964), 435-465.

OESER, D. A. and S. B. Hammond, editors, *Social Structure and Personality in a City,* London: Routledge and Kegan Paul, 1954.

PIKE, Robert M., "Some Social Aspects of Recruitment to Public School Teaching in New South Wales," *Australian and New Zealand Journal of Sociology,* 2 (October, 1966), 94-106.

SHARP, Dan G. and Colin M. Tatz, editors, *Aboriginies in the Economy: Employment, Wages and Training,* Melbourne, Australia: Jacaranda Press, 1966.

TAFT, Ronald, *From Stranger to Citizen: A Survey of Studies of Immigrant Assimilation in Western Australian,* New York: Hu-

AUSTRALIA

manities Press, 1967.

TAFT, Ronald, "The Social Grading of Occupations in Australia," *British Journal of Sociology,* 4 (March, 1953), 181-188.

TIEN, H. Y., "A Profile of the Australian Academic Profession," *Australian Quarterly,* 32 (March, 1960), 66-74.

TIEN, H. Y., *Social Mobility and Controlled Fertility: Family Origins and Structure of the Australian Academic Elite,* New Haven: College and University Press, 1965.

TIEN, H. Y., "The Social Mobility/Fertility Hypothesis Reconsidered: An Empirical Study," *American Sociological Review,* 26 (April, 1961), 247-257.

Miscellaneous

CONGALTON, A. A., "Social Grading of Occupations in New Zealand," *British Journal of Sociology,* 4 (March, 1953), 45-59.

COOPER, James G., "The Social Status of Occupations in Microesia," *Personnel and Guidance Journal,* 41 (November, 1962), 267-269.

DIXON, A. J., *Divorce in New Zealand,* Auckland: Auckland University College Bulletin, No. 46, 1954.

EPSTEIN, A. L., "Occupational Prestige on the Gazelle Peninsula, New Britain," *Australian and New Zealand Journal of Sociology,* 3 (October, 1967), 111-121.

GOLDMAN, Irving, "Status Rivalry and Cultural Evaluation in Polynesia," *American Anthropologist,* 57 (August, 1955), 680-697.

GUIDON, Hubert, "Social Unrest, Social Class and Quebec's Bureaucratic Revolution," *Queen's Quarterly,* 71 (Summer, 1964), 150-162.

JONES, Frank E. and Wallace E. Lambert, "Occupational Rank and Attitudes Toward Immigrants," *Public Opinion Quarterly,* 29 (Spring, 1965), 137-144. Deals with Canada.

KEYFITZ, Nathan, "Differential Fertility in Ontario: An Application of Factorial Design to a Demographic Problem," *Population Studies,* 6 (November, 1952), 123-134.

MARSHALL, T. H., "Class and Power in Canada," *Canadian Review of Sociology and Anthropology,* 2 (November, 1966), 215-222.

MISCELLANEOUS

PAVALKO, Ronald M. and David R. Bishop, "Socioeconomic Status and College Plans: A Study of Canadian High School Students," *Sociology of Education,* 39 (Summer, 1966), 288-298.

PINEO, Peter C. and John Porter, "Occupational Prestige in Canada," *Canadian Review of Sociology and Anthropology,* 4 (1967), 24-40.

PORTER, John, "The Economic Elite and the Social Structure in Canada," in B. Blishen, *et al., Canadian Society,* New York: Free Press, 1961.

PORTER, John, "Elite Groups: A Scheme for the Study of Power in Canada," *Canadian Journal of Economics and Political Science,* (November, 1955), 498-512.

PORTER, John, *The Vertical Mossic: An Analysis of Social Class and Power in Canada,* Toronto: University of Canada Press, 1965.

RICHMOND, Anthony H., "Social Mobility of Immigrants in Canada," *Population Studies,* 18 (July, 1964), 53-69.

SAHLINS, Marshall D., *Social Stratification in Polynesia,* Seattle: University of Washington Press, 1958.

SUTTLES, Wayne, "Private Knowledge, Morality, and Social Classes Among the Coast Salish," *American Anthropologist,* 60 (June, 1958), 497-507.

TUCKMAN, Jacob, "Social Status of Occupations in Canada," *Canadian Journal of Psychology,* 1 (June, 1947), 71-74.

USEEM, John, "Structure of Power in Palau," *Social Forces,* 29 (December, 1950), 141-148.

VAN DER VEUR, Paul W., "Occupational Prestige Among Secondary School Students in West New Guinea (West Irian)," *Australian and New Zealand Journal of Sociology,* 2 (October, 1966), 107-110.

Part II

SOCIAL MOBILITY

and the CORRELATES of STRATIFICATION

This section deals with various kinds of culture, attitudes, behavior, life styles, and life chances that vary with income, power, prestige, or some other stratification variable. In some cases, the stratification variable seems to exercise influence upon the correlated variable, whereas in other cases, the probable line of causation is the other way around, or the influence seems to be reciprocal. In still other cases, there is no probable direct line of causation between the correlated variables. Generally speaking, the studies reported here treat dimensions of stratification as the independent variables, but we do no exclude studies that do not do so.

Characteristics of Lower Strata

This section includes much of the vast literature on the consequences and bases of poverty as well as treatments of the more prosperous and skilled members of the "blue-collar" or "working" class. Publications that merely describe the extent of poverty are listed under "Income Distribution."

ABBOTT, Joan, "Students' Social Class in Three Northern Universities," *British Journal of Sociology,* 16 (September, 1965), 206-220.

ANDERSON, Nels, *The Hobo: The Sociology of the Homeless Man,* Chicago: University of Chicago Press, 1923.

ARNATI, Oscar, *Poverty Amid Affluence,* New York: Twentieth Century Fund, 1966.

BABCHUK, Nicholas and C. Wayne Gordon, *The Voluntary Assocciation in the Slum,* Lincoln: University of Nebraska Press, 1962.

BAHR, Howard M., "The Gradual Disappearance of Skid Row," *Social Problems,* 15 (Summer, 1967), 41-45.

BAHR, Howard M., "Worklife Mobility Among Bowery Men," *Social Science Quarterly,* 49 (June, 1968), 128-141.

BAHR, Howard M. and Stephen J. Langfur, "Social Attachment and Drinking in Skid-Row Life Histories," *Social Problems,* 14 (Spring, 1967), 464-472.

BALAGH, Thomas, *The Economics of Poverty,* New York: Macmillan, 1966.

BANFIELD, Edward, *The Moral Basis of a Backward Society,* New York: Free Press, 1958.

BEAN, Lee L., Jerome K. Myers, and Max P. Pepper, "Social Class and Schizophrenia: A Ten-Year Follow-Up," in Arthur B. Shostak and William Gomberg, editors, *Blue-Collar World: Studies of the American Worker,* Englewood Cliffs, New Jersey: Prentice Hall, 1964.

BECK, Bernard, "Bedbugs, Stench, Dampness, and Immorality: A Review Essay on Recent Literature About Poverty," *Social Problems,* 15 (Summer, 1967), 101-114.

BELL, Daniel, "The Invisible Unemployed," *Fortune,* 58 (July, 1958).

BELL, Robert R., "Lower Class Negro Mothers' Aspirations for Their Children," *Social Forces,* 43 (May, 1965), 493-500.

BENDER, Lloyd D., Daryl J. Hobbs, and James F. Golden, "Congruence between Aspirations and Capabilities of Youth in a Low-income Rural Area," *Rural Sociology,* 32 (September, 1967), 278-289.

BENDINER, Elmer, *The Bowery Man,* New York: Nelson, 1961.

BENNETT, H. S., *Life on the English Manor: A Study of Peasant Conditions, 1150-1400,* London: Cambridge University Press, 1960.

BEQIRAJ, Mehmet, *Peasantry in Revolution,* Ithica: Center for International Studies, Cornell University, 1966.

BERG, Ivar and David Rogers, "Former Blue-Collarites in Small Business," in Arthur B. Shostak and William Gomberg, editors, *Blue-Collar World: Studies of the American Worker,* Englewood Cliffs, New Jersey: Prentice Hall, 1964.

BERGER, Bennett M., *Working Class Suburb,* Berkeley: University of California Press, 1960.

BLAKE, Judith, "Family Instability and Reproductive Behavior in Jamaica," *Current Research in Human Fertility,* New York: Milbank Memorial Fund, 1955.

BLAKE, Judith, *Family Structure in Jamaica,* New York: Free Press, 1961.

BLAUNER, Robert, *Alienation and Freedom: The Factory Worker and His Industry,* Chicago: University of Chicago Press, 1964.

BLUM, Alan F., "Lower-Class Negro Television Spectators: The Concept of Pseudo-Jovial Scepticism," in Arthur B. Shostak and William Gomberg, editors, *Blue-Collar World: Studies of the American Worker,* Englewood Cliffs, New Jersey: Prentice Hall, 1964.

BLUM, Alan F., "Social Structure, Social Class, and Participation in Primary Relationships," in Arthur B. Shostak and William Gomberg, editors, *Blue-Collar World: Studies of the American Worker,* Englewood Cliffs, New Jersey: Prentice Hall, 1964.

BLUM, Jerome, *The European Peasantry from the Fifteenth to*

LOWER STRATA

the Nineteenth Century, Washington, D. C.: American Historical Association, 1960.

BLUM, Jerome, *Lord and Peasant in Russia from the Ninth to
the Nineteenth Century,* Princeton, New Jersey: Princeton
University Press, 1961.

BLUMER, Herbert, "Early Industrialization and the Laboring
Class," *Sociological Quarterly,* 1 (January, 1960), 5-14.

BOGART, Leo, "The Mass Media and the Blue-Collar Worker,"
in Arthur B. Shostak and William Gomberg, editors, *Blue-Collar
World: Studies of the American Worker,* Englewood Cliffs, New
Jersey: Prentice Hall, 1964.

BOGUE, Donald J., *Skid Row in American Cities,* Chicago: Community and Family Study Center, University of Chicago, 1963.

BOISEN, A. T., "Religion and Hard Times: A Study of the Holy
Rollers," *Social Action,* (March 15, 1939), 8-35.

BOWEN, Don R., Elinor R. Bowen, Sheldon R. Gawiser, and
Louis H. Masotti, "Deprivation, Mobility, and Orientation Toward Protest of the Urban Poor," *American Behavioral Scientist,* 11 (March-April, 1968), 20-24.

BOWER, Robert T., "New York City's Labor Vote," *Public Opinion
Quarterly,* (Winter, 1947-1948), 614-615.

BOWMAN, Claude C., "Mental Health in the Worker's World," in
Arthur B. Shostak and William Gomberg, editors, *Blue-Collar
World: Studies of the American Worker,* Englewood Cliffs, New
Jersey: Prentice Hall, 1964.

BRAITHWAITE, Lloyd, "Sociology and Demographic Research
in the British Caribbean," *Social and Economic Studies,* 6
(December, 1957), 541-550.

BRENNAN, T., "The Working Class in the British Social Structure,"
Transactions of the Third World Congress of Sociology, 3 (1956),
96-105.

BRIEFS, Goetz A., *The Proletariat,* New York: McGraw-Hill, 1937.

BRODERSEN, Arvid, *The Soviet Worker: Labor and Government
in Soviet Society,* New York: Random House, 1966.

BROWN, W. O., "Role of the Poor White in Race Contacts of the
South," *Social Forces,* 19 (December, 1940), 258-268.

BULLOCK, Paul, "Poverty in the Ghetto—The View from Watts,"
Monthly Labor Review, (February, 1967), 31-35.

BURCHINAL, Lee G. and Hilda Siff, "Rural Poverty," *Journal of
Marriage and the Family,* 26 (November, 1964), 399-405.

BURGESS, Elaine and Daniel O. Price, *An American Dependency
Challenge,* Chicago: American Public Welfare Association, 1963.

CANCIAN, Frank, "The Southern Italian Peasant: World View and Political Behavior," *Anthropological Quarterly,* 34 (1961), 1-18.

LOWER STRATA
CAPLOVITZ, David, "The Problems of Blue-Collar Consumers," in Arthur B. Shostak and William Gomberg, editors, *Blue-Collar World: Studies of the American Worker,* Englewood Cliffs, New Jersey: Prentice Hall, 1964.

CAPLOVITZ, David, *The Poor Pay More,* revised edition, New York: Free Press, 1967.

CARLIN, Jerome E., Jan Howard, and Sheldon L. Messinger, "Civil Justice and the Poor: Issues for Sociological Research," *Law and Society Review,* 1 (November, 1966), 9-89.

CARTER, Michael, *Into Work,* Baltimore: Penguin, 1966.

CAUDILL, Harry, *Night Comes to the Cumberland: A Biography of a Depressed Area,* Boston: Little, Brown, 1963.

CENTERS, Richard, "Nominal Variation and Class Identification: The Working and Laboring Classes," *Journal of Abnormal and Social Psychology,* 45 (1950), 195-215.

CHAMPION, Phyllis, "A Pilot Study of the Success or Failure of Low-Income Negro Families in the Use of Birth Control," in Donald Bogue, editor, *Sociological Contributions to Family Planning Research,* Community and Family Study Center, University of Chicago, 1967.

CHAPLIN, David, "Domestic Service and the Negro," in Arthur B. Shostak and William Gomberg, editors, *Blue-Collar World: Studies of the American Worker,* Englewood Cliffs, New Jersey: Prentice Hall, 1964.

CHEN, Ta, "Basic Problems of the Chinese Working Classes," *American Journal of Sociology,* 53 (November, 1947), 184-191.

CHICAGO TENANTS RELOCATION BUREAU, *The Homeless Man on Skid Row,* Chicago: 1961.

CHILMAN, Catherine S., "The Crisis and Challenge of Low-Income Families in the 1960's: Implications for Parent Education," *Journal of Marriage and the Family,* 26 (February, 1964), 39-43.

CHILMAN, Catherine S., "Economic and Social Deprivation: Its Effects on Children and Families in the United States—A Selected Bibliography," *Journal of Marriage and the Family,* 26 (November, 1964), 495-497.

CHILMAN, Catherine S., "Fertility and Poverty in the United States: Some Implications for Family-Planning Programs, Evaluations, and Research," *Journal of Marriage and the Family,* 30 (May, 1968), 207-227.

CHILMAN, Catherine S., *Growing Up Poor,* United States Department of Health, Education, and Welfare, Washington, D. C.:

United States Government Printing Office, 1966.

CHILMAN, Catherine S., "Population Dynamics and Poverty in the United States," *Welfare in Review,* (April, 1966).

CHILMAN, Catherine S., "Poverty and Family Planning in the United States: Some Social and Psychological Aspects and Implications, for Programs and Policy," *Welfare in Review,* 5 (April, 1967), 3-15.

CHILMAN, Catherine S., and Marvin B. Sussman, "Poverty in the United States in the Mid-Sixties," *Journal of Marriage and the Family,* 26 (November, 1964), 391-395.

CHINOY, Ely, *Automobile Workers and the American Dream,* Garden City, New York: Doubleday, 1955.

CHINOY, Ely, "The Tradition of Opportunity and the Aspirations of Automobile Workers," *American Journal of Sociology,* 57 (March, 1952), 453-459.

CLARK, Kenneth, *Dark Ghetto,* New York: Harper and Row, 1965.

CLINARD, Marshall B., *Slums and Community Development: Experiments in Self-help,* New York: Free Press, 1966.

COHEN, Albert K., *Delinquent Boys,* New York: Free Press, 1955.

COHEN, Albert K. and Harold M. Hodges, Jr., "Characteristics of the Lower-Blue-Collar Classes," *Social Problems,* 10 (Spring, 1963), 303-334.

COHN, Bernard S., "Changing Traditions of a Low Caste," *Journal of American Folklore,* 71 (1958), 413-421.

COHN, Werner, "Jehovah's Witnesses as a Proletarian Movement," *American Scholar,* 24 (Summer, 1955), 281-298.

COLE, G. D. H. and A. W. Filson, editors, *British Working Class Movements,* New York: Macmillan, 1965.

COLE, G. D. H. and Raymond Postgate, *The Common People,* London: Methuen, 1948.

CONANT, James Bryant, *Slums and Suburbs,* New York: McGraw-Hill, 1961.

COSER, Lewis A., "The Sociology of Poverty—To the Memory of George Simmel," *Social Problems,* 13 (Fall, 1965), 140-148.

COUSENS, F. R., "Indigenous Leadership in Two Lower-Class Neighborhood Organizations," in Arthur B. Shostak and William Gomberg, editors, *Blue-Collar World: Studies of the American Worker,* Englewood Cliffs, New Jersey: Prentice Hall, 1964.

CROOK, Isabel and David Crook, *Revolution in a Chinese Village: Ten Mile Inn,* London: Routledge and Kegan Paul, 1959.

DAILEY, John T., "Education and Emergence from Poverty," *Journal of Marriage and the Family,* 26 (November, 1964), 430-434.

LOWER STRATA

DALTON, George, editor, *Tribal and Peasant Economics: Readings in Economic Anthropology,* Garden City, New York: Natural History Press, 1967.

DALTON, Melville, "Worker Response and Social Background," *Journal of Political Economy,* 55 (1947), 323-332.

DANIEL, Walter G., "Problems of Disadvantaged Youth, Urban and Rural," *Journal of Negro Education,* 33 (Summer, 1964), 218-224.

DANSEREAU, H. Kirk, "Work and the Teen-age Blue-Collarite," in Arthur B. Shostak and William Gomberg, editors, *Blue-Collar World: Studies of the American Worker,* Englewood Cliffs, New Jersey: Prentice Hall, 1964.

DAVENPORT, John, "In the Midst of Plenty," *Fortune,* 63 (March, 1961), 107-240.

DAVIS, Allison, "The Motivation of the Underprivileged Worker," in William F. Whyte, editor, *Industry and Society,* New York: McGraw-Hill, 1946.

DAVIS, Allison, "Socialization and Adolescent Personality," in Guy E. Swanson, *et al.,* editors, *Readings in Social Psychology,* New York: Holt, 1954.

DAVIS, Ethelyn, "Careers as Concerns of Blue-Collar Girls," in Arthur B. Shostak and William Gomberg, editors, *Blue Collar World: Studies of the American Worker,* Englewood Cliffs, New Jersey: Prentice Hall, 1964.

DAVIS, Kingsley, "Some Demographic Aspects of Poverty in the United States," in Margaret S. Gordon, editor, *Poverty in America,* San Francisco: Chandler, 1965.

DELMO, Della-Dora, "The Culturally Disadvantaged: Further Observations," *Exceptional Children,* 29 (January, 1963), 226-237.

DENTLER, Robert A. and Mary Ellen Warshauer, *Big City Drop-Outs,* New York: Center for Urban Education, 1965.

DEUTSHER, Irwin and Elizabeth J. Thompson, editors, *Among the People: Encounters with the Poor,* New York: Basic Books, 1968.

DOTSON, Floyd, "Patterns of Voluntary Association Among Urban Working Class Families," *American Sociological Review,* 16 (October, 1951), 687-693.

DRAKE, St. Clair and Horace R. Cayton, *Black Metropolis,* New York: Harcourt Brace, 1945.

DUBIN, Robert, "Industrial Workers' Worlds: A Study of the

Central Life Interests of Industrial Workers," in Erwin O. Smigel, editor, *Work and Leisure,* New Haven: College and University Press, 1963.

DUNCAN, Beverly, "Dropouts and the Unemployed," *Journal of Political Economy,* 73 (April, 1965), 221-234.

DUNN, Stephen P. and Ethel Dunn, *The Peasants of Central Russia,* New York: Holt, Rinehart, and Winston, 1967.

DUNNE, George H., *Poverty in Plenty,* Washington, D. C.: Kennedy, 1964.

DYER, William G., "The Interlocking of Work and Family Social Systems Among Lower Occupational Families," *Social Forces,* 34 (March, 1956), 230-233.

EDWARDS, G. Franklin, "Community and Class Realities: The Ordeal of Change," *Daedalus,* 95 (Winter, 1966), 1-21.

EICHHORN, Robert L. and Edward G. Ludwig, "Poverty and Health," in Hanna Meissner, editor, *Poverty in the Affluent Society,* New York: Harper and Row, 1966.

ELKAN, Walter, *Migrants and Proletarians: Urban Labour in the Economic Development of Uganda,* New York: Oxford University Press, 1960.

ENDLEMAN, Robert, "Moral Perspectives of Blue-Collar Workers," in Arthur B. Shostak and William Gomberg, editors, *Blue-Collar World: Studies of the American Worker,* Englewood Cliffs, New Jersey: Prentice Hall, 1964.

ENGELS, Friedrich, *The Condition of the Working Class in England,* New York: Macmillan, 1958.

ENGELS, Friedrich, "On the Early History of Christianity," in Karl Marx and Friedrich Engels, *On Religion,* Moscow: Foreign Languages Publishing House, 1957.

ENTWISLE, Doris R., "Developmental Sociolinguistics: Inner-City Children," *American Journal of Sociology,* 74 (July, 1968), 37-49.

EPSTEIN, Lenore, "Effects of Low Income on Children and their Families," in Robert E. Will and Harold G. Vatter, *Poverty in Affluence,* New York: Harcourt, Brace and World, 1965.

FERMAN, Louis A., "Sociological Perspectives in Unemployment Research," in Arthur B. Shostak and William Gomberg, editors, *Blue-Collar World: Studies of the American Worker,* Englewood Cliffs, New Jersey: Prentice Hall, 1964.

FERMAN, Louis A. and Michael J. Aiken, "The Adjustment of the Older Worker to Job Displacement," in Arthur B. Shostak and William Gomberg, editors, *Blue-Collar World: Studies of the American Worker,* Englewood Cliffs, New Jersey: Prentice Hall, 1964.

FERMAN, Louis A., Joyce L. Kornbluh, and Alan Haber, editors, *Poverty in America,* Ann Arbor: University of Michigan Press, 1966.

FISHMAN, Leo, editor, *Poverty Amid Affluence,* New Haven: Yale University Press, 1966.

FLIEGEL, Frederick C., "Aspirations of Low Income Farmers and their Performance and Potential for Change," *Rural Sociology,* 24 (September, 1959), 205-214.

FLIEGEL, Frederick C., "Obstacles to Change for the Low-Income Farmer," *Rural Sociology,* 25 (September, 1960), 347-351.

FORD, Thomas R., editor, *The Southern Appalachian Region: A Survey,* Lexington, Kentucky: University of Kentucky Press, 1962.

FORM, William H. and James A. Geschwender, "Social Reference Basis of Job Satisfaction: The Case of Manual Workers," *American Sociological Review,* 27 (April, 1962), 228-237.

FOSTER, George M., "Interpersonal Relations in Peasant Society," *Human Organization,* 21 (1960-1961), 174-178.

FOSTER, George M., *Tzintzuntzan: Mexican Peasants in a Changing World,* Boston: Little, Brown 1967.

FOSTER, George M., "Peasant Society and the Image of Limited Good," *American Anthropologist,* 67 (1965), 296-311.

FOSTER, William Z., *Pages from a Worker's Life,* New York: International Publishers, 1939.

FREEDMAN, Lawrence, "Psychopathology and Poverty," in Arthur B. Shostak and William Gomberg, editors, *Blue-Collar World: Studies of the American Worker,* Englewood Cliffs, New Jersey: Prentice Hall, 1964.

FREEMAN, Howard E. and Gene G. Kassebaum, "The Illiterate in American Society: Some General Hypotheses," *Social Forces,* 42 (May, 1956), 371-375.

FREEMAN, Howard E. and Camille Lambert, Jr., "The Identification of 'Lower-Class' Families in an Urban Community," in Arthur B. Shostak and William Gomberg, editors, *Blue-Collar World: Studies of the American Worker,* Englewood Cliffs, New Jersey: Prentice Hall, 1964.

FREY, Frederick W., "Surveying Peasant Attitudes in Turkey," *Public Opinion Quarterly,* 27 (Fall, 1963), 335-355.

FRIEDENBERG, Edgar, "An Ideology of School Withdrawal," in Arthur B. Shostak and William Gomberg, editors, *Blue-Collar World: Studies of the American Worker,* Englewood Cliffs, New Jersey: Prentice Hall, 1964.

FULTON, Robert, Everett Keach, Jr. and William E. Gardner,

editors, *Education and Social Crisis Perspectives on Teaching Disadvantaged Youth,* New York: Wiley, 1967.

FUSSELL, G. E., *The English Rural Laborer,* London: Batchworth Press, 1949.

GANS, Herbert J., *The Urban Villagers: Group and Class in the Life of Italian-Americans,* New York: Free Press, 1962.

GEISEL, Paul N., "The Meaning of Work and Mental Illness," in Arthur B. Shostak and William Gomberg, editors, *Blue-Collar World: Studies of the American Worker,* Englewood Cliffs, New Jersey: Prentice Hall, 1964.

GILMORE, Harlan W., *The Beggar,* Chapel Hill: University of North Carolina Press, 1940.

GIROD, Robert and Firouz Tofigh, "Family Background and Income, School Career and Social Mobility of Young Males of Working-Class Origin A Geneva Survey," *Acta Sociologica,* 9 (1965), 94-109.

GLAZER, Nathan, "A Sociologist's View of Poverty," in Margaret S. Gordon, editor, *Poverty in America,* San Francisco: Chandler, 1965.

GLAZER, Mona Y. and Carol Creeden, *Children of the Poor,* Chicago: Rand-McNally, 1967.

GOLDKIND, Victor, "Social Stratification in the Peasant Community: Redfield's Chan Kom Reinterpreted," *American Anthropologist,* 67 (August, 1965), 863-884.

GOLDSTEIN, Bernard, *Low Income Youth in Urban Areas: A Critical Review of the Literature,* New York: Holt, Rinehart and Winston, 1967.

GOLDTHORPE, John H., and David Lockwood, "Affluence and the British Class Structure," *Sociological Review,* 11 (July, 1963), 133-163.

GOLDTHORPE, John H., David Lockwood, Frank Bechhofer, and Jennifer Platt, "The Affluent Worker and the Thesis of Embougeoisement: Some Preliminary Research Findings," in Joseph Kahl, editor, *Comparative Perspectives on Stratification,* Boston: Little, Brown, 1968.

GOMBERG, Adeline, "The Working-Class Child of Four and Television," in Arthur B. Shostak and William Gomberg, editors, *Blue-Collar World: Studies of the American Worker,* Englewood Cliffs, New Jersey: Prentice Hall, 1964.

GOODE, William J., "Illegitimacy in the Caribbean Social Structure," *American Sociological Review,* 25 (February, 1960), 21-30.

GORDON, Margaret S., editor, *Poverty in America,* San Francisco: Chandler, 1965.

GORDON, Milton M. and Charles H. Anderson, "The Blue-Collar Worker at Leisure," in Arthur B. Shostak and William Gomberg, editors, *Blue-Collar World: Studies of the American Worker,* Englewood Cliffs, New Jersey: Prentice Hall, 1964.

LOWER STRATA

GORDON, R. A., "An Economist's View of Poverty," in Margaret S. Gordon, editor, *Poverty in America,* San Francisco: Chandler, 1965.

GROSS, Ronald, "The Future of Toil," in Arthur B. Shostak and William Gomberg, editors, *Blue-Collar World: Studies of the American Worker,* Englewood Cliffs, New Jersey: Prentice Hall, 1964.

HACKLER, James C., "The Integration of a Lower-Class Culture: Some Social Implications of a Rigid Class Structure," *Sociological Quarterly,* 2 (July, 1961), 203-214.

HAGGSTROM, Warren C., "The Power of the Poor," in Frank Riessman, Jerome Cohen, and Arthur Pearl, editor, *Mental Health of the Poor,* New York: Free Press, 1964.

HAMILTON, Richard F., *Affluence and the French Worker in the Fourth Republic,* Princeton: Princeton University Press, 1967.

HAMILTON, Richard F., "Affluence and the Worker: The West German Case," *American Journal of Sociology,* 71 (September, 1965), 144-152.

HAMILTON, Richard F., *Class and Politics in the United States,* New York: Wiley, 1969.

HAMILTON, Richard F., "The Income Difference Between Skilled and White-Collar Workers," *British Journal of Sociology,* 38 (December, 1963), 363-373.

HAMILTON, Richard F., "The Behavior and Values of Skilled Workers," in Arthur B. Shostak and William Gomberg, editors, *Blue-Collar World: Studies of the American Worker,* Englewood Cliffs, New Jersey: Prentice Hall, 1964.

HANDEL, Gerald and Lee Rainwater, "Persistence and Change in Working Class Life Style," *Sociology and Social Research,* 48 (April, 1964), 281-288.

HANDEL, Gerald and Lee Rainwater, *Status of the Working Class in Changing American Society,* Chicago: Social Research, 1961.

HARRINGTON, Michael, *The Other America,* New York: Macmillan, 1962.

HARRINGTON, Michael, "The Other America: Definitions" in Reinhard Bendix and Seymour M. Lipset, editors, *Class, Status and Power,* revised edition, New York: Free Press, 1966.

HARRINGTON, Michael, "A Social Reformer's View of Poverty," in Margaret S. Gordon, editor, *Poverty in America,* San Francisco: Chandler, 1965.

HARRIS, Sara and Donald Bogue, *Skid Row, United States of America,* Garden City, New York: Doubleday, 1956.

HARRISON, Royden, "The British Working Class and the General Election of 1868," parts I and II, *International Review of Social History,* 5 and 6 (1960-1961), 424-455 and 74-109.

HARROLD, H., "Religious Institutions and the Culture of Poverty," *Journal of Religious Thought,* 21 (1964), 81-94.

HASKINS, W. G., *The Midland Peasant: The Economic and Social History of a Leicestershire Village,* London: Macmillan, 1957.

HATHWAY, Marion, *The Migratory Worker and Family Life,* Chicago: University of Chicago Press, 1934.

HAUSKNECHT, Murray, "The Blue-Collar Joiner," in Arthur B. Shostak and William Gomberg, editors, *Blue-Collar World: Studies of the American Worker,* Englewood Cliffs, New Jersey: Prentice Hall, 1964.

HAVIGHURST, Robert, "Who are the Socially Disadvantaged?", *Journal of Negro Education,* 33 (Summer, 1964), 210-217.

HEAL, Florence L. D., "Values in a Group of Lower Socio-Economic Students," *Marriage and Family Living,* 22 (November, 1960), 370-373.

HECHT, Joseph Jean, *The Domestic Servant Class in Eighteenth-Century England,* London: Routledge and Kegan Paul, 1956.

HECKSHER, Bridget Tancock, "Household Structure and Achievement Orientation in Lower Class Barbadian Families," *Journal of Marriage and the Family,* 29 (August, 1967), 521-526.

HERZOG, Elizabeth, "Some Assumptions About the Poor," *Social Service Review,* 37 (1963), 389-403.

HESS, Robert D., "Educability and Rehabilitation: The Future of the Welfare Class, *Journal of Marriage and the Family,* 26 (November, 1964), 422-429.

HILDEBRAND, George H., *Poverty, Income Maintenance and the Negative Income Tax,* Ithaca: New York State School of Industrial and Labor Relations, 1967.

HIMES, Joseph S., "Some Work-Related Cultural Deprivations of Lower-Class Negro Youth," *Journal of Marriage and the Family,* 26 (November, 1964), 447-449.

HINES, Ralph, "Social Expectations and Cultural Deprivation," *Journal of Negro Education,* 33 (Spring, 1964), 136-142.

HOBSHAWN, E. J., *Labouring Men: Studies in the History of Labour,* Garden City, New York: Doubleday 1967.

HOGGART, Richard, *The Uses of Literacy,* New York: Oxford University Press, 1957.

HOLLINGSHEAD, August B. and Lloyd H. Rogler, "Lower Socioeconomic Status and Mental Illness," *Sociology and Social Research,* 46 (July, 1962), 387-396.

HOROWITZ, Michael M., *Morne-Paysant: Peasant Village in Martinique,* New York: Holt, Rinehart and Winston, 1967.

HOULT, Thomas F. and Albert J. Mayer, "The Blue-Collarite Abandoned in the Big City," in Arthur B. Shostak and William Gomberg, editors, *Blue-Collar World: Studies of the American Worker,* Englewood Cliffs, New Jersey: Prentice Hall, 1964.

HUNTER, David R., *The Slums: Challenge and Response,* New York: Free Press, 1964.

HURVITZ, Nathan, "Marital Strain in the Blue-Collar Family," in Arthur B. Shostak and William Gomberg, editors, *Blue-Collar World: Studies of the American Worker,* Englewood Cliffs, New Jersey: Prentice Hall, 1964.

HYMAN, Herbert and Paul B. Sheatsley, "Some Reasons Why Information Campaigns Fail," *Public Opinion Quarterly,* 11 (Fall, 1947), 412-423.

INGLIS, K. S., *Churches and the Working Classes in Victorian England,* London: Routledge and Kegan Paul, 1963.

INMAN, Buis T., *Rural Poverty: Causes, Extent, Location and Trends,* Washington, D.C.: United States Department of Agriculture, 1964.

IRELAN, Lola M., editor, *Low Income Life Styles,* Washington, D. C.: United States Government Printing Office, 1966.

JACKSON, Brian, *Working Class Community,* London: Routledge and Kegan Paul, 1968.

JACKSON, Brian and Dennis Marsden, *Education and the Working Class,* London: Routledge and Kegan Paul, 1962.

JAFFE, Frederick S., *Family Planning and Rural Poverty: An Approach to Programming of Services,* National Advisory Commission on Rural Poverty, 1967.

JAFFE, Frederick S. and Steven Polgar, "Family Planning and Public Policy: 'Is the Culture of Poverty' the New Cop-out?" *Journal of Marriage and the Family,* 30 (May, 1968), 228-235.

JACKSON, Joan K. and Ralph Conner, "The Skid Row Alcoholic," *Quarterly Journal of Studies on Alcohol,* 14 (1953), 468-486.

JEFFERS, Camille, *Living Poor: A Participant Observer Study of Priorities and Choices,* Ann Arbor, Michigan: Ann Arbor Publishers, 1967.

JOHN, Vera P., "The Intellectual Development of Slum Children: Some Preliminary Findings," *American Journal of Orthopsychiatry,* 33 (October, 1963), 813-822.

JOHNSON, Sheila K., "Hong Kong's Resettled Squatters: A Statistical Analysis," *Asian Survey,* 6 (November, 1966), 643-646.

KARACKI, Larry and Jackson Toby, "The Uncommitted Adolescent: Candidate for Gang Socialization, " in Arthur B. Shostak and William Gomberg, editors, *Blue-Collar World: Studies of the American Worker,* Englewood Cliffs, New Jersey: Prentice Hall, 1964.

KATZ, Phyllis A., "Acquisiton and Retention of Discrimination Learning Sets In Lower-Class Preschool Children," *Journal of Educational Psychology,* 58 (August, 1967), 253-258.

KELL, Leone and Esther Herr, "Reaching Low Income Students in Home Economics Classes," *Marriage and Family Living,* 25 (May, 1963), 214-218.

KELSO, Robert W., *Poverty,* Longmans Green, 1929.

KEYSERLING, Leon H., *Poverty and Deprivation in the United States: The Plight of Two-Fifths of a Nation,* Washington, D. C.: The Conference on Economic Progress, 1962.

KEYSERLING, Leon H., *Progress or Poverty: The United States at the Crossroads,* Washington, D. C.: The Conference on Economic Progress, 1964.

KNUPFER, Geneviere, "Portrait of the Underdog," *Public Opinion Quarterly,"* (Spring, 1947), 103-114.

KOGAN, Norman, "Italian Communism, the Working Class and Organized Catholicism," *Journal of Politics,* 28 (August, 1966), 531-555.

KOMAROVSKY, Mirra, *Blue-Collar Marriage,* New York: Random House, 1962.

KORNHAUSER, A. J., A. J. Mayer, and H. L. Sheppard, *When Labor Votes,* New York: University Books, 1956.

KRAUSS, Irving, "Sources of Educational Aspirations Among Working-Class Youth," *American Sociological Review,* 29 (December, 1964), 867-879.

LOWER STRATA

LANE, Robert E., *Political Ideology: Why the American Common Man Believes What He Does,* New York: Free Press, 1967.

LANGDON, Frank C., "The Catholic Anti-Communist Role Within Australian Labor," *Western Political Quarterly,* 9 (December, 1956), 884-899.

LANTZ, Herman R., "Resignation, Induatrialization, and the Problem of Social Change: A Case History of a Coal-Mining Community," in Arthur B. Shostak and William Gomberg, editors, *Blue-Collar World: Studies of the American Worker,* Englewood Cliffs, New Jersey: Prentice Hall, 1964.

LARNER, Jeremy and Irving Howe, editors, *Poverty: Views from the Left,* New York: Morrow, 1968.

LARSON, Richard and James L. Olson, "A Method of Identifying Culturally Deprived Kindergarten Children," *Exceptional Children,* 3 (November, 1963), 130-137.

LAWTON, Denis, *Social Class, Language and Education,* London: Routledge and Kegan Paul, 1968.

LEFTON, Mark, "The Blue-Collar Worker and the Middle Class Ethic," *Sociology and Social Research,* 51 (January, 1967), 158-170.

LEGGETT, John C., "Sources and Consequences of Working-Class Consciousness," in Arthur B. Shostak and William Gomberg, editors, *Blue-Collar World: Studies of the American Worker,* Englewood Cliffs, New Jersey: Prentice Hall, 1964.

LEGGETT, John C., "Working-Class Consciousness, Race, and Political Choice," *American Journal of Sociology,* 69 (September, 1963), 171-176.

LEVENS, Helene, "Organizational Affiliation and Powerlessness: A Case Study of the Welfare Poor," *Social Problems,* 16 (Summer, 1968), 18-32.

LEVINE, Gene, *When Workers Vote,* Totowa, New Jersey: Bedminster, 1963.

LEVINSON, Boris M., "The Socioeconomic Status, Intelligence, and Psychometric Pattern of Native-Born White Homeless Men," *Journal of Genetic Psychology,* 91 (December, 1957).

LEWIS, Harold, "Etiology of Poor Housekeeping Among Low Income Public Housing Families," *Journal of Marriage and the Family,* 26 (May, 1964), 224-225.

LEWIS, Oscar, *The Children of Sanchez,* New York: Random House, 1961.

LEWIS, Oscar, "The Culture of Poverty," *Scientific American,* 215 (October, 1966), 19-25.

LEWIS, Oscar, *Five Families: Mexican Case Studies in the Culture of Poverty,* New York: Basic Books, 1959.

LEWIS, Oscar, "I'm Proud to be Poor," *Commentary*, (August, 1966), 44-47.

LEWIS, Oscar, *La Vida: A Puerto Rican Family in the Culture of Poverty—San Juan and New York*, New York: Random House, 1966.

LEWIS, Oscar and Ruth Lewis, "A Day in the Life of a Mexican Peasant Family," *Journal of Marriage and the Family*, 18 (February, 1956), 3-13.

LIEBOW, Elliot, *Tally's Corner: A Study of Negro Streetcorner Men*, Boston: Little, Brown, 1967.

LIPSET, Seymour M., "Democracy and Working-Class Authoritarianism," *American Sociological Review*, 24 (August, 1959), 482-501.

LIPSET, Seymour M., *Political Man*, Garden City, New York: Doubleday, 1960, Chapter 4.

LIPSET, Seymour M., "Working Class Authoritarianism: A Reply to Miller and Reissman," *British Journal of Sociology*, 12 (September, 1961), 263-276.

LIPSET, Seymour M., Martin Trow, and James S. Coleman, *Union Democracy*, New York: Free Press, 1956.

LIPSITZ, Lewis, "Working-Class Authoritarianism: A Re-Evaluation," *American Sociological Review*, 30 (February, 1965), 103-109.

LIPSITZ, Lewis, "Worklife and Political Attitudes: A Study of Manual Workers," *American Political Science Review*, 58 (December, 1964), 951-962.

LOCKWOOD, David, "The New Working Class," *European Journal of Sociology*, 1 (1960), 248-259.

LOCKWOOD, David, "Sources of Variation in Working Class Images of Society," *Sociological Review*, 14 (November, 1966).

LOETHER, Herman J., "The Meaning of Work and Adjustment to Retirement," in Arthur B. Shostak and William Gomberg, editors, *Blue-Collar World: Studies of the American Worker*, Englewood Cliffs, New Jersey: Prentice Hall, 1964.

LONDON, Jack and Robert Wenkert, "Obstacles to Blue-Collar Participation in Adult Education," in Arthur B. Shostak and William Gomberg, editors, *Blue-Collar World: Studies of the American Worker*, Englewood Cliffs, New Jersey: Prentice Hall, 1964.

LOPREATO, Joseph, "How Would You Like to be a Peasant?" *Human Organization*, 24 (1965), 298-307.

LOPREATO, Joseph, "Interpersonal Relations in Peasant Society: The Peasants' View," *Human Organization*, 21 (1962), 21-24.

LOPREATO, Joseph, *Peasants No More: Social Class and Social Change in Southern Italy,* San Francisco: Chandler, 1967.

LOPREATO, Joseph and Janet Saltzman, "Descriptive Models of Peasant Society: A Reconciliation from Southern Italy," *Human Organization,* 27 (Summer, 1968), 132-142.

LOWE, Jeanne, *Cities in a Race with Time: Progress and Poverty in America's Renewing Cities,* New York: Random House, 1967.

MACDONALD, Dwight, *Our Invisible Poor,* New York: Sidney Hillman Foundation, 1963.

MacIVER, Robert M., editor, *The Assault on Poverty, and Individual Responsibility,* New York: Harper and Row, 1965.

MARSHALL, Ray, *The Negro Worker,* New York: Random House, 1967.

MATZA, David, "The Disreputable Poor," in Reinhard Bendix and Seymour M. Lipset, editors, *Class, Status, and Power,* revised edition, New York: Free Press, 1966.

MAY, Edgar, *The Wasted Americans,* New York: Harper and Row, 1964.

MAYER, John, *Other People's Marital Problems: The "Knowledgeability" of Lower and Middle Class Wives,* New York: Institute of Welfare Research, Community Service Society of New York, 1966.

MAYER, Kurt B. and Sidney Goldstein, "Manual Workers as Small Businessmen," in Arthur B. Shostak and William Gomberg, editors, *Blue-Collar World: Studies of the American Worker,* Englewood Cliffs, New Jersey: Prentice Hall, 1964.

McQUIRE, Carson, "Family Life in Lower and Middle Class Homes," *Marriage and Family Living,* 14 (February, 1952), 1-6.

McKENZIE, R. T. and A. Silver, "Conservatism, Industrialism, and the Working Class Tory in England," *Transactions of the Fifth World Congress of Sociology,* 3 (1964), 191-202.

McMILLAN, Sylvia R., "Aspirations of Low-Income Mothers," *Journal of Marriage and the Family,* 29 (May, 1967), 282-287.

MEISSNER, Hanna H., editor, *Poverty in the Affluent Society,* New York: Harper and Row, 1966.

MILLER, Herman P., "Changes in the Number and Composition of the Poor," in Margaret S. Gordon, editor, *Poverty in America,* San Francisco: Chandler, 1965.

MILLER, Herman P., editor, *Poverty: American Style,* Belmont, California: Wadsworth, 1967.

MILLER, Herman P., *Rich Man, Poor Man,* New York: Crowell, 1964.

MILLER, Kent S. and Charles M. Grigg, editors, *Mental Health and the Lower Social Classes,* Tallahassee: Florida State University, 1966.

MILLER, S. M., "The American Lower Class: A Typological Approach," *Social Research,* 31 (Spring, 1964), 1-22.

MILLER, S. M. "Further Thoughts on Reform," in Arthur B. Shostak and William Gomberg, editors, *Blue-Collar World: Studies of the American Worker,* Englewood Cliffs, New Jersey: Prentice Hall, 1964.

MILLER, S. M., "The 'New' Working Class," in Arthur B. Shostak and William Gomberg, editors, *Blue-Collar World: Studies of the American Worker,* Englewood Cliffs, New Jersey: Prentice Hall, 1964.

MILLER, S. M., "The Outlook of Working-Class Youth," in Arthur B. Shostak and William Gomberg, editors, *Blue-Collar World: Studies of the American Worker,* Englewood Cliffs, New Jersey: Prentice Hall, 1964.

MILLER, S. M., "Poverty and Inequality in America: Implications for the Social Services," *Child Welfare,* 42 (November, 1963), 442-445.

MILLER, S. M., "Some Thoughts on Reform," in Arthur B. Shostak and William Gomberg, editors, *Blue-Collar World: Studies of the American Worker,* Englewood Cliffs, New Jersey: Prentice Hall, 1964.

MILLER, S. M. and Ira E. Harrison, "Types of Dropouts: 'The Unemployables,' " in Arthur B. Shostak and William Gomberg, editors, *Blue-Collar World: Studies of the American Worker,* Englewood Cliffs, New Jersey: Prentice Hall, 1964.

MILLER, S. M. and Martin Rein, "Poverty and Social Change," in E. H. Mizruchi, editor, *The Substance of Sociology,* New York: Appleton-Century-Crofts, 1967.

MILLER, S. M. and Frank Riessman, *Social Class and Social Policy,* New York: Basic Books, 1968.

MILLER, S. M. and Frank Riessman, "Are Workers Middle Class?" *Dissent,* (Autumn, 1961), 507-516.

MILLER, S. M. and Frank Reissman, "Working-Class Authoritarianism: A Critique of Lipset," *British Journal of Sociology,* 12 (September, 1961), 263-276.

MILLER, S. M. and Frank Riessman, "The Working Class Subculture: A New View," *Social Problems,* 9 (Summer, 1961), 86-97.

MILLER, Walter B., "Implications of Urban Lower-Class Culture for Social Work," *Social Service Review,* 33 (September, 1959), 219-236.

MILLER, Walter B., "Lower Class Culture as a Genrating Milieu of Gang Delinquency," *Journal of Social Issues,* 14 (third quarter, 1958), 5-19.

229

MINTZ, Sidney W., "The Folk-Urban Continuum and the Rural Proletarian Community," *American Journal of Sociology,* 59 (September, 1953), 136-143.

LOWER STRATA

MITTELBACH, Frank G. and Grace Marshall, *The Burden of Poverty,* Los Angeles: Graduate School of Business Administration, University of California, 1966.

MIZRUCHI, Ephraim Harold, "Aspirations and Poverty: A Neglected Aspect of Merton's Anomie," *Sociological Quarterly,* 8 (Autumn, 1967), 439-446.

MIZRUCHI, Ephriam Harold, *Success and Opportunity,* New York: Free Press, 1964, Chapter 4.

MOGEY, J. M., "Changes in Family Life Experienced by English Workers Moving from Slums to Housing Estates," *Marriage and Family Living,* 17 (May, 1955), 123-128.

MOGEY, J. M., *Family and Neighborhood,* New York: Oxford University Press, 1956.

MONSON, Astrid, " 'Slums, Semi-Slums, and Super-Slums,' " *Marriage and Family Living,* 17 (May, 1955), 118-122.

MOORE, Barrington, Jr., *Social Origins of Dictatorship and Democracy: Lord and Peasant in the Making of the Modern World,* Boston: Beacon Press, 1966.

MORLAND, J. Kenneth, "Kent Revisited: Blue-Collar Aspirations and Achievements," in Arthur B. Shostak and William Gomberg, editors, *Blue-Collar World: Studies of the American Worker,* Englewood Cliffs, New Jersey: Prentice Hall, 1964.

MYRDAL, Gunnar, *Challenge to Affluence,* New York: Pantheon, 1963.

NASH, Manning, *Primitive and Peasant Economic Systems,* San Francisco: Chandler, 1966.

NEALE, Daniel C. and John M. Proshek, "School Related Attitudes of Culturally Disadvantaged Elementary School Children," *Journal of Educational Psychology,* 58 (August, 1967), 238-244.

NORDLINGER, Eric A., *The Working Class Tories: Authority, Deference, and Stable Democracy,* Berkeley: University of California Press, 1967.

OBERG, Kalervo, "The Marginal Peasant in Rural Brazil," *American Anthropologist,* 67 (December, 1965), 1417-1427.

PADILLA, Elena, *Up from Puerto Rico,* New York: Columbia University Press, 1958.

PALMORE, Erdman B., "Dropouts, Delinquency, and Lower-Class Children," in Robert W. Will and Harold G. Vatter, editors, *Poverty in Affluence,* New York: Harcourt, Brace and World, 1965.

PALMORE, Erdman B., "Factors Associated With School Dropouts and Juvenile Delinquency Among Lower-Class Children," *Social Security Bulletin,* 26 (October, 1963), 4-9.

PALTIEL, Freda L., *Poverty: An Annotated Bibliography and References,* Ottawa: Canadian Welfare Council, 1966.

PASSOW, A. Harry, Miriam Goldbert and Abraham J. Tannenbaun, editors, *Education of the Disadvantaged: A Book of Readings,* New York: Holt, Rinehart and Winston, 1967.

PATTERSON, James M., "Marketing and the Working-Class Family," in Arthur B. Shostak and William Gomberg, editors, *Blue-Collar World: Studies of the American Worker,* Englewood Cliffs, New Jersey: Prentice Hall, 1964.

PAVENSTEDT, Eleanor, editor, *The Drifters: Children of Disorganized Lower-Class Families,* Boston: Little, Brown, 1967.

PETERSON, W. J. and M. A. Maxwell, "The Skid Row 'Wino,' " *Social Problems,* 5 (1958), 308-316.

PINARD, Maurice, "Poverty and Political Movements," *Social Problems,* 15 (Fall, 1967), 250-263.

POPE, Hallowell, "Economic Deprivation and Social Participation in a Group of 'Middle Class' Factory Workers," *Social Problems,* 11 (Winter, 1964), 290-300.

POPE, Liston, *Millhands and Preachers,* New Haven: Yale University Press, 1942.

POTTER, Jack M., May N. Diaz, and George M. Foster, editors, *Peasant Society: A Reader,* Boston: Little, Brown, 1967.

POWLES, William E., "The Southern Appalachian Migrant: Country Boy Turned Blue-Collarite," in Arthur B. Shostak and William Gomberg, editors, *Blue-Collar World: Studies of the American Worker,* Englewood Cliffs, New Jersey: Prentice Hall, 1964.

PRICE, Charlton R. and Harry Levenson, "Work and Mental Health," in Arthur B. Shostak and William Gomberg, editors, *Blue-Collar World: Studies of the American Worker,* Englewood Cliffs, New Jersey: Prentice Hall, 1964.

PURCELL, Theodore V., *Blue-Collar Man: Patterns of Dual Allegiance in Industry,* Cambridge: Harvard University Press, 1960.

PURCELL, Theodore V., "The Hopes of Negro Workers for Their Children," in Arthur B. Shostak and William Gomberg, editors, *Blue-Collar World: Studies of the American Worker,* Englewood Cliffs, New Jersey: Prentice Hall, 1964.

PURCELL, Theodore V., *The Worker Speaks His Mind on Company and Union,* Cambridge: Harvard University Press, 1953.

RAINWATER, Lee, "Crucible of Identity: The Negro Lower-Class Family," in Talcott Parsons and Kenneth B. Clark, editors, *The Negro American,* Boston: Houghton Mifflin, 1966.

RAINWATER, Lee, "Marital Sexuality in Four Cultures of Poverty," *Journal of Marriage and the Family,* 26 (November, 1964), 457-466.

RAINWATER, Lee, "Some Aspects of Lower Class Sex Behavior," *Journal of Social Issues,* 22 (April, 1966), 96-108.

RAINWATER, Lee, Richard P. Coleman, and Gerald Handel, *Workingman's Wife,* New York: Oceana Publications, 1959.

RAINWATER, Lee and Gerald Handel, "Changing Family Roles in the Working Class," in Arthur B. Shostak and William Gomberg, editors, *Blue-Collar World: Studies of the American Worker,* Englewood Cliffs, New Jersey: Prentice Hall, 1964.

RAINWATER, Lee and Karol Kane Weinstein, *And the Poor Get Children,* Chicago: Quadrangle Books, 1960.

RAINWATER, Lee and Karol Kane Weinstein, "A Qualitative Exploration of Family Planning and Contraception in the Working Class," *Marriage and Family Living,* 22 (August, 1960), 238-242.

REDFIELD, Robert, *Peasant Society and Culture,* Chicago: University of Chicago Press, 1956.

RIESSMAN, Frank, *The Culturally Deprived Child,* New York: Harper and Row, 1962.

RIESSMAN, Frank, "Low-Income Culture: The Strengths of the Poor," *Journal of Marriage and the Family,* 26 (November, 1964), 417-421.

RIESSMAN, Frank, "A Portrait of the Underprivileged," in Robert E. Will and Harold G. Vatter, *Poverty in Affluence,* New York: Harcourt Brace, 1965.

RIESSMAN, Frank, Jerome Cohen, and Arthur Pearl, editors, *Mental Health of the Poor,* New York: Free Press, 1964.

ROACH, Jack L., "Sociological Analysis and Poverty," *American Journal of Sociology,* 71 (July, 1965), 68-75.

ROACH, Jack L., "A Theory of Lower-Class Behavior," in Llewellyn Gross, editor, *Sociological Theory: Inquiries and Paradigms,* New York: Harper and Row, 1967.

ROACH, Jack L. and Orville R. Gursslin, "An Evaluation of the Concept, 'Culture of Poverty,' " *Social Forces,* 45 (March, 1967), 383-392.

ROACH, Jack L. and Orville R. Gursslin, "The Lower Class, Status

Frustration, and Social Disorganization," *Social Forces,* 43 (May, 1965), 501-510.

ROBB, J. H., *Working-Class Anti-Semite: A Psychological Study in a London Borough,* London: Travistock Publications, 1954.

ROBERTS, Joan I., editor, *School Children in the Urban Slum,* New York: Free Press, 1967.

RODMAN, Hyman, "Illegitimacy in the Caribbean Social Structure: A Reconsideration," *American Sociological Review,* 31 (October, 1966), 673-683.

RODMAN, Hyman, "The Lower Classes and the Negroes: Implications for Intellectuals," in Arthur B. Shostak and William Gomberg, editors, *Blue-Collar World: Studies of the American Worker,* Englewood Cliffs, New Jersey: Prentice Hall, 1964.

RODMAN, Hyman, "The Lower-Class Value Stretch," *Social Forces,* 42 (December, 1963), 205-215.

RODMAN, Hyman, "Marital Relationships in a Trinidad Village," *Marriage and Family Living,* 23 (May, 1961), 166-170.

RODMAN, Hyman, "Middle-Class Misconceptions About Lower-Class Families," in Arthur B. Shostak and William Gomberg, editors, *Blue-Collar World: Studies of the American Worker,* Englewood Cliffs, New Jersey: Prentice Hall, 1964.

RODMAN, Hyman, "On Understanding Lower-Class Behavior," *Social and Economic Studies,* 8 (December, 1959).

ROMAN, Paul M. and Harrison M. Trice, *Schizophrenia and the Poor,* Ithaca: Cornell University, New York State School of Industrial and Labor Relations, 1967.

ROONEY, J. F., "Group Processes Among Skid Row Winos: A Re-Evaluation of the Under-socialization Hypothesis,"*Quarterly Journal of Studies on Alcohol,* 22 (1961), 444-460.

ROSENBERG, Bernard and Joseph Bensman, "Sexual Patterns in Three Ethnic Subcultures of an American Underclass," *The Annals of the American Academy of Political and Social Science,* 376 (March, 1968), 61-75.

ROSENBLATT, Daniel and Edward A. Suchman, "Blue-Collar Attitudes and Information Toward Health and Illness," in Arthur B. Shostak and William Gomberg, editors, *Blue-Collar World: Studies of the American Worker,* Englewood Cliffs, New Jersey: Prentice Hall, 1964.

ROSENBLATT, Daniel and Edward A. Suchman, "The Underutilization of Medical-Care Services by Blue-Collarites," in Arthur B. Shostak and William Gomberg, editors, *Blue-Collar World: Studies of the American Worker,* Englewood Cliffs, New Jersey: Prentice Hall, 1964.

ROSENGREN, William R., "Social Class and Becoming 'Ill,' " in Arthur B. Shostak and William Gomberg, editors, *Blue-Collar World: Studies of the American Worker,* Englewood Cliffs, New Jersey: Prentice Hall, 1964.

LOWER STRATA   ROSENTHAL, Celia Stopnicka, "Lower Class Family Organization on the Carribbean Coast of Columbia," *Pacific Sociological Review,* 3 (Spring, 1960), 12-17.

ROSS, Arthur M. and Herbert Hill, editors, *Employment, Race, and Poverty,* New York: Harcourt Brace and World, 1968.

ROTH, Guenther, *The Social Democrats in Inperial Germany: A Study in Working Class Isolation and National Integration,* Totowa, New York: Bedminster Press, 1963.

RUBIN, Morton, "Resident Response to Urban Rehabilitation in a Negro Working-Class Neighborhood," in Arthur B. Shostak and William Gomberg, editors, *Blue-Collar World: Studies of the American Worker,* Englewood Cliffs, New Jersey: Prentice Hall,1964.

RUBINGTON, Earl, "Failure as a Heavy Drinker: The Case of the Chronic-Drunkenness Offender on Skid Row," in David J. Pittman and Charles R. Snyder, editors, *Society, Culture and Drinking Patterns,* New York: Wiley, 1962.

SAFA, Helen Icken, *From Shanty Town to Public Housing,* Syracuse, New York: Syracuse University Youth Development Center, 1962.

SCHLESINGER, Benjamin, *Poverty in Canada and the United States: Overview and Annotated Bibliography,* Toronto: University of Toronto Press, 1966.

SCHORR, Alvin L., *Poor Kids: A Report on Children in Poverty,* New York: Basic Books, 1966.

SCHORR, Alvin L., *Slums and Social Insecurity,* Washington, D. C.: United States Government Printing Office, 1964.

SCHREIBER, Daniel, *The School Dropout,* Washington, D. C.: National Education Association, 1964.

SCHULZ, David A., "The Father Role in Negro Lower-Class Families," *Social Science Quarterly,* 49 (December, 1968), 651-659.

SCHWARTZ, Michael and George Henderson, "The Culture of Unemployment: Some Notes on Negro Children," in Arthur B. Shostak and William Gomberg, editors, *Blue-Collar World: Studies of the American Worker,* Englewood Cliffs, New Jersey: Prentice Hall, 1964.

SCHWARZWELLER, Harry K., "Education, Migration, and Economic Life Chances of Male Entrants to the Labor Force from a Low-Income Rural Area," *Rural Sociology,* 29 (June, 1964), 152-167.

SEBALD, Hans, *Adolescence: A Sociological Analysis,* New York: Appleton-Century-Crofts, 1968.

SELIGMAN, Ben B., *Permanent Poverty: An American Syndrome,* Chicago: Quadrangle Books, 1968.

SEXTON, Patricia Cayo, *Spanish Harlem: Anatomy of Poverty,* New York: Harper and Row, 1965.

SEXTON, Patricia Cayo, "Wife of the 'Happy Worker,' " in Arthur B. Shostak and William Gomberg, editors, *Blue-Collar World: Studies of the American Worker,* Englewood Cliffs, New Jersey: Prentice Hall, 1964.

SHEPPARD, Harold L and Nicholas A. Masters, "The Political Attitudes and Preferences of Union Members: The Case of the Detroit Auto Workers," *American Political Science Review,* 53 (June, 1959), 437-447.

SHORT, James F. and Fred L. Strodtbeck, *Group Process and Gang Delinquency,* Chicago: University of Chicago Press, 1965.

SHOSTAK, Arthur B. and William Gomberg, editors, *Blue-Collar World,* Englewood Cliffs, New Jersey: Prentice-Hall, 1964.

SHOSTAK, Arthur B. and William Gomberg, editors, *New Perspectives on Poverty,* Englewood Cliffs, New Jersey: Prentice-Hall, 1965.

SHOTWELL, Louisa R., *The Harvesters: The Story of the Migrant People,* Garden City, New York: Doubleday, 1961.

SIMMEL, Georg, "The Poor," *Social Problems,* 13 (Fall, 1965), 118-140. Translated by Claire Jacobson.

SINGH, Mohinder, *The Depressed Classes: Their Economic and Social Conditions,* Bombay: Hird Kitabs, 1947.

SINGH, Tarlok, "The Landless Labourer and the Pattern of Social and Economic Change," *Transactions of the Third World Congress of Sociology,* 2 (1956), 278-288.

SJOBERG, Gideon, Richard A. Brymer, and Buford Farris, "Bureaucracy and the Lower Class," *Sociology and Social Research,* 50 (April, 1966), 325-337.

SMITH, Luke M. and Irving A. Fowler, "Plant Relocation and Worker Migration," in Arthur B. Shostak and William Gomberg, editors, *Blue-Collar World: Studies of the American Worker,* Englewood Cliffs, New Jersey: Prentice Hall, 1964.

SMITH, Raymond T., *The Negro Family in British Guiana,* London: Routledge and Kegan Paul, 1956.

SMUTS, Robert W., *European Impressions of the American Worker,* New York: King's Crown Press, 1953.

SOGGE, T. M., "Industrial Classes in the United States, 1870 to 1950," *Journal of the American Statistical Association,* 266 (June, 1954), 251-253.

SOLENBURGER, Alice W., *One Thousand Homeless Men,* Philadelphia: Survey Association, 1911.

LOWER STRATA

SPERGEL, Irving, "Male Young Adult Criminality, Deviant Values, and Differential Opportunities in Two Lower-Class Negro Neighborhoods," *Social Problems,* 10 (Winter, 1963), 237-250.

SPINLEY, B. W., *The Deprived and the Privileged,* London: Routledge and Kegan Paul, 1958.

SPINRAD, William, "Blue-Collar Workers as City and Suburban Residents—Effects on Union Membership," in Arthur B. Shostak and William Gomberg, editors, *Blue-Collar World: Studies of the American Worker,* Englewood Cliffs, New Jersey: Prentice Hall, 1964.

STAMLER, Rose, "Acculturation and Negro Blue-Collar Workers," in Arthur B. Shostak and William Gomberg, editors, *Blue-Collar World: Studies of the American Worker,* Englewood Cliffs, New Jersey: Prentice Hall, 1964.

STENDLER, Celia Burns, *Children of Brasstown,* University of Illinois Bulletin, Bureau of Research and Service of the College of Education, 46 (1949), number 59.

STRAUS, Robert, "Alcohol and the Homeless Man," *Quarterly Journal of Studies on Alcohol,* 7 (1946), 360-404.

STRAUS, Robert and Raymond G. McCarthy, "Nonaddictive Pathological Drinking Patterns of Homeless Men," *Quarterly Journal of Studies on Alcohol,* 12 (December, 1951).

STREET, David and John C. Leggett, "Economic Deprivation and Extremism: A Study of Unemployed Negroes," *American Journal of Sociology,* 67 (July, 1961), 53-57.

STYCOS, Joseph M., *Family and Fertility in Puerto Rico: A Study of the Lower Income Group,* New York: Columbia University Press, 1955.

STYS, W., "The Influence of Economic Conditions on the Fertility of Peasant Women," *Population Studies,* 11 (November, 1957), 136-148.

SUMNER, William Graham, *What Social Classes Owe to Each Other,* New York: Harper, 1883.

SURACE, Samuel, *Ideaology, Economic Change and the Working Classes: The Case of Italy,* Berkeley: University of California Press, 1966.

SUTHERLAND, Edwin H. and Harvey J. Locke, *Twenty Thousand Homeless Men: A Study of Unemployed Men in the Chicago Shelter,* Chicago: Lippincott, 1936.

TAYLOR, L. and C. W. Glasgow, *Occupations and Low-Income Rural People: A Southern Regional Study,* Baton Rouge: Louisiana Agricultural Experiment Station, Southern Cooperative Series, Bulletin 90, December, 1963.

THERNSTROM, Stephan, *Poverty and Progress,* Cambridge: Harvard University Press, 1964.

THOMPSON, E. P., *The Making of the English Working Class,* New York: Vintage, 1963.

THUROW, Lester C., "The Causes of Poverty," *Quarterly Journal of Economics,* 81 (February, 1967), 39-57.

TOBY, Jackson, "Orientation to Education as a Factor in the School Adjustment of Lower Class Children," *Social Forces,* 35 (1957), 259-266.

TOWNSEND, Peter, *The Family Life of Old People,* London: Routledge and Kegan Paul, 1957.

TOYNBEE, Philip, editor, *Underdogs, Anguish and Anxiety: Eighteen Men and Women Write Their Own Case Histories,* New York: Horizon Press, 1962.

UNITED STATES BUREAU OF THE CENSUS, Current Population Reports, Series P-20, No. 54, *The Extent of Poverty in the United States: 1959-1966,* United States Government Printing Office, Washington, D. C., 54, 1958, 20.

VADAKIN, James C., *Children, Poverty and Family Allowances,* New York: Basic Books, 1968.

VALENTINE, Charles A., *Culture and Poverty: Critique and Counter-Proposals,* Chicago: University of Chicago Press, 1968.

VALIEN, Preston, "The 'Mentalities' of Negro and White Workers: An 'Experimental School' Interpretation of Negro Trade Unionism," *Social Forces,* 27 (May, 1949), 433-438.

VANDERKOOL, Ronald C., *Skid Row and Its Men: An Exploration of Social Structure, Behavior and Attitudes,* East Lansing: Michigan State University Technical Bulletin B-39, 1963.

VAN DOORN, Jacques A. A., "The Changed Positions of Unskilled Workers in the Social Structure of the Netherlands," *Transactions of the Third World Congress of Sociology,* 3 (1956), 113-125.

VERNON, Glenn M., "Religion and the Blue-Collarite," in Arthur B. Shostak and William Gomberg, editors, *Blue-Collar World: Studies of the American Worker,* Englewood Cliffs, New Jersey: Prentice Hall, 1964.

WALLACE, Samuel E., "The Road to Skid Row," *Social Problems,* 16 (Summer, 1968), 92-105.

WALLACE, Samuel E., *Skid Row as a Way of Life,* Totowa, New Jersey: Bedminster Press, 1965.

WEBB, R. K., *The British Working Class Reader, 1790-1848,* London: Allen and Unwin, 1955.

WEINANDY, Janet E., *Families Under Stress,* New York: Syracuse University Press, 1962.

WEISBROD, Burton A., editor, *The Economics of Poverty: An American Paradox,* Englewood Cliffs, New Jersey: Prentice Hall, 1965.

WHITE, R. Clyde, "Low-Income Classes," *American Journal of Sociology,* 47 (May, 1942), 918-928.

WHYTE, William F., "A Slum Sex Code," *American Journal of Sociology,* 49 (July, 1943), 24-31.

WHYTE, William F., "Social Organization in the Slums," *American Sociological Review,* 8 (February, 1943), 34-39.

WHYTE, William F., *Street Corner Society: The Social Structure of an Italian Slum,* Chicago: University of Chicago Press, 1955.

WILENSKY, Harold L., "The Labor Vote: A Local Union's Impact on the Political Conduct of its Members," *Social Forces,* 35 (December, 1956), 111-120.

WILL, Robert E. and Harold G. Vatter, editors, *Poverty in Affluence: The Social, Political and Economic Dimensions of Poverty in the United States,* New York: Harcourt, Brace and World, 1965.

WILLIE, Charles V. and Janet Weinandy, "The Structure and Composition of 'Problem' and 'Stable' Families in a Low-Income Population," *Marriage and Family Living,* 25 (November, 1963), 439-447.

WILLMOTT, Peter, *Adolescent Boys of East London,* New York: Humanities Press, 1967.

WILLMOTT, Peter and Michael Young, *Family and Class in a London Suburb,* New York: Humanities Press, 1961.

WILLOUGHBY, Gertrude, "The Working Class Family in England," *Transactions of the Third World Congress of Sociology,* 4 (1956), 155-160.

WOLF, Eric R., "Types of Latin-American Peasantry: A Preliminary Discussion," *American Anthropologist,* 57 (June, 1955), 425-471.

WRIGHT, Dale, *They Harvest Despair: The Migrant Farm Worker,* Boston: Beacon Press, 1965.

WRIGHT, Gordon, *Rural Revolution in France: The Peasantry in the Twentieth Century,* Stanford: Stanford University Press, 1964.

YOUMANS, E. G., *The Rural School Drop-Out: A Ten-Year Follow-Up Study of Eastern Kentucky Youth,* Lexington: University of Kentucky, College of Education, Bulletin of the Bureau of School Service, 36, Number 1, September, 1963.

YOUNG, Michael and Peter Willmott, *Family and Kinship in East*

LOWER STRATA

London, New York: Free Press, 1957.

YOUNG, Michael and Peter Willmott, "Social Grading by Manual Workers," *British Journal of Sociology,* 7 (December, 1956), 337-345.

ZEITLIN, Maurice, "Revolutionary Workers and Individual Liberties," *American Journal of Sociology,* 72 (May, 1967), 619-632.

ZOLA, Irving Kenneth, "Illness Behavior of the Working Class: Implications and Recommendations," in Arthur B. Shostak and William Gomberg, editors, *Blue-Collar World: Studies of the American Worker,* Englewood Cliffs, New Jersey: Prentice Hall, 1964.

ZOLA, Irving Kenneth, "Observations on Gambling in a Lower-Class Setting," *Social Problems,* 10 (Spring, 1963), 353-361.

ZWEIG, Ferdinand, *The British Worker,* London: 1952.

ZWEIG, Ferdinand, *The Worker in an Affluent Society,* New York: Free Press, 1962.

ZWEIG, Ferdinand, "Working Classes and the Social Framework in Israel," *Sociological Review,* 5 (December, 1957), 191-206.

Characteristics of Middle Strata

The boundaries between the middle strata and the upper and lower ones are drawn differently by different students of stratification and are largely if not entirely arbitrary. The placement of publications in this section, rather than in the preceding or following one, generally depends upon the terminology of the authors. Therefore, persons interested in this topic may also find relevant material listed under "lower strata" and "upper strata."

Although we do not cover all the literature dealing specifically with any of the social strata, the smaller number of items listed here for the middle than for the lower strata rather accurately reflects the relative size of the two bodies of literature. This results from the "problems" perspective of much of social science and the greater prevalence of socially defined "problem" phenomena in the lower strata.

ABERLE, David F. and Kasper D. Naegele, "Middle Class Fathers' Occupational Role and Attitudes Toward Children," *American Journal of Orthopsychiatry,* 22 (April, 1952), 366-378.

BAGGALEY, Andrew R., "White Collar Employment and Republican Vote," *Public Opinion Quarterly,* 20 (Summer, 1956), 471-473.

MIDDLE STRATA

BANKS, J. A. and Olive Banks, *Feminism and Family Planning in Victorian England,* New York: Schocken, 1964.

BARBER, Elinor G., *The Bourgeoisie in 18th Century France,* Princeton: Princeton University Press, 1955.

BAZELON, David T., "The New Class," *Commentary,* 42 (July, 1966), 48-53.

BEN-DAVID, J., "The Rise of a Salaried Professional Class in Israel," *Transactions of the Third World Congress of Sociology,* 3 (1956), 302-310.

BENDIX, Reinhard, "The Self-Legitimation of an Entrepreneurial Class: The Case of England," *Transactions of the Second World Congress of Sociology,* 2 (1954), 259-282.

BERG, Ivar and David Rogers, "Former Blue-Collarites in Small Business," in Arthur B. Shostak and William Gomberg, editors, *Blue-Collar World: Studies of the American Worker, Englewood Cliffs,* New Jersey: Prentice-Hall, 1964.

BILL, Valentine, *The Forgotten Class: The Russian Bourgeoisie from the Earliest Beginnings to 1900,* New York: Praeger, 1959.

BLACKER, J. G. C., "Social Ambitions of the Bourgeoisie of 18th Century France and their Relation to Family Limitation," *Population Studies,* 11 (1957), 46-63.

BOHLKE, Robert H., "Social Mobility, Stratification Inconsistency and Middle Class Delinquency," *Social Problems,* 8 (1961), 351-363.

BONHAM, John, *The Middle-Class Vote,* London: Faber and Faber, 1954.

BUNZEL, John H., *The American Small Businessman,* New York: Knopf, 1962.

COLE, G. D. H. and Raymond Postgate, *The Common People,* London: Methuem, 1948.

COREY, Lewis, *The Crisis of the Middle Class,* New York, 1935.

COREY, Lewis, "The Middle Class," *The Antioch Review,* 5 (Spring, 1945), 68-87.

CRONER, Fritz, "Salaried Employees in Modern Society," *International Labor Review,* 69 (February, 1954), 97-110.

CROZIER, M., "Classes Sans Conscience," *European Journal of Sociology,* 2 (1961), 18-50.

DAVIS, Allison, *The Psychology of the Child in the Middle Class,* Pittsburg: University of Pittsburgh Press, 1960.

DE GRE, Gerard, "Ideology and Class Consciousness in the Middle Class," *Social Forces,* 29 (December, 1950), 173-179.

DICK, Harry R., "The Office Worker: Attitudes toward Self, Labor, and Management," *Sociological Quarterly,* 3 (January, 1962), 43-56.

ELMER, M. C., "The Growth of a Middle Class in Venezuela," *Social Science,* 38 (1963), 145-147.

FARIS, Robert E. L., "The Middle Class from a Sociological Viewpoint," *Social Forces,* 39 (October, 1960), 1-5.

FERREIRA, J. B., "The Middle Class," *Sociological Bulletin,* 1 (1952), 60-70.

FRAZIER, E. Franklin, "The Negro Middle Class and Desegration," *Social Problems,* 4 (April, 1957), 291-301.

GASTIL, Raymond D., "Middle Class Impediments to Iranian Modernization," *Public Opinion Quarterly,* 22 (Fall, 1958), 325-329.

GINZBERG, Eli, *The Middle-Class Negro in the White Man's World,* New York: Columbia University Press, 1967.

GRAYSON, Henry, *The Crisis of the Middle Class,* New York: Rinehart, 1955.

GREEN, Arnold W., "The Middle Class Male Child and Neurosis," *American Sociological Review,* 11 (February, 1946), 31-41.

GUZZARDI, Walter, Jr., "The Crucial Middle Class," *Fortune,* 65 (February, 1962), 98-214.

HAMILTON, Richard F., *Class and Politics in the United States,* New York: Wiley, 1969.

HAMILTON, Richard F., "The Income Difference Between Skilled and White-Collar Workers," *British Journal of Sociology,* 38 (December, 1963), 363-373.

HAMILTON, Richard F., "The Marginal Middle Class: A Reconsideration," *American Sociological Review,* 31 (April, 1966), 192-199.

HERMANN, Lucille, "The Middle Class in Guaratingueta," *Economic Development and Cultural Change,* 2 (1953), 83-108.

HODGES, Donald Clark, "The 'Intermediate Classes' in Marxian Theory," *Sociology and Social Research,* 28 (Spring, 1961), 23-36.

241

HUNTINGTON, Emily H., *Spending of Middle Income Families,* Berkeley: University of California Press, 1957.

MIDDLE STRATA

INTERNATIONAL INSTITUTE OF DIFFERING CIVILIZATIONS, *Development of a Middle Class in Tropical and Sub-Tropical Countries,* Brussels: 1956.

JOHNSON, John J., "Middle Groups in National Politics in Latin America," *Hispanic American Historical Review,* 37 (1957), 313-329.

JOHNSON, John J., *Political Change in Latin America: The Emergence of the Middle Sectors,* Stanford: Stanford University Press, 1958.

JOHNSON, John J., "The Political Role of the Latin American Middle Sectors," *Annals of American Academy of Political and Social Science,* 334 (1961), 20-29.

KELSALL, R. K., David Lockwood, and A. Trapp, "The New Middle Class in the Power Structure of Great Britain," in *Transactions of the Third World Congress of Sociology,* 3 (1956).

KHURANA, B. K., "A Socio-Economic Study of Clerks, I and II," *Sociological Bulletin,* 6 (March, 1957), 72-79 and 7 (September, 1958), 134-136.

KOOS, Earl L., "Middle-Class Family Crises," *Marriage and Family Living,* 10 (Spring, 1948).

KOTLAR, Sally L., "Middle Class Marital Role Perceptions and Marital Adjustment," *Sociology and Social Research,* 49 (April, 1965), 283-293.

KUPER, Leo, *An African Bourgeoisie: Race, Class, and Politics in South Africa,* New Haven: Yale University Press, 1965.

LADD, Everett C., "Radical Right: The White Collar Extremists," *South Atlantic Quarterly,* 65 (Summer, 1966), 314-324.

LANDES, David, "French Business and the Businessman: A Social and Cultural Analysis," in Edward M. Earle, editor, *Modern France,* Princeton: Princeton University Press, 1951.

LEWIS, Roy and Angus Maude, *Professional People,* London: Phoenix House, 1952.

LEWIS, Roy and Angus Maude, *The English Middle Classes,* New York: Knopf, 1950.

LOCKWOOD, David, *The Blackcoated Worker,* London, 1958.

LUIJCKX, A. W., "Inquiry into the Mobility of Employment in the Dutch Middle Class," *Transactions of the Second World Congress of Sociology,* 2 (1954), 89-90.

MAYER, John E., *Other People's Marital Problems: The Knowledgeability of Lower and Middle Class Wives,* New York: Institute of Welfare Research, Community Service Society of New York, 1966.

MAYER, Kurt B. and Sidney Goldstein, "Manual Workers as Small Businessmen," in Arthur B. Shostak and William Gomberg, editors, *Blue-Collar World: Studies of the American Worker,* Englewood Cliffs, New Jersey: Prentice Hall, 1964.

McGUIRE, Carson, "Family Life in Lower and Middle Class Homes," *Marriage and Family Living,* 14 (February, 1952), 1-6.

MEADOWS, Paul, "Facts and Figures on the White Collar Worker," *Technological Review,* 51 (1949), 508-510 and 522-528.

MERTON, Robert K., "Bureaucratic Structure and Personality," *Social Forces,* 18 (May, 1940), 560-568.

McGINN, Noel F., "Marriage and Family in Middle-Class Mexico," *Journal of Marriage and the Family,* 28 (August, 1966), 305-313.

MILLS, C. Wright, "The Middle Classes in Middle-Sized Cities: The Stratification and Political Position of Small Business and White Collar Strata," *American Sociological Review,* 11 (October, 1946), 520-529.

MILLS, C. Wright, *White Collar: The American Middle Classes,* New York: Oxgord University Press, 1951.

MISRA, B. B., *The Indian Middle Classes,* London: Oxford University Press, 1960.

MORSE, Nancy, *Satisfactions in the White-Collar Job,* Ann Arbor: Survey Research Center, Institute for Social Research, University of Michigan, 1953.

MUSGROVE, F., "Middle Class Families and Schools, 1780-1880," *Sociological Review,* 7 (December, 1959), 169-178.

MYERHOFF, Howard L. and Barbara G. Myerhoff, "Field Observations of Middle Class 'Gangs,'" *Social Forces,* 42 (March, 1964), 328-336.

NELSON, Joel I., "Participation and Integration: The Case of the Small Businessman," *American Sociological Review,* 33 (June, 1968), 427-438.

PARKIN, Frank, *Middle-Class Radicalism: The Social Bases of the British Campaign for Nuclear Disarmament,* New York: Praeger, 1968.

PELZEL, John C., "The Small Industrialist in Japan," *Explorations in Entrepreneurial History,* 7 (1954), 79-93.

PINK, Louis H., "Housing the Middle Income Family," *Journal of Marriage and the Family,* 17 (May, 1955), 152-154.

RANULF, Svend, *Moral Indignation and Middle Class Psychology,* New York: Schocken, 1964.

MIDDLE STRATA

ROGIN, Michael, "Wallace and the Middle Class: The White Backlash in Wisconsin," *Public Opinion Quarterly,* 30 (Spring, 1966), 98-108.

ROSE, Arnold M., "Factors Associated With The Life Satisfaction of Middle-Class, Middle-Aged Persons," *Journal of Marriage and the Family,* 17 (February, 1955), 15-19.

SHANLEY, Fred J., "Middle-Class Delinquency as a Social Problem," *Sociology and Social Research,* 51 (January, 1967), 185-198.

SHOLAM, Shlomo and Meir Hovav, " 'B'Nei-Tovim'–Middle and Upper Class Delinquency in Israel," *Sociology and Social Research,* 48 (July, 1964), 454-468.

SINHA, B., "Disintegration of the Middle Class: Another Indication of West Bengal's Decay," *Modern Review,* 93 (March, 1953), 189-194.

SMITH, T. Lynn, "Observations on the Middle Class in Columbia," in *Materiales para el Estudia de la clase media en la America Latina,* 6, Washington, D. C.: Pan American Union, 1951.

STENDLER, Celia Burns, "The Learning of Certain Secondary Drives by Parisian and American Middle Class Children," *Journal of Marriage and the Family,* 16 (August, 1954), 195-204.

STEVENSON, Elizabeth, *Babbitts and Bohemians,* New York: Macmillan, 1967.

STURMTHAL, Adolf, editor, *White-Collar Trade Unions: Contemporary Developments in Industrialized Societies,* Urbana: University of Illinois Press, 1967.

SUSSMAN, Marvin B., "The Help Pattern of the Middle-Class Family," *American Sociological Review,* 18 (February, 1953), 22-28.

SUTHERLAND, Edwin H., *White Collar Crime,* New York: Holt, Rinehart and Winston, 1949 .

SUTHERLAND, Edwin H., "White-Collar Criminality," *American Sociological Review,* 5 (February, 1940), 1-12.

THRUPP, Sylvia, *The Merchant Class of Medieval London, 1300-1500,* Chicago: University of Chicago Press, 1948.

TREUDLEY, Mary Bosworth, "An Ethnic Group's View of the American Middle Class," *American Sociological*

Review, 11 (December, 1946), 715-724.

VAZ, Edmund W., "Juvenile Delinquency in the Middle-
Class Youth Culture," in Edmund W. Vaz, editor,
Middle-Class Juvenile Delinquency, New York: Harper
and Row, 1967.

VOGEL, Ezra F., *Japan's New Middle Class: The Salary Man
and His Family in a Tokyo Suburb,* Berkeley: University of
California Press, 1963.

WHYTE, William H., Jr., *The Organization Man,* New York:
Simon and Schuster, 1956.

WINCH, Robert F., Scott Greer, and R. L. Blumberg,
"Ethnicity and Extended Familism in an Upper-Middle Class
Suburb," *American Sociological Review,* 32 (April, 1967),
265-272.

WISE, Nancy Barton, "Juvenile Delinquency Among Middle-Class
Girls," in Edmund W. Vaz, editor, *Middle-Class Juvenile Delinquency,* New York: Harper and Row, 1967.

WOLFGANG, Marvin E., "Conformity and the Middle Class,"
Sociology and Social Research, 43 (July-August, 1959),
432-438.

WUNDERLICH, Frieda, "Fascism and the German Middle Class,"
Antioch Review, 5 (1945), 56-67.

Characteristics of Upper Strata

This section includes treatments of variously defined elites. Some of the
publications deal with rather broadly defined upper strata and others deal with very
narrowly defined ones, containing a minute percentage of the people in the society.
Furthermore, all the publications do not use the same stratification variable, or
combination of variables, to delineate the upper strata.

It is apparent that the literature in this area is voluminous, and yet social
scientists have little dependable evidence about many types of values, attitudes, and
behavior in the very uppermost levels. Although social scientists themselves are
placed in the upper strata in some of the publications listed here, few have gained
enough access to the "upper-upper" social circles to gain intimate knowledge of
them.

AARONOVITCH, Sam, *The Ruling Class: A Study of British Finance Capital,* London: Lawrence and Wishart, 1961.

ABEGGLEN, James C., and H. Mannari, "Leaders of Modern Japan: Social Origins and Mobility," *Economic Development and Culture Change,* 9 (1960), 109-134.

ADAMS, Edward L. Jr., William B. Dreffin, Robert B. Kamm, and Dyckman W. Vermidge, "Altitudes With Regard to Minority Groups of a Sample of University Men Students from the Upper Socioeconomic Level," *Journal of Educational Sociology,* 21 (February, 1948), 328-338.

ADAMS, Stuart, "Origins of American Occupational Elites, 1900-1955," *American Journal of Sociology,* 62 (January, 1957), 360-368.

ADAMS, Stuart, "Real and Nominal Origins of Selected Occupational Elites," *Research Studies of the State College of Washington,* 23 (June, 1955), 121-129.

ADAMS, Stuart, "Regional Differences in Vertical Mobility in a High-Status Occupation," *American Sociological Review,* 15 (April, 1950), 228-235.

ADAMS, Stuart, "Trends in Occupational Origins of Business Leaders," *American Sociological Review,* 19 (October, 1954), 541-548.

ADAMS, Stuart, "Trends in Occupational Origins of Physicians," *American Sociological Review,* 18 (August, 1953), 404-409.

AMORY, Cleveland, *The Proper Bostonians,* New York: Dutton, 1947.

AMORY, Cleveland, *Who Killed Society?* New York: Harper and Row, 1960.

ANDERSON, C. Arnold and Bryce Ryan, "Iowa's Contribution to National Leadership: A Study of Iowans in Who's Who," *Rural Sociology,* 12 (March, 1947), 40-48.

ANDERSON, W. A., "The Spacing of Births in the Families of University Graduates," *American Journal of Sociology,* 53 (July, 1947), 23-33.

ANNAN, N. G., "The Intellectual Aristocracy," in J. H. Plumb, editor, *Studies in Social History,* London: Longmans Green, 1955.

ARMSTRONG, John A., *The Soviet Bureaucratic Elite: A Case Study of the Ukranian Apparatus,* London; Stevens, 1959.

ARON, Raymond, "Social Class, Political Class, Ruling Class," in Reinhard Bendix and Seymour M. Lipset, editors, *Class, Status and Power,* 2nd edition, New York: Free Press, 1966.

ARONSON, Sidney H., *Status and Kinship in the Higher Civil Service: Standards of Selection in the Administrations of John Adams, Thomas Jefferson, and Andrew Jackson.* Cambridge: Harvard University Press, 1964.

BAILYN, Bernard, *The New England Merchants in the Seventeenth Century,* Cambridge: Harvard University Press, 1955.

BAINRIDGE, John, *The Super-Americans,* Garden City, New York: Doubleday, 1961.

BALTZELL, E. Digby, *An American Business Aristocracy,* New York: Collier, 1962. A Reissue under a new title of *Philadelphia Gentleman.*

BALTZELL, E. Digby, "The American Aristocrat and Other Direction," in Seymour M. Lipset and Leo Lowenthal, editors, *Culture and Social Character,* New York: Free Press, 1961.

BALTZELL, E. Digby, *Philadelphia Gentlemen: The Making of a National Upper Class,* New York: Free Press, 1958.

BALTZELL, E. Digby, *The Protestant Establishment: Aristocracy and Class in America,* New York: Random House, 1964.

BARKLEY, R., "Theory of the Elite and the Mythology of Power," *Science and Society,* 19 (Spring, 1955), 97-106.

BARLOW, Robin, *et al., Economic Behavior of the Affluent,* Washington, D. C., Brookings Institution, 1966.

BELL, Wendell, "Social Change and Elites in an Emergent Nation," in Herbert R. Barringer, George I. Blanksten, and Raymond W. Mack, editors, *Social Change in Developing Areas,* Cambridge: Schenkman, 1966.

BELOFF, M. "Intellectual Classes and Ruling Classes in France," *Occidente,* 10 (January-February, 1954), 54-65.

BENDIX, Reinhard, *Higher Civil Servants in American Society,* University of Colorado Studies, "Series in Sociology," 1 (July, 1949).

BENDIX, Reinhard and Frank W. Howton, "Social Mobility and the American Business Elite," *British Journal of Sociology,* 9 (March, 1958), 1-14.

BETH, Marian W., "The Elite and The Elites," *American Journal of Sociology,* 47 (March, 1942), 746-755.

BLONDEL, Jean, *Voters, Parties, and Leaders,* Baltimore: Penguin, 1963.

BLOOMFIELD, Paul, *Uncommon People: A Study of England's Elite,* London: Hamish Hamilton, 1955.

BLUM, Jerome, *Lord and Peasant in Russia from the Ninth to the Nineteenth Century,* Princeton: Princeton University Press, 1961.

UPPER STRATA

247

BONILLA, Frank, "Elites and Public Opinion in Areas of High Social Stratification," *Public Opinion Quarterly,* 22 (Fall, 1958) 349-356.

BOTTOMORE, T. B., *Elites and Society,* New York: Basic Books, 1964.

BOTTOMORE, T. B., "Higher Civil Servants in France," *Transactions of the Second World Congress of Sociology,* 2 (1954) 143-152.

BURNHAM, James, *The Managerial Revolution,* London: Putnam, 1943.

CALHOUN, Daniel H., *Professional Lives in America: Structure and Aspiration 1750-1850,* Cambridge: Harvard University Press, 1965.

CARR-SAUNDERS, A. G., and P. A. Wilson, *The Professions,* London: Oxford at the Clarendon Press, 1933.

CARSTAIRS, G. M., *The Twice-Born: A Study of a Community of High-Caste Hindus,* London: Hogarth Press, 1957.

CHANG, Chung-li, *The Chinese Gentry: Studies in their Role in 19th Century Chinese Society,* Seattle: University of Washington Press, 195!

CHANG, Chung-li, *The Income of the Chinese Gentry,* Seattle: University of Washington Press, 1962.

CHARTIER, Barbara, "The Social Role of the Literary Elite," *Social Forces,* 29 (December, 1950) 179-186.

CHOW, Yung-Teh, *Social Mobility in China: Status Careers Among the Gentry in a Chinese Community,* New York: Atherton Press, 1966.

CLAYTON, L. W., "The British Administrative Class," *Personnel Administration,* 14 (1951).

CLIFFORD-VAUGHN, Michalina, "Some French Concepts of Elites," *British Journal of Sociology,* 11 (December, 1960), 319-332.

CLIGNET, Remi, and Philip Foster, *The Fortunate Few: A Study of Secondary Schools and Students in the Ivory Coast,* Evanston: Northwestern University Press, 1966.

COLE, G. D. H., "Elites in British Society," in *Studies in Class Structure,* London: Routledge and Kegan Paul, 1955.

COLE, G. D. H., *Studies in Class Structure,* London: Routledge and Kegan Paul, 1955.

COPEMAN, G. H., *Leaders of British Industry,* London: 1955.

CRAMER, M. Ward, "Leisure Time Activities of Economically Privileged Children," *Sociology and Social Research,* 34 (1949-1950), 444-450.

DALTON, Melville, *Men Who Manage,* New York: Wiley, 1959.

DAVIS, Beverly, "Eminence and Level of Social Origin," *American Journal of Sociology,* 59 (July, 1953), 11-18.

DE HUSZAR, George B., *The Intellectuals: A Controversial Portrait,*

New York: Free Press, 1960.

DJILAS, Milovan, *The New Class: An Analysis of the Communist System,* New York: Praeger, 1959.

DOBLIN, E. M. and C. Pohly, "The Social Composition of the Nazi Leadership," *American Journal of Sociology,* 51 (July, 1945), 42-49.

DOMHOFF, G. William, *Who Rules America?* Englewood Cliffs, New Jersey: Prentice-Hall, 1967.

DUNCAN, Otis Dudley, "Social Origins of Salaried and Self-Employed Professional Workers," *Social Forces,* 44 (December, 1965), 186-189.

EBERHARD, Wolfram, *Conquerors and Rulers: Social Forces in Medieval China,* second edition, Leiden, Netherlands: Brill, 1952.

EDINGER, Lewis J., "Continuity and Change in the Background of German Decision-Makers," *Western Political Quarterly,* 14 (March, 1961), 17-36.

EDINGER, Lewis J. and Donald D. Searing, "Social Background in Elite Analysis: A Methodological Inquiry," *American Political Science Review,* 56 (June, 1967), 428-445.

EDWARDS, G. Franklin, *The Negro Professional Class,* New York: Free Press, 1959.

EISENSTADT, S. N., "The Place of Elites and Primary Groups in the Absorption of New Immigrants in Israel," *American Journal of Sociology,* (November, 1951), 222-231.

ELLIOTT, Osborn, *Men at the Top,* New York: Harper and Row, 1960.

ETZIONI, Amitai, "The Functional Differentiation of Elites in the Kibbutz," *American Journal of Sociology,* 64 (March, 1959), 476-487.

FADIMAN, Clifton, "Is There an Upper-Class American Language?", *Holiday* (October, 1966), 8-10.

FAINSOD, Merle, *How Russia is Ruled,* Cambridge: Harvard University Press, 1953.

FEI, Hsiao-Tung, *China's Gentry,* Chicago: University of Chicago Press, 1953.

EDITORS OF FORTUNE, *The Executive Life,* Garden City, New York: Doubleday, 1956.

FRANK, Myrna E. and Clyde V. Kiser, "Changes in Social and Demographic Attributes of Women in 'Who's Who'," *Milbank Memorial Fund Quarterly,* 43 (January, 1965), 55-75.

FRANKEL, Max, "The 8,708,000 Elite of Russia," *New York Times Magazine,* (May 29, 1960).

UPPER STRATA

FRAZIER, E. Franklin, "Education and the African Elite," *Transactions of the Third World Congress of Sociology,* 5 (1956), 90-96.

UPPER STRATA

GALTON, Francis and Edgar Schuster, *Noteworthy Families,* London: Murray, 1906.

GEIGER, Theodor, "An Historical Study of the Origins and Structure of the Danish Intelligentsia," *British Journal of Sociology,* 1 (1950), 209-220.

GERSTL, Joel E., "Determininants of Occupational Community in High Status Occupations," *Sociological Quarterly,* 2 (January, 1961), 37-48.

GILB, Corine Lathrop, *Hidden Hierarchies: The Professions and Government,* New York: Harper and Row, 1967.

GINI, Corrado, "Real and Apparent Exceptions to the Uniformity of a Lower Natural Increase of the Upper Classes," *Rural Sociology,* 1 (September, 1936).

GINZBERG, Eli, *Life Styles of Educated Women,* New York: Columbia University Press, 1966.

GOLDRICH, Daniel, *Sons of the Establishment: Elite Youth in Panama and Costa Rica,* Chicago: Rand McNally, 1966.

GOODWIN, A., editor, *The European Nobility in the Eighteenth Century,* London: Black, 1953.

GORDON, Milton M., "Social Class and American Intellectuals," *American Association of University Professors Bulletin,* 40 (Winter, 1954-1955), 517-528.

GOULD, Jay M., *The Technical Elite,* New York: Kelley, 1966.

GRANICK, David, *The Red Executive,* Garden City, New York: Doubleday, 1961.

GREGORY, Frances W., and Irene D. Neu, "The American Industrial Elite in the 1870's: Their Social Origin," in William Miller, editor, *Men in Business,* Cambridge: Harvard University Press, 1952.

GUTTSMAN, W. L., *The British Political Elite,* London: MacGibbon and Kee, 1963.

GUTTSMAN, W. L., "The Changing Social Structure of the British Political Elite, 1886-1935," *British Journal of Sociology,* 2 (1951), 122-134.

HACKER, Andrew, "The Elected and the Annointed: Two American Elites," *American Political Science Review,* 55 (September, 1961), 539-549.

HAMON, Leon, "The Members of the French Parliament," *International Social Science Journal,* 13 (1961), 545-567.

HARMON, Lindsey R., *Profiles of Ph.D.'s in the Sciences,* Washington, D. C.: National Academy of Sciences, 1966.

HARTNER, Carl L., "The Power Role of Intellectuals: An Introductory Statement," *Sociology and Social Research,* 48 (January, 1964), 139-154.

HELFRICH, Margaret L., "The Generalized Role of the Executive's Wife," *Journal of Marriage and the Family,* 23 (November, 1961), 384-387.

HENRY, William E., "The Business Executive: The Psycho-Dynamics of a Social Role," *American Journal of Sociology,* 54 (January, 1949), 286-291.

HEXTER, J. H., "The Education of the Aristocracy in the Renaissance," *Journal of Modern History,* 22 (1950), 1-20.

HUNTER, Floyd, *The Big Rich and the Little Rich,* Garden City, New York: Doubleday, 1965.

HUNTER, Floyd, *Top Leadership, United States of America,* Chapel Hill: University of North Carolina Press, 1959.

JANOWITZ, Morris, "Military Elites and the Study of War," *Journal of Conflict Resolution,* 1 (1957), 9-18.

JANOWITZ, Morris, "Social Stratification and the Comparative Analysis of Elites," *Social Forces,* 35 (October, 1956), 81-85.

KATONA, George and John Lansing, "The Wealth of the Wealthy," *Review of Economics and Statistics,* 46 (February, 1964), 1-13.

KAVALER, Lucy, *The Private World of High Society,* New York: McKay, 1960.

KELLER, Suzanne, *Beyond the Ruling Class: Stategic Elites in Modern Society,* New York: Random House, 1963.

KELLER, Suzanne, "Elites," *International Encyclopedia of the Social Sciences,* 5, New York: Free Press, 1968, 26.

KELLY, Sir David, *The Ruling Few,* London: Hollis and Carter, 1952.

KELSALL, R. K., *Higher Civil Servants in Britain,* London: Routledge and Kegan Paul, 1955.

KERSTEINS, T., *The New Elite in Asia and Africa: A Comparative Study of Indonesia and Ghana,* New York: Praeger, 1966.

KINCAID, Harry V. and Margaret Bright, "Interviewing the Business Elite," *American Journal of Sociology,* 63 (November, 1957), 304-311.

KUZNETS, Simon, *Shares of Upper Income Groups in Income and Savings,* New York: National Bureau of Economic Research, 1953.

LADINSKY, Jack, "Occupational Determinants of Geographic Mobility Among Professional Workers," *American Sociological Review,* 32 (April, 1967), 253-264.

UPPER STRATA

LAMPMAN, Robert, *The Share of Top Wealth-Holders in National Wealth: 1922-1956,* Princeton: Princeton University Press, 1962.

LASSWELL, Harold D. and Daniel Lerner, editors, *World Revolutionary Elites: Studies in Coercive Ideological Movements,* Cambridge: Massachusetts Institute of Technology Press, 1965.

LAURIAT, Patience, "Marriage and Fertility Patterns of College Graduates," *Eugenics Quarterly,* 6 (September, 1959), 171-179.

LEE, Shu-Ching, "Intelligentsia of China," *American Journal of Sociology,* 52 (May, 1947), 489-497.

LEHMAN, Harvey C., "The Age of Eminent Leaders: Then and Now," *American Journal of Sociology,* 52 (January, 1947), 342-356.

LEWIS, Gordon F., "A Comparison of Some Aspects of the Backgrounds and Careers of Small Businessmen and American Business Leaders," *American Journal of Sociology,* 65 (January, 1960), 348-355.

LEWIS, R. and Rosemary Stewart, *The Managers: A New Examination of the English, German and American Executive,* New York: Mentor, 1961.

LIPSET, Seymour M., "Aristocracy in America," *Commentary,* 26 (December, 1958), 534-537.

LIPSET, Seymour M., *Political Man,* Chapter 10, "American Intellectuals: Their Politics and Status," London: Heinemann, 1960.

LIPSET, Seymour M., and Aldo Solori, editors, *Elites in Latin America,* New York: Oxford University Press, 1967.

LUNDBERG, Ferdinand, *America's 60 Families,* New York: Citadel, 1946.

LUNDBERG, Ferdinand, *The Rich and the Super-Rich: A Study in the Power of Money Today,* New York: Lyle Stuart, 1968.

MALIA, Martin, "What is the Intelligentsia?" *Daedalus,* (Summer, 1960), 441-459.

MANNHEIM, Karl, "The Problem of the Intelligentsia: An Inquiry into Its Past and Present Role," in his *Essays on the Sociology of Culture,* New York: Oxford University Press, 1956.

MARSH, Robert M., *The Mandarins: The Circulation of Elites in China, 1600-1900,* New York: Free Press, 1961.

MARVICK, Dwaine, editor, *Political Decision-Makers,* New York: Free Press, 1961.

MASUOKA, Edna Cooper, "Motivations for Migration of Southern-born Notables," *Social Forces,* 29 (March, 1951), 290-294.

MATTHEWS, D. R., *The Social Background of Political Decision-Makers,* Garden City, New York: Doubleday, 1954.

McLELLAN, David S. and Charles E. Woodhouse, "The Business Elite and Foreign Policy," *Western Political Quarterly,* 13 (March, 1960), 172-190.

MEIER, August and David Lewis, "History of the Negro Upper Class in Atlanta, Georgia, 1890-1958," *Journal of Negro Education,* 28 (September, 1959), 128-139.

MEISEL, James H., *The Myth of the Ruling Class: Gaetano Mosca and the Elite,* Ann Arbor: University of Michigan Press, 1958.

MERRIAM, Charles, "The Curse of Aristocracy," *American Journal of Sociology,* 43 (May, 1938), 857-877.

MICHELS, Robert, "Intellectuals," in E. R. A. Seligman, editor, *Encyclopedia of the Social Sciences,* 8, New York: Macmillan, 1932, 118-126.

MILLER, William, "American Historians and the Business Elite," *Journal of Economic History,* 9 (1949), 184-208.

MILLER, William, "The Business Elite in Business Bureaucracies," in William Miller, editor, *Men in Business,* Cambridge: Harvard University Press, 1951.

MILLER, William, editor, *Men in Business: Essays on the Historical Role of the Entrepreneur,* revised edition, New York: Harper and Row, 1962.

MILLER, William, "The Recruitment of the American Business Elite," *Quarterly Journal of Economics,* 64 (May, 1950), 242-253.

MILLS, C. Wright, "The American Business Elite: A Collective Portrait," *Journal of Economic History* (Supplement) 5, (1945), 20-44.

MILLS, C. Wright, *The New Men of Power: America's Labor Leaders,* New York: Oxford University Press, 1948.

MILLS, C. Wright, *The Power Elite,* New York, Oxford University Press, 1956.

MILLS, C. Wright, "The Trade Union Leader: A Collective Portrait," *Public Opinion Quarterly,* 9 (Summer, 1945), 158-175.

MOORE, Barrington, Jr., *Social Origins of Dictatorship and Democracy: Lord and Peasant in the Making of the Modern World,* Boston: Beacon Press, 1966.

MOORE, Harry Estill and Sidney R. Warob, "Place of Education and Residence of Eminent Southerners," *Social Forces,* 27 (May, 1949), 408-412.

MOORE, Joan W., "Exclusiveness and Ethnocentrism in a Metropolitan Upper-Class Agency," *Pacific Sociological Review,* 5 (Spring, 1962), 16-20.

UPPER STRATA

MOSCA, Gaetano, *The Ruling Class,* New York: McGraw-Hill, 1939.

MOSKOS, Charles C., Jr., "Social Transformation of the Albanian Elite: From Monarchy to Communism," in Herbert R. Barringer, George Blanksten, and Raymond W. Mack, editors, *Social Change in Developing Areas,* Cambridge: Schenkman, 1966.

MYERS, Gustavus, *History of the Great American Fortunes,* New York: Modern Library, 1937.

NAIR, B. N., *The Dynamic Brahmin,* Bombay, India: Popular Book Depot, 1959.

NAVILLE, Pierre, "Technical Elites and Social Elites," *Sociology of Education,* 37 (Fall, 1963), 27-29.

NEWCOMER, Mabel, *The Big Business Executive: The Factors that Made Him, 1900-1950,* Columbia: Columbia University Press, 1955.

NEWCOMER, Mabel, "The Chief Executives of Large Business Corporations," *Explorations in Entrepreneurial History,* 5 (1952-1953), 1-34.

NORTH, Robert C., "The Chinese Communist Elite," *Annals of the American Academy of Political and Social Science,* (1951), 67-75.

NORTON-TAYLOR, Duncan, "How Top Executives Live," *Fortune,* 52 (July, 1955), 78-169.

PACKARD, Vance, *The Pyramid Climbers,* New York: McGraw-Hill, 1962.

PARETO, Vilfredo, *The Mind and Society,* London: Jonathan Cape, 1935.

PARSONS, Talcott, "The Professions and Social Structure," in his *Essays in Sociological Theory,* revised edition, New York: Free Press, 1954.

PERRUCCI, Carolyn Cummings, "Mobility, Marriage and Child-Spacing Among College Graduates," *Journal of Marriage and the Family,* 30 (May, 1968), 273-282.

PORTER, John, "The Economic Elite and the Social Structure in Canada," in B. Blishen *et al, Canadian Society,* New York: Free Press, 1961.

PORTER, John, "Elite Groups: A Scheme for the Study of Power in Canada," *Canadian Journal of Economics and Political Science,* 21 (November, 1955), 498-512.

READER, W. J., *Professional Men: The Rise of the Professional*

Classes in Nineteenth-Century England, New York: Basic Books, 1967.

ROBERTS, David R., *Executive Compensation,* New York: Free Press, 1953.

ROBINS, Robert S., "Political Elite Formation in Rural India: The Uttar Pradesh *Panchayat* Elections of 1949, 1956, and 1961," *Journal of Politics,* 29 (November, 1967), 838-860.

ROSENBERG, Hans, *Bureaucracy, Aristocracy, and Autocracy: The Prussian Experience, 1660-1815,* Cambridge: Harvard University Press, 1958.

ROSS, Alan S. C., *et al., Noblesse Oblige: An Inquiry into the Identifiable Characteristics of the English Aristocracy,* London: Hamish Hamilton, 1956.

ROSS, Ralph Gilbert, "Elites and The Methodology of Politics," *Public Opinion Quarterly,* 16 (Spring, 1952), 27-32.

ROVERE, Richard, *The American Establishment,* New York: Harcourt, Brace, and World, 1962.

SCHNEIDER, Joseph, "Class Origin and Fame: Eminent English Women," *American Sociological Review,* 5 (October, 1940), 700-712.

SCHNEIDER, Joseph, "The Definition of Eminence and the Social Origins of Famous Men of Genius," *American Sociological Review,* 3 (December, 1938), 834-849.

SCHNEIDER, Joseph, "Social Origin and Fame: The United States and England," *American Sociological Review,* 10 (February, 1945), 52-60.

SELIGMAN, Lester G., "Elite Recruitment and Political Development," *Journal of Politics,* 26 (August, 1964), 612-626.

SERENO, Renzo, *The Rulers,* New York: Praeger, 1962.

SHANNON, J. R., and Maxine Shaw, "Education of Business and Professional Leaders," *American Sociological Review,* 5 (June, 1940), 381-383.

SIMPSON, Alan, *The Wealth of the Gentry, 1540-1660,* London: Cambridge University Press, 1961.

SMITH, James O. and Gideon Sjoberg, "Origins and Career Patterns of Leading Protestant Clergymen," *Social Forces,* 39 (May, 1961), 290-296.

SMYTH, Hugh H., "Nigerian Elite: Role of Education," *Sociology and Social Research,* 45 (October, 1960), 71-73.

SMYTHE, Hugh H. and Mabel M. Smyth, "Africa's New Class," *Queen's Quarterly,* 68 (Summer, 1960), 225-231.

SMYTHE, Hugh H. and Mabel M. Smythe, "The Nigerian Elite: Some Observations," *Sociology and Social Research,* 44 (September-October, 1959), 42-45.

SOELAEMAN, Soemardi, "Some Aspects of the Social Origins of Indonesian Political Decision Makers," *Transactions of the Third World Congress of Sociology,* 3 (1956), 338-348.

STONE, Lawrence, *The Crisis of the Aristocracy: 1558-1641,* New York: Oxford University Press, 1965.

SUTKER, Solomon, "The Jewish Organizational Elite of Atlanta, Georgia," *Social Forces,* 31 (December, 1952), 136-143.

SUTTON, Frances X., *et. al., The American Business Creed,* Cambridge: Harvard University Press, 1956.

SWEEZY, Paul M., "Power Elite or Ruling Class," *Monthly Review,* 8 (September, 1956), 138-150.

SYME, Ronald, *Colonial Elites, Rome, Spain, and the Americas,* London: Oxford University Press, 1958.

TAUSSIG, F. W. and Joslyn, C. S., *Americas Business Leaders,* New York: Macmillan, 1932.

THOENES, Piet, *The Elite in the Welfare State,* translated from the Dutch by John E. Bingham, edited with an introduction by J. A. Banks, New York: Free Press, 1966.

THOMAS, Hugh, editor, *The Establishment: A Symposium,* New York: Potter, 1959.

THOMPSON, Daniel C., *The Negro Leadership Class,* Englewood Cliffs, New Jersey: Prentice-Hall, 1963.

TIEN, H. Y., *Social Mobility and Controlled Fertility: Family Origins and Structure of the Australian Academic Elite,* New Haven: College and University Press, 1965.

TOMASSON, Richard F., "Social Mobility and Family Size in Two High Status Populations," *Eugenics Quarterly,* 13 (June, 1966), 113-121.

TREVOR-ROPER, H. R., *The Gentry, 1540-1640,* London: Cambridge University Press, 1953.

UNESCO, "Symposium on African Elites," *International Social Science Bulletin,* 8 (1956), 413-488.

VAN NIEL, R., *The Emergence of the Modern Indonesian Elite,* The Hague: Van Hoewe, 1960.

VEBLEN, Thorstein, *The Theory of the Leisure Class,* New York: Macmillan, 1899.

VINKE, P., "The Vertical Social Mobility of the Chief Executive Groups in the Netherlands," *Transactions of the Third Congress*

UPPER STRATA

of Sociology, 3 (1956), 219-229.

VISHER, Stephen Sargent, "Environmental Backgrounds of Leading
American Scientists," *American Sociological Review,* 13
(February, 1948), 65-72.

WARBURG, James P., *The Long Road Home,* Garden City, New York:
Doubleday, 1964.

WARNER, W. Lloyd, "The Careers of American Business and Government Executives: A Comparative Analysis," *Social Science Approaches
to Business Behavior,* Homewood, Illinois: Dorsey, 1962.

WARNER, W. Lloyd, "New Look at the Career Civil Service Execut.ve,"
Public Administration Review, 22 (December, 1962), 188-194.

WARNER, W. Lloyd and James C. Abegglen, *Big Business Leaders in America,* revised edition, New York: Atheneum, 1963.

WARNER, W. Lloyd and James C. Abegglen, "Successful Wives of
Successful Executives," *Harvard Business Review,* 34 (March-
April, 1956), 64-70.

WARNER, W. Lloyd, Paul Van Riper, Norman Martin and Orvis Collins,
The American Federal Executive, New Haven: Yale University
Press, 1963.

WARNER, W. Lloyd, *et. al.,* editors, *The Emergent American Society:
Large-Scale Organizations,* New Haven: Yale University Press, 1967.

WECTER, Dixon, *The Saga of American Society,* New York: Scribner,
1937.

WEINBERG, Ian, *The English Public Schools: The Sociology of Elite
Education,* New York: Atherton, 1967.

WEYL, Nathaniel, *The Creative Elite in America,* Washington, D. C.:
Public Affairs Press, 1966.

WILSON, C. S. and T. Lupton, "The Social Background and Connections
of Top Decision Makers," *Manchester School,* 27 (January, 1959),
30-46.

WITTFOGEL, K. A., *Oriental Despotism,* New Haven: Yale University
Press, 1957.

WOLPERT, J. F., "Notes on the American Intelligentsia," *Partisan
Review,* 14 (1947), 472-485.

YAMAMURA, Kozo, "The Role of the Samurai in the Development of
Modern Banking in Japan," *Journal of Economic History,* 27
(June, 1967), 198-220.

ZELENY, L. D., "Characteristics of Group Leaders," *Social Research,*
24 (1939), 140-149.

Mental Health

This section deals with mental illness, reported happiness, anomia, alienation, and related phenomena.

ABRAMSON, J. H., "Emotional Disorder, Status Inconsistency and Migrations: A Health Questionnaire Survey in Jerusalem," *Milbank Memorial Fund Quarterly,* 44 (January, 1966), 23-44.

BAKER, John D., and Nathaniel Wagner, "Social Class and Mental Illness in Children," *Teacher's College Record,"* 66 (1965), 522-536.

BEAN, Lee L., Jerome K. Myers, and Max P. Pepper, "Social Class and Schizophrenia: A Ten-Year Follow-Up", in Arthur B. Shostak and William Gomberg, editors, *Blue-Collar World: Studies of the American Worker,* Englewood Cliffs, New Jersey: Prentice-Hall, 1964.

BELL, Wendell, "Anomie, Social Isolation, and the Class Structure," *Sociometry* 20 (June, 1957), 105-116.

BONJEAN, Charles M., "Mass, Class, and the Industrial Community: A Comparative Analysis of Managers, Businessmen, and Workers," *American Journal of Sociology,* 72 (September, 1966), 149-162.

BOWMAN, Claude C., "Mental Health in the Worker's World," in Arthur B. Shostak and William Gomberg, editors, *Blue-Collar World: Studies of the American Worker,* Englewood Cliffs, New Jersey: Prentice-Hall, 1964.

BRADBURN, Norman M., and David Caplovitz, *Reports on Happiness,* Chicago: Aldine, 1965.

BROWN, Charles A. P., "Social Status' Measured Intelligence, Achieve-*Journal of Educational Sociology,* 25 (November, 1951), 164-168.

BURCHINAL, Lee G., "Social Status Measured Intelligence, Achievement and Personality Adjustment of Rural Iowa Girls," *Sociometry,* 22 (March, 1959), 75-80.

BURCHINAL, Lee G., Bruce Gardner, and Glenn R. Hawkes, "Children's Personality Adjustment and the Socio-Economic Status of Their Families," *Journal of Genetic Psychology,* 92 (June, 1958), 149-159.

CAPLOVITZ, David, and Norman M. Bradburn, *Social Class and Psychological Adjustment,* Study 458, Chicago: National Opinion Research Center, 1964.

CLARK, Robert E., "The Relationship of Alcoholic Psychoses Commitment Rates to Occupational Income and Occupational Prestige," *American Sociological Review,* 14 (August, 1949), 539-543.

CLARK, Robert E., "Psychoses, Income, and Occupational Prestige," *American Journal of Sociology,* 54 (March, 1949), 433-440.

CLARK, Robert E., "The Relationship of Schizophrenia to Occupational Income and Occupational Prestige," *American Sociological Review,* 13 (June, 1948), 325-330.

CLAUSEN, J. A., and Melvin L. Kohn, "Relation of Schizophrenia to the Social Structure of a Small City," in B. Pasamanick, editor, *Epidemiology of Mental Disorder,* Washington, D. C.: American Association for the Advancement of Science, 1959.

CRAMER, Ward, "The Mental Health of Forty-Nine Economically Privileged Children," *Journal of Educational Sociology,* 24 (October, 1950), 93-103.

DEMERATH, N. J., "Adolescent Status Demands and the Student Experiences of Twenty Schizophrenics," *American Sociological Review,* 8 (October, 1943), 513-518.

DOHRENWEND, Bruce P., "Social Status and Psychological Disorder: An Issue of Substance and an Issue of Method," *American Sociological Review,* 31 (February, 1966), 14-34.

DUNHAM, H. Warren, *Community and Schizophrenia: An Epidemiological Analysis,* Detroit: Wayne State University Press, 1965.

DUNHAM, H. Warren, "The Ecology of the Functional Psychoses in Chicago," *American Sociological Review,* 2 (August, 1937), 467-479.

DUNHAM, H. Warren, Patricia Phillips, and Barbara Srinivason, "A Research Note on Diagnosed Mental Illness and Social Class," *American Sociological Review,* 31 (April, 1966), 223-227.

FARRIS, Charles D., "Selected Attitudes on Foreign Affairs as Correlates of Authoritarianism and Political Anomie," *Journal of Politics,* 22 (February, 1960), 50-67.

FARIS, Robert E. L. and H. Warren Dunham, *Mental Disorders in Urban Areas: An Ecological Study of Schizophrenia and Other Psychoses,* Chicago: University of Chicago Press, 1939.

FREEDMAN, Lawrence Zelic, "Psychopathology and Poverty," in Arthur B. Shostak and William Gomberg, editors, *Blue-Collar World: Studies of the American Worker,* Englewood

Cliffs, New Jersey: Prentice Hall, 1964.

FISCHER, Gloria J., "Socio-Economic Factors and Outcome of Released Mental Patients: Influence of Type of Placement, Occupational Adjustment and Type of Hospital," *Journal of Health and Human Behavior,* 6 (Summer, 1965), 105-110.

FRENCH, R. L., "Sociometric Status and Individual Adjustment Among Naval Recruits," *Journal of Abnormal and Social Psychology,* 46 (1951), 64-72.

FRUMKIN, Robert M., "Occupation and Major Mental Disorders," in Arnold Rose, editor, *Mental Health and Mental Disorder,* New York: Norton, 1955.

FRUMKIN, Robert M., "Occupation and Mental Illness," *Ohio Public Welfare Statistics,* (September, 1952), 4-13.

GEISEL, Paul N., "The Meaning of Work and Mental Illness," in Arthur B. Shostak and William Gomberg, editors, *Blue-Collar World: Studies of the American Worker,* Englewood Cliffs, New Jersey: Prentice Hall, 1964.

GLENN, Norval D. and Jon P. Alston, "Cultural Distances Among Occupational Categories," *American Sociological Review,* 33 (August, 1968), pp. 365-382.

GLENN, Norval D. and Jon P. Alston, "Rural-Urban Differences in Reported Attitudes and Behavior," *Southwestern Social Science Quarterly,* 47 (March, 1967), 381-400.

GOLDBERG, E. M. and S. L. Morrison, "Schizophrenia and Social Class," *British Journal of Psychiatry,* 109 (1963), 785-802.

GREEN, Arnold N., "The Middle Class Male Child and Neurosis," *American Sociological Review,* 11 (February, 1946), 31-41.

GREENBLATT, E. L., "Relationship of Mental Health and Social Status," *Journal of Educational Research,* 44 (November, 1950), 193-204.

GURIN, G., J. Veroff, and S. Feld, *Americans View Their Mental Health,* New York: Basic Books, 1960.

GURSSLIN, Orville R., Raymond G. Hunt, and Jack L. Roach, "Social Class and the Mental Health Movement," *Social Problems,* 71 (Winter, 1959-60), 210-217.

HARDT, Robert and Sherwin Feinhandler, "Class and Mental Hospitalization Prognosis," *American Sociological Review,* 24 (December, 1959), 815-821.

HARE, E. H., "Family Setting and the Urban Distribution of Schizophrenia," *Journal of Mental Science,* 102 (October, 1956).

HARE, E. H., "Mental Conditions in Bristol," *Journal of Mental Science,* 102 (April, 1956), 349-357.

HOLLINGSHEAD, August B. and F. C. Redlich, *Social Class and Mental Illness: A Community Study,* New York: Wiley, 1958.

HOLLINGSHEAD, August B. and F. C. Redlich, "Social Stratification and Schizophrenia," *American Sociological Review,* 19 (June, 1954), 302-306.

HOLLINGSHEAD, August B. and F. C. Redlich, "Social Stratification and Psychiatric Disorders," *American Sociological Reivew,* 18 (April, 1953), 163-169.

HOLLINGSHEAD, August B. and Lloyd H. Rogler, "Lower Socioeconomic Status and Mental Illness," *Sociology and Social Research,* 46 (July, 1962), 387-396.

HUNT, Raymond G., Orville Gurrslin, and Jack L. Roach, "Social Status and Psychiatric Service in a Child Guidance Clinic," *American Sociological Review,* 23 (February, 1958), 81-83.

HYDE, R. W. and L. K. Kingsley; "The Relation of Mental Disorders to the Community Socio-economic Level," *New England Journal of Medicine,* 23 (1944), 543.

JACO, E. Gartly, *The Social Epidemiology of Mental Disorders,* New York: Russell Sage, 1960.

JAHODA, Marie, "Environment and Mental Health," *International Social Science Journal,* 11 (1958), 14-23.

KANTOR, Mildred B., editor, *Mobility and Mental Health,* Springfield, Illinois: Thomas, 1965.

KLEINER, Robert J. and Seymour Parker, "Goal-Striving, Social Status, and Mental Disorders: A Research Review," *American Sociological Review,* 29 (April, 1963), 189-203.

KRUPINSKI, Jerzy and Alan Stoller, "Occupational Hierarchy of First Admissions to the Victorian Mental Health Department, 1962-1965," *Australian and New Zealand Journal of Sociology,* 4 (April, 1968), 55-63.

KUHLEN, R. G. and H. S. Bretsch, "Sociometric Status and Personal Problems of Adolescents," *Sociometry,* 10 (1947), 122-132.

LANGNER, Thomas S. and Stanley T. Michael, *Life Stress and Mental Health: The Midtown Manhattan Study,* New York: Free Press, 1963.

LANTZ, Herman R., "Occupational Differences in Mental Disorders," *Social Problems,* 2 (October, 1954), 100-104.

LAPOUSE, Rema, M. Monk, and M. Terris, "The Drift Hypothesis and Socioeconomic Differentials in Schizophrenia," *American Journal of Public Health,* 46 (August, 1956), 978-986.

LEAVY, Stanley A. and L. Z. Freedman, "Psychoneurosis and Economic Life," *Social Problems,* 4 (July, 1956), 55-67.

LEE, Everett, "Socio-Economic and Migration Differentials in Mental Disease in New York State, 1949-1951," *Milbank Memorial Fund Quarterly,* 41 (July, 1963), 249-268.

MENTAL HEALTH

LEFTON, Mark, Shirley Angrist, Simon Dinitz, and Benjamin Pasamanick, "Social Class, Expectations, and Performance of Mental Patients," *American Journal of Sociology,* 68 (July, 1962), 79-87.

LOTSOFF, E. J. and Richard Centers, "Anxiety and Socio-Economic Stratification," *Journal of Clinical Psychology,* 15 (1959), 439-442.

LYSTAD, Mary, "Social Mobility Among Selected Groups of Schizophrenic Patients," *American Sociological Review,* 12 (April, 1957), 288-292.

MEIER, Dorothy and Wendell Bell, "Anomia and Differential Access to the Achievement of Life Goals," *American Sociological Review,* 24 (April, 1959), 189-202.

MEYERS, J. and B. Roberts, *Family and Class Dynamics in Mental Illness,* New York: Wiley, 1959.

MILLER, Kent S. and Charles M. Grigg, editors, *Mental Health and the Lower Social Classes,* Tallahassee: Florida State University Press, 1966.

MISHLER, Elliot G. and Norman A. Scotch, "Sociocultural Factors in the Epidemiology of Schizophrenia," *International Journal of Psychiatry,* 1 (April, 1965), 258-305.

MIZRUCHI, Ephraim H., "Social Structure and Anomia in a Small City," *American Sociological Review,* 25 (October, 1960), 645-654.

MONTAGUE, Joel B., "Social Status and Adjustment in School," *Clearing House,* 27 (September, 1952), 19-24.

MORRIS, J. N., "Health and Social Class," *The Lancet,* (February 7, 1959), 303-305.

MYERS, Jerome K. and Lee L. Bean, with the collaboration of Max Pepper, *A Decade Later: A Follow-Up of Social Class and Mental Illness,* New York: Wiley, 1967.

MYERS, Jerome K., Lee L. Bean, and Max P. Pepper, "Social Class and Psychiatric Disorders: A Ten-Year Follow-Up," *Journal of Health and Human Behavior,* 6 (Summer, 1965), 74-78.

MYERS, Jerome K. and Leslie Schaffer, "Social Stratification and Psychiatric Practice: A Study of an Out-Patient Clinic," *American Sociological Review,* 19 (June, 1954), 307-310.

NOLAN, W. J., "Occupation and Dementia Praecox," *New York State Hospital Quarterly,* 3 (1917), 127-154.

NOLAN, W. J., "Occupation and Manic-Depressive Psychosis," *New York State Hospital Quarterly*, 4 (1918), 75-104.

ODEGAARD, O., "The Incidence of Psychoses in Various Occupations," *International Journal of Social Psychiatry*, 2 (1956), 85-104.

PARKER, Seymour and Robert J. Kleiner, *Mental Illness in the Urban Negro Community*, New York: Free Press, 1966.

POWELL, Edwin H., "Occupation, Status, and Suicide: Toward a Redefinition of Anomie," *American Sociological Review*, 23 (April, 1958), 131-139.

PRICE, Charlton R. and Harry Levinson, "Work and Mental Health," in Arthur B. Shostak and William Gomberg, editors, *Blue-Collar World: Studies of the American Worker*, Englewood Cliffs, New Jersey: Prentice Hall, 1964.

RHODES, Lewis, "Anomia, Aspirations, and Status," *Social Forces*, 42 (May, 1964), 434-440.

RIESSMAN, Frank, *et. al.,* editors, *The Mental Health of the Poor: New Treatment Approaches for Low Income People*, New York: Free Press, 1964.

RINEHART, James W., "Mobility Aspiration, Achievement Discrepancies, and Mental Illness," *Social Problems*, 15 (Spring, 1968), 478-488.

ROBERTS, A. H. and M. Rokeach, "Anomie, Authoritarianism, and Prejudice: A Replication," *American Journal of Sociology*, 61 (January, 1956), 355-358.

ROMAN, Paul M. and Harrison M. Trice, *Schizophrenia and the Poor*, Ithaca, New York: Cornell University Press, 1967.

ROSE, Arnold M., "Class Differences Among the Elderly," *Sociology and Social Research*, 50 (April, 1966), 356-360.

SEWELL, William H. and A. O. Haller, "Factors in the Relationship Between Social Status and the Personality Adjustment of the Child," *American Sociological Review*, 24 (August, 1959), 511-520.

SEWELL, William H. and A. O. Haller, "Social Status and the Personality Adjustment of the Child," *Sociometry*, 19 (June, 1956), 114-125.

SIEGEL, Nathaniel H., Robert L. Kahn, Max Pollack and Max Fink, "Social Class, Diagnosis, and Treatment in Three Psychiatric Hospitals," *Social Problems*, 10 (Fall, 1962), 191-196.

SIMPSON, Richard L., "A Note on Status, Mobility and Anomie," *British Journal of Sociology*, 11 (December, 1960), 370-372.

SIMPSON, Richard L. and H. Max Miller, "Social Status and Anomia," *Social Problems*, 10 (Winter, 1963), 257-264.

SROLE, Leo, Thomas S. Langer, Stanley T. Michael, Marvin K. Opler, and Thomas A. C. Rennie, *Mental Health in the Metropolis,* New York: McGraw-Hill, 1962.

THOMAS, Dorothy Swaine, and Ben Z. Locke, "Marital Status, Education and Occupational Differentials in Mental Disease," *Milbank Memorial Fund Quarterly,* 41 (April, 1963), 145-160.

TIETZE, C., P. Lemkau, and M. Cooper, "Schizophrenia, Manic Depressive Psychosis, and Socioeconomic Status," *American Journal of Sociology,* 47 (September, 1941), 167-175.

TUCKMAN, J. and R. J. Kleiner, "Discrepancy Between Aspiration and Achievement as a Predictor of Schizophrenia,: *Behavioral Scientist,* (October, 1962), 443-447.

TURNER, R. J. and Morton O. Wagenfeld, "Occupational Mobility and Schizophrenia: An Assessment of the Social Causation and Social Selection Hypotheses," *American Sociological Review,* 32 (February, 1967), 104-113.

WASSEF, W. Y., "The Influence of Religion, Socioeconomic Status and Education on Anomie," *Sociological Quarterly,* 8 (Spring, 1967), 233-238.

WILLIAMSON, Robert C., "Social Class Determinants of Perception and Adjustment in an Adolescent and Adult Sample," *Journal of Social Psychology,* 57 (June, 1962), 11-21.

WILNER, Daniel M., Rosabelle Price Walkley, Thomas C. Pinkerton, and Matthew Tayback, *The Housing Environment and Family Life: A Longitudinal Study of the Effects of Housing On Morbidity and Mental Health,* Baltimore: Johns Hopkins Press, 1962.

Suicide

BREED, Warren, "Occupational Mobility and Suicide Among White Males," *American Sociological Review,* 28 (April, 1963), 179-188.

CAVAN, Ruth, *Suicide,* New York: Russell and Russell, 1965.

DOUGLAS, Jack, *The Social Meaning of Suicide,* Princeton: Princeton University Press, 1967.

DUBLIN, Louis I., *Suicide: A Sociological and Statistical Study*, New York: Ronald, 1963.

DUBLIN, Louis I. and Bessie Bunzel, *To Be or Not to Be*, New York: Smith and Haas, 1933.

DURKHEIM, Emile, *Suicide*, New York: Free Press, 1951.

GIBBS, Jack P. and Walter T. Martin, *Status Integration and Suicide*, Eugene: University of Oregon Press, 1964.

HENRY, Andrew F. and James F. Short, Jr., *Suicide and Homicide*, New York: Free Press, 1954.

LABOVITZ, Sanford, "Variation in Suicide Rates," in Jack P. Gibbs, editor, *Suicide*, New York: Harper and Row, 1968.

MAC MAHON, Brian, Samuel Johnson, and Thomas F. Pugh, "Relation of Suicide Rates to Social Conditions," *Public Health Reports*, 78 (April, 1963).

MARIS, Ronald, *Social Forces in Urban Suicide*, Homewood, Illinois: Dorsey, 1968.

MARIS, Ronald, "Suicide, Status, and Mobility in Chicago," *Social Forces*, 46 (December, 1967), 246-256.

MOORE, Merrill, "Cases of Attempted Suicide in a General Hospital: A Problem in Social and Psychological Medicine, *New England Journal of Medicine*, 217 (August 19, 1937).

PORTERFIELD, Austin L. and Jack P. Gibbs, "Occupational Prestige and Social Mobility of Suicides in New Zealand," *American Journal of Sociology*, 66 (September, 1960), 147-152.

POWELL, Elwin, "Occupation, Status, and Suicide," *American Sociological Review*, 23 (April, 1958), 131-134.

ROBINS, Eli, Edwin H. Schmidt, and Patricia O'Neal, "Some Interrelations of Social Factors and Clinical Diagnosis of Attempted Suicide," *American Journal of Psychiatry*, 114 (September, 1957), 221-231.

RUSHING, William A., "Individual Behavior and Suicide," in Jack P. Gibbs, editor, *Suicide*, New York: Harper and Row, 1968.

SAINSBURY, Peter, *Suicide in London*, London: Chapman and Hall, 1955.

SCHMID, Calvin, "Suicide in Minneapolis: 1928-1932," *American Journal of Sociology*, 39 (July, 1933), 30-48.

SEAGER, C. P. and R. A. Flood, "Suicide in Bristol," *British Journal of Psychiatry*, 3 (October, 1965).

STENGEL, Erwin and Nancy G. Cook, "Contrasting Suicide Rates in Industrial Communities," *Journal of Mental Science*, 107 (November, 1961).

SWINSCOW, Douglas, "Some Suicide Statistics," *British Medical Journal,* 1 (June 23, 1951), 1417-1422.

TUCKMAN, Jacob and Martha Lavell, "Study of Suicide in Philadelphia," *Public Health Reports,* 73 (June, 1958), 547-553.

WEISS, James M., "Suicide: An Epidemiologic Analysis," *Psychiatric Quarterly,* 28 (April, 1954), 225-252.

WOOD, Arthur L., "A Socio-Structural Analysis of Murder, Suicide, and Economic Crime in Ceylon," *American Sociological Review,* 26 (October, 1961), 744-753.

Physical Health

ANTONOVSKY, Aaron, "Social Class and Illness: A Reconsideration," *Sociological Inquiry,* 37 (Spring, 1967), 291-295.

BERKSON, D. M., J. Stambler, H. A. Lindberd, W. Miller, H. Mathies, H. Lasky, and Y. Hall, "Socioeconomic Correlates of Atherosclerotic and Hypertensive Heart Disease," *Annals of the New York Academy of Sciences,* 84 (1960), 835-850.

BRIERLY, William B., "Malaria and Socio-Economic Conditions in Mississippi," *Social Forces,* 23 (May, 1945), 451-459.

BURNIGHT, Robert G., "Chronic Morbidity and the Socio-Economic Characteristics of Older Urban Males," *Milbank Memorial Fund Quarterly,* 43 (July, 1965), 311-322.

BURNIGHT, Robert G. and Parker G. Marden, "Social Correlates of Weight in an Aging Population," *Milbank Memorial Fund Quarterly,* 45 (April, 1967), 75-92.

DOUGLAS, James W. B. and Howard R. Simpson, "Height in Relation to Puberty, Family Size and Social Class: A Longitudinal Study," *Milbank Memorial Fund Quarterly,* 42 (July, 1964), 20-35.

EICHHORN, Robert L. and Edward G. Ludwig, "Poverty and Health," in Hanna Meissner, editor, *Poverty in the Affluent Society,* New York: Harper and Row, 1966.

GOLDSTEIN, G. S. and P. F. Wehrle, "The Influence of Socio-economic Factors on the Distribution of Hepatitis in Syracuse, New York," *American Journal of Public Health,* 49 (1959), 473-480.

GRAHAM, Saxon, "Social Factors in Relation to Chronic Illness," in H. E. Freeman, *et al.,* editors, *Handbook of Medical Sociology,* Englewood Cliffs, New Jersey: Prentice-Hall, 1963.

GRAHAM, Saxon, "Socio-Economic Status, Illness and the Use of Medical Services," *Milbank Memorial Fund Quarterly,* 35 (January, 1957), 58-66.

GRAHAM, Saxon, Morton Levin, and Abraham M. Lilienfeld, "The Socioeconomic Distribution of Cancer in Various Sites in Buffalo, New York, 1948-1952," *Cancer,* 13 (January-February, 1960), 180-191.

GUERRIN, Robert F. and Edgar F. Borgatta, "Socio-Economic and Demographic Correlates of Tuberculosis Incidence," *Milbank Memorial Fund Quarterly,* 43 (July, 1965), 269-290.

HINKLE, L. E., Jr., and H. G. Wolff, "Health and the Social Environment," in A. H. Leighton, *et al.,* editors, *Explorations in Social Psychiatry,* New York: Basic Books, 1957.

ILLSLEY, R., "Social Class Selection and Class Differences in Relation to Stillbirth and Infant Deaths," *British Medical Journal,* (December 24, 1955), 1520-1524.

IUTAKA, Sugiyama, "Social Status and Illness in Urban Brazil," *Milbank Memorial Fund Quarterly,* 44 (April, 1966), 97-110.

JACO, E. Gartly, editor, *Patients, Physicians and Illness,* New York: Free Press, 1958.

KADUSHIN, Charles, "Social Class and Ill Health: The Need for Further Research, A Reply to Antonovsky," *Sociological Inquiry,* 37 (Spring, 1967), 291-295.

KADUSCHIN, Charles, "Social Class and the Experience of Ill Health," *Sociological Inquiry,* 34 (Winter, 1964), 67-80.

KLARMAN, Herbert E., *The Economics of Health,* New York: Columbia University Press, 1965.

KODMAN, Frank, Jr., Carl Spies, Kenneth Stockdell and Gordon Sedlacek, "Socio-Economic Status and Observer Identification of Hearing Loss in School Children," *Exceptional Children,* 26 (December, 1959), 176-188.

KOOS, E. L., *The Health of Regionville,* New York: Columbia University Press, 1954.

LAUGHTON, Katherine B., Carol W. Buck and G. E. Hobbs, "Socio-Economic Status and Illness--Introduction," *Milbank Memorial Fund Quarterly,* 36 (January, 1958), 46-57.

267

LAWRENCE, P. S., "Chronic Illness and Socio-Economic Status," in E. Gartly Jaco, editor, *Patients, Physicians and Illness,* New York: Free Press, 1958.

PHYSICAL HEALTH

LEE, Richard E. and Ralph F. Schneider, "Hypertension and Arteriosclerosis in Executive and Non-Executive Personnel," *Journal of the American Medical Association,* 167 (July, 1958), 1447-1450.

LEVINE, G. N., "Anxiety About Illness: Psychological and Social Bases," *Journal of Health and Human Behavior,* 3 (1962), 30-34.

MORRIS, J. N., "Health and Social Class," *The Lancet,* (February 7, 1959), 303-305.

NAGI, Saad Z., "Socioeconomic Stress and Arteriosclerotic Heart Disease," *Rural Sociology,* 27 (December, 1962), 428-437.

REEDER, Leo G., "Social Factors in Heart Disease: A Preliminary Research Report on the Relationship of Certain Social Factors to Blood Pressure in Males," *Social Forces,* 34 (May, 1956), 367-371.

ROSENBLATT, Daniel and Edward A. Suchman, "Blue-Collar Attitudes and Information Toward Health and Illness," in Arthur B. Shostak and William Gomberg, editors, *Blue-Collar World: Studies of the American Worker,* Englewood Cliffs, New Jersey: Prentice-Hall, 1964.

ROSENBLATT, Daniel and Edward A. Suchman, "The Under-utilization of Medical-Care Services by Blue-Collarites," in Arthur B. Shostak and William Gomberg, editors, *Blue-Collar World: Studies of the American Worker,* Englewood Cliffs, New Jersey: Prentice-Hall, 1964.

ROSENGREN, William R., "Social Class and Becoming Ill," in Arthur B. Shostak and William Gomberg, editors, *Blue-Collar World: Studies of the American Worker,* Englewood Cliffs, New Jersey: Prentice-Hall, 1964.

RUESCH, Jurgen, "Social Technique, Social Status, and Social Change in Illness," in C. Kluckhohn, H. Murray, and D. Schneider, editors, *Personality in Nature, Society, and Culture,* New York: Knopf, 1953.

SCHNORE, Leo F. and J. D. Cowhig, "Some Correlates of Reported Health in Metropolitan Areas," *Social Problems,* 3 (1959-1960), 218-226.

SEWELL, William H., "Rural Health: The Health of Farm Families in Relation to their Socioeconomic Status," in Otis Dudley Duncan, editor, *Social Research on Health,* New York: Social Science Research Council, 1946.

STERN, Bernard J., "Socio-Economic Aspects of Heart Disease," *Journal of Educational Sociology,* 24 (April, 1951), 450-462.

WILNER, Daniel M., Rosabelle Price Walkley, Thomas C. Pinkerton, and Matthew Tayback, *The Housing Environment and Family Life: A Longitudinal Study of the Effects of Housing on Morbidity and Mental Health,* Baltimore: John Hopkins Press, 1962.

ZOLA, Irving Kenneth, "Illness Behavior of the Working Class: Implications and Recommendations," in Arthur B. Shostak and William Gomberg, editors, *Blue-Collar World: Studies of the American Worker,* Englewood Cliffs, New Jersey: Prentice-Hall, 1964.

Mortality and Longevity

In addition to the material listed here, the Metropolitan Life Insurance Company periodically reports in its *Statistical Bulletin* differences in mortality from specific causes between its Industrial and its Standard Ordinary policyholders. Since these two kinds of policyholders differ markedly in their average education, income, and occupational status, these reports give important information about the relationship between stratification and mortality and also between stratification and certain kinds of morbidity. Recent reports have dealt with cancer, diabetes, and several other causes of death.

ANDERSON, Odin W., "Infant Mortality and Social and Cultural Factors: Historical Trends and Current Patterns," in E. Gartly Jaco, editor, *Patients, Physicians and Illness,* New York: Free Press, 1958.

ANTONOVSKY, Aaron, "Social Class, Life Expectancy and Overall Mortality," *Milbank Memorial Fund Quarterly,* 45 (April, 1967), 31-73.

DOUGLAS, J. W. B., "Social Class Differences in Health and Survival During the First Two Years of Life: the Results of a National Survey," *Population Studies,* 5 (July, 1951), 35-58.

EICHHORN, Robert L. and Edward G. Ludwig, "Poverty and Health," in Hanna Meissner, editor, *Poverty in the Affluent Society,* New York: Harper and Row, 1966.

ELLIS, John M., "Socio-Economic Differentials in Mortality From Chronic Diseases," *Social Problems,* 5 (July, 1957), 30-36.

FREEDMAN, Ronald, L. C. Coombs, and Judith Friedman, "Social Correlates of Fetal Mortality," *Milbank Memorial Fund Quarterly,* 44 (July, 1966), 327-344.

GURALNICK, Lillian, "The Study of Mortality by Occupation in the United States," Washington, D. C.: National Office of Vital Statistics, (September, 1959).

ILLSLEY, R., "Social Class Selection and Class Differences in Relation to Stillbirth and Infant Deaths," *British Medical Journal,* (December 24, 1955).

MORTALITY
AND LONGEVITY

KILPATRICK, S. J., "Occupational Mortality Indices," *Population Studies,* 16 (November, 1942), 175-185.

LOGAN, W., "Social Class Variations in Mortality," in J. J. Spengler and Otis D. Duncan, editors, *Demographic Analysis: Selected Readings,* New York: Free Press, 1956.

MAYER, Albert J. and Philip Hauser, "Class Differentials in Expectation of Life at Birth," in Reinhard Bendix and Seymour M. Lipset, *Class, Status and Power,* New York: Free Press, 1953.

METROPOLITAN LIFE INSURANCE COMPANY, "Occupational Mortality Diminishing," *Statistical Bulletin,* 49 (April, 1968), 3-4.

PATNO, M. E., "Mortality and Economic Level in an Urban Area," *Public Health Reports,* 27 (1960), 841-851.

PHILLIPS, Harry, "An Inter-Racial Study in Social Conditions and Infant Mortality in Cape Town," *Milbank Memorial Fund Quarterly,* 35 (January, 1957), 7-28.

QUINNEY, Richard, "Mortality Differentials in a Metropolitan Area," *Social Forces,* 43 (December, 1964), 222-230.

SHIPS, Cecil and J. H. Watkins, "Mortality in the Socio-Economic Districts of New Haven," *Yale Journal of Biology and Medicine,* 20 (October, 1947), 51-80.

SILCOCK, H., "The Comparison of Occupational Mortality Rates," *Population Studies,* 13 (November, 1959), 183-192.

SPIEGELMAN, Mortimer, "Mortality Trends for Causes of Death in Countries of Low Mortality," *Demography,* 2 (1965), 115-125.

STOCKWELL, Edward G., "Infant Mortality and Socio-Economic Status: A Changing Relationship," *Milbank Memorial Fund Quarterly,* 40 (January, 1962), 101-111.

TIETZE, Christopher, "Life Tables for Social Classes in England," *Milbank Memorial Fund Quarterly,* 21 (April, 1943), 182-187.

TOMASSON, Richard F., "Patterns in Negro-White Differential Mortality, 1930-1957," *Milbank Memorial Fund Quarterly,* 38 (October, 1960), 362-386.

UPCHURCH, Harley M., "A Tentative Approach to the Study of Mortality Differentials between Educational Strata in the United States," *Rural Sociology,* 27 (June, 1962), 213-217.

WILLIE, Charles, "A Research Note on the Changing Association Between Infant Mortality and Socio-Economic Status," *Social Forces,* 37 (March, 1959), 221-227.

WILLIE, Charles and William B. Rothney, "Racial, Ethnic, and Income Factors in the Epidemiology of Neonatal Mortality," *American Sociological Review,* 27 (August, 1962), 522-526.

YERACARIS, Constantine, "Differential Mortality, General and Cause-Specific, in Buffalo, 1939-1941," *Journal of the American Statistical Association,* 50 (December, 1955), 1235-1247.

Fertility

ABU-LUGHOD, Janet, "The Emergence of Differential Fertility in Urban Egypt," *Milbank Memorial Fund Quarterly,* 43 (April, 1965), 235-253.

ANASTASI, Anne, "Differential Effect of Intelligence and Social Status," *Eugenics Quarterly,* 6 (June, 1959), 84-91.

ANASTASI, Anne, "Intelligence and Family Size," *Psychological Bulletin,* 53 (May, 1956), 187-209.

ANDERSON, W. A., "The Spacing of Births in the Families of University Graduates," *American Journal of Sociology,* 53 (July, 1947), 23-33.

BAJEMA, Carl Jay, "Relation of Fertility to Educational Attainment in a Kalamazoo Public School Population: A Follow-up Study," *Eugenics Quarterly,* 13 (December, 1966), 306-315.

BANKS, J. A. and Olive Banks, *Feminism and Family Planning in Victorian England,* New York: Schocken, 1964.

BARGER, Ben and Everette Hall, "The Interrelationships of Family Size and Socioeconomic Status for Parents of College Students," *Journal of Marriage and the Family,* 28 (May, 1966), 186-187.

BEEBE, Gilbert W., "Differential Fertility by Color for Coal Miners in Logan County, West Virginia," *Milbank Memorial Fund Quarterly,* 19 (April, 1941), 189-195.

BERENT, Jerzy, "Fertility and Social Mobility," *Population Studies,* 5 (March, 1952), 244-260.

BLACKBURN, Julian, "Family Size, Intelligence Score and Social Class," *Population Studies,* 1 (September, 1947), 165-176.

BLACKER, J. G. C., "Population Growth and Differential Fertility in Zanzibar Protectorate," *Population Studies,* 15 (March, 1962), 258-266.

BLACKER, J. G. C., "Social Ambitions of the Bourgeoisie of 18th Century France and their Relation to Family Limitation," *Population Studies,* 11 (1957), 46-63.

FERTILITY

BLAKE, Judith, "Reproductive Ideals and Educational Attainment Among White Americans," *Population Studies,* 21 (September, 1967), 159-174.

BLAU, Peter M. and Otis Dudley Duncan, *The American Occupational Structure,* New York: Wiley, 1967, Chapter 11, "Differential Fertility and Occupational Mobility,"

BOGGS, Stephen T., "Family Size and Social Mobility in a California Suburb," *Eugenics Quarterly,* 4 (December, 1957), 208-213.

BROOKS, Hugh E. and Franklin J. Henry, "An Empirical Study of the Relationships of Catholic Practice and Occupational Mobility to Fertility: Review of the Literature," *Milbank Memorial Fund Quarterly,* 36 (July, 1958), 222-277.

BURT, Cyril, *Intelligence and Fertility: The Effect of the Differential Birth Rate on Inborn Mental Characteristics,* London: Eugenics Society, 1952.

CALDWELL, J. C., "Fertility Differentials as Evidence of Incipient Fertility Decline in a Developing Country," *Population Studies,* 21 (July, 1967), 5-21.

CAMPBELL, Arthur A., "Fertility and Family Planning Among Nonwhite Married Couples in the United States," *Eugenics Quarterly,* 12 (September, 1965), 124-131.

CARLETON, Robert O., "Fertility Trends and Differentials in Latin America," *Milbank Memorial Fund Quarterly,* 43 (October, 1965), 15-35.

CARTER, Cedric O., "Changing Patterns of Differential Fertility in Northwest Europe and North America," *Eugenics Quarterly,* 9 (September, 1962), 147-150.

CHILMAN, Catherine S., "Fertility and Poverty in the United States: Some Implications for Family-Planning Programs, Evaluation, and Research," *Journal of Marriage and the Family,* 30 (May, 1968), 207-227.

CHILMAN, Catherine S., "Population Dynamics and Poverty in the United States," *Welfare in Review,* (April, 1966).

CHILMAN, Catherine S., "Poverty and Family Planning in the United States: Some Social and Psychological Aspects and Implications for Programs and Policy," *Welfare in Review,* 5 (April, 1967), 3-15.

CHAMPION, Phyllis, "A Pilot Study of the Success or Failure of Low-Income Negro Families in the Use of Birth Control," in Donald Bogue, editor, *Sociological Contributions to Family*

Planning Research, Community and Family Study Center, University of Chicago, 1967.

CLEANDRASEKARAN, C. and M. V. George, "Mechanisms Underlying the Differences in Fertility Patterns of Bengalee Women from Three Socio-Economic Groups," *Milbank Memorial Fund Quarterly,* 40 (January, 1962), 59-89.

COMBS, Jerry W., Jr. and Kingsley Davis, "Differential Fertility in Puerto Rico," *Population Studies,* 5 (November, 1951), 104-116.

DAVIS, Kingsley, "Some Demographic Aspects of Poverty in the United States," in Margaret S. Gordon, editor, *Poverty in America,* San Francisco: Chandler, 1965.

De JONG, Gordon F., "Religious Fundamentalism, Socio-Economic Status, and Fertitliy Attitudes in the Southern Appalachians," *Demography,* 2 (1965), 540-548.

DERKSEN, J. B. D., "Statistics of the Distribution of Family Income by Size," *Milbank Memorial Fund Quarterly,* 27 (July, 1949), 324-331.

DICE, Lee R., Philip J. Clark, and Robert I. Gilbert, "Relation of Fertility to Education in Ann Arbor, Michigan, 1951-1954," *Eugenics Quarterly,* 11 (March, 1964), 30-45.

DICE, Lee R., Philip J. Clark, and Robert I. Gilbert, "Relation of Fertility to Occupation and Income in the Male population of Ann Arbor, Michigan, 1951-1954," *Eugenics Quarterly,* 11 (September, 1964), 154-167.

DINKEL, Robert M., "Occupation and Fertility in the United States," *American Sociological Review,* 17 (April, 1952), 178-183.

DODSON, Jack E., "The Differential Fertility of the Negro Population, Houston, Texas, 1940-1950," *Milbank Memorial Fund Quarterly,* 35 (July, 1957), 266-279.

DOOGHE, Gilbert, "Premarital Conception with Married Couples According to Socio-Professional Status," *Journal of Marriage and the Family,* 30 (May, 1968), 324-328.

DORN, Harold F., "Genetic and Social Significance of Differential Fertility, 1. Present Knowledge Concerning the Effects of a Differential Fertility," *Milbank Memorial Fund Quarterly,* 25 (October, 1947), 359-366.

DUNCAN, Otis Dudley, "Farm Background and Differential Fertility," *Demography,* 2 (1965), 240-249.

DUNCAN, Otis Dudley, "Residential Areas and Differential Fertility," *Eugenics Quarterly,* 11 (June, 1964), 82-89.

DUNCAN, Otis Dudley and Robert W. Hodge, "Cohort Analysis of Differential Natality," *International Population Union Conference,* paper no. 4l, New York, 1961.

EDIN, K. A. and E. P. Hutchinson, *Studies of Differential Fertility in Sweden,* London: King, 1935.

FRAZIER, E. Franklin and Eleanor H. Bernert, "Children and Income in Negro Families," *Social Forces,* 25 (December, 1946), 178-182.

FREEDMAN, Deborah S., "The Relation of Economic Status to Fertility," *American Economic Review,* 53 (June, 1963), 414-426.

FREEDMAN, Ronald, "American Studies of Family Planning and Fertility: A Review of Major Trends and Issues," in Clyde V. Kiser, editor, *Research in Family Planning,* Princeton: Princeton University Press, 1962.

FREEDMAN, Ronald and Lolagene Coombs, "Childspacing and Family Economic Position," *American Sociological Review,* 31 (October, 1966), 631-648.

FREEDMAN, Ronald and Lolagene Coombs, "Economic Considerations in Family Growth Decisions," *Population Studies,* 20 (November, 1966).

FREEDMAN, Ronald and Doris Slesinger, "Fertility Differentials for the Indigenous Non-Farm Population of the United States," *Population Studies,* 15 (November, 1961).

FREEDMAN, Ronald, P. K. Whelpton, and Arthur A. Campbell, *Family Planning, Sterility, and Population Growth,* New York: McGraw-Hill, 1959.

GINI, Corrado, "Real and Apparent Exceptions to the Uniformity of a Lower Natural Increase of the Upper Classes," *Rural Sociology,* 1 (September, 1936).

GLASS, David V. and E. Grebenik, *The Trend and Pattern of Fertility in Great Britain,* London: Royal Commission on Population, 1954.

GLENN, Norval D. and Jon P. Alston, "Cultural Distances Among Occupational Categories," *American Sociological Review,* 33 (June, 1968), 365-382.

GLENN, Norval D. and Jon P. Alston, "Rural-Urban Differences in Reported Attitudes and Behavior," *Southwestern Social Science Quarterly,* 47 (March, 1967), 381-400.

GOLDSCHEIDER, Calvin, "Socio-Economic Status and Jewish Fertility," *Jewish Journal of Sociology,* 7 (1965), 221-237.

GOLDSTEIN, Sidney and Kurt B. Mayer, "Residence and Status Differences in Fertility," *Milbank Memorial Fund Quarterly,* 43 (July, 1965), 291-310.

GRABILL, W., Clyde V. Kiser, and P. K. Whelpton, *The Fertility of American Women,* New York: Wiley, 1958.

GROAT, H. Theodore and Arthur G. Neal, "Social Psychological

Correlates of Urban Fertility," *American Sociological Review,* 32 (December, 1967), 945-959.

HAGOOD, Margaret J.,"Changing Fertility Differentials Among Farm-Operator Families in Relation to Economic Size of Farm," *Rural Sociology,* 13 (September, 1947), 137-164.

HAJNAL, John, "The Analysis of Birth Statistics in the Light of the Recent International Recovery of the Birth Rate," *Population Studies,* 1 (September, 1947).

HAJNAL, John, "The Estimation of Total Family Size of Occupation Groups from the Distribution of Births by Order and Duration of Marriage," *Population Studies,* 2 (December, 1948), 305-317.

HAPKIN, W. A. B. and John Hajnal, "Analysis of the Births in England and Wales, 1939, by Father's Occupation. Part I," *Population Studies,* 1 (September, 1947), 187-203.

HILL, R., J. M. Stycos, and K. W. Back, *The Family and Population Control: A Puerto Rican Experiment in Social Change,* Chapel Hill: University of North Carolina Press, 1959.

HUGHES, R. B., "Human Fertility Differentials: The Influence of Industrial Urban Development on Birth Rates," *Population Review,* 3 (July, 1959), 58-69.

HUTCHINSON, Bertram, "Fertility, Social Mobility and Urban Migration in Brazil," *Population Studies,* 14 (March, 1961), 182-189.

INNES, J. W., "Class Birth Rates in England and Wales, 1921-1931," *Milbank Memorial Fund Quarterly,* 19 (January, 1941), 72-96.

INNES, J. W., *Class Fertility Trends in England and Wales,* 1876-1934, Princeton: Princeton University Press, 1938.

JACOBSON, Paul H., "The Trend of the Birth Rate among Persons on Different Economic Levels, City of New York, 1929-1942," *Milbank Memorial Fund Quarterly,* 22 (April, 1944), 131-147.

JAFFE, Frederick S. and Steven Polgar, "Family Planning and Public Policy: Is the 'Culture of Poverty' the New Cop-Out?" *Journal of Marriage and the Family,* 30 (May, 1968), 228-235.

JAFFE, Frederick S., *Family Planning and Rural Poverty: An Approach to Programming of Services,* National Advisory Commission on Rural Poverty, 1967.

KANTNER, John F. and Clyde V. Kiser, "Social and Psychological Factors Affecting Fertility: The Interrelation of Fertility, Fertility Planning, and Intergenerational Social Mobility," *Milbank Memorial Fund Quarterly,* 32 (January, 1954), 69-102.

KEYFITZ, Nathan, "Differential Fertility in Ontario: An Application of Factorial Design to a Demographic Problem," *Population Studies,* 6 (November, 1952), 123-134.

KHAN, A. M. and Harvey M. Choldin, "New 'Family Planners' in Rural East Pakistan," *Demography,* 2 (1965), 1-7.

KISER, Clyde V., "Fertility Trends and Differentials Among Non-whites in the United States," *Milbank Memorial Fund Quarterly,* 36 (April, 1958), 149-197.

KISER, Clyde V., *Group Differences in Urban Fertility,* Baltimore: Wilkins and Wilkins, 1942.

KISER, Clyde V., editor, *Research in Family Planning,* Princeton: Princeton University Press, 1962.

KISER, Clyde V. and M. E. Frank, "Factors Associated with the Low Fertility of Nonwhite Women of College Attainment," *Milbank Memorial Fund Quarterly,* 45 (October, 1967), 427-449.

KISER, Clyde V. and P. K. Whelpton, "Progress Report on the Study of Social and Psychological Factors Affecting Fertility," *American Sociological Review,* 12 (April, 1947), 175-186.

KISER, Clyde V. and P. K. Whelpton, "Social and Psychological Factors Affecting Fertility--II Variations in the Size of Complete Families of 6,551 Mature White Couples in Indianapolis," *Milbank Memorial Fund Quarterly,* 22 (January, 1944), 72-105.

KISER, Clyde V. and P. K. Whelpton, "Social and Psychological Factors Affecting Fertility--IX Fertility Planning and Fertility Rates by Socio-Economic Status," *Milbank Memorial Fund Quarterly,* 27 (April, 1949), 188-244.

KISER, Clyde V. and P. K. Whelpton, "Social and Psychological Factors Affecting Fertility--XI The Interrelationship of Fertility, Fertility Planning and Feeling of Economic Security," *Milbank Memorial Fund Quarterly,* 29 (January, 1951), 467-548.

KITAGAWA, Evelyn M., "Differential Fertility in Chicago, 1920-1940," *American Journal of Sociology,* 58 (March, 1953), 481-492.

KUNZ, Phillip R., "The Relation of Income and Fertility," *Journal of Marriage and the Family,* 27 (November, 1965), 509-513.

LAURIAT, Patience, "Marriage and Fertility Patterns of College Graduates," *Eugenics Quarterly,* 6 (September, 1959), 171-179.

LEE, Everett S. and Anne S. Lee, "The Differential Fertility of the American Negro," *American Sociological Review,* 17 (August, 1952), 437-447.

LEE, Hae Young, Tae Hwon, and Chin Kyum Kim, "Family-Size Value in a Korean Middle Town, Ichon Eup," *Journal of*

Marriage and the Family, 30 (May, 1968), 329-337.

LEWIS-FANING, E., *Family Limitation and Its Influence on Human Fertility During the Past Fifty Years,* Papers of the Royal Commission on Population, I, London, 1949.

LORIMER, Frank and Herbert Roback, "Economics of the Family Relative to Number of Children," *Milbank Memorial Fund Quarterly,* 18 (April, 1940), 114-136.

MATRAS, Judah, "Differential Fertility, Intergenerational Occupational Mobility, and Change in the Occupational Distribution: Some Elementary Interrelationships," *Population Studies,* 15 (November, 1961), 187-197.

MAXWELL, James, "Intelligence, Fertility and the Future: A Report on the 1947 Scottish Mental Survey," *Proceedings of the World Population Conference,* New York: United Nations, 1954.

MAYER, Albert and Carol Klapprodt, "Fertility Differentials in Detroit: 1920-1950," *Population Studies,* 9 (November, 1955), 148-158.

MENDOZA, Elvira, "Socio-economic Correlates of Attitudes Toward Family Size," in Donald Bogue, editor, *Sociological Contributions to Family Planning Research,* Community and Family Study Center, University of Chicago, 1967.

McCORMICK, Thomas C. and Melvin S. Brooks, "Occupational Birth and Marriage Rates, Wisconsin, 1920-1936," *American Sociological Review,* 6 (December, 1941), 806-817.

McGINNIS, Robert, "Similarity in Background Characteristics and Differential Fertility," *Social Forces,* 34 (October, 1955), 67-72.

MITRA, S., "Child-Bearing Pattern of American Women," *Eugenics Quarterly,* 13 (June, 1966), 133-146.

MITRA, S., "Education and Fertility in the United States," *Eugenics Quarterly,* 13 (September, 1966), 214-222.

MITRA, S., "Income, Socio-economic Status, and Fertility in the United States," *Eugenics Quarterly,* 13 (September, 1966), 223-230.

MOBERG, Sven, "Marital Status and Family Size Among Matriculated Persons in Sweden," *Population Studies,* 14 (June, 1950), 115-127.

NATIONAL CENTER FOR HEALTH STATISTICS, *Fertility and Educational Attainment: Puerto Rico–1962,* Washington, D. C.: U. S. Government Printing Office, 1967.

NELSON, Lowry, "Education and the Changing Size of Mormon Families," *Rural Sociology,* 17 (December, 1952), 335-342.

NOTESTEIN, Frank W., "Class Differences in Fertility," *Annals of the American Academy of Political and Social Science,* (November, 1936), 1-11.

PASAMANICK, Benjamin, Simon Dinitz, and Hilda Knobloch, "Socio-Economic and Seasonal Variations in Birth Rates," *Milbank Memorial Fund Quarterly,* 38 (July, 1960), 248-254.

PERRUCCI, Carolyn Cummings, "Social Origins, Mobility Patterns and Fertility," *American Sociological Review,* 32 (August, 1967), 615-625.

POTI, S. J. and D. Subodh, "Pilot Study on Social Mobility and its Association with Fertility in West Bengal in 1956," *Artha Vijnana,* 2 (June, 1960), 85-95.

POWERS, Mary G., "Socioeconomic Status and the Fertility of Married Women," *Sociology and Social Research,* 50 (July, 1966), 472-482.

RAINWATER, Lee, *Family Design: Marital Sexuality, Family Planning and Family Limitation,* Chicago: Aldine, 1964.

RAINWATER, Lee and Karol K. Weinstein, *And the Poor Get Children,* Chicago: Quadrangle Books, 1960.

RAINWATER, Lee and Karol K. Weinstein, "A Qualitative Exploration of Family Planning and Contraception in the Working Class," *Marriage and Family Living,* 22 (August, 1960), 238-242.

RIELE, J. R., "Fertility Differentials in India: Evidence from a Rural Background," *Milbank Memorial Fund Quarterly,* 41 (April, 1963), 183-199.

RIEMER, Ruth and Clyde V. Kiser, "Social and Psychological Factors Affecting Fertility: Economic Tension and Social Mobility in Relation to Fertility Planning and Size of Planned Family," *Milbank Memorial Fund Quarterly,* 32 (April, 1954), 167-231.

ROSENQUIST, Carl M. and Alvin H. Schafft, "Differential Fertility in Rural Texas," *Rural Sociology,* 12 (March, 1947), 21-26.

SAUNDERS, J. V. D., *Differential Fertility in Brazil,* Gainesville, Florida: University of Florida Press, 1958.

SEWELL, William H., "Differential Fertility in Completed Oklahoma Farm Families," *American Sociological Review,* 9 (August, 1944), 427-434.

SCOTT, Wolf, "Fertility and Social Mobility Among Teachers," *Population Studies,* 11 (March, 1958), 251-261.

SINHA, J. N., "Differential Fertility and Family Limitation in an Urban Community of Uttar Pradesh," *Population Studies,* 11 (November, 1957), 157-169.

STYCOS, J. M., "Culture and Differential Fertility in Peru," *Population Studies,* 16 (March, 1963), 257-270.

STYCOS, J. M., *Family and Fertility in Puerto Rico: A Study of the Lower Income Group,* New York: Columbia University Press, 1955.

STYS, W., "The Influence of Economic Conditions on the Fertility of Peasant Women," *Population Studies,* 11 (November, 1957), 136-148.

SYDENSTRIKER, Edgar and Frank W. Notestein, "Differential Fertility According to Social Class," *Journal of the American Statistical Association,* 25 (March, 1930), 9-32.

THOMSON, Sir Godfrey, "Intelligence and Fertility: The Scottish 1947 Survey," *Eugenics Review,* 41 (January, 1950), 163-170.

TIEN, H. Y., *Social Mobility and Controlled Fertility: Family Origins and Structure of the Australian Academic Elite,* New Haven: College and University Press, 1965.

TIEN, H. Y., "The Social Mobility-Fertility Hypothesis Reconsidered: An Empirical Study," *American Sociological Review,* 26 (April, 1961), 247-257.

TIETZE, Christopher, "Differential Reproduction in the United States: Paternity Rates for Occupational Classes Among the Urban White Population," *American Journal of Sociology,* 49 (November, 1943), 242-247.

THOMPSON, Warren S., "Differentials in Fertility and Levels of Living in the Rural Population of the United States," *American Sociological Review,* 13 (August, 1948), 516-534.

TOMASSON, Richard F., "Social Mobility and Family Size in Two High Status Populations," *Eugenics Quarterly,* 13 (June, 1966), 113-121.

WESTOFF, Charles F., "Differential Fertility in the United States: 1900-1952," *American Sociological Review,* 19 (October, 1954), 549-561.

WESTOFF, Charles F., "The Changing Focus of Differential Fertility Research: The Social Mobility Hypothesis," *Milbank Memorial Fund Quarterly,* 31 (January, 1953), 24-38.

WESTOFF, Charles F., Robert G. Potter, Jr., Philip C. Sagi, and Elliott G. Mishler, *Family Growth in Metropolitan America,* Princeton: Princeton University Press, 1961.

WESTOFF, Charles F. and Raymond H. Potvin, *College Women and Fertility Values,* Princeton: Princeton University Press, 1967.

WHELPTON, P. K., "Future Fertility of American Women," *Eugenics Quarterly,* 1 (March, 1954), 4-15.

WHELPTON, P. K., A. A. Campbell, and J. E. Patterson, *Fertility and Family Planning in the United States,* Princeton: Princeton University Press, 1966.

WHELPTON, P. K. and Clyde V. Kiser, "Social and Psychological Factors Affecting Fertility: Differential Fertility Among 41,498 Native-White Couples in Indianapolis," *Milbank Memorial Fund*

Quarterly, 21 (July, 1943), 221-280.

WHELPTON, P. K. and Clyde V. Kiser, *Social and Psychological Factors Affecting Fertility,* 3 volumes, New York: Milbank Memorial Fund, 1946, 1950, and 1953.

WINDLE, Charles and Georges Sabagh, "Social Status and Family Size of Iranian Industrial Employees," *Milbank Memorial Fund Quarterly,* 41 (October, 1963), 436-443.

WOOFTER, T. J., Jr., "Size of Family in Relation to Family Income and Age of Family Head," *American Sociological Review,* 9 (December, 1944), 678-684.

WRONG, Dennis H., "Class Fertility Differentials Before 1850," *Social Research,* 25 (Spring, 1958), 70-86.

WRONG, Dennis H., "Class Fertility Differentials in England and Wales," *Milbank Memorial Fund Quarterly,* 38 (January, 1960), 37-47.

WRONG, Dennis H., "Trends in Class Fertility in Western Nations," *Canadian Journal of Economics and Political Science,* 24 (May, 1958), 216-229.

YANG, Jac Mo, Sook Bang, Myung Ho Kim, and Man Gap Lee, "Fertility and Family Planning in Rural Korea," *Population Studies,* 18 (March, 1965), 237-250.

YASUBA, Yasukichi, *Birth Rates of the White Population in the United States, 1800-1860: An Economic Study,* Baltimore: John Hopkins Press, 1962.

YERACARIS, Constantine A., "Differentials in Ideal Family Size--Buffalo, 1956," *Sociology and Social Research,* 44 (September-October, 1959), 8-11.

YERACARIS, Constantine A., "Differentials in the Relationship Between Values and Practices in Fertility," *Social Forces,* 38 (December, 1959), 153-158.

ZARATE, Alvan O., "Differential Fertility in Monterrey, Mexico: Prelude to Transition?" *Milbank Memorial Fund Quarterly,* 45 (April, 1967), 93-108.

FERTILITY

Deviant Behavior

AKERS, Ronald L., "Socioeconomic Status and Delinquent Behavior: A Re-Test," *Journal of Research in Crime and Delinquency,* 1 (January, 1964), 38-46.

BATES, William, "Caste, Class and Vandalism," *Social Problems,* 9 (Spring, 1962), 349-358.

BLOOM, Bernard L., "A Census Tract Analysis of Socially Deviant Behaviors," *Multivariate Behavioral Research,* 1 (1966), 307-320.

BLUE, John T. Jr., "The Relationship of Juvenile Delinquency, Race, and Economic Status," *Journal of Negro Education,* 17 (Fall, 1948) 469-477.

BOHLKE, Robert H., "Social Mobility, Stratification Inconsistency and Middle Class Delinquency," *Social Problems,* 8 (1961) 351-363.

BORDUA, David J., "Juvenile Delinquency and 'Anomie': An Attempt at Replication," *Social Problems,* 6 (Winter, 1958-1959), 230-238.

BRUNER, Jerome S. and S. J. Korchin, "The Boss and the Vote: A Case Study in City Politics," *Public Opinion Quarterly,* 10 (Spring, 1946), 1-23.

CAMERON, Mary Owen, *The Booster and the Snitch: Department Store Shoplifting,* New York: Free Press, 1964.

CARTWRIGHT, Desmond S. and Kenneth I. Howard, "Multivariate Analysis of Gang Delinquency: I Ecological Influences," *Multivariate Behavioral Research,* 1 (1966), 321-371.

CAVAN, Ruth S., "Negro Family Disorganization and Juvenile Delinquency," *Journal of Negro Education,* 28 (Summer, 1959), 231-238.

CHEIN, Isidor, et al, *The Road to H: Narcotics, Delinquency and Social Policy,* New York: Basic Books, 1964.

CHILTON, Roland J., "Continuity in Delinquency Area Research: A Comparison of Studies for Baltimore, Detroit, and Indianapolis," *American Sociological Review,* 29 (February, 1964), 71-83.

CLARK, John P. and Eugene P. Wenninger, "Socioeconomic Class and Area as Correlates of Illegal Behavior Among Juveniles, *American Sociological Review,* 27 (December, 1962), 826-834.

CLARK, Kenneth B., "Color, Class, Personality, and Juvenile Delinquency," *Journal of Negro Education,* 28 (Summer, 1959), 240-251.

CLAUSEN, J. A., "Social and Psychological Factors in Narcotics Addiction," *Law and Contemporary Problems,* 22 (1957), 34-51.

CLINARD, Marshall, *Sociology of Deviant Behavior,* New York: Rinehart, 1957.

CLOWARD, Richard A., "Illegitimate Means, Anomie, and Deviant Behavior," *American Sociological Review,* 24 (April, 1959), 164-176.

CLOWARD, Richard A. and Lloyd E. Ohlin, *Delinquency and Opportunity: A Theory of Delinquent Gangs,* New York: Free Press, 1961.

COHEN, Albert, *Delinquent Boys: The Culture of the Gang,* New York: Free Press, 1955.

COHEN, Albert K., "The Sociology of the Deviant Act: Anomie Theory and Beyond," *American Sociological Review,* 30 (February, 1965), 5-14.

COHEN, Albert K. and James F. Short, Jr., "Research in Delinquent Subcultures," *Journal of Social Issues,* 14 (third quarter, 1958), 20-37.

CONGER, John Janeway, W. C. Miller, Robert V. Rainey, and Charles R. Walsmith, *Personality, Social Class, and Delinquency,* New York: Wiley, 1966.

DeFLEUR, Lois, "A Cross-Cultural Comparison of Juvenile Offenders and Offenses: Cordoba, Argentina, and the United States," *Social Problems,* 14 (Spring, 1967), 483-492.

DENTLER, Robert A. and Lawrence J. Monroe, "Social Correlates of Early Adolescent Theft," *American Sociological Review,* 26 (October, 1961), 733-743.

DIRKSEN, Cletus, *Economic Factors in Delinquency,* Milwaukee; Bruce, 1948.

DOWNES, David M., *The Delinquent Solution: A Study in Subcultural Theory,* New York: Free Press, 1966.

DRAKE, St. Clair and Horace R. Cayton, *Black Metropolis: A Study of Negro Life in a Northern Metropolis,* New York: Harper and Row, 1944.

DUBIN, Robert, "Deviant Behavior and Social Structure: Continuities in Social Theory," *American Sociological Review,* 24 (April, 1959), 147-164.

ELLIOTT, Delbert S., "Delinquency and Perceived Opportunity," *Sociological Inquiry,* 32 (Spring, 1962), 216-227.

EMPEY, Lamar T. and Maynard L. Erickson, "Class Position, Peers, and Delinquency," *Sociology and Social Research,* 49 (April, 1965), 268-282.

ENDLEMAN, Robert, "Moral Perspectives of Blue-Collar Workers," in Arthur B. Shostak and William Gomberg, editors, *Blue-Collar World: Studies of the American Worker,* Englewood Cliffs, New Jersey: Prentice-Hall, 1964.

FANNIN, Leon F. and Marshall B. Clinard, "Differences in the Conception of Self as a Male Among Lower and Middle Class Delinquents," *Social Problems,* 13 (Fall, 1965), 205-214.

FLEISHER, Belton M., *The Economics of Delinquency,* Chicago: Quadrangle Books, 1966.

GEIS, Gilbert, editor, *White-Collar Criminal: The Offender in Business and the Professions,* New York: Atherton, 1968.

GIBBENS, T.C.N. and T. H. Ahrenfeld, editors, *Cultural Factors in Delinquency,* Philadelphia: Lippincott, 1966.

GLUECK, Sheldon and Eleanor Glueck, *Unraveling Juvenile Delinquency,* Cambridge: Harvard University Press, 1950.

GOLD, Martin, "On Social Status and Delinquency: A Note on Voss's Article," *Social Problems,* 15 (Summer, 1967), 114-116.

GOLD, Martin, *Status Forces in Delinquent Boys,* Ann Arbor: Institute for Social Research, University of Michigan, 1963.

GORDON, Robert A., "Issues in the Ecological Study of Delinquency," *American Sociological Review,* 32 (December, 1967), 927-944.

GORDON, Robert A., "Social Level, Social Disability, and Gang Interaction," *American Journal of Sociology,* 73 (July, 1967), 42-62.

GORDON, Robert A. and James F. Short, "Social Level, Social Disability, and Gang Interaction," Chapter 10 in James F. Short and Fred L. Strodtbeck, *Group Process and Gang Delinquency,* Chicago: University of Chicago Press, 1965.

GUTTENTAG, Marcia, "The Relationship of Unemployment to Crime and Delinquency," *Journal of Social Issues,* 24 (January, 1968).

HAVIGHURST, Robert J., Paul Hoover Bowman, Gordon P. Liddle, Charles V. Matthews, and James V. Pierce, *Growing Up in River City,* New York: Wiley, 1962.

HELLER, Celia S., *Mexican American Youth: Forgotten Youth at the Crossroads,* New York: Random House, 1966.

HENRY, Andrew F. and James F. Short, Jr., *Suicide and Homicide,* New York: Free Press, 1954.

HOLLANDER, E. P., *Leaders, Groups, and Influence,* New York: Oxford University Press, 1964.

KARACHI, Larry and Toby Jackson, "The Uncommitted Adolescent: Candidate for Gang Socialization," in Arthur B.

Shostak and William Gomberg, editors, *Blue-Collar World: Studies of the American Worker,* Englewood Cliffs, New Jersey: Prentice-Hall, 1964.

DEVIANT BEHAVIOR

KITSUSE, John I. and David C. Dietrick, "Delinquent Boys: A Critique," *American Sociological Review,* 24 (April, 1959) 208-215.

KVARACEUS, William, "Juvenile Delinquent Behavior and Social Class," *Journal of Educational Sociology,* 18 (September, 1944), 51-54.

KVARACEUS, William and Walter B. Miller, *Delinquent Behavior: Culture and the Individual,* Washington, D.C.: National Educational Association, 1959.

LANDER, Bernard, *Towards An Understanding of Juvenile Delinquency: A Study of 8,464 Cases of Juvenile Delinquency in Baltimore,* New York: Columbia University Press, 1954.

LEFKOWITZ, M., R. R. Blake, and Jane S. Mouton, "Status Factors in Pedestrian Violation of Traffic Signals," *Journal of Abnormal and Social Psychology,* 51 (1955), 706-708.

LEGGETT, John C. and David Street, "Economic Crisis and Expectations of Violence: A Study of Unemployed Negroes," in Arthur B. Shostak and William Gomberg, editors, *Blue-Collar World: Studies of the American Worker,* Englewood Cliffs, New Jersey: Prentic-Hall, 1964.

MARSHALL, T. F. and A. Mason, "A Framework for the Analysis of Juvenile Delinquency Causation," *British Journal of Sociology,* 19 (June, 1968), 143-159.

MATZA, David, *Delinquency and Drift,* New York: Wiley, 1964.

MERTON, Robert K., "Social Conformity, Deviation, and Opportunity Structures: A Comment on the Contributions of Dubin and Cloward," *American Sociological Review,* 24 (April, 1959), 177-189.

MERTON, Robert K., "Social Structure and Anomie," and "Continuities in the Theory of Social Structure and Anomie," in his *Social Theory and Social Structure,* revised edition, New York: Free Press, 1957.

MILLER, Walter B., "Lower Class Culture as a Generating Milieu of Gang Delinquency," *Journal of Social Issues,* 14 (third quarter, 1958), 5-19.

MILNE, David S., "Economic Factors in Juvenile Delinquency," in Joseph S. Roucek, editor, *Juvenile Delinquency,* New York: Philosophical Library, 1958.

MONACHESI, Elio, "Personality Characteristics and Socio-Economic Status of Delinquents and Non-Delinquents," *Journal of Criminal Law and Criminology,* 40 (1950), 570-583.

MORRIS, Pauline, *Prisoners and Their Families,* New York: Hart, 1965.

MORRIS, Terence, *The Criminal Area: A Study in Social Ecology,* London: Routledge and Kegan Paul, 1957.

MYERHOFF, Howard L. and Barbara G. Myerhoff, "Field Observations of Middle Class 'Gangs,'" *Social Forces,* 42 (March, 1964), 328-336.

NYE, F. Ivan, *Family Relationships and Delinquent Behavior,* New York: Wiley, 1958.

NYE, F. Ivan, James F. Short, Jr., and Virgil J. Olson, "Socio-economic Status and Delinquent Behavior," *American Journal of Sociology,* 63 (January, 1958), 381-389.

PALMORE, Erdman B., "Dropouts, Delinquency, and Lower-Class Children," in Robert E. Will and Harold G. Vatter, editors, *Poverty in Affluence,* New York: Harcourt, Brace and World, 1965.

PALMORE, Erdman B., "Factors Associated With School Dropouts and Juvenile Delinquency Among Lower-Class Children," *Social Security Bulletin,* 26 (October, 1963), 4-9.

PALMORE, Erdman B. and Phillip E. Hammond, "Interacting Factors in Juvenile Delinquency," *American Sociological Review,* 29 (December, 1964), 848-854.

PEARLIN, Leonard I., Marian Radke Yarrow, and Harry A. Scarr, "Unintended Effects of Parental Aspirations: The Case of Children's Cheating," *American Journal of Sociology,* 73 (July, 1967), 73-83.

POLK, Kenneth, "Juvenile Delinquency and Social Areas," *Social Problems,* 5 (1957-1958), 214-217.

PORTERFIELD, Austin, "Delinquency and Its Outcome in Court and College," *American Journal of Sociology,* 49 (September, 1943), 199-204.

PORTERFIELD, Austin, *Youth in Trouble,* Fort Worth: Potishman Foundation, 1946.

QUAY, Herbert C., *Juvenile Delinquency: Research and Theory,* Princeton: Van Nostrand, 1965.

QUINNEY, Earl R., "Occupational Structure and Criminal Behavior: Prescription Violation by Retail Pharmacists," *Social Problems,* 11 (Fall, 1963), 179-185.

REISS, Albert J., Jr. and A. Lewis Rhodes, "The Distribution of Juvenile Delinquency in the Social Class Structure," *American Sociological Review,* 26 (October, 1961), 720-732.

REISS, Albert J., Jr., and A. Lewis Rhodes, "Status Deprivation and Delinquent Behavior," *Sociological Quarterly,* 4 (Spring, 1963), 135-149.

ROBINS, Lee N., Harry Gyman, and Patricia O'Neal, "The Interaction of Social Class and Deviant Behavior," *American Sociological Review,* 27 (August, 1962), 480-492.

ROSEN, Lawrence and Stanley H. Turner, "An Evaluation of the Lander Approach to Ecology of Delinquency," *Social Problems,* 15 (Fall, 1967) 189-200.

SCHMITT, Robert C., "Density, Delinquency and Crime in Honolulu," *Sociology and Social Research,* 41 (March-April, 1957), 274-276.

SCHMITT, Robert C., "Interrelations of Social Problem Rates in Honolulu," *American Sociological Review,* 21 (October, 1956), 617-619.

SCHRAG, Clarence, "Delinquency and Opportunity: Analysis of a Theory," *Sociology and Social Research,* 46 (January, 1962), 167-175.

SCHWARTZ, Edward, "A Community Experiment in the Measurement of Juvenile Delinquency," *National Probation Association Yearbook,* (1945), 157-181.

SHANLEY, Fred J., "Middle-Class Delinquency as a Social Problem," *Sociology and Social Research,* 51 (January, 1967), 185-198.

SHAW, Clifford and Henry D. McKay, *Juvenile Delinquency in Urban Areas,* Chicago: University of Chicago Press, 1942.

SHOHAM, Shlomo, and Meir Hovav, "B'Nei-Lovim' -Middle and Upper Class Delinquency in Israel," *Sociology and Social Research,* 48, (July, 1964), 454-468.

SHORT, James F., "Differential Association and Delinquency," *Social Problems,* 4 (January, 1957), 233-239.

SHORT, James F. and F. Ivan Nye, "Reported Behavior as a Criterion of Deviant Behavior," *Social Problems,* 5 (Winter, 1957-1958), 207-213.

SHORT, James F., Ramon Rivera, and Roy A. Tennyson, "Perceived Opportunities, Gang Membership, and Delinquency," *American Sociological Review,* 30 (February, 1965), 56-67.

SHORT, James F. and Fred L. Strodtbeck, *Group Process and Gang Delinquency,* Chicago: University of Chicago Press, 1965.

SPERGEL, Irving, "Male Young Adult Criminality, Deviant Values, and Differential Opportunities in Two Lower Class Negro Neighborhoods," *Social Problems,* 10 (Winter, 1963), 237-250.

STINCHCOMBE, Arthur L., *Rebellion in High School,* Chicago: Quadrangle Books, 1964.

SUTHERLAND, Edwin H., *White-Collar Crime,* New York: Dryden, 1949.

SUTHERLAND, Edwin H., "White-Collar Criminality," *American Sociological Review,* 5 (February, 1940), 1-12.

SYKES, Gresham, *Crime and Society,* New York: Random House, 1962.

VAZ, Edmund W., "Juvenile Delinquency in the Middle-Class Youth Culture," in Edmund W. Vaz, editor, *Middle-Class Juvenile Delinquency,* New York: Harper and Row, 1967.

VOSS, Harwin L., "Socio-economic Status and Reported Delinquent Behavior," *Social Problems,* 13 (Winter, 1966), 314-324.

WALLENSTEIN, James S. and C. J. Wyle, "Our Law Abiding Law Breakers," *National Probation,* (March-April, 1947), 107-112.

WHITE, Mary Alice and June Cherry, editors, *School Disorder, Intelligence, and Social Class,* New York: Teachers College Press, 1966.

WHYTE, William F., *Street Corner Society,* Chicago: University of Chicago Press, 1943.

WIERS, Paul, *Economic Factors in Michigan Delinquency,* New York: Columbia University Press, 1944.

WILLIE, Charles, "The Relative Contribution of Family Status and Economic Status to Juvenile Delinquency," *Social Problems,* 14 (Winter, 1967), 326-335.

WILLMOTT, Peter, *Adolescent Boys of East London,* New York: Humanities Press, 1967.

WINSLOW, Robert W., "Status Management in the Adolescent Social System: A Reformulation of Merton's Anomie Theory," *British Journal of Sociology,* 19 (June, 1968), 143-159.

WISE, Nancy Barton, "Juvenile Delinquency Among Middle-Class Girls," in Edmund W. Vaz, editor, *Middle-Class Juvenile Delinquency,* New York: Harper and Row, 1967.

WOLF, P., "Crime and Social Class in Denmark," *British Journal of Criminology,* 3 (1962), 5-17.

WOLFGANG, Marvin E., editor, *Studies in Homicide,* New York: Harper and Row, 1967.

WOOD, Arthur L., "A Socio-Structural Analysis of Murder, Suicide, and Economic Crime in Ceylon," *American Sociological Review,* 26 (October, 1961), 744-753.

ZOLA, Irving Kenneth, "Observations on Gambling in a Lower-Class Setting," in Arthur B. Shostak and William Gomberg, editors, *Blue-Collar World: Studies of the American Worker,* Englewood Cliff, New Jersey: Prentice-Hall, 1964.

ABRAMS, Mark, "Class and Politics," *Encounter,* (October, 1961).

ABRAMS, Mark, "Press Polls and Votes in Britain since the 1955 General Elections, *Public Opinion Quarterly,* 21 (1957-1958), 543-547.

ABRAMS, Mark, "Social Class and British Politics," *Public Opinion Quarterly,* 25 (Fall, 1961), 342-350.

ADLER, Kenneth P., "Interest and Influence in Foreign Affairs," *Public Opinion Quarterly,* 20 (Spring, 1956), 89-101.

AGGER, Robert E. and Vincent Ostrom, "Political Participation in a Small Community," in Heinz Eulau, Samuel J. Eldersveld, and Morris Janowitz, editors, *Political Behavior,* New York: Free Press, 1956.

AIKEN, Michael, Louis E. Ferman, and Harold L. Sheppard, *Economic Failure, Alienation, and Extremism,* Ann Arbor: University of Michigan Press, 1968.

ALFORD, Robert R., "The Role of Social Class in American Voting Behavior," *Western Political Quarterly,* 16 (March, 1963), 180-194.

ALFORD, Robert R., "A Suggested Index of the Association of Social Class and Voting," *Public Opinion Quarterly,* 26 (Fall, 1962), 417-425.

ALFORD, Robert R., *Party and Society,* Chicago: Rand McNally, 1963.

ALFORD, Robert R. and Harry M. Scoble, "Community Leadership, Education, and Political Behavior," *American Sociological Review,* 33 (April, 1968), 191-209.

ALLARDT, Erik and Kettil Bruun, "Characteristics of the Finnish Non-Voter," *Transactions of the Westermarck Society,* 3 (1956), 55-76.

ANDERSON, Bo and Morris Zelditch, "Rank Equilibration and Political Behavior," *Archives europennes de sociologie,* 5 (1964), 112-125.

ANDERSON, Dewey and Percy E. Davidson, *Ballots and the Democratic Class Struggle: A Study in the Background of Political Education,* Stanford: Stanford University Press, 1943.

BAGGALEY, Andrew R., "White Collar Employment and Republican Vote," *Public Opinion Quarterly,* 20 (Summer, 1956), 471-473.

BAZELON, David, "The New Class," *Commentary,* 42 (August, 1966), 48-53.

BEER, Samuel M., *British Politics in the Collectivist Age,* New York: Knopf, 1965.

BENDIX, Reinhard, "Social Stratification and the Political Community," *European Journal of Sociology,* 11 (1960).

BENDIX, Reinhard, "Social Stratification and Political Power," *American Political Science Review,* 46 (June, 1952), 357-375.

BENNEY, Mark and Phyllis Geis, "Social Class and Politics in Greenwich," *British Journal of Sociology,* 1 (December, 1950), 310-327.

BENNEY, Mark, A. P. Gray, and R. H. Pear, *How People Vote,* London: Routledge and Kegan Paul, 1956.

BENSON, E. G. and Evelyn Wicoff, "Voters Pick Their Party," *Public Opinion Quarterly,* 8 (Summer, 1944), 165-174.

BERELSON, Bernard R., P. M. Lazarsfeld, and W. N. McPhee, *Voting,* Chicago: University of Chicago Press, 1954.

BIRCH, A. H., *Small-Town Politics,* London: Oxford University Press, 1959.

BIRCH, A. H. and Peter Campbell, "Voting Behavior in a Lancashire Constituency," *British Journal of Sociology,* 1 (September, 1950), 197-208.

BLONDEL, Jean, *Voters, Parties, and Leaders,* Baltimore: Penguin, 1963.

BONHAM, John, *The Middle-Class Vote,* London: Faber and Faber, 1954.

BOWER, Robert T., "New York City's Labor Vote," *Public Opinion Quarterly,"* (Winter, 1947-1948), 614-615.

BRANDMEYER, Gerard, "Status Consistency and Political Behavior: A Replication and Extension of Research," *Sociological Quarterly,* 6 (Summer, 1965), 241-256.

BRENNAN, T., "Class Behavior in Local Politics and Social Affairs," *Transactions of the Second World Congress of Sociology,* 2 (1954), 283-297.

BROOM, Leonard and Norval D. Glenn, "Negro-White Differences in

Reported Attitudes and Behavior," *Sociology and Social Research,* 50 (January, 1966), 187-200.

BROTZ, Howard M., "Social Stratification and the Political Order," *American Journal of Sociology,* 64 (May, 1959), 571-578.

BUTLER, D. E., *The British General Election of 1951,* London: Macmillan, 1951.

CAMPBELL, Angus, Philip E. Converse, W. E. Miller and D. E. Stokes, *The American Voter,* New York: Wiley, 1960.

CAMPBELL, Angus, Gerald Gurin, and Warren E. Miller, *The Voter Decides,* New York: Harper and Row, 1954.

CAMPBELL, Angus and R. L. Kahn, *The People Elect a President,* Ann Arbor: University of Michigan Survey Research Center, 1952.

CANCIAN, Frank, "The Southern Italian Peasant: World View and Political Behavior," *Anthropological Quarterly,* 34 (1961), 1-18.

CENTERS, Richard, *The Psychology of Social Classes,* Princeton: Princeton University Press, 1949.

CONNELLY, G. M. and H. H. Field, "The Non-Voter, Who He Is, and What He Thinks," *Public Opinion Quarterly,* 8 (1944), 175-187.

CONVERSE, Philip E., "The Shifting Role of Class in Political Attitudes and Behavior," in E. Maccoby, T. Newcomb, and E. Hartley, editors, *Readings in Social Psychology,* third edition, New York: Henry Holt, 1958.

CONWAY, Margaret, "The White Backlash Re-Examined: Wallace and the 1964 Northern Primaries," *Social Science Quarterly,* 49 (December, 1968), pp. 710-719.

COOPER, Homer C., "Social Class Identification and Political Party Affiliation," *Psychological Reports,* 5 (June, 1959), 337-340.

DE GRAZIA, Alfred, "The Limits of External Leadership over a Minority Electorate," *Public Opinion Quarterly,* 20 (Spring, 1956), 113-128.

ENGELS, Friedrich, "Why There is No Socialist Party in America," in Lewis E. Feuer, editor, *Basic Writings on Politics and Philosophy,* Garden City, New York: Doubleday, 1959.

ERBE, William, "Social Involvement and Political Activity: A Replication and Elaboration," *American Sociological Review,* 29 (April, 1964), 198-215.

EULAU, Heinz, "Class Identification and Projection in Voting Behavior," *Western Political Quarterly,* 8 (September, 1944), 441-542.

EULAU, Heinz, *Class and Party in the Eisenhower Years,* New York: Free Press, 1962.

EULAU, Heinz, "Identification with Class and Political Perspective," *Journal of Politics,* 18 (May, 1956), 232-253.

EULAU, Heinz, "Identification with Class and Political Role Behavior," *Public Opinion Quarterly,* 20 (Fall, 1956), 515-529.

EULAU, Heinz, "Perceptions of Class and Party in Voting Behavior: 1952," *American Political Science Review,* 49 (June, 1955), 364-384.

EULAU, Heinz and David Koff, ";Occupational Mobility and Political Career," *Western Political Quarterly,* (September, 1962), 507-522.

EULAU, Heinz, Samuel J. Eldersveld, and Morris Janowitz, *Political Behavior,* New York: Free Press, 1956.

EYSENCK, Hans J., *The Psychology of Politics,* London: Routledge and Kegan Paul, 1954.

FILLEY, Walter O., "Social Structure and Canadian Political Parties: The Quebec Case," *Western Political Quarterly,* 9 (December, 1956), 900-914.

GESCHWENDER, James A., "Social Structure and the Negro Revolt: An Examination of Some Hypotheses," *Social Forces,* 43 (December, 1964), 248-256.

GLANTZ, Oscar, "Class Consciousness and Political Solidarity," *American Sociological Review,* 23 (August, 1958), 375-383.

GLENN, Norval D. and Jon P. Alston, "Cultural Distances Among Occupational Categories," *American Sociological Review,* 33 (August, 1968), 365-382.

GLENN, Norval D. and Jon P. Alston, "Rural-Urban Differences in Reported Attitudes and Behavior," *Southwestern Social Science Quarterly,* 47 (March, 1967), 381-400.

GLENN, Norval D. and Michael Grimes, "Aging, Voting, and Political Interest," *American Sociological Review,* 33 (August, 1968), 563-575.

GOFFMAN, Irwin W., "Status Consistency and Preference for Change in Power Distribution," *American Sociological Review,* 22 (June, 1957), 275-281.

GOLDRICH, Daniel and Edward W. Scott, "Developing Political Orientations of Panamanian Students," *Journal of Politics,* 23 (February, 1961), 84-107.

GOSNELL, H. F., *Grass Roots Politics: National Voting Behavior of Typical States,* Washington, D. C.: American Council on Public Affairs, 1942.

GRUSKY, Oscar, "Career Mobility and Managerial Political Behavior," *Political Science Review,* 8 (Fall, 1965), 82-89.

HADDEN, Jeffrey K., "An Analysis of Some Factors Associated with Religious and Political Affiliations in a College Population," *Journal for the Scientific Study of Religion,* 2 (Spring, 1963), 209-216.

HAMILTON, Richard F., *Affluence and the French Worker in the Fourth Republic,* Princeton University Press, 1967.

HAMILTON, Richard F., "Affluence and the Worker: The West German case," *American Journal of Sociology,* 71 (September, 1965), 144-152.

HAMILTON, Richard F., "A Note on Skill Level and Politics," *Public Opinion Quarterly,* 29 (Fall, 1965), 390-399.

HAMILTON, Richard F., *Class and Politics in the United States,* New York: Wiley, 1969.

HAMILTON, Richard F., "The Behavior and Values of Skilled Workers," in Arthur B. Shostak and William Gomberg, editors, *Blue-Collar World,* Englewood Cliffs, New Jersey: Prentice-Hall, 1964.

HAMILTON, Richard F., "The Marginal Middle Class: A Reconsideration," *American Sociological Review,* 31 (April, 1966), 192-199.

HARRISON, Royden, "The British Working Class and the General Election of 1868," parts I and II, *International Review of Social History,* Amsterdam, volumes 5 and 6 (1960, 1961), 424-455; 74-109.

HASTINGS, Philip K., "The Voter and the Non-Voter," *American Journal of Sociology,* 62 (November, 1956), 302-307.

HETZLER, Stanley A., "Social Mobility and Radicalism—Conservatism," *Social Forces,* 33 (December, 1954), 161-166.

JANOWITZ, Morris and Dwaine Marvick, "Authoritarianism and Political Behavior," *Public Opinion Quarterly,* 17 (Summer, 1953), 185-201.

JANOWITZ, Morris and Dwaine Marvick, *Competitive Pressure and Democratic Consent,* Ann Arbor: University of Michigan Press, 1956.

JANOWITZ, Morris and David R. Segal, "Social Cleavage and Party Affiliation: Germany, Great Britain, and the United States," *American Journal of Sociology,* 72 (May, 1967), 601-618.

JENNINGS, M. Kent and Harmon Zeigler, "Class, Party, and Race in Four Types of Elections: The Case of Atlanta," *Journal of Politics,* 28 (May, 1966), 391-407.

JOHNSON, John J., "Middle Groups in National Politics in Latin America," *Hispanic American Historical Review,* 37 (1957), 313-329.

JOHNSON, John J., *Political Change in Latin America: The Emergence of the Middle Sectors,* Stanford, California: Stanford University Press, 1958.

JOHNSON, John J., "The Political Role of the Latin American Middle Sectors," *Annals of American Academy of Political and Social Science,* 334 (1961), 20-29.

KARLSSON, Georg, "Political Attitudes Among Male Swedish Youth," *Acta Sociologica,* 3 (1953), 220-241.

KELLY, K. Dennis and William J. Chambliss, "Status Consistency and Political Attitudes," *American Sociological Review,* 31 (June, 1966), 375-382.

KENKEL, William F., "The Relationship Between Status Consistency and Politico-Economic Attitudes," *American Sociological Review,* 21 (June, 1956), 365-368.

KEY, V. O., Jr., *Politics, Parties, and Pressure Groups,* New York: Crowell, 1968.

KITT, Alice S. and David B. Gleicher, "Determinants of Voting Behavior," *Public Opinion Quarterly,* 14 (Fall, 1950), 393-412.

KOGAN, Norman, "Italian Communism, the Working Class and Organized Catholicism," *Journal of Politics,* 28 (August, 1966), 531-555.

KORNHAUSER, Arthur, H. L. Sheppard, and A. J. Mayer, *When Labor Votes,* New York: University Books, 1956.

KORNHAUSER, William, *The Politics of Mass Society,* New York: Free Press, 1959.

KURODA, Yasumasa, "Measurement, Correlates, and Significance of Political Participation in a Japanese Community," *Western Political Quarterly,* 20 (September, 1967), 660-668.

LADD, Everett C., "Radical Right: The White Collar Extremists," *South Atlantic Quarterly,* 65 (Summer, 1966), 314-324.

LANE, Robert E., *Political Ideology: Why the American Common Man Believes What He Does,* New York: Free Press, 1967.

LANE, Robert E., *Political Life,* New York: Free Press, 1959.

LANGDON, Frank C., "The Catholic Anti-Communist Role Within Australian Labor," *Western Political Quarterly,* 9 (December, 1956), 884-899.

LAZARSFELD, Paul, Bernard Berelson, and Hazel Gaudet, *The People's Choice,* New York: Columbia University Press, 1948.

LEGGETT, John C., "Working-Class Consciousness, Race, and Political Choice," *American Journal of Sociology,* 69 (September, 1963), 171-176.

LENSKI, Gerhard E., "Status Consistency and the Vote: A Four Nations Test," *American Sociological Review,* 32 (April, 1967), 288-301.

LENSKI, Gerhard E., "Status Crystallization: A Non-Vertical Dimension of Social Status," *American Sociological Review,* 19 (August, 1954), 405-413.

LEVINE, Gene, *When Workers Vote,* Totowa, New Jersey: Bedminster, 1963.

LINDENFELD, Frank, "Economic Interest and Political Involvement," *Public Opinion Quarterly,* 28 (Spring, 1964), 104-111.

LINDQUIST, John H., "An Occupational Analysis of Local Politics: Syracuse, New York," *Sociology and Social Research,* 49 (April, 1965), 343-354.

LINDQUIST, John H., "Socioeconomic Status and Political Participation," *Western Political Quarterly,* 17 (December, 1964), 608-614.

LIPSET, Seymour M., *Agrarian Socialism,* Berkeley: University of California Press, 1950.

LIPSET, Seymour M., *Political Man,* Garden City, New York: Doubleday, 1960.

LIPSET, Seymour M., "Social Stratification and 'Right Wing Extremism,'" *British Journal of Sociology,* 10 (December, 1959), 346-382.

LIPSET, Seymour M., "The British Voter--II; Sex, Age, and Education," *New Leader,* (November 21, 1960).

LIPSET, Seymour M., "The Changing Class Structure and Contemporary European Politics," *Daedalus,* (Winter, 1964), 271-303.

LIPSET, Seymour M., "Value Patterns, Class, and the Democratic Policy," in Reinhard Bendix and Seymour M. Lipset, editors, *Class, Status, and Power,* 2nd Edition, New York: Free Press, 1966.

LIPSET, Seymour M., Paul F. Lazarsfeld, Allen H. Barton, and Juan Linz, "The Psychology of Voting: An Analysis of Political Behavior," in Gardner Lindzey, editor, *Handbook of Social Psychology,* Volume II, Reading, Massachusetts: Addison-Wesley, 1954.

LIPSITZ, Lewis, "Work Life and Political Attitudes," *American Political Science Review,* 58 (December, 1964), 951-962.

LOPREATO, Joseph, "Upward Social Mobility and Political Orientation," *American Sociological Review,* 32 (August, 1967), 586-592.

MacRAE, Duncan, Jr., "Occupations and the Congressional Vote,

1940-1950," *American Sociological Review*, 20 (June, 1955), 332-340.

MacRAE, Duncan, Jr., "Religious and Socioeconomic Factors in the French Vote, 1946-56," *American Journal of Sociology*, 64 (November, 1958), 290-298.

MacRAE, Duncan, Jr., and Edith K. MacRae, "Legislators' Social Status and Their Votes," *American Journal of Sociology*, 66 (May, 1961), 599-603.

MARTIN, F. M., "Social Status and Electoral Choice in Two Constituencies," *British Journal of Sociology*, 3 (September, 1952), 231-241.

MARTIN, Roscoe C., "The Municipal Electorate: A Case Study," *Southwestern Social Science Quarterly*, 14 (1933), 193-237.

MARX, Gary T., *Protest and Prejudice: A Study of Belief in the Black Community*, New York: Harper and Row, 1967.

MARX, Karl, *Selected Works of Karl Marx*, New York: International Publishers, 1933.

MATTHEWS, Donald R. and James W. Prothro, *Negroes and the New Southern Politics*, New York: Harcourt, Brace and World, 1966.

MATTHEWS, Donald R. and James W. Prothro, "Social and Economic Factors and Negro Voter Registration in the South," *American Political Science Review*, 57 (March, 1963), 24-44.

McDILL, Edward L. and Jeanne C. Ridley, "Status, Anomie, Political Alienation, and Political Participation," *American Journal of Sociology*, 68 (September, 1962), 205-213.

McIVER, Robert M., *The Web of Government*, New York: Macmillan, 1947.

McKENZIE, R. T. and A. Silver, "Conservatism, Industrialism, and the Working Class Tory in England," *Transactions of the Fifth World Congress of Sociology*, 3 (1964), 191-202.

McLELLAN, David S. and Charles E. Woodhouse, "The Business Elite and Foreign Policy," *Western Political Quarterly*, 13 (March, 1960), 172-190.

MERRIAM, Charles E. and Harold F. Gosnell, *Non-Voting: Causes and Methods of Control*, Chicago: University of Chicago Press, 1924.

MILLER, Warren E., "The Socio-Economic Analysis of Political Behavior," *Midwest Journal of Political Science*, 2 (August, 1958), 239-255.

MILLS, C. Wright, "The Middle Classes in Middle-Sized Cities: The Stratification and Political Position of Small Business and White Collar Strata," *American Sociological Review*, 11 (October, 1946), 520-529.

MITCHELL, Robert Edward, "Class-linked Conflict between Two Dimensions of Liberalism-Conservatism," *Social Problems*, 13 (Spring, 1966), 418-427.

MOSTELLER, F., H. Hyman, P. McCarthy, E. Marks, and D. Truman, *The Pre-Election Polls of 1948*, New York: Social Science Research Council, 1949.

MURPHY, Raymond J. and Richard T. Morris, "Occupational Situs, Subjective Class Identification, and Political Affiliation," *American Sociological Review*, 26 (June, 1961), 383-392.

NORDLINGER, Eric A., *The Working Class Tories: Authority, Deference, and Stable Democracy*, Berkeley: University of California Press, 1967.

NORTH, Cecil C., "Class Structure, Class Consciousness, and Party Alignment," *American Sociological Review*, 2 (June, 1937), 365-371.

O'LESSKER, Karl, "Who Voted for Hitler? A New Look at the Class Basis of Nazism," *American Journal of Sociology*, 74, (July, 1968), 63-69.

ORBELL, John M., "Protest Participation Among Negro College Students," *American Political Science Review*, 61 (June, 1967), 446-456.

ORUM, Anthony M. and Amy W. Orum, "The Class and Status Bases of Negro Student Protest," *Social Science Quarterly*, 49 (December, 1968), 521-533.

PARKIN, Frank, *Middle-Class Radicalism: The Social Bases of the British Campaign for Nuclear Disarmament*, New York: Praeger, 1968.

PARSONS, Talcott, "Voting and the Equilibrium of the American Political System," in E. B. Burdick and A. Brodbeck, editors, *American Voting Behavior*, New York: Free Press, 1959.

PATTERSON, Samuel C., "Inter-Generational Occupational Mobility and Legislative Voting Behavior," *Social Forces*, 43 (October, 1964), 90-93.

PETERSON, Robert L., "Social Structure and the Political Process in Latin America: A Methodological Re-examination," *Western Political Quarterly*, 16 (December, 1963), 885-896.

PETRAS, James and Maurice Zeitlin, "Miners and Agrarian Radicalism," *American Sociological Review*, 32 (August, 1967), 578-586.

PINARD, Maurice, "Poverty and Political Movements," *Social Problems,* 15 (Fall, 1967), 250-263.

POLSBY, Nelson, "Toward an Exploration of McCartyism," in Nelson Polsby, *et al.,* editors, *Politics and Social Life,* Boston: Houghton Mifflin, 1963.

POWELL, Inge B., "The Non-Voter: Some Questions and Hypotheses," *Berkeley Publications in Society and Institutions,* 1 (1955), 25-36.

QUINNEY, Richard, "Political Conservatism Alienation, and Fatalism: Contingencies of Social Status and Religious Fundamentalism," *Sociometry,* 27 (September, 1964), 372-381.

RICE, Stuart A., *Farmers and Workers in American Politics,* New York: Columbia University Press, 1924.

ROGIN, Michael, "Wallace and the Middle Class: The White Backlash in Wisconsin," *Public Opinion Quarterly,* 30 (Spring, 1966), 98-108.

ROSE, Richard, "Class and Party Divisions: Britain as a Test Case," Occasional Paper Number One (1968), Survey Research Center, University of Strathclyde, Glasgow, Scotland.

RUNCIMAN, W. G., "Embourgeoisement, Self-Rated Class, and Party Preference," *Sociological Review,* 12 (July, 1964), 137-154.

RUSH, Gary B., "Status Consistency and Right-Wing Extremism," *American Sociological Review,* 32 (February, 1967), 86-92.

SAENGER, Gerhart H., "Social Status and Political Behavior," *American Journal of Sociology,* 51 (September, 1945), 103-113.

SALISBURY, Robert H. and Gordon Black, "Class and Party in Partisan and Non-Partisan Elections: The Case of Des Moines," *American Political Science Review,* 57 (September, 1963), 584-592.

SEARLES, Ruth and J. Allen Williams, Jr., "Negro College Students' Participation in Sit-Ins," *Social Forces,* 40 (March, 1962), 215-220.

SEEMAN, Melvin, *Social Status and Leadership: The Case of the School Executive,* Columbus: Bureau of Educational Research No. 35, 1960.

SHEPPARD, Harold L. and Nicholas A. Masters, "The Political Attitudes and Preferences of Union Members: The Case of the Detroit Auto Workers," *American Political Science Review,* 53 (June, 1959), 437-447.

SMITH, G. H., "Liberalism and Level of Information," *Journal of Educational Psychology,* 39 (1948), 65-82.

POLITICAL
PHENOMENA

SMITH, G.H., "The Relation of Enlightenment to Liberal-Conservative Opinions," *Journal of Social Psychology,* 28 (1948), 3-17.

SOARES, Glaucio and Robert L. Hamblin, "Socio-economic Variables and Voting for the Radical Left: Chile, 1952," *American Political Science Review,* 56 (December, 1967), 1053-1065.

STARK, Rodney, "Class, Radicalism, and Religious Involvement in Great Britain," *American Sociological Review,* 29 (October, 1964), 698-706.

STOETZEL, Jean, "Voting Behavior in France," *British Journal of Sociology,* 6 (June, 1955), 104-122.

STREET, David and John C. Leggett, "Economic Deprivation and Extremism: A Study of Unemployed Negroes," *American Journal of Sociology,* 67 (July, 1961), 53-57.

THOMPSON, Wayne E. and John E. Horton, "Political Alienation as a Force in Political Action," *Social Forces,* 38 (March, 1960), 190-195.

TINGSTEN, Herbert, *Political Behavior: Studies in Election Statistics,* London: King, 1937.

WATSON, Richard A., *The Politics of Urban Change: The Effect of Middle-Income Apartment Dwellers on Slum Area Politics,* Kansas City: Community Studies, 1963.

WESTBY, David L. and Richard G. Braungart, "Class and Politics in the Family Backgrounds of Student Political Activists," *American Sociological Review,* 31 (October, 1966), 690-692.

WILENSKY, Harold F., "The Labor Vote: A Local Union's Impact on the Political Conduct of its Members," *Social Forces,* 35 (December, 1956), 111-120.

WILKENING, E. A. and Ralph K. Huitt, "Political Participation among Farmers as related to Socioeconomic Status and Perception of the Political Process," *Rural Sociologist,* 26 (December, 1961), 395-408.

WOLFINGER, Raymond E., Barbara Kaye Wolfinger, Kenneth Prewitt, and Sheilah Rosenhack, "America's Radical Right: Politics and Ideology," in David E. Apter, editor, *Ideology and Discontent,* New York: Free Press, 1964.

WOODWARD, Julian L. and Elmo Roper, "Political Activity of American Citizens," *American Political Science Review,* 44 (1950), 874-877.

WUNDERLICH, Frieda, "Fascism and the German Middle Class," *Antioch Review,* 5 (1945), 56-67.

Religious Phenomena

BELL, Wendell and Maryanne Force, "Religious Preference and the Class Structure," *Midwest Sociologist,* 19 (May, 1957), 79-86.

BROOM, Leonard and Norval D. Glenn, "Negro-White Differences in Reported Attitudes and Behavior," *Sociology and Social Research,* 50 (January, 1966), 187-200.

BROWN, James Stephen, "Social Class, Intermarriage, and Church Membership in a Kentucky Community," *American Journal of Sociology,* 57 (November, 1951), 232-242.

BULTENA, Louis, "Church Membership and Church Attendance in Madison, Wisconsin," *American Sociological Review,* 14 (June, 1949), 384-389.

BURCHINAL, L. G., "Some Social Status Criteria and Church Membership and Church Attendance," *Journal of Social Psychology,* 49 (1959), 53-64.

CURTIS, Richard F., "Occupational Mobility and Church Participation," *Social Forces,* 38 (May, 1960), 315-319.

DALTON, Melville, "Worker Response and Social Background," *Journal of Political Economy,* 55 (1947), 323-332.

DeJONG, Gordon F., "Religious Fundamentalism, Socio-Economic Status, and Fertility Attitudes in the Southern Appalachians," *Demography,* 2 (1965), 540-548.

DEMERATH, N. J., III, *Social Class in American Protestantism,* Chicago, Rand McNally, 1965.

DEMERATH, N. J., III, "Social Class, Religious Affiliation, and Styles of Religious Involvement," in Reinhard Bendix and Seymour M. Lipset, editors, *Class, Status, and Power* New York: Free Press, 1966.

DEMERATH, N. J., III, "Social Stratification and Church Involvement: The Church-Sect Distinction Applied to Individual Participation," *Review of Religious Research,* 2 (1961), 146-154.

DILLINGHAM, Harry C., "Protestant Religion and Social Status," *American Journal of Sociology,* 70 (January, 1965), 416-422.

DILLINGHAM, Harry C., "Rejoinder to 'Social Class and Church Participation,'" *American Journal of Sociology,* 73 (July, 1967), 110-114.

DRAKE, St. Clair and Horace R. Cayton, *Black Metropolis,* New York: Harcourt Brace, 1945.

DYNES, Russell, "Church-Sect Typology and Socio-Economic Status," *American Sociological Review,* 20 (October, 1955), 555-560.

FRAZIER, E. Franklin, *Negroes in the United States,* revised edition, New York: Macmillan, 1957.

FUKUYAMA, Yoshio, *Styles of Church Membership,* New York: United Church Board for Homeland Ministries, 1961.

GLENN, Norval D., "Negro Religion and Negro Status in the United States," in Louis Schneider, editor, *Religion, Culture and Society,* New York: Wiley, 1964.

GLENN, Norval D. and Jon P. Alston, "Cultural Distances Among Occupational Categories," *American Sociological Review,* 33 (August, 1968), pp. 365-382.

GLENN, Norval D. and Jon P. Alston, "Rural-Urban Differences in Reported Attitudes and Behavior," *Southwestern Social Science Quarterly,* 47 (March, 1967), 381-400.

GLOCK, Charles Y. and Rodney Stark, *Religion and Society in Tension,* Chicago: Rand McNally, 1965, Chapter 10, "Class, Politics, and Religious Involvement."

GOODE, Eric, "Social Class and Church Participation," *American Journal of Sociology,* 72 (July, 1966), 102-111.

HADDEN, Jeffrey K., "An Analysis of Some Factors Associated with Religious and Political Affiliations in a College Population," *Journal for the Scientific Study of Religion,* 2 (Spring, 1963), 209-216.

HAMILTON, Richard F., "The Behavior and Values of Skilled Workers," in Arthur B. Shostak and William Gomberg, editors, *Blue-Collar World,* Englewood Cliffs, New Jersey: Prentice Hall, 1964.

HAVIGHURST, Robert J., Paul H. Bowman, Gordon P. Liddle, Charles V. Matthews, and James V. Pierce, *Growing Up in River City,* New York: Wiley, 1962.

HOLLINGSHEAD, August B., *Elmtown's Youth,* New York: Wiley, 1949.

INGLIS, K. S., *Churches and the Working Classes in Victorian England,* London: Routledge and Kegan Paul, 1963.

ISAMBERT, Francois-Andre, "Is the Religious Absention of the

Working Classes a General Phenomenon?" in Louis Schneider, editor, *Religion, Culture and Society,* New York: Wiley, 1964.

JOHNSON, Benton, "Theology and Party Preference Among Protestant Clergymen," *American Sociological Review,* 31 (April, 1966), 200-208.

KAUFMAN, Harold F., "Prestige Classes in a New York Rural Community," *Cornell University Agricultural Experiment Station Bulletin,* (March, 1944).

LAZERWITZ, Bernard, "Some Factors Associated with Church Attendance," *Social Forces,* 39 (May, 1961), 301-309.

LENSKI, Gerhard E., "Social Correlates of Religious Interest," *American Sociological Review,* 18 (October, 1953), 533-544.

OBENHAUS, Victor, W. Widick Schroeder, and Charles D. England, "Church Participation Related to Social Class," *Rural Sociology,* 23 (September, 1958), 298-308.

PHOTIADIS, John D. and Jeanne Biggar, "Religiosity, Education, and Ethnic Distance," *American Journal of Sociology,* 67 (May, 1962), 666-672.

PIN, Emile, "Social Classes and Their Religious Approaches," in Louis Schneider, editor, *Religion, Culture and Society,* New York: Wiley, 1964.

POPE, Liston, "Religion and the Class Structure," *Annals of the American Academy of Political and Social Science,* (March, 1948), 84-91.

RANULF, Svend, *Moral Indignation and Middle Class Psychology,* New York: Schocken, 1964.

STARK, Rodney, "Class, Radicalism, and Religious Involvement in Great Britain," *American Sociological Review,* 29 (October, 1964), 698-706.

VERNON, Glenn M., "Background Factors Related to Church Orthodoxy," *Social Forces,* 34 (March, 1956), 252-254.

VERNON, Glenn M. "Religion and the Blue-Collarite," in Arthur B. Shostak and William Gomberg, editors, *Blue-Collar World: Studies of the American Worker.* Englewood Cliffs, New Jersey: Prentice Hall, 1964.

VERNON, Glenn M., "Religious Groups and Social Class—Some Inconsistencies," *Papers of the Michigan Academy of Science, Arts, and Letters,* 45 (1960), 295-301.

Job Satisfaction

BELL, Howard M., *Youth Tell Their Story,* Washington, D. C.: American Council on Education, 1938.

BLAUNER, Robert, *Alienation and Freedom: The Factory Worker and His Industry,* Chicago: University of Chicago Press, 1966.

BLAUNER, Robert, "Work Satisfaction and Industrial Trends in Modern Society," in Walter Galenson and Seymour M. Lipset, editors, *Labor and Trade Unionism: An Interdisciplinary Reader,* New York: Wiley, 1960.

BONJEAN, Charles M., "Mass, Class, and the Industrial Community: A Comparative Analysis of Managers, Businessmen, and Workers," *American Journal of Sociology,* 72 (September, 1966), 149-162.

BONJEAN, Charles M., Grady D. Bruce, and J. Allen Williams, Jr., "Social Mobility and Job Satisfaction: A Replication and Extension," *Social Forces,* 45 (June, 1967), 492-501.

BRADBURN, Norman M. and David Caplovitz, *Reports on Happiness,* Chicago: Aldine, 1965.

BROOM, Leonard and Norval D. Glenn, "Negro-White Differences in Reported Attitudes and Behavior," *Sociology and Social Research,* 50 (January, 1966), 187-200.

BRUCE, Grady D., Charles M. Bonjean, and J. Allen Williams, Jr., "Job Satisfaction Among Independent Businessmen: A Correlative Study," *Sociology and Social Research,* 52 (April, 1968), 195-204.

BULLOCK, Robert P., *Social Factors Related to Job Satisfaction,* Columbus: Bureau of Business Research, The Ohio State University, 1952.

CAPLOW, Theodore, *The Sociology of Work,* Minneapolis: University of Minnesota Press, 1954.

CENTERS, Richard, "Job Satisfaction at Various Occupational Levels," in R.G.S. Kuhlen and G.G. Thompson, editors, *Psychological Studies of Human Development,* New York: Appleton-Century-Crofts, 1952.

CENTERS, Richard, *The Psychology of Social Classes,* Princeton: Princeton University Press, 1949.

DUFFY, N. F., "Occupational Status, Job Satisfaction, and

Levels of Aspiration," *British Journal of Sociology,* 11 (December, 1960), 348-355.

FORM, William H. and James A. Geschwender, "Social Reference Basis of Job Satisfaction: The Case of Manual Workers," *American Sociological Review,* 27 (April, 1962), 228-237.

FRIEDMAN, E. A. and R. J. Havighurst, *The Meaning of Work and Retirement,* Chicago: University of Chicago Press, 1954.

GESCHWENDER, James A., "Status Inconsistency, Social Isolation, and Individual Unrest," *Social Forces,* 46 (June, 1968), 477-483.

GLENN, Norval D. and Jon P. Alston, "Cultural Distances Among Occupational Categories," *American Sociological Review,* 33 (August, 1968), 365-382.

GLENN, Norval D. and Jon P. Alston, "Rural-Urban Differences in Reported Attitudes and Behavior," *Southwestern Social Science Quarterly,* 47 (March, 1967), 381-400.

HERON, Alexander R., *Why Men Work,* Stanford: Stanford University Press, 1948.

HOPPOCK, Robert, *Job Satisfaction,* New York: Harper, 1935.

KORNHAUSER, Arthur, *Detroit as the People See It,* Detroit: Wayne University Press, 1952.

LEHMAN Edward W., "Opportunity, Mobility and Satisfaction Within an Industrial Organization," *Social Forces,* 46 (June, 1968), 492-501.

MORSE, Nancy, *Satisfactions in the White-Collar Job,* Ann Arbor: Survey Research Center, Institute for Social Research, University of Michigan, 1953.

MORSE, Nancy and Robert S. Weiss, "The Function and Meaning of Work and the Job," *American Sociological Review,* 20 (April, 1955), 191-198.

PALMER, Gladys L., "Attitudes Toward Work in an Industrial Community," *American Journal of Sociology,* 63 (May, 1957), 17-26.

RETTIG, S., F. Jacobson, and B. Pasamanick, "Status Overestimation, Objective Status, and Job Satisfaction," *American Sociological Review,* 23 (february, 1958), 75-81.

SUPER, Donald, "Occupational Level and Job Satisfaction," *Journal of Applied Psychology,* 23 (1939), 547-564.

THOMAS, Lawrence G., *The Occupational Structure and Education,* Englewood Cliffs, New Jersey: Prentice-Hall, 1956.

UHRBOCK, R. S., "Attitudes of 4430 Employees, *Journal of Social Psychology,* 5 (1934), 365-377.

Family Structure

ADAMS, Bert N., *Kinship in an Urban Setting,* Chicago: Markham, 1968.

ADAMS, Bert N., "Occupational Position, Mobility, and the Kin of Orientation," *American Sociological Review,* 32 (June, 1967), 364-377.

ADAMS, Bert N. and James E. Butler, "Occupational Status and Husband-Wife Social Participation," *Social Forces,* 45 (June, 1967), 501-508.

ANDERSON, W. A., "Family Social Participation and Social Status Self-Ratings," *American Sociological Review,* 11 (June, 1946), 253-25

BARTH, Ernest A. T. and W. B. Watson, "Social Stratification and the Family in Mass Society," *Social Forces,* 45 (March, 1967), 392-402.

BELL, Wendell and Maryanne Force, "Religious Preference, Familism and the Class Structure," *Midwest Sociologist,* 19 (May, 1957), 79-86.

BERNARD, Jessie, "Marital Stability and Patterns of Status Variables," *Journal of Marriage and the Family,* 28 (November, 1966), 421-439.

BERNARD, Jessie, *Marriage and Family among Negroes,* Englewood Cliffs, New Jersey: Prentice-Hall, 1966.

BLAKE, Judith, "Family Instability and Reproductive Behavior in Jamaica," *Current Research in Human Fertility,* New York: Milbank Memorial Fund, 1955.

BLOOD, Robert O., Jr., and Donald M. Wolfe, *Husbands and Wives: The Dynamics of Married Living,* New York: Free Press, 1960.

BRAITHWAITE, Lloyd, "Sociology and Demographic Research in the British Caribbean," *Social and Economic Studies,* 6 (December, 1957), 541-550.

BROWN, James Stephen, "Social Class, Intermarriage, and Church Membership in a Kentucky Community," *American Journal of Sociology,* 57 (November, 1951), 232-242.

BURCHINAL, Lee G. and Loren E. Chancellor, "Social Status, Religious Af filiation, and Ages at Marriage," *Marriage and Family Living,* 25 (May, 1963), 219-220.

CENTERS, Richard, "Marital Selection and Occupational Strata," *American Journal of Sociology,* 54 (May, 1949), 530-535.

CENTERS, Richard, "Occupational Endogamy in Marital Selection," in Marvin B. Sussman, editor, *Sourcebook in Marriage and the Family,* New York: Houghton Mifflin, 1955.

CHILMAN, Catherine, "Economic and Social Deprivation: Its Effects on Children and Families in the United States: A Selected Bibliography," *Journal of Marriage and the Family,* 26 (November, 1964), 495-497.

CHILMAN, Catherine, "Marital Stability and Patterns of Status Variables: A Comment," *Journal of Marriage and the Family,* 28 (November, 1966), 446-448.

CLARKE, Edith, *My Mother Who Fathered Me,* New York: Humanities Press, 1957.

DAVIS, Allison, "Socialization and Adolescent Personality," in Guy E. Swanson, *et al.,* editors, *Readings in Social Psychology,* New York: Holt, 1954.

DINITZ, Simon, Franklin Banks, and Benjamin Pasamanick, "Mate Selection and Social Class: Changes During the Past Quarter Century," *Marriage and Family Living,* 22 (November, 1960), 348-351.

DIXON, A. J., *Divorce in New Zealand,* Auckland: Auckland University College Bulletin No. 46, 1954.

DOUGHE, Gilbert, "Premarital Conception with Married Couples According to Socio-Professional Status," *Journal of Marriage and the Family,* 30 (May, 1968), 324-328.

DRIVER, Edwin, "Family Structure and Socioeconomic Status in Central India," *Sociological Bulletin,* 11 (March-September, 1962), 112-120.

DYER, William G., "Family Reactions to the Father's Job," in Arthur B. Shostak and William Gomberg, editors, *Blue-Collar World: Studies of the American Worker,* Englewood Cliffs, New Jersey: Prentice-Hall, 1964.

EPSTEIN, Lenore, "Effects of Low Income on Children and their Families," in Robert E. Will and Harold G. Vatter, *Poverty in Affluence,* New York: Harcourt, Brace and World, 1965.

ESHLEMAN, J. Ross and Chester L. Hunt, "Social Class Influences on Family Adjustment Patterns of Married College Students," *Journal of Marriage and the Family*, 29 (August, 1967), 485-491.

FAMILY STRUCTURE

GLENN, Norval D. and Jon P. Alston, "Cultural Distances Among Occupational Categories," *American Sociological Review*, 33 (June, 1968), 365-382.

GLENN, Norval D. and Jon P. Alston, "Rural-Urban Differences in Reported Attitudes and Behavior," *Southwestern Social Science Quarterly*, 47 (March, 1967), 381-400.

GOODE, William J., "Economic Factors and Marital Stability," *American Sociological Review*, 16 (December, 1951), 802-812.

GOODE, William J., "Illegitimacy in the Caribbean Social Structure," *American Sociological Review*, 25 (February, 1960), 21-30.

GOODE, William J., "Marital Satisfaction and Instability: a Cross-Cultural Class Analysis of Divorce Rates," *International Social Science Journal*, 24 (1962), 507-526.

GOODE, William J., "The Meaning of Class Differences in the Divorce Rate," in William J. Goode, *Readings on the Family and Society*, Englewood Cliffs, New Jersey: Prentice-Hall, 1964.

GOVER, David A., "Socio-Economic Differential in the Relationship Between Marital Adjustment and Wife's Employment Status," *Marriage and Family Living*, 25 (November, 1963), 452-458.

HATHWAY, Marion, *The Migratory Worker and Family Life*, Chicago: University of Chicago Press, 1934.

HAVIGHURST, Robert J., "Social Class Differences and Family Life Education at the Secondary Level," *Marriage and Family Living*, 12 (Fall, 1950), 133-135.

HAVIGHURST, Robert J., Paul H. Bowman, Gordon P. Liddle, Charles V. Matthews, and James V. Pierce, *Growing Up in River City*, New York: Wiley, 1962.

HEER, David M., "Dominance and the Working Wife," *Social Forces*, 35 (May, 1958), 341-347.

HENDERSON, Joseph R., "The Effect of One Year's Attendance at College Upon Attitudes Toward Family Living of Students of Different Social Classes," *Marriage and Family Living*, 18 (August, 1956), 209-212.

HOLLINGSHEAD, August B., "Class Differences in Family Stability," *Annals of the American Acedemy of Political and Social Science*, (1950), 39-46.

HOLLINGSHEAD, August B., "Class and Kinship in a Middle Western Community," *American Sociological Review*, 14 (August, 1949), 469-475.

HOLLINGSHEAD, August B., *Elmtown's Youth: The Impact of Social Classes on Adolescents,* New York: Wiley, 1949.

HUANG, Lucy, "Attitude of the Communist Chinese Toward Inter-Class Marriage," *Marriage and Family Living,* 24 (November, 1962), 389-392.

HUNT, Thomas C., "Occupational Status and Marriage Selection," *American Sociological Review,* 5 (August, 1940), 495-504.

HURVITZ, Nathan, "Marital Strain in the Blue-Collar Family," in Arthur B. Shostak and William Gomberg, editors, *Blue-Collar World: Studies of the American Worker,* Englewood Cliffs, New Jersey: Prentice-Hall, 1964.

JONES, Arthur H., "Sex, Educational and Religious Influences on Moral Judgements Relative to the Family," *American Sociological Review,* 8 (August, 1943), 405-411.

KEPHART, William M., "Occupational Level and Marital Disruption," *American Sociological Review,* 20 (August, 1955), 456-465.

KOMAROVSKY, Mirra, *Blue-Collar Marriage,* New York: Random House, 1962.

KOOS, Earl L.,"Class Differences in Family Reactions to Crisis," *Marriage and Family Living,* 12 (Summer, 1950), 77-78.

KOOS, Earl L., "Middle-Class Family Crises," *Marriage and Family Living,* 10 (Spring, 1948).

KORSON, J. Henry, "Dower and Social Class in an Urban Muslim Community," *Journal of Marriage and the Family,* 29 (August, 1967), 527-533.

KOTLAR, Sally L., "Middle Class Marital Role Perceptions and Marital Adjustment," *Sociology and Social Research,* 49 (April, 1965), 283-293.

KUNSTADTER, Peter, "A Survey of the Consanguine and Matri-focal Family," *American Anthropologist,* 65 (February, 1963), 56-66.

LAURIAT, Patience, "Marriage and Fertility Patterns of College Graduates," *Eugenics Quarterly,* 6 (September, 1959), 171-179.

LeMASTERS, E. E., "Social Class Mobility and Family Integration," *Marriage and Family Living,* 16 (August, 1954), 226-232.

LIEBOW, Elliot, *Tally's Corner,* Boston: Little, Brown, 1968.

MAAS, Henry, "Some Social Class Differences in the Family Systems and Group Relations of Pre- and Early Adolescents," *Child Development,* 22 (1951), 145-152.

MARTIN, Jean I., "Marriage, the Family and Class," in A. P. Elkin, editor, *Marriage and the Family in Australia,* Sydney: Angus and Robertson,1957.

McCORMICK, Thomas C. and Melvin S. Brooks, "Occupational Birth and Marriage Rates, Wisconsin, 1900-1936," *American Sociological Review,* 6 (December, 1941), 806-817.

McGINN, Noel F., "Marriage and Family in Middle-Class Mexico," *Journal of Marriage and the Family,* 28 (August, 1966), 305-313.

McGUIRE, Carson, "Family Life in Lower and Middle Class Homes," *Marriage and Family Living,* 14 (February, 1952), 1-6.

McKINLEY, Donald Gilbert, *Social Class and Family Life,* New York: Free Press, 1964.

MIDDLETON, Russell and Snell Putney, "Dominance in Decisions in the Family: Race and Class Differences," *American Journal of Sociology,* 65 (May, 1960), 605-609.

MITTELBACH, Frank G. and Joan W. Moore, "Ethnic Endogamy: The Case of Mexican Americans," *American Journal of Sociology,* 74 (July, 1968), 50-62.

MOGEY, J. M., "Changes in Family Life Experienced by English Workers Moving From Slums to Housing Estates," *Marriage and Family Living,* 17 (May, 1955), 123-128.

MOGEY, J. M., *Family and Neighborhood,* New York: Oxford University Press, 1956.

MONAHAN, Thomas P., "Divorce by Occupational Level," *Marriage and Family Living,* 17 (November, 1955), 322-324.

MONAHAN, Thomas P., "When Married Couples Part: Statistical Trends and Relationships in Divorce," *American Sociological Review,* 27 (October, 1962), 625-633.

MOTZ, Annabelle B., "Conceptions of Marital Roles by Status Groups," *Marriage and Family Living,* 12 (1950), 136-162.

MUKHERJEE, Ramkrishna, "Social Mobility and Age at Marriage," in David V. Glass, editor, *Social Mobility in Britain,* London: Routledge and Kegan Paul, 1954.

NIMKOFF, Meyer F., "Occupational Factors and Marriage," *American Journal of Sociology,* 49 (November, 1943), 248-254.

NYE, Ivan, "Adolescent-Parent Adjustment: Socio-Economic Levels As a Variable," *American Sociological Review,* 16 (June, 1951), 341-349.

OGBURN, William F., "Education, Income, and Family Unity," *American Journal of Sociology,* 53 (May, 1948), 474-476.

OLSEN, Marvin E., "Distribution of Family Responsibility and Social Stratification," *Marriage and Family Living,* 22 (February, 1960), 60-65.

PAVENSTEDT, Eleanor, editor, *The Drifters: Children of Disorganized Lower-Class Families,* Boston: Little, Brown, 1967.

PSATHAS, George, "Ethnicity, Social Class, and Adolescent Independence from Parental Control," *American Sociological Review,* 22 (August, 1957), 415-423.

FAMILY STRUCTURE

RAINWATER, Lee, "Crucible of Identify: The Negro Lower-Class Family," in Talcott Parsons and Kenneth B. Clark, editors, *The Negro American,* Boston: Houghton Mifflin, 1966.

RAINWATER, Lee, *Family Design: Marital Sexuality, Family Planning and Family Limitation,* Chicago: Aldine, 1964.

RAINWATER, Lee, "Marital Sexuality in Four Cultures of Poverty," *Journal of Marriage and the Family,* 26 (November, 1964), 457-466.

RAINWATER, Lee, "Marital Stability and Patterns of Status Variables: A Comment," *Journal of Marriage and the Family,* 28 (November, 1966), 442-445.

RAPOPORT, Robert N., "The Male's Occupation in Relation to His Decision to Marry," *Acta Sociologica,* 8, 68-82.

ROBERTS, Harry W., "Effects of Farm Ownership on Rural Family Life," *Social Forces,* 24 (December, 1945), 185-194.

RODMAN, Hyman, "Illegitimacy in the Carribbean Social Structure: A Reconsideration," *American Sociological Review,* 31 (October, 1966), 673-683.

RODMAN, Hyman, "The Lower-Class Value Stretch," *Social Forces,* 42 (December, 1963), 205-215.

RODMAN, Hyman, "Marital Relationships in a Trinidad Village," *Marriage and Family Living,* 23 (May, 1961).

ROSEN, Bernard, "Social Class and the Child's Perception of the Parent," *Child Development,* 35 (December, 1964), 1147-1153.

ROSENTHAL, Celia Stopnicka, "Lower Class Family Organization on the Carribbean Coast of Columbia," *Pacific Sociological Review,* 3 (Spring, 1960), 12-17.

ROTH, Julius and Robert F. Peck, "Social Class and Social Mobility Factors Related to Marital Adjustment," *American Sociological Review,* 16 (August, 1951), 478-487.

SCANZONI, John, "Occupation and Family Differentiation," *Sociological Quarterly,* 8 (Spring, 1967), 187-198.

SCHERMERHORN, Richard A., "Marital Stability and Patterns of Status Variables: A Comment," *Journal of Marriage and the Family,* 28 (November, 1966), 440-441.

SCHMITT, Robert C., "Demographic Correlates of Interracial Marriage in Hawaii," *Demography,* 2 (1965), 463-473.

SCHMITT, Robert C., "Interracial Marriage and Occupational Status in Hawaii," *American Sociological Review,* 28 (October, 1963), 809-810.

SCHULZ, David A., "The Father Role in Negro Lower-Class Families," *Social Science Quarterly,* 49 (December, 1968), 651-659.

SEXTON, Patricia C., "Wife of the Happy Worker," in Arthur B. Shostak and William Gomberg, editors, *Blue-Collar World: Studies of the American Worker*, Englewood Cliffs, New Jersey: Prentice Hall, 1964.

FAMILY STRUCTURE

SHANAS, Ethel, "Family Help Patterns and Social Class in Three Countries," *Journal of Marriage and the Family*, 29 (May, 1967), 257-266.

SMITH, Raymond T., *The Negro Family in British Guiana*, London: Routledge and Kegan Paul, 1956.

STRAUS, Murray A., "The Influence of Sex of Child and Social Class on Instrumental and Expressive Family Roles in a Laboratory Setting," *Sociology and Social Research*, 52 (October, 1967), 7-21.

SWEETSER, Dorrian Apple, "Intergenerational Ties in Finnish Urban Families," *American Sociological Research*, 33 (April, 1968), 236-246.

SWINEHART, James W., "Socioeconomic Level, Status Aspiration, and Maternal Role," *American Sociological Review*, 28 (June, 1963), 391-399.

TARVER, James D., "Marriage and Divorce Trends in Wisconsin, 1915-1945," *Milbank Memorial Fund Quarterly*, 30 (January, 1952), 5-17.

TOWNSEND, Peter, *The Family Life of Old People*, London: Routledge and Kegan Paul, 1957.

UDRY, J. Richard, "Marital Instability by Race and Income Based on 1960 Census Data," *American Journal of Sociology*, 72 (May, 1967), 673-674.

UDRY, J. Richard, "Marital Instability by Race, Sex, Education, and Occupation Using 1960 Census Data," *American Journal of Sociology*, 72 (September, 1966), 203-209.

WARNER, W. Lloyd and Paul S. Lunt, *The Social Life of a Modern Community*, New Haven: Yale University Press, 1941.

WEEKS, H. Ashley, "Differential Divorce Rates by Occupations," *Social Forces*, 21 (March, 1943), 334-337.

WEINANDY, Janet E., *Families Under Stress*, New York: Syracuse University Press, 1962.

WILLIAMSON, Robert C., "Economic Factors in Marital Adjustment," *Marriage and Family Living*, 14 (November, 1952), 298-300.

WILLMOTT, Peter and Michael Young, *Family and Class in a London Suburb*, New York: Humanities Press, 1961.

WILLOUGHBY, Gertrude, "The Working Class Family in England," *Transactions on the Third World Congress of Sociology*, 4 (1956), 155-160.

WILNER, Daniel M., Rosabelle Price Walkley, Thomas C. Pinkerton, and Matthew Tayback, *The Housing Environment and Family Life: A Longitudinal Study of the Effects of Housing on Morbidity and Mental Health*, Baltimore: Johns Hopkins Press, 1962.

WINCH, Robert F., Scott Greer, and R. L. Blumberg, "Ethnicity and Extended Familism in an Upper-Middle-Class Suburb," *American Sociological Review*, 32 (April, 1967), 265-272.

YOUNG, Michael and Peter Willmott, *Family and Kinship in East London*, New York: Free Press, 1957.

Child Rearing

ABERLE, David F. and Kaspar D. Naegele, "Middle Class Fathers' Occupational Role and Attitudes Toward Children," *American Journal of Orthopsychiatry*, 22 (April, 1952), 366-378.

ANDERSON, H. E., *The Young Child in the Home*, New York: Appleton-Century-Crofts, 1936.

BALDWIN, A. L., J. Kalhorn, and F. H. Breese, *Patterns of Parent Behavior*, Psychological Monographs, 63 (1945).

BLAU, Zena Smith, "Class Structure, Mobility, and Change in Child Rearing," *Sociometry*, 28 (June, 1965), 210-219.

BLAU, Zena Smith, "Exposure to Child-rearing Experts: A Structural Interpretation of Class-Color Differences," *American Journal of Sociology*, 69 (May, 1964), 596-608.

BOEK, Walter E., Marvin B. Sussman, and Alfred Yankauer, "Social Class and Child Care Practices," *Marriage and Family Living*, 20 (November, 1958), 326-333.

BOEK, Walter E., E. D. Lawson, Alfred Yankauer, and Marvin B. Sussman, *Social Class, Maternal Health, and Child Care*, Albany: New York State Department of Health, 1957.

BRONFENBRENNER, Urie, "Socialization and Social Class Through Time and Space," in Eleanor E. Maccoby, Theodore M. Newcomb, and Eugene L. Hartley, editors, *Readings in Social Psychology*, third edition, New York: Holt, 1958, 400-425.

BROOM, Leonard and Norval D. Glenn, "Negro-White Differences in Reported Attitudes and Behavior," *Sociology and Social Research,* 50 (January, 1966), 187-200.

CHILD REARING

DAVIS, Allison, "American Status Systems and the Socialization of the Child," *American Sociological Review,* 6 (June, 1941), 345-356.

DAVIS, Allison, "Child Rearing in the Class Structure of American Society," in Marvin Sussman, editor, *Sourcebook in Marriage and the Family,* New York: Houghton Mifflin, 1963.

DAVIS, Allison and Robert J. Havighurst, "Social Class and Color Differences in Child-Rearing," *American Sociological Review,* 11 (December, 1946), 698-710.

DAVIS, Allison, "Socialization and Adolescent Personality," in Guy E. Swanson, *et al.,* editors, *Readings in Social Psychology,* New York: Holt, 1954.

DUVALL, Evelyn M., "Conceptions of Parenthood," *American Journal of Sociology,* 52 (November, 1946), 193-203.

DYER, William G., "Parental Influence on the Job Attitudes of Children from Two Occupational Strata," *Sociology and Social Research,* 42 (January-February, 1958), 203-206.

ERICSON, Martha C., "Child-rearing and Social Status," *American Journal of Sociology,* 52 (November, 1946), 190-192.

GARFIELD, S. L. and M. M. Helper, "Parental Attitudes and Socio-economic Status," *Journal of Clinical Psychology,* 18 (1962), 171-175.

GLENN, Norval D. and Jon P. Alston, "Cultural Distances Among Occupational Categories," *American Sociological Review,* 33 (June, 1968), 365-382.

GLENN, Norval D. and Jon P. Alston, "Rural-Urban Differences in Reported Attitudes and Behavior," *Southwestern Social Science Quarterly,* 47 (March, 1967), 381-400.

HABER, Lawrence D., "Age and Integration Setting: A Re-Appraisal of *The Changing American Parent,*" *American Sociological Review,* 27 (October, 1962), 682-689.

HAVIGHURST, Robert J. and Allison Davis, "A Comparison of the Chicago and Harvard Studies of Social Class Differences in Child Rearing," *American Sociological Review,* 20 (August, 1955), 438-442.

INKELES, Alex, "Industrial Man: The Relation of Status to Experience, Perception, and Value," *American Journal of Sociology,* 66 (July, 1960), 1-31.

KAMII, Constance K. and Norma L. Radin, "Class Differences in the Socialization Practices of Negro Mothers," *Journal of Marriage and the Family,* 29 (May, 1967), 302-310.

KANTER, M., J. Glidewell, I. Mensh, H. Domke, and M. Deldeg, "Socio-Economic Level and Maternal Attitudes toward Parent Child Relationships," *Human Organization,* 16 (No. 4, 1958), 44-48.

KLATSKIN, E. H., "Shifts in Child Care Practices in Three Social Classes under an Infant Care Program of Flexible Methodology," *American Journal of Orthopsychiatry,* 22 (1952), 52-61.

KOHN, Melvin L., "Social Class and Parental Values," *American Journal of Sociology,* 64 (January, 1959), 337-351.

KOHN, Melvin L., "Social Class and Parent-Child Relationships," *American Journal of Sociology,* 68 (January, 1962), 471-480.

KOHN, Melvin L. and Eleanor E. Carroll, "Social Class and the Allocation of Parental Responsibilities," *Sociometry,* 23 (December, 1960), 372-392.

KOHN, Melvin L., "Social Class and the Exercise of Parental Authority," *American Sociological Review,* 24 (June, 1959), 352-366.

LESLIE, Gerald R. and Kathryn P. Johnsen, "Changed Perceptions of the Maternal Role," *American Sociological Review,* 28 (December, 1963), 919-928.

LITTMAN, Richard A., C. A. Moore, John Pierce-Jones, "Social Class Differences in Child Rearing: A Third Community for Comparison with Chicago and Newton," *American Sociological Review,* 22 (December, 1957), 694-704.

MACCOBY, Eleanor E., Patricia K. Gibbs, and the staff of the Laboratory of Human Development at Harvard University, "Methods of Child Rearing in Two Social Classes," in W. E. Martin and C. B. Standler, editors, *Readings in Child Development,* New York: .
Harcourt Brace, 1954.

McCLELLAND, David C., A. Rindlischbacher, and R. DeCharms, "Religious and Other Sources of Parental Attitudes toward Independence Training," in David McClelland, editor, *Studies in Motivation,* New York: Appleton-Century-Crofts, 1955.

MILLER, D. R. and G. E. Swanson, *The Changing American Parent,* New York: Wiley, 1958.

OPLER, Marvin K., "The Influence of Ethnic and Class Subcultures on Child Care," *Social Problems,* 3 (July, 1955), 12-21.

PEARLIN, Leonard I. and Melvin L. Kohn, "Social Class, Occupation, and Parental Values; A Cross National Study," *American Sociological Review,* 31 (August, 1966), 466-479.

PSATHAS, George, "Ethnicity, Social Class, and Adolescent Independence from Parental Control," *American Sociological Review,* 22 (August, 1957), 415-423.

SEARS, R. R., Eleanor E. Maccoby, and H. Levin, *Patterns of Child Rearing,* New York: Harper and Row, 1957.

SMART, Susan, "Social Class Differences in Parent Behavior in a Natural Setting," *Journal of Marriage and the Family,* 26 (May, 1964), 223-224.

STRODTBECK, Fred L., "Family Interaction, Values, and Achievement," in A. L. Baldwin, U. Bronfenbrenner, David C. McClelland, and Fred L. Strodtbeck, editors, *Talent and Society,* Princeton: Van Nostrand, 1958.

SWINEHART, James W., "Socio-Economic Level, Status Aspiration, and Maternal Role," *American Sociological Review,* 28 (June, 1963), 391-399.

THOMAS, Murray and W. Surachmad, "Social Class Differences in Mothers' Expectations for Children in Indonesia," *Journal of Social Psychology,* 57 (August, 1962), 303-307.

WHITE, Martha Sturn, "Social Class, Child Rearing Practices, and Child Behavior," *American Sociological Review,* 22 (December, 1957), 704-712.

WOLFENSTEIN, M., "Trends in Infant Care," *American Journal of Orthopsychiatry,* 23 (January, 1953), 120-130.

Sex Standards and Behavior

BOWERMAN, Charles E., Donald P. Irish, and Hollowell Pope, *Unwed Motherhood: Personal and Social Consequences,* Chapel Hill: Institute for Research in Social Science, 1966.

BREED, Warren, "Sex, Class and Socialization in Dating," *Marriage and Family Living,* 18 (May, 1956), 137-144.

BROOM, Leonard and Norval D. Glenn, "Negro-White Differences in Reported Attitudes and Behavior," *Sociology and Social Research,* 50 (January, 1966), 187-200.

CLARK, Kenneth, *Dark Ghetto,* New York: Harper and Row, 1965.

DAVIS, Kingsley, "Some Demographic Aspects of Poverty in the United States," in Margaret S. Gordon, editor, *Poverty in America,* San Francisco, Chandler, 1965.

DRAKE, St. Clair and Horace R. Cayton, *Black Metropolis,*
New York: Harcourt Brace, 1945.

EHRMANN, Winston W., *Premarital Dating Behavior,* New York:
Holt, 1959.

FERDINAND, Theodore N., "Sex Behavior and the American Class
Structure: A Mosaic," *The Annals of the American Academy of
Political and Social Science,* 376 (March, 1968), 76-85.

FRAZIER, E. Franklin, *The Negro Family in the United States,*
revised and abridged, New York: Citadel Press, 1948.

GILBERT, Dooghe, "Premarital Conception with Married Couples
According to Socio-Professional Status," *Journal of Marriage
and the Family,* 30 (May, 1968), 324-328.

GLENN, Norval D. and Jon P. Alston, "Rural-Urban Differences
in Reported Attitudes and Behavior," *Southwestern Social
Science Quarterly,* 47 (March, 1967), 381-400.

GOLDSTEIN, Sidney and Kurt B. Mayer, "Illegitimacy, Residence,
and Status," *Social Problems,* 12 (Spring, 1965), 428-436.

GOODE, William J., "Family and Mobility," in Reinhard Bendix
and Seymour M. Lipset, *Class, Status, and Power,* 2nd
Edition, New York: Free Press, 1966.

HOLLINGSHEAD, August B., *Elmtown's Youth,* New York: Wiley,
1949.

HURVITZ, Nathan, "Marital Strain in the Blue-Collar Family," in
Arthur B. Shostak and William Gomberg, *Blue-Collar World,*
Englewood Cliffs, New Jersey: Prentice-Hall, 1964.

KANIN, Eugene and David H. Howard, "Postmarital Consequences
of Premarital Sex Adjustments," *American Sociological Review,*
23 (October, 1958), 556-562.

KANIN, Eugene, "Premarital Sex Adjustments, Social Class, and
Associated Behaviors," *Marriage and Family Living,* 22 (May,
1960), 258-262.

KINSEY, Alfred C., Wardell B. Pomeroy, Clyde E. Martin, *Sexual
Behavior in the Human Female,* Philadelphia: Saunders, 1953.

KINSEY, Alfred C., Wardell B. Pomeroy, and Clyde E. Martin,
Sexual Behavior in the Human Male, Philadelphia, Saunders, 1948.

KOMAROVSKY, Mirra, *Blue-Collar Marriage,* New York: Random House,
1962.

LIEBOW, Elliot, *Tally's Corner,* Boston: Little Brown, 1968.

LINDENFELD, Frank, "A Note on Social Mobility, Religiosity,
and Students' Attitudes Toward Premarital Sexual Relations,"
American Sociological Review, 25 (February, 1960), 81-84.

MADSEN, William, *The Mexican-Americans of South Texas,* New York: Holt, Rinehart and Winston, 1964.

SEX STANDARDS

MONAHAN, Thomas P., "Premarital Pregnancy in the United States: A Critical Review and Some New Findings," *Eugenics Quarterly,* 7 (September, 1960), 133-147.

RAINWATER, Lee, *Family Design: Marital Sexuality, Family Planning and Family Limitation,* Chicago: Aldine, 1964.

RAINWATER, Lee, "Marital Sexuality in Four Cultures of Poverty," *Journal of Marriage and the Family,* 26 (November, 1964), 457-466.

RAINWATER, Lee, "Some Aspects of Lower Class Sexual Behavior," *Journal of Social Issues,* 22 (April, 1966), 96-108.

RAINWATER, Lee and Gerald Handel, "Changing Family Roles in the Working Class," in Arthur B. Shostak and William Gomberg, editors, *Blue-Collar World,* Englewood Cliffs, New Jersey, 1964.

REISS, Ira L., "Premarital Sexual Permissiveness Among Negroes and Whites," *American Sociological Review,* 29 (October, 1964), 688-698.

REISS, Ira L., "Social Class and Campus Dating," *Social Problems,* 13 (Fall, 1965).

REISS, Ira L., "Social Class and Premarital Sexual Permissiveness: A Re-Examination," *American Sociological Review,* 30 (October, 1965), 747-756.

REISS, Ira L., *The Social Context of Premarital Sexual Permissiveness,* New York: Holt, Rinehart and Winston, 1967.

ROSENBERG, Bernard and Joseph Bensman, "Sexual Patterns in Three Ethnic Subcultures of an American Underclass," *The Annals of the American Academy of Political and Social Science,* 376 (March, 1968), 61-75.

SEXTON, Patricia Cayo, "Wife of the 'Happy Worker,'" in Arthur B. Shostak and William Gomberg, editors, *Blue-Collar World,* Englewood Cliffs, New Jersey: Prentice-Hall, 1964.

SLATER, Eliot and Moya Woodside, "Sex in the Lower-Class English Marriage," in William J. Goode, editor, *Readings on the Family and Society,* Englewood Cliffs: Prentice-Hall, 1964.

SMITH, Raymond T., *The Negro Family in British Guiana,* London: Routledge and Kegan Paul, 1956.

VINCENT, Clark E., "The Unwed Mother and Sampling Bias," *American Sociological Review,* 19 (October, 1954), 562-567.

VINCENT, Clark E., *Unmarried Mothers,* New York: Free Press, 1961.

WHYTE, William F., "A Slum Sex Code," *American Journal of Sociology,* 49 (July, 1943), 24-31.

Personality

ADORNO, T. W., Else Frenkel-Brunswick, D. J. Levinson, and R. N. Sanford, *The Authoritarian Personality: Studies in Prejudice,* New York: Harper, 1950.

AIKEN, Michael, Louis E. Ferman, and Harold L. Sheppard, *Economic Failure, Alienation, and Extremism,* Ann Arbor: University of Michigan Press, 1968.

ANGELL, Robert, "Preferences for Moral Norms in Three Problem Areas," *American Journal of Sociology,* 67 (May, 1962), 650-660.

AULD, F., Jr., "Influence of Social Class on Personality Test Response," *Psychological Bulletin,* 49 (1952), 318-332.

BALTZELL, E. Digby, "The American Aristocrat and Other-Direction," in Seymour M. Lipset and Leo Lowenthal, *Culture and Social Character,* New York: Free Press, 1961.

BELL, Wendell, "Anomie, Social Isolation, and the Class Structure," *Sociometry,* 20 (June, 1957), 105-116.

BIERI, James and Robin Lobeds, "Self-Concept Differences in Relation to Identification, Religion, and Social Class," *Journal of Abnormal and Social Psychology,* 62 (1961), 94-98.

BOLTON, Charles D. and Kenneth C. Kammeyer, *The University Student: A Study of Student Behavior and Values,* New Haven: College and University Press, 1967.

BONJEAN, Charles M., "Mass, Class, and the Industrial Community: A Comparative Analysis of Managers, Businessmen, and Workers," *American Journal of Sociology,* 72 (September, 1966), 149-162.

CANCIAN, Frank, "Stratification and Risk-Taking: A Theory Tested on Agricultural Innovation," *American Sociological Review,* 32 (December, 1967), 912-927.

CARNEY, Richard E. and Wilbert J. McKeachie, "Religion, Sex, Social Class, Probability of Success and Student Personality," *Journal for the Scientific Study of Religion,* 3 (Fall, 1963), 32-41.

CONGER, John J., Wilbur C. Miller, Robert V. Rainey, and Charles R. Walsmith, *Personality, Social Class, and Delinquency,* New York: Wiley, 1966.

PERSONALITY

COLEMAN, William and Annie E. Ward, "A Comparison of Davis-Eells and Kuhlman-Finch Scores of Children from High and Low Socio-Economic Status," *Journal of Educational Psychology,* 46 (December, 1955), 465-469.

DAVIS, Allison, "Personality and Social Mobility," *School Review,* 65 (Summer, 1957), 134-143.

DEAN, Dwight, "Alienation: Its Meaning and Measurement," *American Sociological Review,* 26 (October, 1961), 753-758.

ELDER, Glen H., Jr., "Life Opportunity and Personality--Some Consequences of Stratified Secondary Education in Great Britain," *Sociology of Education,* 38 (Spring, 1965), 173-202.

FALK, Gerhard J., "Status Differences and the Frustration–Aggression Hypothesis," *International Journal of Social Psychiatry,* (Winter, 1960), 214-222.

FANNIN, Leon F., and Marshall B. Clinard, "Differences in the Conception of Self as a Male among Lower and Middle Class Delinquents," *Social Problems,* 13 (Fall, 1965), 205-214.

FLIEGEL, Frederick C., "Farm Income and the Adoption of Farm Practices," *Rural Sociology,* 22 (June, 1957), 159-162.

GLENN, Norval D. and Jon P. Alston, "Cultural Distances Among Occupational Categories," *American Sociological Review,* 33 (August, 1968), 365-382.

GLENN, Norval D. and Jon P. Alston, "Rural-Urban Differences in Reported Attitudes and Behavior," *Southwestern Social Science Quarterly,* 47 (March, 1967), 381-400.

GOUGH, Harrison, "A New Dimension of Status, I and II," *American Sociological Review,* 13 (August and October, 1948), 401-409, 534-537.

GOUGH, Harrison, "The Relationship of Socio-Economic Status to Personality Inventory and Achievement Test Scores," *Journal of Educational Psychology,* 37 (1946), 527-540.

GRONLUND, N. E. and L. Anderson, "Personality Characteristics of Socially Rejected Junior High School Pupils," *Educational Administration and Supervision,* 43 (1957), 329-338.

GROSSMANN, Beverly and Joyce Wrighter, "The Relationship between Selection-rejection and Intelligence, Social Status, and Personality Amongst Sixth Grade Children," *Sociometry,* 11 (November, 1948), 346-355.

HALL, M. and R. Keth, "Sex-role Preference among Children in Upper and Lower Social Classes," *Journal of Social Psychology,* 62 (1964), 101-110.

HAVIGHURST, Robert J., "Social Class and Basic Personality Structure," *Sociology and Social Research,* 36 (July-August, 1952), 355-363.

HIMMELWEIT, Hilde T., "Socio-Economic Background and Personality," *International Social Science Bulletin,* 7 (1955), 29-34.

INKELES, Alex, "Industrial Man: The Relation of Status to Experience, Perception, and Value," *American Journal of Sociology,* 66 (July, 1960), 1-31.

JANOWITZ, Morris and Dwaine Marvick, "Authoritarianism and Political Behavior," *Public Opinion Quarterly,* (Summer, 1953), 185-201.

KAUFMAN, Walter C., "Status, Authoritarianism, and Anti-Semitism," *American Journal of Sociology,* 62 (January, 1957), 379-381.

LASSWELL, Harold D., *Power and Personality,* New York: Norton, 1948.

LEMERT, Edwin H., "Paranoia and the Dynamics of Exclusion," *Sociometry,* 25 (1962), 2-20.

LE SHAN, L. L., "Time Orientation and Social Class," *Journal of Abnormal and Social Psychology,* 47 (1952), 589-592.

LIPSET, Seymour M., "Democracy and Working-Class Authoritarianism," *American Sociological Review,* 24 (August, 1959), 482-501.

LIPSET, Seymour M., "Working Class Authoritarianism: A Reply to Miller and Reissman," *British Journal of Sociology,* 12 (September, 1961), 263-276.

LIPSITZ, Lewis, "Working-Class Authoritariansim: A Re-Evaluation," *American Sociological Review,* 30 (February, 1965), 103-109.

LOEB, Martin B., "Implications of Status Differentiation for Personal and Social Development," *Harvard Educational Review,* 23 (Summer, 1953), 168-174.

MacKINNON, William J. and Richard Centers, "Authoritarianism, Social Class and the Iron Curtain Situation," *American Psychologist,* 50 (1955), 350-351.

MacKINNON, William J. and Richard Centers, "Authoritarianism and Urban Stratification," *American Journal of Sociology,* 61 (May, 1956), 610-620.

McARTHUR, Charles, "Personality Differences Between Middle and Upper Classes," *Journal of Abnormal and Social Psychology,*

PERSONALITY

50 (March, 1955), 247-254.

McARTHUR, Charles, "Personalities of Public and Private School Boys," *Harvard Educational Review,* 24 (1954), 256-261.

PERSONALITY McDILL, Edward, "Anomie, Authoritarianism, Prejudice, and Socio-Economic Status: An Attempt at Clarification," *Social Forces,* 39 (March, 1961), 239-245.

McGINN, Noel F., Ernest Harburg, and Gerald P. Ginsburg, "Responses to Interpersonal Conflict by Middle Class Males in Guadalajara and Michigan," *American Anthropologist,* 67 (December, 1965), 1483-1494.

MEHLMAN, Mary R. and James E. Fleming, "Social Stratification--Some Personality Variables," *Journal of General Psychology,* 69 (1963), 3-10.

MEIER, Dorothy L. and Wendell Bell, "Anomia and Differential Access to the Achievement of Life Goals," *American Sociological Review,* 24 (April, 1959), 189-202.

MERTON, Robert K., "Bureaucratic Structure and Personality," *Social Forces,* 18 (May, 1940), 560-568.

MIDDLETON, Russell, "Alienation, Race, and Education," *American Sociological Review,* 28 (December, 1963), 973-977.

MILLER, S. M. and Frank Reissman, "Working Class Authoritarianism: A Critique of Lipset," *British Journal of Sociology,* 12 (September, 1961), 263-276.

MIZRUCHI, Ephraim H., "Social Structure and Anomia in a Small City," *American Sociological Review,* 25 (October, 1960), 645-654.

MUSSEN, Paul, John Conger, and Jerome Kagan, *Child Development and Personality,* New York: Harper and Row, 1963.

NEAL, Arthur G. and Salomon Rettig, "Dimensions of Alienation Among Manual and Non-Manual Workers," *American Sociological Review,* 28 (August, 1963), 599-608.

NEAL, Arthur G. and Melvin Seeman, "Organizations and Powerlessness: A Test of the Mediation Hypothesis," *American Sociological Review,* 29 (April, 1964), 216-226.

PHOTIADIS, John and Jeanne Biggar, "Religiosity, Education, and Social Distance," *American Journal of Sociology,* 67 (May, 1962), 666-672.

RANULF, Svend, *Moral Indignation and Middle Class Psychology,* New York: Schocken, 1964.

ROBERTS, Alan H. and Richard Jessor, "Authoritarianism, Punitiveness, and Perceived Social Status," *Journal of Abnormal and Social Psychology,* (May, 1968), 311-314.

ROBERTS, Alan H. and Milton Rokeach, "Anomie, Authoritarianism, and Prejudice: A Replication," *American Journal of Sociology,* 61 (January, 1956), 355-358.

ROSENHAN, David L., "The Effects of Social Class and Race on Responsiveness to Approval and Disapproval," *Journal of Personality and Social Psychology,* 4 (September, 1966), 253-259.

SEWELL, William H., "Social Class and Childhood Personality," *Sociometry,* 34 (December, 1961), 340-356.

SIGEL, Irving E., Larry M. Anderson, and Howard Shapiro, "Categorization Behavior of Lower and Middle-Class Negro Preschool Children: Differences in Dealing with Representation of Familiar Objects," *Journal of Negro Education,* 35 (Summer, 1966), 218-229.

SIMPSON, Richard L. and H. Max Miller, "Social Status and Anomia," *Social Problems,* 10 (1963), 257-264.

SPAULDING, Charles B., "Social Class and Social Perception," *Sociology and Social Research,* 41 (September-October, 1956), 18-26.

SPINLEY, B. M., *The Deprived and the Privileged: Personality Development in English Society,* London: Routledge and Kegan Paul, 1953.

SROLE, Leo, "Social Integration and Certain Corollaries: An Exploratory Study," *American Sociological Review,* 21 (December, 1956), 709-716.

STRAUS, Murray A., "The Influence of Sex of Child and Social Class on Instrumental and Expressive Family Roles in a Laboratory Setting," *Sociology and Social Research,* 52 (October, 1967), 7-21.

THIBAUT, John and Henry Riecken, "Authoritarianism, Status, and the Communication of Aggression," *Human Relations,* 8 (second quarter, 1955), 95-120.

THOMPSON, Wayne E. and John E. Horton, "Political Alienation as a Force in Political Action," *Social Forces,* 38 (March, 1960), 190-195.

TUMIN, Melvin M. and Ray C. Collins, Jr., "Status, Mobility and Anomie: A Study in Readiness for Desegregation," *British Journal of Sociology,* 10 (September, 1959), 253-267.

WASSEF, W. Y., "The Influence of Religion, Socio-Economic Status and Education on Anomie," *Sociological Quarterly,* 8 (Spring, 1967), 233-238.

Prejudice and Discrimination

ADAMS, Edward L., Jr., William B. Dreffin, Robert B. Kamm, and Dyckman W. Vermilye, "Attitudes with Regard to Minority Groups of a Sample of University Men Students from the Upper Socioeconomic Level," *Journal of Educational Sociology,* 21 (February, 1948), 328-338.

ADORNO, T. W., Else Frenkel-Brunswick, D. J. Levinson, and R. N. Sanford, *The Authoritarian Personality: Studies in Prejudice,* New York: Harper and Row, 1950.

ANGELL, Robert, "Preferences for Moral Norms in Three Problem Areas," *American Journal of Sociology,* 67 (May, 1962), 650-660.

BETTLEHEIM, Bruno and Morris Janowitz, *Social Change and Prejudice,* New York: Free Press, 1964.

BROOM, Leonard and Norval D. Glenn, "Negro-White Differences in Reported Attitudes and Behavior," *Sociology and Social Research,* 50 (January, 1966), 187-200.

BROWN, W. O., "Role of the Poor White in Race Contacts of the South," *Social Forces,* 19 (December, 1940), 258-268.

CAMPBELL, Ernest Q., "On Desegregation and Matters Sociological," *Phylon,* 22 (Summer, 1961).

COHEN, Albert K. and Harold Hodges, Jr., "Characteristics of the Lower-Blue-Collar Class," *Social Problems,* 10 (Spring, 1963).

CONWAY, Margaret, "The White Backlash Re-Examined: Wallace and the 1964 Northern Primaries," *Social Science Quarterly,* 49 (December, 1968), 710-719.

CRAMER, Richard, "School Desegregation and New Industry: The Southern Community Leaders' Viewpoint," *Social Forces,* 41 (May, 1963), 384-389.

DOLLARD, John, *Caste and Class in a Southern Town,* New Haven: Yale University Press, 1937.

DYNES, Wallace, "Education and Tolerance: An Analysis of

Intervening Factors," *Social Forces,* 46 (September, 1967), 22-34.

EYSENCK, H. J., *The Psychology of Politics,* London: Routledge and Kegan Paul, 1954.

GERTH, Hans H., "The Nazi Party: Its Leadership and Composition," *American Journal of Sociology,* 45 (January, 1940), 517-541.

GLENN, Norval D. and Jon P. Alston, "Cultural Distances Among Occupational Categories," *American Sociological Review,* 33 (August, 1968), 365-382.

GLENN, Norval D. and Jon P. Alston, "Rural-Urban Differences in Reported Attitudes and Behavior," *Southwestern Social Science Quarterly,* 47 (March, 1967), 381-400.

GREENBLUM, Joseph and L. I. Pearlin, "Vertical Mobility and Prejudice," in Reinhard Bendix and Seymour M. Lipset, editors, *Class, Status, and Power,* New York: Free Press, 1953.

HAMILTON, Richard F., "The Behavior and Values of Skilled Workers," in Arthur B. Shostak and William Gomberg, editors, *Blue-Collar World,* Englewood Cliffs, New Jersey: Prentic-Hall, 1964.

HAMILTON, Richard F., "The Marginal Middle Class: A Reconsideration," *American Sociological Review,* 31 (April, 1966), 192-199.

HARLAN, Howard H., "Some Factors Affecting Attitude Toward Jews," *American Sociological Review,* 7 (December, 1942), 816-827.

HATT, Paul K., "Class and Ethnic Attitudes," *American Sociological Review,* 13 (February, 1948), 36-43.

HODGE, Robert W. and Donald J. Treiman, "Occupational Mobility and Attitudes Toward Negroes," *American Sociological Review,* 31 (February, 1966), 93-102.

JANOWITZ, Morris and Dwaine Marvick, "Authoritarianism and Political Behavior," *Public Opinion Quarterly,* 17 (Summer, 1953), 185-201.

JONES, Frank E. and Wallace E. Lambert, "Occupational Rank and Attitudes Toward Immigrants," *Public Opinion Quarterly,* 29 (Spring, 1965), 137-144.

KAUFMAN, Walter C., "Status, Authoritarianism, and Anti-Semitism," *American Journal of Sociology,* 62 (January, 1957), 379-382.

KELLY, J. G., J. E. Ferson, and W. H. Holtzman, "The Measurement of Attitudes Toward the Negro in the South," *Journal of Social Psychology,* (November, 1958), 305-317.

KILLIAN, Lewis and John Haer, "Variables Related to Attitudes Regarding School Desegregation Among White Southerners," *Sociometry,* (June, 1958), 159-164.

LEVINSON, Daniel J. and R. Nevitt Sanford, "A Scale for the Measurement of Anti-Semitism," *Journal of Psychology,* 17 (1944), 339-370.

LIPSET, Seymour M., "Democracy and Working-Class Authoritarianism," *American Sociological Review,* 24 (August, 1959), 482-501.

LIPSET, Seymour M., *Political Man,* Garden City, New York: Doubleday, 1960, Chapter 4, "Working-Class Authoritarianism."

LIPSET, Seymour M., "Working Class Authoritarianism: A Reply to Miller and Reissman," *British Journal of Sociology,* 12 (September, 1961), 263-276.

LIPSITZ, Lewis, "Working-Class Authoritarianism: A Re-Evaluation," *American Sociological Review,* 30 (February, 1965), 103-109.

MARTIN, James G. and Frank R. Westie, "The Tolerant Personality," *American Sociological Review,* 24 (August, 1959), 521-528.

McDILL, Edward, "Anomie, Authoritarianism, Prejudice, and Socio-Economic Status: An Attempt at Clarification," *Social Forces,* 39 (March, 1961), 239-245.

MILLER, S. M. and Frank Reissman, "'Working Class Authoritarianism': A Critique of Lipset," *British Journal of Sociology.* 12 (September, 1961), 263-276.

MULLIGAN, Raymond A., "Socioeconomic Background and Minority Attitudes," *Sociology and Social Research,* 45 (April, 1961), 289-294.

NATIONAL PUBLIC OPINION INSTITUTE OF JAPAN, *A Survey Concerning the Protection of Civil Liberties,* Tokyo, 1951.

NOEL, Donald L. and Alphonso Pinkney, "Correlates of Prejudice: Some Racial Differences and Similarities," *American Journal of Sociology,* 69 (May, 1964), 609-622.

PETTIGREW, Thomas F., "Personality and Sociocultural Factors in Intergroup Attitudes: A Cross-National Comparison," *Journal of Conflict Resolution,* 2 (March, 1958), 29-42.

PETTIGREW, Thomas F., "Regional Differences in Anti-Negro Prejudice," *Journal of Abnormal and Social Psychology,* (July, 1959), 28-36.

PETTIGREW, Thomas F. and M. Richard Cramer, "The Demography of Desegregation," *Journal of Social Issues,* 15 (third quarter, 1959), 61-71.

PHOTIADIS, John and Jenne Biggar, "Religiosity, Education, and Social Distance," *American Journal of Sociology,* 67 (May, 1962), 666-672.

RHYNE, Edwin H., "Racial Prejudice and Personality Scales: An Alternative Approach," *Social Forces,* (October, 1962), 44-53.

ROBB, J. H., *Working-Class Anti-Semite: A Psychological Study in a London Borough,* London: Travistock, 1954.

ROGIN, Michael, "Wallace and the Middle Class: The White Backlash in Wisconsin," *Public Opinion Quarterly,* 30 (Spring, 1966), 98-108.

ROSE, Arnold W., *Studies in Reduction of Prejudice,* Chicago: American Council on Race Relations, 1948.

ROSENBLUM, Abraham L., "Ethnic Prejudice as Related to Social Class and Religiosity," *Sociology and Social Research,* 43 (March-April, 1959), 272-275.

SEEMAN, Melvin, Dennis Rohan, and Milton Argeriou, "Social Mobility and Prejudice: A Swedish Replication," *Social Problems,* 14 (Fall, 1966), 188-197.

SILBERSTEIN, F. B. and Melvin Seeman, "Social Mobility and Prejudice," *American Journal of Sociology,* 65 (November, 1959), 258-264.

STEMBER, Charles Herbert, *Education and Attitude Change: The Effect of Schooling on Prejudice Against Minority Groups,* New York: Institute of Human Relations Press, 1961.

STOUFFER, Samuel, *Communism, Conformity, and Civil Liberties,* Garden City, New York: Doubleday, 1955.

TREIMAN, Donald J., "Status Discrepancy, and Prejudice," *American Journal of Sociology,* 72 (March, 1966), 651-664.

TRIANDIS, Harry and Leigh Triandis, "Race, Social Class, Religion, and Nationality as Determinants of Social Distance," *Journal of Abnormal and Social Psychology,* (July, 1960), 110-118.

TUMIN, Melvin, *Desegregation: Resistance and Readiness,* Princeton: Princeton University Press, 1958.

TUMIN, Melvin, Paul Barton, and Bernie Burrus, "Education, Prejudice and Discrimination: A Study in Readiness for Desegregation," *British Journal of Sociology,* 10 (September, 1959), 253-267.

TUMIN, Melvin and Ray C. Collins, Jr., "Status, Mobility, and Anomie: A Study in the Readiness for Desegregation,"

PREJUDICE AND
DISCRIMINATION

British Journal of Sociology, 10 (September, 1959), 253-267.

VANDER ZANDEN, James, "Desegregation and Social Strains in the South," *Journal of Social Issues,* 15 (third quarter, 1959), 53-60.

VANDER ZANDEN, James, "The Klan Revival," *American Journal of Sociology,* 65 (March, 1960), 456-462.

WESTIE, Frank R., "Negro-White Status Differentials and Social Distance," *American Sociological Review,* 17 (October, 1952), 550-558.

WESTIE, Frank R. and Margaret Westie, "The Social Distance Pyramid: Relationships Between Caste and Class," *American Journal of Sociology,* 63 (September, 1957), 190-196.

Values, Attitudes, and Ideology

Public opinion polls provide a wealth of data on this topic. Some of the publications listed here use data from the polls, and in addition poll data by educational, income, and occupational level are reported periodically in the *Gallup Opinion Index,* published monthly by the American Institute of Public Opinion, and in "The Polls" section of each issue of the *Public Opinion Quarterly.*

ALONZO, Angelo A. and John W. Kinch, "Educational Level and Support of Civil Liberties," *Pacific Sociological Review,* 7 (Fall, 1964), 89-93.

ANDERSON, William F., Jr., "Attitudes of Parents of Differing Socio-Economic Status Toward the Teaching Profession," *Journal of Educational Psychology,* 45 (October, 1954), 345-352.

BENE, Eva, "Some Differences Between Middle-Class and Working-Class Grammar School Boys in Their Attitude Toward Education," *British Journal of Sociology,* 10 (June, 1959), 148-152.

BONJEAN, Charles M., "Mass, Class, and the Industrial Community: A Comparative Analysis of Managers, Businessmen, and Workers," *American Journal of Sociology,* 72 (September, 1966), 149-162.

BRIM, Orville G. and Raymond Rorer, "A Note on the Relation of Values and Social Structure to Life Planning," *Sociometry,*

19 (March, 1956), 54-60.

BROOM, Leonard and Norval D. Glenn, Negro-White Differences in Reported Attitudes and Behavior," *Sociology and Social Research,* 50 (January, 1966), 187-200.

CENTERS, Richard, "Attitude, Belief and Occupational Stratification," in Elihu Katz, *et al.,* editors, *Public Opinion and Propaganda,* New York: Dryden, 1954.

CENTERS, Richard, "Attitude and Belief in Relation to Occupational Stratification," *Journal of Social Psychology,* 27 (1948), 159-185.

CENTERS, Richard, "Children of the New Deal: Social Stratification and Adolescent Attitudes," *International Journal of Opinion and Attitude Research,* 4 (1950), 315-335.

CENTERS, Richard, "Social Class, Occupation, and Imputed Belief," *American Journal of Sociology,* 58 (May, 1953), 543-555.

DeGRE, Gerald, "Ideology and Class Consciousness in the Middle Class," *Social Forces,* 29 (December, 1950), 173-179.

DeSHAN, Lawrence H., "Time Orientation and Social Class," *Journal of Abnormal and Social Psychology,* 47 (July, 1952), 589-592.

DIBBLE, Vernon K., "Occupations and Ideologies," *American Journal of Sociology,* 68 (September, 1962), 229-241.

DOHRENWEND, Bruce P. and Edwin Chin-Shong, "Social Status and Attitudes Toward Psychological Disorder: The Problem of Deviance," *American Sociological Review,* 32 (June, 1967), 417-433.

DUBIN, Robert, "Industrial Workers' Worlds: A Study of the 'Central Life Interests' of Industrial Workers," in Erwin O. Smigel, editor, *Work and Leisure,* New Haven: College and University Press, 1963.

DYER, William G., "Parental Influence on the Job Attitudes of Children from Two Occupational Strata," *Sociology and Social Research,* 42 (January-February, 1958), 203-206.

ENDLEMAN, Robert, "Moral Perspectives of Blue-Collar Workers," in Arthur B. Shostak and William Gomberg, editors, *Blue-Collar World: Studies of the American Worker,* Englewood Cliffs, New Jersey: Prentice-Hall, 1964.

EYSENCK, Hans J., "Primary Social Attitudes as Related to Social Class and Political Party," *British Journal of Sociology,* 11 (September, 1951), 198-209.

EYSENCK, Hans J., "Social Attitude and Social Class," *British Journal of Sociology,* 1 (March, 1950), 56-66.

VALUES, ATTITUDES AND IDEOLOGY

FAUNCE, William A., "Social Stratification and Attitude Toward Change in Job Content," *Social Forces*, 39 (December, 1960), 140-148.

FREEMAN, Howard E., "Attitudes Toward Mental Illness Among Relatives of Former Mental Patients," *American Sociological Review*, 26 (February, 1961), 59-66.

FRIEDENBERG, Edgar, "An Ideology of School Withdrawal," in Arthur B. Shostak and William Gomberg, editors, *Blue-Collar World: Studies of the American Worker*, Englewood Cliffs, New Jersey: Prentice-Hall, 1964.

GLENN, Norval D., "Massification Versus Differentiation: Some Trend Data from National Surveys," *Social Forces*, 46 (December, 1967), 172-180.

GLENN, Norval D., "The Trend in Differences in Attitudes and Behavior by Educational Level," *Sociology of Education*, 39 (Summer, 1966), 255-275.

GLENN, Norval D. and Jon P. Alston, "Cultural Distances Among Occupational Categories," *American Sociological Review*, 33 (June, 1968), 365-382.

GLENN, Norval D. and Jon P. Alston, "Rural-Urban Differences in Reported Attitudes and Behavior," *Southwestern Social Science Quarterly*, 47 (March, 1967), 381-400.

GORDON, Milton M., "Kitty Foyle and the Concept of Class as Culture," *American Journal of Sociology*, 53 (November, 1947), 210-217.

GROSS, Llewellyn and Orville Gursslin, "Middle-Class and Lower-Class Beliefs and Values," in Alvin Gouldner and Helen P. Gouldner, editors, *Modern Sociology*, New York: Harcourt, Brace, and World, 1963.

HAER, John L., "Opinions on an Issue in Relation to Selected 'Background' Factors," *Public Opinion Quarterly*, 18 (Summer, 1954), 213-218.

HAER, John L., "Social Stratification in Relation to Attitude toward Sources of Power in a Community," *Social Forces*, 35 (December, 1956), 137-142.

HALL, Marjorie and Robert A. Keith, "Sex Role Preference among Children of Upper and Lower Social Class," *Journal of Social Psychology*, 62 (1964), 101-110.

HAMILTON, Richard F., "The Behavior and Values of Skilled Workers," in Arthur B. Shostak and William Gomberg, editors, *Blue-Collar World: Studies of the American Worker*, Englewood Cliffs, New Jersey: Prentice Hall, 1964.

HAMILTON, Richard F., "The Marginal Middle Class: A Reconsideration," *American Sociological Review,* 31 (April, 1966), 192-199.

HOLLINGSHEAD, August B., *Elmtown's Youth: The Impact of Social Classes on Adolescents,* New York: Wiley, 1949.

HUNT, Chester L., "Class and Behavior," *American Sociological Review,* 23 (June, 1958), 314-315.

HYMAN, Herbert H., "The Value Systems of Different Classes," in Reinhard Bendix and Seymour M. Lipset, editors, *Class, Status, and Power,* revised edition, New York: Free Press, 1966.

INKELES, Alex, "Industrial Man: The Relation of Status to Experience, Perception, and Value," *American Journal of Sociology,* 66 (July, 1960), 1-31.

KAHL, Joseph A., "Social Stratification and Values in Metropoli and Provinces: Brazil and Mexico," *America Latina,* 8 (January-March, 1965), 23-35.

KATZ, F. M., "The Meaning of Success: Some Differences in Value Systems of Social Classes," *Journal of Social Psychology,* 62 (1964), 141-148.

KLUCKHOHN, Clyde and Florence R. Kluckhohn, "American Culture: Generalized Orientations and Class Patterns," in Lyman Bryson, Louis Finkelstein, and R. M. MacIver, editors, *Conflicts of Power in Modern Culture,* New York: Harper, 1947.

KLUCKHOHN, Florence R., "Dominant and Substitute Profiles of Cultural Orientations: Their Significance for the Analysis of Social Stratification," *Social Forces,* 28 (May, 1950), 376-393.

KORNHAUSER, Arthur W., "Public Opinion and Social Class," *American Journal of Sociology,* 55 (January, 1955), 333-345.

KRIESBERG, Louis, "The Relationship between Socio-Economic Rank and Behavior," *Social Problems,* 10 (Spring, 1963), 334-353.

LARSON, Richard F. and Sara Smith Sutker, "Value Differences and Value Consensus by Socioeconomic Levels," *Social Forces,* 44 (June, 1966), 563-569.

LEHMAN, Irvin J., "Some Socio-Cultural Differences in Attitudes and Values," *Journal of Educational Sociology,* 36 (September, 1962), 1-9.

LEWIS, Lionel S., "Class Consciousness and Inter-Class Sentiments," *Sociological Quarterly,* 6 (Autumn, 1965), 325-338.

LYMAN, Elizabeth L., "Occupational Differences in the Value Attached to Work," *American Journal of Sociology,* 61 (September, 1955), 138-144.

LYNES, Russell, "Highbrow, Lowbrow, Middlebrow," *Harper's Magazine,* (February, 1949), 19-28.

MACCOBY, Eleanor E., "Class Differences in Boys' Choices of Authority Roles," *Sociometry,* 25 (March, 1962), 117-119.

MacRAE, Donald G., "Class Relationships and Ideology," *Sociological Review,* 6 (December, 1958), 261-272.

MEHLMAN, B. and Robert G. Warehime, "Social Class and Social Desirability," *Journal of Social Psychology,* 58 (1962), 167-170.

MILLER, S. M., "The Outlook of Working-Class Youth," in Arthur B. Shostak and William Gomberg, editors, *Blue-Collar World: Studies of the American Worker,* Englewood Cliffs, New Jersey: Prentice-Hall, 1964.

MONK, Mary and Theodore M. Newcomb, "Perceived Concensus Within and Among Occupational Classes," *American Sociological Review,* 21 (February, 1956), 71-79.

MUIR, Donal E. and Eugene A. Weinstein, "The Social Debt: An Investigation of Lower-Class and Middle-Class Norms of Social Obligation," *American Sociological Review,* 27 (August, 1962), 532-539.

MURPHY, Mary M., "Values Stressed by Two Social Class Levels at Meetings of Alcoholics Anonymous," *Quarterly Journal of Studies on Alcohol,* 14 (1953), 577-585.

PEARLIN, Leonard I. and Melvin L. Kohn, "Social Class, Occupation, and Parental Values: A Cross National Study," *American Sociological Review,* 31 (August, 1966), 466-479.

PHILLIPS, Derek, "Education, Psychiatric Sophistication and the Rejection of Mentally Ill Help-Seekers," *Sociological Quarterly,* 8 (Winter, 1967), 122-132.

POPE, B., "Socioeconomic Contrasts in Children's Peer Culture Prestige Values," *Genetic Psychology Monographs,* 48 (1953), 157-220.

RANULF, Svend, *Moral Indignation and Middle Class Psychology,* New York: Schocken, 1964.

RETTIG, Salomon and Benjamin Pasamanick, "Moral Value Structure and Social Class," *Sociometry,* 24 (March, 1961), 21-35.

RICH, John Martin, "How Social Class Values Affect Teacher-Pupil Relations," *Journal of Education Sociology,* 33 (May, 1960), 355-359.

RODMAN, Hyman, "Class Culture," *International Encyclopedia of the Social Sciences,* 15, New York: Free Press, 1968.

ROE, Anne, *The Psychology of Occupations,* New York: Wiley, 1956.

VALUES, ATTITUDES
AND IDEOLOGY

ROSEN, Bernard, "Social Class and the Child's Perception of the Parent," *Child Development,* 35 (December, 1964), 1147-1153.

ROSENBERG, Morris, with the assistance of Edward Suchman and Rose Goldsen, *Occupations and Values,* New York: Free Press, 1957.

ROTHMAN, Philip, "Socio-Economic Status and the Values of Junior High School Students," *Journal of Educational Sociology,* 28 (November, 1954), 126-129.

STEINER, Ivan D., "Some Social Values Associated with Objectively and Subjectively Defined Social Class Memberships," *Social Forces,* 31 (May, 1953), 327-332.

STENDLER, Celia B., "Social Class Differences in Parental Attitudes to School at Grade 1 Level," *Child Development,* 22 (1951), 37-46.

SVALASTOGA, Kaare, E. Hogh, M. Pedersen, and E. Schild, "Differential Class Behavior in Denmark," *American Sociological Review,* 21 (August, 1956), 435-439.

SYKES, A. J. M., "Some Differences in the Attitudes of Clerical and of Manual Workers," *Sociological Review,* 13 (November, 1965), 297-310.

TURNER, Ralph H., "Upward Mobility and Class Values," *Social Problems,* 11 (Spring, 1964), 359-371.

WARNER, W. Lloyd and Paul S. Lunt, *The Social Life of a Modern Community,* New Haven: Yale University Press, 1941.

WILLIAMS, Melvin J., "A Socio-Economic Analysis of the Functions and Attitudes of Wartime Youth," *Social Forces,* 24 (December, 1945), 200-210.

WILLIAMS, Warren S., "Class Differences in the Attitudes of Psychiatric Patients," *Social Problems,* 4 (January, 1957), 240-244.

WILLIAMSON, Robert C., "Social Class and Orientation to Change: Some Relevant Variables in a Bogata Sample," *Social Forces,* 46 (March, 1968), 317-328.

WILSON, Everett K., *Sociology: Rules, Roles, and Relationships,* Homewood, Illinois: Dorsey, 1966, Chapter 5, "Class Differences in the Transmission of Culture."

BERNSTEIN, Basil, "Language and Social Class," *British Journal of Sociology,* 11 (September, 1960), 271-276.

BERNSTEIN, Basil, "Social Class and Linguistic Development: A Theory of Social Learning," in A. H. Halsey, J. Floud, and C. A. Anderson, *Education, Economy and Society,* New York: Free Press, 1961.

BERNSTEIN, Basil, "Social Class, Speech Systems, and Psychotherapy," *British Journal of Sociology,* 15 (March, 1964), 55-64.

DEUTSCH, Martin, Alma Malirer, Bert Brown, and Estelle Cherry-Peisach,, *Communication of Information in the Elementary School Classroom,* Washington D. C: Office of Education, 1964.

ELLIS, Dean S., "Speech and Social Status in America," *Social Forces,* 45 (March, 1967), 431-440.

ENTWISLE, Doris R., "Developmental Sociolinguistics: Inner-City Children," *American Journal of Sociology,* 74 (July, 1968), 37-49.

FADIMAN, Clifton, "Is There an Upper-Class American Language?" *Holiday* (October, 1956), 8-10.

GUMPERZ, John J., "Dialect Differences and Social Stratification in a North Indian Village," *American Anthropologist,* 60 (August, 1958), 668-682.

HUFFINE, Carol L., "Inter-Socioeconomic Class Language Differences: A Research Report," *Sociology and Social Research,* 50 (April, 1966), 351-355.

LABOV, William, *The Social Stratification of English in New York City,* Washington, D. C.: Center for Applied Linguistics, 1966.

LASSWELL, Thomas E., *Class and Stratum,* Boston: Houghton-Mifflin, 1965, 147-148 and 215-225.

LAWTON, Denis, *Social Class, Language and Education,* London: Routledge and Kegan Paul, 1968.

ROHRER, John H. and Munro S. Edmonson, editors, *The Eighth Generation,* New York: Harper and Row, 1960, Appendix 4, "Dialect and Society,"

SCHATZMAN, Leonard, and Anselm Strauss, "Social Class and Modes of Communication," *American Journal of Sociology,* 60 (January, 1955), 329-338.

SHRINER, Thomas H. and Lynn Miner, "Morphological Structures in the Language of Disadvantaged and Advantaged Children," *Journal of Speech and Hearing Research,* 11 (September, 1968), 605-610.

Ability and Achievement

ANASTASI, Anne, "Differential Effect of Intelligence and Social Status," *Eugenics Quarterly,* 6 (June, 1959), 84-91.

ANASTASI, Anne, *Differential Psychology,* New York: Macmillan, 1958.

ANDERSON, C. Arnold, "A Skeptical Note on the Relation of Vertical Mobility to Education," *American Journal of Sociology,* 66 (May, 1961), 560-570.

ANDERSON, C. Arnold, James C. Brown, and Mary Jean Bowman, "Intelligence and Occupational Mobility," *Journal of Political Economy,* 60 (June, 1952), 218-239.

BOALT, Gunnar, "Social Mobility in Stockholm: A Pilot Investigation," *Transactions of the Second World Congress of Sociology,* 2 (1954), 67-69.

BOND, Horace Mann, "The Productivity of National Merit Scholars by Occupational Class," *School and Society,* 85 (September 28, 1957), 267-268.

BONNEY, Merl, "Relationships between Social Success, Family Size, Socio-economic Home Background, and Intelligence among School Children in Grades III to V," *Sociometry,* 7 (February, 1944), 26-39.

BRITTON, Joseph H., "Influence of Social Class Upon Performance on The Draw-A-Man Test," *Journal of Educational*

Psychology, 45 (January, 1954), 44-51.

BURT, Cyril, "Class Differences in General Intelligence: III," *British Journal of Statistical Psychology,* 12 (1959), 15-33.

ABILITY AND
ACHIEVEMENT

BURT, Cyril, *Intelligence and Fertility: The Effect of the Differential Birth Rate on Inborn Mental Characteristics,* London: Eugenics Society, 1952.

BURT, Cyril, "Intelligence and Social Mobility," *British Journal of Statistical Psychology,* 14 (1961), 2-24.

CHERRY-PEISACH, Estelle, "Children's Comprehension of Teacher and Peer Speech," *Journal of Speech and Hearing Research* (1969).

CHOWDRY, K. and T. M. Newcomb, "The Relative Abilities of Leaders and Nonleaders to Estimate Opinions of Their own Groups," *Journal of Abnormal and Social Psychology,* 47 (1952), 51-57.

COLEMAN, H. A., "The Relationship of Socio-Economic Status to the Performance of Junior High School Students," *Journal of Experimental Education,* 9 (September, 1940), 61-63.

CONWAY, J., "Class Differences in General Intelligence: II," *British Journal of Statistical Psychology,* 12 (1959), 5-14.

DAVIDSON, Helen H., and D. Bolducci, "Class and Sex Differences In Verbal Facility of Very Bright Children," *Journal of Educational Psychology,* 47 (December, 1956), 476-480.

DAVIS, Allison, "Education for the Conservation of Human Resources," *Progressive Education,* 27 (1950), 221-224.

DEUTSCH, Martin and Estelle Cherry-Peisach, "A Study of Language Patterns," *Instructor,* 75 (March, 1966), 93-96.

DONOVAN, Thomas R., "Socio-economic and Educational Factors Influencing the Achievement Level of Individuals in Large Scale Organizations," *Sociology and Social Research,* 46 (July, 1962), 416-425.

DUNCAN, Otis Dudley, "Is the Intelligence of the General Population Declining?" *American Sociological Review,* 17 (August, 1952), 401-407.

ECKLAND, Bruce K., "Academic Ability, Higher Education, and Occupational Mobility," *American Sociological Review,* 30 (October, 1965), 735-746.

ECKLAND, Bruce K., "Genetics and Sociology: A Reconsideration," *American Sociological Review,* 32 (April, 1967), 173-194.

ECKLAND, Bruce K., "Social Class and College Graduation: Some Misconceptions Corrected," *American Journal of Sociology,* 70 (July, 1964), 36-50.

EELLS, Kenneth, Allison Davis, *et al.*, *Intelligence and Cultural Differences: A Study of Cultural Learning and Problem-Solving*, Chicago: University of Chicago Press, 1951.

FARBER, Bernard, "Social Class and Intelligence," *Social Forces*, 44 (December, 1965), 215-225.

FLOUD, J. E., A. H. Halsey, and F. M. Martin, *Social Class and Educational Opportunity*, London: Heinemann, 1957.

FRYER, D. H., "Occupational Intelligence Standards," *School and Society*, 16 (September, 1922), 273-277.

FULLER, John L., *Nature and Nurture: A Modern Synthesis*, Garden City, New York: Doubleday, 1954.

GETZELS, Jacob W. and Philip W. Jackson, "Family Environment and Cognitive Style: A Study of the Sources of Highly Creative Adolescents," *American Sociological Review*, 26 (June, 1961), 351-359.

GIST, Noel P., C. T. Pihlblad, and C. L. Gregory, "Scholastic Achievement and Occupation," *American Sociological Review*, 7 (December, 1942), 752-763.

GRAY, J. L. and P. Moshinski, *The Nation's Intelligence*, Watts, 1936.

GOUGH, Harrison, "The Relationship of Socio-Economic Status to Personality Inventory and Achievement Test Scores," *Journal of Educational Psychology*, 37 (1946), 527-540.

HAAN, N., "The Relationship of Ego Functioning and Intelligence to Social Status and Social Mobility," *Journal of Abnormal and Social Psychology*, 69 (1964), 594-605.

HALSEY, A. H., "Class Differences in General Intelligence: I," *British Journal of Statistical Psychology*, 12 (1959), 1-4.

HALSEY, A. H., "Genetics, Social Structure, and Intelligence," *British Journal of Sociology*, 9 (1958), 15-28.

HAVIGHURST, Robert J., and Fay H. Breese, "Relations Between Ability and Social Status In a Midwestern Community. III Primary Mental Abilities," *Journal of Educational Psychology*, 38 (April, 1947), 241-247.

HIMMELWEIT, H. T., "Social Status and Secondary Education Since the 1944 Act: Some Data for London," in David V. Glass, editor, *Social Mobility in Britain*, London: Routledge and Kegan Paul, 1954.

ILLSLEY, R., "Social Class Selection and Class Differences in Relation to Stillbirth and Infant Deaths," *British Medical Journal*, (December 24, 1955), 1520-1524.

JANKE, Loeta Long, and Robert J. Havighurst, "Relations

ABILITY AND
ACHIEVEMENT

Between Ability and Social Status In a Midwestern Community: II Sixteen-Year-Old Boys and Girls," *Journal of Educational Psychology,* 36 (November, 1945), 499-509.

ABILITY AND ACHIEVEMENT

JOHN, Vera P., "The Intellectual Development of Slum Children: Some Preliminary Findings," *American Journal of Orthopsychiatry,* 33 (October, 1963), 813-822.

KAHL, Joseph A., "Educational and Oc cupational Aspirations of 'Common Man' Boys," *Harvard Educational Review,* 23 (1953), 186-203.

KARIEL, Patricia, "Social Class, Age, and Educational Group Differences in Childbirth Information," *Journal of Marriage and the Family,* 25 (August, 1963), 353-355.

MAXWELL, James, "Intelligence, Fertility and the Future: A Report on the 1947 Scottish Mental Survey," *Proceedings of the World Population Conference,* New York: United Nations, 1954.

McGURK, Frank C. J., "On White and Negro Test Performance and Socio-economic Factors," *Journal of Abnormal and Social Psychology,* 48 (1953), 448-450.

MINER, John B., *Intelligence in the United States,* New York: Springer, 1957.

MITCHELL, James V., Jr., "A Comparison of the Factorial Structure of Cognitive Functions For a High and Low Status Group," *Journal of Educational Psychology,* 47 (November, 1956), 397-414.

NATIONAL SCIENCE FOUNDATION, *Two Years After the College Degree,* Washington: U. S. Government Printing Office, 1963.

NEFF, W. S. "Socio-Economic Status and Intelligence," *Psychological Bulletin,* 35 (1938), 727-757.

O'DONOVAN, Thomas R., "Socioeconomic and Educational Factors Influencing the Achievement Level of Individuals in Large-Scale Organizations," *Sociology and Social Research,* 46 (July, 1962), 416-425.

PHILLIPS, Beeman N., "Sex, Social Class and Anxiety as Sources of Variation In School Achievement," *Journal of Educational Psychology,* 53 (December, 1962), 316-322.

PHLIBLAD, C. T., and C. L. Gregory, "Occupational Selection and Intelligence in Rural Communities and Small Towns in Missouri," *American Sociological Review,* 21 (February, 1956), 63-71.

POHLMANN, Vernon C., "Relationship Between Ability, Socio-Economic Status and Choice of Secondary School," *Journal of Educational Sociology,* 29 (May, 1956), 392-397.

RYCHMAN, David B., "A Comparison of Information Processing Abilities of Middle and Lower Class Negro Kindergarten Boys," *Exceptional Children,* 33 (April, 1967), 545.

SABAGH, Georges, Harvey F. Dingman, George Tarjan, and Stanley W. Wright, "Social Class and Ethnic Status of Patients Admitted to a State Hospital for the Retarded," *Pacific Sociological Review,* 2 (Fall, 1959), 76-80.

SEWELL, William H., and Bertram L. Ellenbogen, "Social Status and the Measured Intelligence of Small City and Rural Children," *American Sociological Review,* 17 (October, 1952), 612-616.

SEWELL, William H. and Vimal P. Shah, "Socioeconomic Status, Intelligence, and the Attainment of Higher Education," *Sociology of Education,* 40 (Winter, 1967), 1-23.

SCHAIE, Warner K., "Occupational Level and the Primary Mental Abilities," *Journal of Educational Psychology,* 49 (December, 1958), 299-303.

SCHULMAN, Mary Jean, and Robert J. Havighurst, "Relations between Ability and Social Status In a Midwestern Community. IV Size of Vocabulary," *Journal of Educational Psychology,* 38 (November, 1947), 437-442.

SCOTT, Eileen M., R. Illsley, and A. M. Thomson, "A Psychological Investigation of Primigravidae. II: Maternal Social Class, Age, Physique, and Intelligence,". *Journal of Obstetrics and Gynecology of the British Empire,* 63 (1956).

SMITH, Mapheus, "University Student Intelligence and Occupation of Father," *American Sociological Review,* 7 (December, 1942), 764-771.

STACEY, Barrie, "Some Psychological Aspects of Inter-Generation Occupational Mobility." *British Journal of Social and Clinical Psychology,* 4 (December, 1965), 275-286.

STILLER, J., "Socioeconomic Status and Conceptual Thinking," *Journal of Abnormal and Social Psychology,* 55 (July-November, 1957), 365-371.

STRAUS, Murray A., "Communication, Creativity, and Problem-Solving Ability of Middle and Working-Class Families In Three Societies," *American Journal of Sociology,* 73 (January, 1968), 417-430.

STRAUS, Murray A. and Katherine H. Holmberg, "Part-time Employment, Social Class, and Achievement in High School," *Sociology and Social Research,* 52 (April, 1968), 224-230.

SYKES, Gresham M., "The Differential Distribution of Community Knowledge," *Social Forces,* 29 (May, 1951), 376-382.

THOMPSON, J. W., "Genetics, Social Structure, Intelligence, and Statistics," *British Journal of Sociology,* 11 (March, 1960), 44-50.

TYLER, Leona E., *The Psychology of Human Differences,* New York: Appleton-Century-Crofts, 1965.

WADE, Durlyn E., "School Achievement and Parent Employment," *Journal of Educational Sociology,* 36 (October, 1962), 93-96.

WASHBURNE, Norman F., "Socioeconomic Status, Urbanism, and Academic Performance In College," *Journal of Educational Research,* 53 (December, 1959), 138-143.

WHITE, Mary Alice and June Charry, editors, *School Disorder, Intelligence, and Social Class,* New York: Teachers College Press, 1966.

WILSON, Alan B., "Social Stratification and Academic Achievement," in A. Harry Passow, editor, *Education in Depressed Areas,* New York: Teachers College, Columbia University, 1963.

ZIGLER, Edward and Jacques de Labry, "Concept-Switching in Middle-Class, Lower-Class, and Retarded Children," *Journal of Abnormal and Social Psychology, 65 (1962), 267-273.*

Leisure Activities and Consumption Patterns

ALBERT, Robert S. and Harry G. Meline, "The Influence of Social Status on the Uses of Television," *Public Opinion Quarterly,* 22 (Summer, 1958). 145-151.

ALEXIS, Marcus, "Some Negro-White Differences in Consumption," *American Journal of Economics and Sociology,* 21 (January, 1962), 11-28.

AMORY, Cleveland, *Who Killed Society?* New York: Harper and Row, 1961.

BLUM, Alan F., "Lower-Class Negro Television Spectators: The Concept of Pseudo-Jovial Scepticism," in Arthur B. Shostak and William Gomberg, editors, *Blue-Collar World: Studies of* the American Worker, Englewood Cliffs, New Jersey: Prentice-Hall, 1964.

BOGART, Leo, "The Mass Media and the Blue-Collar Worker," in Arthur B. Shostak and William Gomberg, editors, *Blue-Collar World: Studies of the American Worker,* Englewood Cliffs, New Jersey: Prentice-Hall, 1964.

CAPLOVITZ, David, *The Poor Pay More: Consumer Practices of Low-Income Families,* New York: Free Press, 1963.

CAPLOVITZ, David, "The Problems of Blue-Collar Consumers," in Arthur B. Shostak and William Gomberg, editors, *Blue-Collar World: Studies of the American Worker,* Englewood Cliffs, New Jersey: Prentice-Hall, 1964.

CLARKE, Alfred C., "The Use of Leisure and Its Relation to Levels of Occupational Prestige," *American Sociological Review,* 21 (June, 1956), 301-307.

CRAMER, M. Ward, "Leisure Time Activities of Economically Privileged Children," *Sociology and Social Research,* 34 (1949-1950), 444-450.

DEAN, John P., "The Ghosts of Home Ownership," *Journal of Social Issues,* 7 (first quarter, 1951), 59-68.

DeGRAZIA, Sebastian, *Of Time, Work and Leisure,* New York: The Twentieth Century Fund, 1962.

DUBIN, Robert, "Industrial Workers' World: A Study of the Central Life Interests of Industrial Workers," in Erwin O. Smigel, editor, *Work and Leisure,* New Haven: College and University Press, 1963.

EDITORS OF FORTUNE, *Markets of the Sixties,* New York: Harper and Row, 1960.

FORM, William H. and Gregory P. Stone, *The Social Significance of Clothing in Occupational Life,* Technical Bulletin 247, East Lansing: Michigan State University, 1955.

GENTILE, Frank and S. M. Miller, "Television and Social Class," *Sociology and Social Research,* 45 (April, 1961), 259-264.

GLENN, Norval D. and Jon P. Alston, "Cultural Distances Among Occupational Categories, *American Sociological Review,* 33 (June, 1968), 365-382.

GLENN, Norval D. and Jon P. Alston, "Rural-Urban Differences in Reported Attitudes and Behavior," *Southwestern Social Science Quarterly,* 47 (March, 1967), 381-400.

GOLDSTEIN, Sidney, "The Effect of Income Level on the Consumer Behavior of the Aged," *Proceedings of the Seventh International Congress of Gerontology,* Vienna, Austria, 8, 1-6.

GOMBERG, Adeline, "The Working-Class Child of Four and Television," in Arthur B. Shostak and William Gomberg, editors, *Blue-Collar World: Studies of the American Worker,* Englewood Cliffs, New Jersey: Prentice-Hall, 1964.

LEISURE AND CONSUMPTION

GORDON, Milton M. and Charles H. Anderson, "The Blue-Collar Worker at Leisure," in Arthur B. Shostak and William Gomberg, editors, *Blue-Collar World: Studies of the American Worker,* Englewood Cliffs, New Jersey: Prentice-Hall, 1964.

GOTTLIEB, David, "The Neighborhood Tavern and the Cocktail Lounge: A Study of Class Differences," *American Journal of Sociology,* 62 (May, 1957), 559-562.

GROSSACK, Martin M., editor, *Understanding Consumer Behavior,* Boston: Christopher, 1964.

HAMILTON, Richard F., "Affluence and the Worker: The West German Case," *American Journal of Sociology,* 71 (September, 1965), 144-152.

HAMILTON, Richard F., "The Behavior and Values of Skilled Workers," in Arthur B. Shostak and William Gomberg, editors, *Blue-Collar World: Studies of the American Worker,* Englewood Cliffs, New Jersey: Prentice-Hall, 1964.

HARBERGER, Arnold C., editor, *The Demand for Durable Goods,* Chicago: The University of Chicago Press, 1960.

HAVIGHURST, Robert J., "The Leisure Activities of the Middle-Aged," *American Journal of Sociology,* 63 (September, 1957), 152-162.

HOLLINGSHEAD, August B., *Elmtown's Youth: The Impact of Social Classes on Adolescents,* New York: Wiley, 1949.

HUNTINGTON, Emily H., *Spending of Middle Income Families,* Berkeley: University of California Press, 1957.

JACOBI, John E. and S. George Walters, "Social Status and Consumer Choice," *Social Forces,* 36 (March, 1958), 209-214.

KATONA, George, Charles A. Lininger, and Eva Mueller, *1964 Survey of Consumer Finances,* Ann Arbor: Survey Research Center, University of Michigan, 1965.

KATONA, George, *et al., 1965 Survey of Consumer Finances,* Ann Arbor: Survey Research Center, University of Michigan, 1966.

KAVOLIS, Vytautas, "Artistic Preferences of Urban Social Classes," *Pacific Sociological Review,* 8 (Spring, 1965), 43-51.

KNAPP, Robert H., Janet Brimner, and Martha White, "Educational Level, Class Status, and Aesthetic Preference," *Journal of Social Psychology,* 50 (1959), 277-284.

KOSOBUD, Richard and James Morgan, editors, *Consumer Behavior of Individual Families Over Two and Three Years,*

Ann Arbor: Survey Research Center, University of Michigan, 1964.

LOOMIS, Charles P., "Educational Status and Its Relationship to Reading and Other Activities," *Social Forces,* 18 (October, 1939), 56-59.

LUNDBERG, Georga A., Mirra Komarovsky, and M. A. McInery, *Leisure: A Suburban Study,* New York: Columbia University Press, 1934.

LYDALL, H. F., *British Incomes and Savings,* London: 1955.

MacDONALD, Margherita, Carson McGuire, and Robert J. Havighurst, "Leisure Activities and the Socioeconomic Status of Children," *American Journal of Sociology,* 54 (May, 1949), 505-519.

MUELLER, Eva and Gerald Gurin, *Participation in Outdoor Recreation: Factors Affecting Demand Among American Adults,* Ann Arbor: Survey Research Center, University of Michigan, 1962.

MULLIGAN, Raymond A. and Jane C. Dinkins, "Socioeconomic Background and Theatrical Preference," *Sociology and Social Research,* 40 (May-June, 1956), 325-328.

PORTER, James N., Jr., "Consumption Patterns of Professors and Businessmen: A Pilot Study of Conspicuous Consumption and Status," *Sociological Inquiry,* 37 (Spring, 1967), 255-265.

REISSMAN, Leonard, "Class, Leisure, and Social Participation," *American Sociological Review,* 19 (February, 1954), 76-84.

RUNCIMAN, Alexander P., "A Stratification Study of Television Programs," *Sociology and Social Research,* 44 (March-April, 1960), 257-261.

SCHRAMM, Wilbur, Jack Lyle, and Edwin B. Parker, *Television in the Lives of our Children,* Stanford: Stanford University Press, 1961.

SCHUESSLER, Karl F., "Social Background and Musical Taste," *American Sociological Review,* 13 (June, 1948), 330-335.

SEAGOE, Mary V., "Children's Play as an Indicator of Cross-Cultural and Intra-cultural Differences," *Journal of Educational Sociology,* 35 (February, 1962), 278-283.

THOMAS, Lawrence G., "Leisure Pursuits By Socio-Economic Status," *Journal of Educational Sociology,* 29 (May, 1956), 367-377.

TOFFLER, Alvin, *The Culture Consumers: Art and Affluence in America,* Baltimore: Penguin, 1965.

VEBLEN, Thorstein, *The Theory of the Leisure Class,* New

York: Macmillan, 1899.

WARNER, W. Lloyd and William E. Henry, "Radio Daytime Serial: A Symbolic Analysis," *Genetic Psychology Monographs,* 37 (1948), 3-71.

WARNER, W. Lloyd and Paul S. Lunt, *The Social Life of a Modern Community,* New Haven: Yale University Press, 1941.

WHITE, R. Clyde, "Social Class Differences in the Uses of Leisure," *American Journal of Sociology,* 61 (September, 1955), 145-150.

ZOLA, Irving Kenneth, "Observations on Gambling in a Lower-Class Setting," in Arthur B. Shostak and William Gomberg, editors, *Blue-Collar World: Studies of the American Worker,* Englewood Cliffs, New Jersey: Prentice Hall, 1964.

Social Participation

ABRAMSON, S., "Our Status System and Scholastic Rewards," *Journal of Educational Sociology,* 25 (1952), 441-450.

ADAMS, Bert N. and James E. Butler, "Occupational Status and Husband-Wife Social Participation," *Social Forces,* 45 (June, 1967), 501-507.

ALMOND, Gabriel A., *The American People and Foreign Policy,* New York: Harcourt, Brace, 1950.

ANDERSON, C. Arnold and Bryce Ryan, "Social Participation Differences Among Tenure Classes in a Prosperous Commercialized Farming Area," *Rural Sociology,* 8 (September, 1943), 281-290.

ANDERSON, W. A., "Family Social Participation and Social Status Self-Ratings," *American Sociological Review,* 11 (June, 1946), 253-258.

AXELROD, Morris, "Urban Structure and Social Participation," *American Sociological Review,* 21 (February, 1956), 13-18.

BABCHUK, Nicholas and Ralph V. Thompson, "The Voluntary

Associations of Negroes," *American Sociological Review,* 27
(October, 1962), 647-655.

BAILEY, Wilfred C. and Harold F. Kaufman, *Factors Related
to Differential Participation Among Neighborhoods,* Mississippi
State College Agricultural Station, Preliminary Reports in
Sociology and Rural Life No. 3, October, 1956.

BELL, Wendell, "Anomie, Social Isolation, and the Class Structure,"
Sociometry, 20 (June, 1957), 105-116.

BELL, Wendell and Maryanne T. Force, "Social Structure and
Participation in Different Types of Formal Associations,"
Social Forces, 34 (May, 1956), 345-350.

BELL, Wendell and Maryanne T. Force, "Urban Neighborhood
Types and Participation in Formal Associations," *American
Sociological Review,* 21 (February, 1956), 24-34.

BLAU, Peter M., "Social Mobility and Interpersonal Relations,"
American Sociological Review, 21 (June, 1956), 290-295.

BLUM, Alan F., "Social Structure, Social Class, and
Participation in Primary Relationships," in Arthur B. Shostak
and William Gomberg, editors, *Blue-Collar World: Studies
of the American Worker,* Englewood Cliffs, New Jersey:
Prentice-Hall, 1964.

BONJEAN, Charles M., "Mass, Class, and Bureaucracy,"
American Journal of Sociology, 72 (September, 1966), 149-162.

BOTTOMORE, Thomas B., "Social Stratification in Voluntary
Organizations," in David V. Glass, editor, *Social Mobility
in Britain,* London: Routledge and Kegan Paul, 1954.

DOTSON, Floyd, "A Note on Participation in Voluntary Associations in Mexico City," *American Sociological Review,* 18
(August, 1953), 380-386.

DOTSON, Floyd, "Patterns of Voluntary Associations Among
Urban Working Class Families," *American Sociological Review,*
16 (October, 1951), 687-693.

FOSKETT, John M., "Social Structure and Social Participation,"
American Sociological Review, 20 (August, 1955), 431-438.

FREEMAN, Howard, Edwin Novak, and Leo Reeder, "Correlates
of Membership in Voluntary Associations," *American
Sociological Review,* 22 (October, 1957), 528-533.

GALLAGHER, O. R., "Voluntary Associations in France,"
Social Forces, 36 (December, 1957), 153-160.

GESCHWENDER, James A., "Status Inconsistency, Social Isolation and Individual Unrest," *Social Forces,* 46 (June, 1968),
477-483.

HAGEDORN, Robert, and Sanford Labovitz, "An Analysis of Community and Professional Participation Among Occupations," *Social Forces,* 45 (June, 1967), 483-491.

HAGEDORN, Robert and Sanford Labovitz, "Participation in Community Associations by Occupation: A Test of Three Theories," *American Sociological Review,* 33 (April, 1968), 272-283.

HAMILTON, Richard F., "The Behavior and Values of Skilled Workers," in Arthur Shostak and William Gomberg, editors, *Blue-Collar World,* Englewood Cliffs, New Jersey: Prentice-Hall, 1964.

HARDEE, J. Gilbert, "Social Structure and Participation in an Australian Community," *Rural Sociology,* 26 (September, 1961), 240-251.

HAUSKNECHT, Murray, "The Blue-Collar Joiner," in Arthur B. Shostak and William Gomberg, editors, *Blue-Collar World: Studies of the American Worker,* Englewood Cliffs: Prentice-Hall, 1964.

HOLZNER, Burkart, "Institutional Change, Social Stratification and the Direction of Youth Movements," *Journal of Educational Sociology,* 36 (October, 1962), 49-56.

HONKALA, Kauko, "Social Class and Visiting Patterns in Two Finnish Villages," *Acta Sociologica,* 5, 42-49.

JONES, Mary Cover, "A Study of Socialization Patterns at the High School Level," *Journal of Genetic Psychology,* 93 (1958), 87-111.

KATZ, Fred E., "Social Participation and Social Structure," *Social Forces,* 45 (December, 1966), 199-210.

KOMAROVSKY, Mirra, "The Voluntary Associations of Urban Dwellers," *American Sociological Review,* 11 (December, 1946), 686-698.

KORNHAUSER, William, *The Politics of Mass Society,* New York: Free Press, 1959.

KNUPFER, Genevieve, "Portrait of the Underdog," *Public Opinion Quarterly,* 11 (Spring, 1947), 103-309.

LANE, Robert E., *Political Life,* New York: Free Press, 1959.

LAZARSFELD, Paul F., Bernard Berelson, and Hazel Gaudet, *The People's Choice,* New York: Columbia University Press, 1948.

LAZERWITZ, Bernard, "Some Factors Associated with Church Attendance," *Social Forces,* 39 (May, 1961), 306-308.

LUNDBERG, George A., Mirra Komarovsky, and M. A. McInery, *Leisure: A Suburban Study,* New York: Columbia University Press, 1934.

MATHER, William G., "Income and Social Participation," *American Sociological Review*, 6 (June, 1941), 380-383.

NEUGARTEN, Bernice L., "Social Class and Friendship Among School Children," *American Journal of Sociology*, 51 (January, 1946), 305-313.

NOLAN, Francena L., "Relationship of 'Status Groupings' to Differences in Participation," *Rural Sociology*, 21 (September-December, 1956), 298-302.

OBERHAUS, Victor, W. W. Schroeder, and Charles D. England, "Church Participation Related to Social Class, *Rural Sociology*, 23 (September, 1958), 298-308.

ORTMEYER, Carl E., "Social Interaction and Social Stratification," *Rural Sociology*, 17 (September, 1952), 253-260.

POPE, Hallowell, "Economic Deprivation and Social Participation in a Group of 'Middle Class' Factory Workers," *Social Problems*, 11 (Winter, 1964), 290-300.

REISS, Albert J., Jr., "Rural-Urban and Status Differences in Interpersonal Contacts," *American Journal of Sociology*, 65 (September, 1959), 182-195.

REISSMAN, Leonard, "Class, Leisure, and Social Participation," *American Sociological Review*, 19 (February, 1954), 76-84.

SCOTT, John C., Jr., "Membership and Participation in Voluntary Associations," *American Sociological Review*, 22 (June, 1957), 315-326.

SHUVAL, Judith T., "Class and Ethnic Correlates of Casual Neighboring, *American Sociological Review*, 21 (August, 1956), 453-458.

SLATER, Carol, "Class Differences in Definition of Role and Membership in Voluntary Associations among Urban Married Women," *American Journal of Sociology*, 65 (May, 1960), 616-619.

SMITH, P., "A Study of the Selective Character of American Education: Participation in School Activities as Conditioned by Socio-economic Status and Other Factors," *Journal of Educational Psychology*, 36 (1945), 229-246.

SNYDER, Eldon E., "Socioeconomic Variations, Values, and Social Participation Among High School Students," *Journal of Marriage and the Family*, 28 (May, 1966), 174-176.

UZZELL, Odell, "Institution Membership in Relation to Class Levels," *Sociology and Social Research*, 37 (July-August, 1953), 390-394.

WARNER, W. Lloyd and Paul S. Lunt, *The Social Life of a Modern Community*, New Haven: Yale University Press, 1941.

WRIGHT, Charles R. and Herbert H. Hyman, "Voluntary Association Memberships of American Adults: Evidence from National Sample Surveys," *American Sociological Review*, 23 (June, 1958), 284-294.

ZIMMER, Basil B. and Amos H. Hawley, "The Significance of Membership in Associations," *American Journal of Sociology*, 65 (September, 1959), 196-201.

Class Consciousness

and Related Psychological Correlates

The term class consciousness has been used to apply to one or more of a number of related phenomena, all psychological. These range from the awareness of common interests among those who occupy a common "class situation," in the Marxian sense, to awareness of the range of inequality in the distribution of rewards and resources and of one's place in that distribution. The literature in this section covers, in addition to the various dimensions of class consciousness, such phenomena as status concern and more or less disinterested perceptions of the pattern of inequality.

BENDIX, Reinhard and Seymour M. Lipset, "Karl Marx's Theory of Social Classes," in Reinhard Bendix and Seymour M. Lipset, editors, *Class, Status and Power,* revised edition, New York: Free Press, 1966.

BLALOCK, Hubert M., Jr., "Status Consciousness: A Dimensional Analysis," *Social Forces,* 3 (March, 1959), 243-248.

BLUMER, Herbert, "Early Industrialization and the Laboring Class," *Sociological Quarterly,* 1 (January, 1960), 5-14.

BOTT, Elizabeth, "The Concept of Class as a Reference Group," *Human Relations,* 7 (third quarter, 1954), 259-285.

BOTTOMORE, T. B., editor, *Karl Marx: Early Writings,* London: Watts, 1963.

BRIEFS, Goetz A., *The Proletariat,* New York: Mc Graw-Hill, 1937.

BROOKS, Robert F., *When Labor Organizes,* New Haven: Yale University Press, 1942.

BUCHANAN, William and Hadley Cantril, *How Workers See Each Other,* Urbana: University of Illinois Press, 1953.

CANTRIL, Hadley, "The American Class Structure: A Psychological Analysis," in Guy E. Swanson, Theodore M. Newcomb, and Eugene L. Hartley, editors, *Readings in Social Psychology*, revised edition, New York: Holt, 1952.

CANTRIL, Hadley, "Identification With Social and Economic Class," *Journal of Abnormal and Social Psychology*, 38 (January, 1943), 74-80.

CASE, Herman M., "An Independent Test of the Interest-Group Theory of Social Class," *American Sociological Review*, 17 (December, 1952), 751-755.

CENTERS, Richard, "The American Class Structure: A Psychological Analysis," in Guy E. Swanson, Theodore Newcomb, and Eugene L. Hartley, editors, *Readings in Social Psychology*, 2nd Edition, New York: Holt, 1952.

CENTERS, Richard, "Class Consciousness of the American Woman," *International Journal of Opinion and Attitude Research*, 3 (1949), 399-408.

CENTERS, Richard, "Four Studies in Psychology and Social Status," *Psychological Bulletin*, 47 (May, 1950), 263-288.

CENTERS, Richard, "The Intensity Dimension of Class Consciousness and Some Social and Psychological Correlates," *Journal of Social Psychology*, 44 (August, 1956), 101-114.

CENTERS, Richard, "Nominal Variation and Class Identification: The Working and the Laboring Classes," *Journal of Abnormal and Social Psychology*, 45 (April, 1950), 195-215.

CENTERS, Richard, *The Psychology of Social Classes*, Princeton: Princeton University Press, 1949.

CENTERS, Richard, "Social Class Identifications of American Youth," *Journal of Personality*, 18 (1950), 190-302.

CHINOY, Ely, *Automobile Workers and The American Dream*, Garden City, New York: Doubleday, 1955.

COLE, G. D. H., *What Marx Really Meant*, New York: Knopf, 1934.

CRONER, Fritz, "Salaried Employees in Modern Society," *International Labour Review*, 69 (February, 1954), 97-110.

CURTIS, Richard F., "Differential Association and the Stratification of the Urban Community," *Social Forces*, 42 (October, 1963), 68-77.

DAHRENDORF, Ralf, "Social Structure, Class Interests and Social Conflict," *Transactions of the Third World Congress of Sociology*, 3 (1956), 291-296.

DAVIES, A. F., *Images of Class: An Australian Study*, Sydney:

Sydney University Press, 1967.

DeGRE , Gerard, "Ideology and Class Consciousness in the Middle Class," *Social Forces,* 29 (December, 1950), 173-179.

DENISOFF, R. Serge, "Protest Movements: Class Consciousness and the Propaganda Song," *Sociological Quartelry,* 9 (Spring, 1968), 228-247.

ENGELS, Friedrich, "Why There is No Socialist Party in America," in Lewis E. Feuer, editor, *Basis Writings on Politics and Philosophy,* Garden City, New York: Doubleday, 1959.

EULAU, Heinz, "Identification with Class and Political Perspective," *Journal of Politics,* 18 (May, 1956), 232-253.

EULAU, Heinz, "Identification with Class and Political Role Behavior," *Public Opinion Quarterly,* 20 (Fall, 1956), 515-529.

EYSENCK, Hans J., *The Psychology of Politics,* London: Routledge and Kegan Paul, 1954.

FALLERS, Lloyd A., "A Note on the 'Trickle Effect,'" *Public Opinion Quarterly,* 18 (Fall, 1954), 314-321.

FENCHEL, G. H., Jack H. Monderer, and Eugene L. Hartley, "Subjective Status and the Equilibration Hypothesis," *Journal of Abnormal and Social Psychology,* 46 (October, 1951), 476-479.

GALLUP, George and S. F. Rae, *The Pulse of Democracy,* New York: Simon and Schuster, 1940.

GAMSON, William A., *Power and Discontent,* Homewood, Illinois: Dorsey, 1968.

GINSBERG, Morris, "Class Consciousness," *Encyclopedia of the Social Sciences,* New York: Macmillan, 3 (1930), 536-538.

GLANTZ, Oscar, "Class Consciousness and Political Solidarity," *American Sociological Review,* 23 (August, 1958), 375-383.

GLENN, Norval D. and Jon P. Alston, "Cultural Distances Among Occupational Categories," *American Sociological Review,* 33 (June, 1968), 365-382.

GLENN, Norval D. and Jon P. Alston, "Rural-Urban Differences in Reported Attitudes and Behavior," *Southwestern Social Science Quarterly,* 47 (March, 1967), 381-400.

GOLDTHORPE, John H. and David Lockwood, "Affluence and the British Class Structure," *Sociological Review,* 11 (July, 1963), 133-163.

GORDON, Milton M., "A System of Social Class Analysis," *Drew University Bulletin,* 39 (August, 1951), 1-19.

GROSS, Neal, "Social Class Identification in the Urban Community,"

American Sociological Review, 17 (August, 1953), 398-404.

GUEST, Robert H., "Work Careers and Aspirations of Automobile Workers," *American Sociological Review,* 19 (April, 1954), 155-163.

HAER, John L., "An Empirical Study of Social Class Awareness," *Social Forces,* 36 (December, 1957), 117-121.

HALBWACHS, Maurice, *The Psychology of Social Class,* New York: Free Press, 1959.

HAMILTON, Richard F., "Income, Class, and Reference Groups," *American Sociological Review,* 29 (August, 1964), 576-579.

HAMILTON, Richard F., "The Marginal Middle Class: A Reconsideration," *American Sociological Review,* 31 (April, 1966), 192-199.

HARRISON, T., "Notes on Class Consciousness and Unconsciousness," *Sociological Review,* 34 (July-October, 1942), 147-164.

HEBERLE, R., "Recovery of Class Theory," *Pacific Sociological Review,* 2 (Spring, 1959), 18-24.

HOULT, Thomas Ford, "Economic Class Consciousness in American Protestantism," *American Sociological Review,* 15 (February, 1950), 97-100.

HOULT, Thomas Ford, "Economic Class Consciousness in American Protestantism, II," *American Sociological Review,* 17 (June, 1952), 349-350.

HUTCHINSON, Bertram, "Class Self-Assessment in a Rio de Janeiro Population," *American Latina,* 6 (1963), 53-64.

HYMAN, Herbert, *The Psychology of Status,* New York: Archives of Psychology, 269, 1942.

JONES, Alfred W., *Life, Liberty, and Property,* Philadelphia: Lippincott, 1941.

KORNHAUSER, Arthur W., "Analysis of Class Structure of Contemporary American Society—Psychological Bases of Class Divisions," in George Hartmann and Theodore Newcomb, editors, *Industrial Conflict,* New York: Cordon, 1939.

KORNHAUSER, Arthur W., "Public Opinion and Social Class," *American Journal of Sociology,* 55 (January, 1950), 333-345.

KORNHAUSER, Arthur W., Harold L. Sheppard, and Albert J. Mayer, *When Labor Votes,* New York: University Books, 1956.

KORNHAUSER, William, *The Politics of Mass Society,* New York: Free Press, 1959.

LANDECKER, Werner S., "Class Crystallization and Class Consciousness," *American Sociological Review,* 28 (April, 1963), 219-229.

LASSWELL, Thomas E., "The Perception of Social Status," *Sociology and Social Research,* 45 (January, 1961), 170-174.

LASSWELL, Thomas E., "Orientations Toward Social Classes," *American Journal of Sociology,* 65 (May, 1960), 585-587.

LASSWELL, Thomas E., "Social Classes as Affective Categories," *Sociology and Social Research,* 46 (April, 1962), 312-316.

LASSWELL, Thomas E. and P. F. Parshall, "Perception and Social Class," *Sociology and Social Research,* 45 (July, 1961), 407-414.

LAUMANN, Edward O., "Subjective Social Distance and Urban Occupational Stratification," *American Journal of Sociology,* 71 (July, 1965), 26-36.

LEGGETT, John C., *Class, Race, and Labor: Working-Class Consciousness in Detroit,* New York: Oxford University Press, 1968.

LEGGETT, John C., "Economic Insecurity and Working-Class Consciousness," *American Sociological Review,* 29 (October, 1964), 226-234.

LEGGETT, John C., "Sources and Consequences of Working-Class Consciousness," in Arthur B. Shostak and William Gomberg, editors, *Blue-Collar World: Studies of the American Worker,* Englewood Cliffs, New Jersey: Prentice Hall, 1964.

LEGGETT, John C., "Uprootedness and Working-Class Consciousness," *American Journal of Sociology,* 68 (May, 1963), 682-692.

LEGGETT, John C., "Working Class Consciousness, Race, and Political Choice," *American Journal of Sociology,* 69 (September, 1963), 171-176.

LEWIS, Lionel S., "Class Consciousness and Inter-Class Sentiments," *Sociology Quarterly,* 6 (Autumn, 1965), 325-338.

LEWIS, Lionel S., "Class Consciousness and the Salience of Class," *Sociology and Social Research,* 49 (January, 1965), 173-182.

LEWIS, Lionel S., "Class and the Perception of Class," *Social Forces,* 42 (March, 1964), 336-340.

LIPSET, Seymour M., *Revolution and Counterrevolution: Change and Persistence in Social Structures,* New York: Basic Books, 1968.

LIPSET, Seymour M., "Trade Unions and Social Structure," *Industrial Relations,* 1 (October, 1961), 75-89.

LIPSET, Seymour M. and Reinhard Bendix, "Social Status and

CLASS CONSCIOUSNESS

Social Structure: A Re-examination of Data and Interpretations: I," *British Journal of Sociology,* 11 (June, 1951), 150-168.

LIPSET, Seymour M. and Reinhard Bendix, "Social Status and Social Structure: A Re-examination of Data and Interpretations, II," *British Journal of Sociology,* 11 (September, 1951), 230-254.

LOCKWOOD, David, *The Blackcoated Worker: A Study in Class Consciousness,* London: Unwin, 1958.

MANIS, Jerome G. and Bernard N. Meltzer, "Attitudes of Textile Workers to Class Structure," *American Journal of Sociology,* 60 (July, 1954), 30-35.

MANIS, Jerome G. and Bernard N. Meltzer, "Some Correlates of Class Consicousness Among Textile Workers," *American Journal of Sociology,* 69 (September, 1963), 177-184.

MARTIN, F. M., "Some Subjective Aspects of Social Stratification," in David Glass, editor, *Social Mobility in Britain,* London: Routledge and Kegan Paul, 1954.

MARX, Karl, *Capital, The Communist Manifesto, and Other Writings,* Edited by Max Eastman, New York: Modern Library, 1932.

MARX, Karl, *Early Writings,* Translated and edited by T. B. Bottomore, London: Watts, 1963.

MARX, Karl, *German Ideology,* New York: International Publishers, 1960.

MARX, Karl, *Selected Works,* Volumes I and II, Prepared by the Marx-Engels-Lenin Institute, Moscow, under the editorship of V. Adoratsky, London: Lawrence and Wishart, Limited, 1942.

MARX, Karl, *Selected Writings in Sociology and Social Philosophy,* edited by T. B. Bottomore and Maximilien Rubel, London: Watts, 1956.

MARX, Karl and Friedrich Engels, *Basic Writings on Politics and Philosophy,* edited by Lewis S. Feuer, Garden City, New York: Doubleday, 1959.

MARX, Karl and Friedrich Engels, *The Communist Manifesto,* New York: Washington Square Press, 1964.

MARX, Karl and Friedrich Engels, *On Britain,* Moscow: Foreign Languages Publishing House, 1953.

MARX, Karl and Friedrich Engels, *Selected Correspondence: 1846-1895,* Translated by Dona Torr, New York: International Publishers, 1942.

MATHIESEN, Thomas, "Aspects of Social Stratification in a Changing Community," *Acta Sociologica,* 4 (April, 1959), 42-54.

MORRIS, Richard T. and Raymond J. Murphy, "A Paradigm for

the Study of Class Consciousness," *Sociology and Social Research,* 50 (April, 1966), 297-313.

MULFORD, H. A. and W. W. Salisbury II, "Self-Conceptions in a General Population," *Sociological Quarterly,* 5 (Winter, 1964).

MURPHY, Raymond J. and Richard T. Morris, "Occupational Situs, Subjective Class Identification, and Political Affiliation," *American Sociological Review,* 26 (June, 1961), 383-392.

NISBET, Robert A., "The Decline and Fall of Social Class," *Pacific Sociological Review,* 2 (Spring, 1959), 11-17.

NORTH, Cecil C., "Class Structure, Class Consciousness, and Party Alignment," *American Sociological Review,* 2 (June, 1937), 356-371.

OSSOWSKI, Stanislaw, *Class Structure in the Social Consciousness,* translated from the Polish by Sheila Patterson, New York: Free Press, 1963.

OSSOWSKI, Stanislaw, "Different Conceptions of Social Class," in Reinhard Bendix and Seymour M. Lipset, editors, *Class Status and Power,* revised edition, New York: Free Press, 1966.

PENALOSA, Fernando and Edward C. McDonagh, "Education, Economic Status and Social-Class Awareness of Mexican-Americans," *Phylon,* 29 (Summer, 1968), 119-126.

PERLMAN, Selig, *A History of Trade Unionism in the United States,* New York: Macmillan, 1922.

PURCELL, Theodore V., *Blue-Collar Man: Patterns of Dual Allegiance in Industry,* Cambridge: Harvard University Press, 1960.

PURCELL, Theodore V., *The Worker Speaks His Mind on Company and Union,* Cambridge: Harvard University Press, 1953.

RETTIG, Salomon, Frank N. Jacobson, and Benjamin Pasamanick, "Status Overestimation, Objective Status, and Job Satisfaction Among Professions," *American Sociological Review,* 23 (February, 1958), 75-81.

ROBERTS, A. H. and R. Jessor, "Authoritarianism, Punitiveness, and Perceived Social Status," *Journal of Abnormal and Social Psychology,* 56 (1958), 311-314.

ROSE, Arnold M., "The Popular Meaning of Class Designation," *Sociology and Social Research,* 38 (September-October, 1953), 14-21.

ROSENBERG, Morris, "Perceptual Obstacles to Class Consciousness," *Social Forces,* 32 (October, 1953), 22-27.

CLASS CONSCIOUSNESS

ROTHSTEIN, Edward, "Attributes Related to High School Status: A Comparison of the Perceptions of Delinquent and Non-Delinquent Boys," *Social Problems,* 10 (Summer, 1962), 75-83.

RUNCIMAN, W. G., "'Embourgeoisement,' Self-Rated Class and Party Preference," *Sociological Review,* 12 (July, 1942), 137-154.

RUNCIMAN, W. G., *Relative Deprivation and Social Justice: A Study of Attitudes to Social Inequality in Twentieth-Century England,* Berkeley: University of California Press, 1966.

SAFILIOS-ROTHSCHILD, Constantina, "Class Position and Success Stereotypes in Greek and American Cultures," *Social Forces,* 45 (March, 1967), 374-383.

SARGENT, S. Stansfeld, "Class and Class-Consciousness in a California Town," *Social Problems,* 1 (June, 1953), 22-27.

SEGERSTEDT, Torgny T., "An Investigation of Class Consciousness Among Office Employees and Workers in Swedish Factories," *Transactions of the Second World Congress of Sociology,* 2 (1954), 298-308.

STAGNER, R., "Stereotypes of Workers and Executives Among College Men," *Journal of Abnormal and Social Psychology,* 45 (October, 1950), 743-748.

TUCKER, Charles W., "A Comparative Analysis of Subjective Social Class: 1945-1963," *Social Forces,* 46 (June, 1968), 508-514.

WEINSTEIN, Eugene A., "Children's Conceptions of Occupational Stratification," *Sociology and Social Research,* 42 (March-April, 1958), 278-284.

ZWEIG, F., "Analysis of Class Consciousness," *Kyklos,* 13 (1960), 386-396.

General Treatments and Miscellaneous Correlates

ABRAMSON, A., "Our Status System and Scholastic Rewards," *Journal of Educational Sociology,* 25 (1952), 441-450.

ABRAMSON, J. H., "Emotional Disorder, Status Inconsistency and Migration," *Milbank Memorial Fund Quarterly,* 44 (January, 1966), 23-48.

ANDERSON, C. Arnold, "Social Class Differentials in the Schooling of Youth within the Regions and Community-Size Groups of the United States," *Social Forces,* 25 (1947), 434-440.

GENERAL TREATMENTS

ANDERSON, C. Arnold, "Social Class as a Factor in the Assimilation of Women into Higher Education," *Acta Sociologica,* 4 (1959), 27-32.

BECKER, Howard S., "Social Class Variations in the Teacher-Pupil Relationship," *Journal of Educational Sociology,* 25 (April, 1952), 451-465.

BECKER, Howard S., "The Teacher in the Authority System of the Public School," *Journal of Educational Sociology,* 27 (November, 1953), 128-141.

BENNETT, John W., "Food and Social Status in a Rural Society," *American Sociological Review,* 8 (October, 1943), 561-569.

BENTZ, W. Kenneth, "The Relationship between Educational Background and the Referral Role of Ministers," *Sociology and Social Research,* 51 (January, 1967), 199-208.

BERNSTEIN, B., "Some Sociological Determinants of Perception," *British Journal of Sociology,* 9 (June, 1958), 159-174.

BRADBURN, Norman M., *The Structure of Psychological Well Being,* Chicago: Aldine, 1969.

BURNIGHT, Robert G. and Parker G. Marden, "Social Correlates of Weight in an Aging Population," *Milbank Memorial Fund Quarterly,* 45 (April, 1967), 75-92.

BURTON, William H., "Education and Social Class in the United States," *Harvard Educational Review,* 23 (Fall, 1953), 243-256.

CANNON, Kenneth L., "The Relationship of Social Acceptance to Socio-Economic Status and Residence Among High-School Students," *Rural Sociology,* 22 (June, 1957), 142-148.

CHAPIN, F. Stuart, Clarence Johanson, and Arthur L. Johnson, "Rental Rates and Crowding in Dwelling Units in Manhattan," *American Sociological Review,* 15 (February, 1950), 95-97.

CHAPMAN, Dennis, *The Home and Social Status,* London: Routledge and Kegan Paul, 1955.

COLLISON, Peter, "Occupation, Education, and Housing in an English City," *American Journal of Sociology,* 65 (May, 1960), 588-597.

COSTER, John K., "Some Characteristics of High School Pupils From Three Income Groups," *Journal of Educational Psychology,* 50 (April, 1959), 55-62.

DAVIE, James S., "Social Class Factors and School Attendance," *Harvard Educational Review,* 23 (Summer, 1953), 175-185.

DAVIS, Allison, *Social Class Influences Upon Learning,* Cambridge: Harvard University Press, 1948.

DAVIS, Allison, Burleigh Gardner, and Mary R. Gardner, *Deep South,* Chicago: University of Chicago Press, 1941.

DAVIS, Kingsley, "Mental Hygiene and the Class Structure," *Psychiatry,* 1 (February, 1938), 55-65.

DOLLARD, John, "Drinking Mores of the Social Classes," in *Alcohol, Science and Society,* New Haven: Quarterly Journal of Studies on Alcohol, 1945.

DOUGLAS, J. W. B., *The Home and the School,* New York: Hillary House, 1964.

ELLIS, Robert A., "Social Status and Social Distance," *Sociology and Social Research,* 40 (March-April, 1956), 240-246.

FALD, Gerhard J., "The Role of Social Class Differences and Horizontal Mobility in the Etiology of Aggression," *Journal of Educational Sociology,* 33 (September, 1959), 1-10.

FELDMESSER, R. A., "Social Status and Access to Higher Education: A Comparison of the United States and the Soviet Union," *Harvard Educational Review,* 27 (1957), 92-106.

FLOUD, Jean E., A. H. Halsey, and F. M. Martin, editors, *Social Class and Educational Opportunity,* London: Heinemann, 1956.

FREEDMAN, Ronald and Amos H. Hawley, "Education and Occupation of Migrants in the Depression," *American Journal of Sociology,* 56 (September, 1950), 161-166.

FREEMAN, Howard E. and Ozzie G. Simmons, "Social Class and Posthospital Performance Levels," *American Sociological Review,* 24 (June, 1959), 345-351.

GAMSON, William A., *Power and Discontent,* Homewood, Illinois: Dorsey, 1968.

GEORGE, Katherine and Charles H. George, "Roman Catholic Sainthood and Social Status," in Reinhard Bendix and Seymour M. Lipset, editors, *Class, Status and Power,* revised edition, New York: Free Press, 1966.

GLENN, Norval D. and Jon P. Alston, "Cultural Distances Among Occupational Categories," *American Sociological Review,* 33 (June, 1968), 365-382.

GLENN, Norval D. and Jon P. Alston, "Rural-Urban Differences in Reported Attitudes and Behavior," *South-*

western *Social Science Quarterly,* 47 (March, 1967),
381-400.

GOETSCH, Helen B., *Parental Income and College Opportunities,* Teachers College Contributions to Education, No. 795, Columbia University, 1940.

GOFFMAN, Erving, "Symbols of Class Status," *British Journal of Sociology,* 2 (December, 1951), 294-304.

GOLDSTEIN, Sidney and Kurt Mayer, "Demographic Correlates of Status Differences in a Metropolitan Population," *Urban Studies,* 2 (May, 1965), 67-84.

GOLDSTEIN, Sidney and Kurt Mayer, "Migration and Social Status Differentials in the Journey to Work," *Rural Sociology,* 29 (September, 1964), 278-287.

GOODCHILDS, Jacqueline D. and E. E. Smith, "The Effects of Unemployment as Mediated by Social Status," *Sociometry,* 26 (September, 1963), 287-293.

GRAVES, Theodore D., "Acculturation, Access, and Alcohol in a Tri-Ethnic Community," *American Anthropologist,* 69 (June-August, 1967), 306-321.

GREENE, James E., "Demographic Correlates of Educational Status Among Adults," *Journal of Educational Sociology,* 22 (May, 1949), 581-590.

GUSFIELD, Joseph R., *Symbolic Crusade: Status Politics and the American Temperance Movement,* Urbana: University of Illinois Press, 1963.

HAMILTON, Richard F., "Affluence and the Worker: The West German Case," *American Journal of Sociology,* 71 (September, 1965), 144-152.

HAMILTON, Richard F., "A Research Note on the Mass Support for 'Tough' Military Initiatives," *American Sociological Review,* 33 (June, 1968), 439-445.

HAVIGHURST, Robert J., Robert H. Bowman, Gordon P. Liddle, and Charles V. Pierce, *Growing Up in River City,* New York: Wiley, 1962.

HERRIOT, Robert E. and Nancy H. St. John, *Social Class and the Urban School: The Impact of Pupil Backgrounds on Teachers and Principals,* New York: Wiley, 1966.

HOLLINGSHEAD, August B., *Elmtown's Youth,* New York: Wiley, 1949.

HOLLINGSHEAD, August B., "Selected Characteristics of Classes in a Middle Western Community," *American Sociological Review,* 12 (August, 1947), 385-395.

GENERAL
TREATMENTS

HOLLY, D. N., "Profiting from a Comprehensive School: Sex, Class, and Ability," *British Journal of Sociology,* 16 (June, 1965), 150-158.

INKELES, Alex, "Industrial Man: The Relation of Status to Experience, Perception, and Value," *American Journal of Sociology,* 66 (July, 1960), 1-31.

GENERAL
TREATMENTS

JEFFREY, C. Ray, "Social Class and Adoption Petitioners," *Social Problems,* 9 (Spring, 1962), 354-358.

KARPINOS, Bernard D., "School Attendance as Affected by Prevailing Socio-Economic Factors," *School Review,* 51 (January, 1943), 39-49.

KELLER, Suzanne, "Social Class in Physical Planning," *International Social Science Journal,* 18 (1966), 494-512.

KEPHART, William M., "Status After Death," *American Sociological Review,* 15 (October, 1950), 635-643.

KING, Morton B., "Socioeconomic Status and Sociometric Choice," *Social Forces,* 39 (March, 1961), 199-206.

KNUPFER, Genevieve and Robin Room, "Age, Sex, and Social Class as Factors in Amount of Drinking in a Metropolitan Community," *Social Problems,* 12 (Fall, 1964).

KODMAN, Frank, Jr., Carl Spies, Kenneth Stockdell, and Gordon Sedlacek, "Socio-Economic Status and Observer Identification of Hearing Loss in School Children," *Exceptional Children,* 26 (December, 1959), 176-188.

LINN, Erwin L., "Patients' Socio-economic Characteristics and Release from a Mental Hospital," *American Journal of Sociology,* 65 (November, 1959), 280-286.

LINN, Erwin L., "Social Stratification of Discussions about Local Affairs," *American Journal of Sociology,* 72 (May, 1967), 660-668.

LIPSET, Seymour M. and Natalie Rogoff, "Class and Opportunity in Europe and America," *Commentary,* 18 (1954), 562-568.

LITTLE, Alan and John Westergaard, "The Trend of Class Differentials in Educational Opportunity in England and Wales," *British Journal of Sociology,* 15 (December, 1964), 301-316.

LOFLAND, John F. and Robert A. Lejeune, "Initial Interaction of Newcomers in Alcoholics Anonymous: A Field Experiment in Class Symbols and Socialization," *Social Problems,* 8 (Fall, 1960), 102-111.

LONDON, Jack and Robert Wenkert, "Obstacles to Blue-Collar Participation in Adult Education," in Arthur B. Shostak and William Gomberg, editors, *Blue-Collar World: Studies of the American Worker*, Englewood Cliffs, New Jersey: Prentice Hall, 1964.

LOOMIS, Charles P. and Charles Proctor, "The Relationship between Choice Status and Economic Status in Social Systems," *Sociometry*, 13 (November, 1950), 307-313.

LOPREATO, Joseph and Janet Saltzman, "Descriptive Models of Peasant Society: A Reconciliation from Southern Italy," *Human Organization*, 27 (Summer, 1968), 132-142.

LUCHTERHAND, Elmer and Leonard Weller, "Social Class and the Desegregation Movement: A Study of Parents' Decisions in a Negro Ghetto," *Social Problems*, 13 (Summer, 1965), 83-88.

LYNES, Russell, "Highbrow, Lowbrow, Middlebrow," *Harper's Magazine*, 198 (February, 1949), 19-28.

MACK, Raymond W., "Housing as an Index of Social Class," *Social Forces*, 29 (May, 1951), 391-400.

MARSH, Robert M., *Comparative Sociology*, New York: Harcourt, Brace and World, 1967.

MARTIN, John W., "Social Distance and Social Stratification," *Sociology and Social Research*, 47 (January, 1963), 179-186.

MAYER, Albert J. and Thomas Ford Hoult, "Social Stratification and Combat Survival," *Social Forces*, 34 (December, 1955), 155-159.

MULLIGAN, Raymond A., "Socio-Economic Background and College Enrollment," *American Sociological Review*, 16 (April, 1951), 188-196.

PHILLIPS, Walter, "The Influence of Social Class on Education: Some Institutional Imperatives," *Berkeley Journal of Sociology*, 5 (Fall, 1959).

PIHLBLAD, C. T. and C. L. Gregory, "Occupation and Patterns of Migration," *Social Forces*, 36 (October, 1957), 56-64.

REQUENA, B. Mariano, "Social and Economic Correlates of Induced Abortion in Santiago, Chile," *Demography*, 2 (1965), 33-49.

ROEMER, Milton J., "Medical Care and Social Class in Latin America," *Milbank Memorial Fund Quarterly*, 42 (July, 1964), 54-64.

ROSE, Arnold M., "Distance of Migration and Socio-Economic Status of Migrants," *American Sociological Review*, 23 (August, 1958), 420-423.

SABAGH, Georges, Richard K. Eyman, and Donald N. Cogburn, "The Speed of Hospitalization: A Study of a Preadmission Waiting List Cohort in a Hospital for the Retarded," *Social Problems,* 14 (Fall, 1966), 119-128.

SAMPSON, Edward E., "Status Congruence and Cognitive Consistency," *Sociometry,* 26 (June, 1963), 146-162.

SCHAEFER, Janet and Marjorie Allen, "Class and Regional Selection in Fatal Casualties in the First 18-24 Months of World War II," *Social Forces,* 23 (December, 1944), 165-169.

SCHOMMER, C. O., "Socio-Economic Background and Religious Knowledge of Catholic College Students," *American Catholic Sociological Review,* 21 (1960), 229-237.

SCHWARZWELLER, Harry K., "Education, Migration, and Economic Life Chances of Male Entrants to the Labor Force from a Low-Income Rural Area," *Rural Sociology,* 29 (June, 1964), 152-167.

SCHWARZWELLER, Harry K. and James S. Brown, "Social Class Origins, Rural-Urban Migration, and Economic Life Chances: A Case Study," *Rural Sociology,* 32 (March, 1967), 5-19.

SEGAL, Bernard E., "Nurses and Patients: A Case Study of Stratification," *Journal of Health and Human Behavior,* 5 (Spring, 1964), 54-60.

SEXTON, Patricia C., *Education and Income,* New York: The Viking Press, 1961, 72-74.

SEXTON, Patricia C., "Social Class and Pupil Turnover Rates," *Journal of Educational Sociology,* 33 (November, 1959), 131-134.

SIMPSON, Angel P., "Social Class Correlates of Old Age," *Sociology and Social Research,* 45 (January, 1961), 131-139.

SIMS, V. M., "Some Correlates of Social Class Identification Among High-School and College Students," *School Review,* 60 (1952), 160-163.

SJOBERG, Gideon, Richard A. Brymer and Buford Faris, "Bureaucracy and the Lower Class," *Sociology and Social Research,* 50 (April, 1966), 325-337.

SMITH, Benjamin F., "Wishes of Negro High School Seniors and Social Class Status," *Journal of Educational Sociology,* 25 (April, 1952), 466-475.

SMITH, Mapheus, "The Differential Impact of Selective Service Inductions on Occupations in the United States,"; *American Sociological Review,* 11 (October, 1946), 567-572.

SMITH, Mapheus, "Occupational Differentials in Physical Status," *American Sociological Review,* 13 (February, 1948), 72-82.

GENERAL
TREATMENTS

SMITH, P., "A Study of the Selective Character of American Education: Participation in School Activities as Conditioned by Socio-Economic Status and Other Factors," *Journal of Educational Psychology*, 36 (1945), 229-246.

STRAUS, Robert, "Some Sociocultural Considerations In the Care of Patients with Myocardial Infraction," *Journal of Health and Human Behavior*, 1 (Summer, 1960), 119-122.

SUDNOW, David, *Passing On: The Social Organization of Dying*, Englewood Cliffs, New Jersey: Prentice Hall, 1967.

SUTTLES, Wayne, "Private Knowledge, Morality, and Social Classes Among the Coast Salish," *American Anthropologist*, 60 (June, 1958), 497-507.

SVALASTOGA, Kaare, E. Hogh, M. Pederson, and E. Schild, "Differential Class Behavior in Denmark," *American Sociological Review*, 21 (August, 1956), 435-439.

TARVER, James D., "Occupational Migration Differentials," *Social Forces*, 43 (December, 1964), 231-241.

TILLY, Charles, "Occupational Rank and Grade of Residence in a Metropolis," *American Journal of Sociology*, 67 (November, 1961), 323-330.

TRIANDIS, Harry C., Vasso Vassiliou, and Erich K. Thomanek, "Social Status as a Determinent of Respect and Friendship Acceptance," *Sociometry*, 29 (December, 1966), 396-405.

TURNBILL, W. W., "Socio-economic Status and Predictive Test Scores," *Canadian Journal of Psychology*, 5 (1951), 145-149.

VOLBERDING, E., "Out of School Living of 11 Year-Old Boys and Girls from Differing Socio-Economic Groups," *Elementary School Journal*, 49 (February, 1949).

WARNER, W. Lloyd, R. J. Havighurst, and Martin B. Loeb, *Who Shall Be Educated?* New York: Harper, 1945.

WARNER, W. Lloyd and Paul S. Lunt, *The Social Life of a Modern Community*, New Haven: Yale University Press, 1941.

WECKLER, Nora L., "Social Class and School Adjustment in Relation to Character Reputation," in R. J. Havighurst and Hilda Taba, editors, *Adolescent Character and Personality*, New York: Wiley, 1949.

WEINBERG, Carl, "Educational Level and Perceptions of Los Angeles Negroes of Educational Conditions in a Riot Area," *Journal of Negro Education*, 36 (Fall, 1967), 377-384.

WEINSTOCK, S. Alexander, "Role Elements: A Link Between Acculturation and Occupational Status," *British Journal of Sociology*, 14 (June, 1963), 144-149.

WILSON, Everett K., *Sociology: Rules, Roles, and Relationships,* Homewood, Illinois: Dorsey, 1966, Chapter 5, "Class Differences in the Transmission of Culture."

Social Mobility:

General Treatments and Special Topics

A large percentage of the publications listed here deal with rates and trends in inter-generational occupational mobility. Since most studies of vertical mobility deal with inter-generational changes, we do not have a special topic for this kind of study, as we do for treatments of career mobility.

ABEGGLEN, James C., and H. Mannari, "Leaders of Modern Japan: Social Origins and Mobility," *Economic Development and Culture Change,* 9 (1960), 109-134.

ADAMS, Stuart, "Regional Differences in Vertical Mobility in a High-Status Occupation," *American Sociological Review,* 15 (April, 1950), 228-235.

ALLINGHAM, John D., "Class Regression: An Aspect of the Social Stratification Process," *American Sociological Review,* 32 (June, 1967), 442-449.

ANDRZEJEWSKI, Stanislaw, "Vertical Mobility and Technical Progress," *Social Forces,* 29 (October, 1950), 48-51.

ASTROM, Sven-Erik, "Literature on Social Mobility and Social Stratification in Finland: Some Bibliographical Notes," *Transactions of the Westermarck Society,* 2 (1953), 221-227.

BENDIX, Reinhard and Frank W. Howton, "Social Mobility and the American Business Elite," *British Journal of Sociology,* 9 (March, 1958), 1-14.

BENJAMIN, B., "Inter-Generation Differences in Occupation: A Sample Comparison, in England and Wales, of Census and Birth Registration Records," *Population Studies,* 11 (March, 1958), 262-268.

BENNETT, Claude, "Mobility from Full-Time to Part-Time Farming," *Rural Sociology,* 32 (June, 1967), 154-164.

BILLEWICZ, W. Z., "Some Remarks on the Measurement of Social Mobility," *Population Studies,* 9 (July, 1955), 96-100.

BLALOCK, Hubert, M. Jr., "Status Inconsistency, Social Mobility, Status Integration and Structural Effects," *American Sociological Review,* 32 (October, 1967), 790-801.

BLAU, Peter M., "The Flow of Occupational Supply and Recruitment," *American Sociological Review,* 30 (August, 1965), 475-490.

BLAU, Peter M., "Inferring Mobility Trends from a Single Study," *Population Studies,* 16 (July, 1962), 79-85.

BLAU, Peter M. and Otis Dudley Duncan, *The American Occupational Structure,* New York: Wiley, 1967.

BLOOMBAUM, Milton, "The Mobility Dimensions of Status Consistency," *Sociology and Social Research,* 48 (April, 1964), 340-347.

BOALT, Gunnar, "Social Mobility in Stockholm: A Pilot Investigation," *Transactions of the Second World Congress of Sociology,* 2 (1954), 67-73.

BOLTE, Karl Martin, "Some Aspects of Social Mobility in Western Germany," *Transactions of the World Congress of Sociology,* 3 (1956), 183-190.

BOSSARD, James H. S., "Marriage as a Status Achieving Device," *Sociology and Social Research,* 29 (September-October, 1944), 3-10.

BOSSARD, James H. S. and W. P. Sanger, "Social Mobility and the Child: A Case Study," *Journal of Abnormal and Social Psychology,* 44 (April, 1949), 266-271.

BROTZ, Howard M., "A Comparative Study of Social Mobility," *Sociological Quarterly,* 1 (October, 1960), 239-244.

CARLSSON, Gosta, *Social Mobility and Class Structure,* Lund: Gleerup, 1958.

CARLSSON, Gosta, "Sorokin's Theory of Social Mobility," in Philip J. Allen, editor, *Pitirim A. Sorokin in Review,* Durham: Duke University Press, 1963.

CENTERS, Richard, "Marital Selection and Occupational Strata," *American Journal of Sociology,* 54 (May, 1949), 530-535.

CENTERS, Richard, "Occupational Mobility of Urban Occupational Strata," *American Sociological Review,* 13

(April, 1948), 197-203.

CHANDRASHEKARAIYAH, K., "Mobility Patterns Within the Caste," *Sociological Bulletin,* 11(1961) 62-67.

CHINOY, Ely, *Automobile Workers and the American Dream,* Garden City, New York: Doubleday, 1955.

CHINOY, Ely, "Social Mobility Trends in the United States," *American Sociological Review,* 20 (April, 1955), 180-186.

CHOW, Jung-Teh, *Social Mobility in China: Status Careers Among the Gentry in a Chinese Community,* New York: Atherton, 1966.

CLARK, Burton R., "The 'Cooling Out' Function in Higher Education," *American Journal of Sociology,* 65 (May, 1960), 569-576.

COATES, Charles H. and Roland J. Pellegrin, "Executives and Supervisors: A Situational Theory of Differential Occupational Mobility," *Social Forces,* 35 (December, 1956), 121-126.

CROCKETT, Harry J., Jr., "The Achievement Motive and Differential Occupational Mobility in the United States," *American Sociological Review,* 27 (April, 1962), 191-204.

CURTIS, Richard F., "Conceptual Problems in Social Mobility Research," *Sociology and Social Research,* 45 (July, 1961), 387-395.

CURTIS, Richard F., "Occupational Mobility and Urban Social Life," *American Journal of Sociology,* 65 (November, 1959), 296-298.

CUTRIGHT, Phillips, "Occupational Inheritance: A Cross-National Analysis," *American Journal of Sociology,* 73 (January, 1968), 400-416.

CUTRIGHT, Phillips, "Studying Cross National Mobility Rates," *Acta Sociologica,* 11 (1968), 170-176.

DAMLE, Y. B., "Reference Group Theory With Regard to Mobility in Caste," *Social Action,* 13 (1963), 190-199.

DAVIDSON, Percy E. and H. Dewey Anderson, *Occupational Mobility in an American Community,* Stanford: Stanford University Press, 1937.

DEASY, Leila C., "An Index of Social Mobility," *Rural Sociology,* 20, (June, 1955), 149-151.

DOUVAN, Elizabeth and Joseph Adelson, "The Psychodynamics of Social Mobility in Adolescent Boys," *Journal of Abnormal and Social Psychology* 56 (January, 1958), 31-44.

DUNCAN, Otis Dudley, "Methodological Issues in the Analysis of Social Mobility," in Neil J. Smelser and Seymour M. Lipset, editors, *Social Structure and Social Mobility in Economic Development,* Chicago: Aldine, 1966.

DUNCAN, Otis Dudley, "The Trend of Occupational Mobility in the United States," *American Sociological Review,* 30 (August, 1965), 491-498.

EBERHARD, Wolfram, *Social Mobility in Traditional China,* Leiden, Netherlands: Brill, 1962.

EDWARDS, G. Franklin, *The Negro Professional Class,* New York: Free Press, 1959.

EISENSTADT, S. N., "Social Mobility and the Evaluation of Intergroup Leadership," *Transactions of the Second World Congress of Sociology,* 2 (1954), 218-230.

FALLERS, Lloyd A., "A Note on the 'Trickle Effect'," *Public Opinion Quarterly,* 18 (Fall, 1954), 314-321.

FELDMAN, Arnold H., "Economic Development and Social Mobility," *Economic Development and Cultural Change,* 8 (April, 1960), 311-321.

FOLKMAN, William S. and James D. Cowhig, "Intergenerational Occupational Mobility in a Rural Area," *Rural Sociology,* 28 (December, 1963), 405-407.

FOOTE, Nelson N. and Paul K. Hatt, "Social Mobility and Economic Advancement," *American Economic Review,* 43 (May, 1953), 364-378.

FOX, Thomas and S. M. Miller, "Intra-Country Variations: Occupational Stratification and Mobility," in Reinhard Bendix and Seymour M. Lipset, editors, *Class, Status, and Power,* revised edition, Free Press, 1966.

GABOR, Andre, "The Concept of Statistical Freedom and Its Application to Social Mobility," *Population Studies,* 9 (July, 1955), 82-95.

GEIGER, Theodor, "A Dynamic Analysis of Social Mobility," *Acta Sociologica,* 1 (1955), 26-38.

GESCHWENDER, James A., "On the Proper Use of the GOMS," *Social Forces,* 46 (June, 1968), 545-546.

GESCHWENDER, James A., "Theory and Measurement of Occupational Mobility: A Re-examination," *American Sociological Review,* 26 (June, 1961), 451-452.

GLASS, David V., editor, *Social Mobility in Britain,* London: Routledge, and Kegan Paul, 1954.

GLASS, David V., "Social Stratification and Social Mobility,"

International Social Science Bulletin, 6 (1954), 12-24.

GOFFMAN, Erving, "On Cooling the Mark Out: Some Adaptations to Failure," *Psychiatry,* 15 (1952), 451-463.

GOLDNER, Fred H., "Demotion in Industrial Management," *American Sociological Review,* 30 (October, 1965), 714-724.

GOLDNER, Fred H., and R. R. Ritti, "Professionalization as Career Immobility," *American Journal of Sociology,* 72 (March, 1967), 489-502.

GOLDSTEIN, Sidney, *et al, The Morristown Study: An Experiment in Interdisciplinary Research Training,* Philadelphia: University of Pennsylvania Press, 1961.

GOODMAN, Leo A., "On the Statistical Analysis of Mobility Tables," *American Journal of Sociology,* 70 (March, 1965), 564-585.

GOULDNER, Alvin W., *Patterns of Industrial Bureaucracy,* New York: Free Press, 1954.

GUEST, Robert H., "Managerial Succession," *American Journal of Sociology,* 68 (January, 1962), 45-74.

GUPTA, B. K. D., "Caste-Mobility Among the Mahato of South Manbhum," *Man in India,* 42 (1962), 228-236.

HALL, J. R., "A Comparison of the Degree of Social Endogamy in England and Wales and the U. S. A.," in David V. Glass, editor, *Social Mobility in Great Britain,* London: Routledge and Kegan Paul, 1954.

HALL, J. R. and W. A. Ziegel, "A Comparison of Social Mobility Data for England, Wales, Italy, France, and the U. S. A.," in David V. Glass, editor, *Social Mobility in Britain,* London: Routledge and Kegan Paul, 1954.

HALLER, Archibald O., "The Occupational Achievement Process of Farm-Reared Youth in Urban-Industrial Society," *Rural Sociology,* 25 (September, 1960), 321-333.

HALLER, Archibald O., "Research Problems on the Occupational Achievement Levels of Farm-Reared People," *Rural Sociology,* 23 (December, 1958), 355-362.

HALSEY, A. H., "Social Mobility in Britain—A Review," *Sociological Review,* 2 (December, 1954), 169-177.

HARE, Nathan, "Recent Trends in the Occupational Mobility of Negroes, 1930-1960: An Intracohort Analysis," *Social Forces,* 44 (December, 1965), 166-173.

HARGENS, Lowell L. and Warren O. Hagstrom, "Sponsored and Contest Mobility of American Academic Scientists," *Sociology of Education,* 40 (Winter, 1967), 24-38.

HERTZLER, J. O., "Some Tendencies Toward a Closed Class System in the United States," *Social Forces,* 30 (March, 1952), 313-323.

SOCIAL MOBILITY

HIMES, Joseph S., Jr., "The Factor of Social Mobility in Teaching Marriage Courses in Negro Colleges," *Social Forces,* 30 (May, 1952), 439-443.

HO, Ping-Ti, *The Ladder of Success in Imperial China: Aspects of Social Mobility, 1368-1911,* New York: Columbia University Press, 1962.

HSU, Francis L. K., "Social Mobility in China," *American Sociological Review,* 14 (December, 1949), 764-771.

HSU, Francis L. K., *Under the Ancestor's Shadow: Kinship, Personality, and Social Mobility in Village China,* Garden City, New York: Doubleday, 1967.

HUTCHINSON, Bertram, "Social Mobility Rates in Buenos Aires, Montevideo, and Sao Paulo: A Preliminary Comparison," *America Latina,* 5 (1962), 3-20.

HUTCHINSON, Bertram, "Urban Mobility Rates in Brazil Related to Migration and Changing Occupational Structure," *America Latina,* 6, (1963), 47-60.

INKELES, Alex, "Social Stratification and Mobility in the Soviet Union, 1940-1950," *American Sociological Review,* 15 (August, 1950), 465-479.

JACKSON, Brian, *Streaming: An Education System in Miniature,* London: Routledge and Kegan Paul, 1964.

JACKSON, Elton F. and Harry J. Crockett, Jr., "Occupational Mobility in the United States: A Point Estimate and Trend Comparison," *American Sociological Review,* 29 (February, 1964), 5-15.

JAFFE, A. J. and R. O. Carleton, *Occuational Mobility in the United States, 1930-1960,* New York: King's Crown Press, 1954.

JANOWITZ, Morris, "Social Stratification and Mobility in West Germany," *American Journal of Sociology,* 64 (July, 1958), 6-24.

KAUFMAN, Harold F., Kenneth P. Wilkinson, and Lucy W. Cole, *Poverty Programs and Social Mobility,* State College, Mississippi: Social Science Research Center, 1966.

KIDO, Kotaro and Masataka Sugi, "A Report of Research on Social Stratification and Mobility in Tokyo - (III)," *Japanese Sociological Review,* 5 (1954), 74-100.

KNOWLTON, Clark S., "A Study of Social Mobility Among

the Syrian and Lebanese Community of Sao Paulo,"
Rocky Mountain Social Science Journal, 2 (October, 1965),
174-192.

KOLKO, Gabriel, "Economic Mobility and Social Stratification," *American Journal of Sociology,* 63 (July, 1957),
30-38.

KOSA, J., "Patterns of Social Mobility Among American
Catholics," *Social Compass,* 9 (1962), 361-371.

KUBAT, Daniel, "Social Mobility in Czechoslovakia,"
American Sociological Review, 28 (April, 1963), 203-212.

LEE, G. C., "Government and Educational Mobility in a
Democracy," *Harvard Educational Review,* 23 (Summer,
1953), 211-227.

LENSKI, Gerhard E., "Trends in Inter-Generational Occupational Mobility in the United States," *American Sociological Review,* 23 (October, 1958), 514-523.

LIPSET, Seymour M., "Research Problems in the Comparative
Analysis of Mobility and Development," *International
Social Science Journal,* 16 (1964), 35-48.

LIPSET, Seymour M. and Reinhard Bendix, "Ideological
Equalitarianism and Social Mobility in the United States,"
Transactions of the Second World Congress of Sociology,
2 (1954), 34-54.

LIPSET, Seymour M. and Reinhard Bendix, *Social Mobility
in Industrial Society,* Berkeley: University of California
Press, 1959.

LIPSET, Seymour M. and Natalie Rogoff, "Class and Opportunity in Europe and the U. S.: Some Myths and What
the Statistics Show," *Commentary,* 18 (1954), 562-568.

LIPSET, Seymour M. and Hans L. Zetterberg, "A Theory of
Social Mobility," in Reinhard Bendix and Seymour
M. Lipset, editors, *Class, Status and Power,* revised edi-
tion, Free Press, 1966.

LOPREATO, Joseph, *Peasants No More: Social Class and
Social Change in Southern Italy,* San Francisco: Chandler,
1967.

LOPREATO, Joseph, "Social Mobility in Italy," *American
Journal of Sociology,* 71 (November, 1965), 311-314.

LUIJCKX, A. W., "Inquiry into the Mobility of Employment
in the Dutch Middle Class," *Transactions of the Second
World Congress of Sociology,* 2 (1954), 89-90.

LYSTAD, Mary H., "Social Mobility Among Selected Groups
of Schizophrenic Patients," *American Sociological Review,*

22 (June, 1957), 288-292.

MacGAFFEY, Wyatt, " Social Structure and Mobility in Cuba," *Anthropological Quarterly*, 34 (April, 1961), 94-109.

SOCIAL MOBILITY MacPHERSON, J. S., *Eleven-Year-Olds Grow. Up*, London: University of London Press, 1958.

MARSH, Robert M., "Formal Organization and Promotion in a Pre-industrial Society," *American Sociological Review*, 26 (August, 1961), 547-556.

MARSH, Robert M., *The Mandarins: The Circulation of Elites in China, 1600-1900*, New York: Free Press, 1961.

MARSH, Robert M., "Values, Demand and Social Mobility," *American Sociological Review*, 28 (August, 1963), 565-575.

MARSHALL, T. H., "Social Selection in the Welfare State," in *Class, Citizenship, and Social Development*, Garden City, New York: Doubleday, 1965.

MARSHALL, T. H., "Social Selection in the Welfare State," in Reinhard Bendix and Seymour M. Lipset, editors, *Class, Status and Power*, New York: Free Press, 1966.

MATRAS, Judah, "Comparison of Intergenerational Occupational Mobility Patterns: An Application of the Formal Theory of Social Mobility," *Population Studies*, 14 (November, 1960), 163-169.

MATRAS, Judah, "Differential Fertility, Intergenerational Occupational Mobility, and Change in the Occupational Distribution: Some Elementary Inter-relationships," *Population Studies*, 15 (November, 1961), 187-197.

MATRAS, Judah, "Social Mobility and Social Structure: Some Insights from the Linear Models," *American Sociological Review*, 32 (August, 1967), 608-614.

MATRAS, Judah, "Some Data on Intergenerational Occupational Mobility in Israel," *Population Studies*, 17 (November, 1963), 167-186.

MAYER, Kurt B., "Social Mobility: America versus Europe," *Commentary*, 19 (1955), 395-396.

MERTON, Robert K. and Alice Kitt Rossi, "Reference Group Theory and Social Mobility," in Reinhard Bendix and Seymour M. Lipset, editors, *Class, Status, and Power*, 2nd edition, New York: Free Press, 1966.

McGUIRE, Carson, "Social Stratification and Mobility Patterns," *American Sociological Review*, 15 (April, 1950), 195-204.

MILIC, Vojin, "General Trends in Social Mobility in Yugoslavia," *Acta Sociologica*, 9 (1965), 116-136.

MILLER, S. M., "Comparative Social Mobility," *Current Sociology,* 9 (1960), 1-80.

MILLER, S. M., "The Concept of Mobility," *Social Problems,* 3 (October, 1955), 65-73.

MILLER, S. M., "The Concept and Measurement of Mobility," *Transactions of the Third World Congress of Sociology,* 3 (1956), 144-154.

MORRIS, Richard, "Where Success Begins: Rags to Riches- Myth and Reality," *Saturday Review,* (November, 21, 1953), 65-71.

MUKERJEE, Radhakamal, "Mobility, Ecological and Social," *Social Forces,* 21 (December, 1942), 154-159.

MUKHERJEE, Ramkrishna and John R. Hall, "A Note on the Analysis of Data on Social Mobility," in David V. Glass, editor, *Social Mobility in Britain,* London: Routledge and Kegan Paul, 1954.

NEWCOMER, Mabel, *The Big Business Executive,* New York: Columbia University Press, 1955.

NISHIHIRA, Sigeki, "Cross-National Comparative Study on Social Stratification and Social Mobility," *Annals of the Institute of Statistical Mathematics,* 8 (1957), 181-191.

NOEL, Edward, "Sponsored and Contest Mobility in America and England," *Comparative Education Review,* 6 (October, 1962), 148-151.

NOWAKOWSKI, Stefan, "Peasant-Workers: Some Aspects of Social Mobility in Post-War Poland," *Transactions of the Third World Congress of Sociology,* 3 (1956), 330-337.

ODAKA, Kunio and Sigeki Nishihira, "Some Factors Related to Social Mobility in Japan," *Annals of the Institute of Statistical Mathematics,* 10 (1959), 283-288.

ODAKA, Kunio and Sigeki Nishihira, "Social Mobility in Japan: A Report on the 1955 Survey," *East Asian Cultural Studies,* 4 (March, 1965), 83-126.

PALMER, Gladys L. and C. P. Brainerd, *Labor Mobility in Six Cities: A Report on the Survey of Patterns and Factors in Labor Mobility, 1940-1950,* New York: Social Science Research Council, 1954.

PAPE, Ruth H., "Touristry: A Type of Occupational Mobility," *Social Problems,* 11 (Spring, 1964), 336-344.

PARETO, Vilfredo, *The Mind and Society,* London: Jonathan Cape, 1935.

PENALOSA, Fernando and Edward C. McDonagh, "Social

Mobility in a Mexican-American Community," *Social Forces,* 44 (June, 1966), 498-505.

PERROY, E., "Social Mobility Among the French Noblesse in the Later Middle Ages," *Past and Present,* 21(1962), 25-38.

PETERSON, William, "Is America Still the Land of Opportunity? What Recent Studies Show About Social Mobility," *Commentary* (November, 1953), 477-486.

PIHLBLAD, C. T. and C. L. Gregory, "Occupational Mobility in Small Communities in Missouri," *Rural Sociology,* 22 (March, 1957), 40-49.

PORTER, John, "The Future of Upward Mobility," *American Sociological Review,* 33 (February, 1968), 5-19.

PRAIS, S. J., "The Formal Theory of Social Mobility," *Population Studies,* 9 (July, 1955), 72-81.

PRAIS, S. J., "Measuring Social Mobility," *Statistical Journal,* 118 (1955), 56-66.

RAMSOY, Natalie Rogoff, "On the Flow of Talent in Society," *Acta Sociologica,* 9, 152-174.

REISSMAN, Leonard, *Class in American Society,* New York: Free Press, 1959.

RESEARCH COMMITTEE, Japan Sociological Society, *Social Mobility in Japan: An Interim Report on the 1955 Survey of Social stratification and Social Mobility in Japan,* Tokyo: 1956.

RESEARCH COMMITTEE, Japan Sociological Society, "Social Stratification and Mobility in the Six Large Cities of Japan," *Transactions of the Second World Congress of Sociology,* 2 (1954), 414-431.

RICHMOND, Anthony H., "Education, Social Mobility and Racial Relations in the Union of South Africa," *Transactions of the Third World Congress of Sociology,* 5 (1956), 105-114.

RICHMOND, Anthony H., "Social Mobility of Immigrants in Canada," *Population Studies,* 18 (July, 1964), 53-69.

ROGOFF, Natalie, *Recent Trends in Occupational Mobility,* New York: Free Press, 1953.

ROSSER, Colin, "Social Mobility in the Newar Caste System," in Cristoph von Fürer-Haimendorf, editor, *Caste and Kin in Nepal, India and Ceylon,* Bombay: Asia Publishing House, 1966.

SARIOLA, S., *Social Class and Social Mobility in a Costa Rican Town,* Turriabba: Inter-American Institute of Agricultural Sciences, 1954.

SCHNORE, Leo F., "Social Mobility in Demographic Perspective," *American Sociological Review*, 26 (June, 1961), 407-423.

SCOTT, John Finley, "The American College Sorority: Its Role in Class and Ethnic Endogamy," *American Sociological Review*, 30 (August, 1965), 514-527.

SCOTT, W., "Some Remarks on the Measurement of Social Mobility--A Reply," *Population Studies*, 9 (July, 1955), 102-103.

SHARMA, K. N., "Occupational Mobility of Castes in a North Indian Village," *Southwestern Journal of Anthropology*, 17 (Summer, 1961), 146-164.

SIMPSON, George, "Ethnic Groups, Social Mobility and Power in Latin America," *Seminar on Social Structure, Stratification and Mobility, with Special Reference to Latin America*, Washington, D. C., Pan American Union, 1966.

SIMPSON, Richard L., "Parental Influence, Anticipatory Socialization, and Social Mobility," *American Sociological Review*, 27 (August, 1962), 517-522.

SJOBERG, Gideon, "Are Social Classes in America Becoming More Rigid?" *American Sociological Review*, 16 (December, 1951), 775-783.

SMELSER, Neil J. and Seymour M. Lipset, editors, *Social Structure and Mobility in Economic Development*, Chicago: Aldine, 1966.

SMITH, Alfred G., Shirley Chapman, and Alpha M. Bond, "Dimensions of Status Change," *Sociology and Social Research*, 45 (July, 1961), 387-395.

SMITH, Robert J., "Aspects of Mobility in Pre-Industrial Japanese Cities," *Comparative Studies in Society and History*, 5 (July, 1963), 416-423.

SOROKIN, Pitirim A., "Social Mobility," *Encyclopaedia of the Social Sciences*, 11, New York: Macmillan, 1930, 554-555.

SOROKIN, Pitirim A., *Social and Cultural Mobility*, New York: Free Press, 1959.

SOROKIN, Pitirim A., *Social Mobility*, New York: Harper, 1927.

SOVANI, N. V. and Kusum Pradham, "Occupational Mobility in Poona City Between Three Generations," *Indian Economic Review*, 2 (1955), 23-36.

SRIVASTAVA, Kam P., "Tribe-Cast Mobility in India and the Case of Kumaon Bhatias," in Christoph von Furer-Haimendorf, editor, *Caste and Kin in Nepal, India and Ceylon,* Bombay: Asia Publishing House, 1966.

SOCIAL MOBILITY

SVALASTOGA, Kaare, *Prestige, Class and Mobility,* London: Heinemann, 1959.

SVALASTOGA, Kaare, *Social Differentiation,* New York: McKay, 1965, Chapter 6, "Social Mobility,"

SVALASTOGA, Kaare, "Social Mobility: The Western European Model," *Acta Sociologica,* 9, 175-182.

SVALASTOGA, Kaare, and Gosta Carlsson, "Social Stratification and Social Mobility in Scandinavia," *Sociological Inquiry,* 31 (1961), 23-46.

SWIFT, D. F., "Meritocratic and Social Class at Age Eleven," *Educational Research,* 8 (November, 1965), 65-72.

THERNSTROM, Stephan, "Class and Mobility in a Nineteenth-Century City: A Study of Unskilled Laborers," in Reinhard Bendix and Seymour M. Lipset, editors, *Class, Status and Power,* revised edition, New York: Free Press, 1966.

THERNSTROM, Stephan, "Notes on the Historical Study of Social Mobility," *Comparative Studies in Society and History,* 10 (January, 1968).

THERNSTROM, Stephan, *Poverty and Progress: Social Mobility in a Nineteenth Century City,* Cambridge: Harvard University Press, 1964.

TIMASHEFF, Nicholas S., "Vertical Social Mobility in Communist Society," *American Journal of Sociology,* 50 (July, 1944), 9-21.

TOMINAGA, Kenichi, "Occupational Mobility in Tokyo," in Joseph Kahl, editor, *Comparative Perspective on Stratification,* Boston: Little, Brown, 1968.

TUMIN, Melvin M. and Arnold S. Feldman, "Theory and Measurement of Occupational Mobility," *American Sociological Review,* 22 (June, 1957), 281-288.

TURNER, Ralph H., "Acceptance of Irregular Mobility in Britain and the United States," *Sociometry,* 29 (December, 1966), 334-352.

UTECHIN, S. V., "Social Stratification and Social Mobility in the U.S.S.R.," *Transactions of the Second World Congress of Sociology,* 2 (1954), 55-63.

VAN HEEK, F., "The Method of Extreme Types as a Tool for the Study of the Causes of Vertical Mobility," *Transactions of the Second World Congress of Sociology,* 2 (1954), 391-395.

VAN HULTON, Ida, "Summary of a Study of Social Mobility

at the Philips Works, Eindhoven," *Transactions of the Second World Congress of Sociology* 2 (1954), 81-88.

VAN TULDER, J. J. M., "Occupational Mobility in the Netherlands from 1919 to 1954," *Transactions of the Third World Congress of Sociology,* 3 (1956), 209-218.

VINKE, P., "The Vertical Social Mobility of the Chief Executive Groups in the Netherlands," *Transactions of the Third World Congress of Sociology,* 3 (1956), 219-229.

WANCE, William and Richard Butler, "The Effect of Industrial Changes on Occupational 'Inheritance' in Four Pennsylvania Communities," *Social Forces,* 27 (December, 1948), 158-162.

WARNER, W. Lloyd, "Opportunity in America," *Journal of Business,* 23 (July, 1950), 141-153.

WARNER, W. Lloyd and James C. Abegglen, *Big Business, Leaders in America,* New York: Harper and Row, 1955.

WARNER, W. Lloyd and James C. Abegglen, *Occupational Mobility in American Business and Industry,* Minneapolis: University of Minnesota Press, 1955.

WEBER, Max, *The Theory of Social and Economic Organization,* New York: Free Press, 1947.

WESTOFF, Charles F., Marvin Bressler, and Philip C. Sagi, "The Concept of Social Mobility: An Empirical Inquiry," *American Sociological Review,* 25 (June, 1960), 375-385.

WHITE, Harrison C., "Cause and Effect in Social Mobility Tables," *Behavioral Science,* 8 (1963), 14-27.

WIRTH, Louis, "Social Stratification and Social Mobility in the United States," *Current Sociology,* 2 (1953-1954).

WOHL, R. Richard, "The 'Rags to Riches Story,'" in Reinhard Bendix and Seymour M. Lipset, editors, *Class, Status and Power,* 2nd edition, New York: Free Press, 1966.

WONG, Y. C., "Western Impact on Social Mobility in China," *American Sociological Review,* 25 (December, 1960), 843-855.

YASUDA, Saburo, "A Methodological Inquiry into Social Mobility," *American Sociological Review,* 29 (February, 1964), 16-23.

ZELAN, Joseph, Howard R. Freeman, and Arthur H. Richardson, "Occupational Mobility of Spanish-American War Veterans and Their Sons," *Sociology and Social Research,* 52 (April, 1968), 211-223.

Career Mobility

ABU-LABAN, Baha, "Social Origins and Occupational Career Patterns of Community Leaders," *Sociological Inquiry*, 33 (Spring, 1963), 131-140.

ALLINGHAM, John D., "Class Regression: An Aspect of the Social Stratification Process," *American Sociological Review*, 32 (June, 1967), 442-449.

ANDERSON, C. Arnold, "Lifetime Inter-Occupational Mobility Patterns in Sweden," *Acta Sociologica*, 1 (1955), 168-202.

BAHR, Howard M., "Worklife Mobility Among Bowery Men," *Social Science Quarterly*, 49 (June, 1968), 128-141.

BENDIX, Reinhard, Seymour M. Lipset, and Theodore Malin, "Social Origins and Occupational Career Patterns," *Industrial and Labor Relations Review*, 7 (January, 1954), 246-261.

BERLINER, Joseph S., *Factory and Manager in the U. S. S. R.*, Cambridge: Harvard University Press, 1957.

BLAU, Peter M. and Otis Dudley Duncan, *The American Occupational Structure*, New York: Wiley, 1967, Chapter 2.

BOGUE, Donald J., *Skid Row in American Cities*, Chicago: University of Chicago Press, 1963.

BREED, Warren, "Occupational Mobility and Suicide Among White Males," *American Sociological Review*, 28 (April, 1963), 179-188.

BROOM, Leonard, and John H. Smith, "Bridging Occupations," *British Journal of Sociology*, 14 (December, 1963), 321-334.

CAPLOW, Theodore, and Reece J. McGee, *The Academic Market-Place*, New York: Basic Books, *1958.*

CHINOY, Ely, *Automobile Workers and the American Dream*, New York: Random House, 1955.

CHOW, Yung-Teh, *Social Mobility in China: Status Careers Among the Gentry in a Chinese Community*, New York: Atherton, 1966.

COATES, Charles H. and Roland J. Pellegrin, "Executives and Supervisors: Contrasting Definitions of Career Success," *Administrative Science Quarterly,* 1 (1957), 506-517.

COWLES, May L., "Changes in Family Personnel, Occupational Status, and Housing Occurring over the Farm Family's Life Cycle," *Rural Sociology,* 18 (March, 1953), 35-44.

DALTON, Melville, *Men Who Manage,* New York: Wiley, 1959.

ELDER, Glen H., Jr., "Achievement Orientations and Career Patterns of Rural Youth," *Sociology of Education,* 37 (Fall, 1963), 30-58.

EULAU, Heinz, William Buchanan, Leroy C. Ferguson, and John C. Wahlke, "Career Perspectives of American State Legislators," in Dwaine Marvick, editor, *Political Decision Makers,* Baltimore: Johns Hopkins Press, 1961.

FLORO, G. K., "Continuity in City Manager Careers," *American Journal of Sociology,* 61 (November, 1955), 240-246.

FORM, William H., and Delbert C. Miller, "Occupational Career Pattern as a Sociological Instrument," *American Journal of Sociology,* 54 (January, 1949), 317-329.

GINZBERG, Eli and John L. Herma, *Talent and Performance,* New York: Columbia University Press, 1964.

GLASS, David V., *Social Mobility in Britain,* London: Routledge and Kegan Paul, 1954, Chapter 8.

GOLDNER, Fred H., "Demotion in Industrial Management," *American Sociological Review,* 30 (October, 1965), 714-724.

GRUSKY, Oscar, "Career Mobility and Managerial Political Behavior," *Political Science Review,* 8 (Fall, 1965), 82-89.

GRUSKY, Oscar, "Career Mobility and Organizational Commitment," *Administrative Science Quarterly,* 10 (March, 1966), 488-503.

GUSFIELD, Joseph R., "Occupational Roles and Forms of Enterprise," *American Journal of Sociology,* 66 (May, 1961), 571-580.

HALL, Oswald, "The Stages of a Medical Career," *American Journal of Sociology,* 53 (March, 1948), 327-336.

HALLER, A. O., "The Occupational Achievement Process of Farm-Reared Youth in Urban-Industrial Society," *Rural Sociology,* 25 (September, 1960), 321-333.

JAFFE, A. J. and R. O. Carleton, *Occupational Mobility in the United States, 1930-1960,* New York: King's Crown Press, 1954.

CAREER MOBILITY

JANOWITZ, Morris, *The Professional Soldier: A Social and Political Portrait,* New York: Free Press, 1960.

KAPLAN, Sidney J., "Up From the Ranks on a Fast Escalator," *American Sociological Review,* 24 (February, 1959), 79-81.

CAREER MOBILITY

LEEDS, Anthony, "Brazilian Careers and Social Structure: An Evolutionary Model and Case Study," *American Anthropologist,* 66 (1964), 1321-1347.

LEHMAN, Edward W., "Opportunity, Mobility and Satisfaction Within an Industrial Organization," *Social Forces,* 46 (June, 1968), 492-501.

LEVENSON, Bernard, "Bureaucratic Succession," in Amitai Etzioni, editor, *Complex Organizations,* New York: Holt, Rinehart and Winston, 1961.

LEWIS, Gordon F., "A Comparison of Some Aspects of the Backgrounds and Careers of Small Businessmen and American Business Leaders," *American Journal of Sociology,* 65 (January, 1960), 348-355.

LIPSET, Seymour M. and Reinhard Bendix, "Social Mobility and Occupational Career Patterns: I, Stability of Jobholding," *American Journal of Sociology,* 57 (January, 1952), 366-374.

LIPSET, Seymour M. and Reinhard Bendix, "Social Mobility and Occupational Career Patterns: II, Social Mobility," *American Journal of Sociology,* 57 (March, 1952), 494-504.

LIPSET, Seymour M. and Reinhard Bendix, *Social Mobility in Industrial Society,* Berkeley: University of California Press, 1959, Chapter 6.

LORTIE, D. C., "Laymen to Lawmen: Law School, Careers, and Professional Socialization," *Harvard Educational Review,* 29 (1959), 353-369.

MARTIN, Norman H. and Anselm Strauss, "Patterns of Mobility Within Industrial Organizations," in W. Lloyd Warner and Norman H. Martin, editors, *Industrial Man,* New York: Harper, 1959.

MARVICK, Dwaine, *Career Perspectives in a Bureaucratic Setting,* Ann Arbor: University of Michigan Press, 1954.

MERCER, Blaine E., "The Ethics of Academic Status-Striving *Sociology and Social Research,* 47 (October, 1962), 51-56.

MERTON, Robert K., G. C. Reader, and Patricia L. Kendall, *The Student Physician: Introductory Studies in the Sociology of Medical Education,* New York: Free Press, 1957.

MILIC, Vohin, "General Trends in Social Mobility in Yugoslavia," *Acta Sociologica,* 9 (1965), 116-136.

MILLER, Delbert C. and William H. Form, "Measuring Patterns of

Occupational Security," *Sociometry,* 10 (November, 1947), 362-375.

MORE, Douglas M., "Demotion," *Social Problems,* 9 (1962), 213-221.

PALMER, Gladys L., Herbert S. Parnes, Richard C. Wilcock, Mary W. Herman, and Carol P. Brainerd, *The Reluctant Job Changer: Studies in Work Attachments and Aspirations,* Philadelphia: University of Pennsylvania Press, 1962.

PERRUCCI, Robert, "The Significance of Intra-Occupational Mobility: Some Methodological and Theoretical Notes, Together with a Case Study of Engineers," *American Sociological Review,* 26 (December, 1961), 874-883.

REYNOLDS, Lloyd G., *The Structure of Labor Markets,* New York: Harper, 1951.

SIMPSON, Richard L. and Ida Harper Simpson, "Social Origins, Occupational Advice, Occupational Values, and Work Careers," *Social Forces,* 40 (March, 1962), 264-271.

SLOCUM, Walter L., *Occupational Careers: A Sociological Perspective,* Chicago: Aldine, 1966.

SMITH, James O. and Gideon Sjoberg, "Origins and Career Patterns of Leading Protestant Clergymen," *Social Forces,* 39 (May, 1961), 290-296.

STEWART, Rosemary G. and Paul Duncan-Jones, "Educational Background and Career History of British Managers, with Some American Comparisons," *Explorations in Entrepreneurial History,* 9 (December, 1956), 61-71.

STONE, Robert C., "Factory Organization and Vertical Mobility," *American Sociological Review,* 18 (February, 1953), 28-35.

TAUSKY, Curt and Robert Dubin, "Career Anchorage: Managerial Mobility and Motivations," *American Sociological Review,* 30 (October, 1965), 725-735.

U. S. Bureau of the Census, "Lifetime Occupational Mobility of Adult Males: March, 1962," *Current Population Reports,* Series P-23, No. 11, May 12, 1964.

WARNER, W. Lloyd, "The Careers of American Business and Government Executives: A Comparative Analysis," *Social Science Approaches to Business Behavior,* Homewood, Illinois: Dorsey, 1962.

WARNER, W. Lloyd and James C. Abegglen, *Occupational Mobility in American Business and Industry,* Minneapolis: University of Minnesota Press, 1955.

WILENSKY, Harold L., "Orderly Careers and Social Participation," *American Sociological Review,* 26 (August, 1961), 521-539.

WILENSKY, Harold L., "Work, Careers, and Social Integration," *International Social Science Journal,* 12 (1960), 543-560.

WILENSKY, Harold L. and Hugh Edwards, "The Skidders," *American Sociological Review,* 24 (April, 1959), 215-231.

Correlates of Vertical Mobility

Some of the correlates treated by these publications appear to be bases of the mobility and others appear to be consequences. We have not tried to separate the publications dealing with these two kinds of correlates, because often the direction of the causation, if any, is unclear. Undoubtedly, there is sometimes reciprocal influence, and some of the correlations are spurious.

Attempts to determine the consequences of vertical mobility are plagued with essentially the same metholodological problems as the attempts to determine the consequences of status inconsistency. For discussion of the "identification problem" and similar difficulties, see the publications by Blalock under "Status Consistency and Inconsistency."

Family, educational, and religious correlates of mobility are treated in the following three sections rather than here. The correlates of aspiration, motivation, and similar psychological bases of mobility are treated in the publications under the topic "Aspiration, Motivation, and Other Presumed Psychological Bases of Mobility."

ABRAMS, Mark, "Social Class and British Politics," *Public Opinion Quarterly,* 25 (Fall, 1961).

AIKEN, Michael, Louis A Ferman, and Harold L. Sheppard, *Economic Failure, Alienation, and Extremism,* Ann Arbor: University of Michigan Press, 1968.

ALLAN, Philip J., "Childhood Backgrounds of Success in a Profession," *American Sociological Review,* 20 (April, 1955), 186-190.

ANASTASI, Anne, "Intelligence and Family Size," *Psychological Bulletin,* 53 (May, 1956), 187-209.

ANDERSON, C. Arnold, James C. Brown, and Mary Jean Bowman, "Intelligence and Occupational Mobility," *Journal of Political Economy,* 60 (June, 1952), 218-239.

BALAN, Jorge, "Are Farmers' Sons Handicapped in the City?" *Rural Sociology,* 33 (June, 1968), 160-174.

BALTZELL, E. Digby, "Social Mobility and Fertility within an Elite Group," *Milbank Memorial Fund Quarterly,* 31 (October, 1953) 412-420.

BARR, F., "Urban and Rural Differences in Ability and Attainment," *Educational Research,* 1 (February, 1959), 49-60.

BECKER, Howard S., "Some Contingencies of the Professional Dance Musician's Career," *Human Organization,* 12 (Spring, 1953), 22-26.

BEILIN, Harry, "The Pattern of Postponability and Its Relation to Social Class Mobility," *Journal of Social Psychology,* 44 (August, 1956), 33-48.

BEILIN, Harry and Kay V. Bergin, "The Social Mobility of a Limited Urban Group and Some Implications for Counseling," *Personnel and Guidance Journal* 34 (May, 1956), 544-552.

BERENT, Jerzy, "Fertility and Social Mobility," *Population Studies,* 5 (March, 1952), 244-260.

BERGSTEN, B. F., "Social Mobility and Economic Development: The Vital Parameters of the Bolivian Revolution," *Journal of International Studies,* 6 (1964), 367-375.

BETTLEHEIM, Bruno and Morris Janowitz, *Dynamics of Prejudice: A Psychological and Sociological Study of Veterans,* New York: Harper and Row, 1950.

BETTLEHEIM, Bruno and Morris Janowitz, *Social Change and Prejudice,* New York: Free Press, 1964. Revised version of *Dynamics of Prejudice.*

BIERI, J., R. Lobeck and H. Plotnich, "Psychological Factors in Differential Social Mobility," *Journal of Social Psychology,* 58 (October, 1962), 183-200.

BLACKER, J. G. C., "Social Ambitions of the Bourgeoisie of 18th Century France and Their Relation to Family Limitation," *Population Studies,* 11 (1957), 46-63.

BLAU, Peter M., "Occupational Bias and Mobility," *American Sociological Review,* 22 (August, 1957), 392-399.

BLAU, Peter M., "Social Mobility and Interpersonal Relations," *American Sociological Review,* 21 (June, 1956), 290-295.

BLAU, Peter M. and Otis Dudley Duncan, *The American Occupational Structure,* New York: Wiley, 1967, Chapter 11, "Differential Fertility and Occupational Mobility,"

BLAU, Zena Smith, "Class Structure, Mobility, and Change in Child Rearing," *Sociometry,* 28 (June, 1965), 210-219.

BOALT, Gunnar, "Social Mobility in Stockholm: A Pilot Investi-

CORRELATES OF
VERTICAL MOBILITY

gation," *Transactions of the Second World Congress of Sociology,* 2 (1954), 67-69.

BOGGS, Stephen T., "Family Size and Social Mobility in a California Suburb," *Eugenics Quarterly,* 4 (December, 1957), 208-213.

BOHLKE, Robert H., "Social Mobility, Stratification Inconsistency and Middle Class Delinquency," *Social Problems,* 8 (1961), 351-363.

BONJEAN, Charles M., Grady D. Bruce, and J. Allen Williams, Jr., "Social Mobility and Job Satisfaction: A Replication and Extension," *Social Forces,* 45 (June, 1967), 492-501.

BOWEN, Don R., Elinor R. Bowen, Sheldon R. Gawiser, and Louis H. Masotti, "Deprivation, Mobility, and Orientation Toward Protest of the Urban Poor," *American Behavioral Scientist,* 11 (March-April, 1968), 20-24.

BOWLES, Samuel and Henry M. Levine, "The Determinants of Scholastic Achievement--An Appraisal of Some Recent Evidence." *Journal of Human Resources,* 3 (Winter, 1968), 3-24.

BREED, Warren, "Occupational Mobility and Suicide Among White Males," *American Sociological Review,* 28 (April, 1963), 179-188.

BROOKOVER, Wilbur B., Shailer Thomas and Ann Paterson, "Self Concept of Ability and School Achievement," *Sociology of Education,* 37 (Spring, 1964), 271-278.

BROOKS, Hugh E. and Franklin J. Henry, "An Empirical Study of the Relationships of Catholic Practice and Occupational Mobility to Fertility: Review of the Literature," *Milbank Memorial Fund Quarterly,* 36 (July, 1958), 222-277.

BROOM, Leonard, "Intermarriage and Mobility in Hawaii," *Transactions of the Third World Congress of Sociology,* 3 (1956), 277-282.

BRUCE, Grady D., Charles M. Bonjean, and J. Allen Williams, Jr., "Job Satisfaction Among Independent Businessmen: A Correlative Study," *Sociology and Social Research,* 52 (April, 1968), 195-204.

BURT, Cyril, "Intelligence and Social Mobility," *British Journal of Statistical Psychology,* 14 (1961), 2-24.

CARTWRIGHT, Desmond S. and Richard J. Robertson, "Membership in Cliques and Achievement," *American Journal of Sociology,* 66 (March, 1961), 441-445.

CAVE, E. D., "The Effect of the 'Eleven-Plus' Result on the Subsequent Careers of Pupils," *British Journal of Educational Psychology,* 37 (February, 1967).

COLEMAN, James S., "Academic Achievement and the Structure

of Competition," *Harvard Educational Review,* 29 (Fall, 1959), 330-351.

COLEMAN, James S., "The Adolescent Subculture and Academic Achievement," *American Journal of Sociology,* 65 (January, 1960), 337-347.

COLEMAN, James S., "Equality of Educational Opportunity: Reply to Bowles and Levin," *Journal of Human Resources,* 3 (Spring, 1968), 237-246.

COLEMAN, James S., *et al, Equality of Educational Opportunity,* Washington, D. C.: U. S. Office of Education, 1966.

CURTIS, Richard F., "Differential Association and the Stratification of the Urban Community," *Social Forces,* 42 (October, 1963), 68-77.

CURTIS, Richard F., "Income and Occupational Mobility," *American Sociological Review,* 25 (October, 1960), 727-730.

CURTIS, Richard F., "Note on Occupational Mobility and Union Membership in Detroit: A Replication," *Social Forces,* 38 (October, 1959), 69-71.

CURTIS, Richard F., "Occupational Mobility and Church Participation," *Social Forces,* 38 (May, 1960), 315-319.

CURTIS, Richard F., "Occupational Mobility and Membership in Formal Voluntary Associations: A Note on Research," *American Sociological Review,* 24 (December, 1959), 846-848.

CURTIS, Richard F., "Occupational Mobility and Urban Social Life," *American Journal of Sociology,* 65 (November, 1959), 296-298.

DAVIS, Allison, "Personality and Social Mobility, *School Review,* 65 (June, 1957), 134-143.

DAVIS, James A., "Higher Education: Selection and Opportunity," *School Review,* 71 (1963), 249-265.

D'SOUZA, Victor S., "Restriction on Admissions to Higher Education: The Criterion of Selection," *Sociological Bulletin,* 10 (March, 1961), 82-91.

DOUGLAS, James W. B., *The Home and the School: A Study of Ability and Attainment in the Primary School,* London: MacGibbon and Kee, 1964.

DOUVAN, Elizabeth and Joseph B. Adelson, "The Psychodynamics of Social Mobility in Adolescent Boys," *Journal of Abnormal and Social Psychology,* 56 (January, 1958), 31-44.

DOUVAN, Elizabeth and Carol Kaye, "Motivation Factors in College Entrance," in Nevitt Sanford, editor, *The American College,* New York: Wiley, 1962.

ECKLAND, Bruce K., "Academic Ability, Higher Education, and Occupational Mobility," *American Sociological Review*, 30 (October, 1965), 735-746.

ELLIS, Evelyn, "Social Psychological Correlates of Upward Social Mobility Among Unmarried Career Women," *American Sociological Review*, 17 (October, 1952), 558-563.

ELLIS, Robert A. and W. Clayton Lane, "Social Mobility and Career Orientation," *Sociology and Social Research*, 50 (April, 1966), 280-296.

ELLIS, Robert A. and W. Clayton Lane, "Social Mobility and Social Isolation: A Test of Sorokin's Dissociative Hypothesis," *American Sociological Review*, 32 (April, 1967), 237-253.

ELLIS, Robert A. and W. Clayton Lane, "Structural Supports for Upward Mobility," *American Sociological Review*, 28 (October, 1963), 743-756.

EULAU, Heinz and D. Koff, "Occupational Mobility and Political Career," *Western Political Quarterly*, 15 (September, 1962), 507-522.

FARIS, Robert E. L., "Sociological Causes of Genius," *American Sociological Review*, 5 (October, 1940), 689-699.

FORM, William H. and James A. Geschwender, "Social Reference Basis of Job Satisfaction: The Case of Manual Workers," *American Sociological Review*, 27 (April, 1962), 228-237.

FOX, Thomas G. and S. M. Miller, "Economic, Political and Social Determinants of Mobility: An International Comparison," *Acta Sociologica*, 9 (1965), 76-93.

FREEDMAN, Ronald and Lolagene Coombs, "Childspacing and Family Economic Position," *American Sociological Review*, 31 (October, 1966), 631-648.

FREEDMAN, Ronald and Amos H. Hawley, "Migration and Occupational Mobility in the Depression," *American Journal of Sociology*, 55 (September, 1949), 171-177.

FRENCH, Cecil L., "Correlates of Success in Retail Selling," *American Journal of Sociology*, 66 (September, 1960), 128-140.

GILL, Lois J. and Bernard Spilka, "Some Nonintellectual Correlates of Academic Achievement Among Mexican-American Secondary School Students," *Journal of Educational Psychology*, 53 (June, 1962), 144-149.

GINZBERG, Eli and John L. Herma, *Talent and Performance*, New York: Columbia University Press, 1964.

GLASS, David V., editor, *Social Mobility in Britain*, London: Routledge and Kegan Paul, 1954.

GOLDNER, Fred H. and R. R. Ritti, "Professionalization as Career Immobility," *American Journal of Sociology,* 72 (March, 1967), 489-502.

GOLDSTEIN, Sidney, "Migration and Occupational Mobility in Norristown, Pennsylvania," *American Sociological Review,* 20 (August, 1955), 402-408.

GOWAN, J. C., "Factors of Achievement in High School and College," *Journal of Counseling Psychology,* 7 (Summer, 1960), 91-95.

GRAY, George W., "Which Scientists Win Nobel Prizes?" in Bernard Barber and Walter Hirsch, editors, *The Sociology of Science,* New York: Free Press, 1962.

GREENBLUM, Joseph and L. I. Pearlin, "Vertical Mobility and Prejudice," in Reinhard Bendix and Seymour M. Lipset, editors, *Class, Status, and Power,* New York: Free Press, 1953.

GRUSKY, Oscar, "Career Mobility and Managerial Political Behavior," *Pacific Sociological Review,* 8 (Fall, 1965), 82-89.

GRUSKY, Oscar, "Career Mobility and Organizational Commitment," *Administrative Science Quarterly,* 10 (March, 1966), 488-503.

HAAN, N., "The Relationship of Ego Functioning and Intelligence to Social Status and Social Mobility," *Journal of Abnormal and Social Psychology,* 69 (1964), 594-605.

HAVEMANN, Ernest and Patricia West, *They Went to College,* New York: Harcourt Brace, 1952.

HAVIGHURST, Robert J., "The Leisure Activities of the Middle-Aged," *American Journal of Sociology,* 63 (September, 1957), 152-162.

HETZLER, Stanley A., "Social Mobility and Radicalism - Conservatism," *Social Forces,* 33 (December, 1954), 161-166.

HILL, George W. and H. Christensen, "Some Cultural Factors Related to Occupational Mobility Among Wisconsin Farmers," *Rural Sociology,* 7 (June, 1942), 192-200.

HODGE, Robert W. and Donald J. Treiman, "Occupational Mobility and Attitudes Toward Negroes," *American Sociological Review,* 31 (February, 1966), 93-102.

HOGGART, Richard, *The Uses of Literacy: Changing Patterns in English Mass Culture,* Boston: Beacon Press, 1961.

HOLLINGSHEAD, August B., R. Ellis, and E. Kirby, "Social Mobility and Mental Illness," *American Sociological Review,* 19 (October, 1954), 577-591.

HOLLINGSHEAD, August B. and Fredrick Redlich, *Social Class and Mental Illness,* New York: Wiley, 1958.

HORNEY, Karen, *The Neurotic Personality of Our Time,* New York: Norton, 1937.

CORRELATES OF VERTICAL MOBILITY

HUNT, Thomas C., "Occupational Status and Marriage Selection," *American Sociological Review,* 5 (August, 1940), 495-504.

HURVITZ, Nathan, "Sources of Motivation and Achievement of American Jews," *Jewish Journal of Social Studies,* 23 (1961), 217-234.

HUTCHINSON, Bertram, "Fertility, Social Mobility and Urban Migration in Brazil," *Population Studies,* 14 (March, 1961), 182-189.

IANNI, Francis A. J., "Residential and Occupational Mobility as Indices of the Acculturation of an Ethnic Group," *Social Forces,* 36 (October, 1957), 65-72.

ILLSLEY, R., "Social Class Selection and Class Differences in Relation to Stillbirth and Infant Deaths," *British Medical Journal,* (December 24, 1955), 1520-1524.

JACKSON, Brian, *Streaming: An Education System in Miniature,* London: Routledge and Kegan Paul, 1964.

JANOWITZ, Morris, "Some Consequences of Social Mobility in the United States," *Transactions of the Third World Congress of Sociology,* 3 (1956), 191-201.

KANTNER, John F., and Clyde V. Kiser, "Social and Psychological Factors Affecting Fertility: The Interrelation of Fertility, Fertility Planning and Intergenerational Social Mobility," *Milbank Memorial Fund Quarterly,* 32 (January, 1954), 69-102.

KANTOR, Mildred B., editor, *Mobility and Mental Health,* Springfield, Illinois: Thomas, 1965.

KATZ, Elihu, William L. Libby, Jr. and Fred L. Strodtbeck, "Status Mobility and Reactions to Deviance and Subsequent Conformity," *Sociometry,* 27 (September, 1964), 245-260.

KEMPER, Theodore D., "Reference Groups, Socialization, and Achievement," *American Sociological Review,* 33 (February, 1968), 31-45.

KLEINER, Robert J. and Seymour Parker, "Goal-Striving, Social Status, and Mental Disorder: A Research Review," *American Sociological Review,* 28 (April, 1963), 189-203.

KOSA, John, Leo D. Rachiele and Cyril O. Schommer, "The Self-Image and Performance of Socially Mobile College Students," *Journal of Social Psychology,* 56 (1962), 301-316.

KUVLESKY, William P. and R. C. Bealer, "The Relevance of Adolescents' Occupational Aspirations for Subsequent Job Attainments," *Rural Sociology,* 32 (September, 1967), 290-310.

LANE, W. Clayton and Robert A. Ellis, "Social Mobility and Anticipatory Socialization," *Pacific Sociological Review,* 11 (Spring, 1968), 5-14.

LEHMAN, Edward W., "Opportunity, Mobility and Satisfaction Within an Industrial Organization," *Social Forces,* 46 (June, 1968), 492-501.

LeMASTER, E E., "Social Class Mobility and Family Integration," *Marriage and Family Living,* 16 (August, 1954), 226-232.

LEMERT, Edwin H., "Paranoia and the Dynamics of Exclusion," *Sociometry,* 25 (1962), 2-20.

LENSKI, Gerhard E., "Social Correlates of Religious Interest," *American Sociological Review,* 18 (October, 1953), 533-544.

LICHTER, Solomon O., Elsie B. Rapien, Francis M. Seibert, and Morris A. Sklansky, *The Drop-Outs: A Treatment Study of Intellectually Capable Students Who Drop Out of High School,* New York: Free Press, 1962.

LINDENFELD, Frank, "A Note on Social Mobility, Religiosity, and Students' Attitudes Toward Premarital Sexual Relations," *American Sociological Review,* 25 (February, 1960), 81-84.

LIPSET, Seymour M., "Social Mobility and Urbanization," *Rural Sociology,* 20 (September, 1955), 220-228.

LITWAK, Eugene, "Occupational Mobility and Extended Family Cohesion," *American Sociological Review,* 25 (February, 1960), 9-21.

LOPREATO, Joseph, "Upward Social Mobility and Political O-rientation," *American Sociological Review,* 32 (August, 1967), 586-593.

LUCKMAN, Thomas and Peter L. Berger, "Social Mobility and Personal Identity," *European Journal of Sociology,* 5 (1964).

MARIS, Ronald, "Suicide, Status, and Mobility in Chicago," *Social Forces,* 46 (December, 1967), 246-256.

MAXWELL, James, "Intelligence, Fertility and the Future: A Report on the 1947 Scottish Mental Survey," *Proceedings of the World Population Conference,* New York: United Nations, 1954.

McDILL, Edward, Edmund D. Meyers, Jr. and Leo C. Rigsby, "Institutional Effects on the Academic Behavior of High School Students," *Sociology of Education,* 40 (Summer, 1967), 181-189.

MEIER, Dorothy L. and Wendell Bell, "Anomia and Differential Access to the Achievement of Life Goals," *American Sociological Review,* 24 (April, 1959), 189-202.

MIZRUCHI, Ephraim, *Success and Opportunity: A Study of Anomie,* New York: Free Press, 1964.

MORE, Douglas M., "Social Origins and Occupational Adjustment," *Social Forces,* 35 (October, 1956), 16-19.

MUKHERJEE, Ramkrishna, "Social Mobility and Age at Marriage," in David V. Glass, editor, *Social Mobility in Britain,* London: Routledge and Kegan Paul, 1954.

MYERS, Jerome K. and Bertram H. Roberts, *Family and Class Dynamics in Mental Illness,* New York: Wiley, 1959.

NATIONAL SCIENCE FOUNDATION, *Two Years After the College Degree,* Washington, D. C.: U. S. Government Printing Office, 1963.

NEWCOMER, Mabel, *The Big Business Executive: The Factors that Made Him,* New York: Columbia University Press, 1955.

PAPAVASSILIOU, I. T., "Intelligence and Family Size," *Population Studies,* 7 (March, 1954), 222-226.

PARSONS, Talcott, "Revised Analytical Approach to the Theory of Stratification," in Reinhard Bendix and Seymour M. Lipset, *Class, Status, and Power,* New York: Free Press, 1953.

PATTERSON, Samuel C., "Inter-Generational Occupational Mobility and Legislative Voting Behavior," *Social Forces,* 43 (October, 1964), 90-93.

PAVALKO, Ronald M. and Norma Nager, "Contingencies of Marriage to High-Status Men," *Social Forces,* 46 (June, 1968), 523-531.

PELZ, Donald C., "Some Social Factors Related to Performance in a Research Organization," in Bernard Barber and Walter Hirsch, editors, *The Sociology of Science,* New York: Free Press, 1962.

PERUCCI, Carolyn Cummings, "Mobility, Marriage and Child-Spacing Among College Graduates," *Journal of Marriage and the Family,* 30 (May, 1968), 273-282.

PETTIGREW, Thomas F., "Regional Differences in Anti-Negro Prejudice," *Journal of Abnormal and Social Psychology,* (July, 1959), 28-36.

PIHLBLAD, C. T. and C. L. Gregory, "Occupational Selection and Intelligence in Rural Communities and Small Towns in Missouri," *American Sociological Review,* 21 (February, 1956), 63-71.

PHILLIPS, Beeman N., "Sex, Social Class and Anxiety as Sources of Variation in School Achievement," *Journal of Educational Psychology,* 53 (December, 1962), 316-322.

PORTERFIELD, Austin L. and Jack P. Gibbs, "Occupational Prestige and Social Mobility of Suicides in New Zealand." *American Journal of Sociology,* 66 (September, 1960), 147-152.

POTI, S. J. and D. Subodh, "Pilot Study on Social Mobility and its Association with Fertility in West Bengal in 1956," *Artha Vijnana,* 2 (June, 1960), 85-95.

PRESTHUS, Robert, *The Organizational Society: An Analysis and a Theory,* New York: Knopf, 1962.

PUNKE, Harold H., "Factors Affecting the Proportion of High School Graduates Who Enter College," *Bulletin of the National Association of Secondary School Principals,* 38 (November, 1954), 6-27.

QUENSEL, C.T.C., "The Interrelations of Marital Status, Fertility, Family Size, and Intelligence Test Scores," *Population Studies,* 11 (March, 1958), 234-250.

REIMER, Ruth, and Clyde V. Kiser, "Social and Psychological Factors Affecting Fertility: Economic Tension and Social Mobility in Relation to Fertility Planning and Size of Planned Family," *Milbank Memorial Fund Quarterly,* 32 (April, 1954), 167-231.

ROBINS, Lee N., Harry Gyman and Patricia O'Neal, "The Interaction of Social Class and Deviant Behavior," *American Sociological Review,* 27 (August, 1962), 480-492.

ROE, Anne, *The Making of a Scientist,* New York: Dodd, Mead, 1952.

ROGOFF, Natalie, "Local Social Structure and Educational Selection," in A. H. Halsey, Jean Floud, and C. Arnold Anderson, editors, *Education, Economy, and Society,* New York: Free Press, 1961.

ROTH, Julius and Robert F. Peck, "Social Class and Social Mobility Factors Related to Marital Adjustment," *American Sociological Review,* 16 (August, 1951), 478-487.

RUESCH, Jurgen, "Social Technique, Social Status, and Social Change in Illness," in Clyde Kluckhohn and Henry A. Murray, editors, *Personality in Nature, Society, and Culture,* New York: Knopf, 1949.

RUESCH, Jurgen, *et al., Duodenal Ulcer,* Berkeley: University of California Press, 1948.

RUSHING, William A., "Adolescent-Parental Relationships and Mobility Aspirations," *Social Forces,* 43 (December, 1964), 157-166.

SCHNEIDER, Joseph, "Social Class, Historical Circumstances and Fame," *American Journal of Sociology,* 43 (July, 1947), 37-56.

SCOTT, Eileen M., R. Illsley, and A. M. Thomson, "A Psychological Investigation of Primigravidae, II: Maternal Social Class, Age, Physique and Intelligence," *Journal of Obstetrics and Gynecology of the British Empire,* 63 (1956).

SCOTT, Wolf, "Fertility and Social Mobility Among Teachers," *Population Studies,* 11 (March, 1958), 251-261.

SCUDDER, Richard and C. Arnold Anderson, "Migration and Vertical Occupational Mobility," *American Sociological Review,* 19 (June, 1954), 329-334.

SEEMAN, Melvin, "Social Mobility and Administrative Behavior," *American Sociological Review,* 23 (December, 1958), 633-642.

SEEMAN, Melvin, Dennis Rohan, and Milton Argeriou, "Social Mobility and Prejudice: A Swedish Replication," *Social Problems,* 14 (Fall, 1966), 188-197.

SEWELL, William H., "Community of Residence and College Plans," *American Sociological Review,* 29 (February, 1964), 24-38.

SEWELL, William H., and V. P. Shah, "Socioeconomic Status, Intelligence, and the Attainment of Higher Education," *Educational Sociology,* 40 (Winter, 1967), 1-23.

SILBERSTEIN, Fred B., and Melvin Seeman, "Social Mobility and Prejudice," *American Journal of Sociology,* 65 (November, 1959), 258-264.

SIMON, Rita James, Shirley Merritt Clark, and Kathleen Galway, "The Woman Ph.D.: A Recent Profile," *Social Problems,* 15 (Fall, 1967), 221-236.

SIMPSON, Richard L., "A Note on Status, Mobility and Anomie," *British Journal of Sociology,* 11 (December, 1960), 370-372.

SIMPSON, Richard L., "Parental Influence, Anticipatory Socialization and Social Mobility," *American Sociological Review,* 27 (August, 1962), 517-522.

SMITH, Harvey L., "Contingencies of Professional Differentiation," *American Journal of Sociology,* 63 (January, 1958), 410-414.

SOLOMON, David N., "Ethnic and Class Differences Among Hospitals as Contingencies in Medical Careers, *American Journal of Sociology,* 66 (March, 1961), 463-471.

SOROKIN, Pitirim A., *Social Mobility,* New York: Harper, 1927.

SPEIER, Hans, "The Worker Turning Bourgeois," in his *Social Order and the Risks of War,* New York: Steward, 1952.

STACEY, Barrie, "Inter-Generation Mobility and Voting," *Public Opinion Quarterly,* 30 (Spring, 1966), 133-139.

STACEY, Barrie, "Some Psychological Aspects of Inter-Generation Occupational Mobility," *British Journal of Social and Clinical Psychology,* 4 (December, 1965), 275-286.

STRAUS, Murray A. and Katherine H. Holmberg, "Part-time Employment, Social Class, and Achievement in High School," *Sociology and Social Research,* 52 (April, 1958), 224-230.

STRODTBECK, Fred L. and Paul G. Creelan, "The Interaction Linkage Between Family Size, Intelligence, and Sex-Role Identity," *Journal of Marriage and the Family,* 30 (May, 1968), 301-307.

STUCKERT, Robert P., "Occupational Mobility and Family Relationships," *Social Forces,* 41 (March, 1963), 301-307.

SVALASTOGA, Kaare, "An Empirical Analysis of Intrasociety Mobility Determinants," Working Paper Nine submitted to the Fourth Working Conference on Social Stratification and Social Mobility, International Sociological Association, 1957.

SVALASTOGA, Kaare, "Note on the Analysis of Social Mobility Determinants," *Transactions of the Third World Congress of Sociology,* 3 (1956), 178-182.

SYME, Leonard, Merton M. Hyman, and Philip E. Enterline, "Cultural Mobility and the Occurrence of Coronary Heart Disease," *Journal of Health and Human Behavior,* 6 (Winter, 1965), 178-189.

THOMSON, Sir Godfrey, "Intelligence and Fertility: The Scottish 1947 Survey," *Eugenics Review,* 41 (January, 1950), 163-170.

TIEN, H. Yuan, *Social Mobility and Controlled Fertility: Family Origins and Structure of the Australian Academic Elite,* New Haven: College and University Press, 1965.

TIEN, H. Yuan, "The Social Mobility-Fertility Hypothesis Reconsidered: An Empirical Study," *American Sociological Review,* 26 (April, 1961), 247-257.

TIETZE, Christopher, and Patience Lauriat, "Age at Marriage and Educational Attainment in the United States," *Population Studies,* 9 (November, 1955), 159-166.

TOMASSON, Richard F., "Social Mobility and Family Size in Two High Status Populations," *Eugenics Quarterly,* 13 (June, 1966), 113-121.

TUMIN, Melvin M., "Some Unapplauded Consequences of Social Mobility in a Mass Society," *Social Forces,* 36 (October, 1957), 32-37.

TUMIN, Melvin M. and Ray C. Collins, Jr., "Status, Mobility and Anomie: A Study in the Readiness for Desegretation," *British Journal of Sociology,* 10 (September, 1959), 253-267.

TURNER, Ralph H., "Upward Mobility and Class Values," *Social Problems,* 11 (Spring, 1964), 359-371.

TURNER, R. J. and Morton O. Wagenfeld, "Occupational Mobility and Schizophrenia: An Assessment of the Social Causation and Social Selection Hypotheses," *American Sociological Review,* 32 (February, 1967), 104-113.

VISHER, Stephen Sargent, "Environmental Backgrounds of Leading American Scientists," *American Sociological Review,* 13 (February, 1948), 65-72.

WARNER, W. Lloyd and James C. Abegglen, *Big Business Leaders in America,* New York: Atheneum, 1963.

WARNER, W. Lloyd and James C. Abegglen, *Occupational Mobility in American Business and Industry,* Minneapolis: University of Minnesota Press, 1955.

WESTOFF, Charles F., "The Changing Focus of Differential Fertility Research: The Social Mobility Hypothesis," *Milbank Memorial Fund Quarterly,* 31 (January, 1953), 24-38.

WHYTE, William F., *Street Corner Society,* Chicago: University of Chicago Press, 1943.

WILENSKY, Harold L., "Measures and Effects of Mobility," in Neil J. Smelser and Seymour M. Lipset, editors, *Social Structure and Mobility in Economic Development,* Chicago: Aldine, 1966.

WILENSKY, Harold L. and Hugh Edwards, "The Skidder: Ideological Adjustments of Downward Mobile Workers," *American Sociological Review,* 24 (April, 1959), 215-231.

WISPE, Lauren G., "Some Social and Psychological Correlates of Eminence in Psychology," *Journal of the History of the Behavioral Sciences,* 1 (January, 1965).

WRIGHT, Charles R., "Success or Failure in Earning Graduate Degrees," *Sociology of Education,* 38 (Fall, 1964), 73-97.

WRONG, Dennis H., "The Functional Theory of Stratification: Some Neglected Considerations," *American Sociological Review,* 24 (December, 1959), 772-782.

WYLLIE, Irvin G., *The Self Made Man in America,* New Brunswick, New Jersey: Rutgers University Press, 1954.

YOUMANS, E. Grant, "Factors in Educational Attainment," *Rural Sociology,* 24 (March, 1959), 21-28.

ZUCKERMAN, Harriet, "Nobel Laureates in Science: Patterns of Productivity, Collaboration, and Authorship," *American Sociological Review,* 32 (June, 1967), 391-403.

Family Background and Mobility

ADAMS, Bert N., "Occupational Position, Mobility, and the Kin of Orientation," *American Sociological Review,* 32 (June, 1967), 364-377.

ALLEN, Philip J., "Childhood Background of Success in a Profession," *American Sociological Review,* 20 (April, 1955), 186-190.

APPERLY, Frank L., "A Study of American Rhodes Scholars," *Journal of Heredity* 30 (1939), 493-495.

BAYER, Alan E., "Birth Order and Attainment of the Doctorate: A Test of Economic Hypotheses," *American Journal of Sociology,* 72, (March, 1967), 540-550.

BEEZER, R. H. and H. J. Hjilm, *Factors Related to College Attendance,* Office of Education: Cooperative Research Monograph 8, 1961.

BEILIN, Harry, "The Pattern of Postponability and its Relation to Social Class Mobility," *Journal of Social Psychology,* 44 (August, 1956), 33-48.

BELL, Gerald D., "Processes in the Formation of Adolescent Aspirations," *Social Forces,* 42 (December, 1963), 179-185.

BENNETT, William S., Jr. and Noel P. Gist, "Class and Family Influence on Student Aspirations," *Social Forces,* 43, (December, 1964), 167-173.

BERDIE, Ralph F., "Why They Don't Go To College," *Personnel and Guidance Journal,* 31 (March, 1953).

BLAU, Peter M. and Otis Dudley Duncan, *The American Occupational Structure,* New York: Wiley, 1967.

BOGGS, Stephan T., "Family Size and Social Mobility in a California Suburb," *Eugenics Quarterly,* 4 (1957), 208-213.

BORDUA, David J., "Education Aspirations and Parental Stress on College, *Social Forces,* 38 (March, 1960), 262-269.

BRADLEY, William A., "Correlates of Vocational Preferences,"
Genetic Psychology Monographs, 28 (1943), 99-169.

BRONFENBRENNER, Urie, "The Changing American Child,"
Journal of Social Issues, 17 (1961), 6-18.

**FAMILY
BACKGROUND**

CARTER, Harold D., "Vocational Interests and Job Orientation,"
Applied Psychology Monographs, Stanford University Press,
1944.

CHAPMAN, Dwight W. and John Volkman, "A Social Determinant
of the Level of Aspiration," in T. Newcomb, *et al.,* editors,
Readings In Social Psychology, New York: Holt, 1947.

CHILD, Irvin L. and John W. M. Whiting, "Determinants of
Level of Aspiration: Evidence from Everyday Life," *Journal
of Abnormal and Social Psychology,* 44 (1949), 303-314.

CLARK, E. L., *American Men of Letters: Their Nature and
Nurture,* New York: Columbia University Press, 1916.

COHEN, A. K., and H. M. Hodges, Jr., "Characteristics of the
Lower Blue Collar Class," *Social Problems,* 10 (Spring, 1963),
305-323.

COHEN, Elizabeth G., "Parental Factors in Educational Mobility,"
Sociology of Education, 38 (Fall, 1965), 404-425.

COLEMAN, James S., *The Adolescent Society,* New York: Free
Press, 1961.

CUTRIGHT, Phillips, "Students' Decision to Attend College,"
Journal of Educational Sociology, 33 (February, 1960),
292-299.

DAVIS, James A., *Stipends and Spouses,* Chicago: University of
Chicago Press, 1962.

DYER, William G., "Parental Influence on the Job Attitudes
of Children from Two Occupational Strata," *Sociology and
Social Research,* 42 (January-February, 1958), 203-206.

DYNES, Russell R., Alfred C. Clarke, and Simon Dinitz, "Levels
of Occupational Aspiration: Some Aspects of Family Experience as a Variable," *American Sociological Review,* 21
(April, 1956), 212-215.

ELDER, Glen H. Jr., "Family Structure and Educational Attainment: A Cross-National Analysis," *American Sociological Review,* 30 (February, 1965), 81-96.

ELLIS, Havelock, *A Study of British Genius,* London: Hurst and
Blackett, 1904.

ELLIS, Robert A. and W. Clayton Lane, "Structural Supports for
Upward Mobility," *American Sociological Review,* 28 (October,
1963), 743-756.

FARIS, R. E. L., "Sociological Causes of Genius," *American Sociological Review,* 5 (October, 1940), 689-699.

FLOUD, Jean E., editor, *Social Class and Educational Opportunity,* London: Heineman, 1956, 93-95.

GALTON, Francis, *English Men of Science: Their Nature and Nurture,* London: Macmillan, 1874.

GETZELS, Jacob W. and Philip W. Jackson, "Family Environment and Cognitive Style: A Study of the Sources of Highly Intelligent and Highly Creative Adolescents," *American Sociological Review,* 26 (June, 1961), 351-359.

GINI, Corrado, "Superiority of the Eldest," *Journal of Heredity,* 6 (1915), 37-39.

GIST, Noel P. and William Bennett, Jr., "Aspirations of Negro and White Students," *Social Forces,* 42 (October, 1963), 40-48.

GOETSCH, Helen B., *Parental Income and College Opportunities,* Teachers College Contributions to Education, 795, Columbia University, 1940.

GOODE, William J., "Family and Mobility," in Reinhard Bendix and Seymour M. Lipset, editors, *Class, Status and Power,* revised edition, New York: Free Press, 1966.

GOULD, Rosalind, "Some Sociological Determinants of Goal Striving," *Journal of Social Psychology,* 13 (1941), 461-473.

HARRIS, Irving, *The Promised Seed: A Comparative Study of Eminent First and Later Sons,* New York: Free Press, 1964.

HAVEMANN, Ernest and Patricia West, *They Went to College,* New York: Harcourt Brace, 1952.

HUNTINGTON, Ellsworth, *Season of Birth: Its Relation to Human Abilities,* New York: Wiley, 1938.

HURLEY, John R., "Maternal Attitudes and Childrens' Intelligence," *Journal of Clinical Psychology,* 15 (1959), 291-292.

JONES, Harold E., "Order of Birth in Relation to the Development of the Child," in Carl Murchison, editor, *Handbook of Child Psychology,* Worcester, Massachusetts: Clark University Press, 1931.

KAHL, Joseph A., *The American Class Structure,* New York: Rinehart, 1957, 281-289.

KRACKE, E. A., Jr., "Family versus Merit in Chinese Civil Service Examinations Under the Empire," *Harvard Journal of Asiatic Studies,* 10 (1947), 103-123.

FAMILY BACKGROUND

LEES, J. P., "The Social Mobility of a Group of Eldest-Born and Intermediate Adult Males," *British Journal of Psychology,* 43 (August, 1952), 210-221.

LIPSET, Seymour M. and Reinhard Bendix, *Social Mobility In Industrial Society,* Berkeley: University of California Press, 1966, 631-648.

LOWE, Gilbert Antonio, "Education, Occupation of Fathers and Parental Contributions to Educational Expenses as Factors in Career Aspirations Among Male Jamaican Students," *Journal of Negro Education,* 35 (Summer, 1966), 230-236.

MANNINO, Fortune V., "Family Factors Related to School Persistence," *Journal of Educational Sociology,* 35 (January, 1962).

MAXWELL, James, "Intelligence, Fertility and the Future: A Report on the 1947 Scottish Mental Survey," *Proceedings of the World Population Conference,* New York: United Nations, 1954.

MAYER, K. B., *Class and Society,* Garden City, New York: Doubleday, 1955.

McARTHUR, Charles, "Personalities of First and Second Children," *Psychiatry,* 19 (1956), 47-54.

McCLELLAND, David C., editor, *Studies in Motivation,* New York: Appleton-Century-Crofts, 1955.

McCLELLAND, David C., *et. al., The Achievement Motive,* New York: Appleton-Century-Crofts, 1953.

McCLELLAND, David C. *et. al.,* editors, *Talent and Society,* Princeton: Van Nostrand, 1958.

McDILL, Edward L., "Family and Peer Influences in College Plans of High School Students," *Sociology of Education,* 38 (Winter, 1965), 112-126.

McMILLAN, Robert T., "Farm Ownership Status of Parents as a Determinant of the Socioeconomic Status of Farmers," *Rural Sociology,* 9 (June, 1944), 151-160.

MORROW, William R. and Robert C. Wilson, "Family Relations of Bright High-Achieving and Under-Achieving High School Boys," *Child Development,* 32 (1961), 501-510.

MULLIGAN, Raymond A., "Social Characteristics of College Students," *American Sociological Review,* 18 (June, 1953), 305-310.

MULLIGAN, Raymond A., "Socio-Economic Background and College Enrollment," *American Sociological Review,* 16 (April, 1951), 188-196.

NISBET, J. D., *Family Environment: A Direct Effect of Family Size on Intelligence,* London: Eugenics Society, 1953.

OGBURN, William F., "Our Social Heritage," *Survey,* 59 (1927), 277-279.

PAVALKO, Ronald M. and Norma Nager, "Contingencies of Marriage to High-Status Men," *Social Forces,* 46 (June, 1968), 523-531.

PUNKE, Harold H., "Factors Affecting the Proportion of High School Graduates Who Enter College," *Bulletin of the National Association of Secondary School Principals,* 38 (November, 1954), 6-27.

RAMSOY, Natalie Rogoff, *American High Schools at Mid-Century,* New York: Bureau of Applied Social Research, Columbia University, 1961.

ROE, Anne, *The Making of a Scientist,* New York: Dodd-Mead, 1953.

ROE, Anne, "A Psychological Study of Eminent Psychologists and Anthropologists and a Comparison of Biological and Physical Scientists," *Psychological Monographs,* 67 (1953).

ROGOFF, Natalie, "Local Social Structure and Educational Selection," in A. H. Halsey, Jean Floyd, and C. Arnold Anderson, editors, *Education, Economy, and Society,* New York: Free Press, 1961.

ROSEN, Bernard C., "The Achievement Syndrome: A Psychocultural Dimension of Social Stratification, *American Sociological Review,* 21 (April, 1956), 203-211.

ROSEN, Bernard C., "Family Structure and Achievement Motivation," *American Sociological Review,* 26 (August, 1961), 574-585.

ROSEN, Bernard C. and Roy C. de Andrade, "The Psycho-Social Origins of Achievement Motivation," *Sociometry,* 22 (September, 1959), 185-218.

ROSSI, Alice S., "Naming Children in Middle-Class Families," *American Sociological Review,* 30 (August, 1965), 499-513.

SAMPSON, Edward E., "Birth Order, Need Achievement and Conformity," *Journal of Abnormal and Social Psychology,* 64 (1962), 155-159.

SCHACHTER, Stanley, "Birth Order, Eminence and Higher Education," *American Sociological Review,* 28 (October, 1963), 757-768.

SCHACHTER, Stanley, "Birth Order and Sociometric Choice," *Journal of Abnormal and Social Psychology,* 68(1964), 453-456.

SHELDON, Paul M., "The Families of Highly Gifted Children," *Marriage and Family Living,* 16 (February, 1954), 59-60.

SIMPSON, Richard L., "Parental Influence, Anticipatory Socialization and Social Mobility," *American Sociological Review,* 27 (August, 1962), 517-522.

SIMPSON, Richard L. and Ida H. Simpson, "Values, Personal Influence and Occupational Choice," *Social Forces,* 39 (December, 1960) 116-125.

SMELSER, William J., "Adolescent and Adult Occupational Choice as a Function of Family Socioeconomic History," *Sociometry,* 26 (December, 1963), 393-409.

SMITH, Howard P. and M. Abramson, "Racial and Family Experience Correlates of Mobility Aspiration," *Journal of Negro Education,* 31 (Spring, 1962), 117-124.

STAGNER, R. and E. T. Katyoff, "Personality as Related to Birth Order and Family Size," *Journal of Applied Psychology,* 20 (May-June, 1936), 340-346.

STRAUS, Murray A., "Conjugal Power Structure and Adolescent Personality," *Marriage and Family Living,* 24 (February, 1962), 17-25.

STRODBECK, Fred L., "Family Interaction, Values and Achievement," in David C. McClelland, *et. al.,* editors, *Talent and Society,* Princeton: Van Nostrand, 1958.

STROUP, Attlee L. and Katherine Jamison Hunter, "Sibling Position in the Family and Personality of Offspring," *Journal of Marriage and the Family,* 27 (February, 1965), 65-68.

STUBBINS; Joseph, "The Relationship between Level of Vocational Aspiration and Certain Personal Data," *Genetic Psychology Monographs,* 41 (1950), 327-408.

SVALASTOGA, Kaare, "The Family in the Mobility Process," in Nels Anderson, editor, *Recherches sur la Famille,* Gottingen: Vandenhoeck and Ruprecht, 1958.

TERMAN, Lewis, "Mental and Physical Traits of a Thousand Gifted Children," in Lewis Terman, editor, *Genetic Studies of Genius,* Stanford: Stanfordc University Press, 1925.

TERMAN, Lewis and Melita H. Oden, *The Gifted Child Grows Up,* Stanford: Stanford University Press, 1947.

THOMSON, Sir Godfrey, "Intelligence and Fertility: The Scottish 1947 Survey," *Eugenics Review,* 41 (1950).

THURSTONE, L. L. and Richard L. Jenkins, "Birth Order and Intelligence," *Journal of Educational Psychology* 20 (1929), 641-651.

TIEN, H. Y., *Social Mobility and Controlled Fertility: Family Origins and Structure of the Australian Academic Elite,* New Haven: College and University Press, 1965.

TURNER, Ralph H., *The Social Context of Ambition,* San Francisco: Chandler, 1964.

TURNER, Ralph H., "Some Family Determinants of Ambition," *Sociology and Social Research,* 46 (July, 1962), 397-411.

TURNER, Ralph H., "Upward Mobility and Class Values," *Social Problems,* 11 (Spring, 1964), 359-371.

VISHER, Stephen S., "Environmental Backgrounds of Leading American Scientists," *American Sociological Review,* 10 (February, 1945), 52-60.

WARNER, W. Lloyd and James C. Abegglen, *Big Business Leaders in America,* New York: Athenuem, 1955.

WITTY, Paul, editor, *The Gifted Child,* New York: Heath, 1951.

WOEFLE, Dael, *American Resources of Specialized Talent,* New York: Harper, 1954.

YODER, Albert H., "The Study of the Boyhood of Great Men," *Pedagogical Seminary* 3 (1894), 134-156.

Education and Mobility

Additional materials related to this topic can be found under "Interrelations among Stratification Variables."

ANDERSON, C. Arnold, "A Skeptical Note on the Relation of Vertical Mobility to Education," *American Journal of Sociology,* 66 (May, 1961), 560-570.

BENNETT, William S. Jr., "Educational Change and Economic Development," *Sociology of Education,* 40 (Spring, 1967), 101-114.

BURTON, William H., "Education and Social Class in the United States," *Harvard Educational Review,* 23 (Fall, 1953), 243-256.

BUSIA, K. A., "Education and Social Mobility in Economically Underdeveloped Countries," *Transactions of the Third World Congress of Sociology,* 5 (1956), 81-89.

CARLSSON, Gosta and Bengt Gesser, "Universities as Selecting and Socializing Agents: Some Recent Swedish Data," *Acta Sociologica,* 9, 25-39.

CARO, Francis G. and C. Terence Pihlblad, "Social Class, Formal Education, and Social Mobility," *Sociology and Social Research,* 48 (July, 1964), 428-439.

CENTERS, Richard, "Education and Occupational Mobility," *American Sockological Review,* 14 (February, 1949), 143-144.

CLARK, Burton R., "The 'Cooling Out' Function in Higher Education," *American Journal of Sociology,* 65 (May, 1960), 569-576.

CONNELL, W. F., "Education and Social Mobility in Australia," *Transactions of the Third World Congress of Sociology,* 5 (1956), 71-77.

CROCKETT, Harry J. Jr., "Social Class, Education and Motive to Achieve in Differential Occupational Mobility," *Sociological Quarterly*, 5 (Summer, 1964), 231-242.

DAILEY, John T., "Education and Emergence from Poverty," *Journal of Marriage and the Family*, 26 (November, 1964), 430-434.

DAVIE, James S., "Social Class Factors and School Attendance," *Harvard Educational Review*, 23 (Summer, 1953), 175-185.

DONOVAN, Thomas R., "Socioeconomic and Educational Factors Influencing the Achievement Level of Individuals in Large-Scale Organizations," *Sociology and Social Research*, 46 (July, 1962), 416-425.

DUNCAN, Otis Dudley and Robert W. Hodge, "Education and Occupational Mobility: A Regression Anlaysis," *American Journal of Sociology*, 68 (May, 1963), 629-644.

ECKLAND, Bruce K., "Academic Ability, Higher Education, and Occupational Mobility," *American Sociological Review*, 30 (October, 1966), 735-746.

ECKLAND, Bruce K., "A Source of Errors in College Attrition Studies," *Sociology of Education*, 38 (Fall, 1964), 60-72.

FLOUD, J. E., F. M. Martin, and A. H. Halsey, "Educational Opportunity and Social Selection in Britain," *Transactions of the Second World Congress of Sociology*, 2 (1954), 194-208.

FOSTER, Philip J., "Secondary Schooling and Social Mobility in a West African Nation," *Sociology of Education*, 37 (Winter, 1963), 150-171.

GERSTL, Joel, and Robert Perrucci, "Educational Channels and Elite Mobility: A Comparative Analysis," *Sociology of Education*, 38 (Spring, 1965), 224-232.

GLICK, Paul C., "Educational Attainment and Occupational Achievement," *Transactions of the Second World Congress of Sociology*, 2 (1954) 183-193.

HAVEMANN, Ernest and Patricia West, *They Went to College*, New York: Harcourt Brace, 1952.

HAVIGHURST, Robert J., "Education, Social Mobility, and Social Change in Four Societies: Great Britain, U.S.A., Brazil, Australia," *International Review of Education*, 4 (1948), 167-185.

HAVIGHURST, Robert J. and Bernice L. Neugarten, *Society and Education*, Boston: Allyn and Bacon, 1967, 69-94.

HURD, G. E. and T. J. Johnson, "Education and Social Mobility in Ghana," *Sociology of Education*, 40 (Winter, 1967), 55-79.

JACKSON, Brian, *Streaming: An Education Systems in Miniature,* London: Routledge and Kegan Paul, 1964.

MULLIGAN, Raymond A., "Social Mobility and Higher Education," *Journal of Educational Sociology,* 25 (April, 1952), 476-487.

EDUCATION AND MOBILITY

PERRUCCI, Robert, "Education, Stratification, and Mobility," in Donald Hansen and Joel Gerstl, editors, *On Education—Sociological Perspectives,* New York: Wiley, 1967.

ROGOFF, Natalie, "American Public Schools and Equality of Opportunity," in A. H. Halsey, J. Floud, and C. A. Anderson, editors, *Education, Economy and Society,* New York: Free Press, 1961.

SEXTON, Patricia Cayo, *Education and Income,* New York: Viking, 1961.

SHANNON, J. R. and Maxine Shaw, "Education of Business and Professional Leaders," *American Sociological Review,* 5 (June, 1940), 381-385.

SPADY, William G., "Educational Mobility and Access: Growth and Paradoxes," *American Journal of Sociology,* 73 (November, 1967), 273-286.

STEPHENSON, Richard, "Stratification, Education and Occupational Orientation: A Parallel Study and Review," *British Journal of Sociology,* 9 (March, 1958), 42-52.

TURNER, Ralph H., "Sponsored and Contest Mobility and the School System," *American Sociological Review,* 25 (December, 1960), 855-867.

WERTS, Charles E., "Career Changes in College," *Sociology of Education,* 40 (Winter, 1967), 90-95.

WEST, Patricia Salter, "Social Mobility Among College Graduates," in Reinhard Bendix and Seymour M. Lipset, *Class, Status and Power,* New York: Free Press, 1953.

WILSON, Paul B., and R. C. Buck, "The Educational Ladder," *Rural Sociology,* 25 (December, 1960), 404-413.

WINDHAM, Gerald O., "Pre-Adult Socialization and Selected Status Achievement Variables," *Social Forces,* 42 (May, 1964), 456-461.

Religous Preference and Mobility

Most of this literature is in the tradition of Max Weber's *The Protestant Ethic and the Spirit of Capitalism.* A few of the publications deal with degree of religious interest, participation, and commitment as well as with religious affiliation and preference.

BOGUE, Donald J., "Religious Affiliation," *The Population of the United States,* New York: Free Press, 1959, 688-709.

BOISEN, A. T., "Economic Distress and Religious Experience," *Psychiatry,* (May, 1939), 185-194.

BRESSLER, Marvin and Charles F. Westoff, "Catholic Education, Economic Values, and Achievement," *American Journal of Sociology,* 69 (November, 1963), 225-233.

CANTRIL, Hadley, "Education and Economic Composition of Religious Groups: An Analysis of Poll Data," *American Journal of Sociology,* 47 (March, 1943), 574-579.

CARNEY, Richard E. and Wilbert J. McKeachie, "Religion, Sex, Social Class, Probability of Success and Student Personality," *Journal for the Scientific Study of Religion,* 3 (Fall, 1963), 32-41.

CRAMER, Carl, "The Peculiar People Prosper," *New York Times Magazine,* (April 15, 1962).

CURTIS, Richard F., "Occupational Mobility and Church Participation," *Social Forces,* 38 (May, 1960), 315-319.

DATTA, Lois-ellin, "Family Religious Background and Early Scientific Creativity," *American Sociological Review,* 32 (August, 1967), 626-635.

FANFANI, Amitore, *Catholicism, Protestantism, and Capitalism,* New York: Sheed and Ward, 1955.

FAUSET, Arthur H., *Black Gods of the Metropolis,* Philadelphia: University of Pennsylvania Press, 1949.

GLAZER, Nathan, "The American Jew and the Attainment of Middle-Class Rank: Some Trends and Explanations," in Marshall Sklare, editor, *The Jews*, New York: Free Press, 1958.

GLENN, Norval D., "Negro Religion and Negro Status in the United States," in Louis Schneider, editor, *Religion, Culture and Society*, New York: Wiley, 1964.

GLENN, Norval D. and Ruth Hyland, "Religious Preference and Worldly Success: Some Evidence from National Surveys," *American Sociological Review*, 32 (February, 1967), 73-85.

GLOCK, Charles Y., "The Role of Deprivation in the Origin and Evolution of Religious Groups," in Robert Lee and Martin E. Marty, *Religion and Social Conflict*, New York: Oxford University Press, 1964.

GREELEY, Andrew M., "Influence of the 'Religious Factor' on Career Plans and Occupational Values of College Graduates," *American Journal of Sociology*, 68 (May, 1963), 658-671.

GREELEY, Andrew M., "Religion and Academic Career Plans: A Note on Progress, *American Journal of Sociology*, 72 (May, 1967), 668-672.

GREELEY, Andrew M., *Religion and Career: A Study of College Graduates*, New York: Sheed and Ward, 1963.

GREELEY, Andrew and Peter Rossi, *The Education of Catholic Americans*, Chicago: Aldine, 1966.

GREELEY, Andrew M., "The Protestant Ethic: Time for a Moratorium," *Sociological Analysis*, 25 (Spring, 1964), 20-33.

GRONER, F., "The Social Standing of Catholics in the Federal Republic of Germany," *Social Compass*, 9 (1962), 348-355.

HURVITZ, Nathan, "Sources of Middle-Class Values of American Jews," *Social Forces*, 37 (December, 1958), 117-123.

HURVITZ, Nathan, "Sources of Motivitaion and Achievement of American Jews," *Jewish Social Studies,* 23 (1961), 217-234.

JOHNSON, Benton, "Do Holiness Sects Socialize in Dominant Values," *Social Forces*, 39 (May, 1961), 309-316.

JOHNSON, Benton, C. C. Langford, R. H. White, R. B. Jacobsent, and J. D. McCarthy, *Religion and Occupational Be-* University of Oregon, Center for Research in Occupational Planning, 1966.

KEPHART, William M., "What is the Position of Jewish Economy in the United States?" *Social Forces*, 28 (December, 1949), 153-164.

KOSA, J., "Patterns of Social Mobility Among American Catholics," *Social Compass,* 9 (1962), 361-371.

LANE, Ralph, Jr., "Research on Catholics as a Status Group," *Sociological Analysis,* 26 (Summer, 1965).

LAZERWITZ, Bernard, "A Comparison of Major Religious Groups," *Journal of the American Statistical Association,* 56 (September, 1961), 568-579.

LAZERWITZ, Bernard, "Religion and Social Structure in the United States," in Louis Schneider, editor, *Religion, Culture and Society,* New York: Wiley, 1964.

LENSKI, Gerhard, *The Religious Factor,* revised edition, Garden City, New York: Doubleday, 1963.

LINCOLN, C. Eric, *The Black Muslims in America,* Boston: Beacon, 1961.

LIPSET, Seymour M. and Reinhard Bendix, *Social Mobility in Industrial Society,* Berkeley: University of California Press, 1959, 48-56.

MACK, Raymond W., Raymond J. Murphy, and Seymour Yellin, "The Protestant Ethic, Level of Aspiration, and Social Mobility: An Empirical Test," *American Sociological Review,* 21 (June, 1956), 295-300.

MAYER, Albert J. and Harry Sharp, "Religious Preference and Wordly Success," *American Sociological Review,* 27 (April, 1962), 218-227.

McCLELLAND, David C., A. Rindlisbacher and R. DeCharms, "Religious and other Sources of Parental Attitudes toward Independence Training," in David C. McClelland, editor, *Studies in Motivation,* New York: Appleton-Century-Crofts, 1955.

O'DEA, Thomas F., *The Mormans,* Chicago: University of Chicago Press, 1967.

ROBERTSON, H. M., *Aspects of the Rise of Economic Individualism: A Criticism of Max Weber and His School,* Cambridge: Cambridge University Press, 1933.

ROSEN, Bernard C., "Race, Ethnicity, and the Achievement Syndrome," *American Sociological Review,* 24 (February, 1959), 47-60.

SAMUELSSON, Kurt, *Religion and Economic Action: The Protestant Ethic, the Rise of Capitalism, and the Abuses of Scholarship,* New York: Basic Books, 1961.

SCHNEIDER, J., "Social Origin and Fame: The United States

and England," *American Sociological Review,* 10 (February, 1945), 52-60.

SOMBART, Werner, *The Jews and Modern Capitalism,* translated by M. Epstein, London: Unwin, 1913.

RELIGIOUS PREFERENCE

STRODTBECK, Fred L., Margaret R. McDonald, and Bernard C. Rosen, "Evaluation of Occupations: A Reflection of Jewish and Italian Differences," *American Sociological Review,* 22 (October, 1957), 546-553.

STRODTBECK, Fred L., "Family Interaction, Values, and Achievement," in Marshall Sklare, editor, *The Jews,* New York: Free Press, 1958.

TAWNEY, R. H., *Religion and the Rise of Capitalism,* New York: Harcourt Brace, 1926.

THORNER, Isidor, "Ascetic Protestantism and the Development of Science and Technology," *American Journal of Sociology,* 58 (July, 1952), 25-33.

VEROFF, Joseph, Sheila Feld, and Gerald Gurin, "Achievement Motivation and Religious Background," *American Sociological Review,* 27 (April, 1962), 205-217.

WARNER, W. Lloyd and James C. Abbeglen, *Big Business Leaders in America,* New York: Athenuem, 1955.

WEBER, Max, *The Protestant Ethic and the Spirit of Capitalism,* translated by Talcott Parsons, New York: Scribners, 1958.

Aspiration, Motivation, and Other Presumed
Psychological Correlates of Mobility

The publications in this section deal with aspirations, ambition, achievement motivation, expectation of mobility, occupational choice, the ability and willingness to defer gratification, and a number of other psychological phenomena that are believed to affect chances for upward mobility. The literature provides a rich body of evidence on the sources of these characteristics, but unfortunately it provides much less evidence on the relationship of these psychological phenomena to mobility and achievement.

ALEXANDER, C. Norman, Jr. and Ernest Q. Campbell, "Peer Influences on Adolescent Educational aspirations and Attainments," *American Sociological Review,* 29 (August, 1964), 568-575.

ANDERSON, C. LeRoy, "A Preliminary Study of Generational Economic Dependency Orientations," *Social Forces,* 45 (June, 1967), 516-520.

ANDREW, D. C., and Francis Stroup, "Plans of Arkansas High School Seniors," *Personnel and Guidance Journal,* 39 (December, 1960), 300-302.

ANTONOVSKY, Aaron, "Aspirations, Class and Racial-Ethnic Membership," *Journal of Negro Education,* 36 (Fall, 1967), 385-393.

ANTONOVSKY, Aaron and Melvin J. Lerner, "Occupational Aspirations of Lower Class Negro and White Youth," *Social Problems,* 7 (Fall, 1959), 132-138.

BAALI, Fuad, "Educational Aspirations Among College Girls in Iraq," *Sociology and Social Research,* 51 (July, 1967), 485-493.

BANFIELD, Edward C., *The Moral Basis of a Backward Society,* New York: Free Press, 1958.

BAROW, H., "Vocational Development Research: Some Problems

of Logical and Experimental Form," *Personnel and Guidance Journal,* 40 (September, 1961), 21-25.

ASPIRATION AND
MOTIVATION

BEILIN, Harry, "The Pattern of Postponability and its Relation to Social Class Mobility," *Journal of Social Psychology,* 44 (August, 1956), 33-48.

BELL, Robert R., "Lower Class Negro Mothers' Aspirations for their Children," *Social Forces,* 43 (May, 1965), 493-500.

BENDER, Lloyd D., Daryl J. Hobbs, and James F. Golden, "Congruence between Aspirations and Capabilities of Youth in a Low-income Rural Area," *Rural Sociologist,* 32 (September, 1967), 278-289.

BENE, Eva, "Some Differences Between Middle-Class and Working-Class Grammar School Boys in Their Attitude Toward Education," *British Journal of Sociology,* 10 (June, 1959), 148-152.

BENNETT, William S., Jr. and Noel P. Gist, "Class and Family Influences on Student Aspirations," *Social Forces,* 43 (December, 1964), 167-173.

BERTRAND, A. L. and M. B. Smith, *Environmental Factors and School Attendance: A Study in Rural Louisiana,* Baton Rouge: Louisiana Agricultural Experiment Station, Bulletin 533, (May, 1960).

BIRNEY, Robert C., "The Reliability of the Achievement Motive," *Journal of Abnormal and Social Psychology,* 58 (1959), 266-267.

BIRNEY, Robert C., "Research on the Achievement Motive," in Edgar F. Borgatta and William W. Lambert, *Handbook of Personality Theory and Research,* Chicago: Rand McNally, 1968.

BLAU, Peter M., J. W. Gustad, R. Jessor, H. S. Parnes, and R. C. Wilcock, "Occupational Choice: A Conceptual Framework," *Industrial and Labor Relations Review,* 9 (July, 1956), 531-543.

BORDUA, David J., "Educational Aspirations and Parental Stress on College," *Social Forces,* 38 (March, 1960), 262-267.

BOYD, George Felix, "The Levels of Aspiration of White and Negro Children in a Non-Segregated Elementary School," *Journal of Social Psychology,* 36 (August, 1952), 191-196.

BOYKIN, Leander L. and William F. Brazziel, Jr., "Occupational Interests of 1,741 Teacher Education Students as Revealed on the Lee-Thorpe Inventory," *Journal of Negro Education,* 28 (Winter, 1959), 42-48.

BOYLE, Richard P., "The Effect of the High School on Students' Aspirations," *American Journal of Sociology,* 71 (May, 1966), 628-639.

BOYLE, Richard P., "On Neighborhood Context and College Plans," *American Sociological Review,* 31 (October, 1966), 706-707.

BURCHINAL, Lee, "Differences in Educational and Occupational Aspirations of Farm, Small-Town and City Boys," *Rural Sociology,* 26 (June, 1961), 107-121.

BURCHINAL, Lee, editor, *Rural Youth in Crisis: Facts, Myths and Social Change,* Washington, D. C.: Department of Health, Education, and Welfare, 1965.

BURCHINAL, Lee, Marvin Jones, and Archibald O. Haller, *Career Choices of Rural Youth in a Changing Society,* St. Paul: University of Minnesota, North Central Regional Research Bulletin 412, 1962.

CALHOUN, David H., *Professional Lives in America: Structure and Aspiration,* Cambridge: Harvard University Press, 1965.

CAMPBELL, Ernest Q. and C. Norman Alexander, "Structural Effects and Interpersonal Relationships," *American Journal of Sociology,* 71 (November, 1965), 284-289.

CANCIAN, Frank,,"The Southern Italian Peasant: World View and Political Behavior," *Anthropological Quarterly,* 34 (1961), 1-18.

CARDILL, William and George DeVos, "Achievement, Culture, and Personality: The Case of the Japanese Americans," *Anthropological Quarterly,* 58 (1956), 1102-1126.

CARO, Francis G., "Deferred Gratification, Time Conflict, and College Attendance," *Sociology of Education,* 38 (Summer, 1965), 332-341.

CARO, Francis G., "Social Class and Attitudes of Youth Relevant for the Realization of Adult Goals," *Social Forces,* 44 (June, 1966), 492-498.

CARO, Francis G. and C. Terence Pihlblad, "Aspirations and Expectations: A Reexamination of the Bases for Social Class Differences in the Occupational Orientations of Male High School Students," *Sociology and Social Research,* 49 (July, 1965), 465-475.

CASSEL, Russell N. and Randolf G. Sawgstad, "Level of Aspiration and Sociometric Distance," *Sociometry,* 15 (August, 1952), 319-325.

CAUDILL, William and George Devos, "Achievement, Culture and Personality: The Case of the Japanese Americans," *American Anthropologist,* 58 (December, 1956), 1102-1126.

ASPIRATION AND
MOTIVATION

CENTERS, Richard, "Motivational Aspects of Occupational Stratification," *Journal of Social Psychology,* 28 (1948), 187-217.

CENTERS, Richard and Hadley Cantril, "Income Satisfaction and Income Aspiration," *Journal of Abnormal and Social Psychology,* 41 (1946), 64-69.

CHILD, Irvin L. and John W. M. Whiting, "Determinants of Level of Aspiration: Evidence from Everyday Life," *Journal of Abnormal and Social Psychology,* 44 (1949), 303-314.

CHINOY, Ely, *Automobile Workers and the American Dream,* Garden City, New York: Doubleday, 1955.

CHINOY, Ely, "The Tradition of Opportunity and the Aspirations of Automobile Workers," *American Journal of Sociology,* 57 (March, 1952), 453-459.

CHRISTENSEN, Harold T., "Lifetime Family and Occupational Role Projections of High School Students," *Marriage and Family Living,* 23 (May, 1961), 181-182.

CHRISTIANSEN, J. R., J. D. Cowhig, and J. W. Payne, *Educational and Occupational Aspirations of High School Seniors in Three Central Utah Counties,* Provo, Utah: Brigham Young University, Social Science Bulletin 2, August, 1962.

CLARK, Russell A., Richard Teevan, and Henry N. Ricciuti, "Hope of Success and Fear of Failure as Aspects of Need for Achievement," *Journal of Abnormal and Social Psychology,* (September, 1956), 182-186.

CLEVELAND, Stuart, "A Tardy Look at Stouffer's Findings in the Harvard Mobility Project," *Public Opinion Quarterly,* 26 (Fall, 1962), 453-454.

COATES, Charles H. and Roland J. Pellegrin, "Executives and Supervisors: Contrasting Definitions of Career Success," *Administrative Science Quarterly,* 1 (1957), 506-517.

COATES, Charles H. and Roland J. Pellegrin, "Executives and Supervisors: A Situational Theory of Differential Occupational Mobility," *Social Forces,* 35 (December, 1956), 121-126.

COLEMAN, James S., "Academic Achievement and the Structure of Competition," *Harvard Educational Review,* 29 (Fall, 1959), 330-351.

COLEMAN, James S., *The Adolescent Society,* New York: Free Press, 1961.

COLEMAN, James S., "The Adolescent Subculture and Academic Achievement," *American Journal of Sociology,* 65 (January, 1960), 337-347.

CONANT, Bryant *Slums and Suburbs,* New York: McGraw-Hill, 1961.

COOMBS, Robert H. and Vernon Davies, "Social Class, Scholastic Aspiration, and Academic Achievement," *Pacific Sociological Review,* 8 (Fall, 1965), 96-100.

CORWIN, Ronald G., "Role Conception and Career Aspiration: A Study of Identity in Nursing," *Sociological Quarterly,* 2 (April, 1961), 69-86.

COWHIG, J. D., J. Artis, J. A. Beegle, and H. Goldsmith, *Orientation Toward Occupation and Residence: A Study of High School Seniors in Four Rural Counties of Michigan,* East Lansing: Michigan Agricultural Experiment Station, Special Bulletin 428, 1960.

CRAMER, M. Richard, Ernest Q. Campbell, and Charles E. Bowerman, *Social Forces in Educational Achievements and Aspirations among Negro Adolescents,* Volume I: *Demographic Study,* and Volume II: *Survey Study,* Chapel Hill: University of North Carolina, Institute for Social Research, 1966.

CROCKETT, Harry J., "Social Class, Education and Motive to Achieve in Differential Occupational Mobility," *Sociological Quarterly,* 5 (Summer, 1964), 231-242.

CROCKETT, Harry J., "The Achievement Motive and Differential Occupational Mobility in the United States," *American Sociological Review,* 27 (April, 1962), 191-204.

CUTRIGHT, Phillips, "Students' Decisions to Attend College," *Journal of Educational Sociology,* 33 (February, 1960), 292-299.

DANSEREAU, H. Kirk, "Work and the Teen-Age Blue-Collarite," in Arthur B. Shostak and William Gomberg, editors, *Blue-Collar World: Studies of the American Worker,* Englewood Cliffs, New Jersey: Prentice Hall, 1964.

DAVIS, Allison, "The Motivation of the Underprivileged Worker," in William F. Whyte, editor, *Industry and Society,* New York: McGraw-Hill, 1946.

DAVIS, Ethelyn, "Careers as Concerns of Blue-Collar Girls," in Arthur B. Shostak and William Gomberg, editors, *Blue-Collar World: Studies of the American Worker,* Englewood Cliffs, New Jersey: Prentice Hall, 1964.

DAVIS, James A., *Great Aspirations: The Graduate School Plans of America's College Seniors,* Chicago: Aldine, 1964.

DAVIS, James A., *Undergraduate Career Decisions,* Chicago: Aldine, 1965.

ASPIRATION AND
MOTIVATION

deCHARMS, Richard, *et al.,* "Behavioral Correlates of Directly and Indirectly Measured Achievement Motivation," in David C. McClelland, editor, *Studies in Motivation,* New York: Appleton-Century-Crofts, 1955.

DEUTSCH, M., "Some Factors Affecting Membership Motivation and Achievement Motivation in a Group," *Human Relations,* 12 (1959), 81-95.

DOUVAN, Elizabeth and Carol Kaye, "Motivation Factors in College Entrance," in Nevitt Sanford, editor, *The American College,* New York: Wiley, 1962.

DUFFY, N. F., "Occupational Status, Job Satisfaction, and Levels of Aspiration," *British Journal of Sociology,* 11 (December, 1960), 348-355.

DYER, William G., "Parental Influence on the Job Attitudes of Children from Two Occupational Strata," *Sociology and Social Research,* 42 (January-February, 1958), 203-206.

DYNES, Russell R., Alfred C. Clarke, and Simon Dinitz, "Levels of Occupational Aspiration: Some Aspects of Family Experience as a Variable," *American Sociological Review,* 21 (April, 1956), 212-215.

EDLEFSEN, J. B. and M. J. Crowe, *Teen-Agers' Occupational Aspirations,* Pullman: Washington Agricultural Experiment Station, Bulletin 618, July, 1960.

ELDER, Glen H., Jr., "Achievement Orientations and Career Patterns of Rural Youth," *Sociology of Education,* 37 (Fall, 1963), 30-58.

ELDER, Glen H., Jr., *Adolescent Achievement and Mobility Aspirations,* Chapel Hill: University of North Carolina, Institure for Research in Social Science, 1962.

EMPEY, Lamar T., "Social Class and Occupational Aspiration: A Comparison of Absolute and Relative Measurement," *American Sociological Review,* 21 (December, 1956), 703-709.

ESKOLA, Antti, "Level of Aspiration in Career Selection," *Acta Sociologica,* 239-248.

FEATHER, N. T., "The Relationship of Persistence at a Task to Expectation of Success and Achievement Related Motives," *Journal of Abnormal and Social Psychology,* (November, 1961), 552-561.

FICHTER, Joseph H., "Career Preparations and Expectations of Negro College Seniors," *Journal of Negro Education,* 35 (Fall, 1966), 322-335.

FLIEGEL, F. C., "Aspirations of Low-Income Farmers and Their Performance and Potential For Change," *Rural Sociology,* 24 (September, 1959), 205-214.

FOSTER, Philip J., "Secondary School-Leavers in Ghana: Expectations and Reality," *Harvard Educational Review,* 34 (Fall, 1964), 537-558.

FRIEDENBERG, Edgar Z., "An Ideology of School Withdrawal," in Arthur B. Shostak and William Gomberg, editors, *Blue-Collar World: Studies of the American Worker,* Englewood Cliffs, New Jersey: Prentice Hall, 1964.

GALLER, Enid H., "Influence of Social Class on Children's Choices of Occupation," *Elementary School Journal,* 51 (1951), 439-445.

GEORGE, P. M., "A Balance Approach to Occupational Committment, Values, and Perceptions," *Sociological Inquiry,* 37 (Spring, 1967), 291-295.

GINZBERG, Eli, S. W. Ginsburg, S. Axelrad, and J. L. Herma, *Occupational Choice: An Approach to a General Theory,* New York: Columbia University Press, 1951.

GOTTLIEB, David and C. Ramsey, *The American Adolescent,* Homewood, Illinois: Dorsey, 1964, Chapter 8.

GRAVES, Theodore, "Psychological Acculturation in a Tri-Ethnic Community," *Southwestern Journal of Anthropology,* 23 (Winter, 1967), 337-350.

GREELEY, Andrew M., "Influence of the 'Religious Factor' on Career Plans and Occupational Values of College Graduates," *American Journal of Sociology,* 68 (May, 1963), 658-671.

GREELEY, Andrew M., "Religion and Academic Career Plans: A Note on Progress," *American Journal of Sociology,* 72 (May, 1967), 668-672.

GREENBERG, Herbert, C. Marvin, and B. Bivens, "Authoritarianism as a Variable in Motivation to Attend College," *Journal of Social Psychology,* (February, 1959), 81-85.

GRIGG, Charles M. and Russell Middleton, "Community of Oreintation and Occupational Aspirations of Ninth Grade Students," *Social Forces,* 38 (May, 1960), 303-308.

GUEST, Robert H., "Work Careers and Aspirations of Automobile Workers," *American Sociological Review,* 19 (April, 1954), 155-163.

GURIN, Patricia, "Social Class Constraints on the Occupational Aspiration of Students Attending Some Predominately Negro Colleges," *Journal of Negro Education,* 35 (Fall, 1966), 336-350.

HAAS, Eugene, Marvin Taves, and David Shaw, "Primary Group Influence on Vocational Choice," *Sociological Quarterly,* 2 (April, 1961), 87-96.

ASPIRATION AND
MOTIVATION

HALLER, Archie O., "Occupational Choice Behavior of Farm
Boys," *Journal of Cooperative Extension,* 4 (Summer, 1966),
93-102.

HALLER, Archie O., "Planning to Farm: A Social Psychological
Interpretation," *Social Forces,* 37 (March, 1959), 263-268.

HALLER, Archie O., Lee G. Burchinal, and M. J. Taves, *Rural
Youth Need Help in Choosing Occupations,* East Lansing:
Michigan Agricultural Experiment Station, Circular Bulletin,
235, 1963.

HALLER, Archie O. and C. E. Butterworth, "Peer Influences on
Levels of Occupational and Educational Aspiration," *Social
Forces,* 38 (May, 1960), 289-295.

HALLER, Archie O. and Irwin W. Miller, *The Occupational
Aspiration Scale,* East Lansing: Michigan State University
Technical Bulletin 288, 1963.

HALLER, Archie O. and William H. Sewell, "Farm Residence
and Levels of Educational and Occupational Aspiration,"
American Journal of Sociology, 62 (January, 1957), 407-411.

HALLER, Archie O. and William H. Sewell, "Farm Residence
and Levels of Educational and Occupational Aspiration,"
American Journal of Sociology, 62 (January, 1957), 407-411.

HALLER, Archie O. and William H. Sewell, "Occupational
Choices of Wisconsin Farm Boys," *Rural Sociologist,* 32
(March, 1967), 37-55.

HARRIS, Edward E., "Some Comparisons Among Negro-White
College Students: Social Ambitions and Estimated Social
Mobility," *Journal of Negro Education,* 35 (Fall, 1966), 351-
368.

HAVIGHURST, Robert J., "The Influence of Recent Social
Changes on the Desire for Mobility in the United States,"
in Lyman Bryson, Louis Finkelstein, and R. M. McIver,
editors, *Conflicts of Power in Modern Culture,* New York:
Harper, 1947.

HAVIGHURST, Robert J. and Bernice L. Neugarten, *Society
and Education,* Boston: Allyn and Bacon, 1969.

HAVIGHURST, Robert and R. Rodgers, "The Role of Motivation in Attendance at Post-High-School Educational Institutions," in Byron S. Hollinshead, editor, *Who Should Go to
College?,* New York: Columbia University Press, 1952.

HEATH, Clark W., John P. Monks, and William L. Woods, "The
Nature of Career Selection in a group of Harvard Under-
graduates," *Harvard Educational Review,* 17 (Summer, 1947),
190-198.

HECKSHER, Bridget Tancock, "Household Structure and Achievement Orientation in Lower-Class Barbadian Families," *Journal of Marriage and the Family,* 29 (August, 1967), 521-526.

HERRIOTT, Robert E., "Some Social Determinants of Educational Aspiration," *Harvard Educational Review,* 33 (Spring, 1963), 157-177.

HIERONYMUS, A. N., "A Study of Social Class Motivation: Relationahips Between Anxiety For Education and Certain Socio-Economic and Intellectual Variables," *Journal of Educational Psychology,* 42 (April, 1951), 193-205.

HILGARD, E. R., "Success in Relation to Level of Aspiration," *School and Society,* 55 (1942), 423-428.

HOLLOWAY, Robert G. and Joel V. Berreman, "The Educational and Occupational Aspirations and Plans of Negro and White Male Elementary School Students," *Pacific Sociological Review,* 2 (Fall, 1959), 56-60.

HOLT, Robert R., "Effects of Ego-Involvement upon Levels of Aspiration," *Psychiatry,* 8 (1945), 299-317.

HURVITZ, Nathan, "Sources of Motivation and Achievement of American Jews," *Jewish Social Studies,* 23 (1961), 217-234.

HYMAN, Herbert H., "The Value Systems of Different Classes: A Social Psychological Contribution to the Analysis of Stratification," in Reinhard Bendix and Seymour M. Lipset, editors, *Class, Status and Power,* revised edition, New York: Free Press, 1966.

JACOBSEN, R. B., A. L. Flygstad, and R. H. Rodgers, *The Family and Occupational Choice: An Annotated Bibliography,* Eugene, Oregon: University of Oregon, Center for Research in Occupational Planning, 1966.

JAFFE, A. J. and Walter Adams, "College Education for United States Youth: The Attitudes of Parents and Children," *American Journal of Economics and Sociology,* 23 (July, 1964), 269-283.

KAHL, Joseph A., "Educational and Occupational Aspirations of 'Common Man' Boys," *Harvard Educational Review,* 23 (Summer, 1953), 186-203.

KAHL, Joseph A., "Some Measurements of Achievement Orientation," *American Journal of Sociology,* 70 (May, 1965), 669-681.

KALDOR, D. R., E. Eldridge, L. G. Burchinal, and J. W. Arthur, *Occupational Plans of Iowa Farm Boys,* Ames: Iowa Agricultural Experiment Station, Bulletin 508, September, 1962.

ASPIRATION AND
MOTIVATION

KATZ, F. M., "The Meaning of Success: Some Differences in Value Systems of Social Classes," *Journal of Social Psychology,* 62 (1964), 141-148

ASPIRATION AND
MOTIVATION

KELLER, Suzanne and Marisa Zavalloni, "Ambition and Social Class: A Respecification," *Social Forces,* 43 (October, 1964), 58-70.

KEMPER, Theodore D., "Reference Groups, Socialization, and Achievement," *American Sociological Review,* 33 (February, 1968), 31-45.

KRATZ, Lawrence, "The Motivation of the Business Manager," *Behavioral Science,* 5 (October, 1960), 313-316.

KRAUSS, Irving, "Sources of Educational Aspirations Among Working-Class Youth," *American Sociological Review,* 29 (December, 1964), 867-879.

KRIESBERG, Louis, "Rearing Children for Educational Achievement in Fatherless Families," *Journal of Marriage and the Family,* 29 (May, 1967), 288-301.

KRIPPNER, Stanley, "Junior High School Students' Vocational Preferences and Their Parents' Occupational Level," *Personnel and Guidance Journal,* 41 (1963), 590-595.

KROGER, Robert and C. M. Louttit, "The Influence of Fathers' Occupation in Vocational Choices of High School Boys," *Journal of Applied Psychology 19,* (April, 1935), 204-212.

KUVLESKY, W. P. and R. C. Bealer, "A Clarification of the Concept 'Occupational Choice,'" *Rural Sociology,* 31 (September, 1966), 265-276.

KUVLESKY, W. P. and R. C. Bealer, "The Relevance of Adolescents' Occupational Aspirations for Subsequent Job Attainments," *Rural Sociology,* 32 (September, 1967), 290-301.

KUVLESKY, W. P. and G. W. Ohlendorf, *A Bibliography on Educational Orientations of Youth,* College Station: Texas A&M University, Department of Agricultural Economics and Sociology, Information Report 65-5, November, 1965.

KUVLESKY, W. P. and G. W. Ohlendorf, *Occupational Aspirations and Expectations: A Bibliography of Research Literature,* College Station, Texas: Texas A&M University, Department of Agricultural Economics and Sociology, Information Report 66-1, June, 1966.

LADINSKY, Jack, "Higher Education and Work Achievement among Lawyers," *Sociological Quarterly,* 8 (Spring, 1967), 222-232.

LAYTON, Wilber L., "Socioeconomic Status and After-High School Plans," *Personnel and Guidance Journal,* 31 (March, 1953).

LEWIN, Kurt, T. Dembo, Leon Festinger, and David O. Sears, "Level of Aspiration," in J. Hunt, editor, *Personality and the Behavior Disorders,* New York: Ronald, 1944.

LIONBERGER, H. F. and C. L. Gregory with H. C. Chang, *Occupational and College Choices of Farm and Non-Farm Male High School Seniors in Missouri,* Columbia: University of Missouri, Department of Rural Sociology, December, 1965.

LIPSET, Seymour M., "Trade Unions and Social Structure," *Industrial Relations,* 1 (October, 1961), 75-89.

LIPSET, Seymour M. and Reinhard Bendix, *Social Mobility in Industrial Society,* Berkeley: University of California Press, 1959.

LIPSET, Seymour M., Reinhard Bendix, and F. Theodore Malm, "Job Plans and Entry into the Labor Market," *Social Forces,* 33 (March, 1955), 224-232.

LOTT, Albert J. and Bernice E. Lott, *Negro and White Youth: A Psychological Study in a Borderstate Community,* New York: Holt, Rinehart and Winston, 1963.

LYNN, Kenneth S., *The Dream of Success,* London: Constable, 1955.

LYSGAARD, Sverre, "Social Stratification and the Deferred Gratification Pattern," *Transactions of the Second World Congress of Sociology,* 2 (1954), 364-377.

LYSTAD, Mary H., "Family Patterns, Achievements, and Aspirations of Urban Negroes," *Sociology and Social Research,* 45 (April, 1961), 281-288.

MACCOBY, Eleanor E., "Class Differences in Boys' Choices of Authoritative Roles," *Sociometry,* 25 (1962), 117-119.

MAHONE, Charles H., "Fear of Failure and Unrealistic Vocational Aspiration," *Journal of Abnormal and Social Psychology,* 60 (March, 1960), 253-261.

MASLOW, A. H., *Motivation and Personality,* New York: Harper, 1954.

McCLELLAND, David C., "Some Social Consequences of Achievement Motivation," in M. R. Jones, editor, *Nebraska Symposium on Motivation,* Lincoln: University of Nebraska Press, 1955.

McCLELLAND, David C., *The Achieving Society,* Princeton: Van Nostrand, 1961.

McCLELLAND, David C., editor, *Studies in Motivation,* New York: Appleton-Century-Crofts, 1955.

McCLELLAND, David C., *et al., Talent and Society,* New York: Van Nostrand, 1958.

McCLELLAND, David C., J. W. Atkinson, R. A. Clark, and E. L. Lowell, *The Achievement Motive,* New York: Appleton-Century-Crofts, 1953.

ASPIRATION AND MOTIVATION

McDILL, Edward L. and James Coleman, "Family and Peer Influences in College Plans of High School Students," *Sociology of Education,* 38 (Fall, 1964), 112-126.

McDILL, Edward L. and James Coleman, "High School Social Status, College Plans, and Interest in Academic Achievement: A Panel Analysis," *American Sociological Review,* 28 (December, 1963), 905-918.

McMILLAN, Sylvia R., "Aspirations of Low-Income Mothers," *Journal of Marriage and the Family,* 29 (May, 1967), 282-287.

MEADOW, L., "Toward a Theory of Vocational Choice," *Journal of Counseling Psychology,* 2 (1955), 108-112.

MICHAEL, John A., "High School Climates and Plans for Entering College," *Public Opinion Quarterly,* 25 (Winter, 1961), 585-595.

MICHAEL, John A., "On Neighborhood Context and College Plans," *American Sociological Review,* 31 (October, 1966), 702-706.

MIDDLETON, Russell and Charles M. Grigg, "Rural-Urban Differences in Aspirations," *Rural Sociology,* 24 (December, 1959), 347-354.

MILLER, Irwin W. and Archie O. Haller, "A Measure of Level of Occupational Aspirations," *Personnel and Guidance Journal,* 42 (January, 1964), 448-455.

MILLER, Norman, *One Year After Commencement,* Chicago: National Opinion Research Center, Report No. 93, 1963.

MILLER, S. M., "The Outlook of Working-Class Youth," in Arthur B. Shostak and William Gomberg, editors, *Blue-Collar World: Studies of the American Worker,* Englewood Cliffs, New Jersey: Prentice Hall, 1964.

MISCHEL, W., "Delay of Gratification, Need for Achievement, and Acquiescence in Another Culture," *Journal of Abnormal and Social Psychology,* 62 (May, 1961), 543-552.

MIZRUCHI, Ephraim H., "Aspiration and Poverty: A Neglected Aspect of Merton's Anomie," *Sociological Quarterly,* 8 (Autumn, 1967), 439-446.

MIZRUCHI, Ephraim H., *Success and Opportunity,* New York: Free Press, 1964.

MONTAGUE, Joel B. and Edgar G. Epps, "Attitudes Toward

Social Mobility as Revealed By Samples of Negro and White Boys," *Pacific Sociological Review,* 1 (Fall, 1958), 81-84.

MOORE, Wilbert E. and Arnold S. Feldman, editors, *Labor Commitment and Social Change in Developing Areas,* New York: Social Science Research Council, 1960.

MORLAND, J. Kenneth, "Educational and Occupational Aspirations of Mill and Town School Children in a Southern Community," *Social Forces,* 39 (December, 1960), 169-175.

MORLAND, J. Kenneth, "Kent Revisited: Blue-Collar Aspirations and Achievement," in Arthur B. Shostak and William Gomberg, editors, *Blue-Collar World: Studies of the American Worker,* Englewood Cliffs, New Jersey: Prentice Hall, 1964.

MORRISON, Denton E., "Achievement Motivation of Farm Operators: A Measurement Study," *Rural Sociology,* 29 (December, 1964), 367-384.

MOSER, Wilbur E., "The Influence of Certain Cultural Factors Upon The Selection of Vocational Preferences by High School Students," *Journal of Educational Research,* 45 (March, 1952), 523-526.

NASH, R. C., editor, *Rural Youth in a Changing Environment,* Washington, D. C.: National Committee for Children and Youth, 1965.

NEAL, Arthur G. and Melvin Seeman, "Organizations and Powerlessness: A Test of the Mediation Hypothesis," *American Sociological Review,* 29 (April, 1964), 216-226.

NELSON, B. H., *Attitudes of Youth Toward Occupational Opportunities and Social Services in Cherokee County,* College Station: Texas Agricultural Experiment Station, Bulletin 859, May, 1957.

NELSON, R. C., "Knowledge and Interests Concerning Sixteen Occupations Among Elementary and Secondary School Students," *Educational and Psychological Measurement,* 23 (Winter, 1963), 741-754.

NUNALEE, J. H., III, and L. W. Drabick, *Occupational Desires and Expectations of North Carolina High School Seniors,* Raleigh: North Carolina State Educational Research Series, No. 3, June, 1965.

O'DEA, Thomas F., *The Mormans,* Chicago: University of Chicago Press, 1957.

PALMER, Gladys L., Herbert S. Parnes, Richard C. Wilcox, Mary W. Herman, and Carol P. Brainerd, *The Reluctant Job Changer: Studies in Work Attachments and Aspirations,* Phila-

ASPIRATION AND
MOTIVATION

delphia: University of Pennsylvania Press, 1962.

PARSONS, Talcott, "The Motivation of Economic Activities,"
in Talcott Parsons, *Essays in Sociological Theory,* revised
edition, New York: Free Press, 1954.

PARSONS, Talcott, *Social Structure and Personality,* New York:
Free Press, 1964.

PAVALKO, Ronald M. and David R. Bishop, "Socioeconomic
Status and College Plans: A Study of Canadian High School
Students," *Sociology of Education,* 39 (Summer, 1966),
288-298.

PAYNE, Raymond, "Development of Occupational and Migration Expectations and Choices Among Urban, Small Town,
and Rural Adolescent Boys," *Rural Sociology,* 21 (June, 1956),
117-125.

PHILLIPS, Bernard S., "Expected Value Deprivation and Occupational Preference," *Sociometry,* 27 (June, 1964), 151-160.

PHILLIPS, Derek, "Deferred Gratification in a College Setting:
Some Costs and Gains," *Social Problems,* 13 (Winter, 1966), 333-
343.

PIERCE-JONES, John, "Vocational Interest Correlates of Socio-
economic Status in Adolescence," *Educational and Psychological Measurement,* 19 (1959), 65-72.

PIHLBLAD, C. T. and C. L. Gregory, "The Role of Test Intelligence and Occupational Background as Factors in Occupational Choice," *Sociometry,* 19 (September, 1956), 192-199.

PORTER, J. Richard, "Predicting Vocational Plans of High School
Senior Boys," *Personnel and Guidance Journal,* 33 (December,
1954), 6-27.

PSATHAS, George, "Toward a Theory of Occupational Choice
for Women," *Sociology and Social Research,* 52 (January,
1968), 253-268.

PUNKE, Harold H., "Factors Affecting the Proportion of High
School Graduates Who Enter College," *Bulletin of the
National Association of Secondary School Principals,* 38
(November, 1954), 6-27.

PURCELL, Theodore V., "The Hopes of Negro Workers for
Their Children," in Arthur B. Shostak and William Gomberg,
editors, *Blue-Collar World: Studies of the American Worker,*
Englewood Cliffs, New Jersey: Prentice-Hall, 1964.

REHBERG, Richard A., "Adolescent Career Aspirations and Expectations: Evaluation of Two Conflicting Stratification Hypotheses," *Pacific Sociological Review,* 10 (Fall, 1967), 81-90.

REHBERG, Richard A. and Walter E. Schafer, "Participation in Interscholastic Athletics and College Expectations," *American Journal of Sociology,* 73 (May, 1968), 732-740.

REHBERG, Richard A. and David L. Westby, "Parental Encouragement, Occupation, Education and Family Size: Artifactual or Independent Determinants of Adolescent Educational Expectations?" *Social Forces,* 45 (March, 1967), 362-374.

REISSMAN, Leonard, "Levels of Aspiration and Social Class," *American Sociological Review,* 18 (June, 1953), 233-242.

RHODES, Lewis, "Anomia, Aspiration, and Status," *Social Forces,* 42 (May, 1964), 434-440.

ROBIN, E. P. and J. Sardo, *Attitudes and Plans of High School Students in Sedgwick County, Colorado,* Fort Collins: Colorado Agricultural Experiment Station, Technical Bulletin 85, September, 1965.

ROE, Anne, *The Psychology of Occupations,* New York: Wiley, 1956.

ROPER, Elmo, "College Ambitions and Parental Planning," *Public Opinion Quarterly,* 25 (Summer, 1961), 159-166.

ROSEN, Bernard C., "The Achievement Syndrome and Economic Growth in Brazil," *Social Forces,* 42 (March, 1964), 341-354.

ROSEN, Bernard C., "The Achievement Syndrome: A Psychocultural Dimension of Social Stratification," *American Sociological Review,* 21 (April, 1956), 203-211.

ROSEN, Bernard C., "Family Structure and Achievement Motivation," *American Sociological Review,* 26 (August, 1961), 574-585.

ROSEN, Bernard C., "Family Structure and Value Transmission," *Merrill-Palmer Quarterly,* 10 (January, 1964), 59-76.

ROSEN, Bernard C., "Race, Ethnicity, and the Achievement Syndrome," *American Sociological Review,* 24 (February, 1959), 47-60.

ROSEN, Bernard C., "Socialization and Achievement Motivation in Brazil," *American Sociological Review,* 27 (October, 1962), 612-624.

ROSEN, Bernard C., Harry J. Crockett, and Clyde Z. Nunn, editors, *Achievement in American Society,* Cambridge: Schenkman, 1968.

ROSEN, Bernard C. and Roy D'Andrade, "The Psychosocial Origins of Achievement Motivation," *Sociometry,* 22 (September, 1959), 185-218.

ASPIRATION AND
MOTIVATION

ROSENBERG, M. with E. H. Suchman and R. K. Goldsen, *Occupations and Values,* New York: Free Press, 1957.

RUSHING, William A., "Adolescent-Parent Relationships and Mobility Aspirations," *Social Forces,* 43 (December, 1964), 157-166.

ST. JOHN, Nancy Hoyt, "The Effect of Segregation on the Aspirations of Negro Youths," *Harvard Educational Review,* 36 (Summer, 1966), 284-294.

SCANZONI, John, "Socialization, Achievement, and Achievement Values," *American Sociological Review,* 32 (June, 1967), 449-456.

SCHNEIDER, Louis and Sverre Lysgaard, "The Deferred Gratification Pattern: A Preliminary Study," *American Sociological Review,* 18 (April, 1953), 142-149.

SCHWARZWELLER, Harry K., "Community of Residence and Career Choices of German Youth," *Rural Sociology,* 33 (March, 1968), 46-63.

SCHWARZWELLER, Harry K., "Values and Occupational Choice," *Social Forces,* 39 (December, 1960), 126-140.

SCHWARZWELLER, Harry K., "Value Orientations in Educational and Occupational Choices," *Rural Sociology,* 24 (September, 1959), 246-256.

SEWELL, William H., "Community of Residence and College Plans," *American Sociological Review,* 29 (February, 1964), 24-38.

SEWELL, William H., "Essay Review: The Social Context of Ambition," *School Review,* 74 (Summer, 1966), 231-240.

SEWELL, William H. and J. Michael Armer, "Neighborhood Context and College Plans," *American Sociological Review,* 31 (April, 1966), 159-168.

SEWELL, William H. and J. Michael Armer, "Reply to Turner, Michael, and Boyle," *American Sociological Review,* 31 (October, 1966), 707-712.

SEWELL, William H. and Archie O. Haller, "Educational and Occupational Perspectives of Farm and Rural Youth," in Lee G. Burchinal, editor, *Rural Youth in Crisis: Facts, Myths, and Social Change,* Washington, D. C.: Government Printing Office, 1965.

SEWELL, William H., Archie O. Haller, and Murray A. Straus, "Social Status and Educational and Occupational Aspiration," *American Sociological Review,* 22 (February, 1957), 67-73.

SEWELL, William H., D. G. Marshall, Archie O. Haller, and W. A. Dehart, "Factors Associated with Attitude toward High-School

Education in Rural Wisconsin," *Rural Sociology,* 18 (December, 1953), 359–365,

SEWELL, William H. and A. M. Orenstein, "Community of Residence and Occupational Choice," *American Journal of Sociology,* 70 (March, 1965), 551-563.

SEWELL, William H. and Vimal Shah, "Parents' Education and Children's Educational Aspirations and Achievements," *American Sociological Review,* 33 (April, 1968), 191-209.

SEXTON, Patricia, "Negro Career Expectations," *Merrill-Palmer Quarterly,* 9 (October, 1963), 303-316.

SHERIF, Carolyn W., "Self-Radius and Goals of Youth in Different Urban Areas," *Southwestern Social Science Quarterly,* 42 (December, 1961), 259-270.

SIEMENS, L. B., *The Influence of Selected Family Factors on the Educational and Occupational Aspiration Levels of High School Boys and Girls,* Winnipeg, Canada: University of Manitoba, Faculty of Agriculture and Home Economics, June, 1965.

SIMPSON, Richard L., "Parental Influence, Anticipatory Socialization and Social Mobility," *American Sociological Review,* 27 (August, 1962), 517-522.

SISTRUNK, J. L. and J. W. McDavid, "Achievement Motivation Affiliation Motivation, and Task Difficulty as Determinants of Social Conformity," *Journal of Social Psychology,* 66 (1965), 41-50.

SLOCUM, Walter L., "The Influence of Reference Group Values on Educational Aspirations of Rural High School Students," *Rural Sociology,* 32 (September, 1967), 269-277.

SLOCUM, Walter L., *Occupational Careers: A Sociological Perspective,* Chicago: Aldine, 1967.

SLOCUM, Walter L., *Occupational and Educational Plans of High School Seniors From Farm and Non-Farm Homes,* Pullman: Washington Agricultural Experiment Station, Bulletin 564, February, 1956.

SLOCUM, Walter L. and Lamar T. Empey, *Occupational Planning by Young Women,* Pullman: Washington Agricultural Experiment Station, Bulletin 568, August, 1956.

SMELSER, William, "Adolescent and Adult Occupational Choice as a Function of Family Socioeconomic History," *Sociometry,* 26 (December, 1963), 393-409.

SMITH, Charles P., "Achievement-Related Motives and Goal Setting under Different Conditions," *Journal of Personality,* (March, 1963), 124-140.

ASPIRATION AND
MOTIVATION

SPEERY, J. V. and V. R. Kivett, *Educational and Vocational Goals of Rural Youth in North Carolina,* Greensboro: North Carolina Agricultural Experiment Station, Technical Bulletin No. 163, November, 1964.

STAFILIOS-ROTHSCHILD, Constantina, "Class Position and Success Stereotypes in Greek and American Cultures," *Social Forces,* 45 (March, 1967), 374-383.

STEPHENSON, Richard M., "Mobility Orientation and Stratification of 1,000 Ninth Graders," *American Sociological Review* 22 (April, 1957), 204-212.

STRAUS, Murray A., "Deferred Gratification, Social Class, and the Achievement Syndrome," *American Sociological Review,* 27 (June, 1962), 326-335.

STRAUS, Murray A., "Personal Characteristics and Functional Needs in the Choice of Farming as an Occupation," *Rural Sociology,* 21 (September-December, 1956), 257-266.

STRAUS, Murray A., "Societal Needs and Personal Characteristics in the Choice of Farm, Blue Collar, and White Collar Occupations by Farmers' Sons," *Rural Sociology,* 29 (December, 1964), 408-425.

STRODTBECK, Fred L., "Family Interaction, Values, and Achievement," in David C. McClelland, *et al.,* editors, *Talent and Society,* New York: Van Nostrand, 1958.

STRODTBECK, Fred L., Margaret R. McDonald, and Bernard C. Rosen, "Evaluation of Occupations: A Reflection of Jewish and Italian Differences," *American Sociological Review,* 22 (October, 1957), 546-553.

SUPER, D. E., *The Psychology of Careers: An Introduction to Vocational Development,* New York: Harper and Row, 1957.

SUPER, D. E., "A Theory of Vocational Development," *American Psychologist,* 8 (May, 1953), 185-190.

SUPER, D. E. and P. L. Overstreet with C. N. Morris, W. Dubin, and M. B. Heyde, *The Vocational Maturity of Ninth-Grade Boys,* New York: Columbia University, Teachers College, Bureau of Publications, 1960.

SUPER, D. E., J. O. Crites, R. C. Hummel, H. P. Moser, P. L. Overstreet, and C. F. Warnath, *Vocational Development: A Framework for Research,* New York: Columbia University, Teachers College, Bureau of Publications, 1957.

SWIFT, D. F., "Social Class and Achievement Motivation," *Educational Research,* 8 (February, 1966), 83-95.

SWINEHART, James W., "Socio-Economic Level, Status Aspiration, and Maternal Role," *American Sociological Review,* 28 (June, 1963), 391-399.

TAUSKY, Curt and Robert Dubin, "Career Anchorage: Managerial Mobility and Motivations," *American Sociological Review*, 30 (October, 1965), 725-735.

THOMAS, Murray R. and W. Surachmad, "Social Class Differences in Mothers' Expectations for Children in Indonesia," *Journal of Social Psychology*, 57 (August, 1962), 303-307.

TIEDEMAN, D. V., "Decision and Vocational Development: A Paradigm and Its Implications," *Personnel and Guidance Journal*, 40 (September, 1961), 15-21.

TURNER, Ralph H., "On Neighborhood Context and College Plans," *American Sociological Review*, 31 (October, 1966), 698-702.

TURNER, Ralph H., *The Social Context of Ambition: A Study of High School Seniors in Los Angeles*, San Francisco: Chandler, 1964.

TURNER, Ralph H., "Some Aspects of Women's Ambition," *American Journal of Sociology*, 70 (November, 1964), 271-285.

TURNER, Ralph H., "Some Family Determinants of Ambition," *Sociology and Social Reserach*, 46 (July, 1962), 397-411.

TURNER, Ralph H., "Upward Mobility and Class Values," *Social Problems*, 11 (Spring, 1964), 359-371.

UZELL, O., "Occupational Aspirations of Negro Male High School Students," *Sociology and Social Research*, 45 (January, 1961), 202-204.

VERNON, M. D., "The Drives Which Determine the Choice of a Career," *British Journal of Educational Psychology*, 8 (1938), 1-15.

VEROFF, Joseph, Sheila Feld, and Gerald Gurin, "Achievement Motivation and Religious Background," *American Sociological Review*, 27 (April, 1962), 205-217.

VOLKMAN, John, "A Social Determinant of the Level of Aspiration," *Journal of Abnormal and Social Psychology*, 34 (1939), 225-238.

WARKOV, Seymour, "Employment Expectations of Law Students," *Sociological Quarterly*, 6 (Summer, 1965), 222-232.

WATERS, E. W., "Vocational Aspirations, Intelligence, Problems, and Socio-Economic Status of Rural Negro High School Seniors on the Eastern Shore of Maryland: Their Implications For Vocational Guidance," *Journal of Negro Education*, 23 (1954), 502-505.

WEBER, Max, *The Protestant Ethic and the Spirit of Capitalism*, translated by Talcott Parsons, New York: Scribners, 1958.

WENDT, Hans-Werner, "Motivation, Effort, and Performance," in David C. Mc Clelland, editor, *Studies in Motivation,* New York: Appleton-Century-Crofts, 1955.

WERTHEIM, J. and S. A. Mednick, "The Achievement Motive and Field Independence," *Journal of Consulting Psychology,* 22 (February, 1958), 38.

WERTS, Charles E., "Social Class and Initial Career Choice of College Freshmen," *Sociology of Education,* 39 (Winter, 1966), 74-85.

WHYTE, William F., *Street Corner Society,* Chicago: University of Chicago Press, 1943.

WILKENING, Eugene A. and J. C. van Es, "Aspirations and Attainments Among German Farm Families," *Rural Sociology,* 32 (December, 1967), 435-445.

WILSON, Alan B., "Residential Segregation of Social Classes and Aspirations of High School Boys," *American Sociological Review,* 24 (December, 1959), 836-845.

WILSON, Alan B., *The Consequences of Segregation: Academic Achievement in a Northern Community,* Berkeley: The Glendessary Press, 1969.

WINTERBOTTOM, Marian R., "The Relation of Need for Achievement to Learning Experiences in Independence and Mastery," in John W. Atchinson, editor, *Motives in Fantasy, Action, and Society,* Princeton: Van Nostrand, 1958.

WITTY, Paul A. and Harvey C. Lehman, "Drive: A Neglected Trait in the Study of the Gifted," *Psychological Review,* 34 (1927), 364-376.

YOUMANS, E. G., *The Educational Attainment and Future Plans of Rural Youths,* Lexington: Kentucky Agricultural Experiment Station, Bulletin 664, January, 1959.

YOUMANS, E. G., "Occupational Expectations of Twelfth Grade Michigan Boys," *Journal of Experimental Education,* 24 (June, 1956), 259-271.

YOUMANS, E. G., "Social Factors in the Work Attitudes and Interests of 12th Grade Michigan Boys," *Journal of Educational Sociology,* 28 (September, 1954), 35-48.

YOUMANS, E. G., S. E. Grigsby, and H. C. King, *After High School What: Highlights of a Study of Career Plans of Negro and White Rural Youth in Three Florida Counties,* Gainesville: University of Florida, Cooperative Extension Service, 1965.

ZANDER, Alvin and Theodore Curtis, "Effects of Social Power on Aspiration Setting and Striving," *Journal of Abnormal and Social Psychology,* 64 (January, 1962), 63-74.

ASPIRATION AND
MOTIVATION

ZENTNER, Henry, "Factors in the Social Pathology of the
North American Indian Society," *Anthropologica,* 5 (1963),
119-130.

Social Origins Studies

Most inter-generational mobility studies investigate social origins, in that they
start with a sample of people at various levels of the stratification system and
determine the positions of their parents (or fathers) at one or more points in time.
(The obverse procedure, whereby the offspring of a sample of parents are traced to
their eventual positions in the stratification system is much more difficult and is
rarely followed.) However, the term "social origins studies" is sometimes reserved
for research into the background of people in relatively homogeneous groups and
categories, such as a specific occupation, the student body of one university, or a
narrowly defined elite. Many of these studies differ from other inter-generational
mobility studies by investigating a wide range of background factors, in addition to
the status characteristics of the parents.

ABEGGLEN, James C. and Hiroshi Mannari, "Leaders of Modern
Japan: Social Origins and Mobility," *Economic Development
and Cultural Change,* 9 (October, 1960), 109-134.

ABU-LABAN, Baha, "Social Origins and Occupational Career
Patterns of Community Leaders," *Sociological Inquiry,* 33
(Spring, 1963), 131-140.

ADAMS, Stuart, "Origins of American Occupational Elites, 1900-
1955," *American Journal of Sociology,* 62 (January, 1957),
360-368.

ADAMS, Stuart, "Real and Nominal Origins of Selected Occupational Elites," *Reserach Studies of the State College of Washington,* 23 (June, 1955), 121-129.

ADAMS, Stuart, "Regional Differences in Vertical Mobility in a
High-Status Occupation," *American Sociological Review,* 15
(April, 1950), 228-235.

ADAMS, Stuart, "Trends in Occupational Origins of Business
Leaders," *American Sociological Review,* 19 (October, 1954),
541-548.

ADAMS, Stuart, "Trends in the Occupational Origins of Physicians," *American Sociological Review,* 18 (August, 1953), 404-
409.

ALLEN, Philip J., "Childhood Backgrounds of Success in a Profession," *American Sociological Review,* 20 (April, 1955), 186-190.

ANDERSON, C. Arnold and Miriam Schnaper, *School and Society in England: Social Backgrounds of Oxford and Cambridge Students,* Annals of American Research, 1952.

BAMFORD, T. W., "Public Schools and Social Class, 1801-1850," *British Journal of Sociology,* 12 (September, 1961), 224-235.

BASSETT, G. W., "The Occupational Background of Teachers," *Australian Journal of Education,* 2 (1958).

BENDIX, Reinhard and Frank W. Howton, "Social Mobility and the American Business Elite," *British Journal of Sociology,* 8 (December, 1957), 357-369.

BENDIX, Reinhard, Seymour M. Lipset, and Theodore Malin, "Social Origins and Occupational Career Patterns," *Industrial and Labor Relations Review,* 7 (January, 1954), 246-261.

BOGARDUS, Emory, "W. F. Thomas and Social Origins," *Sociology and Social Reserach,* 43 (May-June, 1959), 365-369.

CHARTERS, W. W., Jr., "The Social Background of Teaching," in N. L. Gage, editor, *Handbook of Research on Teaching,* Chicago: Rand McNally, 1963.

COLLINS, Sydney, "Social Mobility in Jamaica, with Reference to Rural Communities and the Teaching Profession," *Transactions of the Third World Congress of Sociology,* 3 (1956), 267-276.

DAVIS, Beverly, "Eminence and Level of Social Origin," *American Journal of Sociology,* 59 (July, 1953), 11-18.

DUNCAN, Beverly, "Education and Social Background," *American Journal of Sociology,* 72 (January, 1967), 363-372.

DUNCAN, Otis Dudley, "Social Origins of Salaried and Self-Employed Professional Workers," *Social Forces,* 44 (December, 1965), 186-189.

EDINGER, Lewis J., "Continuity and Change in the Background of German Decision-Makers," *Western Political Quarterly,* 14 (March, 1961), 17-36.

EDINGER, Lewis J. and Donald D. Searing, "Social Background in Elite Analysis: A Methodological Inquiry," *American Political Science Review,* 61 (June, 1967), 428-445.

EDWARDS, G. Franklin, *The Negro Professional Class,* New York: Free Press, 1959.

GEIGER, T., "Recruitment of University Students," *Acta Sociologica,* 1 (1955), 39-48.

GERSTL, Joel E., "Social Origins of Engineers," *New Society,* (June, 1963), 19-21.

SOCIAL ORIGINS

GILBERT, Jeanne G. and James C. Healey, "The Economic and Social Background of the Unlicensed Personnel of the American Merchant Marine," *Social Forces,* 21 (October, 1942), 40-43.

GIROD, Robert and Firouz Tofigh, "Family Background and Income, School Career and Social Mobility of Young Males of Working-Class Origin—A Geneva Survey," *Acta Sociologica,* 9, 94-109.

GREGORY, Frances W. and Irene D. Neu, "The American Industrial Elite in the 1870's: Their Social Origin," in William Miller, editor, *Men in Business,* Cambridge: Harvard University Press, 1952.

HARGENS, Lowell L. and Warren Hagstrom, "Sponsored and Contest Mobility of American Academic Scientists," *Sociology of Education,* 40 (Winter, 1967), 24-38.

HARMON, Lindsey, *Profiles of Ph.D.'s in the Sciences,* Washington, D. C.: National Academy of Sciences, 1966.

HICKMAN, Martin B. and Neal A. Hollander, "Undergraduate Origin as a Factor in Elite Recruitment and Mobility: The Foreign Service—A Case Study," *Western Political Quarterly,* 19 (June, 1966), 337-353.

HUGHES, Everett C., "The Making of a Physician," *Human Organization,* 21 (Winter, 1956), 21-25.

IRVING, James, "Who Goes to College? A Note on the Social Origins of Students in the Higher Educational Institutions of the Eastern Cape Province," *Journal of Social Research,* 5 (June, 1963), 529-534.

JONES, Frank E., "The Social Origins of High School Teachers in a Canadian City," *Canadian Journal of Economics and Political Science,* 29 (November, 1963), 529-534.

KELSALL, R. K., "The Social Origins of Higher Civil Servants in Great Britain, Now and in the Past," *Transactions of the Second World Congress of Sociology,* 2 (1954), 131-142.

KNAPP, Robert H. and Hubert B. Goodrich, "The Origins of American Scientists," in David C. McClelland, editor, *Studies in Motivation,* New York: Appleton-Century-Crofts, 1955.

KOENIG, Samuel, "Social Backgrounds and Attitudes of Labor Leaders with Special Reference to New Haven and New Britain, Connecticut," *Sociology and Social Reserach,* 25 (January-February, 1941), 264-265.

KUIPER, G., "The Recruitment of the Learned Professions in the Netherlands," *Transactions of the Third World Congress of Sociology,* 3 (1956), 230-238.

KUNKEL, B. W., "A Survey of College Teachers," *Bulletin of the American Association of University Professors,* 24 (1938).

LADINSKY, Jack, "Careers of Lawyers, Law Practice, and Legal Institutions," *American Sociological Review,* 28 (February, 1963), 47-54.

LEWIS, Gordon F., "A Comparison of Some Aspects of the Backgrounds and Careers of Small Businessmen and American Business Leaders," *American Journal of Sociology,* 65 (January, 1960), 348-355.

LEWIS, Gordon F. and C. Arnold Anderson, "Social Origins and Social Mobility of Businessmen in an American City," *Transactions of the Third World Congress of Sociology,* 3 (1956), 253-266.

LOCKWOOD, David, *The Blackcoated Worker: A Study in Class Consciousness,* London: Allen and Unwin, 1958.

MARSH, Robert M., "Values, Demand, and Social Mobility," *American Sociological Review,* 28 (August, 1963), 565-575.

MATTHEWS, Donald R., *The Social Background of Political Decision-Makers,* New York: Doubleday, 1954.

MATTHEWS, Donald R., *U.S. Senators and their World,* Chapel Hill: University of North Carolina Press, 1960.

McMILLAN, Robert T. and Marylee Mason, "Social Background and Farm Ownership, *Rural Sociology,* 10 (December, 1945), 414-416.

MILLER, William, "American Historians and the Business Elite," *Journal of Economic History,* 9 (November, 1949).

MILLER, William, "American Lawyers in Business and Politics," *Yale Law Journal,* 60 (January, 1951), 66-76.

MILLER, William, "The Business Bureaucracies: Careers of Top Executives in the Early Twentieth Century," in William Miller, *Men in Business: Essays in the History of Entrepreneurship,* Cambridge: Harvard University Press, 1952.

MILLER, William, "The Recruitment of the American Business Elite," *Quarterly Journal of Economics,* 64 (May, 1950), 242-253.

MILLS, C. Wright, "The American Business Elite: A Collective Portrait," *Journal of Economic History,* 5 (1945), 20-44.

MOORE, Harry E. and Sidney R. Worob, "Place of Education and Residence of Eminent Southerners," *Social Forces,* 27 (May, 1949), 408-412.

MORE, Douglas M., "A Note on Occupational Origins of Health Service Professions," *American Sociological Review,* 25 (June, 1960), 403-404.

MORE, Douglas M., "Social Origins and Occupational Adjustment," *Social Forces,* 35 (October, 1956), 16-19.

MORE, Douglas M., "Social Origins of Future Dentists," *Midwest Sociologist,* 21 (July, 1959), 70-76.

MUELLER, J. H. and K. H. Mueller, "Socio-economic Background of Women Students at Indiana University," *Educational and Psychological Measurements,* 9 (1949), 321-329.

NEWCOMER, Mabel, *The Big Business Executive: The Factors that Made Him, 1900-1950,* New York: Columbia University Press, 1955.

NEWCOMER, Mabel, "The Chief Executives of Large Business Corporations," *Explorations in Entreprenuerial History,* 5 (1952-1953), 1-34.

NORDAL, Johannes, "The Recruitment of the Professions in Iceland," *Transactions of the Second World Congress of Sociology,* 2 (1954), 153-165.

O'DONOVAN, Thomas and Arthur X. Dregan, "A Comparative Study of the Oreintations of a Selected Group of Church Executives," *Sociology and Social Research,* 48 (April, 1964), 330-339.

ODUM, Howard W., editor, *American Masters of Social Science,* Port Washington, New York: Kennikut Press, 1965.

PALMORE, Erdman, "Sociologists' Class Origins and Political Ideologies," *Sociology and Social Research,* 47 (October, 1962), 45-50.

PERRUCCI, Carolyn Cummings, "Social Origins, Mobility Patterns and Fertility," *American Sociological Review,* 32 (August, 1967), 615-626.

PERRUCCI, Robert, "The Significance of Intra-Occupational Mobility: Some Methodological and Theoretical Notes, Together with a Case Study of Engineers," *American Sociological Review*, 26 (December, 1961), 874-883.

PIKE, Robert M., "Some Social Aspects of Recruitment to Public School Teaching in New South Wales," *Australian and New Zealand Journal of Sociology,* 2 (October, 1966), 94-106.

RAZZELL, P. E., "Social Origins of Officers in the Indian and British Home Army: 1758-1962," *British Journal of Sociology,* 14 (September, 1963), 248-260.

ROE, Anne, *The Making of a Scientist,* New York: Dodd Mead, 1952.

RUCHELMAN, Leonard I., "A Profile of New York State Legislators," *Western Political Quarterly,* 20 (September, 1967), 625-638.

SCHNEIDER, Joseph, "Class Origin and Fame: Eminent English Women," *American Sociological Review,* 5 (October, 1940), 700-712.

SCHNEIDER, Joseph, "Social Origin and Fame: The United States and England," *American Sociological Review*, 10 (February, 1945), 52-60.

SOCIAL ORIGINS   SCHNEIDER, Joseph, "The Definition of Eminence and the Social Origins of Famous English Men of Genius," *American Sociological Review*, 3 (December, 1938), 834-849.

SHANNON, J. R. and Maxine Shaw, "Education of Business and Professional Leaders," *American Sociological Review*, 5 (June, 1940), 381-383.

SIMON, Joan, "The Social Origins of Cambridge Students," *Past and Present*, 26 (November, 1963), 58-67.

SIMPSON, Richard L. and Ida Simpson, "Social Origins, Occupational Advice, Occupational Values and Work Careers," *Social Forces*, 40 (March, 1962), 264-271.

SLOCUM, Walter L., *Occupational Careers: A Sociological Perspective*, Chicago: Aldine, 1967.

SMITH, James O. and Gideon Sjoberg, "Origins and Career Patterns of Leading Protestant Clergymen," *Social Forces*, 39 (May, 1961), 290-296.

SOELAEMAN, Soemardi, "Some Aspects of the Social Origin of Indonesian Political Decision Makers," *Transactions of the Third World Congress of Sociology*, 3 (1956), 338-348.

STEWART, Donald D. and Richard P. Chambers, "The Status Background of the Veteran College Student," *Sociology and Social Research*, 35 (September-October, 1950), 12-21.

STEWART, Rosemary G. and Paul Duncan-Jones, "Educational Background and Career History of British Managers, with Some American Comparisons," *Explorations in Entrepreneurial History*, 9 (December, 1956), 61-71.

TAUSSIG, F. W. and Joslyn, C. S., *American Business Leaders*, New York: Macmillan, 1932.

TIEN, H. Y., "A Profile of the Australian Academic Profession," *Australian Quarterly*, 32 (March, 1960), 66-74.

TIEN, H. Y., *Social Mobility and Controlled Fertility: Family Origins and Structure of the Australian Academic Elite*, New Haven: College and University Press, 1965.

VINKE, P., "The Vertical Social Mobility of the Chief Executive Groups in the Netherlands," *Transactions of the Third World Congress of Sociology*, 3 (1956), 219-229.

VISHER, Stephen S., "Environmental Backgrounds of Leading American Scientists," *American Sociological Review*, 13 (February, 1948), 65-72.

VON FERBER, C., "The Social Background of German University and College Professors Since 1964," *Transactions of the Third World Congress of Sociology,* 3 (1956), 239-244.

WARKOV, Seymour and John F. Marsh, *The Education and Training of America's Scientists and Engineers,* Chicago: National Opinion Research Center, Report No. 104, 1965.

WARNER, W. Lloyd and James C. Abegglen, *Big Business Leaders in America,* New York: Atheneum, 1963.

WEST, S. Stewart, "Origins of Scientists," *Sociometry,* 24 (September, 1961), 251-269.

WILLHELM, Sidney and Gideon Sjoberg, "The Social Characteristics of Entertainers," *Social Forces,* 37 (October, 1958), 71-76.

WILSON, C. S. and T. Lupton, "The Social Background and Connections of Top Decision Makers," *Manchester School,* 27 (January, 1959), 30-46.

WILSON, Logan, *The Academic Man: Sociology of a Profession,* London: Oxford University Press, 1942.

ZELAN, Joseph, "Social Origins and the Recruitment of American Lawyers," *British Journal of Sociology,* 18 (March, 1967), 45-54.

Miscellaneous Publications in Stratification

ALBRECHT, Ruth, "Social Class in Old Age," *Social Forces,* 29 (May, 1951), 400-405.

ANDERSON, C. Arnold, "The Social Status of University Students in Relation to Type of Economy: An International Comparison," *Transactions of the Third World Congress of Sociology,* 5 (1956), 51-63.

ANDERSON, C. Arnold and Mary J. Bowman, "Educational Distributions and Attainment Norms in the United States," *Proceedings, World Population Congress,* 4 (1954), 931-941.

ANDERSON, James G. and Dwight Safar, "The Influence of Differential Community Perceptions on the Provision of Equal Educational Opportunities," *Sociology of Education,* 40 (Summer 1967), 219-230.

ANDERSON, Stuart, "The Economic Status of the Teacher Personnel: Historical Development of the Economic Status of High School Teachers In the United States," *Journal of Educational Research,* 43 (May, 1950), 697-711.

MISCELLANEOUS PUBLICATIONS

BARBER, Bernard, "Areas for Research on Social Stratification," *Sociology and Social Research,* 42 (July-August, 1958), 396-400.

BARTH, Ernest A. T. and Walter B. Watson, "Social Stratification and the Family in Mass Society," *Social Forces,* 45 (March, 1967), 392-402.

BEN-DAVID, Joseph, "The Growth of the Professions and the Class System," *Current Sociology,* 12 (1963-1964), 256-277.

BESHERS, James M., "Urban Social Structure as a Single Hierarchy," *Social Forces,* 41 (March, 1963), 233-239.

BESHERS, James M. and Stanley Reiter, "Social Status and Social Change," *Behavioral Science,* 8 (January, 1963), 1-13.

BIDERMAN, Albert D. and Laure M. Sharp, "The Convergence of Military and Civilian Occupational Structures: Evidence From Studies of Military Retired Employment," *American Journal of Sociology,* 73 (January, 1968) 381-399.

BLACKBURN, R. M., *Union Character and Social Class,* London: Batsford, 1967.

BOGEN, Isidore, "Pupil-Teacher Rapport and the Teacher's Awareness of Status Structures Within the Group," *Journal of Educational Sociology,* 28 (November, 1954), 104-114.

BOTT, Elizabeth, "The Concept of Class as a Reference Group," *Human Relations,* 7 (August, 1954), 259-285.

BROOKOVER, Wilbur B., "Teachers and the Stratification of American Society," *Harvard Educational Review,* 23 (Fall, 1953), 257-267.

BUCK, R. C. and B. L. Bible, *Educational Attainment Among Pennsylvania Rural Youth,* University Park: Pennsylvania Agricultural Experiment Station, Bulletin 686, November, 1961.

BUREAU OF SOCIAL SCIENCE RESEARCH, *Two Years After the College Degree: Work and Further Study Patterns,* Washington, D. C.: Government Printing Office, 1963.

BURNS, Robert K., "Economic Aspects of Aging and Retirement," *American Journal of Sociology,* 59 (January, 1954), 384-390.

BURTON, William H., "Education and Social Class in the United States," *Harvard Educational Review,* 23 (Fall, 1953), 243-256.

CHARTERS, W. W. Jr., "Social Class Analysis and the Control of Public Education," *Harvard Educational Review,* 23 (Fall, 1953), 268-283.

COHN, Werner, "Social Stratification and the Charismatic," *Midwest Sociologist,* 21 (December, 1958), 12-18.

CURTIS, Richard F., "Differential Association and the Stratification of the Urban Community," *Social Forces,* 42 (October, 1963), 68-77.

DESAI, A. R.,"Urbanization and Social Stratification," *Sociological Bulletin,* 9 (September, 1960), 7-14.

DONOVAN, John D., "The American Catholic Hierarchy: A Social Profile," *American Catholic Sociological Review,* 19 (June, 1958), 98-113.

DUNCAN, Otis Dudley,and Jay W. Artis, "Some Problems of Stratification Research," *Rural Sociology,* 16 (March, 1951), 17-29.

DUNCAN, Otis Dudley and Albert J. Reiss, Jr., *Social Characteristics of Urban and Rural Communities, 1950,* New York: Wiley, 1956.

DURHAM, R. and E. S. Cole, "Social Class Structure in Emporia Senior High School," *Midwest Sociologist,* 19 (May, 1957).

ELLIS, Robert A., "Social Stratification and Social Relations: An Empirical Test of the Disjunctiveness of Social Classes," *American Sociological Review,* 22 (October, 1957), 570-578.

FARIS, Robert E. L., "Reflections on the Ability Dimension in Human Society," *American Sociological Review,* 26 (December, 1961), 835-843.

FAUNCE, William A. and Donald A. Clelland, "Professionalization and Stratification Patterns in an Industrial Community," *American Journal of Sociology,* 72 (January, 1967), 341-350.

FOGLER, Sigmund, "The School Socio-Economic Survey," *Journal of Educational Sociology,* 19 (September, 1945), 76-82.

FOOTE, Nelson N., "Destratification and Restratification: An Editorial Foreword," *American Journal of Sociology,* 58 (January, 1953), 325-326.

FOOTE, Nelson N., *et al.,* "Alternative Assumptions in Stratification Research," *Transactions of the Second World Congress of Sociology,* 2 (1954), 378-390.

FORM, William H. and Julius Rivera, "The Place of Returning Migrants in a Stratification System," *Rural Sociology,* 23 (September, 1958), 286-297.

FORM, William H. and Gregory P. Stone, "Urbanism, Anonymity, and Status Symbolism," *American Journal of Sociology,* 62 (March, 1957), 504-514.

GENTILE, Grank and S. M. Miller, "Television and Social Class," *Sociology and Social Research,* 45 (April, 1961), 259-264.

GILB, Corine Lathrop, *Hidden Hierarchies: The Professions and Government,* New York: Harper and Row, 1967.

GOLDENSMITH, Harold F. and S. Young Lee, "Socioeconomic Status Within the Older and Larger 1960 Metropolitan Areas," *Rural Sociology,* 31 (June, 1966), 207-232.

GOLDKIND, Victor, "Social Stratification in the Peasant Community: Redfield's Chan Kom Reinterpreted," *American Anthropologist,* 67 (August, 1965), 863-884.

GOLDNER, Fred H. and R. R. Ritti, "Professionalization as Career Immobility," *American Journal of Sociology,* 72 (March, 1967), 489-502.

GOLDSTEIN, Sidney, "Socio-Economic and Migration Differentials Between the Aged in the Labor Force and the Labor Reserve," *Gerontologist,* 7 (March, 1967), 31-40.

GORDON, Milton M., "A System of Social Class Analysis," *Drew University Studies,* 2 (August, 1951).

GROSS, Llewellyn, "The Use of Class Concepts in Sociological Research," *American Journal of Sociology,* 54 (March, 1949), 262-268.

HAMILTON, C. Horace, "Educational Selectivity of Net Migration from the South," *Social Forces,* 38 (October, 1959), 33-42.

HATT, Paul K., "Occupation and Social Stratification," *American Journal of Sociology,* 55 (May, 1950), 533-543.

HATT, Paul K., and Virginia Ktsanses, "Patterns of American Stratification as Reflected in Selected Social Science Literature," *American Sociological Review,* 17 (December, 1952), 670-679.

HAVIGHURT, Robert J., "Knowledge of Class Status Can Make a Difference," *Progressive Education,* 27 (February, 1950).

HERNANDEZ, David E., "Is the Concept of Social Class Being Missused in Education?" *Journal of Educational Sociology,* 36 (March, 1963).

HERRIOTT, Robert E. and Nancy Hoyt St. John, *Social Class and the Urban School,* New York: Wiley, 1966.

HOCHBAUM, Godfrey, John G. Darley, E. D. Monachesi, and Charles Bird, "Socioeconomic Variables in a Large City," *American Journal of Sociology,* 61 (July, 1955), 31-38.

HOFFERBERT, Richard I., "Socioeconomic Dimensions of the American States," *Midwest Journal of Political Science,* 12 (August, 1968), 401-418.

HOLLY, D. N., "Profiting from a Comprehensive School: Sex, Class, and Ability," *British Journal of Sociology,* 16 (June, 1965), 150-158.

HOLMES, Roger, "Freud and Social Class," *British Journal of Sociology,* 16 (March, 1965), 48-67.

HOROWITZ, Irving Lewis, *Three Worlds of Development: The Theory and Practice of International Stratification,* New York: Oxford University Press, 1966.

HOSELITZ, Bert F., "Social Stratification and Economic Development," *International Social Science Journal,* 16 (1964), 237-251.

JAQUES, Elliott, *Equitable Payment: A General Theory of Work, Differential Payment, and Individual Progress,* New York: Wiley, 1961.

KAUFMAN, Harold F., Otis Dudley Duncan, Neal Gross, and William H. Sewell, "Problems of Theory and Method in the Study of Social Stratification in Rural Society," *Rural Sociology,* 18 (March, 1953), 12-24.

KUGLER, Israel, "Status, Power, and Educational Freedom," *Journal of Educational Sociology,* 25 (May, 1952), 512-515.

LaFLAUD, John F. and Robert A. Lejeune, "Initial Interaction of Newcomers in Alcoholics Anonymous: A Field Experiment in Class Symbols and Socialization," *Social Problems,* 8 (Fall, 1960), 102-110.

LAGOS, Gustavo, *International Stratification and Underdeveloped Countries,* Chapel Hill: University of North Carolina Press, 1963.

LANDIS, Judson, "Factors Contributing to the Dependency of Rural Old People," *Rural Sociology,* 7 (June, 1942), 208-210.

LANDIS, Paul H., "Educational Selectivity of Rural-Urban Migration and its Bearing on Wage and Occupational Adjustments," *Rural Sociology,* 11 (September, 1946), 218-232.

LANE, Robert E., "The Fear of Equality," *American Political Science Review,* 53 (March, 1959), 35-51.

LANG, Kurt, "Mass, Class, and the Reviewer," *Social Problems,* 6 (Summer, 1958), 11-21.

LASSWELL, Thomas E., "Social Class and Size of Community," *American Journal of Sociology,* 64 (March, 1959), 505-508.

LASSWELL, Thomas E., "Social Class and Stereotyping," *Sociology and Social Research,* 42 (March-April, 1958), 256-262.

LAUMANN, Edward O., *Prestige and Association in An Urban*

MISCELLANEOUS
PUBLICATIONS

Community, Indianapolis: Bobbs-Merrill, 1966.

LAUMANN, Edward O., "Subjective Social Distance and Urban Occupational Stratification," *American Journal of Sociology,* 71 (July, 1965), 28-36.

LAUMANN, Edward O. and Louis Guttman, "The Relative Associational Contiguity of Occupations in an Urban Setting," *American Sociological Review,* 31 (April, 1966), 169-178.

LENN, Theodore, "Social Class: Conceptual and Operational Significance for Education," *Journal of Educational Sociology,* 26 (October, 1952), 51-61.

LENNEY, John Joseph, *Caste System in the American Army,* New York: Greenberg, 1949.

LENSKI, Gerhard E. and John C. Leggett, "Caste, Class and Deference in the Research Interview," *American Journal of Sociology,* 65 (March, 1960), 463-467.

LEVINE, Gene Norman and Leila A. Sussmann, "Social Class and Sociability in Fraternity Pledging," *American Journal of Sociology,* 65 (January, 1960), 391-399.

LEWIS, Nahum H., "Application of Social-Class Concepts to Education," *Harvard Educational Review,* 16 (Summer, 1946), 207-224.

LOEB, Martin B., "Implication of Status Differentiation for Personal and Social Development," *Harvard Educational Review,* 23 (Summer, 1953), 168-174.

LOETHER, Herman J., "The Meaning of Work and Adjustment to Retirement," in Arthur B. Shostak and William Gomberg, editors, *Blue-Collar World: Studies of the American Worker,* Englewood Cliffs, New Jersey: Prentice Hall, 1964.

MACHLUP, Fritz, *The Production and Distribution of Knowledge in the United States,* Princeton University Press, 1962.

MAIN, Jackson T., "The Class Structure of Revolutionary America," in Reinhard Bendix and Seymour M. Lipset, editors, *Class, Status, and Power,* Revised edition, New York: Free Press, 1966.

MARTIN, John W., "Social Distance and Social Stratification," *Sociology and Social Research,* 47 (January, 1963), 179-186.

MASON, Philip, *Prospero's Magic: Some Thoughts on Class and Race,* London: Oxgord University Press, 1962.

MATTHEWS, Donald R., "United States Senators and the Class Structure," *Public Opinion Quarterly,* 18 (Spring, 1954), 5-22.

McLEMORE, S. Dale, "The Social Class Position of One Visiting Nurse Association," *Nursing Research,* 12 (1963), 341-346.

MILLER, Alden D., *Principal Components and Curvature in Oc-*

cupational Stratification, Chapel Hill: University of North Carolina, Institute for Research in Social Science, 1967.

MILLER, Herman P., "Lifetime Income and Economic Growth," *American Economic Review,* (September, 1965), 834-844.

MONK, Mary and Theodore M. Newcomb, "Perceived Consensus Within and Among Occupational Classes," *American Sociological Review,* 21 (February, 1956), 71-79.

MOORE, Barrington, Jr., "The Relation Between Social Stratification and Social Control," *Sociometry,* 5 (August, 1942), 230-250.

MOORE, Wilbert E. and Robin M. Williams, "Stratification in the Ante-Bellum South," *American Sociological Review,* 7 (June, 1942), 343-351.

MORRIS, Richard T., *The Two-Way Mirror: National Status in Foreign Students' Adjustment,* Minneapolis: University of Minnesota Press, 1960.

MORRIS, Richard T. and Raymond J. Murphy, "The Situs Dimension in Occupational Structure," *American Sociological Review,* 24 (April, 1959), 231-239.

MURRAY, Walter I., "The Concept of Social Class and Its Implications for Teachers," *Journal of Negro Education,* 20 (Winter, 1951), 16-21.

NAVILLE, P., "The Structure of Employment and Automation," *International Social Science Bulletin,* 10 (1958), 16-28.

NORDHOFF, Charles, *The Communistic Societies in the United States,* New York: Schocken, 1875.

OLSEN, Philip, editor, *America as a Mass Society,* New York: Free Press, 1963.

PAGE, Charles H., *Class and American Sociology: From Ward to Ross,* New York: Dial, 1940.

PATTERN, Thomas H., Jr., "Social Class and the 'Old Soldier,'" *Social Problems,* 8 (Winter, 1960-1961), 263-271.

PELLEGRIN, Roland J. and Charles H. Coates, "Executives and Supervisors: Contrasting Definitions of Career Success," *Administrative Science Quarterly,* 1 (March, 1957), 506-517.

PERLSTADT, Harry, "Some Comments on Professionalization and Stratification," *American Journal of Sociology,* 73 (September, 1967), 245-246.

PIRENNE, Henri, "Stages in the Social History of Capitalism," in Reinhard Bendix and Seymour M. Lipset, editors, *Class, Status, and Power,* 2nd edition, New York: Free Press, 1966.

MISCELLANEOUS PUBLICATIONS

PRICE, Daniel O., "Some Socio-Economic Factors in Internal Migration," *Social Forces,* 29 (May, 1951), 409-415.

RAMSEY, Robert R., Jr., "A Subcultural Approach to Academic Behavior," *Journal of Educational Sociology,* 35 (April, 1962), 355-376.

RATHS, Louis, "Social Class and Education" *Journal of Educational Sociology,* 28 (November, 1954), 124-125.

RATHS, Louis, "Social Class Investigations," *Journal of Educational Sociology,* 25 (April, 1952), 488-492.

REDMON, Edward, "Class Stratification in Industry—Its Social Implications," *Sociology and Social Research,* 33 (January-February, 1949), 212-217.

REISSMAN, Leonard, "Class, The City, and Social Cohesion," *International Review of Community Development,* 7 (1961), 39-51.

RETTIG, Salomon, Leo Despres, and Benjamin Pasamanick, "Status Stratification and Status Equalization," *Journal of Social Psychology,* 52 (August, 1960), 109-117.

RHODES, Albert Lewis, Albert J. Reiss, Jr., and Otis Dudley Duncan, "Occupational Segregation in a Metropolitan School System," *American Journal of Sociology,* 70 (May, 1965), 682-694.

ROGOW, Arnold A., "The Revolt Against Social Equality,"*Dissent,* 4 (1957).

ROSE, Arnold M., "Class Differences Among the Elderly: A Research Report," *Sociology and Social Research,* 50 (April, 1966), 356-360.

ROSE, Arnold M., "The Popular Meaning of Class Designation," *Sociology and Social Research,* 38 (September-October, 1953), 14-21.

SCHNORE, Leo F., "Some Correlates of Urban Size: A Replication," *American Journal of Sociology,* 69 (September, 1963), 185-193.

SHEPPARD, Harold L., "Relationship of an Aging Population to Employment and Occupational Structure," *Social Problems,* 8 (Fall, 1960), 159-162.

SIBLEY, Elbridge, "Some Demographic Clues to Stratification," *American Sociological Review,* 7 (June, 1942), 322-330.

SIMPSON, Ansel P., "Social Class Correlates of Old Age," *Sociology and Social Research,* 45 (January, 1961), 131-139.

SIMS, V. M., "Social Class Affiliation of a Group of Public School Teachers," *School Review,* 59 (September, 1951), 331-338.

SOLOMON, David N., "Ethnic and Class Differences Among Hospitals as Contingencies in Medical Careers," *American Journal of Sociology,* 66 (March, 1961), 463-471.

SPENGLER, Joseph J., "Socioeconomic Theory and Population Policy," *American Journal of Sociology,* 61 (September, 1955), 129-133.

STEPHENSON, Richard, "Education and Stratification," *Journal of Educational Sociology,* 25 (September, 1951), 34-41.

STINCHCOMBE, Arthur L., "Agricultural Enterprise and Rural Class Relations," *American Journal of Sociology,* 6 (September, 1961), 165-176.

SUVAL, Elizabeth M. and C. Horace Hamilton, "Some New Evidence on Educational Selectivity in Migration to and from the South," *Social Forces,* 43 (May, 1965), 536-547.

TERRIEN, Frederic W., "Too Much Room at the Top?" *Social Forces,* 37 (May, 1959), 298-305.

TRIANDIS, Harry C. and Leigh M. Triandis, "Race, Social Class, Religion, and Nationality as Determinants of Social Distance," *Journal of Abnormal and Social Psychology,* 61 (July, 1960), 110-118.

UDRY, J. Richard, "The Importance of Social Class in a Suburban School," *Journal of Educational Sociology,* 33 (April, 1960), 307-310.

VAN DEN BERGHE, Pierre L., "Distance Mechanisms of Stratification," *Sociology and Social Research,* 44 (January-February, 1960), 155-164.

VOGT, E. Z., "Social Stratification in the Rural Middle West: A Structural Analysis," *Rural Sociology,* 12 (December, 1947), 364-375.

WADE, D. E., "Social Class In a Teacher's College," *Journal of Educational Sociology,* 28 (November, 1954), 131-138.

WARNER, W. Lloyd, "The Corporation Man," in Edward S. Mason, editor, *The Corporation in Modern Society,* Cambridge: Harvard University Press, 1959.

WARNER, W. Lloyd, "Profiles of Government Executives," *Business Topics,* 9 (Autumn, 1961), 13-24.

WARNER, W. Lloyd and J. C. Abegglen, "Equal Opportunity and American Business Leaders," *Michigan Business Review,* 8 (March, 1956), 19-23.

WARNER, W. Lloyd, Marchia Meeker and Kenneth Eells, "Social Status in Education," *Phi Delta Kappa,* 30 (December, 1948).

WATNICK, Morris, "The Appeal of Communism to the Peoples of Underdeveloped Areas," in Reinhard Bendix and Seymour

MISCELLANEOUS PUBLICATIONS

M. Lipset, editors, *Class, Status, and Power,* revised edition, New York: Free Press, 1966.

WHITE, Mary Alice and June Charry, editors, *School Disorder, Intelligence, and Social Class,* New York: Teachers College Press, 1966.

WHYTE, William F., "The Social Structure of the Restaurant," *American Journal of Sociology,* 54 (January, 1949), 302-310.

WIGGINS, James A., "Status Differentiation, External Consequences, and Alternative Reward Distributions," *Sociometry,* 29 (June, 1966), 89-103.

WILKINSON, Forrest, "Social Distance Between Occupations," *Sociology and Social Research,* 13 (January-February, 1929), 234-244.

WRIGHT, David McCord, "The Economics of a Classless Society," *American Economic Review,* 39 (May, 1949), 27-36.

WRONG, Dennis H., "Social Inequality Without Social Stratification," *Canadian Review of Sociology and Anthropology,* 1 (1964), 5-16.

MISCELLANEOUS
PUBLICATIONS

AUTHOR INDEX

Blood, R., 108, 304
Bloom, B., 281
Bloom, L., 151
Bloom, R., 136
Bloombaum, M., 119, 362
Bloomberg, W., 21, 42, 85, 88
Bloomfield, P., 159, 247
Blue, J., 279
Blum, A., 214, 338, 343
Blum, J., 28, 167, 214, 215, 247
Blumberg, L., 25, 95
Blumberg, R., 43, 245, 311
Blumenthal, A., 34
Blumer, H., 215, 346
Boek, W., 23, 311
Bogardus, E., 136, 426
Bogart, L., 213, 339
Bogen, I., 432
Boggs, S., 42, 272, 380, 391
Bogue, D., 119, 127, 136, 215, 216, 223, 272, 277, 374, 400
Bohlke, R., 119, 240, 281, 380
Boisen, A., 127, 215, 401
Bolducci, D., 334
Bolte, K., 170, 362
Bolton, C., 317
Bonjean, C., 19, 63, 85, 124, 258, 302, 317, 326, 343, 380
Bonne, A., 50, 193
Bonney, M., 333
Boone, A., 58
Boosard, J., 362
Booth, D., 18, 19, 83, 85
Booth, R., 12
Borah, W., 200
Bordua, D., 281, 391, 406
Borgatta, E., 79, 80, 115, 267, 406
Bose, N., 183
Boskin, J. 136
Boskoff, A., 151
Bott, E., 346, 432
Bottomore, T., 4, 29, 159, 167, 171, 248, 343, 346, 351
Bougle, C., 183
Bouguignon, E., 200
Bouma, D., 109
Bond, H., 333
Bongiorno, A., 105
Bonham, J., 159, 240, 289
Bonilla, F., 248

Bowen, D., 215, 380
Bowen, E., 215, 380
Bower, R., 215, 289
Bowerman, C., 109, 314, 409
Bowers, R., 44
Bowles, S., 380
Bowley, A., 58, 159
Bowman, C., 215, 258
Bowman, L., 151
Bowman, M., 49, 333, 378, 431
Bowman, P., 283, 300, 306
Bowman, R., 36, 65, 356
Boyd, G., 136, 406
Boyd, M., 4
Boykim, L., 151, 406
Boyle, R., 406
Bradburn, N., 119, 258, 259, 302, 354
Braden, C., 127
Brandenburg, F., 100, 200
Bradley, D., 85
Bradley, W., 392
Brady, R., 100
Brainerd, C., 369, 377, 417
Braithwaite, L., 200, 215, 304
Brandmeyer, G., 120, 289
Brandon, A., 120
Braungart, R., 298
Brazer, H., 60
Brazziel, W., Jr., 406
Bredemeier, H., 4
Breed, W., 264, 314, 374, 380
Breese, F., 311, 335
Brennan, T., 159, 215, 289
Bressler, M., 109, 127, 373, 401
Bretsch, H., 261
Bretton, H., 100, 197
Brewer, E., 127
Briefs, G., 215, 346
Brierly, W., 266
Bright, M., 23, 251
Brim, O., 326
Brimmer, J., 340
Britton, J., 333
Brodbeck, A., 296
Brodersen, A., 167, 215
Bronfenbrenner, U., 109, 311, 314, 392
Brookover, W., 380, 432
Brooks, H., 272, 380
Brooks, M., 136
Brooks, M., 277, 307

Brooks, R., 346
Broom, L., 4, 50, 120, 127, 136, 137, 151, 200, 207, 289, 299, 302, 312, 314, 322, 327, 374, 380
Brown, B., 86
Brown, B., 332
Brown, C., 258
Brown, E., 58
Brown, J., 333, 378
Brown, J., 127, 299, 305, 359
Brown, M., 112
Brown, M., 116
Brown, M., 72
Brown, R., 4
Brown, W., 215, 322
Browning, H., 137, 151
Browning, R., 109
Brotz, H., 109, 124, 137, 290, 362
Bruce, G., 302, 380
Bruck, H., 26, 96
Brunner, E., 124
Brutzhus, B., 167
Bruun, K., 170, 288
Brymer, R., 235, 359
Bryson, L., 52, 109, 329, 412
Brzezinski, Z., 100, 167
Buchanan, W., 159, 171, 200, 207, 346, 375
Buck, C., 267
Buck, R., 400, 432
Buckley, W., 14, 15, 79, 200
Bullock, H., 137
Bullock, P., 215
Bullock, R., 302
Bultena, L., 127, 299
Bunzel, B., 160, 265
Bunzel, J., 240
Burchinal, L., 128, 215, 258, 299, 305, 407, 412, 413, 420
Burdick, E., 296
Burgess, E., 44, 45
Burgess, M., 86, 215
Burgin, T., 137
Burke, P., 121
Burma, J., 109, 137, 152, 200
Burnham, J., 50, 100
Burnham, W., 100
Burnight, R., 266, 354
Burns, H., 124, 200
Burns, R., 432
Burns, T., 29, 159
Burnstein, E., 15, 63, 120

Burrus, B., 325
Burt, C., 272, 334, 380
Burton, B., 182
Burton, W., 124, 354, 398, 432
Busia, K., 398
Butler, D., 159, 290
Butler, J., 304, 342
Butler, R., 373
Butterworth, C., 412

C

Cahnman, W., 152
Caldwell, J., 272
Calhoun, D., 248
Calhoun, D., 407
Cameron, M., 281
Camilleri, S., 109
Campbell, A., 290
Campbell, A., 272, 274, 279
Campbell, E., 139, 322, 405, 407, 409
Campbell, P., 159, 289
Cancian, F., 34, 63, 128, 171, 216, 290, 317, 407
Cannetti, E., 109
Cannon, K., 354
Cannon, M., 93, 104
Cantril, H., 58, 100, 128, 159, 167, 171, 200, 207, 346, 347, 401, 408
Caplan, G., 109
Caplovitz, D., 119, 216, 259, 302, 339
Caplow, T., 45, 63, 171, 174, 200, 302, 374
Carlsson, G., 4, 19, 72, 159, 171, 178, 362, 372, 398
Carney, R., 130, 317, 401
Caro, F., 398, 407
Carroll, E., 313
Carr-Saunders, A., 159, 248
Carstairs, G., 183, 248
Carstens, P., 137, 152
Carter, C., 50, 171, 272
Carlson, R., 72
Case, F., 137
Case, H., 347
Cassel, R., 407
Cardill, W., 407
Carleton, R., 200, 272, 366, 375
Carlin, J., 216

Carter, H., 392
Carter, L., 85
Carter, M., 159, 216
Carter, R., 72, 109
Cartter, A., 50, 58, 159
Cartwright, D., 79, 281, 380
Cater, D., 100
Cattell, R., 15, 19, 63, 109
Catton, W., Jr., 7
Caudill, H., 216
Caudill, W., 137, 407
Cavan, R., 264, 281
Cave, E., 380
Cayton, H., 64, 129, 137, 139, 152, 218, 282, 315
Centers, R., 19, 58, 216, 262, 290, 302, 305, 319, 327, 347, 362, 398, 408
Chambers, R., 430
Chambliss, W., 121, 293
Champernowne, D., 58
Champion, P., 216, 272
Chancellor, L., 305
Chandrasekaran, C., 193
Chandrashekaraiyah, K., 183, 363
Chang, C-L., 58, 177, 248
Chang, H., 415
Chapin, S., 19, 20, 354
Chaplin, D., 137, 216
Chapman, D., 159
Chapman, D., 392
Chapman, J., 9
Chapman, S., 371
Charry, J., 287, 338, 440
Charters, W., Jr., 110, 426, 433
Chartier, B., 248
Chattopadhyaya, B., 183
Chein, I., 281
Chen, T., 177, 216
Chen, T., 50, 177
Cherry-Peisach, E., 332, 334
Chicago Tenants Relocation Bureau, 216
Child, I., 392, 408
Chilman, C., 12, 216, 217, 272, 305
Chilton, R., 281
Chinoy, E., 4, 217, 347, 363, 375, 408
Chin-Shong, E., 327
Cho, Y-T., 177
Choldin, H., 276
Chow, J-T., 248, 363, 374
Chowdry, K., 334

Christensen, H., 408
Christensen, H., 383, 408
Christiansen, J., 137, 408
Circourel, A., 110
Clark, B., 363, 398
Clark, E., 392
Clark, E., 128
Clark, K., 110, 137, 139, 145, 148, 217, 232, 281, 309, 314
Clark, J., 281
Clark, P., 273
Clark, R., 259
Clark, R., 20, 68
Clark, R., 408, 416
Clark, S., 42, 128
Clark, S., 388
Clark, T., 86
Clarke, A., 339, 392, 410
Clarke, C., 183
Clarke, E., 305
Clarke, P., 109
Clausen, J., 113, 259, 282
Clayton, H., 34
Clayton, L., 159, 248
Cleandrasekaran, C., 273
Clelland, D., 35, 86, 124, 433
Cleveland, S., 408
Clifford-Vaughn, M., 171, 248
Clignet, R., 197, 248
Clinard, M., 217, 282, 283, 318
Cloward, R., 282
Coates, C., 93, 363, 375, 408, 437
Codere, H., 100, 197
Cogburn, D., 359
Cohen, A., 217, 282, 322, 392
Cohen, A., 110, 118
Cohen, E., 392
Cohen, J., 111, 222, 232
Cohen, J., 110
Cohen, L., 74
Cohen, W., 60
Cohn, B., 50, 183, 217
Cohn, W., 15, 63, 110, 128, 217, 433
Colcord, F., Jr., 86
Cole, E., 64, 433
Cole, G., 4, 29, 159, 160, 217, 240, 248, 347
Cole, J., 63
Cole, L., 366
Cole, S., 63

Coleman, H., 334
Coleman, J., 20, 68, 79, 86,
137, 138, 227, 380, 381,
392, 408, 416
Coleman, J., 20
Coleman, R., 5, 232
Coleman, W., 318
Collins, N., 100
Collins, R., Jr., 321, 325,
389
Collins, S., 200, 426
Collison, P., 45, 165, 354
Colm, G., 58
Combs, J., Jr., 200, 273
Comhaire-Sylvan, J., 200
Conant, J., 217, 409
Congalton, A., 72, 73, 207,
209
Conger, J., 282, 318, 320
Connell, W., 208, 398
Connelly, G., 290
Conner, R., 225
Converse, P., 290
Conway, J., 334
Conway, M., 290, 322
Cook, D., 73, 193
Cook, F., 100
Cook, N., 265
Coombs, L., 269, 274, 382
Coombs, R., 409
Cooper, H., 290
Cooper, J., 73, 209
Cooper, M., 264
Copeman, G., 101, 160, 248
Corey, L., 240
Cornell, J., 179
Corwin, R., 409
Coser, L., 217
Costa, L., 50
Costello, B., 138
Coster, J., 354
Cotgrove, S., 124
Cothran, T., 110, 152
Cottrell, L., Jr., 120
Couch, A., 79
Cough, E., 183
Coughlin, R., 138
Counts, G., 73
Cousens, F., 110
Cousens, R., 217
Coutu, W., 73
Cowhig, J., 45, 124, 138, 268
268, 364, 408, 409
Cowles, M., 375
Cox, O., 5, 29, 138, 183
Crain, R., 63, 86, 114, 124
Cramer, C., 128, 138, 401
Cramer, M., 324, 409

Cramer, M., 248, 259, 339
Cramer, R., 322
Crane, D., 63
Crankshaw, E., 101, 168
Creeden, C., 221
Creelan, P., 389
Cressey, P., 45, 193
Crites, J., 422
Crockett, H., Jr., 363, 366,
399
Crockett, H., 409, 419
Croner, F., 240, 347
Crook, D., 29, 34, 177, 217
Crook, I., 29, 34, 177, 217
Crowe, M., 410
Crowley, D., 200
Crozier, M., 240
Cuber, J., 5, 34, 63
Cunnison, I., 110
Curtis, R., 29, 120, 128,
299, 347, 363, 381, 401,
433
Curtis, T., 118, 424
Cutright, P., 50, 58, 363,
392, 409
Cutter, H., 78, 82

D

Dahl, R., 79, 86, 101
Dahlstrom, E., 79
Dahrendorf, R., 5, 29, 50,
110, 171, 347
Dailey, J., 124, 218, 399
Dakin, R., 86, 110
Dale, G., 20
Dallin, D., 168
Dalton, G., 218
Dalton, M., 128, 218, 248,
299, 375
Damle, Y., 14, 58, 183, 363
D'Andrade, R., 419
Daniel, V., 152
Daniel, W., 218
Daniels, J., 34, 63, 152
Dansereau, H., 218, 409
D'Antonio, W., 20, 87, 88,
201
Danzger, M., 87
Darley, J., 22, 34, 125, 434
Datta, L., 128, 401
Datwyler, D., 143
Davenport, J., 218
David, M., 60
Davidson, H., 334

Davidson, P., 28, 73, 289,
363
Davie, J., 355, 399
Davie, M., 138, 152
Davies, A., 73, 208, 347
Davies, J., 128
Davies, V., 409
Davis, A., 34, 63, 138, 152,
218, 241, 305, 312, 318,
335, 355, 381, 409
Davis, B., 248, 426
Davis, E., 218, 409
Davis, J., 20, 22, 63, 381,
392, 409
Davis, J., 73, 168
Davis, K., 5, 15, 63, 183,
200, 218, 273, 314, 355
Dean, D., 318
Dean, J., 339
Dean, L., 34
de Andrade, R., 395
Deasy, L., 20, 363
Decter, M., 138, 168
de Charmes, R., 313, 403,
410
Deeg, M., 50, 73
Deegan, A., 133
de Fleur, L., 282
de Fleur, M., 73
de Grazia, A., 110, 138, 290
de Grazia, S., 339
de Gre, G., 241, 327, 348
de Grove, J., 90
Dehart, W., 420
de Huszar, G., 248
de Jong, G., 128, 273, 299
de Kadt, E., 29, 101
de Labry, J., 338
Deldeg, M., 313
Delmo, D-D., 218
Demant, V., 128
Dembo, T., 415
Demerath, N., III, 101, 120,
128, 129, 259, 299
Denisoff, R., 348
Denlinger, P., 177
Denney, R., 105
Dennis, C., 354
Dentler, R., 95, 218, 282
Derksen, J., 58, 273
Desai, A., 433
Desai, I., 183
Desai, R., 138, 160
de Shan, L., 327
Despres, L., 438
de Tocqueville, A., 29
Deutsch, M., 136, 332, 334,
410

Greer, S., 42, 43, 89, 141, 245, 311
Gregory, C., 335, 336, 358, 370
Gregory, C., 386, 415, 418
Gregory, F., 250, 427
Gregory, F., 250, 427
Gresser, B., 171
Grigg, C., 228, 262, 411, 416
Grigsby, S., 424
Grimes, M., 291
Grimshaw, A., 29
Groat, H., 274
Groff, P., 74
Groner, F., 130, 402
Gronlund, N., 318
Gross, B., 111
Gross, L., 6, 12, 230, 328, 434
Gross, N., 23, 348, 435
Gross, R., 222
Grossack, M., 340
Grossmann, B., 318
Growther, J., 75
Grusky, O., 111, 291, 375, 383
Gubin, K., 102
Guerrin, R., 267
Guest, R., 349, 365, 411
Guha, U., 185
Guidon, H., 29, 141, 209
Gulick, J., 35
Gumperz, J., 185, 194, 332
Gupta, B., 185, 365
Gupta, R., 30, 185
Guralnick, L., 269
Gurin, G., 134, 260, 290, 341, 404, 423
Gurin, P., 411
Gursslin, O., 12, 232, 260, 261, 328
Gusfield, J., 74, 356, 375
Gustad, J., 406
Guttentag, M., 283
Guttman, L., 22, 37, 436
Guttsman, W., 52, 102, 161, 250
Guzzardi, W., Jr., 241
Gyman, H., 286, 387

H

Haan, N., 335, 383
Haas, E., 411
Haas, M., 65, 194
Habakkuk, H., 161
Haber, A., 220
Haber, L., 312
Hacker, A., 102, 250
Hackler, J., 222
Hadden, J., 130, 292, 300
Haer, J., 22, 65, 89, 324, 328, 349
Hagedorn, R., 344
Haggstrom, W., 111, 222
Hagood, M., 22, 275
Hagstrom. W., 65, 365, 427
Hajnal, J., 275
Halbwachs, M., 6, 349
Hall, E., 271
Hall, J., 74, 75, 161, 172, 365, 369
Hall, M., 319
Hall, M., 328
Hall, O., 375
Hall, Y., 266
Haller, A., 22, 24, 74, 263, 365, 375, 407, 412, 416, 420
Halmos, P., 206
Halpern, J., 35
Halsey, A., 124, 125, 160, 161, 332, 335, 355, 365, 387, 395, 399, 400
Hamblin, R., 108, 206, 298
Hamilton, C., 434, 439
Hamilton, R., 52, 59, 172, 222, 241, 292, 300, 323, 328, 340, 344, 349, 356
Hammond, P., 285
Hammond, S., 35, 208
Hamon, L., 172, 250
Handel, G., 51, 55, 222, 232, 316
Handlin, O., 141
Hanks, L., Jr., 102, 194
Hansen, A., 46, 185, 201
Hansen, D., 111, 400
Hanson, R., 89
Hapgood, H., 153,
Hapkin, W., 275
Harburg, E., 320
Harberger, A., 340

Hardee, J., 208, 344
Hardgrave, R., 185
Hardt, R., 260
Hare, A., 80, 115
Hare, E., 260
Hare, N., 52, 141, 365
Hargens, L., 65, 265, 427
Harlan, H., 325
Harmon, L., 251, 427
Harper, E., 185
Harrington, M., 59, 222, 223
Harris, E., 15, 65, 74, 412
Harris, I., 393
Harris, M., 141
Harris, M., 201
Harris, M., 59
Harris, R., 89, 161
Harris, S., 223
Harrison, I., 229
Harrison, P., 111
Harrison, R., 223, 292
Harrison, S., 185
Harrison, T., 349
Harrold, H., 130, 223
Harter, C., 111, 251
Hartley, E., 113, 117, 120, 208, 290, 311, 347, 348
Hartmann, G., 74, 349
Harvey, O., 69
Harwitz, M., 197
Hatch, D., 22, 65
Hatch, M., 22, 65
Hathway, M., 223, 306
Hatt, P., 6, 36, 65, 74, 76, 125, 325, 364, 434
Haunol, J., 161
Hauser, P., 270
Hausknecht, M., 223, 344
Havemann, E., 125, 383, 393, 399
Havens, A., 69
Havighurst, R., 36, 52, 65, 161, 201, 208, 223, 283, 300, 303, 306, 312, 319, 335, 337, 340, 341, 356, 360, 383, 399, 412, 434
Haskins, W., 161, 223
Hastings, P., 292
Hayden, T., 105
Hayner, N., 46, 201
Hawkins, B., 89
Hawley, A., 44, 46, 89, 98, 179, 194, 346, 355, 382
Hawley, W., 90
Hawthorn, A., 46, 201
Hawthorn, H., 46, 201

Parsons, T., 9, 32, 81, 93, 105, 134, 139, 145, 148, 232, 254, 296, 309, 386, 404, 418, 423
Pasamanick, B., 50, 63, 262, 278, 303, 305, 330, 352, 438
Pashkov, A., 55, 169
Passin, H., 180
Passow, A., 231, 338
Paterson, A., 380
Patnick, N., 188
Patno, M., 270
Patten, T., Jr., 437
Patterson, D., 50, 72, 73
Patterson, J., 279
Patterson, J., 231
Patterson, M., 13
Patterson, S., 296, 386
Patterson, S., 352
Patwardhan, S., 189
Paulus, C., 189
Pavalko, R., 210, 386, 395, 418
Pavenstedt, E., 231, 308
Paydarfar, A., 66
Payne, J., 408
Payne, R., 25, 68, 93, 418
Peabody, R., 81, 89, 114
Peacock, A., 61
Pear, H., 158, 164
Pearl, A., 111, 222
Pearlin, L., 174, 285, 313, 323, 330, 383
Pearsall, M., 23, 91
Peck, R., 309, 387
Peck, S., 105, 115
Pederson, M., 176, 331, 360
Pellegrin, R., 13, 93, 115, 122, 145, 155, 363, 375, 408, 437
Pelz, D., 386
Pelzel, J., 180, 243
Penalosa, F., 55, 145, 155, 352, 369
Pennock, J., 9
Pepper, M., 213, 258
Perlo, V., 55, 61, 105, 145
Perlman, S., 352
Perlstadt, H., 437
Perrow, C., 68
Perroy, E., 175, 370
Perrucci, C., 257, 278, 386, 429
Perrucci, R., 62, 68, 126, 377, 399, 400, 429
Peterson, R., 204, 296
Peterson, W., 230, 370

Petras, J., 205, 296
Petrullo, L., 109, 115
Pettigrew, T., 64, 145, 153, 155, 324, 386
Pfautz, H., 14, 39, 68, 93, 155
Phillips, B., 336, 386
Phillips, B., 418
Phillips, D., 330, 418
Phillips, H., 270
Phillips, H., 195
Phillips, P., 259
Phillips, W., 358
Phillips, W., 110, 152
Photiadis, J., 300, 320, 325
Pierce, C., 356
Pierce, J., 36, 65, 283, 300, 306
Pierce-Jones, J., 313, 418
Pierson, D., 145, 205
Pigors, P., 81
Pihlblad, C., 335, 336, 358, 370, 386, 398, 407, 418
Pike, E., 133
Pike, F., 32, 205
Pike, R., 208, 429
Pilisuk, M., 105
Pin, E., 133, 300
Pinard, M., 32, 230, 268, 297
Pineo, P., 76, 210
Pink, L., 243
Pinkerton, T., 264, 269, 311
Pinkney, A., 324
Pinto, L., 205
Pirenne, H., 437
Pittman, D., 234
Platt, J., 52, 160
Plessner, H., 81
Plotnick, H., 379
Plumb, J., 158
Pocock, D., 189
Pohlman, E., 145
Pohlmann, V., 336
Pohly, C., 171, 249
Polansky, N., 80
Polgar, S., 224, 275
Polk, K., 285
Pollins, H., 140
Polsby, N., 25, 93, 94, 297
Pomeroy, W., 315
Pope, B., 68, 330
Pope, H., 230, 314, 345
Pope, L., 133, 231
Porter, J., 418
Porter, J., 16, 122, 341

Porter, J., 9, 25, 61, 76, 94, 105, 146, 212, 254, 370
Porterfield, A., 265, 285, 387
Postgate, R., 217
Poti, S., 195, 278, 387
Potter, A., 105
Potter, J., 231
Potter, R., Jr., 279
Potvin, R., 279
Powdermaker, H., 39, 68, 146, 155
Powell, E., 263, 265
Powell, I., 297
Powell, R., 38, 67, 204
Powers, M., 122, 145, 278
Powles, W., 231
Prabhu, I., 189
Pradham, K., 190, 371
Prais, S., 25, 370
Prasad, I., 189
Preiss, J., 64
Prentice, N., 146
Present, P., 94
Presthus, R., 94, 387
Preston, L., 100
Prewitt, K., 298
Price, C., 231, 263
Price, D., 55, 146, 215, 438
Price, D., 69
Prince, J., 94
Proctor, C., 358
Proshek, J., 230
Prothro, J., 114, 144, 154, 155, 295
Pryer, M., 108
Psathas, G., 306, 313, 418
Pugh, T., 265
Pundalik, V., 189
Punke, H., 126, 387, 395, 418
Purcell, T., 146, 231, 352, 418
Putney, G., 69
Putney, S., 69, 114, 308

Q

Quay, H., 285
Queen, S., 16
Quensel, C., 387
Quinn, J., 47
Quinney, E., 285
Quinney, R., 270, 297

R

Roth, J., 309, 387
Roth, G., 234
Rothman, P., 331
Rothney, W., 271
Rothstein, E., 353
Rothwell, C., 13
Roucek, J., 69, 115, 146
Rousseau, J., 9
Rovere, R., 106, 255
Rowe, W., 189, 195
Rubel, M., 351
Rubin, M., 146, 234
Rubington, E., 234
Ruchelman, L., 429
Rudolph, L., 189
Rudolph, S., 189
Rudwick, E., 144, 155
Reusch, J., 268, 387
Runciman, A., 341
Runciman, W., 164, 297, 353
Ruschmeyer, D., 25, 175
Rush, G., 122, 297
Rushing, W., 115, 265, 386, 420
Rustow, D., 81
Ryan, B., 55, 189, 246, 342
Rychman, D., 337

S

Sabagh, G., 196, 280, 337, 359
Saboul, A., 32
Saenger, G., 297
Safa, H., 234
Safar, D., 431
Safilios-Rothschild, C., 353
Sagarin, E., 142
Sagi, P., 279, 373
Sahlins, M., 212
Sainsbury, P., 165, 265
Saltzman, J., 173, 358
Salisbury, W., 352
Salisbury, R., 297
Samora, J., 97, 117, 146, 155, 157
Sampson, E., 122, 359, 395
Samuelsson, K., 133, 403
Sanford, F., 115
Sanford, N., 410
Sanford, R., 317, 322
Sangane, V., 55, 189
Sanger, W., 362
Sangstad, R., 407
Sapin, B., 26, 96
Sarana, G., 187

Sarapata, A., 76, 175
Sardo, J., 419
Sargent, S., 353
Sarma, J., 189
Sariola, S., 25, 39, 175, 205, 370
Sasnett, M., 198
Sauer, W., 88
Saunders, J., 278
Sawyer, J., 106
Scanzoni, J., 309, 420
Scarr, H., 285
Schachter, S., 395, 396
Schaefer, J., 359
Schafer, W., 419
Schaffer, L., 262
Schaffer, R., 90
Schafft, A., 278
Schaie, W., 337
Schapiro, L., 106, 169
Schatzman, L., 333
Scheff, T., 115
Schermerhorn, R., 81, 95, 1 106, 115, 147, 309
Scheuch, E., 25, 175
Schild, E., 176, 331, 360
Schlesinger, A., Jr., 115
Schlesinger, B., 14, 234
Schlesinger, R., 169
Schmid, C., 47, 55, 147, 265
Schmidt, E., 265
Schmitt, D., 122
Schmitt, R., 61, 147, 286, 309
Schnaper, M., 426
Schneider, D., 268
Schneider, J., 69, 165, 255, 387, 403, 429, 430
Schneider, L., 129, 131, 132, 133, 140, 143, 153, 154, 300, 301, 402, 403, 420
Schneider, R., 268
Schnore, L., 43, 48, 55, 156, 268, 371, 438
Schoenbaum, D., 69, 106, 175
Schoenfeld, B., 115
Schommer, C., 359, 384
Schoor, A., 234
Schrag, C., 7, 116, 286
Schramm, W., 341
Schreiber, D., 234
Schroeder, W., 132, 301, 345
Schuessler, K., 341
Schuler, E., 39, 70
Schulman, M., 337
Schultz, T., 126
Schulz, D., 234, 309

Schulze, R., 25, 95, 126
Schuman, H., 74
Schumpeter, J., 10, 32, 106
Schuster, E., 250
Schwartz, B., 187, 188, 190
Schwartz, E., 286
Schwartz, M., 74, 147, 234
Schwartz, R., 16, 195
Schwartz, S., 147, 169
Schwarzweller, H., 175, 234, 359, 420
Scotch, N., 262
Scott, E., 291
Scott, E., 165, 337, 388
Scott, J., Jr., 345
Scott, J., 371
Scott, W., 25, 371
Scott, W., 278, 388
Scudder, R., 25, 69, 388
Seager, C., 165, 265
Seagoe, M., 341
Searing, D., 20, 249, 426
Searles, R., 156, 297
Sears, D., 415
Sears, R., 314
Sebald, H., 234
Sedlacek, G., 267, 357
Seeley, J., 39, 43
Seeman, M., 5, 16, 26, 81, 122, 175, 297, 320, 325, 388, 417
Segal, B., 359
Segal, D., 30, 162, 172, 292
Segerstedt, T., 175, 353
Seibert, F., 385
Seidman, J., 116
Seligman, B., 235
Seligman, L., 255
Selznick, P., 4, 116
Sepmeyer, I., 198
Sepulveda, O., 72
Sereno, R., 255
Sewell, W., 14, 23, 26, 263, 268, 278, 321, 337, 388, 412, 420, 421, 435
Sexton, P., 61, 126, 147, 235, 310, 315, 359, 400, 421
Sgan, M., 16
Shah, B., 190
Shah, V., 337, 388, 421
Shahani, S., 14
Shanas, E., 310
Shanley, F., 244, 286
Shannon, L., 126, 143, 147
Shannon, J., 255, 400, 430
Shapiro, H., 321
Sharma, K., 190, 371

Spengler, J., 56, 61, 270, 439

Spergel, I., 236, 286

Spiegelman, M., 270

Spies, C., 267, 357

Spilka, B., 382

Spinley, B., 165, 236, 321

Spinrad, W., 33, 43, 96, 236

Spiro, M., 196

Sprey, J., 148

Srausz-Hupe, R., 96

Srinivas, M., 14, 56, 190, 191

Srinivason, B., 259

Srinivastava, R., 191, 371

Srole, L., 41, 150, 263, 321

St. John, N., 148, 356, 420, 434

Staab, J., 59

Stacey, B., 337, 388, 389

Stafilios-Rothschild, C., 175, 422

Stagner, R., 70, 95, 116, 126, 353, 396

Stambler, J., 266

Stamler, R., 148, 236

Standler, C., 313

Stanton, F., 92, 114

Stark, R., 129, 134, 165, 298, 300, 301

Stavenhagen, R., 206

Steele, M., 38

Stein, M., 40

Stember, C., 325

Stephens, R., 101

Stephenson, R., 4, 126, 400, 422, 439

Steinle, J., 84

Steiner, G., 3

Steiner, I., 331

Stendler, C., 236, 244, 331

Stengel, E., 265

Stern, B., 268

Stern, C., 206

Sterner, R., 148, 155

Stewart, C., 109

Stewart, D., 430

Stewart, F., 96

Stewart, R., 162, 173, 252, 377, 430

Stevenson, E., 244

Stevenson, H., 70, 191

Stiller, J., 337

Stinchcombe, A., 10, 16, 286, 439

Stockdell, K., 267, 357

Stockwell, E., 56, 270

Stoddard, L., 176

Stoetzel, J., 176, 298

Stokes, D., 106

Stokes, D., 290

Stoller, A., 208, 261

Stone, G., 40, 70, 96, 339, 434

Stone, L., 256

Stone, R., 33, 96, 116, 377

Stouffer, S., 325

Straus, M., 117, 310, 321, 337, 389, 396, 420, 422

Straus, R., 236, 360

Strauss, A., 333, 376

Street, D., 143, 236, 284, 298

Strickon, A., 206

Strizower, S., 148, 191

Strodtbeck, F., 76, 112, 134, 148, 235, 283, 286, 314, 384, 389, 396, 404, 422

Stroup, A., 396

Stroup, F., 405

Stroup, H., 134

Stuart, R., 165

Stubbins, J., 396

Stuckert, R., 389

Sturmthal, A., 244

Stycos, J., 201, 218, 236, 275, 278

Stys, W., 236, 279

Subodh, D., 195, 278, 387

Suchman, E., 233, 268, 331, 420

Sudnow, D., 360

Sugi, M., 180, 366

Sumner, W., 33, 236

Sunshine, M., 21, 42, 85, 88

Super, D., 422

Super, D., 303

Surace, S., 176, 236

Surachmad, W., 196, 314, 423

Sussman, L., 67, 436

Sussman, M., 96, 217, 244, 305, 311, 312

Sutherland, E., 236, 244, 287

Sutker, S., 329

Sutker, S., 156, 256

Suttles, W., 212, 360

Sutton, F., 106, 256

Suval, E., 439

Svalastoga, K., 10, 26, 70, 77, 176, 331, 360, 372, 389, 396

Swanson, B., 28, 78, 83, 89, 90, 94, 96

Swanson, G., 208, 218, 305, 312, 313, 347

Sweezy, P., 96, 106, 256

Sweetser, D., 176, 310

Swift, D., 165, 372, 422

Swinehart, J., 310, 314, 422

Swinscow, D., 266

Sydenstriker, E., 279

Sykes, A., 331

Sykes, G., 287, 337

Syme, L., 389

Syme, R., 176, 256

Szczepanski, J., 176

T

Taba, H., 360

Taeuber, A., 43, 48, 56, 156

Taeuber, I., 181

Taeuber, K., 43, 48, 56, 156

Taft, R., 77, 208, 209

Tangent, P., 40, 70

Tannenbaum, A., 26, 82, 96, 117

Tannenbaum, F., 206, 96, 117

Tannenbaum, R., 117

Tarcher, M., 117

Tarjan, G., 337

Tarver, J., 310, 360

Tatz, C., 147, 208

Tausky, C., 10, 16, 377, 423

Taussig, F., 256, 430

Tawney, R., 61, 134, 165, 404

Taves, M., 411, 412

Taylor, L., 236

Taylor, O., 10

Tayback, M., 264, 269, 311

Teevan, R., 408

Tennyson, R., 286

Terman, L., 396

Terrien, F., 439

Terris, M., 261

Thakkar, K., 191

Thernstrom, S., 40, 237, 372

Thibaut, J., 117, 321

Thielans, W., Jr., 67

Thoenes, P., 176, 256

Thomanek, E., 70, 360